Praise for Engineering a Compiler

"Keith Cooper and Linda Torczon are leading compilers researchers who have also built several state-of-the-art compilers. This book adeptly spans both worlds, by explaining both time-tested techniques and new algorithms and by providing practical advice on engineering and constructing a compiler. *Engineering a Compiler* is a rich survey and exposition of the important techniques necessary to build a modern compiler."

—Jim Larus, Microsoft Research

"A wonderful introduction to the theory, practice, and lore of modern compilers. Cooper and Torczon convey the simple joys of this subject that follow from the elegant interplay between compilation and the rest of computer science. If you're looking for an end-to-end tour of compiler construction annotated with a broad range of practical experiences, this is the book."

—Michael D. Smith, Harvard University

"I am delighted to see this comprehensive new book on modern compiler design. The authors have covered the classical material, as well as the important techniques developed in the last 15 years, including compilation of object-oriented languages, static single assignment, region-based register allocation, and code scheduling. Their approach nicely balances the formal structure that modern compilers build on with the pragmatic insights that are necessary for good engineering of a compiler."

—John Hennessy, Stanford University

"Cooper and Torczon have done a superb job of integrating the principles of compiler construction with the pragmatic aspects of compiler implementation. This, along with the excellent coverage of recent advances in the field, make their book ideal for teaching a modern undergraduate course on compilers."

—Ken Kennedy, Rice University

Engineering a Compiler

About the Authors

Dr. Cooper, Professor, Dept. of Computer Science at Rice University, is the leader of the Massively Scalar Compiler Project at Rice, which investigates issues relating to optimization and code generation for modern machines. He is also a member of the Center for High Performance Software Research, the Computer and Information Technology Institute, and the Center for Multimedia Communication—all at Rice. He teaches courses in compiler construction at the undergraduate and graduate level.

Dr. Torczon, Research Scientist, Dept. of Computer Science at Rice University, is a principal investigator on the Massively Scalar Compiler Project at Rice and on the Grid Application Development Software Project sponsored by the Next Generation Software program of the National Science Foundation. She also serves as the executive director of the Center for High Performance Software Research and of the Los Alamos Computer Science Institute.

Engineering a Compiler

Keith D. Cooper and Linda Torczon
Rice University

MORGAN KAUFMANN PUBLISHERS

AN IMPRINT OF ELSEVIER SCIENCE

SAN FRANCISCO   SAN DIEGO   NEW YORK   BOSTON
LONDON   SYDNEY   TOKYO

Senior Editor: Denise E. M. Penrose
Publishing Services Manager: Simon Crump
Project Management: Overton Editorial and Production
Editorial Coordinator: Emilia Thiuri
Cover Design: Ross Carron Design
Cover Image: John Outram
Text Design: Rebecca Evans and Associates
Composition: Integra Software Services Pvt Ltd
Technical Illustration: Dartmouth Publishing, Inc.
Copyeditor: John Hammett
Proofreader: Carol Leyba and Associates
Indexer: Steve Rath
Printer: The Maple-Vail Book Manufacturing Group

Cover Image: "The Landing of the Ark," a vaulted ceiling-design whose iconography was narrated, designed, and drawn by John Outram of John Outram Associates, Architects and City Planners, London, England. To read more visit *www.johnoutram.com/rice.html*

Morgan Kaufmann Publishers
An Imprint of Elsevier Science
500 Sansome Street, Suite 400
San Francisco, CA 94111
www.mkp.com

Library of Congress Cataloging-in-Publication Data Application submitted

ISBN: 1–55860–698-X (hardback)–ISBN 1–55860–699–8 (paperback)

This book is printed on acid-free paper.

We dedicate this volume to

- our parents, who instilled in us the thirst for knowledge and supported us as we developed the skills to follow our quest for knowledge;

- our children, who have shown us again how wonderful the process of learning and growing can be; and

- our spouses, without whom this book would never have been written.

About the Cover

The cover of this book features a portion of the drawing, "The Landing of the Ark," which decorates the ceiling of Duncan Hall at Rice University (see the picture below). Both Duncan Hall and its ceiling were designed by British architect John Outram. Duncan Hall is an outward expression of architectural, decorative, and philosophical themes developed over Outram's career as an architect. The decorated ceiling of the ceremonial hall plays a central role in the building's decorative scheme. Outram inscribed the ceiling with a set of significant ideas—a creation myth. By expressing those ideas in an allegorical drawing of vast size and intense color, Outram created a signpost that tells visitors who wander into the hall that, indeed, this building is not like other buildings.

By using the same signpost on the cover of *Engineering a Compiler*, the authors intend to signal that this work contains significant ideas that are at the core of their discipline. Like Outram's building, this volume is the culmination of intellectual themes developed over the authors' professional careers. Like Outram's decorative scheme, this book is a device for communicating ideas. Like Outram's ceiling, it presents significant ideas in new ways.

By connecting the design and construction of compilers with the design and construction of buildings, we intend to convey the many similarities in these two distinct activities. Our many long discussions with Outram introduced us to the Vitruvian ideals for architecture: commodity, firmness, and delight. These ideals apply to many kinds of construction. Their analogs for compiler construction are consistent themes of this text: function, structure,

and elegance. Function matters; a compiler that generates incorrect code is useless. Structure matters; engineering detail determines a compiler's efficiency and robustness. Elegance matters; a well-designed compiler, in which the algorithms and data structures flow smoothly from one pass to another, can be a thing of beauty.

We are delighted to have John Outram's work grace the cover of this book.

Duncan Hall's ceiling is an interesting technological artifact. Outram drew the original design on one sheet of paper. It was photographed and scanned at 1200 dpi yielding roughly 750 MB of data. The image was enlarged to form 234 distinct 2 x 8 foot panels, creating a 52 x 72 foot image. The panels were printed onto oversize sheets of perforated vinyl using a 12 dpi acrylic-ink printer. These sheets were precision mounted onto 2 x 8 foot acoustic tiles and hung on the vault's aluminum frame.

CONTENTS

PREFACE

Over the last twenty years, the practice of compiler construction has changed dramatically. Front ends have become commodity components; they can be purchased from a reliable vendor or adapted from one of the many public-domain systems. At the same time, processors have become more performance sensitive; the actual performance of compiled code depends heavily on the compiler's ability to optimize for specific processor and system features. These changes affect the way that we build compilers; they should also affect the way that we teach compiler construction.

Compiler development today focuses on optimization and on code generation. A new hire in a compiler group is far more likely to port a code generator to a new processor or modify an optimization pass than to work on a scanner or parser. Preparing students to enter this environment is a real challenge. Successful compiler writers must be familiar with current best-practice techniques in optimization and code generation. They must also have the background and intuition to understand new techniques as they appear during the coming years. Our goal in writing *Engineering a Compiler* (EAC) has been to create a text and a course that exposes students to the critical issues in modern compilers and provides them with the background to tackle those problems.

MOTIVATION FOR STUDYING COMPILER CONSTRUCTION

Compiler construction brings together techniques from disparate parts of computer science. At its simplest, a compiler is just a large computer program. A compiler takes a source-language program and translates it for execution on some target architecture. As part of this translation, the compiler must perform syntax analysis to determine if the input program is valid. To map that input program onto the finite resources of a target computer, the compiler must manipulate several distinct name spaces, allocate several different kinds of resources, and orchestrate the behavior of multiple run-time data structures. For the output program to have reasonable performance, it must manage hardware latencies in functional units, predict the flow of execution and the demand for memory, and reason about the independence and dependence of different machine-level operations in the program.

Open up a modern optimizing compiler and you will find greedy heuristic searches that explore large solution spaces, deterministic finite automata that recognize words in the input, fixed-point algorithms that help reason about program behavior, simple theorem provers and algebraic simplifiers that try to predict the values of expressions, pattern-matchers that map abstract computations to machine-level operations, solvers for diophantine equations and Pressburger arithmetic used to analyze array subscripts, and such classic algorithms and data-structures as hash tables, graph algorithms, and sparse set implementations.

BALANCE

Our primary goal in writing *Engineering a Compiler* (EAC) has been to create a text for use in an introductory course on the design and implementation of compilers. EAC lays out many of the problems that face compiler writers and explores some of the techniques used by compiler writers to solve them. EAC presents a pragmatic selection of practical techniques that you might use to build a modern compiler.

In selecting material for EAC, we have deliberately rebalanced the curriculum for a first course in compiler construction to cover the material that a student will need in the job market. This shift reduces the coverage of front-end issues in favor of increased coverage of optimization and code generation. In these latter areas, EAC focuses on best-practice techniques such as static single-assignment form, list scheduling, and graph-coloring register allocation. These topics prepare students for the algorithms that they will encounter in a modern commercial or research compiler.

The book also includes material for the advanced student or the practicing professional. Most chapters include an *Advanced Topics* section that discusses issues and techniques that are beyond a typical undergraduate course. In addition, Chapters 9 and 10 introduce data-flow analysis and scalar optimization in greater depth than a typical undergraduate course will cover. Including this material in EAC makes it available to the more advanced or curious student; professionals may also find these chapters useful as they try to implement some of the techniques.

APPROACH

Compiler construction is an exercise in engineering design. The compiler writer must choose a path through a design space that is filled with diverse alternatives, each with distinct costs, advantages, and complexity. Each decision has an impact on the resulting compiler. The quality of the end product depends on informed decisions at each step along the way.

Thus, there is no single right answer for many of the design decisions in a compiler. Even within "well understood" and "solved" problems, nuances in design and implementation have an impact on both the behavior of the compiler and the quality of the code that it produces. Many considerations play into each decision. As an example, the choice of an intermediate representation for the compiler has a profound impact on the rest of the compiler, from time and space requirements through the ease with which different algorithms can be applied. The decision, however, is often given short shrift. Chapter 5 examines the space of intermediate representations and some of the issues that should be considered in selecting one. We raise the issue again at several points in the book—both directly in the text and indirectly in the exercises.

EAC tries to explore the design space and convey both the depth of the problems and the breadth of the possible solutions. It presents some of the ways that problems have been solved, along with the constraints that made those solutions attractive. A student needs to understand both the parameters of the problems and their solutions, as well as the impact of those decisions on other facets of the compiler's design. Only then can the compiler writer make informed and intelligent choices.

PHILOSOPHY

This text exposes our philosophy for how compilers should be built, developed in more than twenty years each of research, teaching, and practice. For example, intermediate representations should expose those details that matter in the final code; this belief leads to a bias toward low-level representations. Values should reside in registers until the allocator discovers that it cannot keep them there; this practice produces examples that use virtual registers and store values to memory only when it cannot be avoided. It also increases the importance of effective algorithms in the compiler's back end. Every compiler should include optimization; it simplifies the rest of the compiler.

EAC departs from some of the accepted conventions for compiler construction textbooks. For example, we use several different programming languages in the examples. It makes little sense to describe call-by-name parameter passing in c, so we use Algol-60. It makes little sense to describe tail-recursion in FORTRAN, so we use Scheme. This multilingual approach is realistic; over the course of the reader's career, the "language of the future" will change several times.[1] Algorithms in EAC are presented at a reasonably high level of abstraction. We assume that the reader can fill in the details and that those details might be tailored to the specific environment in which the code will run.

ORGANIZING THE TEXT

In writing EAC, our overriding goal has been to create a textbook that prepares a student to work on real compilers. We have taught the material in this text for a decade or more, experimenting with the selection, depth, and order. The course materials available on the website show how we adapt and teach the contents of EAC in the undergraduate course at Rice University.

The desire to teach modern code generation techniques complicates the problem of ordering the material. Modern code generators rely heavily on ideas from optimization, such as data-flow analysis and static single-assignment form. This dependence suggests teaching optimization before covering back-end algorithms. Covering optimization before any discussion of code generation means that a student may not see the code generated for a case statement, a loop, or an array reference before trying to improve that code.

Since no linear ordering of the material is perfect, EAC presents the material, to the extent possible, in the order that the algorithms execute at compile time. Thus, optimization follows the front end and precedes the back end, even though the discussion of code shape is part of the back end material. The chapter opening graphic serves as a reminder of this order. In practice, an undergraduate course will take some of the material out of order.

---

1. Over the past thirty years, Algol-68, APL, PL/I, Smalltalk, C, Modula-3, C++, Java, and even ADA have been hailed as the language of the future.

Content

After the introduction (Chapter 1), the text divides into four sections.

Front End. Successive chapters in the first section present scanning, parsing, and context-sensitive analysis. Chapter 2 introduces recognizers, finite automata, regular expressions, and the algorithms for automating the construction of a scanner from a regular expression. Chapter 3 describes parsing, with context-free grammars, top-down recursive-descent parsers, and bottom-up, table-driven, LR(1) parsers. Chapter 4 introduces type systems as an example of a practical problem that is too complex to express in a context-free grammar. It then shows both formal and ad hoc techniques for solving such context-sensitive problems.

These chapters show a progression. In scanning, automation has replaced hand coding. In parsing, automation has dramatically reduced the programmer's effort. In context-sensitive analysis, automation has not replaced ad hoc, hand-coded methods. However, those ad hoc techniques mimic some of the intuitions behind one of the formal techniques, the use of attribute grammars.

Infrastructure. The second section brings together material that is often scattered throughout the course. It provides background knowledge needed to generate intermediate code in the front end, to optimize that code, and to transform it into code for a target machine.

Chapter 5 describes a variety of intermediate representations that compilers use, including trees, graphs, linear codes, and symbol tables. Chapter 6 introduces the run-time abstractions that a compiler must implement with the code that it generates, including procedures, name spaces, linkage conventions, and memory management. Chapter 7 provides a prelude to code generation, focusing on what kind of code the compiler should generate for various language constructs rather than on the algorithms to generate that code.

Optimization. The third section covers issues that arise in building an optimizer, a compiler's middle section. Chapter 8 provides an overview of the problems and techniques of optimization by working one problem at several different scopes. Chapter 9 introduces iterative data-flow analysis and presents the construction of static single-assignment form. Chapter 10 shows an effects-based taxonomy for scalar optimization and then populates the taxonomy with selected examples.

This division reflects the fact that a full treatment of analysis and optimization may not fit into a single-semester course, while making the material available in the book for the more advanced or curious student. In teaching this material, we cover Chapter 8 and then move on to code generation. During code generation, we refer back to specific sections in Chapters 9 and 10 as the need or interest arises. We also use this section of the book, augmented with a selection of papers, to teach a second course on scalar optimization.

Code Generation. The final section looks at the three primary problems in code generation. Chapter 11 covers instruction selection; it begins with tree-pattern matching and then delves into peephole-style matchers. Chapter 12 examines instruction scheduling; it focuses on list scheduling and its variants. Chapter 13 presents register allocation; it gives an in-depth treatment of algorithms for both local and global allocation. The algorithms that EAC presents are techniques that a student might find used inside a modern compiler.

For some students, these chapters are the first time that they must approximate the solution to an NP-complete problem rather than prove it equivalent to three-satisfiability. The chapters emphasize best-practice approximation algorithms. The exercises give students the opportunity to work tractable examples.

Crosscutting Ideas. Compiler construction is a complex, multifaceted discipline. Due to the sequential flow of information in a compiler, solutions chosen for one problem determine the input that later phases see and the opportunities that those phases have to improve the code. Small changes made in the front end can hide opportunities for optimization; the results of optimization have a direct impact on the code generator (changing, for example, the demand for registers). The complex, interrelated nature of design decisions in a compiler are one reason that this material is often used in a capstone course for undergraduates.

These complex relationships also arise in a compiler construction course. Solution techniques appear again and again in the course. Fixed-point algorithms play a critical role in the construction of scanners and parsers. They are a primary tool for the analyses that support optimization and code generation. Finite automata arise in scanning. They play a key role in the LR(1) table construction and, again, in pattern matchers for instruction selection. By identifying and emphasizing these common techniques, EAC makes them familiar. Thus, when a student encounters the iterative data-flow algorithm in

Chapter 8, it is just another fixed-point algorithm and, thus, familiar. Similarly, the discussion on the scope of optimization in Chapter 8 is reinforced by the transition from local algorithms to regional or global algorithms in Chapters 12 and 13.

ORGANIZING THE COURSE

A class in compiler construction offers both student and teacher the opportunity to explore all these issues in the context of a concrete application—one whose basic functions are well understood by any student with the background for a compiler construction course. In some curricula, the course serves as a capstone course for seniors, tying together concepts from many other courses in a practice-oriented project course. Students in such a class might write a complete compiler for a simple language or add support for a new language feature to an existing compiler such as GCC or the ORC compiler for the IA-64. This class might present the material in a linear order that closely follows the text's organization.

If other courses in the curriculum give students the experience of large projects, the teacher can focus the compiler construction course more narrowly on algorithms and their implementation. In such a class, the labs can focus on abstracted instances of truly hard problems, such as register allocation and scheduling. This class might skip around in the text, adjusting the order of presentation to meet the needs of the labs. For example, any student who has done assembly-language programming can write a register allocator for straightline code. We have often used a simple register allocator as the first lab.

In either scenario, the course should draw material from other classes. Obvious connections exist to computer organization and assembly-language programming, operating systems, computer architecture, algorithms, and formal languages. Although the connections from compiler construction to other courses may be less obvious, they are no less important. Character copying, as discussed in Chapter 7, plays a critical role in the performance of applications that include network protocols, file servers, and web servers. The techniques developed in Chapter 2 for scanning have applications that range from text editing through URL-filtering. The bottom-up local register allocator in Chapter 13 is recognizable as a cousin of the optimal offline page replacement algorithm.

Supporting Materials

Morgan Kaufmann's website for the book contains a variety of resources that should help you adapt the material presented in EAC to your course. The web site includes

1. a complete set of lectures for the course as taught at Rice University;

2. example lab assignments from a capstone-project version of the course;

3. example lab assignments from the course as taught at Rice;

4. an instructor's manual that contains solutions for the exercises;

5. a glossary of abbreviations, acronyms, and terms defined in EAC;

6. single-page copies of the line art from the book; and

7. the syllabus and lectures for a course on scalar optimization taught from the optimization section of EAC and a selection of recent papers.

THE ART AND SCIENCE OF COMPILER CONSTRUCTION

The lore of compiler construction includes both amazing success stories about the application of theory to practice and humbling stories about the limits of what we can do. On the success side, modern scanners are built by applying the theory of regular languages to automatic construction of recognizers. LR parsers use the same techniques to perform the handle-recognition that drives a shift-reduce parser. Data-flow analysis (and its cousins) apply lattice theory to the analysis of programs in ways that are both useful and clever. The approximation algorithms used in code generation produce good solutions to many instances of truly hard problems.

On the other side, compiler construction exposes some complex problems that defy good solutions. The back end of a compiler for a modern superscalar machine must approximate the solution to two or more interacting NP-complete problems (instruction scheduling, register allocation, and, perhaps, instruction and data placement). These NP-complete problems, however, look easy next to problems such as algebraic reassociation of expressions (see, for example, Figure 7.1). This problem admits a huge number of solutions; to make matters worse, the desired solution depends on the other transformations that the compiler applies. While the compiler attempts to solve these problems (or approximate their solutions), it must run in a reasonable amount of time and consume a modest amount of space. Thus, a good compiler for a modern superscalar machine must artfully blend theory, practical knowledge, engineering, and experience.

In this book, we have tried to convey both the art and the science of compiler construction. EAC includes a sufficiently broad selection of material to show the reader that real tradeoffs exist and that the impact of those choices can be both subtle and far-reaching. EAC omits techniques that have been rendered less important by changes in the marketplace, in the technology of languages and compilers, or in the availability of tools. Instead, EAC provides a deeper treatment of optimization and code generation.

ACKNOWLEDGMENTS

Many people have provided us with useful feedback on the form, content, and exposition of EAC. Among these are L. Almagor, Saman Amarasinghe, Thomas Ball, Preston Briggs, Corky Cartwright, Carolyn Cooper, Christine Cooper, Anshuman Das Gupta, Jason Eckhardt, Stephan Ellner, Mike Fagan, Matthias Felleisen, Alex Grosul, John Greiner, Dan Grossman, Timothy Harvey, James Larus, Ken Kennedy, Shriram Krishnamurthy, Ursula Kuterbach, Robert Morgan, Guilherme Ottoni, Vishal Patel, Norm Ramsey, Steve Reeves, Martin Rinard, L. Taylor Simpson, Reid Tatge, Dan Wallach, Todd Waterman, and Christian Westbrook.

Steve Carr served as exercise editor; he coordinated a team that produced the exercises. His team included Chen Ding, Rodolfo Jardim de Azevedo, Zhiyuan Li, Guilherme Ottoni, and Sandra Rigo. Aaron Smith, Ben Hardekopf, and Paul A. Navratil checked the exercise solutions. The manuscript went through many rounds of review and revision; Saman Amarasinghe, Guido Araujo, Preston Briggs, Steve Carr, James Larus, Gloria Melara, Kathryn McKinley, Robert Morgan, Thomas Murtagh, Gordon Novak, Santosh Pande, Allan Porterfield, Martin Rinard, Mark Roberts, Michael Smith, and Hongwei Xi all served as reviewers. Wilson Hsieh, Jurek Jaromczyk, Tevfik Bultan, Chau-Wen Tseng, Mahmut Kandemir, and Zhiyuan Li all tested the book in their classrooms, as did several members of the exercise team and the reviewing team. Their work improved this volume, changing its style and its contents and improving its accuracy.

Michael Scott and Steve Muchnick each reviewed the complete manuscript several times. Their attention to detail, their patience, and their suggestions substantially improved this book.

The editorial and production team that Morgan Kaufmann put together for this book has been wonderful. The team, led by Denise Penrose and Yonie Overton, includes John Hammet, Carol Leyba, Rebecca Evans, Steve Rath, Emilia Thiuri, and Lauren Wheelock. The illustrations were redrawn by a team at Dartmouth Publishing; the composition work was done by a team at Integra. As authors, we could not ask for a more flexible, skilled, or patient group of people. Their suggestions and insights improved the book; their professionalism made the process of producing it substantially easier.

Finally, many people have provided us with intellectual and emotional support over the last five years. First and foremost, our families and our colleagues at Rice have encouraged us at every step of the way. In addition, Regina Brooks and Janice Bordeaux encouraged us to start this effort. Denise Penrose and Yonie Overton made it possible for us to finish it. We are deeply indebted to Kathryn O'Brien for undertaking the many administrative tasks that arise in a project of this size and for keeping a sense of humor through it all. Finally, Ken Kennedy and Scott Warren have both shaped the way that we think about programming, about language issues, and about compilation.

CHAPTER 1

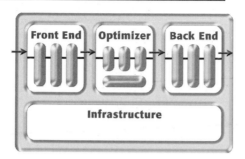

Overview of Compilation

1.1 INTRODUCTION

The role of computers in daily life is growing each year. Modern microprocessors are found in cars, microwave ovens, dishwashers, mobile telephones, GPS navigation systems, video games, and personal computers. These computers perform their jobs by executing programs—sequences of operations written in a "programming language." The programming language is a formal language with mathematical properties and well-defined meanings, as opposed to a natural language with evolved properties and ambiguities. Programming languages are designed for expressiveness, conciseness, and clarity. Programming languages are designed to specify computations—to record a sequence of actions that perform a particular computational task or produce a specific computational result.

Before a program can execute, it must be translated into a set of operations that are defined on the target computer. This translation is done by a specialized program called a *compiler*. The compiler takes as input the specification for an executable program and produces as output the specification for another, equivalent executable program. Of course, if it finds errors in the input program, the compiler should produce an appropriate set of error messages. Viewed as a black box, a compiler might look like this:

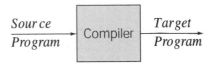

Typically, the "source" language that the compiler accepts is a programming language, such as FORTRAN, C, C++, Ada, Java, or ML. The "target" language is usually the instruction set of some computer system.

Some compilers produce a target program written in a full-fledged programming language rather than the assembly language of some computer. The programs that these compilers produce require further translation before they can execute directly on a computer. Many research compilers produce C programs as their output. Because compilers for C are available on most computers, this makes the target program executable on all those systems, at the cost of an extra compilation for the final target. Compilers that target programming languages rather than the instruction set of a computer are often called *source-to-source translators*.

Many other systems qualify as compilers. For example, a typesetting program that produces PostScript can be considered a compiler. It takes as input a specification for how the document should look on the printed page and it produces as output a PostScript file. PostScript is simply a language for describing images. Since the typesetting program takes an executable specification and produces another executable specification, it is a compiler.

The code that turns PostScript into pixels is typically an *interpreter*, not a compiler. An interpreter takes as input an executable specification and produces as output the result of executing the specification.

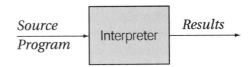

Interpreters can be used to implement programming languages as well. For some languages, such as Perl, Scheme, and APL, interpreters are more common than compilers.

Interpreters and compilers have much in common. They perform many of the same tasks. Both examine the input program and determine whether or not it is a valid program. Both build an internal model of the structure and meaning of the program. Both determine where to store values during execution. However, interpreting the code to produce a result is quite different from emitting a translated program that can be executed to produce the result. This book focuses on the problems that arise in building compilers. However, an implementor of interpreters may find much of the material relevant.

1.2 WHY STUDY COMPILER CONSTRUCTION?

A compiler is a large, complex program. Compilers often include hundreds of thousands, if not millions, of lines of code. Their many parts have complex interactions. Design decisions made for one part of the compiler have important ramifications for other parts. Thus, the design and implementation of a compiler is a substantial exercise in software engineering.

A good compiler contains a microcosm of computer science. It makes practical application of greedy algorithms (register allocation), heuristic search techniques (list scheduling), graph algorithms (dead-code elimination), dynamic programming (instruction selection), finite automata and push-down automata (scanning and parsing), and fixed-point algorithms (data-flow analysis). It deals with problems such as dynamic allocation, synchronization, naming, locality, memory hierarchy management, and pipeline scheduling. Few software systems make as many complex and diverse components work together to achieve a single purpose. Working inside a compiler provides practical experience in software engineering that is hard to obtain with smaller, less intricate systems.

Compilers play a fundamental role in the central activity of computer science: preparing problems for solution by computer. Most software is compiled; the correctness of that process and the efficiency of the resulting code have a direct impact on our ability to build large systems. Most students are not satisfied with reading about these ideas; many of the ideas must be implemented to be appreciated. Thus, the study of compiler construction is an important component of a computer science education.

The lore of compiler construction includes many success stories. Formal language theory has led to tools that automate the production of scanners and parsers. These same tools and techniques find application in text searching, website filtering, word processing, and command-language interpreters. Type checking and static analysis apply results from lattice theory, number theory, and other branches of mathematics to understand and improve programs. Code generators uses algorithms for tree-pattern matching, parsing, dynamic programming, and text matching to automate the selection of instructions.

At the same time, the history of compiler construction includes its share of humbling experiences. Compilation includes problems that are truly hard. Attempts to design a high-level, universal, intermediate representation have foundered on complexity. Several parts of the process have resisted automation—at least, automatic techniques have not yet replaced hand-coded solutions. In many cases, we have had to resort to ad hoc methods. The dominant method for instruction scheduling is a greedy algorithm with several layers of tie-breaking heuristics. While it is obvious that the compiler can use commutativity and associativity to improve the code, most compilers that try to do so simply rearrange the expression into some canonical order.

Building a successful compiler requires a blend of algorithms, engineering insights, and careful planning. Good compilers approximate the solutions to hard problems. They emphasize efficiency—in their own implementations and in the code they generate. They have internal data structures and knowledge representations that expose the right level of detail—enough to allow strong optimization, but not enough to force the compiler to wallow in detail.

1.3 THE FUNDAMENTAL PRINCIPLES OF COMPILATION

Compilers are engineered objects—large software systems built with distinct goals. Building a compiler requires myriad design decisions, each of which has an impact on the resulting compiler. While many issues in compiler design are amenable to several different solutions, there are two principles that should not be compromised. The first principle that a compiler must observe is inviolable.

The compiler must preserve the meaning of the program being compiled.

Correctness is a fundamental issue in programming. The compiler must preserve correctness by faithfully implementing the "meaning" of its input program. This principle lies at the heart of the social contract between the compiler writer and compiler user. If the compiler can take liberties with meaning, then why not simply generate a nop or a return? If an incorrect translation is acceptable, why expend the effort to get it right?

The second principle that a compiler must observe is practical.

The compiler must improve the input program in some discernible way.

A traditional compiler improves upon the input program by making it directly executable on some target machine. Other "compilers" improve their input in different ways. For example, tpic is a program that takes the specification for a drawing written in the graphics language pic and converts it into LaTeX; the "improvement" lies in LaTeX's greater availability and generality. Some compilers produce output programs in the same language as their input; we call these source-to-source translators. In general, these systems rewrite a program in a way that will lead to an improvement when the program is finally translated into code for some target machine. If the compiler does not improve the code in some way, why should anyone invoke it?

1.4 COMPILER STRUCTURE

A compiler is a large and complex software system. The compiler community has been building compilers since 1955; over those years, we have learned many lessons about how to structure a compiler. Earlier, we depicted a compiler as a single box that translates a source program into a target program. Reality, of course, is more complex than that simple picture.

As this single-box model suggests, a compiler must both understand the source program presented for compilation and map its functionality to the target machine. The distinct nature of these two tasks suggests a division of labor and leads to a design that decomposes compilation into two major pieces: a *front end* and a *back end*.

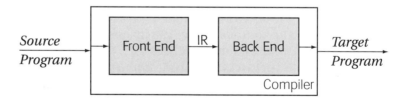

The front end focuses on understanding the source-language program. The back end focuses on mapping programs to the target machine. This separation of concerns has several important implications for the design and implementation of compilers.

The front end must encode its knowledge of the source program in some structure for later use by the back end. This *intermediate representation* (IR) becomes the compiler's definitive representation for the code it is translating. At each point in compilation, the compiler will have a definitive representation. It may, in fact, use several different IRs as compilation progresses, but at each point, one representation will be the definitive IR. We think of the definitive IR as the version of the program passed between independent phases of the compiler, like the IR passed from the front end to the back end in the preceding drawing.

In a two-phase compiler, the front end must ensure that the source program is well formed, and it must map that code into the IR. The back end must map the IR program into the instruction set and the finite resources of the target machine. Since the back end only processes IR created by the front end, it can assume that the IR contains no syntactic or semantic errors.

The compiler can make multiple passes over the IR form of the code before emitting the target program. This should lead to better code; the compiler can, in effect, study the code in its first phase and record relevant details. Then, in the second phase, it can use these recorded facts to improve the quality of translation. (This idea is not new. The original FORTRAN compiler made several passes over the code.) This strategy requires that knowledge derived in the first pass be recorded in the IR where the second pass can find and use it.

Finally, the two-phase structure may simplify the process of retargeting the compiler. We can easily envision constructing multiple back ends for a single front end to produce compilers that accept the same language but target different machines. Similarly, we can envision front ends for different languages producing the same IR and using a common back end. Both scenarios assume that one IR can serve for several combinations of source and target; in practice, both language-specific and machine-specific details usually find their way into the IR.

Introducing an IR makes it possible to add more phases to compilation. The compiler writer can insert a third phase between the front end and the back end. This middle section, or *optimizer*, takes an IR program as its input and produces an equivalent IR program as its output. By using the IR as an interface, the compiler writer can insert this third phase with minimal disruption to the front end and the back end. This leads to the following compiler structure, termed a *three-phase compiler*.

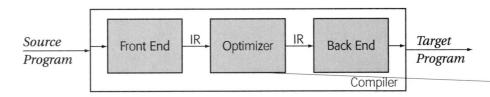

The optimizer is an IR-to-IR transformer that tries to improve the IR program in some way. (Notice that these transformers are, themselves, compilers according to our definition in Section 1.1.) The optimizer can make one or more passes over the IR, analyze the IR, and rewrite the IR. The optimizer may rewrite the IR in a way that is likely to produce a faster target program from the back end or a smaller target program from the back end. It may have other objectives, such as a program that produces fewer page faults or uses less power.

Conceptually, this three-phase structure represents the classic optimizing compiler. In practice, the phases are divided internally into a series of passes. The front end consists of two or three passes that handle the details of recognizing valid source-language programs and producing the initial IR form of the program. The middle section contains several passes that perform different optimizations. The number and purpose of these passes vary from compiler to compiler. The back end consists of a series of passes, each of which takes the IR program one step closer to the target machine's instruction set. The three phases and their individual passes share a common infrastructure. This structure is shown in Figure 1.1.

In practice, the conceptual division of a compiler into three phases, a front end, a middle section, and a back end, is useful. The problems addressed by these phases are different. The front end is concerned with understanding the source program and recording the results of its analysis into IR form. The middle section focuses on improving the IR form. The back end must map the transformed IR program onto the bounded resources of the target machine in a way that leads to efficient use of those resources.

Of these three phases, the middle section has the murkiest description. The term *optimization* implies that the compiler discovers an optimal solution to some problem. The issues and problems that arise in optimization are so complex and so interrelated that they cannot, in practice, be solved

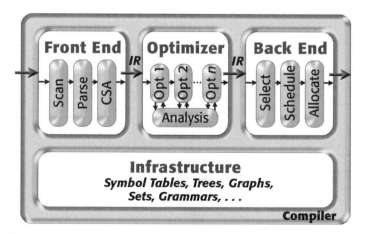

FIGURE 1.1   Structure of a Typical Compiler

optimally. Furthermore, the actual behavior of the compiled code depends on interactions among all of the techniques applied in the optimizer and the back end. Thus, even if a single technique can be proved optimal, its interactions with other techniques may produce less than optimal results. As a result, a good optimizing compiler can improve the quality of the code, relative to an unoptimized version. It will almost always fail to produce optimal code.

The middle section can be a single monolithic pass that applies one or more optimizations to improve the code, or it can be structured as a series of smaller passes with each pass reading and writing IR. The monolithic structure may be more efficient. The multipass structure may lend itself to a less complex implementation and a simpler approach to debugging the compiler. It also creates the flexibility to employ different sets of optimization in different situations. The choice between these two approaches depends on the constraints under which the compiler is built and operates.

1.5 HIGH-LEVEL VIEW OF TRANSLATION

To gain a better understanding of the tasks that arise in compilation, consider what must be done to generate executable code for the following expression:

$$w \leftarrow w \times 2 \times x \times y \times z$$

where w, x, y, and z are variables, $\leftarrow$ indicates an assignment, and $\times$ is the operator for multiplication. To learn what facts the compiler must discover and what questions it must answer, we will trace the path that a compiler takes to turn such a simple program into executable code.

1.5.1 Understanding the Input

The first step in compiling $w \leftarrow w \times 2 \times x \times y \times z$ is to determine whether or not these characters form a legal sentence in the programming language. This job falls to the compiler's front end. It involves both form, or *syntax*, and meaning, or *semantics*. If the program is well formed in both these respects, the compiler can continue with translation, optimization, and code generation. If it is not well formed, the compiler should report back to the user with a clear error message that isolates the problems with the sentence, to the extent possible.

NOTATION

Compiler books are, in essence, about notation. After all, a compiler translates a program written in one notation into an equivalent program written in another notation. A number of notational issues will arise in your reading of this book. In some cases, these issues will directly affect your understanding of the material.

Expressing Algorithms We have tried to keep the algorithms concise. Algorithms are written at a relatively high level, assuming that the reader can supply implementation details. They are written in a *slanted, sans-serif font*. Indentation is both deliberate and significant; this matters most in an *if-then-else* construct. Indented code after a *then* or an *else* forms a block. In the following code fragment

```
if Action [s,word] = "shift sᵢ" then
    push word
    push sᵢ
    word ← NextWord()
else if · · ·
```

all the statements between the *then* and the *else* are part of the *then* clause of the *if-then-else* construct. When a clause in an *if-then-else* construct contains just one statement, we write the keyword *then* or *else* on the same line as the statement.

Writing Code In some examples, we show actual program text written in some language chosen to demonstrate a particular point. Actual program text is written in a `typewriter` font.

Arithmetic Operators Finally, we have forsaken the traditional use of $*$ for $\times$ and of $/$ for $\div$, except in actual program text. The meaning should be clear to the reader.

Checking Syntax

To check the syntax of the input program, the compiler must compare the program's structure against a definition for the language. This requires an appropriate formal definition, an efficient mechanism for testing whether or not the input meets that definition, and a plan for how to proceed on an illegal input.

Mathematically, the source language is a set, usually infinite, of strings defined by some finite set of rules, called a *grammar*. In a compiler's front end, the scanner and the parser determine whether the input program is, in fact, an element of that set of valid strings. The engineering challenge is to make this membership test efficient.

Grammars for programming languages usually refer to words by their parts of speech, or syntactic categories. Basing the grammar rules on parts of speech lets a single rule describe many sentences. For example, in English, many sentences have the form

Sentence → *Subject* verb *Object* endmark

where verb and endmark are parts of speech, and *Sentence*, *Subject*, and *Object* are syntactic variables. *Sentence* represents any string with the form described by this rule. The symbol "→" reads "derives" and means that an instance of the right-hand side can be abstracted to the syntactic variable on the left-hand side.

To apply this rule, the user must map words to their parts of speech. For example, verb represents the set of all English-language verbs, and endmark represents all sentence-ending punctuation marks, such as a period, a question mark, or an exclamation point. For English, the reader generally recognizes several thousand words and knows the possible parts of speech that each can fulfill. For an unfamiliar word, the reader consults a dictionary. Thus, the syntax of this example is described with a set of rules, or grammar, and a system for finding words and classifying them into syntactic categories.

This specification-based approach to defining syntax is critical to compilation. We cannot build a front end that contains an infinite set of rules or an infinite set of sentences. Instead, we need a finite set of rules that generate or specify the sentences in our language. As we shall see in Chapters 2 and 3, the finite nature of a grammar does not limit the expressiveness of the language.

To understand whether the sentence "Compilers are engineered objects." is, in fact, a valid English sentence, we first establish that each word exists in English with a dictionary lookup. Next, each word is replaced by its syntactic category to create a somewhat more abstract representation of the sentence:

```
noun verb adjective noun endmark
```

Finally, we try to fit this sequence of abstracted words into the rules for an English sentence. A working knowledge of English grammar might include the following rules:

1	*Sentence*	→	*Subject* verb *Object* endmark
2	*Subject*	→	noun
3	*Subject*	→	*Modifier* noun
4	*Object*	→	noun
5	*Object*	→	*Modifier* noun
6	*Modifier*	→	adjective
	. . .		

By inspection, we can discover the following *derivation* for our example sentence:

Rule	Prototype Sentence
—	*Sentence*
1	*Subject* verb *Object* endmark
2	noun verb *Object* endmark
5	noun verb *Modifier* noun endmark
6	noun verb adjective noun endmark

The derivation starts with the syntactic variable *Sentence*. At each step, it rewrites one term in the prototype sentence, replacing the term with a right-hand side that can be derived from that rule. The first step uses Rule 1 to replace *Sentence*. The second uses Rule 2 to replace *Subject*. The third replaces *Object* using Rule 5, while the final step rewrites *Modifier* with adjective according to Rule 6. At this point, the prototype sentence generated by the derivation matches the abstract representation of our input sentence.

This derivation proves that "Compilers are engineered objects." belongs to the language described by Rules 1 through 6. The process of discovering words in a string of characters and classifying them according to their parts of speech is called *scanning*. Discovering whether a stream of classified words has a derivation in some set of grammatical rules is called *parsing*. Scanning and parsing are the first two steps in compiling a program.

Of course, the scanner and parser might discover that the input is not a valid sentence. In this case, the compiler must report the error back to the user. It should provide concise and useful feedback that lets the user isolate and correct the syntactic error.

Checking Meaning

Syntactic correctness depends purely on parts of speech and the map from a word to its part of speech. It ignores the meanings of the words. The grammatical rules do not differentiate between two nouns, such as "compilers" and "rocks." Thus, the sentence "Rocks are engineered objects." is grammatically indistinguishable from "Compilers are engineered objects.", even though they have significantly different meanings. To understand the difference between these two sentences requires contextual knowledge about both software systems and geological objects.

Before the front end can translate an input program into the compiler's IR, it must determine that the program has a well-defined meaning. Syntax analysis can determine that the sentences are well formed, at the level of checking parts of speech against grammatical rules. Correctness and meaning, however, go deeper than that. In an English sentence, the reader must understand the words' definitions, their denotations, and their connotations. In a programming language, the compiler must ensure that variable names are used in a fashion consistent with their declarations. In both contexts, the analysis must look beyond the spelling of a word and its syntactic category.

A well-formed computer program specifies some computation. There are many ways in which the expression

$$w \leftarrow w \times 2 \times x \times y \times z$$

might be ill formed, beyond the obvious, syntactic ones. For example, one or more of the names might not be defined. The variable x might not have been declared. The variables y and z might be of different types that cannot be multiplied together.

In a compiler, such errors are discovered by *semantic analysis* or *context-sensitive analysis*. The latter term emphasizes the notion that the meaning of some part of the input may depend on the context that precedes it or follows it or both. A compiler's front end may contain a separate pass that performs semantic analysis, or that analysis may be folded into the parser. In either case, the process of examining the input for semantic errors derives critical information about the meaning of the program that shapes the IR form of the program generated by the compiler's front end.

Roadmap

Chapters 2 through 4 describe the algorithms and techniques that a compiler's front end uses to analyze the input program and determine whether it is well formed and to construct a representation of the code in some internal form. Chapter 5 and Appendix B explore the issues that arise in designing and implementing the internal structures used throughout the compiler. The front end builds many of these structures.

1.5.2 Creating and Maintaining the Run-Time Environment

A compiler implements the abstractions defined by the source language. Finding efficient ways to create these abstractions is an overarching concern in compilation. Consider our example, $w \leftarrow w \times 2 \times x \times y \times z$. It showcases one particular abstraction, symbolic names. The expression refers to w, x, y, and z. These names are not just values; w occurs on both the right-hand side and left-hand side of the assignment operator. It clearly has one value before execution of the expression and another afterward (unless $x \times y \times z = \frac{1}{2}$). Thus, w refers to the value stored in a named location, rather than to a specific value, such as 15.

The memories of modern computers are organized by numerical addresses, not textual names. Within the address space of an executing program, these addresses correspond uniquely to storage locations. In a source-level program, however, the programmer may create many distinct variables that have the same textual name. For example, many programs define the variables i, j, and k in several different procedures; they are common names for loop index variables. The compiler is responsible for mapping each use of the name j to the appropriate instance of j and, from there, to the storage location set aside for that instance of j. Computers do not have this kind of name space for storage locations; it is an abstraction created by the language designer and maintained by the compiler-generated code and its run-time environment.

To translate $w \leftarrow w \times 2 \times x \times y \times z$, the compiler must assign a storage location to each name. (We assume, for the moment, that the constant 2 needs no memory location, since it is a small integer and can probably be obtained using a load immediate instruction.) The compiler might keep the values for these names in memory by assigning each name an address, such as $\langle w, 0 \rangle$, $\langle x, 4 \rangle$, $\langle y, 8 \rangle$, and $\langle z, 12 \rangle$, assuming each value takes four bytes. Alternately, the compiler might elect to keep the variables in machine registers with a series of assignments such as $\langle w, r_1 \rangle$, $\langle x, r_2 \rangle$, $\langle y, r_3 \rangle$, and $\langle z, r_4 \rangle$.

The choice of storage location both depends on surrounding context and has an impact on it. Keeping w in a register will likely lead to faster execution. Unfortunately, the target machine provides only a limited set of registers; thus, there may not be enough registers to hold w. Alternately, the program may use w in a way that prevents the compiler from keeping it in a register.

Names are just one abstraction maintained by the compiler. Each programming language defines many abstractions, and programmers write code using those abstractions. (Implementations of QuickSort in Scheme, Java, and FORTRAN may look quite different.) These abstractions insulate programmers from the low-level details of the computer systems they use. Some abstractions are easy to implement; the mnemonic names in an assembly language map directly to target machine opcodes. Others are much harder to implement; the set-based abstractions in SETL require the compiler to infer efficient algorithms from high-level, set-theoretic operators.

To handle a complete programming language, the compiler must create and support a variety of abstractions. Procedures, parameters, names, lexical scopes, and control-flow operations are all abstractions designed into the source language. The compiler, in cooperation with other system software, creates and maintains an implementation of these abstractions on the target machine. The compiler must emit the appropriate instructions at compile time; the remainder involves interactions between the compiled code and the run-time environment that supports that code.

Designing and implementing a compiler involves the construction of a set of mechanisms that will create and maintain the necessary abstractions at run time. These mechanisms must deal with the layout and allocation of memory, with the transfer of control between procedures, with the transmission of values and the mapping of name spaces at procedure borders, and with interfaces to the world outside the compiler's control, including input and output devices, the operating system, and other running programs.

Roadmap

Chapter 6 explores the abstractions that the compiler must maintain to bridge the gap between the programming model embodied in the source language and the facilities provided by the operating system and the actual hardware. It describes algorithms and techniques that compilers use to implement the various abstractions contained in language definitions. It explores some of the issues that arise on the boundary between the compiler's realm and that of the operating system.

Chapter 7 creates a base of knowledge for the rest of the book. Optimization and code generation can only exploit details that the IR program exposes. Thus, specific decisions about what to represent and how to represent it have a strong impact on the effectiveness of the optimizer and on the quality of code that the code generator can produce. This chapter focuses on "code shape" and the set of choices that the compiler writer makes about how to implement particular source-language constructs.

```
                                            x ← · · ·
         x ← · · ·                          y ← · · ·
         y ← · · ·                          w ← 1
         w ← 1                              t ← 2 × x × y
         for i = 1 to n                     for i = 1 to n
           read z                             read z
           w ← w × 2 × x × y × z              w ← w × z × t
         end                                end

       Surrounding Context                Improved Code
```

FIGURE 1.2   Context Makes a Difference

1.5.3 Improving the Code

Often, a compiler can use contextual knowledge to improve the quality of code that it generates for a statement. If, as shown on the left side of Figure 1.2, the statement in our continuing example was embedded in a loop, the contextual information might let the compiler significantly improve the code. The compiler could recognize that the subexpression $2 \times x \times y$ is invariant in the loop—that is, its value does not change between iterations. Then the compiler could rewrite the code as shown on the right side of the figure. The transformed code performs many fewer operations in the loop body. If the loop executes more than once, the transformed code should run faster than the original.

This process of analyzing code to discover facts from context and using that knowledge to improve the code is often called *code optimization*. Roughly speaking, optimization consists of two distinct activities: analyzing the code to understand its run-time behavior and transforming the code to capitalize on knowledge derived during analysis. These techniques play a critical role in the performance of compiled code; the presence of a good optimizer can have a major impact on the design and implementation of the rest of the compiler.

Analysis

Compilers use several kinds of analysis to support transformations. *Data-flow analysis* involves reasoning, at compile time, about the flow of values at run time. Data-flow analyzers typically solve a system of simultaneous set equations that are derived from the structure of the code being translated. *Dependence analysis* uses number-theoretic tests to reason about the values that can be assumed by subscript expressions. It is used to disambiguate references to array elements.

Transformation

Many distinct transformations have been invented that try to improve the time or space requirements of executable code. Some, like discovering loop-invariant computations and moving them to less frequently executed locations, improve the running time of the program. Others make the code more compact. Transformations vary in their effect, the scope over which they operate, and the analysis required to support them. Often, a transformation is packaged together with the analysis needed to determine when it can be safely and profitably applied. We refer to this combination as an *optimization*.

Roadmap

Chapters 8 through 10 provide an introduction to the workings of an optimizer. Chapter 8 introduces the terminology of optimization through a detailed example, eliminating redundant computations. It presents algorithms that work across different scopes and that work in different ways. Chapter 9 provides an introduction to the field of data-flow analysis. It also presents an algorithm for building the static single-assignment form of a program. Chapter 10 presents a taxonomy for scalar transformations along with example optimizations from most categories in the taxonomy.

1.5.4 Creating the Output Program

The final stage of compilation is code generation. During code generation, the compiler traverses the IR form of the code and emits equivalent code for the target machine. It selects target-machine operations to implement each IR operation in the code. It chooses an order in which the operations will execute efficiently. It decides which values will reside in registers and which values will reside in memory and inserts code to enforce those decisions.

Instruction Selection

Instruction selection is the first stage of code generation. The code generator selects a sequence of machine instructions to implement the code being

About ILOC

Throughout the book, low-level examples are written in a notation that we call ILOC—an acronym derived from "intermediate language for an optimizing compiler." Over the years, this notation has undergone many changes. The version used in this book is described in detail in Appendix A.

Think of ILOC as the assembly language for a simple RISC machine. It has a standard set of operations. Most operations take arguments that are registers. The memory operations, loads and stores, transfer values between memory and the registers. To simplify the exposition in the text, most examples assume that all data consists of integers.

Each operation has a set of operands and a target. The operation is written in five parts: an operation name, a list of operands, a separator, a list of targets, and an optional comment. Thus, to add registers 1 and 2, leaving the result in register 3, the programmer would write

```
add r₁,r₂ ⇒ r₃    // example instruction
```

The separator, $\Rightarrow$, precedes the target list. It is a visual reminder that information flows from left to right. In particular, it disambiguates cases where a person reading the assembly-level text can easily confuse operands and targets. (See loadAI and storeAI in the following table.)

The example in Figure 1.3 only uses four ILOC operations:

ILOC Operation	Meaning
loadAI $r_1, c_2 \Rightarrow r_3$	Memory$(r_1 + c_2) \rightarrow r_3$
loadI $c_1 \Rightarrow r_2$	$c_1 \rightarrow r_2$
mult $r_1, r_2 \Rightarrow r_3$	$r_1 \times r_2 \rightarrow r_3$
storeAI $r_1 \Rightarrow r_2, c_3$	$r_1 \rightarrow$ Memory$(r_2 + c_2)$

Appendix A contains a more detailed description of ILOC. The examples consistently use the name r_{arp} as a register that contains the start of data storage for the current procedure or the *activation record pointer*.

compiled. In preparing the statement w ← w × 2 × x × y × z, to execute on an ILOC virtual machine, the compiler might choose the operations shown in Figure 1.3. This code assumes that w, x, y, and z are located at offsets @w, @x, @y, and @z from an address contained in the register r_{arp}.

```
loadAI    r_arp, @w ⇒ r_w        // load 'w'
loadI     2         ⇒ r_2        // constant 2 into r_2
loadAI    r_arp, @x ⇒ r_x        // load 'x'
loadAI    r_arp, @y ⇒ r_y        // load 'y'
loadAI    r_arp, @z ⇒ r_z        // load 'z'
mult      r_w, r_2  ⇒ r_w        // r_w ← w × 2
mult      r_w, r_x  ⇒ r_w        // r_w ← (w × 2) × x
mult      r_w, r_y  ⇒ r_w        // r_w ← (w × 2 × x) × y
mult      r_w, r_z  ⇒ r_w        // r_w ← (w × 2 × x × y) × z
storeAI   r_w       ⇒ r_arp, 0   // write r_w back to 'w'
```

FIGURE 1.3   Code for $w \leftarrow x \times 2 \times y \times z$ in ILOC

This sequence is straightforward. It loads all of the relevant values into registers, performs the multiplications in order, and stores the result to the memory location for w. It assumes an unlimited supply of registers and names them with symbolic names such as r_w to hold w and r_{arp} to hold the address where the data storage for our named values begins. Implicitly, the instruction selector relies on the register allocator to map these symbolic register names, or virtual registers, to the actual registers of the target machine.

Depending on the properties of the target machine, the instruction-selection pass might make other choices. For example, if an immediate-multiply operation (multI) is available, the operation $mult\ r_w, r_2 \Rightarrow r_w$ could be replaced with $multI\ r_w, 2 \Rightarrow r_w$, eliminating the need for the operation $loadI\ 2 \Rightarrow r_2$ and reducing the number of registers needed. If addition is faster than multiplication, that operation could be replaced with $add\ r_w, r_w \Rightarrow r_w$, avoiding both the loadI and its use of r_2, as well as replacing the mult with a faster add.

Register Allocation

During instruction selection, the compiler deliberately ignored the fact that the target machine has a limited set of registers. Instead, it used an unlimited set of *virtual registers* and assumed that "enough" registers existed. In practice, the earlier stages of compilation may create many more virtual registers than the hardware can support. The task of mapping those virtual registers to actual target-machine registers falls to the register allocator.

The register allocator decides which values should reside in the target machine's registers at each point in the code. It then modifies the code to reflect its decisions. For example, a register allocator that tried to minimize the number of registers used might rewrite the code from Figure 1.3 as follows:

```
loadAI   r_arp, @w ⇒ r_1          // load 'w'
add      r_1, r_1  ⇒ r_1          // r_1 ← w × 2
loadAI   r_arp, @x ⇒ r_2          // load 'x'
mult     r_1, r_2  ⇒ r_1          // r_1 ← (w × 2) × x
loadAI   r_arp, @y ⇒ r_2          // load 'y'
mult     r_1, r_2  ⇒ r_1          // r_1 ← (w × 2 × x) × y
loadAI   r_arp, @z ⇒ r_2          // load 'z'
mult     r_1,r_2   ⇒ r_1          // r_1 ← (w × 2 × x × y) × z
storeAI  r_1       ⇒ r_arp, @w    // write r_w back to 'w'
```

This sequence uses three registers instead of six.

Minimizing register use may be counterproductive. If, for example, any of the named values, w, x, y, or z, are already in registers, the code should reference those registers directly. If all are in registers, the sequence could be implemented so that it required no additional registers. Alternatively, if some nearby expression also computed w × 2, it might be better to preserve that value in a register than to recompute it later. This would increase demand for registers but eliminate a later instruction.

The problem of allocating an arbitrary set of values to a bounded set of machine registers in a way that minimizes loads and stores is NP-complete. Thus, we should not expect the compiler to discover optimal solutions to the problem unless we allow exponential time for some compilations. In practice, compilers use approximation techniques to discover good solutions to this problem; the solutions may not be optimal, but the approximation techniques ensure that some solution is found in a reasonable amount of time.

Instruction Scheduling

To produce code that executes quickly, the code generator may need to reorder operations to reflect the target machine's specific performance constraints. The execution time of the different operations can vary widely. Memory access operations can take tens or hundreds of cycles, while some arithmetic operations, particularly multiply, take several cycles. The impact of these longer latency operations on the performance of compiled code can be dramatic.

TERMINOLOGY

A careful reader will notice that we use the word *code* in many places where either *program* or *procedure* might naturally fit. This is a deliberate affectation; compilers can be invoked to translate fragments of code that range from a single reference through an entire system of programs. Rather than specify some scope of compilation, we will continue to use the ambiguous, but more general, term, *code*.

Assume, for the moment, that a `loadAI` or `storeAI` operation requires three cycles, a `mult` requires two cycles, and all other operations require one cycle. The following table shows how the previous code fragment performs under these assumptions. The **Start** column shows the cycle in which each operation begins execution and the **End** column shows the cycle in which it completes.

Start	End				
1	3	loadAI	r_{arp}, @w $\Rightarrow$ r_1		// load 'w'
4	4	add	r_1, r_1 $\Rightarrow$ r_1		// $r_1 \leftarrow$ w × 2
5	7	loadAI	r_{arp}, @x $\Rightarrow$ r_2		// load 'x'
8	9	mult	r_1, r_2 $\Rightarrow$ r_1		// $r_1 \leftarrow$ (w × 2) × x
10	12	loadAI	r_{arp}, @y $\Rightarrow$ r_2		// load 'y'
13	14	mult	r_1, r_2 $\Rightarrow$ r_1		// $r_1 \leftarrow$ (w × 2 × x) × y
15	17	loadAI	r_{arp}, @z $\Rightarrow$ r_2		// load 'z'
18	19	mult	r_1, r_2 $\Rightarrow$ r_1		// $r_1 \leftarrow$ (w × 2 × x × y) × z
20	22	storeAI	r_1 $\Rightarrow$ r_{arp}, @w		// write r_w back to 'w'

This nine-operation sequence takes twenty-two cycles to execute. Minimizing register use did not lead to rapid execution.

Many modern processors have the property that they can initiate new operations while a long-latency operation executes. As long as the results of a long-latency operation are not referenced until the operation completes, execution proceeds normally. If, however, some intervening operation tries to read the result of the long-latency operation prematurely, the processor "stalls," or waits until the long-latency operation completes. An operation cannot begin to execute until its operands are ready, and its results are not ready until the operation terminates.

The instruction scheduler reorders the operations in the code. It attempts to minimize the number of cycles wasted in stalls. Of course, the scheduler must ensure that the new sequence produces the same result as the original. In many cases, the scheduler can drastically improve on the performance of "naive" code. For our example, a good scheduler might produce the following sequence:

Start	End			
1	3	loadAI r_{arp}, @w $\Rightarrow r_1$	// load 'w'
2	4	loadAI r_{arp}, @x $\Rightarrow r_2$	// load 'x'
3	5	loadAI r_{arp}, @y $\Rightarrow r_3$	// load 'y'
4	4	add r_1, r_1 $\Rightarrow r_1$	// $r_1 \leftarrow$ w × 2
5	6	mult r_1, r_2 $\Rightarrow r_1$	// $r_1 \leftarrow$ (w × 2) × x
6	8	loadAI r_{arp}, @z $\Rightarrow r_2$	// load 'z'
7	8	mult r_1, r_3 $\Rightarrow r_1$	// $r_1 \leftarrow$ (w × 2 × x) × y
9	10	mult r_1, r_2 $\Rightarrow r_1$	// $r_1 \leftarrow$ (w × 2 × x × y) × z
11	13	storeAI r_1 $\Rightarrow r_{arp}$, @w	// write r_w back to 'w'

This version of the code requires just thirteen cycles to execute. The code needs one more register than the minimal number. It starts an operation in every cycle except eight, ten, and twelve. This schedule is not unique; several equivalent schedules are possible, as are equal-length schedules that use more registers.

Instruction scheduling is, like register allocation, a hard problem. In its general form, it is NP-complete. Because variants of this problem arise in so many fields, it has received a great deal of attention in the literature.

Interactions

Most of the truly hard problems that occur in compilation arise during code generation. To make matters more complex, these problems interact. For example, instruction scheduling moves load operations away from the arithmetic operations that depend on them. This can increase the period over which the values are needed and, correspondingly, increase the number of registers needed during that period. Similarly, the assignment of particular values to specific registers can constrain instruction scheduling by creating a "false" dependence between two operations. (The second operation cannot be

MAY YOU STUDY IN INTERESTING TIMES ...

This is an exciting era in the design and implementation of compilers. In the 1980s almost all compilers were large, monolithic systems. They took as input one of a handful of languages and produced assembly code for some particular computer. The assembly code was pasted together with the code produced by other compilations—including system libraries and application libraries—to form an executable. The executable was stored on a disk; at the appropriate time, the final code was moved from disk to main memory and executed.

Today, compiler technology is being applied in many different settings. As computers find application in diverse places, compilers must cope with new and different constraints. No longer is speed the sole criterion for judging the compiled code. Today, code might be judged on how small it is, on how much power it consumes, on how well it compresses, or on how many page faults it generates when it runs.

At the same time, compilation techniques have escaped from the monolithic systems of the 1980s. They are appearing in many new places. Java compilers take partially compiled programs (in Java "byte-code" format) and translate them into native code for the target machine. In this environment, success requires that the sum of compile time plus run time must be less than the cost of interpretation. Techniques to analyze whole programs are moving from compile time to link time, where the linker can analyze the assembly code for the entire application and use that knowledge to improve the program. Finally, compilers are being invoked at run time to generate customized code that capitalizes on facts that cannot be known any earlier. If the compilation time can be kept small and the benefits are large, this strategy can produce noticeable improvements.

scheduled until the first completes, even though the values in the common register are independent. Renaming the values can eliminate this false dependence, at the cost of using more registers.)

Roadmap

Chapters 11 through 13 describe the issues that arise in code generation and present a variety of techniques to address these issues. Chapter 11 discusses algorithms for instruction selection—how to map a particular code shape into the target machine's instruction set. Because the order of execution can have a strong impact on the performance of compiled code, Chapter 12 delves into algorithms for instruction scheduling. Finally, Chapter 13 looks at the problem of deciding which values to keep in registers and explores algorithms that compilers use to make these decisions.

1.6   DESIRABLE PROPERTIES OF A COMPILER

The fundamental principles tell us what a compiler must do. They do not, however, describe all of the properties and behaviors that the compiler should have. While specific compilers may have their own priorities and constraints, we tend to judge compilers based on their performance in five distinct areas.

1. *Speed* At any point in time, there are applications that need more performance than they can easily obtain. For example, our ability to simulate the behavior of digital circuits, like microprocessors, always lags far behind the demand for such simulation. Similarly, large physical problems such as climate modeling have an insatiable demand for computation. For these applications, the run-time performance of the compiled code is a critical issue. Achieving predictably good performance requires additional analysis and transformation at compile time. This extra work typically requires longer compilations.

2. *Space* Many applications impose tight restrictions on the size of compiled code. These constraints usually arise from either physical or economic factors. For example, the power consumption of a handheld computer depends, in part, on the amount of memory it contains. Code is often committed to *read-only memory* (ROM); code size determines the ROM that a device needs. In environments ranging from Grid computing to web pages with embedded applets, executables are transmitted between computers before they run; this places a premium on the size of compiled code. Compilers can, by design, focus on producing compact code. However, a tension may exist between the desire for compact code and the desire for fast code.

3. *Feedback* When the compiler encounters an incorrect program, it must report that fact back to the user. The amount of information provided to the user can vary widely. For example, the early Unix compilers often

produced a simple and uniform message, "syntax error." At the other end of the spectrum the Cornell PL/C system and the UW-Pascal system, which were designed as "student" compilers, made concerted efforts to correct every syntax error in a program and, then, to execute it.

4. *Debugging* Unfortunately, most programs do not run correctly the first time that they are compiled. Thus, programmers place a high value on the ability to use a source-level debugger with compiled code. If the debugger tries to relate the state of the broken executable to the source code, the complexities introduced by radical program transformations can cause the debugger to mislead the programmer. Thus, both the compiler writer and the user may be forced to choose between efficiency in the compiled code and transparency in the debugger. This is why many compilers have a "debug" flag that prevents the compiler from applying transformations that obscure the relationship between the source code and the executing program.

5. *Compile-Time Efficiency* Compilers are heavily used. In many cases, the compiler user waits for the results, so compilation speed can be an important issue. In practice, no one likes to wait for a compiler to finish. Some users will be more tolerant of slow compilations, especially when code quality is a serious issue. However, given the choice between a slow compiler and a fast compiler that produces the same results, the user will undoubtedly choose the faster one.

Before reading the rest of this book, you should write down a prioritized list of the qualities that you want in a compiler. You might apply the traditional standard from software engineering—evaluate features as if you were paying for them with your own money! Examining your list will tell you a great deal about how you would make the various tradeoffs in building your own compiler.

1.7 SUMMARY AND PERSPECTIVE

Compiler construction is a complex task. A good compiler combines ideas from formal language theory, from the study of algorithms, from artificial intelligence, from systems design, from computer architecture, and from the theory of programming languages and applies them to the problem of translating a program. A compiler brings together greedy algorithms, heuristic techniques, graph algorithms, dynamic programming, DFAs and NFAs, fixed-point algorithms, allocation and naming, synchronization and locality, and pipeline management. Many of the problems that confront the compiler are too hard for it to solve optimally; thus, compilers use approximations, heuristics, and rules of thumb. This produces complex interactions that can lead to surprising results—both good and bad.

To place this activity in an orderly framework, most compilers are organized into three major phases: a front end, an optimizer, and a back end. Each phase has a different set of problems to tackle; the approaches used to solve those problems differ, too. The front end focuses on translating source code into some IR. Front ends rely on results from formal language theory and type theory, with a healthy dose of algorithms and data structures. The middle section, or optimizer, translates one IR program into another, with the goal of producing an IR program that executes efficiently. Optimizers analyze programs to derive knowledge about their run-time behavior and then use that knowledge to transform the code and improve its behavior. The back end maps an IR program to the instruction set of a specific processor. A back end approximates the answers to hard problems in allocation and scheduling; the quality of its approximation has a direct impact on the speed and size of the compiled code.

This book explores each of these phases. Chapters 2 through 4 deal with the algorithms used in a compiler's front end. Chapters 5 through 7 describe background material for the discussion of optimization and code generation. Chapter 8 provides an introduction to code optimization; Chapters 9 and 10 provide more detailed treatment of analysis and optimization for the interested reader. Finally, Chapters 11 through 13 cover the techniques used by back ends for instruction selection, scheduling, and register allocation.

CHAPTER NOTES

The first compilers appeared in the 1950s. These early systems showed surprising sophistication. The original FORTRAN compiler was a multipass system that included a distinct scanner, parser, and register allocator, along with some optimizations [26, 25]. The Alpha system, built by Ershov and his colleagues at Novosibirsk, performed local optimization [131] and used graph coloring to reduce the amount of memory needed for data items [132, 133].

Knuth provides some interesting recollections of compiler construction in the early 1960s [221]. Randell and Russell describe early implementation efforts for Algol 60 [282]. Allen describes the history of compiler development inside IBM with an emphasis on the interplay of theory and practice [14].

Many influential compilers were built in the 1960s and 1970s. These include the classic optimizing compiler FORTRAN H [243, 297], the Bliss-11 and Bliss-32 compilers [339, 67], and the portable BCPL compiler [289]. These compilers produced high-quality code for a variety of CISC machines. Compilers for students, on the other hand, focused on rapid compilation, good diagnostic messages, and error correction [92, 139].

The advent of RISC architecture in the 1980s led to another generation of compilers; these focused on strong optimization and high-quality code generation [84, 23, 76, 194]. These compilers featured full-blown optimizers structured as shown in Figure 1.1. Modern RISC compilers still follow this model.

During the 1990s, compiler-construction research focused on reacting to the rapid changes taking place in microprocessor architecture. The decade began with Intel's *i*860 processor challenging compiler writers to manage pipelines and memory latencies directly. At its end, compilers confronted challenges that ranged from multiple functional units to long memory latencies to parallel code generation. The structure and organization of 1980s RISC compilers proved flexible enough for these new challenges, so researchers built new passes to insert into the optimization and code-generation phases of their compilers.

CHAPTER 2

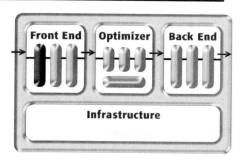

Scanning

INTRODUCTION

Scanning is the first stage of a three-part process that the compiler uses to understand the input program. The scanner, or lexical analyzer, takes as input a stream of characters and produces as output a stream of words along with their associated syntactic categories. It aggregates symbols to form words and applies a set of rules to determine whether or not each word is legal in the source language. If the word is valid, the scanner assigns it a syntactic category, or part of speech. To make this process efficient, compilers use specialized recognizers.

This chapter describes the mathematical tools and the programming techniques that are commonly used to perform lexical analysis. Most of the work in scanner construction has been automated; indeed, this is a classic example of the application of theoretical results to solve an important practical problem—specifying and recognizing patterns in strings. The problem of specifying patterns has a natural mathematical formulation, in a notation called *regular expressions*. The mathematics leads directly to recognizers, called *finite automata*, that scan a stream of symbols to find the specified patterns. Readily available tools build efficient, customized recognizers from specifications, taking advantage of the theoretical connection between regular expressions and finite automata. This technique has been applied in many settings, from tools such as the Unix grep program, to website filtering software, to the regular-expression "find" commands in text editors, word processing tools, and command shells.

Scanners look at a stream of characters and recognize words. The rules that govern the lexical structure of a programming language, sometimes called its *microsyntax*, are simple and regular. This leads to highly efficient specialized recognizers for scanning. Typically, a compiler's front end uses a scanner to recognize and classify words. The scanner's output is a stream of words, each annotated with its syntactic category or part of speech. The parser consumes these words, in order. It determines whether or not the words form a syntactically correct sentence in the programming language—a program. Once the compiler knows that the input is syntactically correct, it subjects that program to deeper analysis, sometimes called *context-sensitive analysis*, to see if the program has a consistent meaning. Many of the details that determine whether or not a program has meaning are not easily expressed in syntax; thus the compiler must use more-complex techniques to examine them.

Conceptually, these three kinds of analysis are separate tasks. In practice, they often run in an interleaved fashion, with the parser calling the scanner to produce classified words on demand and invoking the context-sensitive analysis as it recognizes various syntactic subparts of the code. Together, these different analyzers form the compiler's front end, as depicted in Figure 1.1 or in the graphic at the start of each chapter.

Separating microsyntax from syntax simplifies the compiler in three ways.

1. The description of syntax used in the parser is written in terms of words and syntactic categories, rather than letters, numbers, and blanks. This lets the parser ignore irrelevant issues such as absorbing extraneous blanks, newlines, and comments. These issues are hidden inside the scanner, where they are handled cleanly and efficiently.

2. Scanner construction is almost completely automated. The lexical rules are encoded in a formal notation and fed to a scanner generator. The result is an executable program that produces the input for the parser. Scanners generated from high-level specifications are efficient.

3. Every rule moved into the scanner shrinks the parser. Parsing is harder than scanning; the size of the parser grows as the grammar grows. Since building a parser requires more direct effort from the programmer, shrinking the parser reduces the compiler writer's effort.

As a final point, well-implemented scanners have lower overhead (measured by instructions executed per input symbol) than well-implemented parsers. The scanner aggregates characters into words so that the parser can treat each word as a symbol. This reduces the number of words that the parser must handle.

This chapter examines techniques to recognize words in a stream of characters and to identify each word's syntactic category. It shows how to specify concisely the kinds of words that arise in programming languages. It presents methods to derive scanners directly from these specifications. Finally, it shows some examples that demonstrate how language design can complicate the task of recognizing and categorizing words.

2.2   RECOGNIZING WORDS

When describing algorithms for recognizing words, a character-by-character formulation can sometimes makes things clear. For simple algorithms, the structure of the code can provide some insight into the underlying problem. Consider the problem of recognizing the word fee. Assuming the presence of a routine *NextChar* that returns the next character, the code might look like the following fragment.

```
c ← NextChar()
if (c ≠ 'f')
   then do something else
   else
        c ← NextChar()
        if (c ≠ 'e')
           then do something else
           else
                c ← NextChar()
                if (c ≠ 'e')
                   then do something else
                   else report success
```

The code tests for f followed by e followed by e. At each step, failure to match the appropriate character causes the code to reject the string and do something else. (If the sole purpose of the program was to recognize the word fee, then the appropriate behavior would be to print an error message or return failure. Scanners rarely recognize only one word, as we shall see, so we leave this "error path" deliberately vague at this point.)

This simple code fragment performs one test per character, encoded as an *if-then-else* construct. We can represent this code fragment using the simple diagram shown to the right of the code. The circles, or nodes, represent abstract states of the computation, numbered from zero to three. The initial state, or start state, is labelled s_0. Throughout this chapter, s_0 will be the start state, unless explicitly stated. A valid final state, such as s_3 in this example, is drawn with a double circle. The arrows represent transitions from state to state based on the input character. If we start in the topmost state and see the characters f, e, and e, the transitions take us to the bottommost state. What happens on any other input, such as f, i, and e? The f takes us to the second state. The i does not match the edge leaving the second state, so we know that the input word is not fee. All of the cases that do not match fee are implemented as *do something else* in the code. We can think of this as a transition to an error state.

Using the same implementation strategy, a fragment that recognizes the word while can be encoded into a series of five nested *if-then-else* constructs. Since the code would be tedious to read, we simply present the transition diagram:

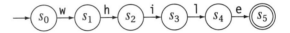

If we start the code in state s_0 and it reaches s_5, we know that the first five characters of the input stream were while.

To recognize more than one word, we can begin to fill in the *do something else* path in the code. A fragment to recognize both fee and fie can be represented like this:

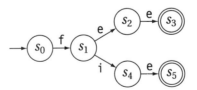

This fragment uses a common test for f that moves it from s_0 to s_1. If the second character is e, it takes the transition $s_1 \xrightarrow{e} s_2$. If, instead, the second character is i, it makes the move $s_1 \xrightarrow{i} s_4$. Finally, if it encounters an e in s_2, it takes $s_2 \xrightarrow{e} s_3$. An e in s_4 produces the move $s_4 \xrightarrow{e} s_5$. In this fragment, both s_3 and s_5 are final states.

We can combine our fragment that recognizes fee and fie with the one that recognizes while by merging their initial states and renumbering the other states, as needed. This produces the following transition diagram:

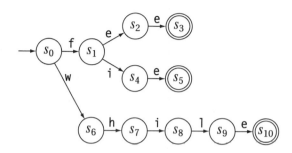

Now, s_0 has transitions for f and w, and there are three final states. If any state encounters an input character that does not match one of its transitions, it indicates an error.

2.2.1 A Formalism for Recognizers

These transition diagrams serve as abstractions of the code that would be required to implement them. They can also be viewed as formal mathematical objects, called *finite automata*, that specify recognizers. A finite automaton (FA) is a finite collection of states, a set of transitions between those states, an alphabet, a start state (s_0), and one or more designated final states.

Formally, an FA is a five-tuple $(S, \Sigma, \delta, s_0, S_F)$, where

- S is the set of states. It contains every state in the transition diagram, along with the designated error state s_e. S must be finite.

- Σ is the alphabet, or character set, used by the recognizer. Typically, Σ is the union of the edge labels in the transition diagram. Σ must be finite.

- $\delta(s, c)$ is a function that takes two arguments, a state $s \in S$ and a character $c \in \Sigma$. It encodes the transitions of the FA. When the FA is in state s and sees a c, it makes a transition to the state $\delta(s, c)$.

- $s_0 \in S$ is the designated start state.

- S_F is the set of final states. $S_F \subseteq S$. Each state in S_F is drawn with a double circle in the transition diagram.

To make this more concrete, let's revisit the last FA of the previous section, which recognizes `fee` or `fie` or `while`. Casting this FA into the formalism yields

$$S = \{s_0, s_1, s_2, s_3, s_4, s_5, s_6, s_7, s_8, s_9, s_{10}, s_e\}$$

$$\Sigma = \{\texttt{e}, \texttt{f}, \texttt{i}, \texttt{h}, \texttt{l}, \texttt{w}\}$$

$$\delta = \left\{ \begin{array}{llllll} s_0 \xrightarrow{f} s_1, & s_0 \xrightarrow{w} s_6, & s_1 \xrightarrow{e} s_2, & s_1 \xrightarrow{i} s_4, & s_2 \xrightarrow{e} s_3, \\ s_4 \xrightarrow{e} s_5, & s_6 \xrightarrow{h} s_7, & s_7 \xrightarrow{i} s_8, & s_8 \xrightarrow{l} s_9, & s_9 \xrightarrow{e} s_{10} \end{array} \right\}$$

$$s_0 = s_0$$

$$S_F = \{s_3, s_5, s_{10}\}$$

This quintuple is equivalent to the transition diagram; given one, we can easily re-create the other. In some sense, the transition diagram is a picture of the corresponding FA.

If the FA is in state s with character c, and $\delta(s, c)$ is not defined, this indicates an erroneous input string. In this case, $\delta(s, c)$ should return an indication of error. Alternatively, we can view this as returning an explicit error state, s_e, with the provision that $s_e \xrightarrow{c} s_e, \forall c \in \Sigma$.

An FA accepts a string x if and only if, starting in s_0, the string takes it through a series of transitions that leaves it in a final state when the entire string has been consumed. This corresponds to our intuition for the transition diagram. For the string `fee`, our example recognizer runs through the transitions $s_0 \xrightarrow{f} s_1$, $s_1 \xrightarrow{e} s_2$, and $s_2 \xrightarrow{e} s_3$. Since $s_3 \in S_F$, and no input remains, the FA accepts the string `fee`. For the string `foe`, the behavior is different. The initial transition, $s_0 \xrightarrow{f} s_1$, is the same. In s_1, however, there is no normal transition on `o`, so δ returns s_e.

To be more formal, if the string x is composed of characters $x_1 x_2 x_3 \ldots x_n$, then the FA $(S, \Sigma, \delta, s_0, S_F)$ accepts x if and only if

$$\delta(\delta(\ldots \delta(\delta(\delta(s_0, x_1), x_2), x_3) \ldots, x_{n-1}), x_n) \in S_F.$$

Intuitively, this corresponds to a repeated application of δ to a pair composed of some state $s \in S$ and an input symbol x_i. The base case is $\delta(s_0, x_1)$, which corresponds to the initial state of the FA. The state produced by this application of δ is then used as input, along with x_2, to δ to produce the next state, and so on, until all the input has been consumed. The result of the final application of δ is, again, a state. If that state is in S_F, then the FA accepts $x_1 x_2 x_3 \ldots x_n$.

Two other cases are possible. The FA might encounter an error while processing the string—that is, it might encounter character x_j while it is in state s_i and find that $\delta(s_i, x_j)$ is undefined. This indicates a lexical error. The string $x_1 x_2 x_3 \ldots x_j$ is not a valid prefix for any legal word in the language accepted by the FA. Alternately, the FA might reach x_n, process it, and be in a nonfinal state. In this case, the input string is a proper prefix of some word accepted by the FA. Again, this indicates an error and should be reported to the end user.

2.2.2 Recognizing More-Complex Words

The character-by-character model shown in the original recognizer for fee extends easily to handle arbitrary collections of fully specified words. How could we recognize a number with such a recognizer? A specific number, such as 113.4, is easy.

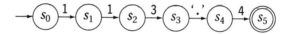

To be useful, however, we need a transition diagram (and the corresponding code fragment) that can recognize any number. For simplicity's sake, let's limit the discussion to unsigned integers. In general, an integer is either zero, or it is a series of one or more digits where the first digit is from one to nine, and the subsequent digits are from zero to nine. (This rules out leading zeros.) How would we draw a transition diagram for this definition?

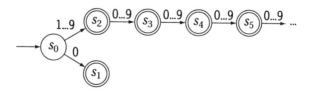

The transition $s_0 \xrightarrow{0} s_1$ handles the case for zero. The other path, from s_0 to s_2, to s_3, and so on, handles the case for an integer greater than zero. This path, however, presents several problems. First, it does not end. This violates the requirement that an FA have a finite set of states. Second, all of the states on the path beginning with s_3 are equivalent—they have the same labels on their input and output transitions, and they are all final states.

$$S = \{s_0, s_1, s_2\}$$

char ← *NextChar()*
state ← s_0

$$\Sigma = \{0,1,2,3,4,5,6,7,8,9\}$$

while (char ≠ eof and state ≠ s_e)
    state ← *δ(state,char)*
    char ← *NextChar()*

$$\delta = \left\{ \begin{array}{c} s_0 \overset{0}{\to} s_1,\ s_0 \overset{1-9}{\to} s_2 \\ s_2 \overset{0-9}{\to} s_2 \end{array} \right\}$$

if (state ∈ S_F)
    then report acceptance
    else report failure

$$S_F = \{s_1, s_2\}$$

FIGURE 2.1   A Recognizer for Unsigned Integers

We can simplify the FA significantly if we allow the transition diagram to include cycles. We can replace the entire chain of states beginning at s_2 with a single transition from s_2 back to itself, like this:

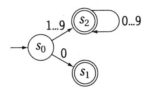

This transition diagram makes sense as an FA. From an implementation perspective, however, it is more complex than the acyclic diagrams shown earlier. We cannot translate this directly into a set of nested *if-then-else* constructs. The introduction of a cycle in the transition graph creates the need for cyclic control flow. We can implement this with a *while* loop, as shown in Figure 2.1. We can specify δ efficiently using a table:

δ	0	1	2	3	4	5	6	7	8	9	Other
s_0	s_1	s_2	s_2	s_2	s_2	s_2	s_2	s_2	s_2	s_2	s_e
s_1	s_e	s_e	s_e	s_e	s_e	s_e	s_e	s_e	s_e	s_e	s_e
s_2	s_2	s_2	s_2	s_2	s_2	s_2	s_2	s_2	s_2	s_2	s_e
s_e	s_e	s_e	s_e	s_e	s_e	s_e	s_e	s_e	s_e	s_e	s_e

Changing the table allows the same basic code skeleton to implement other recognizers. Notice that this table has ample opportunity for compression. The

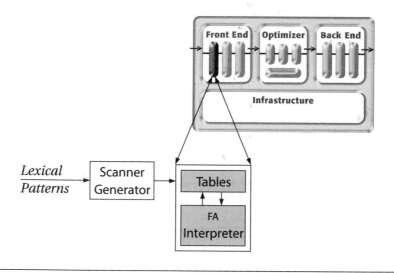

FIGURE 2.2 Automatic Scanner Generation

columns for the digits 1 through 9 are identical, so they could be represented once. This leaves a table with three columns: 0, 1 . . . 9, and *other*. Close examination of the code skeleton shows that it reports failure as soon as it enters s_e, so it never references that row of the table. The implementation can elide the entire row, leaving a table with three rows and three columns in place of the original table of four rows and eleven columns.

We can develop similar FAs for signed integers, real numbers, and complex numbers. In each case, the FA recognizes an unlimited set of words. While the FAs can be viewed as specifications for a recognizer, they are not particularly concise specifications. To simplify scanner implementation, we would like a concise notation for specifying the lexical structure of words, and a set of automatic techniques for turning those specifications into an FA and into code that implements the FA. The remaining sections of this chapter develop those notations and techniques.

2.2.3 Automating Scanner Construction

Tools that automatically build scanners from specifications are widely available. The basic structure of these tools is shown in Figure 2.2. The compiler writer supplies the tool with a set of lexical patterns that describe the various words in a specific source language. The scanner generator analyzes these patterns and produces a recognizer that becomes the heart of the scanner. The recognizer can be encoded into a set of tables or directly into executable code.

Either way, it derives a correct, efficient scanner from the patterns. Because these tools produce good scanners, compiler writers rarely construct scanners by hand.

2.3 REGULAR EXPRESSIONS

The set of words accepted by a finite automaton, $\mathcal{F}$, forms a language, denoted $L(\mathcal{F})$. The transition diagram of the FA specifies, in precise detail, that language. It is not, however, a specification that humans find intuitive. For any FA, we can also describe its language using a notation called a *regular expression*.

Regular expressions (REs) are equivalent to the finite automata (FAS) described in the previous section. (We will prove this with a construction in Section 2.4.) Simple recognizers have simple RE specifications.

- The language consisting of the single word fee can be described by an RE written as *fee*. Writing two characters next to each other implies that they are expected to appear in that order. The expression *fee* is an RE for the language.

- The language consisting of the two words fee or while can be written as *fee* or *while*. To avoid possible misinterpretation of *or*, we write this using the symbol | to mean *or*. Thus, we write the RE as *fee* | *while*.

- The language consisting of fee or fie can be written as *fee* | *fie*. A second RE is possible, *f(e|i)e*. The RE *f(e|i)e* might reflect the structure of the FA more closely than *fee* | *fie*.

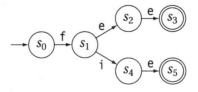

To make this concrete, consider some examples from programming languages. Punctuation marks, such as colons, semicolons, commas, and various brackets, can be represented by their character representations. Thus, we might find the following REs in the lexical specification for a typical programming language:

$$: \quad ; \quad ? \quad => \quad (\quad) \quad \{ \quad \} \quad [\quad]$$

Similarly, keywords have simple REs.

if   while   this   integer   instanceof

To model more complex constructs, such as integers or identifiers, we need a notation that can capture the essence of the cyclic edge in an FA.

The FA for an unsigned integer had three states, an initial state, s_0, a final state s_1 for the unique integer zero, and a final state s_2 for all other integers.

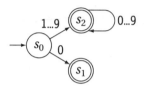

The key to this FA's power is the transition from s_2 back to itself that occurs on each additional digit. State s_2 folds the specification back on itself, creating a rule to derive a new unsigned integer from an existing one: add another digit to the right end of the existing number. Another way of stating this rule is, an unsigned integer is either a zero, or a nonzero digit followed by zero or more digits. To capture the essence of this FA, we need a notation for this notion of "zero or more occurrences" of an RE. For the RE x, we write this as x^*, with the meaning "zero or more occurrences of x." We call the * operator *Kleene closure*, or *closure* for short. Using the closure operator, we can write an RE for this FA: *0 | (1|2|3|4|5|6|7|8|9) (0|1|2|3|4|5|6|7|8|9)**.

2.3.1 Formalizing the Notation

To work with regular expressions in a rigorous way, we must define them more formally. A regular expression describes a set of strings over the characters contained in some alphabet, Σ, augmented with a character ϵ that represents the empty string. We call the set of strings a *language*. For a given regular expression, *r*, we denote the language that it specifies as $L(r)$. A regular expression is built up from three basic operations:

1. *Alternation* The alternation, or union, of two sets R and S, denoted $R \mid S$, is $\{s \mid s \in R \text{ or } s \in S\}$.

REGULAR EXPRESSIONS IN VIRTUAL LIFE

Regular expressions are used in many applications to specify patterns in character strings. Some of the early work on translating regular expressions into code was done to provide a flexible way of specifying strings in the "find" command of a text editor. From that early genesis, the notation has crept into many different applications.

In Unix, and many other operating systems, the asterisk can be used as a wildcard to match substrings against file names. Here, $*$ is a shorthand for the regular expression Σ^*, specifying zero or more characters drawn from the entire alphabet of legal characters. (Since few keyboards have a Σ key, the shorthand has stayed with us.) Many systems use ? as a wildcard that matches a single character.

The grep family of tools, and their kin in non-Unix systems, implement regular expression pattern matching. (In fact, grep is an acronym for global regular-expression pattern match and print.)

Regular expressions have found widespread use because they are easily written and easily understood. They are one of the techniques of choice when a program must recognize a fixed vocabulary. They work well for languages that fit within their limited rules. They are easily translated into an executable form; and the resulting recognizer is fast.

2. *Concatenation*   The concatenation of two sets R and S, denoted RS, is $\{st \mid s \in R \text{ and } t \in S\}$. We will sometimes write R^2 for RR, the concatenation of R with itself, and R^3 for RRR (or RR^2).

3. *Closure*   The Kleene closure of a set R, denoted R^*, is $\bigcup_0^\infty R^i$. This is just the union of the concatenations of R with itself, zero or more times.

It is sometimes convenient to talk about the *positive closure* of R, denoted R^+ and defined as $\bigcup_1^\infty R^i$. Since R^+ can always be rewritten as RR^*, we ignore it in the discussion that follows.

Using these three operations, we can define the set of regular expressions over an alphabet Σ as follows:

1. If $a \in \Sigma$, then a is also an RE denoting the set containing only a.

2. If r and s are REs, denoting sets $L(r)$ and $L(s)$, respectively, then

     (r) is an RE denoting $L(r)$,

> *r* | *s* is an RE denoting the union, or alternation, of *L(r)* and *L(s)*,
>
> *rs* is an RE denoting the set of concatenations of strings in *L(r)* and *L(s)*, respectively, and
>
> *r** is an RE denoting the Kleene closure of *L(r)*.

3. ϵ is an RE denoting the set containing only the empty string.

To eliminate any ambiguity, closure has highest precedence, followed by concatenation, followed by alternation.

As a convenient shorthand, we will specify ranges of characters with the first and the last element, connected by an ellipsis. To make this abbreviation stand out, we will always surround it with a pair of square brackets. Thus, *[0...9]* represents the set of decimal digits. It can always be rewritten with the full set as *(0 | 1 | 2 | 3 | 4 | 5 | 6 | 7 | 8 | 9)*.

2.3.2 Examples

The goal of this chapter is to show how we can use formal techniques to automate the construction of high-quality scanners and how we can encode the microsyntax of programming languages into that formalism. Before proceeding further, some examples from real programming languages are in order.

1. Algol and its descendants define an identifier as a single alphabetic character followed by zero or more alphanumeric characters. We can write this in RE form as *[a...z] ([a...z] | [0...9])**, if we assume that all letters are lowercase[1] Many languages also allow a few special characters, such as the underscore (_), the percent sign (%), or the ampersand (&), in identifiers.

2. An unsigned integer can be described as either zero or a nonzero digit followed by zero or more digits. The RE, *0 | [1...9][0...9]**, is more concise. In practice, many implementations admit a larger class of strings as integers, accepting the language *[0...9]+*.

3. Real numbers are more complex than integers. A real number might be described as *(0 | [1...9][0...9]*) (ϵ | . [0...9]*)*. The first part is just the RE for an integer. The rest generates either the empty string or a decimal point followed by zero or more digits.

---

1. If the programming language ignores case, the scanner can fold all characters to lowercase. If it is case sensitive, the REs become more complex, in obvious ways.

Programming languages often extend this to scientific notation, with an RE such as $(0 \mid [1 \ldots 9][0 \ldots 9]^*) \, (. \, [0 \ldots 9]^* \mid \epsilon) \, E \, (+ \mid - \mid \epsilon) \, (0 \mid [1 \ldots 9][0 \ldots 9]^*)$. This RE describes a real number, followed by an E, followed by an integer to specify the exponent.

4. Quoted character strings have their own complexity. In most languages, any character can appear inside a string. This can include blanks, tabs, newlines, and even the character used to delimit the string. To represent the set $\{\Sigma - c\}$, we use the notation *[ˆc]*, taken from the lex scanner generator. A character string in C might be described as *"[ˆ"]*"*.

The use of escape characters, such as \n for newline and \" for " in C simplifies handling of strings. The alternative to escape characters was to double the character in question. Thus, to place the character " in a string, the programmer would write "". This complicated the RE for character string constants.

5. Comments appear in a number of forms. Some languages allow a delimiter, such as # or //, that indicates a comment running to the end of the current line. This produces an RE such as *//[ˆ\n]*, where \n represents the newline character. Other languages use distinct delimiters for the start and end of a comment. Pascal uses { and } as comment delimiters, which produces an RE such as *{ [ˆ}]* }*. Java and C allow two-character delimiters /* and */; this creates a more complex RE.

Each of these examples admits an unbounded set of words. Limiting the set of words often produces a longer or more complex RE. For example, some languages limit the length of an identifier. This leads to a longer regular expression than the one presented. Limiting the preceding, Algol-like identifiers to a maximum of six characters produces the RE

$$[a \ldots z] \, ([a \ldots z] \mid [0 \ldots 9]) \, ([a \ldots z] \mid [0 \ldots 9]) \, ([a \ldots z] \mid [0 \ldots 9]) \, ([a \ldots z] \mid [0 \ldots 9]) \, ([a \ldots z] \mid [0 \ldots 9])$$

The corresponding FA has more states than the FA for identifiers of unbounded length. We can introduce the notion of a limited closure, c^k, that specifies zero to k copies of c. This would let us write the RE for six-character identifiers as $[a \ldots z]([a \ldots z][0 \ldots 9])^5$. It simplifies and shortens the RE, but does nothing to simplify the corresponding FA.

Trying to be specific with an RE can also lead to complex expressions. Consider, for example, that the register specifier in a typical assembly language consists of the letter r followed by a small integer. While the RE $r[0\ldots9]^+$ describes the register names allowed in ILOC, it admits an unlimited set of register names. The corresponding recognizer looks like:

This recognizer accepts r29, and rejects s29. It also accepts r99999, even though no currently available computer has 100,000 registers.

On a real computer, however, the set of register names is severely limited—say, 32, 64, or 128 registers. Rather than writing code to convert each register name into an integer and compare it against the range 0 to 31, we could build a more precise RE for the register specifier. One such RE might be

$$r\left(\,(0|1|2)\;([0\ldots9]\,|\,\epsilon)\,|\,(4|5|6|7|8|9)\,|\,(3\,(0|1|\epsilon))\,\right)$$

This expression is carefully crafted to accept r0, r29, r31, but not r32 or r99999. It might be used to define the syntactic category for register names. It specifies a much smaller language, limited to registers from 0 to 31 with an optional leading 0 on single-digit register names. The corresponding FA looks like:

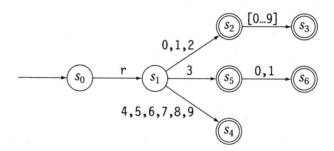

Which FA is better? Either FA makes a single transition on each input character. Thus, they both make the same number of transitions, even though the more complicated FA checks a more complex microsyntactic specification. The more complex FA has more states and more transitions, so its representation requires more space. However, its operating cost is, essentially, the same.

This is critical: the cost of operating an FA is proportional to the length of the input string, not to the length or complexity of the regular expression that generated the recognizer. Increased complexity in the regular expression can increase the number of states in the corresponding FA. This, in turn, increases the space needed to represent the FA and the cost of automatically constructing it, but the cost of operation remains one transition per input character.

Can we improve our description of the register specifier? The RE is both complex and counterintuitive. An alternative RE might be

$$r0 \mid r00 \mid r1 \mid r01 \mid r2 \mid r02 \mid r3 \mid r03 \mid r4 \mid r04 \mid r5 \mid r05 \mid r6 \mid r06 \mid r7 \mid r07 \mid r8 \mid r08 \mid$$
$$r9 \mid r09 \mid r10 \mid r11 \mid r12 \mid r13 \mid r14 \mid r15 \mid r16 \mid r17 \mid r18 \mid r19 \mid r20 \mid r21 \mid r22 \mid r23 \mid$$
$$r24 \mid r25 \mid r26 \mid r27 \mid r28 \mid r29 \mid r30 \mid r31$$

This expression is conceptually simpler, but much longer than the previous version. The resulting FA will still require one transition per input symbol. Thus, if we can keep the space requirements from growing too much, we might prefer this version of the register specifier because it is clear and obvious.

2.3.3 Properties of REs

The set of languages that can be expressed with REs is called the set of *regular languages*. The regular languages have been studied extensively; they have many interesting and important properties. Some of those properties play an important role in the use of regular expressions to generate scanners.

Regular expressions are closed under many operations—that is, if we apply the operation to an RE or a collection of REs, the result is an RE. Obvious examples are concatenation, union, and closure. The concatenation of two REs, x and y, is just xy. Their union is $x \mid y$. The Kleene closure of x is x^*. All of these follow from the definition of REs.

The fact that REs are closed plays a critical role in the use of REs to build scanners. Assume that we have an RE for each syntactic category in the source language, $a_1, a_2, a_3 \ldots, a_n$. We can construct an RE for the language of all valid words by joining the individual REs with alternation as $a_1 \mid a_2 \mid a_3 \mid \cdots \mid a_n$. Since REs are closed under union, the result must be an RE. Anything that we can do to an RE for a single syntactic category will be equally applicable to the RE for the entire set of words in the language.

Closure under concatenation allows us to build complex REs from simpler ones by concatenating them. This property seems both obvious and unimportant. However, it lets us piece together REs in systematic ways. Closure ensures that ab is an RE as long as both a and b are REs. Thus, any techniques that can be applied to either a or b can be applied to ab; this includes constructions that automatically generate a recognizer from REs.

PROGRAMMING LANGUAGES VERSUS NATURAL LANGUAGES

Lexical analysis highlights one of the subtle ways in which a programming language differs from a natural language, such as English or Chinese. In natural languages, the relationship between a word's representation—its spelling or its pictogram—and its meaning is not obvious. In English, *are* is a verb while *art* is a noun, even though they differ only in the final character. Furthermore, not all combinations of characters are legitimate words. For example, *arz* differs minimally from *are* and *art*, but does not occur as a word in normal English usage.

A scanner for English could use FA-based techniques to recognize potential words, since all English words are drawn from a restricted alphabet. After that, however, it must look up the prospective word in some sort of dictionary to see if it is, in fact, a word. If the word can be classified as only one part of speech, the lookup can also resolve that issue. However, many English words can be classified as any of several parts of speech. Examples include *buoy* and *stress*; both can be either a noun or a verb. For these words, the part of speech depends on the surrounding context. In some cases, understanding the grammatical context suffices to classify the word. In other cases, it requires an understanding of meaning, for both the word in question and its surrounding context.

In contrast, the words in a programming language are almost always specified lexically. Thus, any string in $(1 \ldots 9)(0 \ldots 9)^*$ is a positive integer. Any string of $[a \ldots z]([a \ldots z]|[0 \ldots 9])^*$ is an Algol identifier. The string *arz* is as valid as *are*, and no lookup is required to verify its legality. To be sure, some identifiers may be reserved as keywords. However, these exceptions can be specified lexically, as well. No context is required.

This is a deliberate decision in programming language design. The choice to make spelling imply a unique part of speech simplifies scanning, simplifies parsing, and, apparently, gives up little in the expressiveness of the language. Some languages have allowed words with dual parts of speech—for example, PL/I has no reserved keywords. The fact that languages designed later abandoned the idea suggests that the complications outweighed the extra linguistic flexibility.

The closure property for Kleene closure allows us to specify particular kinds of infinite sets with finite patterns. This is critical; infinite patterns are of little use to an implementor. Since the Algol identifier rule does not limit the length of a name, the rule admits an infinite set of words. This lets the programmer write identifiers of arbitrary, but finite, length. Closure allows us to write concise rules for such a set without specifying a maximum length.

The next section shows how to build an FA that recognizes the language specified by an RE and an algorithm that constructs an RE for the language accepted by an FA. Together, these constructions establish the equivalence of REs and FAs. The fact that REs are closed under alternation, concatenation, and closure is critical to these constructions.

The equivalence between REs and FAs also suggests other closure properties. For example, given an FA, we can construct an FA that recognizes all words w that are not in $L(\text{FA})$—called the complement of $L(\text{FA})$. To build the FA for the complement, we can make all nonfinal states final and all final states nonfinal. This suggests that we can add a complement operator to our notation for regular expressions without changing the underlying properties. Many practical systems that use regular expressions have such an operator.

2.4 FROM REGULAR EXPRESSION TO SCANNER AND BACK

The goal of our work with finite automata is to automate the derivation of executable scanners from a collection of regular expressions. This section develops the constructions that transform an RE into an FA that is suitable for direct implementation and an algorithm that derives an RE for the language accepted by an FA. Figure 2.3 shows the relationship between all of these constructions.

To present these constructions, we must first introduce two subclasses of FAs, called *nondeterministic* FAs (or NFAs), and *deterministic* FAs (or DFAs). Section 2.4.1 introduces NFAs and distinguishes them from DFAs. Next, we present the construction in three steps. Thompson's construction derives an NFA from an RE. The subset construction builds a DFA that simulates an NFA. Hopcroft's algorithm, presented in Section 2.4.4, minimizes a DFA. Section 2.4.5 presents Kleene's algorithm for deriving an RE that describes the language accepted by a DFA. It plays a crucial role in establishing that FAs are equivalent to REs by completing the cycle of constructions. Section 2.5 presents several schemes for implementing a DFA.

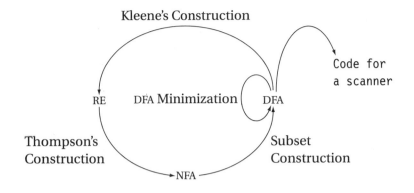

FIGURE 2.3   The Cycle of Constructions

2.4.1 Nondeterministic Finite Automata

Recall from the definition of a regular expression that we designated the empty string, ϵ, as an RE. None of the FAs that we built by hand included ϵ, but some of the REs did. What role does ϵ play in an FA? We can use transitions on ϵ to combine FAs and form FAs for more complex REs. For example, assume that we have FAs for the REs m and n, called FA_m and FA_n, respectively.

We can build an FA for mn by adding a transition on ϵ from the final state of FA_m to the initial state of FA_n, renumbering the states, and using FA_n's final states as the final states for the new FA.

With a transition on ϵ, the definition of acceptance must change slightly to allow one or more ϵ-transitions between any two characters in the input string. For example, in s_1, the FA takes the transition $s_1 \overset{\epsilon}{\to} s_2$ on no input. This is a minor change, but it seems intuitive.

By inspection, we can see that states s_1 and s_2 can be combined and the transition on ϵ eliminated.

Merging two FAs with an ϵ-transition can complicate our model of how FAs work. Consider the FAs for the languages a^* and ab.

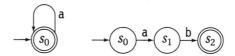

We can combine them with an ϵ-transition to form an FA for a^*ab.

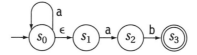

The ϵ transition, in effect, gives the FA two distinct transitions out of s_0 on the letter a. It can take the transition $s_0 \xrightarrow{a} s_0$, or the two transitions $s_0 \xrightarrow{\epsilon} s_1$ and $s_1 \xrightarrow{a} s_2$. Which transition is correct? Consider the strings aab and ab. The DFA should accept both strings. For aab, it should move $s_0 \xrightarrow{a} s_0$, $s_0 \xrightarrow{\epsilon} s_1$, $s_1 \xrightarrow{a} s_2$, and $s_2 \xrightarrow{b} s_3$. For ab, it should move $s_0 \xrightarrow{\epsilon} s_1$, $s_1 \xrightarrow{a} s_2$, and $s_2 \xrightarrow{b} s_3$.

As these two strings show, the correct transition out of s_0 on a depends on the character that follows the a. At each step, an FA examines the current character. Its state encodes the left context—the characters that it has already processed. Because the FA must make a transition before examining the next character, a state such as s_0 violates our notion of the behavior of a sequential algorithm. An FA that includes states such as s_0 that have multiple transitions on a single character is called a *nondeterministic finite automaton* (NFA). In contrast, an FA with unique character transitions in each state is called a *deterministic finite automaton* (DFA).

To make sense of an NFA, we need a new set of rules that describe its behavior. Historically, two distinct models have been given for the behavior of an NFA.

1. Each time the NFA encounters a nondeterministic choice, it follows the transition that leads to an accepting state for the input string, if such a transition exists. This model, using an omniscient NFA, is appealing because it maintains (on the surface) the well-defined accepting mechanism of the DFA.

2. Each time the NFA encounters a nondeterministic choice, the NFA clones itself to pursue each possible transition. Thus, for a given input character, the NFA is in a specific set of states, taken across all of its clones. We call

this set of states the *configuration* of the NFA. When the NFA reaches a configuration in which it has exhausted the input and one or more of the clones has reached a final state, it accepts the string. This model, while somewhat more complex, follows paths through the NFA's transition graph until it either achieves success or exhausts the set of paths.

In either model, it is worthwhile to formalize the acceptance criteria for an NFA. An NFA $(S, \Sigma, \delta, s_0, S_F)$ halts on an input string $x_1 x_2 x_3 \ldots x_k$ if and only if there exists at least one path through the transition diagram that starts in s_0 and ends in some $s_k \in S_F$ such that the edge labels along the path spell out the input string. (Edges labelled with ϵ are omitted.) In other words, the ith path label must be x_i. This definition is consistent with either model of the NFA's behavior.

One consequence of the cycle of constructions in this section is that NFAS and DFAS are equivalent. Any DFA is a special case of an NFA. Thus, an NFA is at least as powerful as a DFA. Any NFA can be simulated by a DFA—a fact established by the subset construction in Section 2.4.3. The intuition behind this idea is simple; the construction is a little more complex.

Consider the state of an NFA when it has reached some point in the input string. Under the second model of NFA behavior, the NFA has some finite number of clones. The number of these configurations can be bounded; for each state, the configuration either includes a clone in that state or it does not. If the NFA has n states, it produces at most 2^n configurations.

To simulate the behavior of the NFA, we need a DFA with a state for each configuration of the NFA. Thus, the DFA may have exponentially more states than the original NFA. (We will denote the set of all subsets of N as 2^N, called the *powerset* of N.) Thus, S_{DFA} might be as large as $2^{S_{NFA}}$. But, $2^{S_{NFA}}$ is finite. Furthermore, the DFA still makes one transition per input symbol. Thus, the DFA that simulates the NFA still runs in time that grows linearly with the length of the input string. The simulation of an NFA on a DFA has a potential space problem, but not a time problem.

Since NFAS and DFAS are equivalent, we should be able to construct a DFA for $a^* ab$. The following DFA will work.

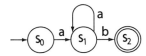

Notice that $a^* ab$ specifies the same set of words as $aa^* b$. This FA has a structure that resembles the RE $aa^* b$.

2.4.2 Regular Expression to NFA: Thompson's Construction

The first step in moving from an RE to an implemented scanner is deriving an NFA from the RE. Thompson's construction follows a straightforward idea. It has a template for building the NFA that corresponds to a single-letter RE, and transformations on the NFAs to represent the impact of the RE operators: concatenation, alternation, and closure. Figure 2.4 shows the trivial NFAs for the REs *a* and *b*, as well as the transformations to form NFAs for the REs *ab*, *a*|*b*, and *a** from the NFAs for *a* and *b*. Arbitrary NFAs can be used in place of the NFAs for *a* and *b*.

The construction begins by building trivial NFAs for each character in the input RE. Next, it applies the transformations for alternation, concatenation,

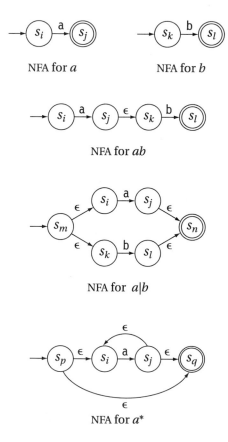

NFA for *a*   NFA for *b*

NFA for *ab*

NFA for *a*|*b*

NFA for *a**

FIGURE 2.4   Trivial NFAs for Regular Expression Operators

and closure to the collection of trivial NFAs in the order dictated by precedence and parentheses. For the RE $a(b|c)^*$, the construction would proceed by building NFAs for a, b, and c. Since parentheses have highest precedence, it next builds the NFA for $b|c$. Closure is next, so it builds the NFA for $(b|c)^*$. Finally, it applies the concatenation operator to build an NFA for $a(b|c)^*$. Figure 2.5 shows this sequence of transformations.

The construction depends on several properties of REs. It relies on the obvious and direct correspondence between the RE operators and the transformations on the NFAs. It combines this with the closure properties on REs for assurance that the transformations produce valid NFAs. Finally, it uses ϵ-moves to connect the NFAs for the subexpressions; this permits the transformations to be simple templates.

The NFAs derived from this construction have several useful properties.

1. Each NFA has a single start state and a single final state. The only transition that enters the start state is the initial transition. No transitions leave the final state.

2. An ϵ-move always connects two states that were, earlier in the process, the start state or final state of an NFA for a component RE.

3. A state has at most two entering and two exiting ϵ-moves, and at most one entering and one exiting move on a symbol in the alphabet.

These properties simplify an implementation of the construction. For example, instead of iterating over all the final states in the NFA for some arbitrary subexpression, the construction only needs to deal with a single final state.

Notice the large number of states in the NFA that Thompson's construction built for $a(b|c)^*$. A human would likely produce a much simpler NFA, such as the following:

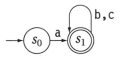

We could directly remove many of the ϵ-moves present in the NFA built by Thompson's construction. This would radically shrink the size of the NFA. However, later stages in the construction will remove them, so we leave a general algorithm for eliminating ϵ-moves as an exercise for the reader.

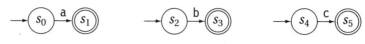

NFAs for *a*, *b* and *c*

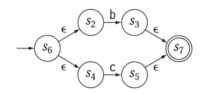

NFA for *b|c*

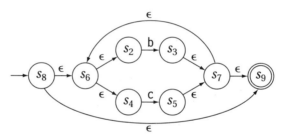

NFA for *(b|c)**

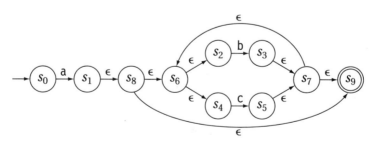

NFA for *a(b|c)**

FIGURE 2.5   Applying Thompson's Construction to *a(b|c)**

2.4.3 NFA to DFA: The Subset Construction

Thompson's construction produces an NFA that recognizes the language specified by an RE. Since neither model for NFA execution lends itself to an obvious and efficient implementation, the next step is to convert the NFA to a DFA that has a simple and efficient implementation. From an NFA, denoted $(N, \Sigma, \delta_n, n_0, n_F)$, the conversion must produce a DFA, denoted $(D, \Sigma, \delta_D, d_0, D_F)$. The key step in this process is deriving D and δ_D from the NFA. (Σ is the same in the NFA and the DFA, and both d_0 and D_F emerge from construction of D and δ_D.) The algorithm that constructs this DFA is called the subset construction. Figure 2.6 gives a high-level version of the algorithm.

The subset construction builds a set Q whose elements, q_i, are sets of states that are subsets of N—that is, each $q_i \in 2^N$. When it is done, each $q_i \in Q$ will correspond to a state in the DFA. The construction builds the various q_i by following the set of all transitions that the NFA can make on a given input. Thus, a set q_i contains precisely the set of states in the NFA that can be reached in response to a particular set of inputs. Each q_i represents a valid configuration of the NFA.

To build Q, the algorithm builds an initial set, q_0, that consists of n_0 and any states in the NFA that can be reached from n_0 by following paths containing only ϵ-transitions. Those states are all equivalent since they can be reached with an empty input.

The code uses the function ϵ-closure: $2^N \rightarrow 2^N$ to construct q_0 from n_0. It starts with a set $n = \{n_0\}$ and systematically adds to n those states that can be reached by following an ϵ-transition from some state already in n. If m is a collection of states that can be reached from n_0 by following paths labelled

$$q_0 \leftarrow \epsilon\text{-}closure(\,n_0)$$
$$Q \leftarrow \{q_0\}$$
$$WorkList \leftarrow q_0$$

$$while\ (WorkList \neq \emptyset)$$
$$\quad remove\ q\ from\ WorkList$$
$$\quad for\ each\ character\ c \in \Sigma$$
$$\quad\quad t \leftarrow \epsilon\text{-}closure(Delta(q,c))$$
$$\quad\quad T[q,c] \leftarrow t$$
$$\quad\quad if\ t \notin Q\ then$$
$$\quad\quad\quad add\ t\ to\ Q\ and\ to\ WorkList$$

FIGURE 2.6 The Subset Construction

with abc, then ϵ-*closure(m)* contains all the states whose paths from n_0 are labelled with abcϵ^*.

The algorithm uses a second function, *Delta:* $2^N \times \Sigma \to 2^N$, to compute transitions for a set of NFA states. *Delta*(q_i, c) applies the NFA's transition function to each element of q_i. It returns a set of NFA states, computed as the union, for each $n \in q_i$, of $\delta_n(n,c)$.

To build the rest of Q, the construction picks a set q_i and uses *Delta* to find the set of states reachable from q_i along transitions labelled c. It computes the ϵ-*closure* of this set and assigns it a temporary name t. It records the transition from q_i to t in a table, T. If $t \notin Q$, it adds t to Q. It repeats this process for every $q_i \in Q$ and every symbol $c \in \Sigma$.

The *while* loop repeatedly removes a set q_i from the worklist and processes it. q_i represents a configuration of the NFA. The algorithm finds each NFA configuration reachable from q_i by iterating through Σ and applying *Delta* and ϵ-*closure*. It adds any new sets that it finds to both Q and the worklist. Since the NFA has at most $|2^N|$ configurations, this process must halt.

Unfortunately, Q can become large—as large as $|2^N|$ distinct states. The degree of nondeterminism found in the input NFA determines how much state expansion occurs. However, the resulting DFA still makes one transition per input character, independent of the size of D. Thus, using nondeterminism to specify and build the NFA increases the space required to represent the corresponding DFA, but not the time required to recognize an input string.

From Q to D

When the algorithm halts, it has constructed both a set of valid NFA configurations, Q, and a table, T, that records potential transitions between elements of Q. Together, Q and T form a model of a DFA that simulates the original NFA. Building the DFA from Q and T is straightforward. Each set $q_i \in Q$ generates a representer state $d_i \in D$. If q_i contained a final state of the NFA, then d_i is a final state of the DFA. The transition function, δ_D, can be constructed directly from T by observing the mapping from q_i to d_i. Finally, the state constructed from q_0 becomes d_0, the initial state of the DFA.

Example

Consider the NFA built for $a(b|c)^*$ in Section 2.4.2. This NFA is shown at the top of Figure 2.7. The states have been renumbered. The table in the center of the figure sketches the steps followed by the subset construction. The first column

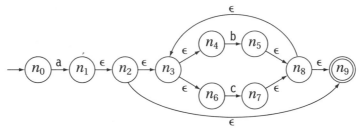

(a) NFA for $a(b|c)^*$ (with states renumbered)

Set Name	DFA States	NFA States	ϵ-closure(Delta(q,*))		
			a	**b**	**c**
q_0	d_0	n_0	$\{n_1, n_2, n_3, n_4, n_6, n_9\}$	– none –	– none –
q_1	d_1	$\{n_1, n_2, n_3, n_4, n_6, n_9\}$	– none –	$\{n_5, n_8, n_9, n_3, n_4, n_6\}$	$\{n_7, n_8, n_9, n_3, n_4, n_6\}$
q_2	d_2	$\{n_5, n_8, n_9, n_3, n_4, n_6\}$	– none –	q_2	q_3
q_3	d_3	$\{n_7, n_8, n_9, n_3, n_4, n_6\}$	– none –	q_2	q_3

(b) Iterations of the Subset Construction

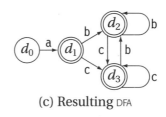

(c) Resulting DFA

FIGURE 2.7   Applying the Subset Construction to the DFA from Figure 2.5

shows the name of the set in Q being processed in a given iteration. The second column shows the name of the corresponding state in the new DFA. The third column shows the set of NFA states contained in the current set from Q. The final three columns show results of computing the ϵ-*closure* of *Delta* on the state for each character in Σ.

The algorithm takes the following steps:

1. The initialization sets q_0 to ϵ-*closure*($\{n_0\}$). The first iteration computes ϵ-*closure(Delta(q_0,* a$))$, ϵ-*closure(Delta(q_0,* b$))$, and ϵ-*closure(Delta(q_0,* c$))$.

   The columns show the result of taking the ϵ-*closure* of the sets returned by those *Delta* computations.

2. Next, the algorithm follows the same process for q_1, computed in the first iteration. This produces two sets, which become q_2 and q_3.

3. In the third and fourth iterations, the algorithm tries to construct new states from q_2 and q_3. These produce sets that are identical to q_2 and q_3, as shown in the table.

The lowest third of the figure shows the resulting DFA; the states correspond to the DFA states from the table and the transitions are given by the *Delta* operations that generate those states. Since the sets q_1, q_2, and q_3 all contain n_9 (the final state of the NFA), all three become final states in the DFA.

Fixed-Point Computations

The subset construction is an example of a *fixed-point computation*, a particular style of computation that arises regularly in computer science. These computations are characterized by iterated application of a monotone function to some collection of sets drawn from a domain whose structure is known. (A function $f : D \rightarrow D$, for a domain D, is *monotone* if, $\forall\, x \in D, f(x) \geq x$.) These computations terminate when they reach a state where further iteration produces the same answer—a "fixed point" in the space of successive iterates produced by the algorithm. Fixed-point computations play an important and recurring role in compiler construction.

Termination arguments for fixed-point algorithms usually depend on the known properties of the domain. In the case of the subset construction, the domain D is 2^{2^N}, since $Q = \{q_0, q_1, q_2, \ldots, q_k\}$, where each $q_1 \in 2^N$. Since N is finite, 2^N and 2^{2^N} are also finite. The *while* loop adds elements to Q; it cannot remove an element from Q. (The *while* loop is monotone increasing; the comparison operator $\geq$ is $\supseteq$ and D.) Since Q can have at most $\mid 2^N \mid$ distinct elements, the *while* loop can iterate at most $\mid 2^N \mid$ times. It may, of course, reach a fixed point and halt more quickly.

Computing ε-*closure* Offline

A straightforward implementation of the subset construction might compute ε-*closure()* by following paths in the transition graph of the NFA as needed. However, we should consider another approach: an offline algorithm that computes ε-*closure({n})* for each state *n* in the NFA's transition graph:

> *for each state* $n \in N$
> $E(n) \leftarrow \{n\}$
>   *WorkList* $\leftarrow N$
> *while (WorkList* $\neq \emptyset$)
>   *remove n from WorkList*
> $t \leftarrow \{ n \} \cup \bigcup_{n \xrightarrow{\epsilon} m \in \delta_n} E(m)$
>   *if* $t \neq E(n)$ *then*
> $E(n) \leftarrow t$
>   *WorkList* $\leftarrow$ *WorkList* $\cup \{ k \mid k \xrightarrow{\epsilon} n \in \delta_N \}$

This is another fixed-point computation.

The termination argument for this algorithm is more complex than that for the algorithm in Figure 2.6. The algorithm halts when the worklist is empty. Initially, the worklist contains N. Each time a set changes, the algorithm adds its predecessors in the transition graph to the worklist.

The $E(n)$ sets grow monotonically. Thus, each $E(n)$ set can change at most $|N|$ times. Each time it changes, its predecessors are added to the worklist. Each set has a fixed number of successors that can place it on the list $|N|$ times. Thus, the worklist eventually becomes empty and the computation halts.

To obtain a time bound, observe that each ε-transition $n \xrightarrow{\epsilon} m$ can force n onto the worklist at most $|E(m)|$ times. Since $|E(m)| \leq |N|$, and the number of ε-transitions is bounded by the number of edges in the transition graph, $|\delta_n|$, the number of nodes on the worklist, summed over the entire algorithm, must be bounded by $|\delta_n| \cdot |N|$. Since each node on the worklist requires one iteration of the while loop, this bounds the number of iterations, too.

2.4.4   DFA to Minimal DFA: Hopcroft's Algorithm

As a final refinement to the RE→DFA conversion, we can add a step that minimizes the DFA built by the subset construction. The DFA that emerges from the subset construction can have a large set of states. While this does not increase

$$P \leftarrow \{ D_F, \{D - D_F\} \}$$
while (P is still changing)
  $T \leftarrow \emptyset$
  for each set $p \in P$
    $T \leftarrow T \cup Split(p)$
  $P \leftarrow T$

Split(S)
  for each $c \in \Sigma$
    if c splits S into s_1 *and* s_2
      then return $\{ s_1, s_2 \}$
  return S

FIGURE 2.8   DFA Minimization Algorithm

the time needed to scan a string, it does increase the size of the recognizer in memory. On modern computers, the speed of memory accesses often governs the speed of computation. A smaller recognizer uses less space on disk, in random-access memory (RAM), and in the processor's cache. Each of those can be an advantage.

To minimize the size of a DFA, $(D, \Sigma, \delta, d_0, D_F)$, we need a technique for recognizing when two states are equivalent—that is, they produce the same behavior on any input string. The algorithm in Figure 2.8 partitions the states in a DFA into sets that represent equivalence classes based on their behavior.

The algorithm constructs a collection, p, of sets $p_1, p_2, p_3, \ldots p_m$, where each p_i contains a set of one or more DFA states. We say that p partitions D because:

1. Each $p_i \in P$ contains one or more states of the DFA, and

2. Each $d_i \in D$ is a member of exactly one $p_j \in P$.

Together, the sets in p cover D: $\bigcup_{1 \leq i \leq m} p_i = D$. These properties define a partition of D.

To minimize a DFA, the algorithm constructs a particular partition of the original DFA's states. It builds a partition that groups states together by their behavior. For any set $p_l \in P$, any two states d_i and d_j in p_l must have the same behavior in response to any input string. To minimize a DFA, each set $p_l \in P$ should be as large as possible, within the constraint of behavioral equivalence.

To construct the partition that represents a minimal DFA, the algorithm begins with an initial rough partition that obeys all the properties *except* behavioral equivalence and iteratively refines that partition to enforce behavioral equivalence. The initial partition contains two sets, $p_0 = D_F$ and $p_1 = \{D - D_F\}$. Separating the final states into p_0 ensures that no set in the final partition contains both final states and nonfinal states, since the algorithm never combines two partitions.

The algorithm refines this initial partition by repeatedly examining each $p_l \in P$ to look for states that should not occupy the same set p_l. Clearly, it cannot trace the behavior of the DFA on every string. It can, however, simulate the behavior of a given state in response to a single input character. This leads to a simple condition for refining the partition: a symbol $c \in \Sigma$ must produce the same behavior for every state $d_j \in p_l$.

This splitting action is the key to understanding the algorithm. For d_i and d_j to remain in the same set p_l, they must take equivalent transitions on each character $c \in \Sigma$. That is, $\forall c \in \Sigma$, $d_i \xrightarrow{c} d_x$ and $d_j \xrightarrow{c} d_y$, where d_x and d_y are in the same $p_t \in P$. Any state $d_a \in p_l$ where $d_k \xrightarrow{c} d_z$, $d_z \notin p_t$, cannot remain in the same partition of d_i and d_j. Similarly, if d_k has no transition on c, it cannot remain in the same partition with d_i and d_j.

Figure 2.9 makes this concrete. The states in $p_1 = \{d_i, d_j, d_k\}$ are equivalent if and only if their transitions, $\forall c \in \Sigma$, take them to states that are, themselves, in an equivalence class. As shown, each state has a transition on c: $d_i \xrightarrow{c} d_x$, $d_j \xrightarrow{c} d_y$, and $d_k \xrightarrow{c} d_z$. If d_x, d_y, and d_z are in the same set in the current partition, as shown on the left, then d_i, d_j, and d_k should remain in the same set, and c does not split p_1. If, on the other hand, two of d_x, d_y, and d_z are in different sets, as shown on the right, then c splits p_1. The algorithm must construct two new sets $\{d_x\}$ and $\{d_y, d_z\}$ to reflect the potential for different outcomes with

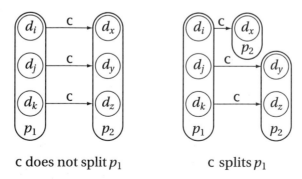

c does not split p_1 c splits p_1

FIGURE 2.9   Splitting a Partition around c

strings that have an initial symbol c. The same split would result if state d_i had no transition on c.

To refine a partition P, the algorithm examines each $p \in P$ and each $c \in \Sigma$. If c splits p, the algorithm constructs two new sets from p and adds them to T. (It could split p into more than two sets, all having internally consistent behavior on c. However, creating one consistent state and lumping the rest of p into another state will suffice. If the latter state is inconsistent in its behavior on c, the algorithm will split it in a later iteration.) The algorithm repeats this process until it finds a partition where it can split no sets.

To construct the new DFA from the final partition p, we can create a single state to represent each set $p \in P$ and add the appropriate transitions between these new representative states. For the state representing p_l, we add a transition to the state representing p_m on c if some $d_j \in p_l$ has a transition on c to some $d_k \in p_m$. From the construction, we know that if d_j has such a transition, so does every other state in p_l; if this were not the case, the algorithm would have split p_l around c. The resulting DFA is minimal; the proof is beyond our scope.

Consider again the DFA for $a\,(b\mid c)^*$ produced by Thompson's construction and the subset construction:

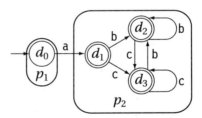

The algorithm constructs an initial partition $p_1 = \{d_0\}$ and $p_2 = \{d_1, d_2, d_3\}$. Since p_1 has only one state, it cannot be split. When the algorithm examines p_2, it finds no transitions on a from any state in p_2. For b, each state has a transition to p_2. Similarly, c always produces a transition to p_2. Thus, no symbol in Σ splits p_2, and the partition $P = \{\{d_0\}, \{d_1, d_2, d_3\}\}$ minimizes the DFA.

Choosing represener states for p_1 and p_2 and adding the transitions produces the following DFA:

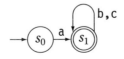

Recall that this is the DFA that we suggested a human would derive. After minimization, the automatic techniques produce the same result.

$$
\begin{aligned}
&\textit{for } i = 0 \textit{ to } |D| - 1 \\
&\quad \textit{for } j = 0 \textit{ to } |D| - 1 \\
&\qquad R_{ij}^0 \;=\; \{a \mid \delta(d_i, a) = d_j\} \\
&\qquad \textit{if } (i = j) \textit{ then} \\
&\qquad\quad R_{ij}^0 \;=\; R_{ij}^0 \mid \{\epsilon\} \\
&\textit{for } k = 1 \textit{ to } |D| - 1 \\
&\quad \textit{for } i = 0 \textit{ to } |D| - 1 \\
&\qquad \textit{for } j = 0 \textit{ to } |D| - 1 \\
&\qquad\quad R_{ij}^k \;=\; R_{ik}^{k-1} (R_{kk}^{k-1})^* R_{kj}^{k-1} \mid R_{ij}^{k-1} \\
&L = \mid_{s_j \in S_F} \; R_{0j}^{|D|-1}
\end{aligned}
$$

FIGURE 2.10   Deriving a Regular Expression from a DFA

This algorithm is another example of a fixed-point computation. P is finite; at most, it can contain $|D|$ elements. The *while* loop splits sets in P but never combines them. Thus, $|P|$ grows monotonically. The loop halts when some iteration splits no sets in P. The worst-case behavior occurs when each state in the DFA has different behavior; in that case, the *while* loop halts when P has a distinct set for each $d_i \in D$. This occurs when the algorithm is applied to a minimal DFA.

2.4.5 DFA to Regular Expression

The final step in the cycle of constructions, shown in Figure 2.3, is to construct a regular expression from a DFA. The combination of Thompson's construction and the subset construction provide a constructive proof that DFAs are at least as powerful as REs. This section presents Kleene's construction, which builds an RE to describe the set of strings accepted by an arbitrary DFA. This algorithm establishes that REs are at least as powerful as DFAs.

Consider the transition diagram of a DFA as a graph with labelled edges. The problem of deriving an RE that describes the language accepted by the DFA corresponds to a path problem over the DFA's transition diagram. The set of strings in $L(\text{DFA})$ consists of the set of edge labels for every path from d_0 to $d_i, \forall\, d_i \in D_F$. For any DFA with a cyclic transition graph, the set of such paths is infinite. Fortunately, REs have the Kleene closure operator to handle this case and summarize the complete set of subpaths created by a cycle.

Figure 2.10 shows one algorithm to compute this path expression. It assumes that the DFA has states numbered from 0 to $|D| - 1$, with d_0 as the start state. It generates an expression that represents the labels along all paths between two nodes, for each pair of nodes in the transition diagram. As a final step, it combines the expressions for each path that leaves d_0 and reaches some final state, $d_i \in D_F$. In this way, it systematically constructs the path expressions for all paths.

The algorithm computes a set of expressions, denoted R_{ij}^k, for all the relevant values of i, j, and k. R_{ij}^k is an expression that describes all paths through the transition graph, from state i to state j without going through a state numbered higher than k. Here, *through* means both entering and leaving, so that $R_{1,16}^2$ can be nonempty if an edge runs directly from 1 to 16.

Initially, the algorithm sets R_{ij}^0 to contain the labels of all edges that run directly from i to j, since direct paths go through no nodes. Over successive iterations, it builds up longer paths by adding to R_{ij}^{k-1} the paths that pass through k on their way from i to j. Given R_{ij}^{k-1}, the set of paths added by going from $k-1$ to k is exactly the set of paths that run from i to k using no state higher than $k-1$, concatenated with the paths from k to itself that pass through no state higher than $k-1$, followed by the paths from k to j that pass through no state higher than $k-1$. That is, each iteration of the loop on k adds the paths that pass through k to each set R_{ij}^{k-1}.

When the k loop terminates, the various R_{ij}^k expressions account for all paths in the transition graph. The final step computes the set of paths that start with d_0 and end in some final state, $d_j \in d_F$, as the alternation of the appropriate path expressions.

2.4.6 Using a DFA as a Recognizer

Thus far, we have developed the mechanisms to construct a DFA implementation from a single RE. To be useful, a compiler's scanner must recognize all the syntactic categories that appear in the grammar for the source language. What we need, then, is a recognizer that can handle all the REs for the language's microsyntax. Given the REs for the various syntactic categories, $r_1, r_2, r_3, \ldots, r_k$, we can construct a single RE for the entire collection by forming $(r_1|r_2|r_3|\ldots|r_k)$.

If we run this RE through the entire process, building NFAs for the subexpressions, joining them with ϵ-transitions, coalescing states, constructing the DFA that simulates the NFA, and turning the DFA into executable code, we get a scanner that recognizes the next word that matches one of the r_i's. That is, when we invoke it on some input, it will run through the characters one at a time and accept the string if it is in a final state when it exhausts the input.

Since most real programs contain more than one word, we need to transform either the language or the recognizer.

At the language level, we can insist that each word end with some easily recognizable delimiter, like a blank or a tab. This is deceptively attractive. Taken literally, it would require delimiters surrounding commas, operators such as + and -, and parentheses.

At the recognizer level, we can change the implementation of the DFA and its notion of acceptance. To find the longest word that matches one of the REs, the DFA should run until it reaches the point where the current state, s, has no outgoing transition on the next character. At that point, the implementation must decide which RE it has matched. Two cases arise; the first is simple. If s is a final state, then the DFA has found a word in the language and should report the word and its syntactic category.

If s is not a final state, matters are more complex. If the DFA passed through one or more final states on its path to s, then the recognizer should report the last final state that it encountered—corresponding to the longest keyword that it matched. To accomplish this, the implementation can track the most recent final state, along with its position in the input string. Then, when it reaches a state s where it has no legal transition, it can report the most recent final state—either s or an earlier state. If the recognizer has encountered no final states on its path to s, then the input does not begin with a valid word and the recognizer should report the error to the user.

As a final complication, a final state in the DFA may represent several final states in the original NFA. For example, if the lexical specification includes REs for keywords as well as an RE for identifiers, then a keyword such as new might match two REs. The recognizer must decide which syntactic category to return: identifier or the singleton category for the keyword new.

Most scanner-generator tools allow the compiler writer to specify a priority among patterns. When the recognizer matches multiple patterns, it returns the syntactic category of the highest-priority pattern. This mechanism resolves the problem in a simple way. The lex scanner generator, distributed with many Unix systems, assigns priorities based on position in the list of regular expressions. The first RE has highest priority; the last RE has lowest priority.

2.5 IMPLEMENTING SCANNERS

A straightforward scanner generator would take as input a set of REs, construct the NFA for each RE, combine the NFAs using ϵ-transitions (using the pattern for $a|b$ in Thompson's construction), perform the subset construction to create

```
char ← NextChar()
state ← s0
while (char ≠ eof)
    state ← δ(state,char)
    char ← NextChar()
if (state ∈ SF)
    then report acceptance
    else report failure
```

δ	r	0,1,2,3,4 5,6,7,8,9	Other
s_0	s_1	s_e	s_e
s_1	s_e	s_2	s_e
s_2	s_e	s_2	s_e
s_e	s_e	s_e	s_e

FIGURE 2.11   Scanner for Register Names

the corresponding DFA, and then minimize the DFA. At that point, the scanner generator must construct executable code for the DFA.

This section covers several issues that arise in implementing scanners from DFAs. The first two subsections present different strategies for constructing executable code from a DFA. The remaining subsections describe low-level issues that arise in scanner design and implementation.

2.5.1   Table-Driven Scanners

To convert a DFA into an executable program, the scanner generator uses a skeleton scanner, parameterized by a table that implements the transition function, δ. Changing the language recognized by the scanner requires replacing the table. Recall the FA for our initial ILOC register specification $(r[0 \ldots 9][0 \ldots 9]^*)$.

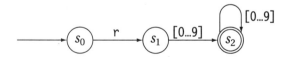

Figure 2.11 shows a table-driven implementation of this DFA. The table encodes the transition function, δ.

In representing the table, we have compressed the columns for the digits zero through nine into a single column. This suggests the kind of compaction that can be achieved with simple schemes, such as combining identical columns. Using a compressed table, however, requires a further translation on the input character. Typically, this takes one additional memory reference per character; the tradeoff between the cost of that extra memory reference and the cost of larger tables depends on the target machine.

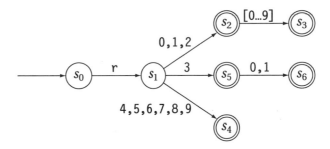

The DFA

δ	r	0,1	2	3	4...9	Other
s_0	s_1	s_e	s_e	s_e	s_e	s_e
s_1	s_e	s_2	s_2	s_5	s_4	s_e
s_2	s_e	s_3	s_3	s_3	s_3	s_e
s_3	s_e	s_e	s_e	s_e	s_e	s_e
s_4	s_e	s_e	s_e	s_e	s_e	s_e
s_5	s_e	s_6	s_e	s_e	s_e	s_e
s_6	s_e	s_e	s_e	s_e	s_e	s_e
s_e	s_e	s_e	s_e	s_e	s_e	s_e

The Transition Table

FIGURE 2.12   Implementing the Refined Register Specification

The extent to which the table can be compressed depends on the underlying structure of the DFA. For example, the more refined register specification

$$r\ ((0\,|\,1\,|\,2)\ ([0\ldots 9]\,|\,\epsilon)\ |\ (4\,|\,5\,|\,6\,|\,7\,|\,8\,|\,9)\ |\ (3\,(0\,|\,1\,|\,\epsilon)))$$

produced a seven-state DFA, shown with its table in Figure 2.12. This table has more information content than the table in Figure 2.11; consequently, it cannot be compressed as tightly.

Generating tables from a description of the DFA is straightforward. For each state, in order, the code examines each outbound transition and emits the appropriate row in the table.

$$goto\ s_0$$

s_0: *char* ← *NextChar()*
 if (char = 'r')
  then goto s_1
  else goto s_e

s_1: *char* ← *NextChar()*
 if ('0'≤char≤'9')
  then goto s_2
  else goto s_e

s_2: *char* ← *NextChar()*
 if ('0'≤char≤'9')
  then goto s_2
  else if (char = eof)
   then report acceptance
   else goto s_e

s_e: *report failure*

FIGURE 2.13   A Direct-Coded Recognizer for "r *digit digit**"

2.5.2 Direct-Coded Scanners

The table-driven scanner uses an explicit variable, *state*, to hold the current state of the DFA. The *while* loop tests *char* against *eof*, computes a new state, advances the input stream, and branches back to the top of the loop. The implementation spends a large part of its time manipulating or testing the state.

Table accesses also incur some overhead; in particular, the address calculation requires a multiply and an add (see Section 7.5). We can avoid much of this overhead by encoding the state information implicitly in the program counter. In this model, each state checks the next character against its transitions and branches directly to the next state. This creates a program with complex control flow. Figure 2.13 shows a version of the skeleton recognizer written in this style; it implements the FA for Figure 2.11. The code is longer and more complicated than the table-driven version. Because it incurs less overhead per character, it should also be faster than that version.

Of course, this implementation paradigm violates many of the precepts of structured programming. In a small example like this one, the code may be comprehensible. As the RE specification becomes more complex and generates both more states and more transitions, the added complexity can make the code difficult for a human to follow. If the code is generated directly from a collection of REs, using automatic tools, there is little reason for a human to read or debug the scanner code at all. The additional speed obtained from lower overhead and better memory locality makes direct coding an attractive option.

2.5.3 Handling Keywords

We have consistently assumed that keywords in the input language should be recognized by including explicit REs for them in the description that generates the DFA and the recognizer. Many authors have proposed an alternative strategy: having the DFA classify them as identifiers and testing each identifier to determine whether or not it is a keyword.

This strategy made sense in the context of a hand-implemented scanner. The additional complexity added by checking explicitly for keywords causes a significant expansion in the number of DFA states. This added implementation burden matters in a hand-coded program. With a reasonable hash table (see Section B.4), the expected cost of each lookup should be constant. In fact, this scheme has been used as a classic application for *perfect hashing*. In perfect hashing, the implementor ensures, for a fixed set of keys, that the hash function generates a compact set of integers with no collisions. This lowers the cost of lookup on each keyword. If the table implementation takes into account the perfect hash function, a single probe serves to distinguish keywords from identifiers. If it retries on a miss, however, the behavior can be much worse for non-keywords than for keywords.

If the compiler writer uses a scanner generator to construct the recognizer, then the added complexity of recognizing keywords in the DFA is handled by the tools. The extra states that this adds consume memory, but not compile time. Using the DFA mechanism to recognize keywords avoids a table lookup on each identifier. It also avoids the overhead of implementing a keyword table and its support functions. In most cases, folding keyword recognition into the DFA makes more sense than using a separate lookup table.

2.5.4 Specifying Actions

In building a scanner generator, the designer can allow actions for each transition in the DFA or only in the final states of the DFA. This choice has a strong impact on the efficiency of the resulting DFA. Consider, for example, our earlier RE for unsigned integers; $0 \mid [1 \ldots 9][0 \ldots 9]^*$. A scanner generator that allows actions only in accepting states will force the user to rescan the string to compute its actual value. Thus, the scanner will step through each character of the already recognized word, performing some appropriate action to convert the text into a decimal value. Worse yet, if the system provides a built-in mechanism for the conversion, the programmer will likely use it, adding the

REPRESENTING STRINGS

The scanner classifies words in the input program into a small set of categories. From a functional perspective, each word in the input stream becomes a pair ⟨*word,type*⟩, where *word* is the actual text that forms the word and *type* represents its syntactic category.

For many categories, having both *word* and *type* is redundant. The words + , × , and for have only one spelling. For identifiers, numbers, and character strings, however, the compiler will repeatedly use the *word*. Unfortunately, many compilers are written in languages that lack an appropriate representation for the *word* part of the pair. We need a representation that is compact and offers a fast equality test for two words.

A common practice to address this problem has the scanner create a single hash table (see Section B.4) to hold all the distinct strings used in the input program. The compiler then uses either the string's index in this "string table" or a pointer to its stored image in the string table as a proxy for the string. Information derived from the string, such as the length of a character constant or the value and type of a numerical constant, can be computed once and referenced quickly through the table. Since most computers have storage-efficient representations for integers and pointers, this reduces the amount of memory used internally in the compiler. By using the hardware comparison mechanisms on the integer or pointer proxies, it also simplifies the code used to compare them.

overhead of a procedure call to this simple and frequently executed operation. (On Unix systems, many lex-generated scanners contain an action that invokes sscanf() to perform precisely this function.)

If, however, the scanner generator allows actions for each transition, the compiler writer can implement the ancient assembly language trick for this conversion. On recognizing an initial digit, the accumulator is set to the value of the recognized digit. For each subsequent digit, the accumulator is multiplied by ten and the new digit added to it. This algorithm avoids touching the character twice; it produces the result quickly and inline using the well-known conversion algorithm; and it eliminates the string manipulation overhead implicit in the first solution. (The scanner probably copies characters from the input buffer into a result string for each transition in the first scenario.)

In general, the scanner should avoid processing each character multiple times. The more freedom that it allows the compiler writer in the placement of actions, the simpler it becomes to implement effective and efficient algorithms that avoid copying characters and examining them several times. In a typical compiler, this level of inefficiency may not be noticed. However, in applications where DFA-based pattern matching is a time-critical component, doubling the amount of data-manipulation can be significant.

2.6   ADVANCED TOPICS

This chapter has dealt, largely, with the theory of specifying and automatically generating scanners. The development of this theory has affected the design of programming languages. Thus, most modern programming languages have a simple lexical structure that makes them amenable to scanning with DFA-based recognizers. To find features that are hard to scan, we must consider older languages.

FORTRAN 77 has a number of properties that make it difficult to scan. Blanks and tabs are not significant; the programmer can add them or omit them without changing the meaning of a statement. (Algol 68 had a similar rule.) The programmer can specify the same variable as anint, an int, and an int. Identifiers are limited to six characters, and the language relies on this property to make some constructs recognizable. Keywords are not reserved; the programmer can use them as identifiers. (PL/I has a similar rule.) Thus, the scanner must use surrounding context to classify some words. Finally, FORTRAN supported several distinct ways of writing literal constant strings.

The FORTRAN fragment shown in Figure 2.14 shows some of the difficulties in scanning FORTRAN. The statement labelled 10 contains three words, integer, function, and a. To discover this, the scanner must apply the six-character limit on identifiers. Statement 20 declares a and b as "parameters"—named manifest constants that can be used in place of literal constants. With statement 20 as context, the declaration character*(a-b) in statement 30 expands to character*4.

Statement 50 is a format statement because the sequence 4H is a prefix that designates)=(3 as a literal string, called a *Hollerith constant*. It contains four words: the keyword format, (, the string constant)=(3, and). Statement 60 is an assignment to the fourth element of the integer array format. The difference

Fortran Code	Explanation
10 integerfunctiona	6-character rule
20 parameter(a=6,b=2)	changes next statement
30 implicit character*(a-b)(c-d)	*(a-b) becomes *4
40 integer format(10),if(10),d09e1	
50 format(4h)=(3)	format statement
60 format(4)=(3)	assignment to format
70 do9e1=12	assignment to do9e1
80 do9e1=1,2	header of a do loop
	9e1 scans as 9 and e1
90 if(x)=1	assignment to if
100 if(x)h=1	
110 if(x)120,130	
120 end	
c This is a comment	must look past comment
$file(1)	$ is in continuation field
130 end	

FIGURE 2.14 Scanning FORTRAN

in syntactic category for format depends on the presence or absence of the character h after the 4.[2]

Context also differentiates statements 70 and 80. The first is an assignment to the integer variable do9e1, while the comma in the second makes it the header of a do loop. Statements 90, 100, and 110 are also similar in form. However, in 90, if is an identifier, while it is a keyword in 100 and 110.

Statement 120 appears to be an end statement, denoting the end of a procedure. It is followed, however, by a comment; the c in the first column marks a comment line. The line after the comment, however, contains a character (the $) in column six, which makes it a continuation of the previous statement. This makes the letters file part of the statement labelled 120. Since blanks, newlines, and intervening comment lines are not significant, the

---

2. While Hollerith constants were dropped from the language with the 1977 standard, almost all FORTRAN 77 compilers support them to provide backward compatibility with the 1966 FORTRAN standard.

first word in 120 is endfile, split across an internal comment. (The number of comment lines that can appear in the middle of a statement [or in the middle of a keyword] is unbounded.) Statement 130 marks the actual end of the procedure.

Two-Pass Scanners

Many FORTRAN compilers use two-pass scanners. Some of these, like the scanner built for the PFC system at Rice, have two explicit passes. Others, such as the scanner for the original Unix f77 compiler and f2c, perform some scanning and simplification as part of the input buffering. Both of these approaches scan some parts of the text multiple times.

The first pass of the PFC scanner performed ad hoc analysis to classify each statement and rewrote the text in ways that simplified the second pass. The key to correctly dividing the text into words is distinguishing assignment statements and comments from other statements. An assignment statement begins with an identifier. All other FORTRAN statements begin with a keyword.

To discover assignment statements, the PFC scanner used several rules. An operator is considered "free" if it is not inside one or more sets of parentheses. An assignment statement must contain a free =. A free slash before the first free = proves that the the statement is not an assignment. A free comma in the statement indicates that it is not an assignment.

The final rule is complex. If the scanner encounters parentheses before finding a free = and the first character after the parenthetical expression is neither = nor (, then the statement is not an assignment. If the character after the parenthetical expression is =, then the statement is an assignment (as with 90 in the example). If the character is (, it might be a substring expression; in this case, the = must immediately follow the second parenthetical expression. Finally, if the character after the parenthetical expression is neither = nor (, the statement is not an assignment, as with 100 and 110 in the example.

The first pass of the PFC scanner labelled each statement with a label indicating its type. It removed all comments. It discovered string constants and rewrote them with a uniform, recognizable syntax. It expanded each use of a parameter. With these changes, the code was much easier to scan.

The second pass looked at the code on a statement-by-statement basis. It looked at the statement's type and invoked an appropriate recognizer on the remainder of the statement. The syntax of the format statement differs wildly from other statements.

Some context is still required during scanning. For example, the string do9e1 is one word in statement 70 and three in statement 80. After handling the do in 80, the scanner encounters 9e1 and recognizes the label 9 and the identifier e1, instead of the floating-point number 9e1.

Using Right Context

Some scanner generators include a notation for specifying right context. Some of the difficulties of FORTRAN can be handled using right context in the recognizer. Consider an RE for the right context of the do keyword. It must recognize a label, followed by an identifier, an =, a number, and a comma.

$$[0...9]^* \quad ([A...Z] \mid [0...9])^* = [0...9]^* \, ,$$

If we add the keyword do to the front of this expression, it will match statement 80 but not 70.[3] By giving this RE a higher priority than the RE for the identifier and having the recognizer mark the end of the matching string at the end of the initial do, the compiler writer can use an RE-based recognizer to find the do keyword. Similar right context would let the recognizer distinguish the 9e1 as a label and an identifier in statement 80, rather than a floating-point number.

Using right context lets the compiler writer handle many of the complications of FORTRAN. Some problems, however, are not easily handled with this mechanism. Internal comments, like the one in statement 120, require an unbounded right context that can contain any character—as long as it occurs in a line with the character c in the first column. To deal with internal comments, we could add the regular expression for a comment between any two symbols in the RE. This would make the RE both larger and more difficult to devise. Comments and string recognition can be handled with a lightweight mechanism in the code that buffers the input; the scanner for f77 and f2c uses this approach.

In contrast, the complications posed by parameter expansion can be deferred to the parser. In this approach, the scanner recognizes a use of a parameter constant as an identifier. The parser uses a looser grammar for the language. For example, the grammar would need to allow an expression containing identifiers in the expression for a character string length. (The standard specifies that the expression must be an unsigned integer constant, an integer constant expression that evaluates to a positive integer, or an asterisk.) The parser would build a small expression tree for the expression, evaluate it, and rewrite it as an integer value.

---

3. We have simplified the expression by assuming that the initial value of the loop-index variable is a positive integer.

2.7 SUMMARY AND PERSPECTIVE

The widespread use of regular expressions for searching and scanning is one of the success stories of modern computer science. These ideas were developed as an early part of the theory of formal languages and automata. They are routinely applied in tools ranging from text editors to web filtering engines to compilers as a means of concisely specifying groups of strings that happen to be regular languages. Anytime that a finite collection of words must be recognized, DFA-based recognizers deserve serious consideration.

Most modern compilers use generated scanners. The properties of deterministic finite automata match closely the demands of a compiler. The cost of recognizing a word is proportional to its length. The overhead per character is small in a careful implementation. The number of states can be reduced with the widely used minimization algorithm. Direct encoding of the states provides a speed boost over a table-driven interpreter. Because the widely available scanner generators are good, hand implementation can rarely, if ever, be justified.

CHAPTER NOTES

Originally, the separation of lexical analysis, or scanning, from syntax analysis, or parsing, was justified with an efficiency argument. Since the cost of scanning grows linearly with the number of characters, and the constant costs are low, pushing analysis from the parser into a separate scanner lowered the cost of compiling. The advent of efficient parsing techniques weakened this argument, but the practice of building scanners persists because it provides a clean separation of concerns between lexical structure and syntactic structure.

Because scanner construction plays a small role in building an actual compiler, we have tried to keep this chapter brief. Thus, the chapter omits many theorems on regular languages and finite automata that the ambitious reader might enjoy. The many good texts on this subject can provide a much deeper treatment of finite automata, regular expressions, and their many useful properties [184, 222, 307].

Kleene [213] established the equivalence of REs and FAs. Both Kleene closure and the RE→DFA algorithm bear his name. McNaughton and Yamada showed one construction that relates REs to NFAs [256]. The construction in this chapter is patterned after Thompson's work [321], which was motivated by the implementation of a textual search command for an early text editor.

Johnson describes the first application of this technology to automate scanner construction [197]. The DFA minimization algorithm is due to Hopcroft [183]. It has found application to many different problems, including detecting when two program variables always have the same value [21].

Preston Briggs pointed out the negative impact of perfect hashing [248] for reserved words on scanner performance. The FORTRAN code in Figure 2.14 is taken from a talk given by F. K. Zadeck, while he was a graduate student.

CHAPTER 3

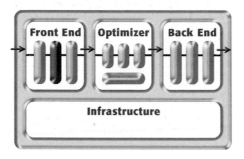

Front End   Optimizer   Back End

Infrastructure

Parsing

3.1   INTRODUCTION

A compiler's parser has the primary responsibility for recognizing syntax—that is, for determining if the program being compiled is a valid sentence in the syntactic model programming language. The parser works with an abstracted version of the program, a stream of words and parts of speech produced by the scanner. If this stream of words forms a valid program, then the parser builds a concrete model of the program for use by the later phases of the compiler. Those later phases analyze this concrete model, in semantic elaboration and translation. The results of that analysis are recorded as part of the compiler's internal model of the program. If the input does not form a valid program, the parser should report the problems back to the user, along with useful diagnostic information.

Parsing has much in common with scanning. In particular, parsing is another area where extensive study of the underlying mathematics has led directly to the creation of efficient recognizers, or parsers, for large classes of languages. Tools that automate most of parser construction are widely available. In this chapter, we will study how to express the syntax of a programming language, using context-free grammars, and how to produce robust and efficient parsers from such grammars. The later parts of the chapter focus on three specific parsing techniques. The primary focus is on top-down, recursive-descent parsing and bottom-up, LR(1) parsing. Both methods lead to high-quality parsers for typical programming languages. Top-down, recursive-descent parsing, as presented here, leads to the systematic construction of a hand-coded parser. Recursive-descent parsers are typically compact and efficient. Because the same insights lead directly to table-driven LL(1) parsers, the chapter briefly describes them. Bottom-up, LR(1) parsing, as presented here, leads to automatic construction of efficient, accurate, table-driven parsers. All three techniques are used in commercial compilers.

Many other parsing methods appear in practice, in the research literature, and in other textbooks. We focus on recursive-descent to illustrate top-down parsing because of the intuitive relationship between the code and the underlying grammar and the ease with which efficient recursive-descent parsers can be built. To illustrate bottom-up parsing, we selected the canonical LR(1) parser because of its generality. Other LR(1) techniques, notably SLR(1) and LALR(1), are easily understood as either simplifications or extensions of the canonical LR(1) construction.

The first section of this chapter introduces context-free grammars and explores some of the issues that can arise while encoding a programming language into the form of a context-free grammar. The second major section develops the insights that underlie top-down parsing and describes the construction of recursive-descent parsers by using handwritten code in a grammar-structured framework. The third major section introduces a style of bottom-up parsing called shift-reduce parsing, develops the somewhat subtle mathematics that drives these parsers, and shows an example LR(1) parser. The next section shows how to derive the parse tables that form the heart of an LR(1) parser; in practice, these algorithms are implemented in a parser-generator system so that the compiler writer need not execute them by hand. The final section addresses a series of pragmatic issues that arise in designing and building top-quality parsers.

3.2 EXPRESSING SYNTAX

A parser is, essentially, an engine that determines whether or not the input program is a syntactically valid sentence in the source language. To answer this question, we need both a formal mechanism for specifying the syntax of the input language and a systematic method of determining membership in this formally specified language. This section describes one mechanism for expressing syntax: a simple variation on the Backus-Naur form for writing formal grammars. The remainder of the chapter discusses techniques to determine membership in the language described by a formal grammar.

3.2.1 Context-Free Grammars

To describe the syntax of a programming language, we need a notation that can capture the syntactic structure of such languages and that leads to efficient recognizers. The regular expressions of Chapter 2 are not sufficiently expressive to capture the syntax of a language such as Java or C. We need a more powerful notation. The traditional notation for expressing syntax is a *grammar*—a collection of rules that define, mathematically, which strings of symbols are valid sentences. A class of grammars called *context-free grammars* provides this power. Fortunately, large subclasses of the context-free grammars have the property that they lead to efficient recognizers.

A context-free grammar, G, is a set of rules that describe how to form sentences; the collection of sentences that can be derived from G is called the *language defined by* G, and denoted $L(G)$. An example may help. Consider the following grammar, which we call *SN*:

$$
\begin{aligned}
\textit{SheepNoise} \quad &\rightarrow \quad \text{baa } \textit{SheepNoise} \\
&\mid \quad \text{baa}
\end{aligned}
$$

The first rule, or *production*, reads "*SheepNoise* can derive the word baa followed by more *SheepNoise*." Here *SheepNoise* is a syntactic variable representing the set of strings that can be derived from the grammar. We call these syntactic variables *nonterminal symbols*. We refer to words in the language defined by a grammar as *terminal symbols*. The second rule reads "*SheepNoise* can also derive the string baa."

To understand the relationship between the *SN* grammar and $L(SN)$, we need to specify how to apply the rules in the grammar to derive sentences in $L(SN)$. To begin, we must identify the *goal symbol* or *start symbol* of *SN*. The goal symbol represents the set of all strings in $L(SN)$. As such, it cannot be one of the words in the language. Instead, it must be one of the syntactic variables introduced to add structure and abstraction to the language. Since *SN* has only one syntactic variable, *SheepNoise* must be the goal symbol.

To derive a sentence, we start with the goal symbol, *SheepNoise*. We pick a syntactic variable, α, in our prototype string, choose a grammar rule, $\alpha \rightarrow \beta$, and replace the selected occurrence of α with β. We repeat this process until the string contains no more syntactic variables; at this point, the string consists entirely of words and is a sentence in the language.

BACKUS-NAUR FORM

The traditional notation used by computer scientists to represent a context-free grammar is called Backus-Naur form, or BNF. BNF denoted nonterminal symbols by wrapping them in angle brackets, like ⟨SheepNoise⟩. Terminal symbols were underlined. The symbol ::= means "derives," and the symbol | means "also derives." In BNF, the sheep noise grammar becomes:

⟨SheepNoise⟩   ::=   baa ⟨SheepNoise⟩

              | baa

This is completely equivalent to our grammar *SN*.

BNF has its origins in the late 1950s and early 1960s. The syntactic conventions of angle brackets, underlining, ::=, and | arose in response to the limited typographic options available to people writing language descriptions. (For an extreme example, see David Gries' book *Compiler Construction for Digital Computers*, which was printed entirely on a standard lineprinter [166].) Throughout this book, we use a typographically updated form of BNF. Nonterminals are written in *italics*. Terminals are written in the typewriter font. We use the symbol → for "derives."

At each point in this derivation process, the string is a collection of symbols in the grammar. The symbols can be either terminal or nonterminal symbols. Such a string is called a *sentential form* if it occurs in some step of a valid derivation—that is, it can be derived from the start symbol and a valid sentence can be derived from it, each in zero or more steps. If we begin with *SheepNoise* and apply successive rewrites using the two rules, at each step in the process the string is a sentential form.[1] When we have reached the point where the string contains only words (no syntactic variables), the string is a sentence in $L(SN)$.

For *SN*, we must begin with the string *SheepNoise*. Using rule 2, we can rewrite *SheepNoise* as baa. Since the sentential form contains only terminal symbols, no further rewrites are possible. Thus, the sentential form baa is

---

1. At each step, we can apply any rule whose left-hand side appears in the sentential form. The rules give us no way to constrain the application of a rule based on prior context. For this reason, we call the grammar a context-free grammar. When we define context-free grammars more formally, this notion will take concrete form as a restriction on the form of each rule in the grammar.

a valid sentence in the language defined by our grammar. We can represent this derivation in tabular form.

Rule	Sentential Form
	SheepNoise
2	baa

We can also begin with *SheepNoise* and apply rule 1 to obtain the sentential form baa *SheepNoise*. Next, we can use rule 2 to derive the sentence baa baa.

Rule	Sentential Form
	SheepNoise
1	baa *SheepNoise*
2	baa baa

As a notational convenience, we will build on this interpretation of the symbol →; when convenient, we will write →⁺ to mean "derives in one or more steps." Thus, we might write *SheepNoise* →⁺ baa baa.

Of course, we can apply rule 1 in place of rule 2 to generate an even longer string of baas. Repeated application of this pattern of rules, in a sequence (*rule 1*)* *rule 2*, will derive the language consisting of one or more occurrences of the word baa. This corresponds to the set of noises that a sheep makes, under normal circumstances. These derivations all have the same form.

Rule	Sentential Form
	SheepNoise
1	baa *SheepNoise*
1	baa baa *SheepNoise*
	. . . and so on . . .
1	baa . . . baa *SheepNoise*
2	baa baa . . . baa

More formally, a context-free grammar G is a quadruple, (T, NT, S, P), where

T is the set of terminal symbols, or words, in the language. In a compiler, the terminal symbols correspond to words discovered in lexical analysis. Terminal symbols are the fundamental units of grammatical sentences.

NT is the set of nonterminal symbols that appear in the rules of the grammar. NT consists of all the symbols mentioned in the rules other than those in T. Nonterminal symbols are syntactic variables used by the grammar writer to provide abstraction and structure in the set of rules.

s is a designated member of NT called the goal symbol or start symbol. The language that G describes, denoted $L(G)$, contains exactly those sentences that can be derived from s. In other words, s represents the set of sentences in $L(G)$.

P is a set of productions or rewrite rules. Formally, $P : NT \rightarrow (T \cup NT)^*$, or P maps an element of NT into an element of $(T \cup NT)^*$. Notice that the definition allows only a single nonterminal on the left-hand side. This restriction ensures that the grammar is context free.

The rules in P encode the syntactic structure of the grammar.

We can derive T, NT, and P directly from the grammar rules. For SN, these sets have the following values:

$$
\begin{aligned}
T &= \{\text{baa}\} & s &= \{\textit{SheepNoise}\} \\
NT &= \{\textit{SheepNoise}\} & P &= \left\{ \begin{array}{l} \textit{SheepNoise} \rightarrow \text{baa } \textit{SheepNoise} \\ \textit{SheepNoise} \rightarrow \text{baa} \end{array} \right\}
\end{aligned}
$$

In SN, *SheepNoise* must be the start symbol, s, since NT contains only one symbol. In general, discovering the start symbol is not possible. Consider, for example, the grammar

$$
\begin{array}{llll}
\textit{Paren} & \rightarrow & (\quad \textit{Bracket} \quad) & \qquad \textit{Bracket} \rightarrow [\quad \textit{Paren} \quad] \\
& | & (\qquad\qquad\quad) & \qquad\qquad\qquad | \quad [\qquad\qquad]
\end{array}
$$

The grammar describes the set of sentences consisting of balanced pairs of alternating parentheses and square brackets. It is not clear, however, if the outermost pair should be parentheses or square brackets. Designating *Paren* as *s* forces outermost parentheses. Designating *Bracket* as *s* forces outermost square brackets. If the intent is that either can serve as the outermost pair of symbols, we need two additional productions:

$$Start \quad \rightarrow \quad Paren$$
$$| \quad Bracket$$

Now, the grammar has an unambiguous goal symbol, *Start*, which does not appear in the right-hand side of any production. Some tools that manipulate grammars require that a grammar have a *Start* symbol that appears in no production's right-hand side. They use this property to simplify the process of discovering *s*. Others simply assume that *s* is the left-hand side of the first production. As the example suggests, we can always create a unique start symbol by adding one more nonterminal and a few simple productions.

3.2.2 Constructing Sentences

To explore the power and complexity of context-free grammars, we need a more involved example than *SN*. Consider the following grammar:

1	*Expr*	$\rightarrow$	*Expr Op* num
2		|	num
3	*Op*	$\rightarrow$	+
4		|	-
5		|	×
6		|	÷

The grammar defines a set of expressions over nums and the four operators +, -, ×, and ÷. Using the grammar as a rewrite system, we can derive a large set of expressions. For example, applying rule 2 produces the trivial expression consisting solely of num. Using the sequence 1, 3, 2 produces the expression num + num.

Rule	Sentential Form
	Expr
1	*Expr Op* num
3	*Expr* + num
2	num + num

Longer rewrite sequences produce more complex expressions. For example, 1, 5, 1, 4, 2 derives the sentence num - num × num.

Rule	Sentential Form
	Expr
1	*Expr Op* num
5	*Expr* × num
1	*Expr Op* num × num
4	*Expr* - num × num
2	num - num × num

We can depict this derivation graphically.

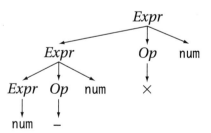

This derivation tree, or parse tree, represents each step in the derivation, in some order.

So far, our derivations have always expanded the rightmost nonterminal symbol remaining in the string. Other choices are possible; an obvious alternative is to select the leftmost nonterminal for expansion at each point. Using leftmost choices would produce a different derivation sequence for the same sentence. For num - num × num, the leftmost derivation would be

Rule	Sentential Form
	Expr
1	*Expr Op* num
1	*Expr Op* num *Op* num
2	num *Op* num *Op* num
4	num - num *Op* num
5	num - num × num

This "leftmost" derivation uses the same set of rules as the "rightmost" derivation, but applies them in a different order. The corresponding parse tree looks like:

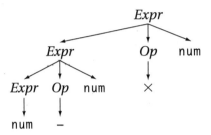

It is identical to the tree for the rightmost derivation! The tree represents all the rules applied in the derivation, but not their order of application.

We want the rightmost (or leftmost) derivation for a given sentence to be unique. If multiple rightmost (or leftmost) derivations exist for some sentence, then, at some point in the derivation, multiple distinct expansions of the rightmost (leftmost) nonterminal lead to the same sentence. This would produce multiple derivations and, possibly, multiple parse trees. Since later stages of translation will associate meaning with the detailed shape of the parse tree, having a grammar that produces a unique rightmost (leftmost) derivation is an important issue in translation.

A grammar G is *ambiguous* if and only if there exists a sentence in $L(G)$ that has multiple rightmost (or leftmost) derivations. Since grammatical structure is an important clue to the underlying meaning of the sentence, ambiguity is often undesirable. If the compiler cannot be sure of the meaning of a sentence, it cannot translate it into a definitive code sequence.

The classic example of an ambiguous construct in the grammar for a programming language is the if-then-else construct of many Algol-like languages. The straightforward grammar for if-then-else might be

1	*Statement*	$\rightarrow$	if *Expr* then *Statement* else *Statement*
2		|	if *Expr* then *Statement*
3		|	*Assignment*
4		|	... *other statements* ...

This fragment shows that the else part is optional. Unfortunately, with this grammar the code fragment

if $Expr_1$ then if $Expr_2$ then $Assignment_1$ else $Assignment_2$

has two distinct rightmost derivations. The difference between them is simple. Using indentation to convey the relationship among the various parts of the statements, we have

<pre>
if Expr₁   if Expr₁
    then if Expr₂   then if Expr₂
            then Assignment₁   then Assignment₁
            else Assignment₂   else Assignment₂
</pre>

The version on the left has $Assignment_2$ controlled by the inner if, so it executes if $Expr_1$ is true and $Expr_2$ is false. The version on the right associates the else clause with the first if, so that $Assignment_2$ executes if $Expr_1$ is false, independent of the value of $Expr_2$. Clearly, the difference in derivations will produce different behaviors for the compiled code.

To remove this ambiguity, the grammar must be modified to encode a rule that determines which if controls an else. To fix the if-then-else grammar, we can rewrite it as

1	*Statement*	$\rightarrow$	if *Expr* then *Statement*
2		|	if *Expr* then *WithElse* else *Statement*
3		|	*Assignment*
4	*WithElse*	$\rightarrow$	if *Expr* then *WithElse* else *WithElse*
5		|	*Assignment*

The solution restricts the set of statements that can occur in the then part of an if-then-else construct. It accepts the same set of sentences as the original grammar, but ensures that each else has an unambiguous match to a specific if. It encodes into the grammar a simple rule—bind each else to the innermost unclosed if. It has only one rightmost derivation for the example.

Rule	Sentential Form
	Statement
1	if *Expr* then *Statement*
2	if *Expr* then if *Expr* then *WithElse* else *Statement*
3	if *Expr* then if *Expr* then *WithElse* else *Assignment*
5	if *Expr* then if *Expr* then *Assignment* else *Assignment*

The rewritten grammar eliminates the ambiguity.

The if-then-else ambiguity arises from a shortcoming in the original grammar. The solution resolves the ambiguity in a way by imposing a rule that is easy for the programmer to remember. (To avoid the ambiguity entirely, some language designers have restructured the if-then-else construct by introducing elseif and endif.) In Section 3.6.3, we will look at other kinds of ambiguity and systematic ways of handling them.

3.2.3 Encoding Meaning into Structure

The if-then-else ambiguity points out the relationship between grammatical structure and meaning. However, ambiguity is not the only situation where grammatical structure and meaning interact. Consider again the parse tree for our simple expression, num - num × num.

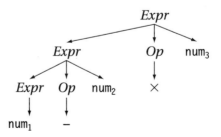

We have added subscripts to the instances of number to clarify the discussion. A natural way to evaluate the expression is with a simple postorder treewalk. This would first compute num_1 - num_2 and multiply that result by num_3, producing (num_1 - num_2) × num_3. This evaluation order contradicts the rules of algebraic precedence taught in algebra classes. Standard precedence would evaluate this expression as

$$\text{num}_1 - (\text{num}_2 \times \text{num}_3).$$

Since the ultimate goal of parsing the expression is to produce code that will implement it, the expression grammar should have the property that it builds a tree whose "natural" treewalk evaluation produces the correct result.

The problem lies in the structure of the grammar. All of the arithmetic operators derive the same way, at the same level of the grammar. To make the parse trees encode algebraic precedence, we must restructure the grammar so that it incorporates the correct precedence.

To introduce precedence, we must identify the appropriate levels of precedence in the language. For our simple expression grammar, we have two levels of precedence: lower precedence for + and -, and higher precedence for × and ÷. We associate a distinct nonterminal with each level of precedence and isolate the corresponding part of the grammar.

1	*Expr*	→	*Expr* + *Term*
2		|	*Expr* - *Term*
3		|	*Term*
4	*Term*	→	*Term* × num
5		|	*Term* ÷ num
6		|	num

Here, *Expr* represents the lower level of precedence for + and -, while *Term* represents the higher level for × and ÷ . This grammar derives $\text{num}_1 - \text{num}_2 \times \text{num}_3$ in an order that is consistent with the relative precedence of - and × :

Rule	Sentential Form
	Expr
2	*Expr* - *Term*
4	*Expr* - *Term* × num_3
6	*Expr* - num_2 × num_3
3	*Term* - num_2 × num_3
6	num_1 - num_2 × num_3

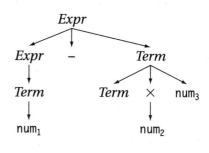

1	*Expr*	$\rightarrow$	*Expr + Term*
2		|	*Expr - Term*
3		|	*Term*
4	*Term*	$\rightarrow$	*Term × Factor*
5		|	*Term ÷ Factor*
6		|	*Factor*
7	*Factor*	$\rightarrow$	*(Expr)*
8		|	num
9		|	ident

FIGURE 3.1   The Classic Expression Grammar

A postorder tree walk over this parse tree will first evaluate $num_2 \times num_3$ and then subtract the result from num_1. This implements the standard rules of arithmetic precedence. Notice that the addition of nonterminals to enforce precedence adds interior nodes to the tree. Similarly, substituting the individual operators for occurrences of *Op* removes interior nodes from the tree.

To add parentheses to the grammar requires another level of precedence. Parentheses have a higher level of precedence than either × or ÷; this forces evaluation of an expression enclosed in parentheses before any operator that either precedes or follows the parenthetic expression. Thus, a × (b - c) evaluates b - c to a value and multiplies that value by a. To work this into the grammar, we add another nonterminal, *Factor*. The resulting grammar, shown in Figure 3.1, correctly represents the relative precedence of +, -, × , ÷, and parenthetic expressions. We refer to this grammar as the *classic expression grammar*.

Other operations require high precedence. For example, array subscripts should be applied before standard arithmetic operations. This ensures, for example, that x + y[i] evaluates y[i] to a value before adding it to ×, as opposed to treating i as a subscript on some array whose location is computed as x + y. Similarly, operations that change the type of a value, known as *type casts* in languages such as C or Java, have higher precedence than arithmetic but lower precedence than parentheses or subscripting operations.

If the language allows assignment inside expressions, the assignment operator should have low precedence. This ensures that the code completely evaluates both the left-hand side and the right-hand side of the assignment before performing the assignment. If assignment ($\leftarrow$) had the same precedence as addition, for example, the expression x $\leftarrow$ y + z would assign y's value to × before performing the addition, assuming a left-to-right evaluation.

3.2.4 Discovering a Specific Derivation

We have seen how to discover sentences that are in $L(G)$ for our grammar G. In contrast, a compiler must infer a derivation for a given input string, or determine that no such derivation exists. The process of constructing a derivation from a specific input sentence is called *parsing*.

A parser takes, as input, an alleged program written in some source language. The program appears to the parser as a stream of words and their syntactic categories. Thus, the expression x - 2 × y from the language generated by the classic expression grammar might be rendered as

$$\langle \text{ident, x} \rangle \quad - \quad \langle \text{num, 2} \rangle \quad \times \quad \langle \text{ident, y} \rangle$$

As output, the parser produces either a derivation for the input program or an indication that the input is not a valid program. Since parse trees are equivalent to derivations for unambiguous languages, we can think of parsing as building the parse tree from the input string. Thus, a parser for the classic expression grammar might produce the following parse tree for x - 2 × y:

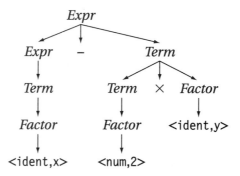

Constructing a derivation is equivalent to building a parse tree. The root and leaves of the parse tree are known. The root must be a single node that represents s. The leaves must be, in order from left to right, nodes that match the stream of words returned by the scanner. The hard part of this problem is using the language's structure, as embodied by the grammar, to connect the leaves with the root. Two distinct and opposite approaches for constructing the tree suggest themselves.

1. *Top-down parsers* begin with the root and proceed by growing the tree toward the leaves. At each step, a top-down parser selects some

nonterminal node on the lower fringe of the tree and extends the tree downward from that node.

2. *Bottom-up parsers* begin with the leaves and proceed by growing the tree toward the root. At each step, a bottom-up parser adds nodes that extend the partially built tree upward.

In either scenario, the parser makes a series of choices about which productions to apply. Most of the intellectual complexity in parsing lies in the mechanisms for making these choices.

3.2.5 Context-Free Grammars versus Regular Expressions

To understand the differences between regular expressions and context-free grammars, contrast the classic expression grammar against the following regular expression:

$$((ident \mid num) \; (+ \mid - \mid x \mid \div))^* \; (ident \mid num)$$

Both the regular expression and the context-free grammar describe the same set of expressions.

To make the difference between regular expressions and context-free grammars clear, consider the notion of a *regular grammar*. Regular grammars have the same expressive power as regular expressions—that is, they can describe exactly the full set of regular languages.

A regular grammar is a quadruple, $R = (T, NT, S, P)$, with the components having the same meanings as for a context-free grammar. In a regular grammar, however, productions in P are restricted to two forms, either $A \rightarrow \mathsf{a}$, or $A \rightarrow \mathsf{a}B$, where $A, B \in NT$ and $\mathsf{a} \in T$. (This restriction on the form of the production gives rise to another name for the regular grammars—they are often called *left-linear grammars*.)

In contrast, a context-free grammar allows productions with right-hand sides that contain an arbitrary set of symbols from $(T \cup NT)$. Thus, regular grammars are a proper subset of context-free grammars. The same relationship holds for the languages described by regular grammars, called regular languages, and those described by context-free grammars, called context-free languages. The regular languages are a proper subset of the context-free languages. The *SheepNoise* grammar used earlier in this chapter is a regular grammar.

Of course, we should ask: are there interesting programming language constructs that can be expressed by a context-free grammar but not by a regular

CLASSES OF CONTEXT-FREE GRAMMARS AND THEIR PARSERS

We can partition the set of all context-free grammars into a hierarchy based on the difficulty of parsing the grammars. This hierarchy has many levels. This chapter mentions four of them, namely, arbitrary context-free grammars, the LR(1) grammars, the LL(1) grammars, and the regular grammars (RG). These sets are nested: context-free grammars $\supset$ LR(1) $\supset$ LL(1) $\supset$ RG, as shown in the diagram.

Arbitrary context-free grammars require more time to parse than the restricted sets LR(1) or LL(1). For example, Earley's algorithm parses context-free grammars in $\mathbf{O}(n^3)$ time, worst case, where n is the number of words in the input stream. Of course, the actual running time may be better. Historically, compiler writers have shied away from "universal" techniques because of their perceived inefficiency.

The LR(1) grammars include a large subset of the unambiguous context-free grammars. LR(1) grammars can be parsed, bottom-up, in a linear scan from left to right, looking at most one word ahead of the current input symbol. Several algorithms exist to derive LR(1) parsers from grammars. The widespread availability of tools that automate this process has made LR(1) parsers "everyone's favorite parsers."

The LL(1) grammars are an important subset of the LR(1) grammars. LL(1) grammars can be parsed, top-down, in a linear scan from left to right, with a single-word lookahead. Two distinct styles of parser for LL(1) grammars are popular—hand-coded recursive-descent parsers and table-driven parsers called LL(1) parsers. Many interesting programming languages are easily expressed with LL(1) grammars.

Regular grammars encode precisely those languages that can be recognized by a DFA. The primary use for regular languages in compiler construction is to specify scanners.

Almost all programming-language constructs can be expressed in LR(1) form (and, often, in LL(1) form). Thus, most compilers use a fast parsing algorithm based on one of these two restricted classes of context-free grammars.

grammar? Many important features of modern programming languages fall into this gap between context-free grammars and regular grammars. Examples include matching brackets, such as parentheses, braces, and pairs of keywords (for example, begin and end). Equally important, the compiler writer can encode notions like the precedence of operators or the structure of an if-then-else construct into a context-free grammar. Parsing × - 2 × y with the classic expression grammar yields a parse tree that encodes the expected evaluation order (× before -). Recognizing the same string with the regular expression provides no insight into evaluation order.

Since context-free grammars can recognize any construct specified by a regular expression, why use regular expressions at all? The compiler writer could encode the lexical structure of the language directly into its grammar. Two factors argue in favor of separate scanners and parsers. First, DFA-based recognizers are efficient. They take time proportional to the length of the input string. With reasonable implementation techniques, even the constants in the asymptotic complexity are small. A parser that can handle reasonable subsets of the context-free grammars is more complex than a scanner, and the overhead per input symbol is higher, as well. Second, scanners simplify the input text in ways that dramatically reduce the complexity of the context-free grammar. For example, scanners typically discover comments and remove them from the input stream. Imagine extending the classic expression grammar to allow a comment between any two terminal symbols; it is far simpler to recognize and remove comments in the scanner. The same issues arise for text strings.

Thus, compiler writers use DFA-based scanners for efficiency and for convenience. Moving microsyntax into the context-free grammar would enlarge the grammar, lengthen the derivations, and make the front end slower. In general, regular expressions are used to classify words, to match regular patterns, and to remove objects that, themselves, have an internal lexical structure. When higher-level structure is needed, to match brackets, to impart structure, or to match across intervening context, context-free grammars are the tool of choice.

3.3 TOP-DOWN PARSING

A top-down parser begins with the root of the parse tree and systematically extends the tree downward until its leaves match the classified words returned by the scanner. At each point, the process considers a partially built parse tree. It selects a nonterminal symbol on the lower fringe of the tree and extends it by adding children that correspond to the right-hand side of some production for that nonterminal. It cannot extend the frontier from a terminal. This process continues until either:

    a. the fringe of the parse tree contains only terminal symbols, and the input stream has been exhausted; or

    b. a clear mismatch occurs between the fringe of the partially built parse tree and the input stream.

In the first case, the parse succeeds. In the second case, two possibilities exist. The parser may have selected the wrong production at some earlier step in the process, in which case backtracking will lead it to the correct choice. Alternatively, the input string may not be a valid sentence in the language being parsed; in this case, backtracking will fail, and the parser should report the syntactic error to the user.

One key insight makes top-down parsing efficient: *there exists a large subset of the context-free grammars for which backtracking is never needed.* The latter part of this section presents techniques that can help transform an arbitrary grammar into a backtrack-free, or predictive grammar. First, however, we present an example to showcase the ideas behind top-down parsing and to illustrate some of the problems that can arise with unconstrained context-free grammars.

3.3.1 Example

Figure 3.2 shows a simple algorithm for top-down parsing. The process works entirely on the lower fringe of the parse tree—which always corresponds to a sentential form. We have chosen, at each step, to expand the leftmost nonterminal. This corresponds to a leftmost derivation because the parser considers words in the left-to-right order in which the scanner produces them.

To understand the top-down parsing algorithm, consider the steps that the parser goes through to recognize x - 2 × y using the classic expression grammar. The goal symbol of the grammar is *Expr*; thus the parser begins with a tree rooted in *Expr*. To show the parser's actions, we will expand our tabular representation of a derivation. The leftmost column shows the grammar rule used to reach each state; the center column shows the lower fringe of the partially constructed parse tree, which is the most recently derived sentential form. On the right, we have added a representation of the input stream. The ↑ shows

word ← *NextWord( )*
root ← *start_symbol*
node ← *root*

loop forever
    if node ∈ *T & node matches word then*
        advance node to the next node on the fringe
        word ← *NextWord( )*

    else if node ∈ *T & node does not match word then*
        backtrack

    else if node ∈ *NT then*
        pick a rule "node→β"
        extend tree from node by building β
        node ← *leftmost symbol in β*

    if node is empty & word is eof then
        accept and exit the loop

    else if node is empty & word is not eof then
        backtrack

FIGURE 3.2   A Leftmost, Top-Down Parsing Algorithm

the position of the scanner; it precedes the current input symbol. We have added two actions to the rule column, → and ←, to represent advancing the input pointer and backtracking through the set of productions, respectively. The first several moves that the parser might take are

Rule	Sentential Form	Input
	Expr	↑x – 2 × y
1	*Expr + Term*	↑x – 2 × y
1	*Expr + Term + Term*	↑x – 2 × y
1	*Expr + Term +* ···	↑x – 2 × y
1	···	↑x – 2 × y

It begins with the start symbol, *Expr*, and expands it with the first right-hand side for *Expr* in the grammar. This produces a fringe *Expr + Term*. To produce a leftmost derivation, the parser must expand the leftmost nonterminal on the fringe, which is still *Expr*. If it chooses rule 1 consistently, this leads to an infinite sequence of expansions, each of which makes no progress. This suggests a problem with the form of the expression grammar.

A production is left-recursive if the first symbol on its right-hand side is the same as the symbol on its left-hand side. Left recursion can occur in less direct ways, as we will see in Section 3.3.3. Grammars that exhibit left recursion can cause a top-down parser to expand forever while making no progress.

To sidestep the issue of left recursion and illustrate another potential problem with top-down parsers, we will let the parser choose productions in an arbitrary manner. A real implementation would undoubtedly make these choices in a deterministic and consistent way. For example, the parser might try to rewrite *Expr* into ident. This produces the expansion sequence: rule 3 (*Expr* → *Term*), rule 6 (*Term* → *Factor*), and rule 9 (*Factor* → ident).

Rule	Sentential Form	Input
–	*Expr*	↑x - 2 × y
3	*Term*	↑x - 2 × y
6	*Factor*	↑x - 2 × y
9	ident	↑x - 2 × y
→	ident	x ↑- 2 × y

At this point, the leftmost symbol on the fringe is a terminal symbol, so the parser checks whether that symbol matches the current input symbol, held in *word*. Since they match, it advances one symbol rightward on the fringe and advances the input stream by calling *NextWord*. Unfortunately, the parse tree's fringe ends with ident even though the input stream continues, with -. This mismatch shows that the steps taken so far do not lead to a valid parse. Either the parser made an incorrect choice at some earlier expansion, or the input string is not a valid sentence for the expression grammar.

The parser handles this situation by backtracking. If the parser were making systematic choices, it would retract the most recent action—expansion by rule 9—and try the other possibilities for *Factor*. When these failed, it would retract the expansion by rule 6 and try the other possibilities for *Term*. Finally, it would retry the alternatives for the expansion by rule 3 and discover that the first step should have been an expansion by rule 2, *Expr* → *Expr* - *Term*.

From that point, the parser can work forward, applying the sequence 3, 6, 9 to derive ident from the *Expr* in the first position on the fringe. Moving ahead on the fringe and in the input stream, it discovers that the - sign in the input matches the - on the fringe.

Rule	Sentential Form	Input
–	*Expr*	↑x - 2 × y
2	*Expr - Term*	↑x - 2 × y
3	*Term - Term*	↑x - 2 × y
6	*Factor - Term*	↑x - 2 × y
9	ident - *Term*	↑x - 2 × y
→	ident - *Term*	x ↑- 2 × y
→	ident - *Term*	x - ↑2 × y

At this point, the parser should expand by the sequence 4, 6, 8 to match the num and leave the appropriate right context on the fringe. It can match num against the fringe, then advance and match the × . The final expansion uses rule 9 to place an ident on the fringe to match the final input symbol.

Rule	Sentential form	Input
4	ident - *Term* × *Factor*	x - ↑2 × y
6	ident - *Factor* × *Factor*	x - ↑2 × y
8	ident - num × *Factor*	x - ↑2 × y
→	ident - num × *Factor*	x - 2 ↑ × y
→	ident - num × *Factor*	x - 2 × ↑y
9	ident - num × ident	x - 2 × ↑y
→	ident - num × ident	x - 2 × y↑

At this point, the lower fringe contains only terminal symbols and the input has been exhausted. In the parser, *node* is empty and *word* is *eof*, so it reports success and halts.

(Note that we could have made erroneous expansions at many points in the parse, triggering additional backtracking. For the sake of clarity and brevity, we did not. The reader should, however, consider how much backtracking would occur if rules were chosen deterministically—in ascending order by rule number, for example.)

3.3.2 Complications in Top-Down Parsing

As the previous example demonstrated, several problems can complicate the use of top-down parsers. Grammars with left recursion cause termination problems. Choosing the wrong expansion necessitates backtracking. In general, the key issue is ensuring that, at each step, the parser can choose the correct production to expand the growing fringe of the parse tree.

Writing a backtrack-free grammar requires some care. The grammar must avoid left recursion. It must also ensure that a single-symbol lookahead suffices to determine the correct expansion, at each step. The next two subsections delve into these issues in more detail.

3.3.3 Eliminating Left Recursion

Left-recursive grammars can cause a deterministic top-down parser to loop indefinitely by expanding the fringe without generating a leading terminal symbol. Since backtracking is only triggered by a mismatch between a terminal symbol on the fringe and the current input symbol, the parser cannot recover from the expansion induced by left recursion.

Fortunately, we can mechanically transform a grammar to remove left recursion. For an immediate left recursion, like the one shown on the left, we can rewrite it to use right recursion, shown on the right.

$$
\begin{array}{rcl}
Fee & \rightarrow & Fee\ \alpha \\
& | & \beta
\end{array}
\qquad\qquad
\begin{array}{rcl}
Fee & \rightarrow & \beta\ Fie \\
Fie & \rightarrow & \alpha\ Fie \\
& | & \epsilon
\end{array}
$$

The transformation introduces a new nonterminal, *Fie*, and transfers the recursion onto *Fie*. It also adds the rule *Fie*→ϵ, where ϵ represents the empty string. This ϵ-production requires careful interpretation in the parsing algorithm. If the parser expands by the rule *Fie*→ϵ, the effect is to advance the current *node* along the tree's fringe by one position.

In the expression grammar, immediate left recursion appears in the productions for both *Expr* and *Term*.

1	*Expr*	$\rightarrow$	*Term Expr'*
2	*Expr'*	$\rightarrow$	*+ Term Expr'*
3				*- Term Expr'*
4				ϵ
5	*Term*	$\rightarrow$	*Factor Term'*
6	*Term'*	$\rightarrow$	*× Factor Term'*
7				*÷ Factor Term'*
8				ϵ
9	*Factor*	$\rightarrow$	*(Expr)*
10				num
11				ident

FIGURE 3.3   Right-Recursive Variant of the Classic Expression Grammar

	Original			Transformed	
Expr	$\rightarrow$	*Expr + Term*	*Expr*	$\rightarrow$	*Term Expr'*
		Expr - Term	*Expr'*	$\rightarrow$	*+ Term Expr'*
		Term			*- Term Expr'*
					ϵ
Term	$\rightarrow$	*Term × Factor*	*Term*	$\rightarrow$	*Factor Term'*
		Term ÷ Factor	*Term'*	$\rightarrow$	*× Factor Term'*
		Factor			*÷ Factor Term'*
					ϵ

Plugging these replacements back into the classic expression grammar yields a right-recursive variant of the grammar, shown in Figure 3.3. This grammar describes the same set of expressions as the classic expression grammar, but uses right recursion. It works well with a top-down parser.

The transformation eliminates immediate left recursion. Left recursion can also occur indirectly, when a chain of rules such as $\alpha \rightarrow \beta$, $\beta \rightarrow \gamma$, and $\gamma \rightarrow \alpha\delta$ combines to create the situation that $\alpha \rightarrow^{+} \alpha\delta$. Such indirect left recursion is not always obvious; it can be obscured by a long chain of productions.

To convert these indirect left recursions into right recursion, we need a more systematic approach than inspection followed by application of our transformation. Figure 3.4 shows an algorithm that achieves this goal. It assumes that the original grammar has no cycles ($A \rightarrow^+ A$) and no ϵ-productions ($A \rightarrow \epsilon$).

The algorithm imposes an arbitrary order on the nonterminals. The outer loop cycles through the nonterminals in this order. The inner loop looks for any production that expands A_i into a right-hand side that begins with A_j, for $j < i$. Such an expansion may lead to an indirect left recursion. To avoid this, the algorithm replaces the occurrence of A_j with all the alternative right-hand sides that can derive from A_j. That is, if the inner loop discovers a production $A_i \rightarrow A_j\gamma$, and $A_j \rightarrow \delta_1|\delta_2|\cdots|\delta_k$, then it replaces the former production with a set of productions $A_i \rightarrow \delta_1\gamma|\delta_2\gamma|\cdots|\delta_k\gamma$. This eventually converts each indirect left recursion into a direct left recursion. The final step in the outer loop converts any direct left recursion on A_i to right recursion using the simple transformation shown earlier. Because new nonterminals are added at the end and only involve right recursion, the loop can ignore them—they do not need to be checked and converted.

Considering the loop invariant for the outer loop may make this clearer. At the start of the ith outer loop iteration

$$\forall\, k < i,\, \nexists\; a\; production\; expanding\; A_k\; with\; A_l\; in\; its\; rhs, for\; l < k.$$

At the end of this process, ($i = n$), all indirect left recursion has been eliminated through the repetitive application of the inner loop, and all immediate left recursion has been eliminated in the final step of each iteration.

---

assume the nonterminals are ordered arbitrarily
    $A_1,\ A_2,\ \ldots,\ A_n$
for $i \leftarrow 1$ to n
    for $j \leftarrow 1$ to i - 1
        if $\exists$ a production $A_i \rightarrow A_j\gamma$ then
            replace it with one or more productions
            that expand A_j
    use the direct transformation to eliminate
        any immediate left recursion on A_i

FIGURE 3.4   Removal of General Left Recursion

3.3.4 Eliminating the Need to Backtrack

With the right-recursive expression grammar, a top-down parser can handle the string x - 2 × y without backtracking. In fact, the right-recursive expression grammar avoids all need to backtrack. To see this, consider how the parser makes a decision that it must retract through backtracking.

The critical choice occurs when the parser selects a production with which to expand the lower fringe of the partially constructed parse tree. When it tries to expand some nonterminal A, it must pick a rule $A{\rightarrow}\beta$. The algorithm shown in Figure 3.2 picks that rule arbitrarily. If, however, the parser could always pick the appropriate rule, it could avoid backtracking.

In the right-recursive expression grammar, the parser can always make the correct choice by comparing the next word in the input stream against the alternative right-hand sides for the leftmost nonterminal on the fringe. Following this discipline produces the following parse for x - 2 × y with the right-recursive variant of the expression grammar.

Rule	Sentential Form	Input
	Expr	↑ x - 2 × y
1	*Term Expr'*	↑ x - 2 × y
5	*Factor Term' Expr'*	↑ x - 2 × y
11	ident *Term' Expr'*	↑ x - 2 × y
→	ident *Term' Expr'*	x ↑ - 2 × y
8	ident *Expr'*	x ↑ - 2 × y
3	ident - *Term Expr'*	x ↑ - 2 × y
→	ident - *Term Expr'*	x - ↑ 2 × y
5	ident - *Factor Term' Expr'*	x - ↑ 2 × y
10	ident - num *Term' Expr'*	x - ↑ 2 × y
→	ident - num *Term' Expr'*	x - 2 ↑ × y
6	ident - num × *Factor Term' Expr'*	x - 2 ↑ × y
→	ident - num × *Factor Term' Expr'*	x - 2 × ↑ y
11	ident - num × ident *Term' Expr'*	x - 2 × ↑ y
→	ident - num × ident *Term' Expr'*	x - 2 × y ↑
8	ident - num × ident *Expr'*	x - 2 × y ↑
4	ident - num × ident	x - 2 × y ↑

The first two expansions are obvious; in both cases, the grammar has only one rule for expanding the leftmost nonterminal. Expanding *Factor* to ident requires a choice; looking at the current word in the input stream makes the choice clear. At that point, the parser faces an expansion of *Term'* with - as the current word. Rules 6 and 7 do not match, so it selects rule 8. Now, the parser faces an expansion of *Expr'* with the input -. This matches rule 3, so the parser expands using three's right-hand side. This process continues, with the input symbol dictating the choice, until the parser reaches its accepting state.

We can formalize the property that makes the right-recursive expression grammar backtrack-free. At each point in the parse, the choice of an expansion is obvious because each alternative for the leftmost nonterminal leads to a distinct terminal symbol. Comparing the next word in the input stream against those choices reveals the correct expansion.

The intuition is clear. FIRST is defined over $T \cup NT \cup \{\epsilon\}$. For a symbol α, define FIRST(α) as the set of words that can appear as the first symbol in some string derived from α. Consider the rules for *Expr'*:

2	*Expr'*	$\rightarrow$	+ *Term Expr'*
3		|	- *Term Expr'*
4		|	ϵ

Each of these productions has a unique FIRST set. For the terminals, + and -, their FIRST sets contain exactly one element—the symbol itself. The ϵ-production poses a tougher problem. It cannot derive any terminal symbols, so FIRST(ϵ) contains only ϵ. But, ϵ never appears in the input stream.

For the ϵ-production, the parser must compare the next word against the set of symbols that can appear on the fringe immediately to the right of the ϵ (or, equivalently, to the right of the *Expr'*). In this case, that should be the set of symbols that can be derived from any symbol that follows *Expr'* in the right-hand side of some production. If the symbol to the right of *Expr'* can derive ϵ, then the parser must also consider symbols to its right, and so on until it finds a symbol that cannot derive ϵ. Let FOLLOW(A) be the set of symbols that can occur immediately after some nonterminal A in a valid sentence. In this grammar, FOLLOW(*Expr'*) is $\{eof\}$.

The backtrack-free condition relies on the FIRST and FOLLOW sets. Figure 3.5 shows algorithms that compute the sets. FIRST sets must be computed before FOLLOW sets because the latter computation relies on the FIRST sets. Both computations are formulated as fixed-point computations.

We can formulate the condition for a backtrack-free grammar precisely in terms of FIRST and FOLLOW sets. Define the set FIRST$^+(\alpha)$ as FIRST(α) if

$for\ each\ \alpha\ \in\ (T \cup \epsilon)$
$\quad \text{FIRST}(\alpha) \leftarrow \alpha$
$for\ each\ A\ \in\ NT$
$\quad \text{FIRST}(A) \leftarrow \emptyset$
$while\ (\text{FIRST}\ sets\ are\ still\ changing)$
$\quad for\ each\ p \in P,\ where\ p\ has\ the\ form\ A{\rightarrow}\beta$
$\quad\quad if\ \beta\ is\ \beta_1\beta_2\ldots\beta_k,\ where\ \beta_i \in T \cup NT,\ then$
$\quad\quad\quad \text{FIRST}(A) \leftarrow \text{FIRST}(A) \cup (\text{FIRST}(\beta_1) - \{\epsilon\})$
$\quad\quad\quad i \leftarrow 1$
$\quad\quad\quad while\ (\epsilon \in \text{FIRST}(\beta_i)\ and\ i \leq k\text{-}1)$
$\quad\quad\quad\quad \text{FIRST}(A) \leftarrow \text{FIRST}(A) \cup (\text{FIRST}(\beta_{i+1}) - \{\epsilon\})$
$\quad\quad\quad\quad i \leftarrow i + 1$
$\quad\quad\quad if\ i = k\ and\ \epsilon \in \text{FIRST}(\beta_k)$
$\quad\quad\quad\quad then\ \text{FIRST}(A) \leftarrow \text{FIRST}(A) \cup \{\epsilon\}$

$for\ each\ A \in NT$
$\quad \text{FOLLOW}(A) \leftarrow \emptyset$
$\text{FOLLOW}(S) \leftarrow \{eof\}$
$while\ (\text{FOLLOW}\ sets\ are\ still\ changing\ )$
$\quad for\ each\ p \in P\ of\ the\ form\ A \rightarrow \beta_1\beta_2\cdots\beta_k$
$\quad\quad \text{FOLLOW}(\beta_k) \leftarrow \text{FOLLOW}(\beta_k) \cup \text{FOLLOW}(A)$
$\quad\quad \text{TRAILER} \leftarrow \text{FOLLOW}(A)$
$\quad\quad for\ i \leftarrow k\ down\ to\ 2$
$\quad\quad\quad if\ \epsilon \in \text{FOLLOW}(\beta_i)\ then$
$\quad\quad\quad\quad \text{FOLLOW}(\beta_{i-1}) \leftarrow \text{FOLLOW}(\beta_{i-1}) \cup$
$\quad\quad\quad\quad\quad\quad\quad\quad\quad\quad \{\text{FIRST}(\beta_i) - \epsilon\} \cup \text{TRAILER}$
$\quad\quad\quad else$
$\quad\quad\quad\quad \text{FOLLOW}(\beta_{i-1}) \leftarrow \text{FOLLOW}(\beta_{i-1}) \cup \text{FIRST}(\beta_i)$
$\quad\quad\quad\quad \text{TRAILER} \leftarrow \emptyset$

FIGURE 3.5 Computing FIRST and FOLLOW Sets

FIRST(α) does not include ϵ, and as FIRST$(\alpha) \cup$ FOLLOW(α) otherwise. Then, for any nonterminal A with multiple right-hand sides, $A{\rightarrow}\beta_1 \mid \beta_2 \mid \cdots \mid \beta_n$, it must be true that

$$\text{FIRST}^+(\beta_i) \cap \text{FIRST}^+(\beta_j) = \emptyset,\ \ \forall\, 1 \leq i < j \leq n$$

for the grammar to have the backtrack-free property. Since FIRST is defined over grammar symbols rather than strings of grammar symbols, we interpret

FIRST(β_i) as the FIRST set of the initial symbol in β_i. This rule captures the backtrack-free property.

Consider, for example, extending the right-recursive expression grammar to include syntax for scalar variable references, array-element references, and function calls. To extend it, we can replace the production *Factor*→ident with a set of productions that describe the syntax for scalar variable references, array-element references, and function calls.

11	*Factor*	→	ident
12		|	ident [*ExprList*]
13		|	ident (*ExprList*)
14	*ExprList*	→	*Expr* , *ExprList*
15		|	*Expr*

These productions use square brackets to denote an array reference and parentheses to denote a function call.

This fragment of the grammar fails the backtrack-free condition because productions 11, 12, and 13 all begin with ident. The FIRST sets of their right-hand sides are identical. When the parser tries to expand a *Factor* on the parse tree's lower fringe, it cannot distinguish between 11, 12, and 13 by looking ahead only one word. (Of course, looking ahead two words would allow it to predict the correct expansion.)

As with many grammars that fail the backtrack-free condition, we can rewrite the grammar in a way that does not change the language, but does make the grammar backtrack free. The following revision will work:

11	*Factor*	→	ident *Arguments*
12	*Arguments*	→	[*ExprList*]
13		|	(*ExprList*)
14		|	ϵ
15	*ExprList*	→	*Expr* , *ExprList*
16		|	*Expr*

This version of the grammar breaks the derivation into two steps, one that recognizes the common prefix of the three original right-hand sides (ident) and the other that contains the three distinct alternatives. To accomplish this, we introduced a new nonterminal, *Arguments*, and pushed [, (, and ϵ down into

for each $A \in NT$
if a common prefix exists for two or more
right-hand sides for A then
find the longest common prefix α
left-factor α out of the right-hand sides for A

repeat until no common prefixes remain

FIGURE 3.6   Left-Factoring a Grammar

the right-hand sides for *Arguments*. We call this transformation *left-factoring* the productions for ident.

We can apply this transformation to an arbitrary grammar. Figure 3.6 shows a simple algorithm that does this. The algorithm systematically identifies nonterminals that have two or more productions with a common prefix and factors the productions that expand that nonterminal. Thus, if it finds a nonterminal A that has productions

$$A \rightarrow \alpha\beta_1 \mid \alpha\beta_2 \mid \cdots \mid \alpha\beta_n \mid \gamma_1 \mid \gamma_2 \mid \cdots \mid \gamma_j$$

where α is a common prefix and the γ_i's represent right-hand sides that do not begin with α, it will replace those productions with a set of productions

$$A \quad \rightarrow \quad \alpha B \mid \gamma_1 \mid \gamma_2 \mid \cdots \mid \gamma_j$$
$$B \quad \rightarrow \quad \beta_1 \mid \beta_2 \mid \cdots \mid \beta_n$$

where B is a new nonterminal. B will be considered for further left-factoring in the next iteration of the *repeat* loop. The algorithm stops when it can find no more common prefixes.

Left-factoring can convert some grammars that require backtracking into backtrack-free grammars. However, not all context-free languages can be expressed by backtrack-free grammars. Using left-recursion elimination and left-factoring, we may be able to transform a grammar to the point where it can be predictively parsed. In general, however, it is undecidable whether or not a backtrack-free grammar exists for an arbitrary context-free language.

3.3.5 Top-Down Recursive-Descent Parsers

Given a predictive grammar G, we can construct a hand-coded parser for G that operates by recursive descent. A recursive-descent parser is structured as a set of mutually recursive routines, one for each nonterminal in the grammar.

PREDICTIVE PARSERS VERSUS DFAS

Predictive parsing is the natural extension of DFA-style reasoning to parsers. A DFA makes its transition based on the next input character. A predictive parser requires that the expansions be uniquely determined by the next word in the input stream. Thus, for each nonterminal in the grammar, there must be a unique mapping from the first word in any acceptable input string to a specific production that leads to a derivation for that string. The real difference in power between a DFA and a predictively parsable, or LL(1), grammar derives from the fact that one prediction may lead to a right-hand side with many symbols, whereas, in a regular grammar, it predicts only a single symbol. This lets predictive grammars include productions such as $p \rightarrow (\ p\ )$, which are beyond the power of a regular expression to describe. (Recall that a regular expression can recognize $(^+ \Sigma^*)^+$, but this does not specify that the numbers of opening and closing parentheses must match.)

Of course, a hand-constructed, recursive-descent parser can use arbitrary tricks to disambiguate production choices. For example, if a particular left-hand side cannot be predicted with a single-symbol lookahead, the parser could use two symbols. Done judiciously, this should not cause problems.

The routine for nonterminal A recognizes an instance of A in the input stream. To accomplish this, the routine invokes other routines to recognize the various nonterminals on A's right-hand side.

Consider a set of productions $A \rightarrow \beta_1 \mid \beta_2 \mid \epsilon$ in G. Since G is predictive, the parser can select the appropriate right-hand side (one of β_1, β_2, or ϵ) using only the input word and the FIRST$^+$ sets. Thus, the routine that recognizes A should include code to check for each alternate right-hand side. This might look like:

```
/* find an A */
if (word ∈ FIRST⁺(β₁)) then
    look for a β₁
else if (word ∈ FIRST⁺(β₂)) then
    look for a β₂
else if (word ∈ FOLLOW(A)) then
    return true
else
    report an error
    return false
```

The parser must handle the ϵ-production in a different manner than the other right-hand sides.

The code for each right-hand side, β_i, must recognize each of the grammar symbols in β_i, in order. If the symbol is a terminal, the parser can test the input word directly against the terminal. A match lets the parse continue; a mismatch indicates an error. If the symbol is a nonterminal, the parser invokes the routine that recognizes that nonterminal. It returns either true or false to indicate success or failure. Again, success lets the parse continue. If it returns false, the current routine should return false, too. The routine that discovers the mismatch can immediately report the error.

For a right-hand side $\beta_1 = cDE$, with $c \in T$ and $D, E \in NT$, the code needs to recognize a c, then a D, and, finally, an E. In the code fragment, we abstracted away these actions with the words "*look for a β_1*". The code in routine *Parse_A* to handle β_1 might look like:

```
if (word ∈ FIRST⁺(β₁)) then
    if (word ≠ c) then
        report an error finding c in cDE
        return false
    else  /* word is c */
        word ← NextWord()
        if (Parse_D() = true)
            then return Parse_E()
            else return false
```

Parse_A contains a fragment like this for each alternate right-hand side for A.

The strategy for constructing a complete recursive-descent parser is clear. For each nonterminal, we construct a routine that recognizes that nonterminal. Each routine relies on the other routines to recognize nonterminals and directly tests the terminal symbols that arise in its own right-hand sides. Figure 3.7 shows a top-down recursive-descent parser for the predictive grammar that we derived in Section 3.3.3. The code for similar right-hand sides has been combined. The routine *NextWord()* provides an incremental interface to the scanner.

Automating the Process

Top-down recursive-descent parsing is usually considered a technique for hand-coding a parser. Of course, we could build a parser generator that automatically emits top-down recursive-descent parsers for suitable grammars. The parser generator would construct the FIRST and FOLLOW sets for the grammar, check each nonterminal to ensure that each of its alternative right-hand sides has a set of initial terminal symbols that are disjoint from all the other alternatives, and emit a suitable parsing routine for each nonterminal symbol in the grammar. The resulting parser would have the advantages of top-down recursive-descent parsers, such as speed, code-space locality, and good error detection. It would also have the advantages of a grammar-generated system, such as a concise, high-level specification and reduced implementation effort.

The cost of predictive parsing is proportional to the size of the parse tree, plus the amount of time spent selecting the correct right-hand side at each expansion. To reduce this latter cost, the compiler writer might convert the nest of *if* statements into a case statement that switches on the current word. This can produce more efficient code if the case statement is translated in an appropriate way.

Alternatively, the compiler writer might construct a table that encodes these actions. With the right-recursive variant of the expression grammar, for example, the parser has three expansions for a *Factor*, as follows: (*Expr*), ident, and num. In tabular form, this might look like:

	+	-	×	÷	(	)	ident	num	*eof*
Factor	–	–	–	–	9	–	11	10	–

where terminal symbols are arrayed across the columns of the table, and the entries are either a rule number or a dash (–) indicating a syntax error. This table predicts the appropriate expansions for *Factor* as a function of the current input symbol.

If we expand the table to include all the nonterminals, then the algorithm in Figure 3.8 can use the table to perform a top-down, table-driven parse. The resulting parser is a table-driven, LL(1) parser. The name LL(1) derives from the fact that these parsers scan their input left to right, construct a leftmost derivation, and use 1 symbol of lookahead. Grammars that work in an LL(1) scheme are often called LL(1) grammars. LL(1) grammars are, by definition, backtrack free.

```
Main()
    /* Goal → Expr */
    word ← NextWord();
    if (Expr() and word = eof)
        then proceed to the next step
        else return false

Expr()
    /* Expr → Term Expr' */
    if (Term() = false)
        then return false
        else return EPrime()

EPrime()
    /* Expr' → + Term Expr'*/
    /* Expr' → - Term Expr'*/
    if (word = + or word = -) then
        word ← NextWord()
        if (Term() = false)
            then return false
            else return EPrime()
    /* Expr' → ε */
    return true

Term()
    /* Term → Factor Term' */
    if (Factor() = false)
        then return false
        else return TPrime()
```

```
TPrime()
    /* Term' → × Factor Term' */
    /* Term' → ÷ Factor Term' */
    if (word = × or word = ÷ ) then
        word ← NextWord()
        if (Factor() = false)
            then return false
            else return TPrime()
    /* Term' → ε */
    return true

Factor()
    /* Factor → ( Expr ) */
    if (word = ( ) then
        word ← NextWord()
        if (Expr() = false)
            then return false
            else if (word ≠ ) ) then
                report syntax error
                return false
    /* Factor → num */
    /* Factor → ident */
    else if (word ≠ num and
                word ≠ ident) then
        report syntax error
        return false
    word ← NextWord()
    return true
```

FIGURE 3.7   Recursive-Descent Parser for Expressions

To build the table for an LL(1) parser, the compiler writer must compute FIRST and FOLLOW sets and then fill in each entry in the table. For $Table[X, y]$, where x is a nonterminal and y is a terminal symbol, the entry should be the rule number of a production $x \to \beta$ if $y \in \text{FIRST}^+(\beta)$. If $x \to \epsilon$ is also in the grammar, then the entry for every terminal symbol in $\text{FOLLOW}(X)$ should be the rule number associated with this ϵ-production. Any entries not defined by one of these rules becomes an error entry. If any entry is defined multiple times, then the construction fails.

Any grammar for which this construction succeeds is an LL(1) grammar. The resulting table can be used directly to drive a parser based on the

```
word ← NextChar()
push eof onto stack
push Start Symbol onto stack
TOS ← top of stack
loop forever
    if TOS = eof and word = eof
        then report success and exit the loop

    else if TOS is a terminal or eof then
        if TOS matches word then
            pop the stack
            word ← NextWord()
        else
            report an error looking for TOS

    else /* TOS is a nonterminal */
        if Table[TOS,word] is A → B₁B₂ ··· Bₖ then
            pop the stack
            for i ← k to 1 by -1
                push Bᵢ onto the stack
        else
            report an error expanding TOS
    TOS ← top of stack
```

FIGURE 3.8   A Skeleton LL(1) Parser

skeleton parser in Figure 3.8. The grammar is also suitable for use in a top-down, recursive-descent parser.

Wrap-Up

Predictive parsing is important because most programming-language constructs can be expressed by backtrack-free grammars. In practice, the restriction that the alternate right-hand sides for a nonterminal have distinct FIRST sets does not seriously limit the usefulness of LL(1) grammars. The parsers that we can build for these grammars are compact and efficient. They lend themselves to high-quality diagnostic messages for erroneous inputs. For small languages and for situations in which good error messages are critical, top-down, recursive-descent parsers are a viable choice.

3.4 BOTTOM-UP PARSING

A bottom-up parser builds the parse tree starting with its leaves and working toward its root. As it encounters each word in the input stream, it constructs a leaf node. These form the base of the parse tree. To construct a derivation, it adds layers of nonterminals on top of the leaves, in a structure dictated by both the grammar and the input stream. The upper edge of this partially constructed parse tree is called its *upper frontier*. This process extends the frontier upward, toward the tree's root.

At each step, the parser looks for a section of the upper frontier that matches the right-hand side of some production in the grammar. When it finds a match, the parser builds a node to represent the nonterminal symbol on the production's left-hand side and adds edges to the nodes that represent the symbols on the right-hand side. Since productions have only one nonterminal on their left-hand sides, these upward extensions replace one or more symbols on the frontier with a single symbol. The parser repeats this process until one of two conditions occurs:

1. The upper frontier reduces to a single node that represents the grammar's start symbol. If the parser has matched all the words in the input, then the input is a valid sentence in the language. If some words remain, then the input is not a valid sentence. Instead, it is a valid sentence followed by extra words, and the parser should report this error to the user.

2. No match can be found. Since the parser has been unable to build a derivation for the input stream, the input is not a valid sentence. The parser should report the failure to the user. The upper fringe of the parse tree contains information that can be used to construct a diagnostic message.

A successful parse runs through every step of the derivation. A failed parse halts when it can find no further steps, at which point it can use the context accumulated in the tree to produce a meaningful error message. In many cases, it can recover from the error and continue parsing so that it discovers as many syntactic errors as possible in a single parse (see Section 3.6.1).

Derivations in a bottom-up parser begin with the goal symbol and work toward a sentence. Because the parser builds the parse tree bottom up, it discovers derivation steps in reverse order. If the derivation consists of a series of steps that produces the sentential forms

$$S_0 = \gamma_0 \rightarrow \gamma_1 \rightarrow \gamma_2 \rightarrow \cdots \rightarrow \gamma_{n-1} \rightarrow \gamma_n = \textit{sentence,}$$

the bottom-up parser will discover $\gamma_{n-1}\rightarrow\gamma_n$ before it discovers $\gamma_{n-2}\rightarrow\gamma_{n-1}$. The bottom-up construction of the tree forces this order. The parser must add the nodes implied by $\gamma_{n-1}\rightarrow\gamma_n$ to the frontier before it can discover any matches that involve those nodes. Thus, it can only discover the nodes in an order consistent with the reverse derivation.

Because the scanner finds the words in the input stream in left-to-right order, the parser should look at the leaves from left to right. This suggests a derivation order that produces terminals from right to left, so that its reverse order matches the scanner's behavior. This leads, rather naturally, to bottom-up parsers that construct, in reverse, a rightmost derivation. At each point, the parser will operate on the frontier of the partially constructed parse tree; the current frontier is a prefix of the corresponding sentential form in the derivation. Because each sentential form occurs in a rightmost derivation, the unexamined suffix consists entirely of terminal symbols.

Bottom-up parsing is easier if the grammar is unambiguous. With an unambiguous grammar, the rightmost derivation is unique. For a large class of unambiguous grammars, γ_{i-1} can be determined from γ_i and a limited amount of context. This leads to an efficient class of bottom-up parsers.

In this section, we consider a specific class of bottom-up parsers called LR(1) parsers. These parsers scan the input from left to right, the order in which scanners return classified words. These parsers build a rightmost derivation, in reverse. LR(1) parsers make decisions, at each step in the parse, based on the history of the parse so far and a lookahead of, at most, one symbol. The name LR(1) derives from these three properties: left-to-right scan, reverse-rightmost derivation, and 1 symbol of lookahead. Informally, we will say that a language has the LR(1) property if it can be parsed in a single left-to-right scan, to build a reverse-rightmost derivation, using only one symbol of lookahead to determine parsing actions.[2]

3.4.1 Shift-Reduce Parsing

The key to constructing efficient top-down parsers is discovering the correct right-hand side to use at each step. In bottom-up parsing, the critical step is developing an efficient mechanism that finds matches along the tree's current

---

2. The theory of LR parsing defines a family of parsing techniques, the LR(k) parsers, for arbitrary $k \geq 0$. Here, k denotes the amount of lookahead that the parser needs. LR(1) parsers accept the same set of languages as LR(k) parsers for any $k > 1$; however, the LR(1) grammar for a language may be more complicated than a grammar that requires more lookahead.

upper frontier. Formally, the parser must find some substring, β, of the upper frontier where

1. β is the right-hand side of some production $A \rightarrow \beta$, and

2. $A \rightarrow \beta$ is one step in the rightmost derivation of the input stream.

For the sake of efficiency, we want the parser to accomplish this while looking no more than one word beyond the right end of β.

We can represent each potential match as a pair $\langle A{\rightarrow}\beta, k \rangle$, where $A{\rightarrow}\beta$ is a production in G and k is the position on the tree's current frontier of the right end of β. If replacing this occurrence of β with A is the next step in the reverse-rightmost derivation of the input string, then $\langle A{\rightarrow}\beta, k \rangle$ is called a *handle* of the bottom-up parse. A handle concisely represents the next step in building the reverse rightmost derivation.

A bottom-up parser operates by repeatedly locating handles on the frontier of the current partial parse tree and performing the reductions that they specify. When the frontier does not contain a handle, the parser calls the scanner to obtain the next word, builds the corresponding leaf, and makes it the rightmost leaf in the partially constructed tree. This extends the frontier by one leaf node.

To see how this works, consider parsing the string x - 2 × y with the classic expression grammar from Figure 3.1. The state of the parser, at each step, is summarized in Figure 3.9. Figure 3.10 shows the corresponding partial parse tree for each step in the process; the trees are drawn with their frontier elements justified along the top of each drawing. At each step, the parser either finds a handle on the frontier, or it adds to the frontier.

As the example shows, the parser only needs to examine the upper frontier of the partially constructed parse tree. Using this fact, we can build a particularly clean form of bottom-up parser called a *shift-reduce* parser. These parsers use a stack to hold the frontier; this simplifies the algorithm in two ways. First, the stack trivializes the problem of managing space for the frontier. To extend the frontier, the parser simply pushes the current input symbol onto the top of the stack. Second, it ensures that all handles occur with their right end at the top of the stack. This eliminates the need explicitly to represent the handle's position—simplifying the representation and making the set of handles finite.

Figure 3.11 shows a simple shift-reduce parser. To begin, it shifts a designated symbol, *invalid*, onto the stack and gets the first input symbol from the scanner. Then, it follows a simple discipline: it shifts symbols from the input onto the stack until it discovers a handle, and it reduces handles as soon as they are found. It halts when the top of the stack contains *Goal* and the parser has consumed all the input.

	Next Word	Frontier	Handle	Action
1	ident		— none —	*extend*
2	-	ident	$\langle Factor \rightarrow ident, 1 \rangle$	*reduce*
3	-	*Factor*	$\langle Term \rightarrow Factor, 1 \rangle$	*reduce*
4	-	*Term*	$\langle Expr \rightarrow Term, 1 \rangle$	*reduce*
5	-	*Expr*	— none —	*extend*
6	num	*Expr* -	— none —	*extend*
7	×	*Expr* - num	$\langle Factor \rightarrow num, 3 \rangle$	*reduce*
8	×	*Expr* - *Factor*	$\langle Term \rightarrow Factor, 3 \rangle$	*reduce*
9	×	*Expr* - *Term*	— none —	*extend*
10	ident	*Expr* - *Term* ×	— none —	*extend*
11	*eof*	*Expr* - *Term* × ident	$\langle Factor \rightarrow ident, 5 \rangle$	*reduce*
12	*eof*	*Expr* - *Term* × *Factor*	$\langle Term \rightarrow Term \times Factor, 5 \rangle$	*reduce*
13	*eof*	*Expr* - *Term*	$\langle Expr \rightarrow Expr - Term, 3 \rangle$	*reduce*
14	*eof*	*Expr*	$\langle Goal \rightarrow Expr, 1 \rangle$	*reduce*
15	*eof*	*Goal*	— none —	*accept*

FIGURE 3.9   States of the Bottom-Up Parser on x - 2 × y

The algorithm discovers syntax errors when the handle-discovery mechanism fails. Since Figure 3.11 describes handle-finding only in an abstract way, "*if a handle for $A \rightarrow \beta$ is on top of the stack,*" the details of error detection are not clear. In fact, the figure suggests that an error can occur only when all the input has been shifted onto the stack. As we explore the mechanism for handle-finding, we will see that it discovers syntax errors much earlier in the process. For example, the input string × + ÷ y is not in the language described by the classic expression grammar. The handle-finder should recognize this as soon as it sees that the ÷ follows a +.

Using the algorithm in Figure 3.11, we can reinterpret Figure 3.9 to show the actions of our shift-reduce parser on the input stream x - 2 × y. The column labelled "Next Word" shows the contents of the variable *word* in the algorithm. The column labelled "Frontier" depicts the contents of the stack at each step; the stack top is to the right. Finally, the action *extend* indicates a shift; *reduce* still indicates a reduction.

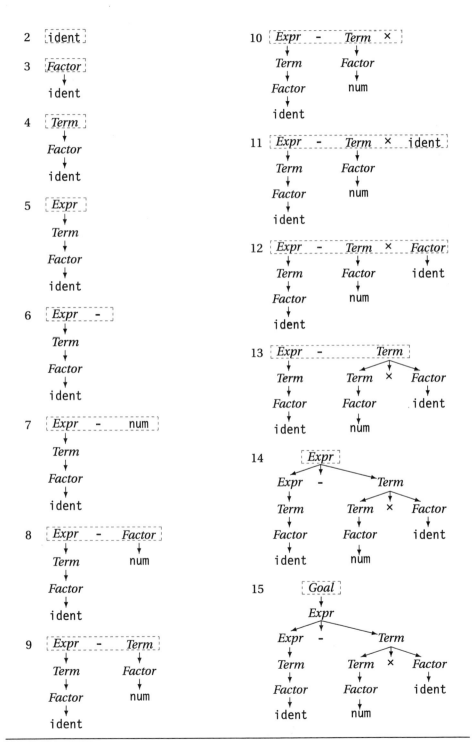

FIGURE 3.10   Partial Parse Trees for a Bottom-Up Parse of x - 2 × y

```
push invalid
word ← NextWord()

repeat until (word = eof & the stack contains
        exactly Goal on top of invalid)
    if a handle for A→β is on top of the stack then
        /* reduce by A→β */
        pop | β | symbols off the stack
        push A onto the stack
    else if (word ≠ eof) then
        /* shift word onto the stack */
        push word
        word ← NextWord()
    else /* no handle, no input */
        report syntax error & halt
```

FIGURE 3.11   Shift-Reduce Parsing Algorithm

For an input stream of length s, this shift-reduce parser performs s shifts. It performs a reduction for each step in the derivation, for r steps. It looks for a handle on each iteration of the *repeat until* loop, so it must perform $s + r$ handle-finding operations. This is equivalent to the number of nodes in the parse tree; each shift and each reduce creates one new node in the parse tree.

For a fixed grammar, r must be $\mathbf{O}(s)$, so the number of handle-finding operations is proportional to the length of the input string. If we can keep the cost of handle-finding to a small constant, the parser will operate in time proportional to $s + r$. Of course, constraining the cost of handle-finding in this way rules out any technique that traverses the entire stack on each handle-finding operation. It places a premium on efficient handle-finding.

3.4.2 Finding Handles

The handle-finding mechanism is the key to efficient bottom-up parsing. As it processes an input string, the parser must find and track all the potential handles. For example, every legal input eventually reduces the entire frontier to the grammar's goal symbol. In the classic expression grammar, *Goal→Expr* is the only production that reduces to *Goal*. It must be the last reduction in any successful parse. If the entire frontier is reduced to *Goal*, then the position in the handle must be 1. Thus, $\langle Goal{\rightarrow}Expr,1 \rangle$ is a potential handle at the start of every parse.

As the parser builds a derivation, it discovers other handles. At each step, the set of potential handles should represent the different suffixes that, if seen, lead to a reduction. Given the part of the derivation already constructed, each potential handle represents a string of grammar symbols that, if seen, would complete the right-hand side of some production in the grammar. Figure 3.9 shows the nine complete handles that the shift-reduce parser found while processing x - 2 × y.

The handles at steps three and eight in that parse both specify a reduction by *Term→Factor*. The handles have different position fields, specifying where on the frontier the symbol *Factor* occurs. In a shift-reduce parser, however, that portion of the frontier shown in the table always resides on the stack, with the most recently recognized symbol on top. In both steps three and eight, the position field in the handle specifies the symbol on the top of the stack. In fact, for each handle that the parser recognizes, the position field specifies the top of the stack. If we treat the position field as relative to the top of the stack, we can drastically reduce the number of distinct handles—to one handle per production in the grammar.

Pushing this notion further, we can represent the potential handles that the shift-reduce parser should track. If we use the placeholder • to represent the top of the stack, then the nine handles in Figure 3.9 become:

$$\langle \textit{Factor} \rightarrow \texttt{ident} \bullet \rangle \qquad \langle \textit{Term} \rightarrow \textit{Factor} \bullet \rangle \qquad \langle \textit{Expr} \rightarrow \textit{Term} \bullet \rangle$$

$$\langle \textit{Factor} \rightarrow \texttt{num} \bullet \rangle \qquad \langle \textit{Term} \rightarrow \textit{Factor} \bullet \rangle \qquad \langle \textit{Factor} \rightarrow \texttt{ident} \bullet \rangle$$

$$\langle \textit{Term} \rightarrow \textit{Term} \times \textit{Factor} \bullet \rangle \qquad \langle \textit{Expr} \rightarrow \textit{Expr} - \textit{Term} \bullet \rangle \qquad \langle \textit{Goal} \rightarrow \textit{Expr} \bullet \rangle$$

This notation shows that the second and fifth handles are identical, as are the first and sixth. It also creates a way to represent the potential of discovering a handle in the future.

Consider the parser's state in step six, with the input symbol num and the frontier *Expr* -. From the table, we know that the next reduction will be $\langle \textit{Factor} \rightarrow \texttt{num} \bullet \rangle$, followed by further shifts and reductions to recognize the symbols × and ident. What, however, of the current frontier? The parser has recognized *Expr* -. It needs to recognize, eventually, a *Term* before it can reduce this part of the frontier. Using this stack-relative notation, we can represent the parser's state as *Expr→Expr* - • *Term*. The parser has already recognized an *Expr* and a -, with the - on top of the stack. If it reaches a state where it shifts a *Term* on top of *Expr*-, it will complete the handle *Expr→Expr* - *Term* •.

With a concrete notation for representing both handles and potential handles, we can ask the question, how many potential handles must the parser recognize? The right-hand side of each production can have a placeholder at its start, at its end, and between any two consecutive symbols. If the right-hand side has k symbols, it has $k + 1$ placeholder positions. The number of potential handles for the grammar is simply the sum of the lengths of the right-hand sides of all the productions. The number of complete handles is simply the number of productions. These two facts lead to the critical insight behind LR(1) parsers.

> *A given grammar generates a finite set of handles (and potential handles) that the parser must recognize.*

From Chapter 2, we have an appropriate tool to recognize finite collections of words — the DFA. The LR(1) parsers use a handle-recognizing DFA to efficiently find handles on the top of the parse stack. The table-construction algorithm builds a model of this DFA and encodes it into a pair of tables.

Careful examination of the parse in Figure 3.9 reveals one flaw in this reasoning. Consider the parser's action at step nine. The frontier is *Expr - Term*, suggesting a handle $\langle Expr \rightarrow Expr$ - $Term \bullet \rangle$. However, the parser decides to extend the frontier by shifting × onto the stack, rather than reducing the frontier to *Expr*. Clearly, this is the correct move for the parser. No potential handle contains *Expr* followed by ×.

To determine the correct action, the parser can recognize the distinct actions required by different right contexts—the symbols that come later in the input stream. At step nine, the set of potential handles is

$$\langle Expr \rightarrow Expr - Term \bullet \rangle \quad \langle Term \rightarrow Term \bullet \times Factor \rangle \quad \langle Term \rightarrow Term \bullet \div Factor \rangle$$

The next input symbol × clearly matches the second choice and rules out the third choice. The parser needs a basis for deciding between the first and second choices. This requires more context than the parser has in the frontier.

To choose between reducing *Expr - Term* to *Expr* and shifting × in an attempt to recognize *Term × Factor*, the parser must recognize which symbols can occur to the right of *Expr* and *Term* in valid parses. Looking at the grammar, + and - immediately follow *Expr* in productions one and two. From productions four and five, × and ÷ can follow *Term*. Thus, in step nine, the parser can choose the correct action by looking at the next symbol: On + or -, it should reduce; on × or ÷, it should shift. Since the next symbol is ×, the parser shifts.

The LR(1) parsers can recognize precisely those languages in which a one-symbol lookahead suffices to determine whether to shift or reduce. The LR(1) construction algorithm builds a handle-recognizing DFA; the parsing algorithm uses this DFA to recognize handles and potential handles on the parse stack. It uses a shift-reduce parsing framework to guide the application of the DFA. The framework can invoke the DFA recursively; to accomplish this, it stores information about the DFA's internal state on the stack, interleaved with the grammar symbols that represent the upper frontier of the parse tree.

3.4.3 LR(1) Parsers

The LR(1) parsers, including the restricted forms known as SLR(1) and LALR(1) parsers, are the most widely used family of parsers. Table-driven LR(1) parsers are efficient. Tools that automate construction of the tables are widely available. The grammars that these tools accept allow most programming-language constructs to be expressed in a natural way. This section explains how LR(1) parsers work and shows how to construct the parse tables for one kind of LR(1) parser, namely, a canonical LR(1) parser.

Figure 3.12 shows the structure of a typical LR(1) parser-generator system. The compiler writer creates a grammar that describes the source language. The parser generator consumes that grammar and produces a pair of tables that drive the LR(1) parser. The tables encode all of the grammatical knowledge needed for parsing; in some sense, the parser generator precompiles into the tables all the knowledge required to identify handles, to decide when to shift, and to decide when to reduce and which rule to use in the reduction. In most such systems, the compiler writer can also provide a snippet of code for each production that will execute on a reduction. These ad hoc "actions" provide

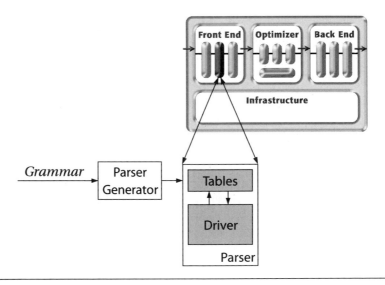

FIGURE 3.12   Structure of an LR(1) Parser Generator System

*push **invalid***
push start state, s_0
word ← NextWord()

while (true)
  s ← top of stack

  *if Action[s,word] = "**shift** s_i" then*
    push word
    push s_i
    word ← NextWord()

  *else if Action[s,word] = "**reduce** $A \rightarrow \beta$" then*
    pop $2 \times |\beta|$ symbols
    s ← top of stack
    push A
    push Goto[s, A]

  *else if Action[s,word] = "**accept**" then*
    return

  else report syntax error and halt

FIGURE 3.13   The Driver for an LR(1) Parser

a mechanism to perform syntax-driven computation at parse time. Chapter 4 explores some of the uses for such ad hoc actions.

LR(1) table construction is an elegant application of theory to practice. The construction systematically builds up a model of the handle-recognizing DFA and then translates that model into a pair of tables that drive the skeleton parser. However, the construction is a complex undertaking that requires painstaking attention to detail. It is precisely the kind of task that should be automated—parser generators are better at following these long chains of computations than are humans. That notwithstanding, a skilled compiler writer should understand the table-construction algorithms because they provide insight into how the parsers work, what kinds of errors the parser generator can encounter, how those errors arise, and how they can be remedied.

As shown in Figure 3.12, an LR(1) parser consists of a driver and a pair of tables that drive the parser. Figure 3.13 shows the driver. A pair of tables, called the *Action* and *Goto* tables, encode all the grammatical knowledge needed by the driver. Figures 3.14 and 3.15 show these tables for the classic expression grammar. To simplify the table-construction algorithm, we have augmented the grammar with a goal production and renumbered the rest of the productions accordingly. The resulting grammar follows:

1	*Goal*	$\rightarrow$ *Expr*
2	*Expr*	$\rightarrow$ *Expr + Term*
3		| *Expr - Term*
4		| *Term*
5	*Term*	$\rightarrow$ *Term × Factor*
6		| *Term ÷ Factor*
7		| *Factor*
8	*Factor*	$\rightarrow$ (*Expr*)
9		| num
10		| ident

The skeleton parser resembles the shift-reduce parser shown in Figure 3.11. At each step, it pushes two objects onto the stack: a grammar symbol from the frontier and a state from the handle recognizer. It has four actions.

1. *shift*   Extend the frontier by shifting the lookahead word onto the stack, along with a new state for the handle recognizer. This may result in a recursive invocation of the recognizer.

2. *reduce*   Shrink the frontier by replacing the current handle with its left-hand side. It discards all the intermediate states used to recognize the handle by popping off two stack items for each symbol in the handle's right-hand side. Next, it uses the state underneath the handle and the left-hand side to find a new recognizer state and pushes both the left-hand side and the new state onto the stack.

3. *accept*   Report success. This state is reached only when the parser has reduced the frontier to the goal symbol and the lookahead symbol is *eof*.

4. *error*   Report a syntax error. This state is reached any time the *Action* table contains an entry other than *shift, reduce,* or *accept*. In the figure, these entries are left blank.

Entries in the *Action* table are encoded using the letters *s* for *shift* and *r* for *reduce*. Thus, the entry *s 3* indicates the action "shift and go to state s_3," while *r 5* indicates "*reduce* by production 5." The *Goto* table encodes the transition that must be taken after a *reduce* action. Its sparsity reflects the fact that relatively few states represent reductions.

Action **Table**

State	eof	+	–	×	÷	(	)	num	ident
0						s 4		s 5	s 6
1	acc	s 7	s 8						
2	r 4	r 4	r 4	s 9	s 10				
3	r 7	r 7	r 7	r 7	r 7				
4						s 14		s 15	s 16
5	r 9	r 9	r 9	r 9	r 9				
6	r 10	r 10	r 10	r 10	r 10				
7						s 4		s 5	s 6
8						s 4		s 5	s 6
9						s 4		s 5	s 6
10						s 4		s 5	s 6
11		s 21	s 22				s 23		
12		r 4	r 4	s 24	s 25		r 4		
13		r 7	r 7	r 7	r 7		r 7		
14						s 14		s 15	s 16
15		r 9	r 9	r 9	r 9		r 9		
16		r 10	r 10	r 10	r 10		r 10		
17	r 2	r 2	r 2	s 9	s 10				
18	r 3	r 3	r 3	s 9	s 10				
19	r 5	r 5	r 5	r 5	r 5				
20	r 6	r 6	r 6	r 6	r 6				
21						s 14		s 15	s 16
22						s 14		s 15	s 16
23	r 8	r 8	r 8	r 8	r 8				
24						s 14		s 15	s 16
25						s 14		s 15	s 16
26		s 21	s 22				s 31		
27		r 2	r 2	s 24	s 25		r 2		
28		r 3	r 3	s 24	s 25		r 3		
29		r 5	r 5	r 5	r 5		r 5		
30		r 6	r 6	r 6	r 6		r 6		
31		r 8	r 8	r 8	r 8		r 8		

FIGURE 3.14   Action Table for the Classic Expression Grammar

	Goto **Table**				*Goto* **Table**		
State	**Expr**	**Term**	**Factor**	**State**	**Expr**	**Term**	**Factor**
0	1	2	3	16			
1				17			
2				18			
3				19			
4	11	12	13	20			
5				21		27	13
6				22		28	13
7		17	3	23			
8		18	3	24			29
9			19	25			30
10			20	26			
11				27			
12				28			
13				29			
14	26	12	13	30			
15				31			

FIGURE 3.15   *Goto* Table for the Classic Expression Grammar

To understand this parser, consider again our simple example. Figure 3.16 shows the succession of states that the LR(1) parser takes to parse the expression x - 2 × y. The parser begins by shifting *invalid*, and state zero, represented by 0, onto the stack. Next, it shifts ident onto the stack, then reduces it to a *Factor*, to a *Term*, and to an *Expr*. Next, it shifts the -, followed by the num. At this point, it reduces num to *Factor*, then *Factor* to *Term*. Next, it shifts × and then ident onto the stack. Finally, it reduces ident to *Factor*, *Term × Factor* to *Term*, and then *Expr - Term* to *Expr*. At this point, with *Expr* on the stack and EOF as the next word, it accepts the input string. This is similar to the sequence portrayed in Figure 3.9.

The key to building an LR(1) parser is constructing the *Action* and *Goto* tables. These tables encode the actions of the handle-recognizing DFA, along with the information necessary to use limited right context to decide whether to shift, reduce, or accept. While it is possible to construct these tables by hand, the algorithm requires manipulation of lots of detail, as well as scrupulous

	Current Symbol	Stack	Action
1	ident	*invalid* 0	*shift*
2	–	*invalid* 0 ident 6	*reduce 10*
3	–	*invalid* 0 *Factor* 3	*reduce 7*
4	–	*invalid* 0 *Term* 2	*reduce 4*
5	–	*invalid* 0 *Expr* 1	*shift*
6	num	*invalid* 0 *Expr* 1 - 8	*shift*
7	×	*invalid* 0 *Expr* 1 - 8 num 5	*reduce 9*
8	×	*invalid* 0 *Expr* 1 - 8 *Factor* 3	*reduce 7*
9	×	*invalid* 0 *Expr* 1 - 8 *Term* 18	*shift*
10	ident	*invalid* 0 *Expr* 1 - 8 *Term* 18 × 9	*shift*
11	*eof*	*invalid* 0 *Expr* 1 - 8 *Term* 18 × 9 ident 6	*reduce 10*
12	*eof*	*invalid* 0 *Expr* 1 - 8 *Term* 18 × 9 *Factor* 19	*reduce 5*
13	*eof*	*invalid* 0 *Expr* 1 - 8 *Term* 18	*reduce 3*
14	*eof*	*invalid* 0 *Expr* 1	*accept*

FIGURE 3.16 LR(1) Parser States for x - 2 × y

bookkeeping. Building LR(1) tables is a prime example of the kind of task that should be automated and relegated to a computer program.

3.5 BUILDING LR(1) TABLES

To construct *Action* and *Goto* tables, an LR(1) parser generator builds a model of the handle-recognizing DFA and uses that model to fill in the tables. The model uses a set of LR(1) items, described in the next subsection, to represent each parser state; these sets are constructed using a systematic technique. The model is called *the canonical collection of sets of LR(1) items*, $CC = \{CC_0, CC_1, CC_2, \ldots, CC_n\}$. Each set in CC represents a state in the eventual parser.

To explain the construction, we will use two examples. The first is our *SheepNoise* grammar, *SN*, augmented with a unique goal symbol. It is small enough to use as a running example to clarify the individual steps in the process.

1	*Goal*	$\rightarrow$	*SheepNoise*
2	*SheepNoise*	$\rightarrow$	baa *SheepNoise*
3		$|$	baa

In building the tables, we will explicitly include the symbol *eof* as a terminal symbol. It occurs at the end of the input stream. In the grammar, it implicitly occurs at the end of the goal production.

Our second example, in Section 3.5.4, will be an abstracted version of the classic if-then-else ambiguity. This example is more complex than *SN*. Because the grammar is ambiguous, the actual table construction fails. However, the failure occurs late in the process, so the example shows the more complex parts of the construction. It highlights the kinds of situations that lead to errors.

3.5.1   LR(1) Items

The LR(1)-table construction needs a concrete representation for the handles and potential handles, and their associated lookahead symbols. We call this representation an LR(1) item. An LR(1) item is a pair $[A{\rightarrow}\beta\bullet\gamma, a]$, where $A{\rightarrow}\beta\bullet\gamma$ represents a handle or potential handle using the placeholder $\bullet$ to indicate the position of the stack top and $a \in T$ is a word in the source language. Individual LR(1) items describe configurations of a bottom-up parser; they represent potential handles that are consistent with the left context that the parser would already have seen.

For a production $A{\rightarrow}\beta\gamma$ and a lookahead symbol $a \in T$, the placeholder can generate three distinct items, each with its own interpretation. In each case, the presence of the item in the set associated with some parser state indicates that the input that the parser has seen is consistent with the occurrence of an A followed by an a in the grammar. The position of $\bullet$ in the item provides more information.

$[A{\rightarrow}\bullet\beta\gamma,a]$ Indicates that an A would be valid and that recognizing a β at this point would be one step toward discovering an A. We call such an item a *possibility*, because it represents a possible completion for the input already seen.

$[A{\rightarrow}\beta \bullet \gamma,a]$ Indicates that the parser has progressed from the state where an A would be valid by recognizing β. The β is consistent with recognizing an A. The next step would be to recognize a γ. We call such an item *partially complete*.

[$A{\rightarrow}\beta\gamma{\bullet}$,a] Indicates that the parser has found $\beta\gamma$ in a context where an A followed by an a would be valid. If the lookahead symbol is a, the parser can reduce $\beta\gamma$ to A, and the item is a handle. Such an item is *complete*.

In an LR(1) item, the $\bullet$ encodes left context—the history of the parse so far. The lookahead symbol encodes potential right context. If the parser moves the $\bullet$ to the end of the production and finds that the next symbol matches the item's lookahead symbol, then it should reduce by the item's production.

The *SheepNoise* grammar produces the following LR(1) items:

[$Goal \rightarrow \bullet\ SheepNoise$, eof]	[$SheepNoise \rightarrow \bullet$ baa $SheepNoise$, eof]
[$Goal \rightarrow SheepNoise\ \bullet$, eof]	[$SheepNoise \rightarrow$ baa $\bullet$ $SheepNoise$, eof]
[$SheepNoise \rightarrow \bullet$ baa, eof]	[$SheepNoise \rightarrow$ baa $SheepNoise\ \bullet$, eof]
[$SheepNoise \rightarrow$ baa $\bullet$, eof]	[$SheepNoise \rightarrow \bullet$ baa $SheepNoise$, baa]
[$SheepNoise \rightarrow \bullet$ baa, baa]	[$SheepNoise \rightarrow$ baa $\bullet$ $SheepNoise$, baa]
[$SheepNoise \rightarrow$ baa $\bullet$, baa]	[$SheepNoise \rightarrow$ baa $SheepNoise\ \bullet$, baa]

The item [$Goal{\rightarrow}SheepNoise\ \bullet$, eof] represents a configuration in which the parser has already recognized a string that reduces to *Goal*, and it has exhausted the input, indicated by the lookahead *eof*. If the stack below *Goal* is empty (that is, the symbol *invalid* is below *Goal*), then the parse succeeds.

3.5.2   Constructing the Canonical Collection

The construction of $\mathcal{CC}$ begins by building a model of the parser's initial state. This state consists of the set of items that represent the parser's initial state, along with any items that must also hold in the initial state. To simplify the task of building this initial state, the construction requires that the grammar have a unique goal symbol, as the augmented SN grammar does.

The item [$Goal{\rightarrow}\bullet SheepNoise$, eof] describes the parser's initial state. It represents a configuration in which recognizing *SheepNoise* followed by *eof* would be a valid parse. This item becomes the core of the first state in $\mathcal{CC}$, labelled CC_0. If the grammar has several distinct productions for the goal symbol, each of them generates an item in this initial core of CC_0.

The *closure* Procedure

To compute the initial state of the parser, CC_0, the construction starts with the initial items for each alternative right-hand side of the goal symbol. To complete the state, it must add all of the items implied by those initial items. The procedure *closure* does this.

```
closure(s)
    while (s is still changing)
        for each item [A→β • Cδ,a] ∈ s
            for each production C→γ ∈ P
                for each b ∈ FIRST(δa)
                    s ← s ∪ {[C→•γ,b]}
    return s
```

The *closure* procedure iterates over the items in set s. If the placeholder • in an item immediately precedes some nonterminal C, then *closure* must add one or more items for every production that can derive C. These items have the • at the start of the production's right-hand side.

The rationale for this is clear. If $[A→β•Cδ,a] ∈ s$, then one potential completion for the left context is to find a string that reduces to C, followed by $δa$. This completion should cause a reduction to A, since it fills out the production's right-hand side ($Cδ$) and follows it with a valid lookahead symbol.

For a production $C→γ$, *closure* must insert the placeholder before $γ$ and add the appropriate lookahead symbols—all terminals that can appear as the initial symbol in $δa$. This includes every terminal in FIRST($δ$). If $ε ∈$ FIRST($δ$), it also includes a. The notation FIRST($δa$) in the algorithm represents this extension of the FIRST set to a string in this way. If $δ$ is $ε$, this devolves into FIRST(a) = { a }.

For SN, the initial item is [*Goal* → • *SheepNoise, eof*]. Taking its closure adds two items to the set: [*SheepNoise* → • baa *SheepNoise, eof*] from production two and [*SheepNoise* → • baa, *eof*] from production three. Since the terminal symbol baa follows the • in each item, they generate no more new items. These three items form the first set, CC$_0$.

The *closure* computation is another fixed-point computation. At each point, the triply nested loop either adds items to s or leaves s intact. It never removes an item from s. Since the set of LR(1) items is finite, this loop must halt. The triply nested loop looks expensive. However, close examination reveals that each item in s needs to be processed only once. The outer loop needs to consider only items added in the previous iteration of the outer loop. The middle loop iterates over the set of alternative right-hand sides for a single nonterminal, while the inner loop iterates over FIRST($δa$). If $δ$ is $ε$, the inner loop looks only at one symbol, a. Thus, this computation is faster than it first appears.

The goto Procedure

The second critical step in the construction is to derive the other parser states from CC_0. To accomplish this, we compute, for each state CC_i and each grammar symbol x, the state that would arise if the parser recognized an x while in state CC_i. The procedure *goto* does this.

```
goto(s, x)
    moved ← ∅
    for each item i ∈ s
        if the form of i is [α→β • xδ, a] then
            moved ← moved ∪ {[α→βx • δ, a]}
    return closure(moved)
```

The goto Procedure takes two arguments, a set of LR(1) items s and a grammar symbol x. It iterates over the items in s. When it finds one in which the • immediately precedes x, it creates a new item by moving the • rightward past x. This new item represents the state that results from recognizing x. The *goto* procedure places these new items in the set *moved*, and returns *closure(moved)*.

Given the set CC_0 from *SN*, we can derive the state of the parser after recognizing an initial terminal symbol, baa, by computing *goto* (CC_0, baa). Moving the • past baa produces two items: [*SheepNoise* → baa • *SheepNoise, eof*] from item 2 in CC_0, and [*SheepNoise* → baa •, *eof*] from item 3 in CC_0. Applying *closure* to this set adds two more items: [*SheepNoise* → • baa *SheepNoise, eof*] and [*SheepNoise* → • baa, *eof*]. Both of these derive from the • preceding *SheepNoise* in the first item.

The construction uses *goto* to find the set of states that derive directly from some state such as CC_0. To do this, it computes *goto*(CC_0, x) for each x that occurs after a • in an item in CC_0. This produces all the sets that are one symbol away from CC_0. To compute the complete canonical collection, we simply iterate this process to a fixed point.

The Algorithm

To construct the canonical collection of sets of LR(1) items, the algorithm computes the initial set, CC_0, and then systematically finds all of the sets of LR(1) items that are reachable from CC_0. It repeatedly applies *goto* to the new sets in CC; *goto*, in turn, uses *closure*. If the goal production is $S' \rightarrow s$, the construction is

$$\text{CC}_0 \leftarrow \textit{closure}(\{[S' \rightarrow \bullet S, eof]\})$$
$$CC \leftarrow \{\text{CC}_0\}$$
while (new sets are still being added to CC)
  for each unmarked set $\text{cc}_j \in CC$
    mark cc_j *as processed*
    for each x following a • *in an item in* cc_j
      $temp \leftarrow \textit{goto}(\text{cc}_j, x)$
      if $temp \notin CC$
        then $CC \leftarrow CC \cup \{temp\}$
      record transition from cc_j *to temp on x*

It begins by initializing CC to contain CC_0, as described earlier. Next, it systematically extends CC by looking for any transition from a state in CC to a state not yet in CC. It does this constructively, by building each possible state, *temp*, and testing *temp* for membership in CC. If *temp* is new, it adds *temp* to CC. Whether or not *temp* is new, it records the transition from cc_j to *temp* for later use in building the *Goto* table.

To ensure that the algorithm processes each set cc_i only once, it uses a simple marking scheme. It creates each set in an unmarked condition and marks the set as it is processed. This drastically reduces the number of times that it invokes *goto* and *closure*.

Like the other computations in the construction, this is a fixed-point computation. The canonical collection, CC, is a subset of the powerset of the LR(1) items, 2^{ITEMS}. The while loop is monotonic; it can only add new sets to CC. Since CC can grow no larger than 2^{ITEMS}, the computation must halt.

Canonical Collection for *SN*

The computation of the canonical collection for the augmented *SheepNoise* grammar proceeds as follows:

CC_0 is computed as *closure*$([Goal \rightarrow \bullet \, SheepNoise, eof])$.

$$\text{CC}_0 = \left\{ \begin{array}{l} [Goal \rightarrow \bullet \, SheepNoise, eof], \quad [SheepNoise \rightarrow \bullet \, \text{baa} \, SheepNoise, eof], \\ [SheepNoise \rightarrow \bullet \, \text{baa}, eof] \end{array} \right\}.$$

Since each item has the • at the start of its right-hand side, CC_0 contains only possibilities. This is appropriate, since it is the parser's initial state. The first iteration of the *while* loop produces two sets, CC_1 and CC_2.

	Item	Goal	SheepNoise	baa	eof
1	CC_0	$\emptyset$	CC_1	CC_2	$\emptyset$
2	CC_1	$\emptyset$	$\emptyset$	$\emptyset$	$\emptyset$
	CC_2	$\emptyset$	CC_3	CC_2	$\emptyset$
3	CC_3	$\emptyset$	$\emptyset$	$\emptyset$	$\emptyset$

FIGURE 3.17   Trace of the LR(1) Construction on the *SheepNoise* Grammar

goto(CC_0, *SheepNoise*) is CC_1.

$$CC_1 = \{\ [Goal \rightarrow SheepNoise \bullet, eof]\ \}.$$

If the lookahead symbol is *eof*, then the item [*Goal* → *SheepNoise* •, *eof*] is a handle, and the parser should accept the input string.

goto(CC_0, baa) is CC_2.

$$CC_2 = \left\{ \begin{array}{ll} [SheepNoise \rightarrow \bullet\, \text{baa}\ SheepNoise, eof], & [SheepNoise \rightarrow \bullet\, \text{baa}, eof], \\ [SheepNoise \rightarrow \text{baa} \bullet SheepNoise, eof], & [SheepNoise \rightarrow \text{baa} \bullet, eof] \end{array} \right\}.$$

The second iteration of the *while* loop tries to derive new sets from CC_1 and CC_2. *Goto*(CC_1, *x*) produces the empty set for any grammar symbol *x*. *Goto*(CC_2, *x*) produces the empty set with *eof* and *Goal* as *x*. With *SheepNoise* as *x*, it produces a new set, designated CC_3.

goto(CC_2, *SheepNoise*) is CC_3.

$$CC_3 = \{\ [SheepNoise \rightarrow \text{baa}\ SheepNoise \bullet, eof]\ \}.$$

Finally, *goto*(CC_2, baa) is CC_2, which is already in $\mathcal{CC}$. Since iteration three adds no additional sets to $\mathcal{CC}$, the process halts.

Figure 3.17 shows the progress of the construction of the canonical collection. The first column shows the iteration number. The construction computes CC_0 and uses *goto* to construct more sets for $\mathcal{CC}$. The first iteration builds CC_1 from *SheepNoise* and CC_2 from baa. The second iteration cannot derive any sets from CC_1. From CC_2, it builds CC_3 from *SheepNoise* and CC_2 from baa. The third iteration cannot derive any sets from CC_3.

The canonical collection represents the states of a handle-recognizing DFA. Each set in the collection becomes a state in the DFA. The transitions follow

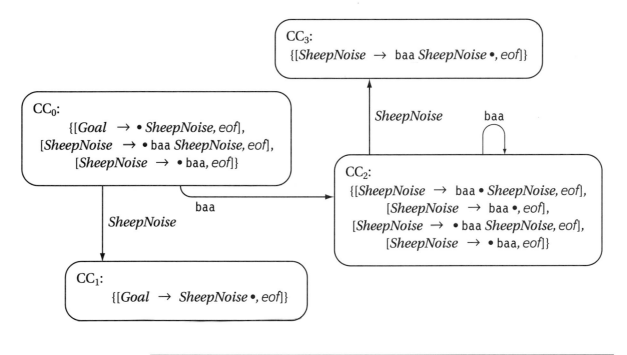

FIGURE 3.18   Handle-recognizing DFA for the *SheepNoise* Grammar, SN

the actions that generated the set. For example, *goto*(CC$_2$,*SheepNoise*) is CC$_3$. This indicates a transition from the state for CC$_2$ to the state for CC$_3$ on the grammar symbol *SheepNoise*. Figure 3.18 shows the handle-recognizing DFA that we built for SN.

3.5.3 Filling in the Tables

Given the canonical collection of sets of LR(1) items for *SN*, the parser generator can fill in the *Action* and *Goto* tables by iterating through $\mathcal{CC}$ and examining the items in each CC$_j$ $\in$ $\mathcal{CC}$. Each CC$_j$ becomes a parser state. Its items generate the nonempty elements of one row of *Action*; the corresponding transitions recorded during construction of $\mathcal{CC}$ specify the nonempty elements of *Goto*. Three cases generate entries in the *Action* table.

1. An item of the form $[A{\rightarrow}\beta{\bullet}c\gamma,a]$ indicates that encountering the terminal symbol c would be a valid next step toward discovering the nonterminal A. Thus, it generates a *shift* item on c in the current state. The next

$$\textit{for each } \mathbf{cc}_i \in \mathcal{CC}$$
$$\quad \textit{for each item } I \in \mathbf{cc}_i$$
$$\quad\quad \textit{if } I \textit{ is } [A{\rightarrow}\beta \bullet \mathsf{c}\gamma, \mathsf{a}] \textit{ and } goto(\mathbf{cc}_i, \mathsf{c}) = \mathbf{cc}_j \textit{ then}$$
$$\quad\quad\quad Action[i, \mathsf{c}] \leftarrow \textit{"shift j"}$$
$$\quad\quad \textit{else if } I \textit{ is } [A{\rightarrow}\beta\bullet, \mathsf{a}] \textit{ then}$$
$$\quad\quad\quad Action[i, \mathsf{a}] \leftarrow \textit{"reduce } A{\rightarrow}\beta\textit{"}$$
$$\quad\quad \textit{else if } I \textit{ is } [S'{\rightarrow}S\bullet, eof] \textit{ then}$$
$$\quad\quad\quad Action[i, eof] \leftarrow \textit{"accept"}$$
$$\quad \textit{for each } n \in NT$$
$$\quad\quad \textit{if } goto(\mathbf{cc}_i, n) = \mathbf{cc}_j \textit{ then}$$
$$\quad\quad\quad Goto[i, n] \leftarrow j$$

Figure 3.19   LR(1) Table-Filling Algorithm

state for the recognizer is the state generated by computing *goto* on the current state with the terminal c. Either β or γ can be ϵ.

2. An item of the form $[A{\rightarrow}\beta\bullet, \mathsf{a}]$ indicates that the parser has recognized a β, and if the lookahead is a, then the item is a handle. Thus, it generates a *reduce* item for the production $A{\rightarrow}\beta$ on a in the current state.

3. The item $[S'{\rightarrow}S\bullet, eof]$ is unique. It indicates the accepting state for the parser; the parser has recognized an input stream that reduces to the goal symbol and the lookahead symbol is *eof*. Thus, this item generates an *accept* action on *eof* in the current state.

Figure 3.19 makes this concrete. For an LR(1) grammar, it should uniquely define the non-error entries in the *Action* and *Goto* tables.

Notice that the table-filling algorithm essentially ignores items where the $\bullet$ precedes a nonterminal symbol. Shift actions are generated when $\bullet$ precedes a terminal. Reduce and accept actions are generated when $\bullet$ is at the right end of the production. What if $\mathbf{cc}_i$ contains an item $[A{\rightarrow}\beta \bullet \gamma\delta, \mathsf{a}]$, where $\gamma \in NT$? While this item does not generate any table entries itself, its presence in the set forces the *closure* procedure to include items that generate table entries. When *closure* finds a $\bullet$ that immediately precedes a nonterminal symbol γ, it adds productions that have γ as their left-hand side, with a $\bullet$ preceding their right-hand sides. This process instantiates FIRST(γ) in $\mathbf{cc}_i$. The *closure* procedure will find each $x \in$ FIRST(γ) and add the items into $\mathbf{cc}_i$ to generate shift items for each x.

Of course, the table-filling actions can be integrated into the construction of the canonical collection of sets of LR(1) items.

For the *SheepNoise* grammar, the construction produces these two tables:

Action **Table**				*Goto* **Table**	
State	*eof*	**baa**		**State**	**SheepNoise**
0		s 2		0	1
1	*accept*			1	
2	r 3	s 2		2	3
3	r 2			3	

These tables can be used with the driver in Figure 3.13 to create an LR(1) parser for *SN*.

3.5.4 Errors in the Table Construction

As a second example of the LR(1) table construction, consider the ambiguous grammar for the classic *if-then-else* construct. Abstracting away the details of the controlling expression and all other statements (by treating them as terminal symbols) produces the following four-production grammar:

1	*Goal*	→	*Stmt*
2	*Stmt*	→	if expr then *Stmt*
3		|	if expr then *Stmt* else *Stmt*
4		|	assign

It has two nonterminal symbols, *Goal* and *Stmt*, and six terminal symbols, if, expr, then, else, assign, and the implicit *eof*.

The construction begins by initializing CC_0 to the item [*Goal* → • *Stmt*, *eof*] and taking its *closure* to produce the first set:

$$CC_0 = \left\{ \begin{array}{l} [\textit{Goal} \rightarrow \bullet \textit{Stmt}, \textit{eof}], [\textit{Stmt} \rightarrow \bullet\, \texttt{if expr then}\, \textit{Stmt}, \textit{eof}], \\ [\textit{Stmt} \rightarrow \bullet\, \texttt{if expr then}\, \textit{Stmt}\, \texttt{else}\, \textit{Stmt}, \textit{eof}], [\textit{Stmt} \rightarrow \bullet\, \texttt{assign}, \textit{eof}] \end{array} \right\}.$$

From this set, the construction begins deriving the remaining members of the canonical collection of sets of LR(1) items.

Figure 3.20 shows the progress of the construction. The first iteration examines the transitions out of CC_0 for each grammar symbol. This produces three

Item	Goal	Stmt	if	expr	then	else	assign	eof
1	CC_0	$\emptyset$	CC_1	CC_2	$\emptyset$	$\emptyset$	$\emptyset$	CC_3	$\emptyset$
2	CC_1	$\emptyset$	$\emptyset$	$\emptyset$	$\emptyset$	$\emptyset$	$\emptyset$	$\emptyset$	$\emptyset$
	CC_2	$\emptyset$	$\emptyset$	$\emptyset$	CC_4	$\emptyset$	$\emptyset$	$\emptyset$	$\emptyset$
	CC_3	$\emptyset$	$\emptyset$	$\emptyset$	$\emptyset$	$\emptyset$	$\emptyset$	$\emptyset$	$\emptyset$
3	CC_4	$\emptyset$	$\emptyset$	$\emptyset$	$\emptyset$	CC_5	$\emptyset$	$\emptyset$	$\emptyset$
4	CC_5	$\emptyset$	CC_6	CC_7	$\emptyset$	$\emptyset$	$\emptyset$	CC_8	$\emptyset$
5	CC_6	$\emptyset$	$\emptyset$	$\emptyset$	$\emptyset$	$\emptyset$	CC_9	$\emptyset$	$\emptyset$
	CC_7	$\emptyset$	$\emptyset$	$\emptyset$	CC_{10}	$\emptyset$	$\emptyset$	$\emptyset$	$\emptyset$
	CC_8	$\emptyset$	$\emptyset$	$\emptyset$	$\emptyset$	$\emptyset$	$\emptyset$	$\emptyset$	$\emptyset$
6	CC_9	$\emptyset$	CC_{11}	CC_2	$\emptyset$	$\emptyset$	$\emptyset$	CC_3	$\emptyset$
	CC_{10}	$\emptyset$	$\emptyset$	$\emptyset$	$\emptyset$	CC_{12}	$\emptyset$	$\emptyset$	$\emptyset$
7	CC_{11}	$\emptyset$	$\emptyset$	$\emptyset$	$\emptyset$	$\emptyset$	$\emptyset$	$\emptyset$	$\emptyset$
	CC_{12}	$\emptyset$	CC_{13}	CC_7	$\emptyset$	$\emptyset$	$\emptyset$	CC_8	$\emptyset$
8	CC_{13}	$\emptyset$	$\emptyset$	$\emptyset$	$\emptyset$	$\emptyset$	CC_{14}	$\emptyset$	$\emptyset$
9	CC_{14}	$\emptyset$	CC_{15}	CC_7	$\emptyset$	$\emptyset$	$\emptyset$	CC_8	$\emptyset$
10	CC_{15}	$\emptyset$	$\emptyset$	$\emptyset$	$\emptyset$	$\emptyset$	$\emptyset$	$\emptyset$	$\emptyset$

FIGURE 3.20   Trace of the LR(1) Construction on the If-Then-Else Grammar

new sets for the canonical collection from CC_0: CC_1 for *Stmt*, CC_2 for if, and CC_3 for assign. These sets are

$$CC_1 = \left\{ \; [Goal \rightarrow Stmt \bullet, eof] \; \right\},$$

$$CC_2 = \left\{ \begin{array}{l} [Stmt \rightarrow \text{if} \bullet \text{ expr then } Stmt, eof], \\ [Stmt \rightarrow \text{if} \bullet \text{ expr then } Stmt \text{ else } Stmt, eof] \end{array} \right\}, \text{ and}$$

$$CC_3 = \left\{ \; [Stmt \rightarrow \text{assign} \bullet, eof] \; \right\}.$$

The second iteration examines transitions out of these three new sets. Only one combination produces a new set, looking at CC_2 with the symbol expr.

$$CC_4 = \left\{ \begin{array}{l} [Stmt \rightarrow \texttt{if expr} \bullet \texttt{then } Stmt, eof], \\ [Stmt \rightarrow \texttt{if expr} \bullet \texttt{then } Stmt \texttt{ else } Stmt, eof] \end{array} \right\}.$$

The third iteration examines transitions out of CC_4 and creates CC_5 with the symbol then:

$$CC_5 = \left\{ \begin{array}{l} [Stmt \rightarrow \texttt{if expr then} \bullet Stmt, eof], \\ [Stmt \rightarrow \texttt{if expr then} \bullet Stmt \texttt{ else } Stmt, eof], \\ [Stmt \rightarrow \bullet \texttt{if expr then } Stmt, \{eof, \texttt{else}\}], \\ [Stmt \rightarrow \bullet \texttt{assign}, \{eof, \texttt{else}\}], \\ [Stmt \rightarrow \bullet \texttt{if expr then } Stmt \texttt{ else } Stmt, \{eof, \texttt{else}\}] \end{array} \right\}.$$

The fourth iteration examines transitions out of CC_5. It creates new sets for *Stmt*, for if, and for assign:

$$CC_6 = \left\{ \begin{array}{l} [Stmt \rightarrow \texttt{if expr then } Stmt\bullet, eof], \\ [Stmt \rightarrow \texttt{if expr then } Stmt \bullet \texttt{else } Stmt, eof] \end{array} \right\},$$

$$CC_7 = \left\{ \begin{array}{l} [Stmt \rightarrow \texttt{if} \bullet \texttt{expr then } Stmt, \{eof, \texttt{else}\}], \\ [Stmt \rightarrow \texttt{if} \bullet \texttt{expr then } Stmt \texttt{ else } Stmt, \{eof, \texttt{else}\}] \end{array} \right\}, \text{ and}$$

$$CC_8 = \{ \ [Stmt \rightarrow \texttt{assign} \bullet, \{eof, \texttt{else}\}] \ \}.$$

The fifth iteration examines CC_6, CC_7, and CC_8. While most of the combinations produce the empty set, two combinations lead to new sets. The transition on else from CC_6 leads to CC_9, and the transition on expr from CC_7 creates CC_{10}.

$$CC_9 = \left\{ \begin{array}{l} [Stmt \rightarrow \texttt{if expr then } Stmt \texttt{ else } \bullet Stmt, eof], \\ [Stmt \rightarrow \bullet \texttt{if expr then } Stmt, eof], \\ [Stmt \rightarrow \bullet \texttt{if expr then } Stmt \texttt{ else } Stmt, eof], \\ [Stmt \rightarrow \bullet \texttt{assign}, eof] \end{array} \right\}, \text{ and}$$

$$CC_{10} = \left\{ \begin{array}{l} [Stmt \rightarrow \texttt{if expr} \bullet \texttt{then } Stmt, \{eof, \texttt{else}\}], \\ [Stmt \rightarrow \texttt{if expr} \bullet \texttt{then } Stmt \texttt{ else } Stmt, \{eof, \texttt{else}\}] \end{array} \right\}.$$

When the sixth iteration examines the sets produced in the fifth iteration, it creates two new sets, CC_{11} from CC_9 on *Stmt* and CC_{12} from CC_{10} on then. It also creates duplicate sets for CC_2 and CC_3 from CC_9.

$$\text{CC}_{11} = \{\ [Stmt \rightarrow \texttt{if expr then } Stmt \texttt{ else } Stmt \bullet, eof]\ \}, \text{and}$$

$$\text{CC}_{12} = \left\{ \begin{array}{l} [Stmt \rightarrow \texttt{if expr then} \bullet Stmt, \{eof, \texttt{else}\}], \\ {}[Stmt \rightarrow \texttt{if expr then} \bullet Stmt \texttt{ else } Stmt, \{eof, \texttt{else}\}], \\ {}[Stmt \rightarrow \bullet \texttt{if expr then } Stmt, \{eof, \texttt{else}\}], \\ {}[Stmt \rightarrow \bullet \texttt{if expr then } Stmt \texttt{ else } Stmt, \{eof, \texttt{else}\}], \\ {}[Stmt \rightarrow \bullet \texttt{assign}, \{eof, \texttt{else}\}] \end{array} \right\}.$$

Iteration seven creates CC_{13} from CC_{12} on *Stmt*, along with duplicates for CC_7 and CC_8.

$$\text{CC}_{13} = \left\{ \begin{array}{l} [Stmt \rightarrow \texttt{if expr then } Stmt \bullet, \{eof, \texttt{else}\}], \\ {}[Stmt \rightarrow \texttt{if expr then } Stmt \bullet \texttt{ else } Stmt, \{eof, \texttt{else}\}] \end{array} \right\}.$$

Iteration eight finds one new set, CC_{14} from CC_{13}, on the transition for else.

$$\text{CC}_{14} = \left\{ \begin{array}{l} [Stmt \rightarrow \texttt{if expr then } Stmt \texttt{ else } \bullet Stmt, \{eof, \texttt{else}\}], \\ {}[Stmt \rightarrow \bullet \texttt{if expr then } Stmt, \{eof, \texttt{else}\}], \\ {}[Stmt \rightarrow \bullet \texttt{if expr then } Stmt \texttt{ else } Stmt, \{eof, \texttt{else}\}], \\ {}[Stmt \rightarrow \bullet \texttt{assign}, \{eof, \texttt{else}\}] \end{array} \right\}.$$

Iteration nine generates CC_{15} from CC_{14} on the transition for *Stmt*, along with duplicates of CC_7 and CC_8.

$$\text{CC}_{15} = \{\ [Stmt \rightarrow \texttt{if expr then } Stmt \texttt{ else } Stmt \bullet, \{eof, \texttt{else}\}]\ \}.$$

The final iteration looks at CC_{15}. Since the $\bullet$ lies at the end of every item in CC_{15}, it can only generate empty sets. At this point, no additional sets of items can be added to the canonical collection, so the algorithm has reached a fixed point. It halts.

The ambiguity in the grammar becomes apparent during the table-filling algorithm. The items in states CC_0 through CC_{12} generate no conflicts. State CC_{13} contains four items:

1. $[Stmt \rightarrow \texttt{if expr then } Stmt \bullet, \texttt{else}]$,

2. $[Stmt \rightarrow \texttt{if expr then } Stmt \bullet, eof]$,

3. [*Stmt* → i f expr then *Stmt* • el se *Stmt*, el se], and

4. [*Stmt* → i f expr then *Stmt* • el se *Stmt*, *eof*].

Item 1 generates a reduce entry for CC_{13} and the lookahead el se. Item 3 generates a shift entry for the same location in the table. Clearly, the table entry cannot hold both actions. This shift-reduce conflict indicates that the grammar is ambiguous. Items 2 and 4 generate a similar shift-reduce conflict with a lookahead of *eof*. When the table-filling algorithm encounters such a conflict, the construction has failed. The table generator should report the problem—a fundamental ambiguity between the productions in the specific LR(1) items—to the compiler writer.[3]

In this case, the conflict arises because production two in the grammar is a prefix of production three. The table generator can resolve this conflict in favor of shifting; that forces the parser to recognize the longer production and binds the el se to the innermost i f.

An ambiguous grammar can also produce a reduce-reduce conflict. This occurs if the grammar contains two productions $A{\to}\gamma\delta$ and $B{\to}\gamma\delta$, for the same right-hand side $\gamma\delta$. If a state contains the items $[A{\to}\gamma\delta \bullet,a]$ and $[B{\to}\gamma\delta \bullet,a]$, then it will generate two conflicting reduce actions for the lookahead a—one for each production. Again, this conflict reflects a fundamental ambiguity in the underlying grammar; the compiler writer must reshape the grammar to eliminate it (see Section 3.6.3).

Since parser generators that automate this process are widely available, the method of choice for determining whether a grammar has the LR(1) property is to invoke an LR(1) parser generator on it. If the process succeeds, the grammar has the LR(1) property.

3.6 PRACTICAL ISSUES

Even with automatic parser generators, the compiler writer must manage several issues to produce a robust, efficient parser for a real programming language. This section addresses several issues that arise in practice.

---

3. Typically, the error message includes the LR(1) items that generate the conflict—another reason to study the table construction.

3.6.1 Error Recovery

Programmers often compile code that contains syntax errors. In fact, compilers are widely accepted as the fastest way to discover such errors. In this application, the compiler must find as many syntax errors as possible in a single attempt at parsing the code. This requires attention to the parser's behavior in error states.

All of the parsers shown in this chapter have the same behavior when they encounter a syntax error: they report the problem and halt. This prevents the compiler from wasting time trying to translate an incorrect program. However, it ensures that the compiler finds at most one syntax error per compilation. Such a compiler would make finding syntax errors a potentially long and painful process.

A parser should find as many syntax errors as possible in each compilation. This requires a mechanism that lets the parser recover from an error by moving to a state where it can continue parsing. A common way of achieving this is to select one or more words that the parser can use to synchronize the input with its internal state. When the parser encounters an error, it discards input symbols until it finds a synchronizing word and then resets its internal state to one consistent with the synchronizing word.

In an Algol-like language, with semicolons as statement separators, the semicolon is often used as a synchronizing word. When an error occurs, the parser calls the scanner repeatedly until it finds a semicolon. It then changes state to one that would have resulted from successful recognition of a complete statement, rather than an error.

In a recursive-descent parser, the code can simply discard words until it finds a semicolon. At that point, it can return control to the point where the routine that parses statements reports success. This may involve manipulating the run-time stack or using a nonlocal jump like C's `setjmp longjmp` construct.

In an LR(1) parser, this kind of resynchronization is more complex. The parser discards input until it finds a semicolon. Next, it scans backward down the parse stack until it finds a state *s* such that *Goto*[*s*, *Statement*] is a valid, nonerror entry. The first such state on the stack represents the statement that contains the error. The error recovery routine then pushes the state *Goto*[*s*, *Statement*] onto the stack and resumes normal parsing.

In a table-driven parser, either LL(1) or LR(1), the compiler needs a way of telling the parser generator where to synchronize. This can be done using error productions—a production whose right-hand side includes a reserved word that indicates an error synchronization point and one or more synchronizing tokens. With such a construct, the parser generator can construct error-recovery routines that implement the desired behavior.

Of course, the error-recovery routines should take steps to ensure that the compiler does not try to generate and optimize code for a syntactically invalid program. This requires simple handshaking between the error-recovery apparatus and the high-level driver that invokes the various parts of the compiler.

3.6.2 Unary Operators

The classic expression grammar includes only binary operators. Standard algebraic notation, however, includes both a unary minus, or negation, operator and an absolute-value operator. Other unary operators arise in programming languages, including boolean complement, autoincrement, autodecrement, typecasts, address-of, and dereference. Adding unary operators to the expression grammar requires some care.

Consider adding a unary absolute-value operator, ‖, to the classic expression grammar. Absolute value should have higher precedence than either × or ÷. However, it needs a lower precedence than *Factor* to force evaluation of parenthetic expressions before application of ‖. This leads to a grammar such as

$$
\begin{array}{rcl}
Expr & \rightarrow & Expr + Term \\
& | & Expr - Term \\
& | & Term \\
Term & \rightarrow & Term \times Value \\
& | & Term \div Value \\
& | & Value \\
Value & \rightarrow & \| \ Factor \\
& | & Factor \\
Factor & \rightarrow & (\ Expr\ ) \\
& | & \texttt{num} \\
& | & \texttt{ident}
\end{array}
$$

With these additions, the grammar is still LR(1). It lets the programmer form the absolute value of a number, of an identifier, or of a parenthesized expression. The string ‖x - 3 produces the following parse tree:

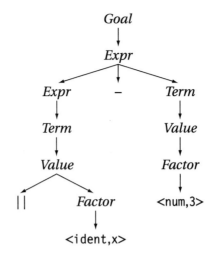

which correctly shows that the code must evaluate ‖x before performing the subtraction. The grammar does not allow the programmer to write ‖‖x, as that makes little mathematical sense. It does, however, allow ‖(‖x), which makes as little sense as ‖‖x.

The inability to write ‖‖x hardly limits the expressiveness of the language. With other unary operators, however, the issue seems more serious. For example, a C programmer might need to write **p to dereference a variable declared as char **p;. We can add a dereference production for *Value* as well: *Value* → * *Value*. The resulting grammar is still an LR(1) grammar, even if we replace the × operator in *Term* → *Term* × *Value* with *, overloading the operator "*" in the way that C does. This same approach works for unary minus.

3.6.3 Handling Context-Sensitive Ambiguity

Using one word to represent two different meanings can create a syntactic ambiguity. One example of this problem arose in the definitions of several early programming languages, including FORTRAN, PL/I, and Ada. These languages used parentheses to enclose both the subscript expressions of an array reference and the argument list of a subroutine or function. Given a textual reference, such as fee(i,j), the compiler cannot tell if fee is a two-dimensional array or a procedure that must be invoked. Differentiating between these two cases requires knowledge of fee's declared type. This information is not syntactically obvious. The scanner undoubtedly classifies fee as an ident in either case. A function call and an array reference can appear in many of the same situations.

Neither of these constructs appears in the classic expression grammar. We can add productions that derive them from *Factor*.

$$
\begin{array}{rcl}
\textit{Factor} & \rightarrow & \textit{FunctionReference} \\
 & | & \textit{ArrayReference} \\
 & | & (\ \textit{Expr}\ ) \\
 & | & \texttt{num} \\
 & | & \texttt{ident} \\
\textit{FunctionReference} & \rightarrow & \texttt{ident}\ (\ \textit{ExprList}\ ) \\
\textit{ArrayReference} & \rightarrow & \texttt{ident}\ (\ \textit{ExprList}\ )
\end{array}
$$

Since the last two productions have identical right-hand sides, this grammar is ambiguous. This creates a reduce-reduce conflict for an LR(1) table builder.

Resolving this ambiguity requires extrasyntactic knowledge. In a recursive-descent parser, the compiler writer can simply combine the code for *FunctionReference* and *ArrayReference* and add the extra code required to check the ident's declared type. In a table-driven parser built from tools, the solution must work within the tools.

Two different approaches have been used to solve this problem over the years. The compiler writer can rewrite the grammar to combine both the function invocation and the array reference into a single production. In this scheme, the issue is deferred until a later step in translation, when it can be resolved with information from the declarations. The parser must construct a representation that preserves all the information needed by either resolution; the later step will then rewrite the reference to its appropriate form as an array reference or as a function invocation.

Alternatively, the scanner can classify identifiers based on their declared types, rather than their microsyntactic properties. This requires some hand-shaking between the scanner and the parser; the coordination is not hard to arrange as long as the language has a define-before-use rule. Since the declaration is parsed before the use occurs, the parser can make its internal symbol table available to the scanner to resolve identifiers into distinct classes, such as variable-name and function-name. The relevant productions become

$$
\begin{array}{rcl}
\textit{FunctionReference} & \rightarrow & \texttt{function-name}\ (\ \textit{ExprList}\ ) \\
\textit{ArrayReference} & \rightarrow & \texttt{variable-name}\ (\ \textit{ExprList}\ )
\end{array}
$$

Rewritten in this way, the grammar is unambiguous. Since the scanner returns a distinct syntactic category in each case, the parser can distinguish between these two cases.

3.6.4 Left versus Right Recursion

As we have seen, top-down parsers need right-recursive grammars rather than left-recursive grammars. Bottom-up parsers can accommodate both left recursion and right recursion. Thus, the compiler writer has a choice between left recursion and right recursion in laying out the grammar for a bottom-up parser. Several factors play into this decision.

Stack Depth

In general, left recursion can lead to smaller stack depths. Consider two alternate grammars for a simple list construct. (Notice the similarity to the *Sheep-Noise* grammar.)

$$
\begin{array}{rcl}
List & \to & List \ \texttt{elt} \\
     & | & \texttt{elt}
\end{array}
\qquad\qquad
\begin{array}{rcl}
List & \to & \texttt{elt} \ List \\
     & | & \texttt{elt}
\end{array}
$$

Using each grammar to produce a list of five elements, we produce the following derivations:

List	*List*
List $\texttt{elt}_5$	$\texttt{elt}_1$ *List*
List $\texttt{elt}_4$ $\texttt{elt}_5$	$\texttt{elt}_1$ $\texttt{elt}_2$ *List*
List $\texttt{elt}_3$ $\texttt{elt}_4$ $\texttt{elt}_5$	$\texttt{elt}_1$ $\texttt{elt}_2$ $\texttt{elt}_3$ *List*
List $\texttt{elt}_2$ $\texttt{elt}_3$ $\texttt{elt}_4$$\texttt{elt}_5$	$\texttt{elt}_1$ $\texttt{elt}_2$ $\texttt{elt}_3$ $\texttt{elt}_4$ *List*
$\texttt{elt}_1$ $\texttt{elt}_2$ $\texttt{elt}_3$ $\texttt{elt}_4$ $\texttt{elt}_5$	$\texttt{elt}_1$ $\texttt{elt}_2$ $\texttt{elt}_3$ $\texttt{elt}_4$ $\texttt{elt}_5$

Since the parser constructs these sequences in reverse, reading each derivation from the bottom line to the top line allows us to follow the parser's actions.

1. *Left Recursion* This grammar shifts elt_1 onto its stack and immediately reduces it to *List*. Next, it shifts elt_2 onto the stack and reduces it to *List*. It proceeds until it has shifted each of the five elt_is onto the stack and reduced them to *List*. Thus, the stack reaches a maximum depth of two and an average depth of $\frac{10}{6} = 1\frac{2}{3}$.

2. *Right Recursion* This version shifts all five elt_is onto its stack. Next, it reduces elt_5 to *List* using rule two, and the remaining elt_is using rule one. Thus, its maximum stack depth will be five and its average will be $\frac{20}{6} = 3\frac{1}{3}$.

The right-recursive grammar requires more stack space; in fact, its maximum stack depth is bounded only by the length of the list. In contrast, the maximum stack depth of the left-recursive grammar is a function of the grammar rather than the input stream.

For short lists, this is not a problem. If, however, the list represents the statement list in a long run of straight-line code, it might have hundreds of elements. In this case, the difference in space can be dramatic. If all other issues are equal, the smaller stack height is an advantage.

Associativity

Left recursion naturally produces left associativity, and right recursion naturally produces right associativity. In some cases, the order of evaluation makes a difference. Consider the abstract syntax trees (ASTs) for the five-element lists constructed earlier. (An AST eliminates many of the nodes in a parse tree.)

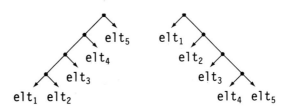

The left-recursive grammar reduces elt_1 to a *List*, then reduces *List* elt_2, and so on. This produces the AST shown on the left. Similarly, the right-recursive grammar produces the AST on the right.

With a list, neither of these orders is obviously correct, although the right-recursive AST may seem more natural. Consider, however, the result if we replace the list constructor with arithmetic operations, as in the grammars

Expr	$\rightarrow$	*Expr* + Operand	*Expr*	$\rightarrow$	Operand + *Expr*
	|	*Expr* - Operand		|	Operand - *Expr*
	|	Operand		|	Operand

For the string $x_1 + x_2 + x_3 + x_4 + x_5$, the left-recursive grammar implies a left-to-right evaluation order, while the right-recursive grammar implies a right-to-left evaluation order. With some number systems, such as floating-point arithmetic on a computer, these two evaluation orders can produce different results.[4] If any of the terms in the operation is a function call, then the order of evaluation may be important. If the function call changes the value of a variable in the expression, then changing the evaluation order might change the result.

In a string with subtractions, such as $x_1 - x_2 + x_3$, changing the evaluation order can produce incorrect results. Left associativity evaluates, in a postorder tree walk, to $(x_1 - x_2) + x_3$, the expected result. Right associativity, on the other hand, implies an evaluation order of $x_1 - (x_2 + x_3)$. The compiler must, of course, preserve the evaluation order dictated by the language definition. The compiler writer can accomplish this in either of two ways—namely, writing the expression grammar so that it produces the desired order, or taking care to generate the intermediate representation to reflect the correct order and associativity, as described in Section 4.5.2.

3.7 ADVANCED TOPICS

To build a satisfactory parser, the compiler writer must understand the basics of engineering a grammar and a parser. Given a working parser, there are often ways of improving its performance. This section looks at two specific issues in parser construction—namely, optimizing a grammar to reduce the

---

4. Since floating-point numbers have a small mantissa relative to the range of the exponent, addition becomes an identity operation for the larger of two numbers that are far enough apart in magnitude. If, for example, x_4 is much smaller than x_5, the processor will compute $x_4 + x_5 = x_5$. For some values of the arguments, this effect can cascade, leading to different answers from left-to-right and right-to-left evaluations.

length of derivations (and increase the speed of parsing) and ways of reducing the size of the *Action* and *Goto* tables in an LR(1) parser.

3.7.1 Optimizing a Grammar

While syntax analysis no longer consumes a major share of compile time, the compiler should not waste undue time in parsing. The actual form of a grammar has a direct effect on the amount of work required to parse it. Both top-down and bottom-up parsers construct derivations. A top-down parser performs an expansion for every production in the derivation. A bottom-up parser performs a reduction for every production in the derivation. A grammar that produces shorter derivations takes less time to parse.

The compiler writer can often rewrite the grammar to reduce the height of the parse tree. This reduces the number of expansions in a top-down parser and the number of reductions in a bottom-up parser. Optimizing the grammar cannot change the parser's asymptotic behavior; after all, the parse tree must have a leaf node for each symbol in the input stream. Still, reducing the constants in heavily used portions of the grammar, such as the expression grammar, can make enough difference to justify the effort.

Consider, again, the classic expression grammar from Section 3.2.3. To enforce the desired precedence among operators, we added two nonterminals, *Term* and *Factor*, and reshaped the grammar into its present form.

1	*Expr*	→	*Expr* + *Term*
2		|	*Expr* - *Term*
3		|	*Term*
4	*Term*	→	*Term* × *Factor*
5		|	*Term* ÷ *Factor*
6		|	*Factor*
7	*Factor*	→	(*Expr*)
8		|	num
9		|	ident

This leads to rather large parse trees, even for simple expressions. As we saw in Figure 3.10, the parse tree for x - 2 × y has fourteen nodes, five of which are leaves. (We cannot optimize away the leaves. Changing the grammar cannot shorten the input program!)

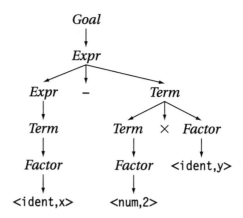

Any node that has a single child is a candidate for optimization. The sequence of nodes *Expr* to *Term* to *Factor* to ⟨ident,x⟩ uses four nodes for a single word in the input stream. We can eliminate at least one layer, the layer of *Factor* nodes, by folding the alternative expansions for *Factor* upward in the grammar. This replaces each occurrence of *Factor* on the right-hand side of a production with each of its three alternatives.

$$
\begin{array}{rlcll}
Term & \rightarrow & Term \times (\,Expr\,) & |\quad Term \times \mathtt{ident} & |\quad Term \times \mathtt{num} \\
& | & Term \div (\,Expr\,) & |\quad Term \div \mathtt{ident} & |\quad Term \div \mathtt{num} \\
& | & (\,Expr\,) & |\quad \mathtt{ident} & |\quad \mathtt{num}
\end{array}
$$

It multiplies by three the number of alternatives for *Term*, but shrinks the parse tree by one layer.

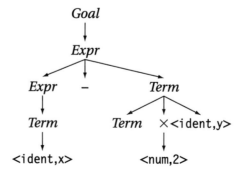

In a top-down, recursive-descent parser, this eliminates three of fourteen procedure calls. In an LR(1) parser, it eliminates three of nine reduce actions, and leaves the five shifts intact.

In general, any production that has a single symbol on its right-hand side can be folded away. These productions are called *useless productions.* Sometimes, useless productions serve a purpose—making the grammar more compact and, perhaps, more readable, or forcing the derivation to assume a particular shape. (Recall that the simplest of our expression grammars accepts x - 2 × y but does not encode any notion of precedence into the parse tree.) As we shall see in Chapter 4, the compiler writer may include a useless production simply to create a point in the derivation where a particular action can be performed.

This transformation, folding away useless productions, has its costs. In an LR(1) parser, it can make the tables larger. In our example, eliminating *Factor* removes one column from the *Goto* table, but the extra productions for *Term* increase the size of *CC* from thirty-two sets to forty-six sets. Thus, the tables have one fewer column, but an extra fourteen rows. The resulting parser does fewer reductions (and runs faster), but has larger tables.

In a hand-coded, recursive-descent parser, the larger grammar may increase the number of alternatives that must be compared before expanding some left-hand side.[5] The compiler writer may be able to compensate for this increased cost by combining cases. For example, the code for both nontrivial expansions of *Expr'* in Figure 3.7 is identical. The compiler writer could combine them with a test that matches *word* against either + or -. Alternatively, the compiler writer could assign both + and - to the same syntactic category, have the parser inspect the syntactic category, and use the actual text of the word to differentiate between the two when needed.

3.7.2 Reducing the Size of LR(1) Tables

As Figures 3.14 and 3.15 show, the LR(1) tables generated for relatively small grammars can be large. Many techniques exist for shrinking these tables. This section describes three approaches to reducing table size.

---

5. Do not let this discussion mislead you into thinking that the classic expression grammar, modified in this way, is LL(1). Recall that the grammar required modifications to make it predictively parsable. The same transformation, in spirit, can be applied to the current version of the grammar.

Combining Rows or Columns

If the table generator can find two rows, or two columns, that are identical, it can combine them. In Figure 3.14, the rows for states 0 and 7 through 10 are identical, as are rows 4, 14, 21, 22, 24, and 25. The table generator can implement each of these sets once, and remap the states accordingly. This would remove nine rows from the table, reducing its size by 28 percent. To use this table, the skeleton parser needs a mapping from a parser state to a row index in the *Action* table. The table generator can combine identical columns in the analogous way. A separate inspection of the *Goto* table will yield a different set of state combinations—in particular, all of the rows containing only zeros should condense to a single row.

In some cases, the table generator can discover two rows or two columns that differ only in cases where one of the two has an "error" entry (denoted by a blank in our figures). In Figure 3.14, the column for *eof* and for num differ only where one or the other has a blank. Combining these columns produces a table that has the same behavior on correct inputs. It will change the parser's behavior on erroneous inputs and may decrease the parser's ability to provide accurate and helpful error messages.

Combining rows and columns produces a direct reduction in table size. If this space reduction adds an extra indirection to every table access, the cost of those memory operations must trade off directly against the savings in memory. The table generator could also use other techniques to represent sparse matrices—again, the implementor must consider the tradeoff of memory size against any increase in access costs.

Shrinking the Grammar

In many cases, the compiler writer can recode the grammar to reduce the number of productions it contains. This usually leads to smaller tables. For example, in the classic expression grammar, the distinction between a number and an identifier is irrelevant to the productions for *Goal*, *Expr*, *Term*, and *Factor*. Replacing the two productions *Factor* → num and *Factor* → ident with a single production *Factor* → val shrinks the grammar by a production. In the *Action* table, each terminal symbol has its own column. Folding num and ident into a single symbol, val, removes a column from the *Action* table. To make this work, in practice, the scanner must return the same syntactic category, or word, for both num and ident.

Similar arguments can be made for combining × and ÷ into a single terminal `muldiv`, and for combining + and - into a single terminal `addsub`. Each of these replacements removes a terminal symbol and a production. These three changes produce the following reduced expression grammar:

1	*Goal*	$\rightarrow$	*Expr*
2	*Expr*	$\rightarrow$	*Expr* `addsub` *Term*
3				*Term*
4	*Term*	$\rightarrow$	*Term* `muldiv` *Factor*
5				*Factor*
6	*Factor*	$\rightarrow$	(*Expr*)
7				`val`

This grammar produces a smaller $\mathcal{CC}$, removing rows from the table. Because it has fewer terminal symbols, it has fewer columns as well.

The resulting *Action* and *Goto* tables are shown in Figure 3.21. The *Action* table contains 132 entries and the *Goto* table contains 66 entries, for a total of 198 entries. This compares favorably with the tables for the original grammar, with their 384 entries. Changing the grammar produced a 48 percent reduction in table size. Note, however, that the tables still contain duplicate rows, such as 0, 6, and 7 in the *Action* table, and 4, 11, 15, and 17 in the *Action* table, and identical rows in the *Goto* table also. If table size is a serious concern, these techniques should be used together.

Other considerations may limit the compiler writer's ability to combine productions. For example, the × operator might have multiple uses that make combining it with ÷ impractical. Similarly, the parser might use separate productions to let the parser handle two syntactically similar constructs in different ways.

Directly Encoding the Table

As a final improvement, the parser generator can abandon completely the table-driven skeleton parser in favor of a hard-coded implementation. Each state becomes a small case statement or a collection of if–then–else statements that test the type of the next symbol and either shift, reduce, accept, or report an error. The entire contents of the *Action* and *Goto* tables can be encoded in this way. (A similar transformation for scanners is discussed in Section 2.5.2.)

		Action **Table**							*Goto* **Table**		
	eof	add-sub	mul-div	(	)	val		Expr	Term	Factor
0				s 4		s 5	0	1	2	3
1	acc	s 6					1			
2	r 3	r 3	s 7				2			
3	r 5	r 5	r 5				3			
4				s 11		s 12	4	8	9	10
5	r 7	r 7	r 7				5			
6				s 4		s 5	6		13	3
7				s 4		s 5	7			14
8		s 15			s 16		8			
9		r 3	s 17		r 3		9			
10		r 5	r 5		r 5		10			
11				s 11		s 12	11	18	9	10
12		r 7	r 7		r 7		12			
13	r 2	r 2	s 7				13			
14	r 4	r 4	r 4				14			
15				s 11		s 12	15		19	10
16	r 6	r 6	r 6				16			
17				s 11		s 12	17			20
18		s 15			s 21		18			
19		r 2	s 17		r 2		19			
20		r 4	r 4		r 4		20			
21		r 6	r 6		r 6		21			

FIGURE 3.21 Tables for the Reduced Expression Grammar

The resulting parser avoids directly representing all of the "don't care" states in the *Action* and *Goto* tables, shown as blanks in the figures. This space savings may be offset by larger code size, since each state now includes more code. The new parser, however, has no parse table, performs no table lookups, and lacks the outer loop found in the skeleton parser. While its structure makes it almost unreadable by humans, it should execute more quickly than the corresponding table-driven parser. With appropriate code-layout techniques, the resulting parser can exhibit strong locality in both the instruction cache and the paging system. The classic example places all the routines for the expression grammar together on a single page, where they cannot conflict with one another.

Using Other Construction Algorithms

Several other algorithms to construct LR-style parsers exist. Among these techniques are the SLR(1) construction, for simple LR(1), and the LALR(1) construction, for lookahead LR(1). Both of these constructions produce smaller tables than the canonical LR(1) algorithm.

The SLR(1) algorithm accepts a smaller class of grammars than the canonical LR(1) construction. These grammars are restricted so that the lookahead symbols in the LR(1) items are not needed. The algorithm uses FOLLOW sets, to distinguish between cases in which the parser should shift and those in which it should reduce. In practice, this mechanism is powerful enough to resolve many grammars of practical interest. By using FOLLOW sets, the algorithm eliminates the need for lookahead symbols. This produces a smaller canonical collection and a table with correspondingly fewer rows.

The LALR(1) algorithm capitalizes on the observation that some items in the set representing a state are critical and that the remaining ones can be derived from the critical items. The LALR(1) table construction only represents the critical items; again, this produces a canonical collection that is equivalent to the one produced by the SLR(1) construction. The details differ, but the table sizes are the same.

The LR(1) construction presented earlier in the chapter is the most general of these table-construction algorithms. It produces the largest tables, but accepts the largest class of grammars. With appropriate table reduction techniques, the LR(1) tables can approximate the size of those produced by the more limited techniques. However, in a mildly counterintuitive result, any language that has an LR(1) grammar also has an LALR(1) grammar and an SLR(1) grammar. The grammars for these more restrictive forms will be shaped in a way that allows their respective construction algorithms to resolve the situations in which the parser should shift and those in which it should reduce.

3.8 SUMMARY AND PERSPECTIVE

Almost every compiler contains a parser. For many years, parsing was a subject of intense interest. This led to the development of many different techniques for building efficient parsers. The LR(1) family of grammars includes all of the context-free grammars that can be parsed in a deterministic fashion. The tools produce efficient parsers with provably strong error-detection properties. This combination of features, coupled with the widespread availability of parser generators for LR(1), LALR(1), and SLR(1) grammars, has decreased interest in other automatic parsing techniques (such as LL(1) and operator precedence).

Top-down, recursive-descent parsers have their own set of advantages. They are, arguably, the easiest hand-coded parsers to construct. They provide excellent opportunities to detect and repair syntax errors. The compiler writer can more easily finesse ambiguities in the source language that might trouble an LR(1) parser—such as a language in which keyword names can appear as identifiers. Top-down, recursive-descent parsers are efficient; in fact, a well-constructed top-down, recursive-descent parser can be faster than a table-driven LR(1) parser. (The direct encoding scheme for LR(1) may overcome this speed advantage.) A compiler writer who wants to construct a hand-coded parser, for whatever reason, is well advised to use the top-down, recursive-descent method.

More general parsing algorithms are available. In practice, however, the restrictions placed on context-free grammars by the LR(1) and LL(1) classes do not cause problems for most programming languages.

In choosing between LR(1) and LL(1) grammars, the choice becomes one of available tools. In practice, however, few, if any, programming-language constructs fall in the gap between LR(1) grammars and LL(1) grammars. Thus, starting with an available parser generator is always better than implementing a parser generator from scratch.

CHAPTER NOTES

The earliest compilers used hand-coded parsers [26, 304, 221]. The syntactic richness of Algol 60 challenged early compiler writers. They tried a variety of schemes to parse the language; Randell and Russell give a fascinating overview of the methods used in a variety of Algol 60 compilers [282, Chapter 1].

Irons was one of the first to separate the notion of syntax from translation [191]. Lucas appears to have introduced the notion of recursive-descent parsing [246]. Conway applies similar ideas to an efficient single-pass compiler for COBOL [91].

The ideas behind LL and LR parsing appeared in the 1960s. Lewis and Stearns introduced LL(k) grammars [236]; Rosenkrantz and Stearns described their properties in more depth [294]. Foster developed an algorithm to transform a grammar into LL(1) form [144]. Wood formalized the notion of left-factoring a grammar and explored the theoretical issues involved in transformating a grammar to LL(1) form [336, 337, 338].

Knuth laid out the theory behind LR(1) parsing [217]. DeRemer and others made these techniques practical with the advent of the SLR and LALR table constructions [113, 114]. Waite and Goos describe a technique for automatically eliminating useless productions during the LR(1) table-construction algorithm [326]. Penello suggested direct encoding of the tables into executable code [272]. Aho, Johnson, and Ullman [7] is a definitive reference on both LL and LR parsing.

Several algorithms for parsing arbitrary context-free grammars appeared in the 1960s and early 1970s. Algorithms by Cocke and Schwartz [86] and Younger [341], by Kasami [201], and by Earley [126] all had similar computational complexity. Earley's algorithm deserves particular note because of its similarity to the LR(1) table-construction algorithm. Earley's algorithm derives the set of possible parse states at parse time, rather than at run time, where the LR(1) techniques precompute these in a parser generator. From a high-level view, the LR(1) algorithms might appear as a natural optimization of Earley's algorithm.

CHAPTER 4

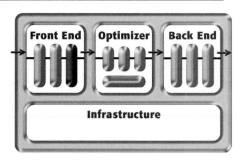

Context-Sensitive Analysis

4.1 INTRODUCTION

The compiler's ultimate task is to translate the input program into a form that can execute directly on the target machine. Before it can translate the program into target-machine operations, it must build up a large base of knowledge about the details encoded in the program. It must know how values are represented and how they flow between variables. It must understand the structure of the computation. It must analyze how the program interacts with external files and devices. All of these facts can be derived from the source code, with some contextual knowledge. However, this requires that the compiler look deeper than scanning and parsing can.

Consider a single variable; let's call it x. Before the compiler can emit executable target-machine code for computations involving x, it must have answers to many questions.

- *What kind of value is stored in x?* Modern programming languages use a plethora of data types, including several types of numbers, characters, boolean values, pointers to other objects, literals, sets (such as {red, yellow, green}), and others. Most languages include compound objects that aggregate individual values; these include arrays, structures, sets, and strings.

- *How big is x?* Because the compiler must manipulate x, it needs to know the length of x's representation on the target machine. If x is a number, it might be one word (an integer or floating-point number), two words (a double-precision floating-point number or a complex number), or four words (a quad-precision floating-point number or a double-precision complex number). For arrays and strings, the number of elements might be fixed at compile time or it might be determined at run time.

- *If x is a procedure, what arguments does it take? What kind of value, if any, does it return?* Before the compiler can generate code to invoke a procedure, it must know how many arguments the code for the called procedure expects, where it expects to find those arguments, and what kind of value it expects in each argument. If the procedure returns a value, where will the calling routine find that value, and what kind of data will it be? (The compiler must ensure that the calling procedure uses the value in a consistent and safe manner. If the calling procedure assumes that the return value is a pointer that it can dereference, and the called procedure returns an arbitrary character string, the results may not be predictable, safe, or consistent.)

- *How long must x's value be preserved?* The compiler must ensure that x's value remains accessible for any part of the computation that can legally reference it. If x is a local variable in Pascal, the compiler can easily overestimate x's interesting lifetime by preserving its value for the duration of the procedure that declares x. If x is a global variable that can be referenced anywhere, or if it is an element of a structure explicitly allocated by the program, the compiler may have a harder time determining its lifetime. The compiler can always preserve x's value for the entire computation; however, more precise information about x's lifetime might let the compiler reuse its space for other values with nonconflicting lifetimes.

- *Who is responsible for allocating space for x? (and initializing it?)* Is space allocated for x implicitly, or does the program explicitly allocate space for it? If the allocation is explicit, then the compiler must assume that x's address cannot be known until the program runs. If, on the other hand, the compiler allocates space for x in one of the run-time data structures that it manages, then it knows more about x's address. This knowledge may let it generate more efficient code.

The compiler must derive the answers to these questions, and more, from the source program and the rules of the source language. In an Algol-like language, such as Pascal or C, most of these questions can be answered by examining the declarations for x. If the language has no declarations, as in APL, the compiler must either derive this kind of information by analyzing the program, or it must generate code that can handle any case that might arise.

Many, if not all, of these questions reach beyond the syntax of the source language, as expressed in a context-free grammar. For example, the parse trees for x ← y and x ← z differ only in the text of the ident on the right-hand side of the assignment. If x and y are numbers while z is a character string, the compiler may need to emit different code for x ← y than for x ← z. To distinguish between these cases, the compiler must delve into the program's meaning. Scanning and parsing deal solely with the program's form; the analysis of meaning is the realm of *context-sensitive analysis.*

To see this difference between syntax and meaning more clearly, consider the structure of a program in most Algol-like languages. These languages require that every variable be declared before it is used and that all uses of a variable be consistent with its declaration.

The compiler writer can structure the syntax to ensure that all declarations occur before any executable statement. A production such as

$$ProcedureBody \rightarrow Declarations \ Executables$$

where the nonterminals have the obvious meanings, ensures that all declarations occur before any executable statements. This does nothing to check the deeper rule—that the program actually declares each variable before its first use in an executable statement. Neither can it handle the simpler case of a language like C++ which requires declaration before use for some categories of variables, but lets the programmer intermix declarations and executable statements.

Enforcing the "declare before use" rule requires a deeper level of knowledge than can be encoded in the context-free grammar. The context-free grammar deals with syntactic categories rather than specific words. Thus, the grammar can specify the positions in an expression where a variable name may occur. The parser can recognize that the grammar allows a variable name to occur, and it can tell that one has occurred. However, the grammar has no way to match one instance of a variable name with another; that would require the grammar to specify a much deeper level of analysis—an analysis that can account for context and that can examine and manipulate information at a deeper level than context-free syntax.

This chapter explores some of the problems that necessitate context-sensitive analysis and the frameworks used to perform it. It uses type checking as a continuing example to illustrate both the need for context-sensitive analysis and the issues that can arise in performing context-sensitive analysis. We begin with an overview of type systems and the need for type inference in Section 4.2. To perform type inference, and similar context-sensitive syntax-oriented computations, we introduce two frameworks: the attribute-grammar formalism in Section 4.3 and an ad hoc style of syntax-directed translation in Section 4.4. The advanced topics section briefly describes situations that lead to harder problems in type inference and type checking; it also shows one final example of an ad hoc syntax-directed translation scheme.

4.2 AN INTRODUCTION TO TYPE SYSTEMS

Most programming languages associate a collection of properties with each data value. We call this collection of properties the value's *type*. The type specifies a set of properties held in common by all values of that type. Types can be specified by membership; for example, an integer might be any whole number i in the range $-2^{31} \le i < 2^{31}$, or red might be a value in an enumerated type colors, defined as the set {red, orange, yellow, green, blue, brown, black, white}. Types can be specified by rules; for example, the declaration of a structure in C defines a type. In this case, the type includes any object with the declared fields in the declared order; the individual fields have types that specify the allowable ranges of values and their interpretation. (We represent the type of a structure as the product of the types of its constituent fields, in order.) Some types are predefined by a programming language; others are constructed by the programmer. The set of types in a programming language, along with the rules that use types to specify program behavior, are collectively called a *type system*.

4.2.1 The Purpose of Type Systems

Programming-language designers introduce type systems so that they can specify program behavior at a more precise level than is possible in a context-free grammar. The type system creates a second vocabulary for describing both the form and behavior of valid programs. Analyzing a program from the perspective of its type system yields information that cannot be obtained using the techniques of scanning and parsing. In a compiler, this information is typically used for three distinct purposes: safety, expressiveness, and run-time efficiency.

Ensuring Run-Time Safety

A well-designed type system helps the compiler detect and avoid run-time errors. The type system should ensure that programs are well behaved—that is, the compiler and run-time system can identify all ill-formed programs before they execute an operation that causes a run-time error. In truth, the type system cannot catch all ill-formed programs; the set of ill-formed programs is not computable. Some run-time errors, such as dereferencing an out-of-bounds pointer, have obvious (and often catastrophic) effects. Others, such as mistakenly interpreting an integer as a floating-point number, can have subtle and cumulative effects. The compiler should eliminate as many run-time errors as it can using type-checking techniques.

To accomplish this, the compiler must first infer a type for each expression. These inferred types expose situations in which a value is incorrectly interpreted, such as using a floating-point number in place of a boolean value. Second, the compiler must check the types of the operands of each operator against the rules that define what the language allows. In some cases, these rules might require the compiler to convert values from one representation to another. In other circumstances, they may forbid such a conversion and simply declare that the program is ill formed and, therefore, not executable.

In many languages, the compiler can infer a type for every expression. FORTRAN 77 has a particularly simple type system with just a handful of types. Figure 4.1 shows all the cases that can arise for the + operator. Given an expression a + b and the types of a and b, the table specifies the type of a + b. For an integer a and a double-precision b, a + b produces a double-precision result.

+	integer	real	double	complex
integer	integer	real	double	complex
real	real	real	double	complex
double	double	double	double	*illegal*
complex	complex	complex	*illegal*	complex

FIGURE 4.1   Result Types for **+** in FORTRAN 77

If, instead, a were complex, a + b would be illegal. The compiler should detect this situation and report it before the program executes—a simple example of type safety.

For some languages, the compiler cannot infer types for all expressions. APL, for example, lacks declarations, allows a variable's type to change at any assignment, and lets the user enter arbitrary code at input prompts. While this makes APL powerful and expressive, it ensures that the implementation must do some amount of run-time type inference and checking.[1]

Safety is a strong reason for using typed languages. A language implementation that guarantees to catch most type-related errors before they execute can simplify the design and implementation of programs. A language in which every expression can be assigned an unambiguous type is called a *strongly typed* language. If every expression can be typed at compile time, the language is *statically typed*; if some expressions can only be typed at run time, the language is *dynamically typed*. Two alternatives exist: an *untyped* language, such as assembly language or BCPL, and a *weakly typed* language—one with a poor type system.

Improving Expressiveness

A well-constructed type system allows the language designer to specify behavior more precisely than is possible with context-free rules. This capability lets the language designer include features that would be impossible to specify in a context-free grammar. An excellent example is operator overloading, which gives context-dependent meanings to an operator. Many programming languages use + to signify several kinds of addition. The interpretation of + depends on the types of its operands. In typed languages, many operators are overloaded. The alternative, in an untyped language, is to provide lexically different operators for each case.

For example, in BCPL, the only type is a "cell." A cell can hold any bit pattern; the interpretation of that bit pattern is determined by the operator applied to the cell. Because cells are essentially untyped, operators cannot be overloaded. Thus, BCPL uses + for integer addition and #+ for floating-point addition. Given two cells a and b, both a + b and a #+ b are valid expressions, neither of which performs any conversion on its operands.

In contrast, even the oldest typed languages use overloading to specify complex behavior. As described in the previous section, FORTRAN has a single addition operator, + , and uses type information to determine how it should be

---

1. The alternative, of course, is to assume that the program behaves well and ignore such checking. In general, this leads to bad behavior when a program goes awry. In APL, many of the advanced features rely heavily on the availability of type and dimension information.

implemented. ANSI C uses function prototypes—declarations of the number and type of a function's parameters and the type of its returned value—to convert arguments to the appropriate types. Type information determines the effect of autoincrementing a pointer in C; the amount of the increment is determined by the pointer's type. Object-oriented languages use type information to select the appropriate implementation at each procedure call. For example, Java selects between a default constructor and a specialized one by examining the constructor's argument list.

Generating Better Code

A well-designed type system provides the compiler with detailed information about every expression in the program—information that can often be used to produce more efficient translations. Consider implementing addition in FORTRAN 77. The compiler can completely determine the types of all expressions, so it can consult a table similar to the one in Figure 4.2. The code on the right shows the ILOC operation for the addition, along with the conversions specified in the FORTRAN standard for each mixed-type expression. The full table would include all the cases from Figure 4.1.

In a language with types that cannot be wholly determined at compile time, some of this checking might be deferred until run time. To accomplish this, the compiler needs to emit code similar to the pseudo-code in Figure 4.3.

Type of			Code
a	**b**	**a + b**	
integer	integer	integer	iADD r_a, r_b $\Rightarrow$ r_{a+b}
integer	real	real	i2f r_a $\Rightarrow$ r_{a_f}
			fADD r_{a_f}, r_b $\Rightarrow$ r_{a_f+b}
integer	double	double	i2d r_a $\Rightarrow$ r_{a_d}
			dADD r_{a_d}, r_b $\Rightarrow$ r_{a_d+b}
real	real	real	fADD r_a, r_b $\Rightarrow$ r_{a+b}
real	double	double	r2d r_a $\Rightarrow$ r_{a_d}
			dADD r_{a_d}, r_b $\Rightarrow$ r_{a_d+b}
double	double	double	dADD r_a, r_b $\Rightarrow$ r_{a+b}

FIGURE 4.2 Implementing **+** in FORTRAN 77

$$switch\ (\ type\ of\ \mathtt{a}\ )\ \{$$

$$\begin{aligned}
&case\ \mathtt{integer:}\\
&\quad switch\ (\ type\ of\ \mathtt{b}\ )\ \{\\
&\qquad case\ \mathtt{integer:}\ \mathtt{iADD}\ r_a, r_b\ \Rightarrow\ r_{a+b}\\
&\qquad\qquad\qquad\qquad\quad break\\
&\qquad case\ \mathtt{real:}\quad\ \mathtt{i2f}\ r_a\ \Rightarrow\ r_{a_f}\\
&\qquad\qquad\qquad\qquad\quad \mathtt{fADD}\ r_{a_f}, r_b\ \Rightarrow\ r_{a_f+b}\\
&\qquad\qquad\qquad\qquad\quad break\\
&\qquad case\ \mathtt{double:}\ \ \mathtt{i2d}\ r_a\ \Rightarrow\ r_{a_d}\\
&\qquad\qquad\qquad\qquad\quad \mathtt{dADD}\ r_{a_d}, r_b\ \Rightarrow\ r_{a_d+b}\\
&\qquad\qquad\qquad\qquad\quad break\\
&\qquad default:\qquad\quad signal\ a\ run\text{-}time\ type\ error\\
&\qquad\qquad\qquad\qquad\quad break\\
&\quad \}\\
&\quad break
\end{aligned}$$

$$\begin{aligned}
&case\ \mathtt{real:}\\
&\quad switch\ (\ type\ of\ \mathtt{b}\ )\ \{\\
&\qquad case\ \mathtt{integer:}\ \mathtt{i2f}\ r_b\ \Rightarrow\ r_{b_f}\\
&\qquad\qquad\qquad\qquad\quad \mathtt{fADD}\ r_a, r_{b_f}\ \Rightarrow\ r_{a+b_d}\\
&\qquad\qquad\qquad\qquad\quad break\\
&\qquad case\ \mathtt{real:}\quad\ \mathtt{fADD}\ r_a, r_b\ \Rightarrow\ r_{a+b}\\
&\qquad\qquad\qquad\qquad\quad break\\
&\qquad case\ \mathtt{double:}\ \ \mathtt{f2d}\ r_a\ \Rightarrow\ r_{a_d}\\
&\qquad\qquad\qquad\qquad\quad \mathtt{dADD}\ r_{a_d}, r_b\ \Rightarrow\ r_{a_d+b}\\
&\qquad\qquad\qquad\qquad\quad break\\
&\qquad default:\qquad\quad signal\ a\ run\text{-}time\ type\ error\\
&\qquad\qquad\qquad\qquad\quad break\\
&\quad \}\\
&\quad break
\end{aligned}$$

$$\begin{aligned}
&case\ \mathtt{double:}\\
&\quad switch\ (\ type\ of\ \mathtt{b}\ )\ \{\\
&\qquad case\ \mathtt{integer:}\ \mathtt{i2d}\ r_b\ \Rightarrow\ r_{b_d}\\
&\qquad\qquad\qquad\qquad\quad \mathtt{dADD}\ r_a, r_{b_d}\ \Rightarrow\ r_{a+b_d}\\
&\qquad\qquad\qquad\qquad\quad break\\
&\qquad case\ \mathtt{real:}\quad\ \mathtt{f2d}\ r_b\ \Rightarrow\ r_{b_d}\\
&\qquad\qquad\qquad\qquad\quad \mathtt{dADD}\ r_a, r_{b_d}\ \Rightarrow\ r_{a+b_d}\\
&\qquad\qquad\qquad\qquad\quad break\\
&\qquad case\ \mathtt{double:}\ \ \mathtt{dADD}\ r_a, r_b\ \Rightarrow\ r_{a+b}\\
&\qquad\qquad\qquad\qquad\quad break\\
&\qquad default:\qquad\quad signal\ a\ run\text{-}time\ type\ error\\
&\quad \}\\
&\quad break\\
&default:\ \ signal\ a\ run\text{-}time\ type\ error\\
&\qquad\qquad break\\
&\}
\end{aligned}$$

Figure 4.3 Run-Time Checking and Conversion for + Using fortran 77 Rules

(It shows the same subset of cases as Figure 4.2.) While this ensures run-time safety, it adds significant overhead to each operation. One goal of compile-time checking is to provide such safety without paying the price at run time.

The code in Figure 4.3 relies on the implicit assumption that the running code can determine the types of both operands, a and b. To accomplish this, the compiler and run-time system must tag each value with its type, so that *type of* a becomes a reference to a value stored alongside a's actual value. After the operand has been converted, the code must also set the tag field for the resulting value. (We have omitted the code for tag manipulation from Figure 4.3.) The overhead for the tag manipulation is large relative to the cost of the addition. Each operation runs through two case statements. The code for the selected case performs any needed conversion, along with the actual addition. It reads two tags and writes a third. If a and b are stored in registers, their tags should also be in registers. This decreases the cost of the tag accesses but increases demand for registers. (An alternative is to use part of the space in a and b for tag storage and to reduce the range of values that they can represent.)

Performing type inference and checking at compile time eliminates this kind of overhead. It can replace the control flow and tests of Figure 4.3 with the faster, more compact code of Figure 4.2. These operations are unavoidable, in the general case. (Additional knowledge can further simplify the code. For example, if the compiler knows that one operand of an addition is zero, it can eliminate the addition.)

Type Checking

To achieve these benefits, the compiler must analyze the program and assign a type to each expression that it calculates. It must check these types to ensure that they are used in contexts where they are legal. Taken together, these activities are often called *type checking*. This is an unfortunate misnomer, because it lumps together the separate activities of assigning, or inferring, types and of checking for type-related errors.

The programmer should be aware of the manner in which type checking is performed. A strongly typed, statically checkable language might be implemented with dynamic checking (or no checking at all). An untyped language might be implemented in a way that catches certain kinds of errors. Both ML and Modula-3 are good examples of strongly typed languages that can be statically checked. Common Lisp has a strong type system that must be checked dynamically. ANSI C is a typed language for which the implementations often do a poor job of checking for type violations.

The theory underlying type systems encompasses a large and complex body of knowledge. This section provides an overview of type systems and introduces some simple problems in type checking. Subsequent sections use simple problems of type inference as one example of a context-sensitive computation.

4.2.2 Components of a Type System

A type system for a typical modern language has four major components: a set of base types, or built-in types; rules for constructing new types from the existing types; a method for determining if two types are equivalent or compatible; and rules for inferring the type of each source-language expression. Many languages also include rules for the implicit conversion of values from one type to another based on context. This section describes each of these in more detail, with examples from popular programming languages.

Base Types

Most programming languages include base types for some, if not all, of the following kinds of data: numbers, characters, and booleans. These types are directly supported by most processors. Numbers typically come in several forms, such as integers and floating-point numbers. Individual languages add other base types. Lisp includes both a rational number type and a recursive list type. Rational numbers are, essentially, pairs of integers interpreted as ratios. Lists are defined as either the designated value nil or a pair (f r) where f is an object and r is a list.

The precise definitions for these base types, and the operators defined for them, vary from language to language. Some languages refine these base types to create more; for example, many languages distinguish between several types of numbers in their type systems. Other languages lack one or more of these base types; for example, C lacks a string type. Instead, C implements a character string as a pointer to an array of characters. Almost all languages include facilities to construct more complex types from their base types.

Numbers Almost all programming languages include one or more kinds of numbers as base types. Typically, this includes support for both limited-range integers and approximate real numbers, often called *floating-point* numbers. Many programming languages expose the underlying hardware implementation by creating distinct types for different hardware implementations. For example, C, C++, and Java distinguish between signed and unsigned integers.

FORTRAN, PL/I, Ada, and C expose the length of integers. In PL/I, the programmer specifies a length in bits; the compiler then maps this length onto one of the hardware representations for integers. The IBM 370 implementation of PL/I mapped a fixed binary(15) variable to a 16-bit integer, while a fixed binary(31) became a 32-bit integer. In contrast, C and FORTRAN specify length in relative terms. C's long is twice the length of a short. The same relationship holds between a double and a real in FORTRAN. Both language definitions, however, leave to the compiler the mapping from a length specifier to a specific bit length.

Some languages specify implementations in detail. For example, Java defines distinct types for signed integers with lengths of 8, 16, 32, and 64 bits. Respectively, they are byte, short, int, and long. Similarly, Java's float type specifies a 32-bit IEEE floating-point number, while its double type specifies a 64-bit IEEE floating-point number. This approach ensures identical behavior on different architectures.

Scheme takes a different approach. The language definition includes a hierarchy of number types but lets the implementor select a subset to support. However, the standard draws a careful distinction between exact numbers and inexact numbers and specifies a set of operations that should return an exact number when all of its arguments are exact. This provides a degree of flexibility to the implementer, while allowing the programmer to reason about when and where approximation can occur.

Characters Many languages include a character type. In the abstract, a character is a single letter. For years, due to the limited size of the Western alphabets, this led to a single-byte (8-bit) representation for characters, usually mapped into the ASCII character set (or EBCDIC on IBM machines). Recently, more implementations—both operating system and programming language—have begun to support larger character sets expressed in the Unicode standard format, which requires 16 bits. Most languages assume that the character set is ordered, so that standard comparison operators, such as <, =, and >, work intuitively, enforcing lexicographic ordering. Few other operations make sense on character data.

Booleans Most programming languages include a boolean type that takes on two values: true and false. Standard operations provided for booleans include and, or, xor, and not. Boolean values, or boolean-valued expressions, are often used to determine the flow of control. C considers boolean values as a subrange of the unsigned integers, restricted to the values zero (false) and one (true).

Compound and Constructed Types

While the base types of a programming language usually provide an adequate abstraction of the actual kinds of data handled directly by the hardware, they are often inadequate as a vocabulary for representing the information domain needed by programs. Programs routinely deal with more complex data structures, such as graphs, trees, tables, arrays, lists, and stacks. These structures consist of one or more objects, each with its own type. The ability to construct new types for these compound or aggregate objects is an essential feature of many programming languages. It lets the programmer organize information in novel, program-specific ways. Tying these organizations to the type system improves the compiler's ability to detect ill-formed programs. It also lets the language express higher-level operations, such as a whole-structure assignment.

Take, for example, Lisp, which provides extensive support for programming with lists. Lisp's list is a constructed type. A list is either the designated value nil or (cons f r) where f is an object, r is a list, and cons is a constructor that creates a list from its two arguments. A Lisp implementation can check each call to cons to ensure that its second argument is, in fact, a list.

Arrays Arrays are the most common aggregate objects. An array groups together multiple objects of the same type and gives each a distinct name— albeit an implicit, computed name rather than an explicit, programmer-designated, name. The C declaration int a[100][200]; sets aside space for 20,000 integers and ensures that they can be addressed using the name a. The references a[1][17] and a[2][30] access distinct and independent memory locations. The essential property of an array is that the program can compute names for each of its elements by using numbers (or some other ordered, discrete type) as subscripts.

Support for operations on arrays varies widely. FORTRAN 90, PL/I, and APL all support assignment of whole or partial arrays. These languages support element-by-element application of arithmetic operations to arrays. For 10 × 10 arrays x, y, and z, the statement x = y + z would overwrite each element of x with the sum of the corresponding elements of y and z. APL takes this further than most languages; it includes operators for inner product, outer product, and several kinds of reductions. (The sum reduction of x, written +/x, computes the sum of all the elements of x.)

An array can be viewed as a constructed type because we construct an array by specifying the type of its elements. Thus, a 10 × 10 array of integers has type *two-dimensional array of integers*. Some languages include the array's dimensions in its type; thus a 10 × 10 array of integers has a different type than a 12 × 12 array of integers. This lets the compiler catch array operations in which dimensions are incompatible as a type error. Most languages allow arrays of any base type; some languages allow arrays of constructed types as well.

Strings   Some programming languages treat strings as a constructed type. For example, PL/I has both bit strings and character strings. The properties, attributes, and operations defined on both of these types are similar; they are properties of a string. The range of values allowed in any position differs between a bit string and a character string. Thus, viewing them as *string of bit* and *string of character* is appropriate. (Most languages that support strings limit the built-in support to a single string type—the character string.) Other languages support character strings by handling them as arrays of characters.

A true string type differs from an array type in several important ways. Operations that make sense on strings, such as concatenation, translation, and computing the length, may not have analogs for arrays. Conceptually, string comparison should work from lexicographic order, so that "a" < "boo" and "fee" < "fie". The standard comparison operators can be overloaded and used in the natural way. Implementing comparison for an array of characters suggests an equivalent comparison for an array of numbers or an array of structures, where the analogy to strings may not hold. Similarly, the actual length of a string may differ from its allocated size, while most uses of an array use all the allocated elements.

Enumerated Types   Many languages allow the programmer to create a type that contains a specific set of constant values. This notion, introduced in Pascal, lets the programmer use self-documenting names for small sets of constants. Classic examples include days of the week and months. In C syntax, these might be

```
enum WeekDay {Monday, Tuesday, Wednesday,
              Thursday, Friday, Saturday, Sunday};

enum Month {January, February, March, April,
            May, June, July, August, September,
            October, November, December};
```

The compiler maps each element of an enumerated type to a distinct value. The elements of an enumerated type are ordered, so comparisons between elements of the same type make sense. In the examples, Monday < Tuesday and June < July. Operations that combine different enumerated types make no sense—for example, Tuesday > September should produce a type error. Pascal ensures that each enumerated type behaves as if it were a subrange of the

AN ALTERNATIVE VIEW OF STRUCTURES

The classical view of structures treats each distinct kind of structure as a distinct type. This approach to structure types follows the treatment of other aggregates, such as arrays and strings. It seems natural. It makes distinctions that are useful to the programmer. For example, a tree node with two children probably should have a different type than a tree node with three children; presumably, they are used in different situations. A program that assigns a three-child node to a two-child node should generate a type error and a warning message to the programmer.

From the perspective of the run-time system, however, treating each structure as a distinct type complicates the picture. With distinct structure types, the heap contains an arbitrary set of objects drawn from an arbitrary set of types. This makes it difficult to reason about programs that deal directly with the objects on the heap, such as a garbage collector. To simplify such programs, their authors sometimes take a different approach to structure types.

This alternate model considers all structures in the program as a single type. Individual structure declarations each create a variant form of the type *structure*. The type *structure*, itself, is the union of all these variants. This approach lets the program view the heap as a collection of objects of a single type, rather than a collection of many types. This makes code that manipulates the heap much simpler to analyze and optimize.

integers. For example, the programmer can declare an array indexed by the elements of an enumerated type.

Structures and Variants Structures group together multiple objects of arbitrary type. The elements, or members, of the structure are typically given explicit names. For example, a programmer implementing a parse tree in C might need nodes with one and two children.

```
struct Node1 {                  struct Node2 {
  struct   Node1 *left;           struct   Node2 *left;
  unsigned Operator;              struct   Node2 *right;
  int      Value                  unsigned Operator;
}                                 int      Value
                                }
```

The type of a structure is the ordered product of the types of its elements. Thus, we might describe the type of a Node1 as (Node1 *) × unsigned × int, while a Node2 would be (Node2 *) × (Node2 *) × unsigned × int. These new types have the same essential properties that a base type has. Autoincrementing a pointer to a Node1 or casting a pointer into a Node1 * has the desired effect—the behavior is analogous to what happens for a base type.

Many programming languages allow the creation of a type that is the union of other types. For example, some variable x can have the type integer or boolean or WeekDay. In Pascal, this is accomplished with variant records—a *record* is the Pascal term for a structure. In C, this is accomplished with a union. The type of a union is the alternation of its component types; thus our variable x has type integer ∪ boolean ∪ WeekDay. Unions can also include structures of distinct types, even when the individual structure types have different lengths. The language must provide a mechanism to reference each field unambiguously.

Pointers To let the programmer manipulate arbitrary data structures, many languages include pointer types. Pointers abstract addresses. They allow a program to save an address and to examine later the object that it addresses. Pointers are created when objects are created (new in Java or malloc in C). Some languages also include an operator that returns the address of an object, such as C's & operator. (The address operator, when applied to an object of type *t*, returns a value of type *pointer to t*.)

To protect the programmer from some kinds of pointer-related errors, such as using a pointer of type *t* to reference a structure of type *s*, some programming languages restrict pointer assignment to "equivalent" types. In these languages, the pointer on the left-hand side of an assignment must have the same type as the expression on the right-hand side. A program can legally assign a *pointer to integer* to a variable declared as *pointer to integer* but not to one declared as *pointer to pointer to integer* or *pointer to boolean*.

Of course, the mechanism for creating new objects should return an object of the appropriate type. Thus, Java's new explicitly creates a typed object; other languages use a polymorphic routine that takes the return type as a parameter. ANSI C handles this in an unusual way; the standard allocation routine malloc returns a *pointer to* void. This forces the programmer to cast the value returned by each call to malloc.

Some languages allow more complex pointer manipulation. Arithmetic on pointers, including autoincrement and autodecrement, allow the program to construct new pointers. C uses the type of a pointer to determine the magnitude of the increment or decrement. The programmer can set a pointer to the start of an array; autoincrementing advances the pointer from one element in the array to the next element.

Type safety with pointers relies on an implicit assumption that addresses correspond to typed objects. The ability to construct new pointers makes that assumption tenuous and seriously reduces the ability of both the compiler and its run-time system to reason about pointer-based computations. (See, for example, Section 8.3).

Type Equivalence

A critical component of any type system is the mechanism that it uses to decide whether or not two different type declarations are equivalent. Consider the following two declarations in C:

```
struct TreeNode {                struct SearchTree {
   struct TreeNode *left;           struct SearchTree *left;
   struct TreeNode *right;          struct SearchTree *right;
   int value                        int value
}                                }
```

Are TreeNode and SearchTree the same type? Are they equivalent? Any programming language that has a nontrivial type system must include an unambiguous rule to answer this question for arbitrary types.

Historically, two general approaches have been tried. The first, *name equivalence*, asserts that two types are equivalent if and only if they have the same name. Philosophically, this rule assumes that the programmer can select any name for a type; if the programmer chooses different names, the language and its implementation should honor that deliberate act. Unfortunately, once a program has multiple authors or multiple files, maintaining consistent names becomes impractical.

The second approach, *structural equivalence*, asserts that two types are equivalent if and only if they have the same structure. Philosophically, this rule asserts that two objects are interchangeable if they consist of the same set of fields, in the same order, and those fields all have equivalent types. Structural equivalence examines the essential properties that define the type.

Each policy has strengths and weaknesses. Name equivalence assumes that identical names occur as a deliberate act; in a large programming project, this requires discipline to avoid unintentional clashes. Structural equivalence assumes that interchangeable objects can be used safely in place of one another; if some of the values have "special" meanings, this can create problems. (Imagine two hypothetical, structurally identical types. The first holds a system I/O control block, while the second holds the collection of information about a bit-mapped image on the screen. Treating them as distinct types

REPRESENTING TYPES

As with most objects that a compiler must manipulate, types need an internal representation. Some languages, such as FORTRAN 77, have a small fixed set of types. For these languages, a small integer tag is both efficient and sufficient. However, many modern languages have open-ended type systems. For these languages, the compiler writer needs to design a structure that can represent arbitrary types.

If the type system is based on name equivalence, any number of simple representations will suffice, as long as the compiler can use the representation to trace back to a representation of the actual structure. If the type system is based on structural equivalence, the representation of the type must encode its structure. Most such systems build trees to represent types. They construct a tree for each type declaration and compare tree structures to test for equivalence.

would allow the compiler to detect a misuse—passing the I/O control block to a screen refresh routine—while treating them as the same type would not.)

Inference Rules

In general, type inference rules specify, for each operator, the mapping between the operand types and the result type. For some cases, the mapping is simple. An assignment, for example, has one operand and one result. The result, or left-hand side, must have a type that is compatible with the type of the operand, or right-hand side. (In Pascal, the subrange 1..100 is compatible with the integers since any element of the subrange can be assigned safely to an integer.) This rule allows assignment of an integer value to an integer variable. It forbids assignment of a structure to an integer variable, without an explicit conversion that makes sense of the operation.

The relationship between operand types and result types is often specified as a recursive function on the type of the expression tree. The function computes the result type of an operation as a function of the types of its operands. The functions might be specified in tabular form, similar to the table in Figure 4.1. Sometimes, the relationship between operand types and result types is specified by a simple rule. In Java, for example, adding two integer types of different precision produces a result of the more precise (longer) type.

The inference rules can identify type errors. In the FORTRAN table, some combinations are forbidden, such as double with complex. This combination produces a type error; the program is ill formed. In Java, assigning a number to a character is forbidden. Both of these type errors should result in error messages to the programmer.

Some languages require the compiler to fix certain type errors related to mixed-type expressions. When the compiler finds such an error, it must insert conversions that create values of compatible types. In FORTRAN 77, the addition of an integer and a floating-point number requires coercion of the integer to a floating-point value before addition. Similarly, Java's rule for integer addition of values with different precision coerces the less precise value to the form of the more precise value. Integer assignment in Java can force coercion. If the right-hand side is less precise, it is converted to the more precise type of the left-hand side. If, however, the left-hand side is less precise than the right-hand side, the assignment produces a type error (unless the programmer inserts an explicit cast operation to change its type and coerce its value).

Declarations and Inference As previously mentioned, many programming languages include a "declare before use" rule. With mandatory declarations, each variable has a well-defined type. The compiler needs a way to assign types to constants. Two approaches are common. Either a constant's form implies a specific type—for example, 2 is an integer and 2.0 is a floating-point number—or the compiler infers a constant's type from its usage—$sin(2)$ implies that 2 is a floating-point number, while $x \leftarrow 2$, for integer x, implies that 2 is an integer.[2] With declared types for variables, implied types for constants, and a complete set of type-inference rules, the compiler can assign types to any expression over variables and constants. Function calls complicate the picture, as we shall see.

Some languages absolve the programmer from writing any declarations. In these languages, the problem of type inference becomes substantially more intricate. Section 4.5 describes some of the problems that this creates and some of the techniques that compilers use to address them.

Inferring Types for Expressions

The goal of type inference is to assign a type to each expression that occurs in a program. The simplest case for type inference occurs when the compiler can assign a type to each base element in an expression—that is, to each leaf in the parse tree for an expression. This requires declarations for all variables, inferred types for all constants, and type information about all functions.

---

2. Unfortunately, this means that "2" means different things in different contexts. Experience suggests that programmers are good at understanding this kind of overloading.

CLASSIFYING TYPE SYSTEMS

Many terms are used to describe type systems. In the text, we have introduced the terms *strongly typed*, *untyped*, and *weakly typed* languages. Other distinctions between type systems and their implementations are important.

Checked versus Unchecked Implementations   The implementation of a programming language may elect to perform enough checking to detect and to prevent all run-time errors that result from misuse of a type. (This may actually exclude some value-specific errors, such as division by zero.) Such an implementation is called *strongly checked*. The opposite of a strongly checked implementation is an *unchecked implementation*—one that assumes a well-formed program. Between these poles lies a spectrum of *weakly checked implementations* that perform partial checking.

Compile-Time versus Run-Time Activity   A strongly typed language may have the property that all inference and all checking can be done at compile time. An implementation that actually does all this work at compile time is called *statically typed* and *statically checked*. Some languages have constructs that must be typed and checked at run time. We term these languages *dynamically typed* and *dynamically checked*. To confuse matters further, of course, a compiler writer can implement a strongly typed, statically typed language with dynamic checking. Java is an example of a language that could be statically typed and checked, except for an execution model that keeps the compiler from seeing all the source code at once. This forces it to perform type inference as classes are loaded and to perform some of the checking at run time.

Conceptually, the compiler can assign a type to each value in the expression during a simple postorder tree walk. This should let the compiler detect every violation of an inference rule, and report it *at compile time*. If the language lacks one or more of the features that make this simple style of inference possible, the compiler will need to use more sophisticated techniques. If compile-time type inference becomes too difficult, the compiler writer may need to move some of the analysis and checking to run time.

Type inference for expressions, in this simple case, directly follows the expression's structure. The inference rules describe the problem in terms of the source language. The evaluation strategy operates bottom up on the parse tree. For these reasons, type inference for expressions has become a classic example problem to illustrate context-sensitive analysis.

Interprocedural Aspects of Type Inference

Type inference for expressions depends, inherently, on the other procedures that form the executable program. Even in the simplest type systems, expressions contain function calls. The compiler must check each of those calls. It must ensure that each actual parameter is type compatible with the corresponding formal parameter. It must determine the type of any returned value for use in further inference.

To analyze and understand procedure calls, the compiler needs a *type signature* for each function. The type signature specifies the types of the formal parameters and the return value. For example, the strlen function in C's standard library takes an operand of type char * and returns an int that contains its length in bytes, excluding the null termination character. In C, the programmer can record this fact with a *function prototype* that looks like:

$$\text{unsigned int strlen(const char *s);}$$

This prototype asserts that strlen takes an argument of type char *, which it does not modify, as indicated by the the const attribute. The function returns a nonnegative integer. Writing this in a more abstract notation, we might say that

$$\text{strlen : const char * } \rightarrow \text{ unsigned int}$$

which we read as "strlen is a function that takes a constant-valued character string and returns an unsigned integer." As a second example, the classic Scheme function filter has the type signature

$$\text{filter: } (\alpha \rightarrow boolean) \times list\ of\ \alpha \rightarrow list\ of\ \alpha$$

That is, filter is a function that takes two arguments. The first should be a function that maps some type α into a boolean, written $(\alpha \rightarrow boolean)$, and the second should be a list whose elements are of the same type α. Given arguments of those types, filter returns a list whose elements have type α. The function filter exhibits *parametric polymorphism*: its result type is a function of its argument types.

To perform accurate type inference, the compiler needs a type signature for every function. It can obtain that information in several ways. The compiler can eliminate separate compilation—requiring that the entire program be presented for compilation as a unit. The compiler can require the programmer to provide a type signature for each function; this usually takes the form of mandatory function prototypes. The compiler can defer type checking until either link time, or run time, when all such information is available. Finally, the compiler writer can embed the compiler in a program-development system that gathers the requisite information and makes it available to the compiler on demand. All of these approaches have been used in real systems.

4.3 THE ATTRIBUTE-GRAMMAR FRAMEWORK

One formalism that has been proposed for performing context-sensitive analysis is the *attribute grammar*, or attributed context-free grammar. An attribute grammar consists of a context-free grammar augmented by a set of rules that specify a computation. Each rule defines one value, or *attribute*, in terms of the values of other attributes. The rule associates the attribute with a specific grammar symbol; each instance of the grammar symbol that occurs in a parse tree has a corresponding instance of the attribute. Because of the relationship between attribute instances and nodes in the parse tree, implementations are often described as adding fields for the attributes to the nodes of the parse tree.

To make these notions concrete, consider a context-free grammar for signed binary numbers. The grammar $SBN = (T,NT,S,P)$ is defined as follows:

$$T = \{\texttt{+, -, 0, 1}\}$$

$$NT = \{Number,\ Sign,\ List, Bit\}$$

$$S = \{Number\}$$

$$P = \left\{ \begin{array}{ll} Number \to Sign\ List & \\ Sign \to \texttt{+} & Sign \to \texttt{-} \\ List \to List\ Bit & List \to Bit \\ Bit \to \texttt{0} & Bit \to \texttt{1} \end{array} \right\}$$

$L(SBN)$ includes all signed binary numbers, such as -101, +11, -01, and +11111001100. It excludes unsigned binary numbers, such as 10.

From *SBN*, we can build an attribute grammar that annotates *Number* with the value of the signed binary number that it represents. To build an attribute grammar from a context-free grammar, we must decide what attributes each node needs, and we must elaborate the productions with rules that define values for these attributes. For our attributed version of *SBN*, the following attributes are needed:

Symbol	Attributes
Number	*value*
Sign	*negative*
List	*position, value*
Bit	*position, value*

In this case, no attributes are needed for the terminal symbols.

Figure 4.4 shows the productions of *SBN* elaborated with attribution rules. Subscripts are added to grammar symbols whenever a specific symbol appears multiple times in a single production. This disambiguates references to that symbol in the rules. Thus, the occurrences of *List* in production five have subscripts, both in the production and in the corresponding rules.

The rules specify the value of an attribute in terms of attributes of any other symbols mentioned in the production, along with literal constants. This permits rules that pass information from the left-hand side to the right-hand side; it also permits information flow in the other direction. Production four relies on information flow in both directions. The first rule sets *Bit.position* to *List.position*, while the second rule sets *List.value* to *Bit.value*. Simpler attribution schemes exist; we have chosen this one specifically to show bidirectional attribute flow.

Given a string in the context-free grammar, the attribution rules set *Number.value* to the decimal value of the binary input string. For example, the string -101 causes the attribution shown on the left side of Figure 4.5. (Attribute names are abbreviated.) Notice that *Number.value* has the value -5.

To evaluate an attributed parse tree for some sentence in $L(SBN)$, the attributes specified in the various rules are instantiated for each node in the parse tree. This creates, for example, an attribute instance for both *value* and *position* in each *List* node. Each rule implicitly defines a set of dependences; the attribute being defined depends on each argument to the rule. Taken over the entire parse tree, these dependences form an *attribute-dependence graph*. Edges in the graph follow the flow of values in the evaluation of a rule; an edge from $node_i.field_j$ to $node_k.field_l$ indicates that the rule defining $node_k.field_l$

	Production	Attribution Rules
1	$Number \rightarrow Sign\ List$	$List.position \leftarrow 0$
		if Sign.negative
		then $Number.value \leftarrow - List.value$
		else $Number.value \leftarrow List.value$
2	$Sign \rightarrow +$	$Sign.negative \leftarrow false$
3	$Sign \rightarrow -$	$Sign.negative \leftarrow true$
4	$List \rightarrow Bit$	$Bit.position \leftarrow List.position$
		$List.value \leftarrow Bit.value$
5	$List_0 \rightarrow List_1\ Bit$	$List_1.position \leftarrow List_0.position + 1$
		$Bit.position \leftarrow List_0.position$
		$List_0.value \leftarrow List_1.value + Bit.value$
6	$Bit \rightarrow 0$	$Bit.value \leftarrow 0$
7	$Bit \rightarrow 1$	$Bit.value \leftarrow 2^{Bit.position}$

FIGURE 4.4   Attribute Grammar for Signed Binary Numbers

uses the value of $node_i.field_j$ as one of its inputs. The right side of Figure 4.5 shows the dependence graph induced by the parse tree for the string -101.

The bidirectional flow of values that we noted earlier (in, for example, production four) shows up in the dependence graph, where arrows indicate both flow upward toward the root (*Number*) and flow downward toward the leaves. The *List* nodes show this effect most clearly. We distinguish between attributes based on the direction of value flow.

1. *Synthesized Attributes*   In general, attributes of a node whose values are defined wholly in terms of the attributes of the node's children are called synthesized attributes. The values used to compute synthesized attributes flow bottom-up in the parse tree. (Leaf nodes cannot have synthesized attributes.)

2. *Inherited Attributes*   Attributes whose values are defined in terms of the node's own attributes, those of its siblings, and those of its parent, are called inherited attributes. The values used to compute inherited attributes flow top-down and laterally in the parse tree. (The root node can have no inherited attributes.)

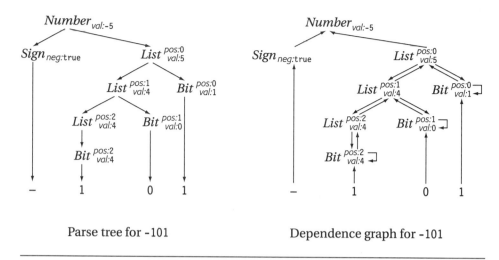

Parse tree for -101 · Dependence graph for -101

FIGURE 4.5   Attributed Tree for the Signed Binary Number −101

In the example from Figure 4.5, the *value* and *negative* attributes are synthesized, while the *position* attributes are inherited.

Any scheme for evaluating attributes must respect the relationships encoded implicitly in the attribute-dependence graph. Each attribute must be defined by some rule. If that rule depends on the values of other attributes, it cannot be evaluated until all those values have been defined. If the rule depends on no other attribute values, then it must produce its value from a constant or some external source. As long as no rule relies on its own value, the rules should uniquely define each value.

Of course, a rule can reference its own result, either directly or indirectly. An attribute grammar containing such rules is called *circular*. For the moment, we will ignore circularity; Section 4.3.2 addresses this issue.

The dependence graph captures the flow of values that an evaluator must respect in evaluating an instance of an attributed tree. If the grammar is non-circular, it imposes a partial order on the attributes. This partial order determines when the rule defining each attribute can be evaluated. Evaluation order is unrelated to the order in which the rules appear in the grammar.

Consider the evaluation order for the rules associated with the uppermost *List* node—the right child of *Number*. The node results from applying production five, *List* → *List Bit*; applying that production adds three rules to the evaluation. The two rules that set inherited attributes for the *List* node's children must execute first. They depend on the value of *List.position* and set the *position* attributes for the node's subtrees. The third rule, which sets the *List* node's *value* attribute, cannot execute until the two subtrees both have defined *value* attributes. Since those subtrees cannot be evaluated until the first two rules at the *List* node have been evaluated, the evaluation sequence will include the first two rules early and the third rule much later.

To create and use an attribute grammar, the compiler writer determines a set of attributes for each symbol in the grammar and designs a set of rules to compute their values. These rules specify a computation for any valid parse tree. To create an implementation, the compiler writer must create an evaluator; this can be done with an ad hoc program or by using an evaluator generator—the more attractive option. The evaluator generator takes as input the specification for the attribute grammar. It produces the code for an evaluator as its output. This is the attraction of attribute grammars for the compiler writer; the tools take a high-level, nonprocedural specification and automatically produce an implementation.

One critical insight behind the attribute-grammar formalism is the notion that the attribution rules can be associated with productions in the context-free grammar. Since the rules are functional, the values that they produce are independent of evaluation order, for any order that respects the relationships embodied in the attribute-dependence graph. In practice, any order that evaluates a rule only after all of its inputs have been defined respects the dependences.

4.3.1 Evaluation Methods

The attribute grammar model has practical use only if we can build evaluators that interpret the rules to evaluate an instance of the problem automatically—a specific parse tree, for example. Many attribute evaluation techniques have been proposed in the literature. In general, they fall into three major categories.

1. *Dynamic Methods* These techniques use the structure of a particular attributed parse tree to determine the evaluation order. Knuth's original paper on attribute grammars proposed an evaluator that operated in a manner similar to a dataflow computer architecture—each rule "fired" as soon as all its operands were available. In practical terms, this might be implemented using a queue of attributes that are ready for evaluation. As each attribute is evaluated, its successors in the attribute dependence graph are checked for "readiness" (see the description of "list scheduling" in Section 12.3). A related scheme would build the attribute dependence graph, topologically sort it, and use the topological order to evaluate the attributes.

2. *Oblivious Methods* In these methods, the order of evaluation is independent of both the attribute grammar and the particular attributed parse tree. Presumably, the system's designer selects a method deemed appropriate for both the attribute grammar and the evaluation environment. Examples of this evaluation style include repeated left-to-right passes (until all attributes have values), repeated right-to-left passes, and alternating left-to-right and right-to-left passes. These methods have simple implementations and relatively small run-time overheads. They lack, of course, any improvement that can be derived from knowledge of the specific tree being attributed.

3. *Rule-Based Methods* The rule-based methods rely on a static analysis of the attribute grammar to construct an evaluation order. In this framework, the evaluator relies on grammatical structure; thus, the parse tree guides the application of the rules. In the signed binary number example, the evaluation order for production four should use the first rule to set *Bit.position*, recurse downward to *Bit*, and, on return, use *Bit.value* to set *List.value*. Similarly, for production five, it should evaluate the first two rules to define the *position* attributes on the right-hand side, then recurse downward to each child. On return, it can evaluate the third rule to set the *List.value* field of the parent *List* node. Tools that perform the necessary static analysis offline can produce fast rule-based evaluators.

4.3.2 Circularity

Circular attribute grammars can give rise to cyclic attribute-dependence graphs. Our models for evaluation fail when the dependence graph contains a cycle. A failure of this kind in a compiler causes serious problems—for example, the compiler might not be able to generate code for its input. The catastrophic impact of cycles in the dependence graph suggests that this issue deserves close attention.

If a compiler uses attribute grammars, it must handle circularity in an appropriate way. Two approaches are possible.

1. *Avoidance* The compiler writer can restrict the attribute grammar to a class that cannot give rise to circular dependence graphs. For example, restricting the grammar to use only synthesized attributes eliminates any possibility of a circular dependence graph. More general classes

of noncircular attribute grammars exist; some, like *strongly noncircular attribute grammars,* have polynomial-time tests for membership.

2. *Evaluation* The compiler writer can use an evaluation method that assigns a value to every attribute, even those involved in cycles. The evaluator might iterate over the cycle until the values reach a fixed point. Such an evaluator would avoid the problems associated with a failure to fully attribute the tree.

In practice, most attribute-grammar systems restrict their attention to non-circular grammars. The rule-based evaluation methods may fail to construct an evaluator if the attribute grammar is circular. The oblivious methods and the dynamic methods will attempt to evaluate a circular dependence graph; they will simply fail to define some of the attribute instances.

4.3.3 Extended Examples

To better understand the strengths and weaknesses of attribute grammars as a tool for specifying computations over the syntax of a language, we will work through two more detailed examples—inferring types for expression trees in a simple, Algol-like language, and estimating the execution time, in cycles, for a straight-line sequence of code.

Inferring Expression Types

Any compiler that tries to generate efficient code for a typed language must confront the problem of inferring types for every expression in the program. This problem relies, inherently, on context-sensitive information; the type associated with an ident or num depends on its identity—its textual name—rather than its syntactic category.

Consider a simplified version of the type inference problem for expressions derived from the classic expression grammar given in Chapter 3. Assume that the expressions are represented as parse trees, and that any node representing an ident or a num already has a *type* attribute. (Later, we will explore the problem of getting the type information into these *type* attributes.) For each arithmetic operator in the grammar, we need a function that maps the two operand types to a result type. We will call these functions $\mathcal{F}_+$, $\mathcal{F}_-$, $\mathcal{F}_\times$, and $\mathcal{F}_\div$; they encode the information found in tables such as the one shown in Figure 4.1. With these assumptions, we can write simple attribution rules that define a *type* attribute for each node in the tree. Figure 4.6 shows the attribution rules.

Productions			Attribution Rules
$Expr_0$	$\rightarrow$	$Expr_1 + Term$	$Expr_0.type \leftarrow \mathcal{F}+(Expr_1.type, Term.type)$
	|	$Expr_1 - Term$	$Expr_0.type \leftarrow \mathcal{F} - (Expr_1.type, Term.type)$
	|	$Term$	$Expr_0.type \leftarrow Term.type$
$Term_0$	$\rightarrow$	$Term_1 \times Factor$	$Term_0.type \leftarrow \mathcal{F} \times (Term_1.type, Factor.type)$
	|	$Term_1 \div Factor$	$Term_0.type \leftarrow \mathcal{F} \div (Term_1.type, Factor.type)$
	|	$Factor$	$Term_0.type \leftarrow Factor.type$
$Factor$	$\rightarrow$	$(Expr)$	$Factor.type \leftarrow Expr.type$
	|	num	num.*type is already defined*
	|	ident	ident.*type is already defined*

FIGURE 4.6   Attribute Grammar to Infer Expression Types

If x has type integer (denoted $\mathcal{I}$) and y has type real (denoted $\mathcal{R}$), then this scheme generates the following attributed parse tree for the input string x - 2 × y:

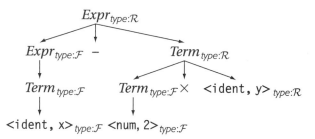

The leaf nodes have their *type* attributes initialized appropriately. The remainder of the attributes are defined by the rules from Figure 4.6, with the assumption that $\mathcal{F}_+$, $\mathcal{F}_-$, $\mathcal{F}_\times$, and $\mathcal{F}_\div$ reflect the FORTRAN 77 rules.

A close look at the attribution rules shows that all the attributes are synthesized attributes. Thus, all the dependences flow from a child to its parent in the parse tree. Such grammars are sometimes called *S-attributed grammars*. This style of attribution has a simple, rule-based evaluation scheme. It meshes well with bottom-up parsing; each rule can be evaluated when the parser reduces by the corresponding right-hand side. The attribute-grammar paradigm fits this problem well. The specification is short. It is easily understood. It leads to an efficient evaluator.

Careful inspection of the attributed expression tree shows two cases in which an operation has an operand whose type is different from the type of the operation's result. In FORTRAN 77, this requires the compiler to insert a conversion operation between the operand and the operator. For the *Term* node that represents the multiplication of 2 and y, the compiler would convert 2 from an integer representation to a real representation. For the *Expr* node at the root of the tree, the compiler would convert x from an integer to a real. Unfortunately, changing the parse tree does not fit well into the attribute-grammar paradigm.

To represent these conversions in the attributed tree, we could add an attribute to each node that holds its converted type, along with rules to set the attributes appropriately. Alternatively, we could rely on the process that generates code from the tree to compare the two types—parent and child—during the traversal and insert the necessary conversion. The former approach adds some work to the attribute-evaluation pass; this localizes all of the information needed for a conversion to a single parse-tree node. The latter approach defers that work until code generation, but does so at the cost of distributing the knowledge about types and conversions across two separate parts of the compiler. Either approach will work; the difference is largely a matter of taste.

A Simple Execution-Time Estimator

As a second example, consider the problem of estimating the execution time of a sequence of assignment statements. We can generate a sequence of assignments by adding three new productions to the classic expression grammar

$$
\begin{aligned}
Block \quad &\rightarrow \quad Block\ Assign \\
&\mid \quad Assign \\
Assign \quad &\rightarrow \quad \texttt{ident} = Expr;
\end{aligned}
$$

where *Expr* is from the expression grammar. The resulting grammar is simplistic in that it allows only simple identifiers as variables and it contains no function calls. Nonetheless, it is complex enough to convey the complications that arise in estimating run-time behavior.

Figure 4.7 shows an attribute grammar that estimates the execution time of a block of assignment statements. The attribution rules estimate the total cycle count for the block, assuming a single processor that executes one operation at a time. This grammar, like the one for inferring expression types, uses only synthesized attributes. The estimate appears in the *cost* attribute of the topmost

Production			Attribution Rules
$Block_0$	$\rightarrow$	$Block_1\ Assign$	$\{\ Block_0.cost \leftarrow Block_1.cost\ +$ $Assign.cost\ \}$
	$\vert$	$Assign$	$\{\ Block_0.cost \leftarrow Assign.cost\ \}$
$Assign$	$\rightarrow$	$\mathtt{ident} = Expr;$	$\{\ Assign.cost \leftarrow Cost(\mathtt{store})\ +$ $Expr.cost\ \}$
$Expr_0$	$\rightarrow$	$Expr_1 + Term$	$\{\ Expr_0.cost \leftarrow Expr_1.cost\ +$ $Cost(\mathtt{add}) + Term.cost\ \}$
	$\vert$	$Expr_1 - Term$	$\{\ Expr_0.cost \leftarrow Expr_1.cost\ +$ $Cost(\mathtt{sub}) + Term.cost\ \}$
	$\vert$	$Term$	$\{\ Expr_0.cost \leftarrow Term.cost\ \}$
$Term_0$	$\rightarrow$	$Term_1 \times Factor$	$\{\ Term_0.cost \leftarrow Term_1.cost\ +$ $Cost(\mathtt{mult}) + Factor.cost\ \}$
	$\vert$	$Term_1 \div Factor$	$\{\ Term_0.cost \leftarrow Term_1.cost\ +$ $Cost(\mathtt{div}) + Factor.cost\ \}$
	$\vert$	$Factor$	$\{\ Term_0.cost \leftarrow Factor.cost\ \}$
$Factor$	$\rightarrow$	$(Expr)$	$\{\ Factor.cost \leftarrow Expr.cost\ \}$
	$\vert$	$\mathtt{num}$	$\{\ Factor.cost \leftarrow Cost(\mathtt{loadI})\ \}$
	$\vert$	$\mathtt{ident}$	$\{\ Factor.cost \leftarrow Cost(\mathtt{load})\ \}$

FIGURE 4.7   Simple Attribute Grammar to Estimate Execution Time

Block node of the parse tree. The methodology is simple. Costs are computed bottom up; to read the example, start with the productions for *Factor* and work your way up to the productions for *Block*. The function *Cost* returns the latency of a given ILOC operation.

Improving the Execution-Cost Estimator

To make this example more realistic, we can improve its model for how the compiler handles variables. The initial version of our cost-estimating attribute grammar assumes that the compiler naively generates a separate load operation for each reference to a variable. For the assignment x = y + y;, the model counts two load operations for y. Few compilers would generate a redundant load for y. More likely, the compiler would generate a sequence such as

$$
\begin{array}{lll}
\texttt{loadAI} & r_{arp}, \texttt{@y} & \Rightarrow r_y \\
\texttt{add} & r_y, r_y & \Rightarrow r_x \\
\texttt{storeAI} & r_x & \Rightarrow r_{arp}, \texttt{@x}
\end{array}
$$

that loads y once. To approximate the compiler's behavior better, we can modify the attribute grammar to charge only a single load for each variable used in the block. This requires more complex attribution rules.

To account for loads more accurately, the rules must track references to each variable by the variable's name. These names are extragrammatical, since the grammar tracks the syntactic category ident rather than individual names such as x, y, and z. The rule for ident should follow the general outline:

> *if (*ident *has not been loaded)*
> *then Factor.cost ← Cost(*load*);*
> *else Factor.cost ← 0;*

The key to making this work is the test "ident *has not been loaded*."

To implement this test, the compiler writer can add an attribute that holds the set of all variables already loaded. The production *Block → Assign* can initialize the set. The rules must thread the expression trees to pass the set through each assignment. This suggests augmenting each node with two sets, *Before* and *After*. The *Before* set for a node contains the names of all idents that occur earlier in the *Block*; each of these must have been loaded already. A node's *After* set contains all the names in its *Before* set, plus any idents that would be loaded in the subtree rooted at that node.

The expanded rules for *Factor* are shown in Figure 4.8. The code assumes that it can obtain the textual name of each ident. The first production, which derives (*Expr*), copies the *Before* set down into the *Expr* subtree and copies the *After* set up to the *Factor*. The second production, which derives num, simply copies its parent's *Before* set into its parent's *After* set. num must be a leaf in the tree; therefore, no further actions are needed. The final production, which derives ident, performs the critical work. It tests the *Before* set to determine whether or not a load is needed and updates the parent's *cost* and *After* attributes accordingly.

Production	Attribution Rules
Factor → (*Expr*)	{ *Factor.cost* ← *Expr.cost;*
	Expr.Before ← *Factor.Before;*
	Factor.After ← *Expr.After* }
| num	{ *Factor.cost* ← *Cost(*loadI*);*
	Factor.After ← *Factor.Before* }
| ident	{ *if (*ident.*name* ∉ *Factor.Before)*
	then
	Factor.cost ← *Cost(*load*);*
	Factor.After ← *Factor.Before*
	∪ { ident.*name* }
	else
	Factor.cost ← *0;*
	Factor.After ← *Factor.Before* }

FIGURE 4.8   Rules to Track Loads in *Factor* Productions

To complete the specification, the compiler writer must add rules that copy the *Before* and *After* sets around the parse tree. These rules, sometimes called copy rules, connect the *Before* and *After* sets of the various *Factor* nodes. Because the attribution rules can reference only local attributes—defined as the attributes of a node's parent, its siblings, and its children—the attribute grammar must explicitly copy values around the parse tree to ensure that they are local. Figure 4.9 shows the required rules for the other productions in the grammar. One additional rule has been added; it initializes the *Before* set of the first *Assign* statement to ∅.

This model is much more complex than the simple model. It has over three times as many rules; each rule must be written, understood, and evaluated. It uses both synthesized and inherited attributes; the simple bottom-up evaluation strategy will no longer work. Finally, the rules that manipulate the *Before* and *After* sets require a fair amount of attention—the kind of low-level detail that we would hope to avoid by using a system based on high-level specifications.

Production	Attribution Rules
$Block_0 \rightarrow Block_1\ Assign$	{ $Block_0.cost \leftarrow Block_1.cost +$ $Assign.cost;$ $Assign.Before \leftarrow Block_1.After;$ $Block_0.After \leftarrow Assign.After$ }
$\mid Assign$	{ $Block_0.cost \leftarrow Assign.cost;$ $Assign.Before \leftarrow \emptyset;$ $Block_0.After \leftarrow Assign.After$ }
$Assign \rightarrow Identifier = Expr;$	{ $Assign.cost \leftarrow Cost(\mathtt{store}) +$ $Expr.cost;$ $Expr.Before \leftarrow Assign.Before;$ $Assign.After \leftarrow Expr.After$ }
$Expr_0 \rightarrow Expr_1 + Term$	{ $Expr_0.cost \leftarrow Expr_1.cost +$ $Cost(\mathtt{add}) + Term.cost;$ $Expr_1.Before \leftarrow Expr_0.Before;$ $Term.Before \leftarrow Expr_1.After;$ $Expr_0.After \leftarrow Term.After$ }
$\mid Expr_1 - Term$	{ $Expr_0.cost \leftarrow Expr_1.cost +$ $Cost(\mathtt{sub}) + Term.cost;$ $Expr_1.Before \leftarrow Expr_0.Before;$ $Term.Before \leftarrow Expr_1.After;$ $Expr_0.After \leftarrow Term.After$ }
$\mid Term$	{ $Expr_0.cost \leftarrow Term.cost;$ $Term.Before \leftarrow Expr_0.Before;$ $Expr_0.After \leftarrow Term.After$ }
$Term_0 \rightarrow Term_1 \times Factor$	{ $Term_0.cost \leftarrow Term_1.cost +$ $Cost(\mathtt{mult}) + Factor.cost;$ $Term_1.Before \leftarrow Term_0.Before;$ $Factor.Before \leftarrow Term_1.After;$ $Term_0.After \leftarrow Factor.After$ }
$\mid Term_1 \div Factor$	{ $Term_0.cost \leftarrow Term_1.cost +$ $Cost(\mathtt{div}) + Factor.cost;$ $Term_1.Before \leftarrow Term_0.Before;$ $Factor.Before \leftarrow Term_1.After;$ $Term_0.After \leftarrow Factor.After$ }
$\mid Factor$	{ $Term_0.cost \leftarrow Factor.cost;$ $Factor.Before \leftarrow Term_0.Before;$ $Term_0.After \leftarrow Factor.After$ }

FIGURE 4.9   Copy Rules to Track Loads

Back to Inferring Expression Types

In the initial discussion about inferring expression types, we assumed that the ident.*type* and num.*type* attributes were already defined by some external mechanism. To fill in those values using an attribute grammar, the compiler writer would need to develop a set of rules for the portion of the grammar that handles declarations.

Those rules would need to record the type information for each variable in the productions associated with the declaration syntax. The rules would need to collect and aggregate that information so that a small set of attributes contained the necessary information on all the declared variables. The rules would need to propagate that information up the parse tree to a node that is an ancestor of all the executable statements, and then to copy it downward into each expression. Finally, at each leaf that is an ident or num, the rules would need to extract the appropriate facts from the aggregated information.

The resulting set of rules would have much the same flavor as those that we developed for tracking loads but would be more complex at the detailed level. These rules also create large, complex attributes that must be copied around the parse tree. In a naive implementation, each instance of a copy rule would create a new copy. Some of these copies could be shared, but many of the versions created by merging information from multiple children will differ (and, thus, need to be distinct copies). The same problem arises with the *Before* and *After* sets in the previous example.

A Final Improvement to the Execution-Cost Estimator

While tracking loads improved the fidelity of the estimated execution costs, many further refinements are possible. Consider, for example, the impact of finite register sets on the model. So far, our model has assumed that the target computer provides an unlimited set of registers. In reality, computers provide small register sets. To model the capacity of the register set, the estimator could limit the number of values allowed in the *Before* and *After* sets.

As a first step, we must replace the implementation of *Before* and *After*. They were implemented with arbitrarily sized sets; in this refined model, the sets should hold exactly k values, where k is the number of registers available to hold the values of variables. Next, we must rewrite the rules for the production *Factor* $\rightarrow$ ident to model register occupancy. If a value has not been loaded, and a register is available, it charges for a simple load. If a load is needed, but no register is available, it can evict a value from some register and charge for the load. The choice of which value to evict is complex; it is discussed in

Chapter 13. Since the rule for *Assign* always charges for a store, the value in memory will be current. Thus, no store is needed when a value is evicted. Finally, if the value has already been loaded and is still in a register, then no cost is charged.

This model complicates the rule set for *Factor* → ident and requires a slightly more complex initial condition (in the rule for *Block* → *Assign*). It does not, however, complicate the copy rules for all the other productions. Thus, the accuracy of the model does not add significantly to the complexity of using an attribute grammar. All of the added complexity falls into the few rules that directly manipulate the model.

4.3.4 Problems with the Attribute-Grammar Approach

The preceding examples illustrate many of the computational issues that arise in using attribute grammars to perform context-sensitive computations on parse trees. Some of these pose particular problems for the use of attribute grammars in a compiler. In particular, most applications of attribute grammars in the front end of a compiler assume that the results of attribution must be preserved—typically in the form of an attributed parse tree. This section details the impact of the problems that we have seen in the preceding examples.

Handling Nonlocal Information

Some problems map cleanly onto the attribute-grammar paradigm, particularly those problems in which all information flows in the same direction. However, problems with a complex pattern of information flow can be difficult to express as attribute grammars. An attribution rule can name only values associated with a grammar symbol that appears in the same production; this constrains the rule to using only nearby, or local, information. If the computation requires a nonlocal value, the attribute grammar must include rules that explicitly copy those values to the point in the parse tree where they are used.

These copy rules can swell the size of an attribute grammar; compare Figure 4.7 against Figures 4.8 and 4.9. The implementor must write each of those rules. In the evaluator, each of the rules must be executed, creating new attributes and additional work. When information is aggregated, as in the declare-before-use rule or the framework for estimating execution times, a new copy of the information must be made each time a rule changes an aggregate's value. These copy rules add another layer of work to the tasks of writing and evaluating an attribute grammar.

Storage Management

For realistic examples, evaluation produces large numbers of attributes. The use of copy rules to move information around the parse tree can multiply the number of attribute instances that evaluation creates. If the grammar aggregates information into complex structures—to pass declaration information around the parse tree, for example—the individual attributes can be large. The evaluator must manage storage for attributes; a poor storage-management scheme can have a disproportionately large negative impact on the resource requirements of the evaluator.

If the evaluator can determine which attribute values can be used after evaluation, it may be able to reuse some of the attribute storage by reclaiming space for values that can never again be used. For example, an attribute grammar that evaluated an expression tree to a single value might return that value to the process that invoked it. In this scenario, the intermediate values calculated at interior nodes might be dead—never used again—and, thus, candidates for reclamation. On the other hand, if the tree resulting from attribution is persistent and subject to later inspection—as might be the case in an attribute grammar for type inference—then the evaluator must assume that a later phase of the compiler can traverse the tree and inspect arbitrary attributes. In this case, the evaluator cannot reclaim the storage for any of the attribute instances.

(This problem actually reflects a clash between the functional nature of the attribute-grammar paradigm and the imperative use to which it might be put in the compiler. The possible uses of an attribute in later phases of the compiler have the effect of adding dependences from that attribute to uses not specified in the attribute grammar. This bends the functional paradigm and removes one of its strengths—the ability to automatically manage attribute storage.)

Instantiating the Parse Tree

An attribute grammar specifies a computation relative to the parse tree for a valid sentence in the underlying grammar. The paradigm relies, inherently, on the availability of the parse tree. The evaluator might simulate the parse tree, but it must behave as if the parse tree exists. While the parse tree is useful for discussions of parsing, few compilers actually build a parse tree.

Some compilers use an abstract syntax tree (AST) to represent the program being compiled. The AST has the essential structure of the parse tree but eliminates many of the internal nodes that represent nonterminal symbols in the grammar (see Section 5.3.1). If the compiler builds an AST, it could use an attribute grammar tied to a grammar for the AST. However, if the compiler has no other use for the AST, then the programming effort and compile-time cost associated with building and maintaining the AST must be weighed against the benefits of using the attribute-grammar formalism.

Locating the Answers

One final problem with attribute-grammar schemes for context-sensitive analysis is more subtle. The result of attribute evaluation is an attributed tree. The results of the analysis are distributed over that tree, in the form of attribute values. To use these results in later passes, the compiler must traverse the tree to locate the desired information.

The compiler can use carefully constructed traversals to locate a particular node; this still requires walking from the root of the parse tree down to the appropriate location—on each access. This makes the code both slower and harder to write—the compiler must execute each of these traversals and the compiler writer must construct each of them. The alternative is to copy the important answers to a point in the tree where they are easily found, typically the root. This introduces more copy rules, exacerbating that problem.

Breakdown of the Functional Paradigm

One way to address all of these problems is to add a central repository for attributes. In this scenario, an attribute rule can record information directly into a global table, where other rules can read the information. This hybrid approach can eliminate many of the problems that arise from nonlocal information. Since the table can be accessed from any attribution rule, it has the effect of providing local access to any information already derived.

Adding a central repository for facts complicates matters in another way. If two rules communicate through a mechanism other than an attribution rule, the implicit dependence between them is removed from the attribute dependence graph. The missing dependence should constrain the evaluator to ensure that the two rules are processed in the correct order; without it, the evaluator may be able to construct an order that, while correct for the grammar, has unintended behavior because of the removed constraint. For example, passing information between the declaration syntax and an executable expression through a table might allow the evaluator to process declarations after some or all of the expressions that use the declared variables. If the grammar uses copy rules to propagate that same information, those rules constrain the evaluator to orders that respect the dependences embodied by those copy rules.

Summary

Attribute grammars are not the right abstraction for every context-sensitive analysis. Advocates of attribute-grammar techniques argue that the problems with attribute grammars are manageable, and that the advantages of a high-level, nonprocedural specification outweigh the problems. However, the attribute-grammar approach has never achieved widespread popularity for a number of mundane reasons. Large problems, such as the difficulty of performing nonlocal computation and the need to traverse the parse tree to discover answers to simple questions, have discouraged the adoption of these ideas. Myriad small problems, such as space management for short-lived attributes, efficiency of evaluators, and the lack of high-quality, inexpensive tools, have also made these tools and techniques less attractive.

Still, the simplicity of the attribute-grammar paradigm is attractive. If attribute flow can be constrained to a single direction, either synthesized or inherited, the resulting attribute grammar is simple and the evaluator is efficient. For example, the paradigm works well on expression evaluation in a calculator or an interpreter. The flow of values follows the parse tree from leaves to root, so both the rules and the evaluator are straightforward. Similarly, applications that involve only local information often have good attribute-grammar solutions.

4.4 AD HOC SYNTAX-DIRECTED TRANSLATION

The rule-based evaluators for attribute grammars introduce a powerful idea that serves as the basis for the ad hoc techniques used for context-sensitive analysis in many compilers. In the rule-based evaluators, the compiler writer specifies a sequence of actions that are associated with productions in the grammar. The underlying observation, that the actions required for context-sensitive analysis can be organized around the structure of the grammar, leads to a powerful, albeit ad hoc, approach to incorporating this kind of analysis into the process of parsing a context-free grammar. We refer to this approach as ad hoc syntax-directed translation.

In this scheme, the compiler writer provides snippets of code that execute at parse time. Each snippet, or *action*, is directly tied to a production in the grammar. Each time the parser recognizes that it is at a particular place in the grammar, the corresponding action is invoked to perform its task. To implement this in a top-down, recursive-descent parser, the compiler writer simply adds the appropriate code to the parsing routines. The compiler writer has complete control over when the actions execute. In a bottom-up, shift-reduce parser, the actions are performed each time the parser performs a reduce action. This is more restrictive, but still workable.

To make this concrete, consider reformulating the signed binary number example in an ad hoc syntax-directed translation framework. Figure 4.10 shows one such framework. Each grammar symbol has a single value associated with it, denoted *val* in the code snippets. The code snippet for each rule defines the value associated with the symbol on the rule's left-hand side. Rule 1 simply multiplies the value for *Sign* with the value for *List*. Rules 2 and 3 set the value for *Sign* appropriately, just as rules 6 and 7 set the value for each instance of *Bit*. Rule 4 simply copies the value from *Bit* to *List*. The real work occurs in rule 5, which multiplies the accumulated value of the leading bits (in *List.val*) by two, and then adds in the next bit.

So far, this looks quite similar to an attribute grammar. However, it has two key simplifications. Values flow in only one direction—from leaves to root. It allows only a single value per grammar symbol. Even so, the scheme in Figure 4.10 correctly computes the value of the signed binary number. It leaves that value at the root of the tree, just like the attribute grammar for signed binary numbers.

These two simplifications make possible an evaluation method that works well with a bottom-up parser, such as the LR parsers described in Chapter 3.

	Production	Code Snippet
1	$Number \rightarrow Sign\ List$	$Number.val \leftarrow Sign.val \times List.val$
2	$Sign \rightarrow +$	$Sign.val \leftarrow 1$
3	$Sign \rightarrow -$	$Sign.val \leftarrow -1$
4	$List \rightarrow Bit$	$List.val \leftarrow Bit.val$
5	$List_0 \rightarrow List_1\ Bit$	$List_0.val \leftarrow 2 \times List_1.val + Bit.val$
6	$Bit \rightarrow 0$	$Bit.val \leftarrow 0$
7	$Bit \rightarrow 1$	$Bit.val \leftarrow 1$

FIGURE 4.10 Ad Hoc Syntax-Directed Translation for Signed Binary Numbers

Since each code snippet is associated with the right-hand side of a specific production, the parser can invoke the action each time it reduces by that production. This requires minor modifications to the reduce action in the LR(1) parser driver shown in Figure 3.13.

> *else if Action[s,word] = "**reduce** A→β" then*
> *invoke the appropriate reduce action*
> *pop 2 × |β| symbols*
> *s ← top of stack*
> *push A*
> *push Goto[s, A]*

The parser generator can gather the syntax-directed actions together, embed them in a case statement that switches on the number of the production being reduced, and execute the case statement just before it pops the right-hand side from the stack.

The translation scheme shown in Figure 4.10 is simpler than the scheme used to explain attribute grammars. Of course, we can write an attribute grammar that applies the same strategy. It would use only synthesized attributes. It would have fewer attribution rules and fewer attributes than the one shown in Figure 4.4. We chose the more complex attribution scheme to illustrate the use of both synthesized and inherited attributes.

4.4.1 Implementing Ad Hoc Syntax-Directed Translation

To make ad hoc syntax-directed translation work, the parser must include mechanisms to pass values from their definitions in one action to their uses in another, to provide convenient and consistent naming, and to allow for actions that execute at other points in the parse. This section describes mechanisms for handling these issues in a bottom-up, shift-reduce parser. Analogous ideas will work for top-down parsers. We adopt a notation introduced in the YACC system, an early and popular LALR(1) parser generator distributed with the Unix operating system. The Yacc notation has been adopted by many subsequent systems.

Communicating between Actions

To pass values between actions, the parser must have a methodology for allocating space to hold the values produced by the various actions. The mechanism must make it possible for an action that uses a value to find it. An attribute grammar associates the values (attributes) with nodes in the parse tree; tying the attribute storage to the tree nodes' storage makes it possible to find attribute values in a systematic way. In ad hoc syntax-directed translation, the parser may not construct the parse tree. Instead, the parser can integrate the storage for values into its own mechanism for tracking the state of the parse—its internal stack.

Recall that the skeleton LR(1) parser stored two values on the stack for each grammar symbol: the symbol and a corresponding state. When it recognizes a handle, such as a *List Bit* sequence to match the right-hand side of rule 5, the first pair on the stack represents the *Bit*. Underneath that lies the pair representing the *List*. We can replace these ⟨*symbol, state*⟩ pairs with triples, ⟨*value, symbol, state*⟩. This provides a single value attribute per grammar symbol—precisely what the simplified scheme needs. To manage the stack, the parser pushes and pops more values. On a reduction by $A \rightarrow \beta$, it pops $3 \times |\beta|$ locations from the stack, rather than $2 \times |\beta|$ locations. It pushes the value along with the symbol and state.

This approach stores the values at easily computed locations relative to the top of the stack. Each reduction pushes its result onto the stack as part of the triple that represents the left-hand side. The action reads the values for the right-hand side from their relative positions in the stack; the ith symbol on the right-hand side has its value in the ith triple from the top of the stack. Values are restricted to a fixed size; in practice, this limitation means that more complex values are passed using pointers to structures.

To save storage, the parser could omit the actual grammar symbols from the stack. The information necessary for parsing is encoded in the state. This shrinks the stack and speeds up the parse by eliminating the operations that stack and unstack those symbols. On the other hand, the grammar symbol can help in error reporting and in debugging the parser. This tradeoff is usually decided in favor of not modifying the parser that the tools produce—such modifications must be reapplied each time the parser is regenerated.

Naming Values

To simplify the use of stack-based values, the compiler writer needs a notation for naming them. Yacc introduced a concise notation to address this problem. The symbol *$$* refers to the result location for the current production. Thus, the assignment *$$ = 0;* would push the integer value zero as the result corresponding to the current reduction. This assignment could implement the action for rule 6 in Figure 4.10. For the right-hand side, the symbols *$1, $2,* ..., *$n* refer to the locations for the first, second, through n^{th} symbols in the right-hand side, respectively.

Rewriting the example from Figure 4.10 in this notation produces the following specification:

	Production	Code Snippet
1	$Number \rightarrow Sign\ List$	$\$\$ \leftarrow \$1 \times \$2$
2	$Sign \rightarrow +$	$\$\$ \leftarrow 1$
3	$Sign \rightarrow -$	$\$\$ \leftarrow -1$
4	$List \rightarrow Bit$	$\$\$ \leftarrow \$1$
5	$List_0 \rightarrow List_1\ Bit$	$\$\$ \leftarrow 2 \times \$1 + \$2$
6	$Bit \rightarrow 0$	$\$\$ \leftarrow 0$
7	$Bit \rightarrow 1$	$\$\$ \leftarrow 1$

Notice how compact the code snippets are.

This scheme has an efficient implementation; the symbols translate directly into offsets from the top of the stack. The notation $\$1$ indicates a location $3 \times |\beta|$ slots below the top of the stack, while $\$i$ designates the location $3 \times (|\beta| - i + 1)$ slots from the top of the stack. Thus, the positional notation allows the action snippets to read and write the stack locations directly. (If we optimize the parser so that it does not stack the actual grammar symbols, the multiplier becomes 2 rather than 3.)

Actions at Other Points in the Parse

Compiler writers might also need to perform an action in the middle of a production or on a shift action. To accomplish this, compiler writers can transform the grammar so that it performs a reduction at each point where an action is needed. To reduce in the middle of a production, they can break the production into two pieces around the point where the action should execute. A higher-level production that sequences the first part, then the second part, is added. When the first part reduces, the parser invokes the action. To force actions on shifts, a compiler writer can either move them into the scanner or add a production to hold the action. For example, to perform an action whenever the parser shifts the terminal symbol *Bit*, a compiler writer can add a production

$$ShiftedBit \rightarrow Bit$$

and replace every occurrence of *Bit* with *ShiftedBit*. This adds an extra reduction for every terminal symbol. Thus, the additional cost is directly proportional to the number of terminal symbols in the program.

4.4.2 Examples

To understand how ad hoc syntax-directed translation works, consider rewriting the execution-time estimator using this approach. The primary drawback of the attribute-grammar solution lies in the proliferation of rules to copy information around the tree. This creates many additional rules in the specification and duplicates attribute values at many nodes.

To address these problems in an ad hoc syntax-directed translation scheme, the compiler writer typically introduces a central repository for information about variables, as suggested earlier. This eliminates the need to copy values around the trees. It also simplifies the handling of inherited values. Since the parser determines evaluation order, we do not need to worry about breaking dependences between attributes.

Most compilers build and use such a repository, called a *symbol table*. The symbol table maps a name into a variety of annotations such as a type, the size of its run-time representation, and the information needed to generate a run-time address. The table may also store a number of type-dependent fields, such as the type signature of a function or the number of dimensions and their bounds for an array. Sections 5.7 and B.4 delve into symbol-table design more deeply.

Load Tracking, Revisited

Consider, again, the problem of tracking load operations that arose as part of estimating execution costs. Most of the complexity in the attribute grammar for this problem arose from the need to pass information around the tree. In an ad hoc syntax-directed translation scheme that uses a symbol table, the problem is easy to handle. The compiler writer can set aside a field in the table to hold a boolean that indicates whether or not that identifier has already been charged for a load. The field is initially set to *false*. The critical code is associated with the production *Factor* → ident. If the ident's symbol table entry indicates that it has not been charged for a load, then cost is updated and the field is set to *true*.

Figure 4.11 shows this case, along with all the other actions. Because the actions can contain arbitrary code, the compiler can accumulate *cost* in a single variable, rather than creating a *cost* attribute at each node in the parse tree.

Production			Syntax-Directed Actions
$Block_0$	$\rightarrow$	$Block_1$ $Assign$	
	|	$Assign$	
$Assign$	$\rightarrow$	$Identifier = Expr$;	{ $cost = cost + Cost($store$)$ }
$Expr_0$	$\rightarrow$	$Expr_1 + Term$	{ $cost = cost + Cost($add$)$ }
	|	$Expr_1$ - $Term$	{ $cost = cost + Cost($sub$)$ }
	|	$Term$	
$Term_0$	$\rightarrow$	$Term_1 \times Factor$	{ $cost = cost + Cost($mult$)$ }
	|	$Term_1 \div Factor$	{ $cost = cost + Cost($div$)$ }
	|	$Factor$	
$Factor$	$\rightarrow$	($Expr$)	
	|	num	{ $cost = cost + Cost($loadI$)$ }
	|	ident	{ *if* ident*'s symbol table field*
			indicates that it has not been loaded
			then
			$cost = cost + Cost($load$)$;
			set the field to true }

FIGURE 4.11   Tracking Loads with Ad Hoc Syntax-Directed Translation

This scheme requires fewer actions than the attribution rules for the simplest execution model, even though it can provide the accuracy of the more complex model.

Notice that several productions have no actions. The remaining actions are simple, except for the action taken on reduction by ident. All of the complication introduced by tracking loads falls into that single action; contrast that with the attribute-grammar version, where the task of passing around the *Before* and *After* sets came to dominate the specification. The ad hoc version is cleaner and simpler, in part because the problem fits nicely into the evaluation order dictated by the reduce actions in a shift-reduce parser. Of course, the compiler writer must implement the symbol table or import it from some library of data-structure implementations.

Of course, some of these strategies could also be applied in an attribute-grammar framework. However, it violates the functional nature of the attribute grammar. It forces critical parts of the work out of the attribute-grammar framework and into an ad hoc setting.

The scheme in Figure 4.11 ignores one critical issue: initializing *cost*. The grammar, as written, contains no production that can appropriately initialize *cost* to zero. The solution, as described earlier, is to modify the grammar in a way that creates a place for the initialization. An initial production, such as *Start → CostInit Block*, along with *CostInit → ε*, does this. The framework can perform the assignment *cost ← 0* on the reduction from ε to *CostInit*.

Type Inference for Expressions, Revisited

The problem of inferring types for expressions fit well into the attribute-grammar framework, as long as we assumed that leaf nodes already had type information. The simplicity of the solution shown in Figure 4.6 derives from two principal facts. First, because expression types are defined recursively on the expression tree, the natural flow of information runs bottom up from the leaves to the root. This biases the solution toward an *S*-attributed grammar. Second, expression types are defined in terms of the syntax of the source language. This fits well with the attribute-grammar framework, which implicitly requires the presence of a parse tree. All the type information can be tied to instances of grammar symbols—which correspond precisely to nodes in the parse tree.

We can reformulate this problem in an ad hoc framework, as shown in Figure 4.12. The resulting framework looks similar to the attribute grammar for the same purpose from Figure 4.6. The ad hoc framework provides no real advantage for this problem.

	Productions	Syntax-Directed Actions
Expr →	*Expr + Term*	{ $$ ← $\mathcal{F}_+($1,3)$ }
|	*Expr − Term*	{ $$ ← $\mathcal{F}_-($1,3)$ }
|	*Term*	{ $$ ← $1 }
Term →	*Term × Factor*	{ $$ ← $\mathcal{F}_\times($1,3)$ }
|	*Term ÷ Factor*	{ $$ ← $\mathcal{F}_\div($1,3)$ }
|	*Factor*	{ $$ ← $1 }
Factor →	*(Expr)*	{ $$ ← $2 }
|	num	{ $$ ← *type of the* num }
|	ident	{ $$ ← *type of the* ident }

FIGURE 4.12 Ad Hoc Framework for Inferring Expression Types

Building an Abstract Syntax Tree

Compiler front ends must build an intermediate representation of the program for use in the compiler's middle part and its back end. Abstract syntax trees are a common form of tree-structured IR (see Section 5.3.1). The task of building an AST fits neatly into an ad hoc syntax-directed translation scheme.

Assume that the compiler has a series of routines named *MakeNode$_i$*, for $0 \leq i \leq 3$. The routine takes, as its first argument, a constant that uniquely identifies the grammar symbol that the new node will represent. The remaining i arguments are the nodes that head each of the i subtrees. Thus, *MakeNode$_0$* (*number*) constructs a leaf node and marks it as representing a num. Similarly,

$$MakeNode_2(Plus, MakeNode_0(number), MakeNode_0(number))$$

	Productions	Syntax-Directed Actions
Expr	$\rightarrow$ *Expr* + *Term*	{ *$$* ← *MakeNode$_2$* (plus, *$1*, *$3*); *$$.type* ← $\mathcal{F}+$(*$1.type*,*$3.type*) }
	| *Expr* − *Term*	{ *$$* ← *MakeNode$_2$*(minus, *$1*, *$3*); *$$.type* ← $\mathcal{F}-$(*$1.type*,*$3.type*) }
	| *Term*	{ *$$* ← *$1* }
Term	$\rightarrow$ *Term* × *Factor*	{ *$$* ← *MakeNode$_2$*(times, *$1*, *$3*); *$$.type* ← $\mathcal{F}\times$(*$1.type*,*$3.type*) }
	| *Term* ÷ *Factor*	{ *$$* ← *MakeNode$_2$*(divide, *$1*, *$3*); *$$.type* ← $\mathcal{F}\div$(*$1.type*,*$3.type*) }
	| *Factor*	{ *$$* ← *$1* }
Factor	$\rightarrow$ (*Expr*)	{ *$$* ← *$2* }
	| num	{ *$$* ← *MakeNode$_0$*(number); *$$.text* ← *scanned text*; *$$.type* ← *type of the number* }
	| ident	{ *$$* ← *MakeNode$_0$*(identifier); *$$.text* ← *scanned text*; *$$.type* ← *type of the identifier* }

FIGURE 4.13   Building an Abstract Syntax Tree and Inferring Expression Types

builds an AST rooted in a node for *plus* with two children, each of which is a leaf node for num.[3]

To build an abstract syntax tree, the ad hoc syntax-directed translation scheme follows two general principles:

1. For an operator, it creates a node with a child for each operand. Thus, 2 + 3 creates a binary node for + with the nodes for 2 and 3 as children.

2. For a useless production, such as *Term → Factor*, it reuses the result from the *Factor* action as its own result.

In this manner, it avoids building tree nodes that represent syntactic variables, such as *Factor, Term*, and *Expr*. Figure 4.13 shows a syntax-directed translation scheme that incorporates these ideas.

Generating ILOC for Expressions

As a final example of manipulating expressions, consider an ad hoc framework that generates ILOC rather than an AST. We will make several simplifying assumptions. The example limits its attention to integers; handling other types adds complexity, but little insight. The example also assumes that all values can be held in registers—both that the values fit in registers and that the ILOC implementation provides more registers than the computation will use.

Code generation requires the compiler to track many small details. To abstract away most of these bookkeeping details (and to defer some deeper issues to following chapters), the example framework uses four supporting routines.

1. *Address* takes a variable name as its argument and returns a register number. It ensures that the register contains the variable's address. If necessary, it generates code to compute that address.

2. *Emit* handles the details of creating a concrete representation for the various ILOC operations. It might format and print them to a file. Alternatively, it might build an internal representation for later use.

3. *NextRegister* returns a new register number. A simple implementation could increment a global counter.

---

3. The *MakeNode_i* routines can implement the tree in any appropriate way. For example, they might map the structure onto a binary tree. See the discussion in Section B.31.

Productions			Syntax-Directed Actions
Expr	→	*Expr* + *Term*	{ *$$* ← *NextRegister;*
			Emit(add, $1, $3, $$)
	|	*Expr* − *Term*	{ *$$* ← *NextRegister;*
			Emit(sub, $1, $3, $$)
	|	*Term*	{ *$$* ← *$1* }
Term	→	*Term* × *Factor*	{ *$$* ← *NextRegister;*
			Emit(mult, $1, $3, $$)
	|	*Term* ÷ *Factor*	{ *$$* ← *NextRegister;*
			Emit(div, $1, $3, $$)
	|	*Factor*	{ *$$* ← *$1* }
Factor	→	(*Expr*)	{ *$$* ← *$2* }
	|	num	{ *$$* ← *Value(scanned text);* }
	|	ident	{ *$$* ← *Address(scanned text);* }

FIGURE 4.14   Emitting ILOC for Expressions

4. *Value* takes a number as its argument and returns a register number. It ensures that the register contains the number passed as its argument. If necessary, it generates code to move that number into the register.

Figure 4.14 shows the syntax-directed framework for this problem. The actions communicate by passing register names in the parsing stack. The actions pass these names to *Emit* as needed, to create the operations that implement the input expression.

Processing Declarations

Of course, the compiler writer can use syntax-directed actions to fill in much of the information that resides in the symbol table. For example, the grammar fragment shown in Figure 4.15 describes a limited subset of the syntax for declaring variables in C. (It omits typedefs, structs, unions, the type qualifiers const, restrict, and volatile, and the details of the initialization syntax. It also leaves several nonterminals unelaborated.) Consider the actions required to build symbol-table entries for each declared variable. Each *Declaration* begins

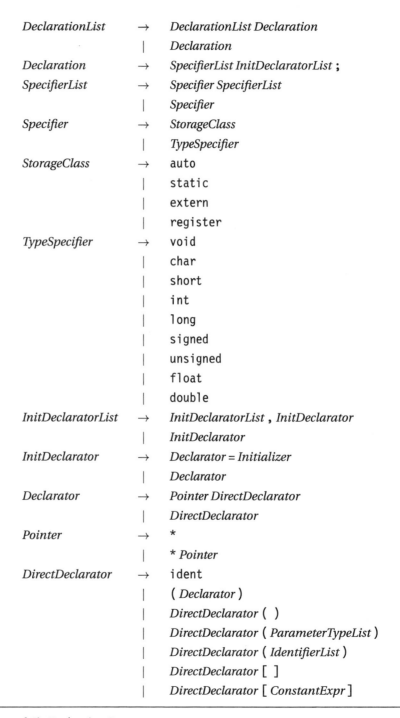

DeclarationList	→	*DeclarationList Declaration*
	|	*Declaration*
Declaration	→	*SpecifierList InitDeclaratorList* ;
SpecifierList	→	*Specifier SpecifierList*
	|	*Specifier*
Specifier	→	*StorageClass*
	|	*TypeSpecifier*
StorageClass	→	auto
	|	static
	|	extern
	|	register
TypeSpecifier	→	void
	|	char
	|	short
	|	int
	|	long
	|	signed
	|	unsigned
	|	float
	|	double
InitDeclaratorList	→	*InitDeclaratorList* , *InitDeclarator*
	|	*InitDeclarator*
InitDeclarator	→	*Declarator = Initializer*
	|	*Declarator*
Declarator	→	*Pointer DirectDeclarator*
	|	*DirectDeclarator*
Pointer	→	*
	|	* *Pointer*
DirectDeclarator	→	ident
	|	(*Declarator*)
	|	*DirectDeclarator* ( )
	|	*DirectDeclarator* (*ParameterTypeList*)
	|	*DirectDeclarator* (*IdentifierList*)
	|	*DirectDeclarator* [ ]
	|	*DirectDeclarator* [*ConstantExpr*]

FIGURE 4.15   A Subset of C's Declaration Syntax

with a set of one or more qualifiers that specify the variable's type and storage class. These qualifiers are followed by a list of one or more variable names; each variable name can include specifications about indirection (one or more occurrences of *), about array dimensions, and about initial values for the variable.

For example, the *StorageClass* production allows the programmer to specify information about the lifetime of a variable's value; an auto variable has a lifetime that matches the lifetime of the block that declares it, while static variables have lifetimes that span the program's entire execution. The register specifier suggests to the compiler that the value should be kept in a location that can be accessed quickly—historically, a hardware register. The extern specifier tells the compiler that declarations of the same name in different compilation units are to be linked as a single object.

The compiler must ensure that each declared name has at most one storage class attribute. The grammar places the specifiers before a list of one or more names. The compiler can record the specifiers as it processes them and apply them to the names when it later encounters them. The grammar admits an arbitrary number of *StorageClass* and *TypeSpecifier* keywords; the standard limits the ways that the actual keywords can be combined.[4] For example, it allows only one *StorageClass* per declaration. The compiler must enforce this restriction through context-sensitive checking. Similar restrictions apply to *TypeSpecifier*s. For example, short is legal with int but not with float.

To process declarations, the compiler must collect the attributes from the qualifiers, add any indirection, dimension, or initialization attributes, and enter the variable in the table. The compiler writer might set up a properties structure whose fields match those of a symbol-table entry. At the end of a *Declaration*, it can initialize the values of each field in the structure. As it reduces the various productions in the declaration syntax, it can adjust the values in the structure accordingly.

- On a reduction of auto to *StorageClass*, it can check that the field for storage class has not already been set, and then set it to auto. Similar actions for static, extern, and register complete the handling of those properties of a name.

- The type specifier productions will set other fields in the structure. They must include checks to insure that only valid combinations occur.

---

4. This kind of restriction can be enforced grammatically. The authors of the standard chose not to handle it this way. Adding the restriction would complicate an already large grammar. Since the compiler must track similar restrictions on combinations of *TypeSpecifier*s, the overhead for checking it extrasyntactically is low.

WHAT ABOUT CONTEXT-SENSITIVE GRAMMARS?

Given the progression of ideas from the previous chapters, it might seem natural to consider the use of context-sensitive languages to perform context-sensitive checks, such as type inference. After all, we used regular languages to perform lexical analysis and context-free languages to perform syntax analysis. A natural progression might suggest the study of context-sensitive languages and their grammars. Context-sensitive grammars can express a larger family of languages than can context-free grammars.

However, context-sensitive grammars are not the right answer for two distinct reasons. First, the problem of parsing a context-sensitive grammar is P-space complete. Thus, a compiler that used such a technique could run *very* slowly. Second, many of the important questions are difficult, if not impossible, to encode in a context-sensitive grammar. For example, consider the issue of declaration before use. To write this rule into a context-sensitive grammar would require the grammar to encode each distinct combination of declared variables. With a sufficiently small name space (for example, Dartmouth BASIC limited the programmer to single-letter names, with an optional single digit), this might be manageable; in a modern language with a large name space, the set of names is too large to encode in a context-sensitive grammar.

- Reduction from ident to *DirectDeclarator* should trigger an action that creates a new symbol-table entry for the name and copies the current settings from the properties structure into that entry.

- Reducing by the production

  InitDeclaratorList → *InitDeclaratorList* , *InitDeclarator*

  it can reset the properties fields that relate to the specific name, including those set by the *Pointer*, *Initializer*, and *DirectDeclarator* productions.

By coordinating a series of actions across the productions in the declaration syntax, the compiler writer can arrange to have the properties structure contain the appropriate settings each time a name is processed.

When the parser finishes building the *DeclarationList*, it has built a symbol-table entry for each variable declared in the current scope. At that point, it may need to perform some housekeeping chores, such as assigning storage locations to declared variables. This can be done in an action for the production that reduces the *DeclarationList*. If necessary, that production can be split to create a convenient point for the action.

4.5 ADVANCED TOPICS

This chapter has introduced the basic notions of type theory and used them as one motivating example for both attribute-grammar frameworks and for ad hoc syntax-directed translation. A deeper treatment of type theory and its applications could easily fill an entire volume.

The first subsection lays out some language design issues that affect the way that a compiler must perform type inference and type checking. The second subsection looks at a problem that arises in practice: rearranging a computation during the process of building the intermediate representation for it.

4.5.1 Harder Problems in Type Inference

Strongly typed, statically checked languages can help the programmer produce valid programs by detecting large classes of erroneous programs. The same features that expose errors can improve the compiler's ability to generate efficient code for a program by eliminating run-time checks and exposing where the compiler can specialize special case code for some construct to eliminate cases that cannot occur at run time. These facts account, in part, for the growing role of type systems in modern programming languages.

Our examples, however, have made assumptions that do not hold in all programming languages. For example, we assumed that variables and procedures are declared—the programmer writes down a concise and binding specification for each name. Varying these assumptions can radically change the nature of both the type-checking problem and the strategies that the compiler can use to implement the language.

Some programming languages either omit declarations or treat them as optional information. Scheme programs lack declarations for variables. Smalltalk programs declare classes, but an object's class is determined only when the program instantiates that object. Languages that support separate compilation—compiling procedures independently and combining them at link time to form a program—may not require declarations for independently compiled procedures.

In the absence of declarations, type checking is harder because the compiler must rely on contextual clues to determine the appropriate type for each name. For example, if i is used as an index for some array a, that might constrain i to have a numeric type. The language might allow only integer subscripts; alternatively, it might allow any type that can be converted to an integer.

Typing rules are specified by the language definition. The specific details of those rules determine how difficult it is to infer a type for each variable. This, in turn, has a direct effect on the strategies that a compiler can use to implement the language.

Type-Consistent Uses and Constant Function Types

Consider a declaration-free language that requires consistent use of variables and functions. In this case, the compiler can assign each name a general type and narrow that type by examining each use of the name in context. For example, a statement such as x ← y * 3.14159 provides evidence that x and y are numbers and that x must have a type that allows it to hold a decimal number. If y also appears in contexts where an integer is expected, such as an array reference a(y), then the compiler must choose between a non-integer number (for y * 3.14159) and an integer (for a(y)). With either choice, it will need a conversion for one of the uses.

If functions have return types that are both known and constant—that is, a function fee always returns the same type—then the compiler can solve the type inference problem with an iterative fixed-point algorithm operating over a lattice of types.

Type-Consistent Uses and Unknown Function Types

If the type of a function varies with the function's arguments, then the problem of type inference becomes more complex. This situation arises in Scheme, for example. Scheme's library procedure map takes as arguments a function and a list. It returns the result of applying the function argument to each element of the list. That is, if the argument function takes type α to β, then map takes a list of α to a list of β.[5] We would write its type signature as

$$\text{map: } (\alpha \rightarrow \beta) \times \textit{list of } \alpha \rightarrow \textit{list of } \beta$$

5. Map can also handle functions with multiple arguments. To do so, it takes multiple argument lists and treats them as lists of arguments, in order.

Since map's return type depends on the types of its arguments, a property known as parametric polymorphism, the inference rules must include equations over the space of types. (With known, constant return types, functions return values in the space of types.) With this addition, a simple iterative fixed-point approach to type inference is not sufficient.

The classic approach to checking these more complex systems relies on unification, although clever type-system design and type representations can permit the use of simpler or more efficient techniques.

Dynamic Changes in Type

If a variable's type can change during execution, other strategies may be required to discover where type changes occur and to infer appropriate types. In principle, a compiler can rename the variables so that each definition site corresponds to a unique name. It can then infer types for those names based on the context provided by the operation that defines each name.

To infer types successfully, such a system would need to handle points in the code where distinct definitions must merge due to the convergence of different control-flow paths, as with ϕ-functions in static single assignment form (see Sections 5.5 and 9.3). If the language includes parametric polymorphism, the type-inference mechanism must handle it, as well.

The classic approach to implementing a language with dynamically changing types is to fall back on interpretation. Lisp, Scheme, Smalltalk, and APL all have similar problems. The standard implementation practice for these languages involves interpreting the operators, tagging the data with their types, and checking for type errors at run time.

In APL, the programmer can easily write a program where a × b multiplies integers the first time it executes and multiplies multidimensional arrays of floating-point numbers the next time. This led to a body of research on check elimination and check motion. The best APL systems avoided most of the checks that a naive interpreter would need.

4.5.2 Changing Associativity

As we saw in Section 3.6.4, associativity can make a difference in numerical computation. Similarly, it can change the way that data structures are built. We can use syntax-directed actions to build representations that reflect a different associativity than the grammar would naturally produce.

In general, left-recursive grammars naturally produce left associativity, while right-recursive grammars naturally produce right associativity. To see this, consider the left-recursive and right-recursive list grammars, augmented with syntax-directed actions to build lists, shown at the top of Figure 4.16. The actions associated with each production build a list representation. Assume that $L(x,y)$ is a list constructor; it can be implemented as $MakeNode_2(cons,x,y)$. The lower part of the figure shows the result of applying the two translation schemes to an input consisting of five elts.

The two trees are, in many ways, equivalent. An in-order traversal of both trees visits the leaf nodes in the same order. If we add parentheses to reflect the tree structure, the left-recursive tree is $((((elt_1,elt_2),elt_3,)elt_4),elt_5)$ while the right-recursive tree is $(elt_1,(elt_2,(elt_3,(elt_4,elt_5))))$. The ordering produced by left recursion corresponds to the classic left-to-right ordering for algebraic operators. The ordering produced by right recursion corresponds to the notion of a list found in Lisp and Scheme.

Sometimes, it is convenient to use different directions for recursion and associativity. To build the right-recursive tree from the left-recursive grammar, we could use a constructor that adds successive elements to the end of the list. A straightforward implementation of this idea would have to walk the list on each reduction, making the constructor itself take $O(n^2)$ time, where n is the length of the list. To avoid this overhead, the compiler can create a list header node that contains pointers to both the first and last nodes in the list. This introduces an extra node to the list. If the system constructs many short lists, the overhead may be a problem.

A solution that we find particularly appealing is to use a list header node during construction and discard it after the list has been built. Rewriting the grammar to use an ϵ-production makes this particularly clean.

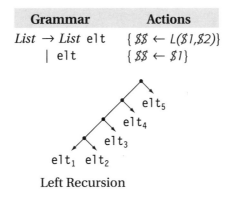

Grammar	**Actions**
List → *List* elt	{ $\$\$$ ← $L(\$1,\$2)$}
| elt	{ $\$\$$ ← $\$1$}

Left Recursion

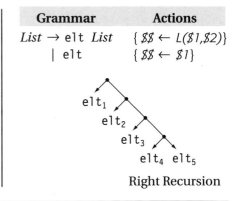

Grammar	**Actions**
List → elt *List*	{ $\$\$$ ← $L(\$1,\$2)$}
| elt	{ $\$\$$ ← $\$1$}

Right Recursion

FIGURE 4.16   Recursion versus Associativity

Grammar			Actions
List	→	ϵ	{ $\$\$ \leftarrow$ *MakeListHeader()* }
	|	*List* elt	{ $\$\$ \leftarrow$ *AddToEnd($1,$2)* }
Quux	→	*List*	{ $\$\$ \leftarrow$ *RemoveListHeader($1)* }

A reduction with the ϵ-production creates the temporary list header node; with a shift-reduce parser, this reduction occurs first. The *List* → *List* elt production invokes a constructor that relies on the presence of the temporary header node. When *List* is reduced on the right-hand side of any other production, the corresponding action invokes a function that discards the temporary header and returns the first element of the list.

This approach lets the parser reverse the associativity at the cost of a small constant overhead in both space and time. It requires one more reduction per list, for the ϵ-production. The revised grammar admits an empty list, while the original grammar did not. To remedy this problem, *RemoveListHeader* can explicitly check for the empty case and report the error.

4.6 SUMMARY AND PERSPECTIVE

In Chapters 2 and 3, we saw that much of the work in a compiler's front end can be automated. Regular expressions work well for lexical analysis. Context-free grammars work well for syntax analysis. In this chapter, we examined two ways to perform context-sensitive analysis: the attribute-grammar formalism and an ad hoc approach. For context-sensitive analysis, unlike scanning and parsing, the formalism has not displaced the ad hoc approach.

The formal approach, using attribute grammars, offers the hope of writing high-level specifications that produce reasonably efficient executables. While attribute grammars are not the solution to every problem in context-sensitive analysis, they have found application in several domains, ranging from theorem provers to program analysis. For problems in which the attribute flow is mostly local, attribute grammars work well. Problems that can be formulated entirely in terms of one kind of attribute, either inherited or synthesized, often produce clean, intuitive solutions when cast as attribute grammars. When the problem of directing the flow of attributes around the tree with copy rules comes to dominate the grammar, it is probably time to step outside the functional paradigm of attribute grammars and introduce a central repository for facts.

The ad hoc technique, syntax-directed translation, integrates arbitrary snippets of code into the parser and lets the parser sequence the actions and pass values between them. This approach has been widely embraced, because of its flexibility and its inclusion in most parser-generator systems. The ad hoc approach sidesteps the practical problems that arise from nonlocal attribute flow and from the need to manage attribute storage. Values flow in one direction alongside the parser's internal representation of its state (synthesized values for bottom-up parsers and inherited for top-down parsers). These schemes use global data structures to pass information in the other direction and to handle nonlocal attribute flow.

In practice, the compiler writer often tries to solve several problems at once, such as building an intermediate representation, inferring types, and assigning storage locations. This tends to create significant attribute flows in both directions, pushing the implementor toward an ad hoc solution that uses some central repository for facts, such as a symbol table. The justification for solving many problems in one pass is usually compile-time efficiency. However, solving the problems in separate passes can often produce solutions that are easier to understand, to implement, and to maintain.

This chapter introduced the ideas behind type systems as an example of the kind of context-sensitive analysis that a compiler must perform. The study of type theory and type-system design is a significant scholarly activity with a deep literature of its own. This chapter scratched the surface of type inference and type checking, but a deeper treatment of these issues is beyond the scope of this text. In practice, the compiler writer needs to study the type system of the source language thoroughly and to engineer the implementation of type inference and type checking carefully. The pointers in this chapter are a start, but a realistic implementation requires more study.

Chapter Notes

Type systems have been an integral part of programming languages since the original FORTRAN compiler. While the first type systems reflected the underlying machine resources, significant levels of abstraction in type systems soon appeared, in languages such as Algol 68 and Simula 67. The theory of type systems has been actively studied for decades, producing a string of languages that embodied important principles. These include Russell [43] (parametric polymorphism), CLU [239] (abstract data types), Smalltalk [157] (subtyping through inheritance), and ML [258] (thorough and complete treatment of types as first-class objects). Cardelli has written an excellent overview of type systems [64]. The APL community produced a series of classic papers that dealt with techniques to eliminate run-time checks [1, 32, 257, 331].

Attribute grammars, like many ideas in computer science, were first proposed by Knuth [218, 219]. The literature on attribute grammars has focused on evaluators [193, 327], on circularity testing [327], and on applications of attribute grammars [152, 287]. Attribute grammars have served as the basis for several successful systems, including Intel's Pascal compiler for the 80286 [135, 136], the Cornell Program Synthesizer [286], and the Synthesizer Generator [188, 288].

Ad hoc syntax-directed translation has always been a part of the development of real parsers. Irons described the basic ideas behind syntax-directed translation to separate a parser's actions from the description of its syntax [191]. Undoubtedly, the same basic ideas were used in hand-coded precedence parsers before the advent of syntax-directed parsers. The style of writing syntax-directed actions that we describe was introduced by Johnson in Yacc [195]. The same notation has been carried forward into more recent systems, including bison from the Gnu project.

CHAPTER 5

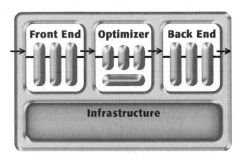

Intermediate Representations

5.1 INTRODUCTION

As we have seen, compilers are organized as a series of passes, each of which plays a distinct role. This structure creates the need for an intermediate representation for the code being compiled. Thus, it must use some internal form—an intermediate representation or IR—to represent the code being analyzed and translated. Most passes consume IR; most passes produce IR. Many compilers use more than one IR during the course of compilation. In this scheme, the intermediate representation becomes the primary, or definitive, representation of the code.

For this to work, the IR must be expressive enough to record all of the useful facts that might be passed between passes of the compiler. During translation, the compiler derives facts that have no representation in the source code—for example, the addresses of variables and procedures. Typically the compiler augments the IR with a set of tables that record additional information. We consider these tables to be part of the IR.

In designing algorithms, a critical distinction arises between problems that must be solved online and those that can be solved offline. In general, compilers work offline—that is, they can make more than a single pass over the code being translated. Making multiple passes over the code should improve the quality of code generated by the compiler. The compiler can gather information in some passes and use that information to make decisions in later passes.

Selecting an appropriate IR for a compiler project requires an understanding of both the source languages and the target machines and of the properties of programs that will be presented for compilation. Thus, a source-to-source translator might keep its internal information in a form quite close to the source. In contrast, a compiler that produces assembly code for a microcontroller might use an internal form close in form to the target machine's instruction set.

Designing a specific IR requires consideration of the kinds of information that the compiler must record, analyze, and manipulate. Thus, a compiler for C might need additional information about pointer values that are not needed in a compiler for Perl. Similarly, a compiler for Java needs information about the class hierarchy that has no equivalent in a C compiler.

Finally, implementing an IR forces the compiler writer to examine several practical considerations. The IR should provide inexpensive ways to perform operations that the compiler does frequently. It should have concise ways to express the full range of constructs that might arise during compilation. Finally, the implementation should provide mechanisms that let humans, particularly compiler writers, examine the IR program easily and directly.

The compiler writer should never overlook this final point. A clean, readable external format for the IR pays for itself. Sometimes, syntax can be added to improve readability. The ⇒ symbol in ILOC is an example. It serves no purpose except to help the reader separate operands from results.

5.2 TAXONOMY

To organize our thinking about IRs, we should recognize that there are two major axes along which we can place a specific design. First, the IR has a structural organization. Broadly speaking, IRs fall into three organizational categories:

- *Graphical* IRs encode the compiler's knowledge in a graph. The algorithms are expressed in terms of nodes and edges, or lists or trees. The parse trees used to depict derivations in Chapter 3 are a graphical IR.

- *Linear* IRs resemble pseudocode for some abstract machine. The algorithms iterate over simple, linear sequences of operations. The ILOC code used throughout the book is a form of linear IR.

- *Hybrid* IRs combine elements of both structural and linear IRs, in an attempt to capture the strengths and avoid the weaknesses of both kinds of IRs. A common hybrid representation uses a low-level linear IR to represent blocks of straight-line code and a graph to represent the flow of control among those blocks.

The structural organization of an IR has a strong impact on how the compiler writer thinks about analysis, optimization, and code generation. For example, treelike IRs lead naturally to passes that embed their operations into some variety of tree walk. Similarly, linear IRs lead naturally to passes that operate in linear scans over all the instructions.

The second axis of our IR taxonomy is the level of abstraction at which the IR represents operations. This can range from a near-source representation in which a procedure call is represented by a single node to a very low-level representation in which several IR operations must be combined to form a single target-machine operation.

To illustrate the possibilities, consider how the compiler might represent the reference A[i,j] in a source-level tree and in ILOC. Assume that A is a two-dimensional array with ten elements per dimension.

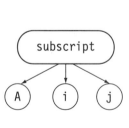

Source-Level Tree

```
loadI  1         ⇒ r_1
sub    r_j, r_1  ⇒ r_2
loadI  10        ⇒ r_3
mult   r_2, r_3  ⇒ r_4
sub    r_i, r_1  ⇒ r_5
add    r_4, r_5  ⇒ r_6
loadI  @A        ⇒ r_7
add    r_7, r_6  ⇒ r_8
load   r_8       ⇒ r_{A_{ij}}
```

ILOC Code

In the source-level AST, the compiler can easily recognize that the computation is an array reference; examining the low-level code, we find that simple fact fairly well obscured. In a compiler that tries to determine when two different references can touch the same memory location, the higher level of abstraction in the AST may prove valuable. In contrast, recognizing the low-level code as an array reference is hard, particularly if the IR has been subjected to optimizations that move individual operations to other parts of a procedure or eliminate them altogether. On the other hand, if the compiler is optimizing the code generated for the array-address calculation, the low-level code exposes operations that remain implicit in the AST. In this case, the lower level of abstraction may result in more efficient code for the address calculation.

The high level of abstraction is not an inherent property of tree-based IRs; it is implicit in the notion of a parse tree. However, low-level expression trees have been used in many compilers to represent all the details of computations, such as the address calculation for A[i,j]. Similarly, linear IRs can have relatively high-level constructs. For example, many linear IRs have included a byte-copying operation to encode string-to-string copy as a single operation.

On some simple RISC machines, the best encoding of a string copy involves clearing out the entire register set and iterating through a tight loop that does a multiword load followed by a multiword store. Some preliminary logic is needed to deal with alignment and the special case of overlapping strings. By using a single IR instruction to represent this complex operation, the compiler writer can make it easier for the optimizer to move the copy out of a loop or to discover that the copy is redundant. In later stages of compilation, the single instruction is expanded, in place, to code that performs the copy or to a call to some system or library routine that performs the copy.

The costs of generating and manipulating an IR should concern the compiler writer, since they directly affect a compiler's speed. The data-space requirements of different IRs vary over a wide range. Since the compiler typically touches all of the space that is allocated, data space usually has a direct relationship to running time. To make this discussion concrete, consider the IRs used in two different research systems that we built at Rice University.

- The $\mathcal{R}^n$ Programming Environment built an abstract syntax tree for FORTRAN. Nodes in the tree occupied 92 bytes each. The parser built an average of eleven nodes per FORTRAN source line, for a size of just over 1,000 bytes per source-code line.

- The research compiler produced by our group uses a full-scale implementation of ILOC. (The ILOC in this book is a simple subset.) ILOC operations take from 23 to 25 bytes. The compiler generates an average of roughly fifteen ILOC operations per source-code line. Optimization drops this to just over three operations per source-code line.

Finally, the compiler writer should consider the expressiveness of the IR—its ability to accommodate all the facts that the compiler needs to record.

This can include the sequence of actions that defines a procedure, along with the results of static analysis, profiles of previous executions, and information needed by the debugger. All should be expressed in a way that makes clear their relationship to specific points in the IR.

5.3 GRAPHICAL IRS

Many IRs represent the code being translated as a graph. Conceptually, all the graphical IRs consist of nodes and edges. The differences among them lie in the relationship between the graph and the source language program, and in the structure of the graph.

5.3.1 Syntax-Related Trees

The parse trees shown in Chapter 3 are graphs that represent the source-code form of the program. Many compilers use treelike IRs in which the structure of the tree corresponds to the syntax of the source code.

Parse Trees

The *parse tree*, sometimes called a *syntax tree*, is a graphical representation for the derivation, or parse, that corresponds to the input program. Figure 5.1 shows the grammar on the left and a parse tree for $x \times 2 + x \times 2 \times y$ on the right. It represents the complete derivation, with a node for each grammar symbol in the derivation. The compiler must allocate memory for each node and each edge. Similarly, the compiler will traverse all of those nodes and edges several times. Thus, it is worth considering ways to shrink this parse tree.

Minor transformations on the grammar, as described in Section 3.7.1, can eliminate some of the steps in the derivation and their corresponding syntax-tree nodes. A more effective technique is to abstract away those nodes that serve no real purpose in the rest of the compiler. This approach leads to a simplified version of the parse tree.

Parse trees are used primarily in discussions of parsing, and in attribute-grammar systems, where they are the primary IR. In most other applications

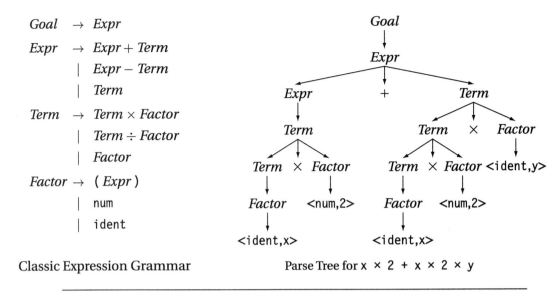

Classic Expression Grammar | Parse Tree for x × 2 + x × 2 × y

FIGURE 5.1   Parse Tree Using the Classic Expression Grammar

in which a source-level tree is needed, compiler writers tend to use one of the more concise alternatives, described in the remainder of this subsection.

Abstract Syntax Trees

The *abstract syntax tree* (AST) retains the essential structure of the parse tree but eliminates the extraneous nodes. The precedence and meaning of the expression remain, but extraneous nodes have disappeared.

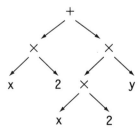

Abstract Syntax Tree for x × 2 + x × 2 × y

The AST is a near source-level representation. Because of its rough correspondence to a parse tree, it is easily built in a parser (see Section 4.4.2).

ASTs have been used in many practical compiler systems. Source-to-source systems, including programming environments and automatic parallelization tools, generally rely on an AST from which source code can easily be regenerated. (This process is often called *prettyprinting*; it reproduces the source text during an in order tree walk on the AST.) The S-expressions found in Lisp and Scheme implementations are, essentially, ASTs.

Even when the AST is used as a near source-level representation, the specific representations chosen and the abstractions used can be an issue. The AST in the $\mathcal{R}^n$ Programming Environment used the subtree on the left below to represent a complex constant in FORTRAN, written (c_1, c_2). This choice worked well for the syntax-directed editor, in which the programmer was able to change c_1 and c_2 independently; the pair node corresponded to the parentheses and the comma.

AST for Editing   AST for Compiling

However, this abstraction proved problematic for the compiler. Every part of the compiler that dealt with constants needed to include special-case code to handle complex constants. The other constants all had a single constant node that contained a pointer to a textual string recorded in a table. The compiler might have been better served by using that representation for the complex constant, as shown on the right. It would have simplified the compiler by eliminating much of the special-case code.

Abstract syntax trees have found widespread use in systems that must represent source-level information. These include language-based editors, source-to-source translators, and interpreters. Many compilers use ASTs as an IR; the level of abstraction varies widely. If the compiler targets another programming language as its output, the AST typically has relatively high-level abstractions. In compilers that generate assembly code for some target machine, the final version of the AST is usually at or below the abstraction level of the machine's instruction set.

STORAGE EFFICIENCY AND GRAPHICAL REPRESENTATIONS

Many practical systems have used abstract syntax trees to represent the source text being translated. A common problem encountered in these systems is the size of the AST relative to the input text. Large data structures can limit the size of programs that the tools can handle.

The AST nodes in the $\mathcal{R}^n$ Programming Environment were large enough that they posed a problem for the limited memory systems of 1980s workstations. The cost of disk I/O for the trees slowed down all the $\mathcal{R}^n$ tools.

No single problem leads to this explosion in AST size. $\mathcal{R}^n$ had only one kind of node, so that structure included all the fields needed by any node. This simplified allocation but increased the node size. (Roughly half the nodes were leaves, which need no pointers to children.) In other systems, the nodes grow through the addition of myriad minor fields used by one pass or another in the compiler. Sometimes, the node size increases over time, as new features and passes are added.

Careful attention to the form and content of the AST can shrink its size. In $\mathcal{R}^n$, we built programs to analyze the contents of the AST and how the AST was used. We combined some fields and eliminated others. (In some cases, it was less expensive to recompute information than to write it and read it.) In a few cases, we used hash linking to record unusual facts—using one bit in the field that stores each node's type to indicate the presence of additional information stored in a hash table. (This avoided allocating fields that were rarely used.) To record the AST on disk, we converted it to a linear representation with a preorder tree walk; this eliminated the need to record any internal pointers.

In $\mathcal{R}^n$, the combination of all these things reduced the size of ASTs in memory by roughly 75 percent. On disk, after the pointers were removed, the files were about half the size of their memory representation. These changes let $\mathcal{R}^n$ handle larger programs and made the tools more responsive.

Directed Acyclic Graphs

While the AST is more concise than a syntax tree, it faithfully retains the structure of the original source code. For example, the AST for x × 2 + x × 2 × y contains two distinct copies of the expression x × 2. A *directed acyclic graph*

(DAG) is a contraction of the AST that avoids this duplication. In a DAG, nodes can have multiple parents, and identical subtrees are reused. This makes the DAG more compact than the corresponding AST.

For expressions without assignment, textually identical expressions must produce identical values. The DAG for x × 2 + x × 2 + x × y reflects this fact by using only one copy of x × 2, as follows.

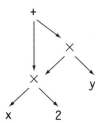

The DAG encodes into its shape an explicit hint about the expression. If the value of x does not change between the uses of x × 2, then the compiler can generate code that evaluates the subtree once and uses the result twice. This can lead to better code for the whole expression. The compiler must, however, prove to itself that x's value does not change. If the expression contains neither assignment nor calls to other procedures, this proof is easy. Since either an assignment or a procedure call can change the value associated with a name, the DAG construction must invalidate subtrees as the values of their operands change. DAG construction is described in Section 8.3.1

DAGs are used in real systems for two reasons. Some systems benefit from the smaller memory footprint of a DAG. In particular, memory constraints often limit the size of programs that a compiler can handle. DAGs can help reduce this limitation. Other systems use a DAG to expose potential redundancies. Here, the benefit lies in better compiled code. These systems tend to use the DAG as a derivative IR—building it, transforming the definitive IR, and discarding it.

Level of Abstraction

All of our examples of trees have shown ones that closely resemble the source code. Trees can also be used to represent low-level detail in the code. Tree-based techniques for optimization and code generation, in fact, may require such detail. As an example, consider the statement w ← x - 2 × y. A source-level AST captures the statement in a concise form, as follows.

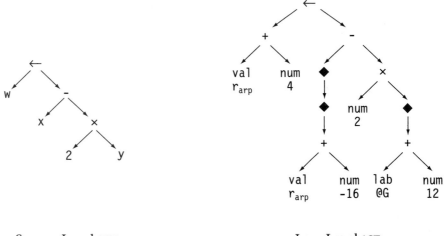

Source-Level AST   Low-Level AST

However, the source-level tree lacks much of the detail needed to translate the statement into assembly code. A low-level tree, shown on the right, can make that detail explicit. This tree introduces four new node types. A val node represents a value already in a register. A num node represents a known constant. A lab node represents an assembly-level label, typically a relocatable symbol. Finally, ◆ is an operator that dereferences a value; it treats the value as a memory address and returns the contents of the memory at that address.

The low-level tree reveals the address calculations for the three variables. w is stored at offset 4 from the pointer in r_{arp}, which holds the pointer to the data area for the current procedure. The double dereference of y shows that it is a call-by-reference formal parameter accessed through a pointer stored 16 bytes before r_{arp}. Finally, y is stored at offset 12 after the label @G.

Notice that w evaluates to an address because it is on the left-hand side of the assignment. In contrast, both x and y evaluate to values because of the ◆ operator.

5.3.2 Graphs

While trees provide a natural representation for the grammatical structure of the source code discovered by parsing, their rigid structure makes them less useful for representing other properties of programs. To model these aspects of program behavior, compilers often use more general graphs as IRs. The DAG introduced in the previous section is one example of a graphical IR.

Control-Flow Graph

A *control-flow graph* (CFG) models flow of control in the program. A CFG is a directed graph, $G = (N, E)$. Each node $n \in N$ corresponds to a *basic block*. A basic block is a sequence of operations that always execute together. Control always enters a basic block at its first operation and exits at its last operation. Each edge $e = (n_i, n_j) \in E$ corresponds to a possible transfer of control from block n_i to block n_j.

To simplify the discussion of program analysis in Chapters 8 and 9, we assume that each CFG has a unique entry node, n_0, and a unique exit node, n_f. In the CFG for a procedure, n_0 corresponds to the procedure's entry point. If a procedure has multiple entries, the compiler can insert a unique n_0 and add edges from n_0 to each actual entry point. Similarly, n_f corresponds to the procedure's exit. Multiple exits are more common than multiple entries, but the compiler can easily add a unique n_f and connect each of the actual exits to it.

The CFG provides a graphical representation of the possible run-time control-flow paths. Figure 5.2 shows two examples: a loop and a simple conditional. This differs from the syntax-oriented IRs, such as an AST, in which the edges show grammatical structure. Thus, the CFG for the *while* loop contains a cycle where its AST would be acyclic. The CFG for the conditional is acyclic, as expected. It shows that control always flows from $stmt_1$ and $stmt_2$ to $stmt_3$. In an AST, that connection is implicit, rather than explicit.

Compilers typically use a CFG in conjunction with another IR. The CFG represents the relationships among blocks, while the operations inside a block are represented with another IR, such as an expression-level AST, a DAG, or linear three-address code. The combination might be considered a hybrid IR.

One tradeoff in CFG implementation is deciding how much code each block contains. The two most common granularities are single-statement blocks and basic blocks. Single-statement blocks are sometimes used to simplify algorithms for analysis and optimization.

Using single-statement blocks produces a larger CFG than using a basic block. Many optimization and code-generation techniques annotate the nodes and edges in the CFG. Since the single-statement CFG has more nodes and edges, it can require more space for those annotations and more time and effort to create them and to copy them from block to block.

A CFG that uses basic blocks has fewer nodes and edges than the single-statement CFG. In this model, the compiler must find the beginning and end

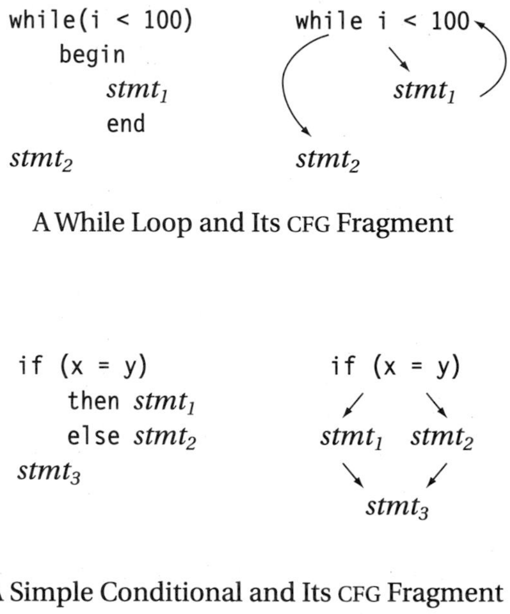

```
while(i < 100)                 while i < 100
      begin
           stmt₁                           stmt₁
      end
stmt₂                          stmt₂
```

A While Loop and Its CFG Fragment

```
if (x = y)                     if (x = y)
      then stmt₁
      else stmt₂               stmt₁    stmt₂
stmt₃
                                    stmt₃
```

A Simple Conditional and Its CFG Fragment

FIGURE 5.2   Control-Flow Graph Fragments

of each block, an issue that is trivial with single statement blocks.[1] This model reduces the space required to hold annotations. However, the algorithms for computing and using the annotations must deal with the aggregation implicit in larger blocks. Some interpretation may be required to determine which facts hold true at a specific point inside a block.

Many different activities in a compiler rely on a control-flow graph, either explicitly or implicitly. Analysis to support optimization generally begins with control-flow analysis and the construction of a CFG (Chapter 9). Instruction scheduling requires a CFG to understand how the scheduled code for individual blocks flows together (Chapter 12). Global register allocation relies on a CFG to understand how often each operation might execute and where to place operations that move values between registers and memory (Chapter 13).

---

1. Generally, basic blocks begin with labelled statements, since they can be reached along multiple paths. The first operation in a procedure, labelled or not, also begins a block. Blocks end with branches or jumps. Predicated operations end blocks, too, since they create, in effect, two paths through the code.

Dependence Graph

Compilers use graphs to encode the flow of values from the point where a value is created, a *definition point*, to points where it is used, *use points*. A *data-dependence graph* directly encodes this relationship.

Nodes in a data-dependence graph represent operations. Most operations both use values and define new values. An edge in a data-dependence graph connects two nodes, one of which uses the result defined by the other. We draw dependence graphs with the edges running from definition to use.

To make this concrete, Figure 5.3 reproduces the example from Figure 1.3 and shows its data-dependence graph. The graph has a node for each statement in the block. Each edge shows the flow of a single value. For example, the edge from 3 to 7 reflects the definition of r_x in statement 3 and its subsequent use in statement 7. Uses of r_{arp} refer to its implicit definition at the start of the procedure; we have shown them in bold.

The edges in the graph represent real constraints on the sequencing of operations—a value cannot be used until it has been defined. However, the dependence graph does not fully capture the program's control flow. For example, the graph requires that 1 and 2 precede 6. Nothing, however, requires that 1 or 2 precedes 3. Many execution sequences preserve the dependences shown in the code, including $\langle 1,2,3,4,5,6,7,8,9,10 \rangle$ and $\langle 2,1,6,3,7,4,8,5,9,10 \rangle$. The freedom in this partial order is precisely what an "out-of-order" processor exploits.

At a higher level, consider the code fragment shown in Figure 5.4. References to a[i] are shown deriving their values from a node representing prior

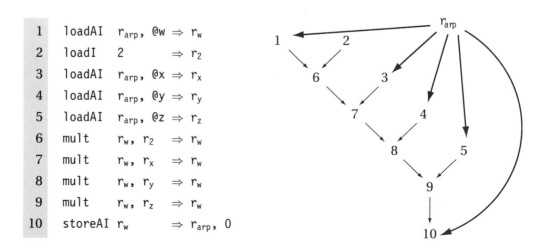

1	loadAI	r_{arp}, @w	$\Rightarrow$	r_w
2	loadI	2	$\Rightarrow$	r_2
3	loadAI	r_{arp}, @x	$\Rightarrow$	r_x
4	loadAI	r_{arp}, @y	$\Rightarrow$	r_y
5	loadAI	r_{arp}, @z	$\Rightarrow$	r_z
6	mult	r_w, r_2	$\Rightarrow$	r_w
7	mult	r_w, r_x	$\Rightarrow$	r_w
8	mult	r_w, r_y	$\Rightarrow$	r_w
9	mult	r_w, r_z	$\Rightarrow$	r_w
10	storeAI	r_w	$\Rightarrow$	r_{arp}, 0

FIGURE 5.3 An ILOC Basic Block and Its Dependence Graph

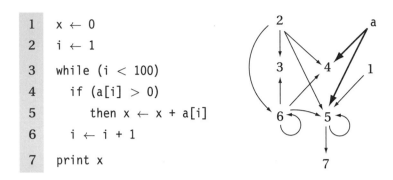

```
1    x ← 0

2    i ← 1

3    while (i < 100)

4      if (a[i] > 0)

5        then x ← x + a[i]

6      i ← i + 1

7    print x
```

FIGURE 5.4   Interaction between Control Flow and the Dependence Graph

definitions of a. This connects all uses of a together through a single node. Without sophisticated analysis of the subscript expressions, the compiler cannot differentiate between references to individual array elements.

This dependence graph is more complex than the previous example. Nodes 5 and 6 both depend on themselves; they use values that they may have defined in a previous iteration. Node 6, for example, can take the value of i from either 2 (in the initial iteration) or from itself (in any subsequent iteration). Nodes 4 and 5 also have two distinct sources for the value of i: nodes 2 and 6.

Data-dependence graphs are often used as a derivative IR—constructed from the definitive IR for a specific task, used, and then discarded. They play a central role in instruction scheduling (Chapter 12). They find application in a variety of optimizations, particularly transformations that reorder loops to expose parallelism and to improve memory behavior; these typically require sophisticated analysis of array subscripts to determine more precisely the patterns of access to arrays. In more sophisticated applications of the data-dependence graph, the compiler may perform extensive analysis of array subscript values to determine when references to the same array can overlap.

5.4 LINEAR IRS

The alternative to a graphical IR is a linear IR. An assembly-language program is a form of linear code. It consists of a sequence of instructions that execute in their order of appearance (or in an order consistent with that order).

Instructions may contain more than one operation; if so, those operations execute in parallel. The linear IRs used in compilers resemble the assembly code for an abstract machine.

The logic behind using a linear form is simple. The source code that serves as input to the compiler is a linear form, as is the target-machine code that it emits. Several early compilers used linear IRs; this was a natural notation for their authors, since they had previously programmed in assembly code.

Linear IRs impose a clear and useful ordering on the sequence of operations. For example, in Figure 5.3, contrast the ILOC code with the data-dependence graph. The ILOC code has an implicit order; the dependence graph imposes a partial ordering that allows many different execution orders.

If a linear IR is used as the definitive representation in a compiler, it must include a mechanism to encode transfers of control among points in the program. Control flow in a linear IR usually models the implementation of control flow on the target machine. Thus, linear codes usually include conditional branches and jumps. Control flow demarcates the basic blocks in a linear IR; blocks end at branches, jumps, or just before labelled operations.

In the ILOC used throughout this book, we include a branch or jump at the end of every block. In ILOC, the branch operations specify a label for the taken path and the not-taken path. This eliminates any fall-through paths at the end of a block. Together, these stipulations make it easier to find basic blocks and to reorder them.

Many kinds of linear IRs have been used in compilers. Some have fallen into disuse because the architectures that they model are no longer used. One-address codes modelled the behavior of accumulator machines. These codes exposed the computer's limited name space to the compiler so that it could tailor the code for those constraints. Similarly, two-address code modelled machines with destructive operations in which one argument served as both an operand and the destination for the operation's result. Two-address codes gave the compiler an IR in which the choice between destroying one operand or the other was explicit. As computers moved away from these instruction formats, compilers moved away from the corresponding IRs.

This section describes two linear IRs that are used in modern compilers: stack-machine code and three-address code. Stack-machine code offers a compact, storage-efficient representation. In applications in which IR size matters, such as a Java applet transmitted over a network before execution, stack-machine code makes sense. Three-address code models the instruction format of a modern RISC machine; it has distinct names for two operands and a result. You are already familiar with one three-address code: the ILOC used in this book.

push 2	$t_1 \leftarrow 2$
push y	$t_2 \leftarrow y$
multiply	$t_3 \leftarrow t_1 \times t_2$
push x	$t_4 \leftarrow x$
subtract	$t_5 \leftarrow t_4 - t_1$
Stack-Machine Code	Three-Address Code

FIGURE 5.5   Linear Representations of x - 2 × y

5.4.1   Stack-Machine Code

Stack-machine code, sometimes called one-address code, assumes the presence of an operand stack. Most operations take their operands from the stack and push their results back onto the stack. For example, an integer subtract operation would remove the top two elements from the stack and push their difference onto the stack. The stack discipline creates a need for some new operations. Stack IRs usually include a swap operation that interchanges the top two elements of the stack. Several stack-based computers have been built; this IR seems to have appeared in response to the demands of compiling for these machines. The left column of Figure 5.5 shows the expression x - 2 × y in one-address code.

Stack-machine code is compact. The stack creates an implicit name space and eliminates many names from the IR. This shrinks the size of a program in IR form. Using the stack, however, means that all results and arguments are transitory, unless the code explicitly moves them to memory.

Stack-machine code is simple to generate and to execute. Languages such as Smalltalk 80 and Java have used bytecodes, which are abstract stack-machine code to encode programs. The bytecodes either run on an interpreter implemented for the target machine or are translated into target-machine code just prior to execution. This creates a system with a compact form of the program for distribution and a reasonably simple scheme for porting the language to a new target machine (implementing the interpreter).

5.4.2   Three-Address Code

In three-address code, most operations have the form x ← y op z, with an operator (op), two operands (y and z) and one result (x). Some operators, such as an immediate load and a jump, will need fewer arguments. Sometimes, an operation with more than three addresses is needed. The rightmost column of Figure 5.5 shows x − 2 × y in a three-address code.

Three-address code is attractive for several reasons. First, the absence of destructive operators gives the compiler freedom to reuse names and values. Translating a program into three-address code introduces a new set of compiler-generated names—names that hold the results of the various operations. A carefully chosen name space can reveal new opportunities to improve the code. Second, three-address code is reasonably compact. Most operations consist of four items: an operation and three names. Both the operation and the names are drawn from limited sets. Operations typically require 1 or 2 bytes. Names are typically represented by integers or table indices; in either case, 4 bytes is usually enough. Finally, since many modern processors implement three-address operations, a three-address code models their properties well.

Within three-address codes, the set of specific operators represented and their level of abstraction can vary widely. Often, a three-address IR will contain mostly low-level operations, such as jumps, branches, and simple memory operations, alongside more complex operations like mvcl, max, or min. Representing these complex operations directly makes them easier to analyze and optimize.

For example, mvcl (move characters long) takes a source address, a destination address, and a character count. It copies the specified number of characters from memory beginning at the source address to memory beginning at the destination address. Some machines, like the IBM 370, implement this functionality in a single instruction (mvcl is a 370 opcode). On machines that do not implement the operation in hardware, it may require many operations to perform such a copy.

Adding mvcl to the three-address code lets the compiler use a compact representation for this complex operation. It allows the compiler to analyze, optimize, and move the operation without concern for its internal workings. If the hardware supports an mvcl-like operation, then code generation will map the IR construct directly to the hardware operation. If the hardware does not, then the compiler can translate mvcl into a sequence of lower-level IR operations before final optimization and code generation.

5.4.3 Representing Linear Codes

Many data structures have been used to implement linear IRs. The choices that a compiler writer makes affect the costs of various operations on IR code. Since a compiler spends most of its time manipulating the IR form of the code, these

IRS IN ACTUAL USE

In practice, compilers use a variety of IRs. IBM's FORTRAN H compilers used quadruples and a control-flow graph to represent the code for optimization. Since the compiler was written in FORTRAN, the data structure that held the three-address code was an array.

The portable C compiler, PCC, has its parser emit assembly code for the control structures and build low-level trees for expressions. It does a careful job of generating code for the expression trees, based on the assumption that most time is spent in expression evaluation.

GCC has long relied on a very low-level IR, called register transfer language (RTL). RTL is well suited to detailed optimization of address calculations and scalar arithmetic operations. It obscures some of the abstractions, such as array references, needed for high-level memory optimizations. To address these issues, the G++ front-end for GCC uses an AST for some C++ specific optimizations before it generates the RTL form for more general optimization and code generation.

The IBM PL.8 compiler used a low-level, linear IR that was slightly below the level of abstraction in the IBM 801 processor's instruction set. This exposed calculations that might later be folded into an address-mode computation. This compiler had several front ends and back ends; all used the same IR. The HP PA-RISC compilers have a similar structure.

The Open64 compiler, an open-source compiler for the IA-64 architecture, uses a family of five related IRs, called WHIRL. The initial translation in the parser produces a near-source-level WHIRL. Subsequent phases of the compiler introduce more detail to the WHIRL program, lowering the level of abstraction toward the actual machine code. This lets the compiler use a source-level AST for dependence-based transformations on the source text and a low-level IR for the late stages of optimization and code generation.

costs deserve some attention. While this discussion focuses on three-address codes, most of the points apply equally to stack-machine code (or any other linear form).

Three-address codes are often implemented as a set of quadruples. Each quadruple is represented with four fields: an operator, two operands (or sources), and a destination. To form blocks, the compiler needs a mechanism to connect individual quadruples. Compilers implement quadruples in a variety of ways.

Figure 5.6 shows three different schemes for implementing the three-address code from Figure 5.5. The simplest scheme, shown on the left, uses a short array to represent each basic block. Often, the compiler writer places the array inside a node in the CFG. (This may be the most common form of hybrid IR.) The scheme shown in the center uses an array of pointers to group quadruples into a block; the pointer array can be contained in a CFG node. The final scheme, on the right, links the quadruples together to form a list. It requires less storage in the CFG node, at the cost of restricting accesses to sequential traversals.

Consider the costs incurred in rearranging the code in this block. The first operation loads a constant into a register; on most machines this translates directly into an immediate load operation. The second and fourth operations load values from memory, which on most machines might incur a multicycle delay unless the values are already in the primary cache. To hide some of the delay, the instruction scheduler might move the loads of y and x in front of the immediate load of 2.

In the simple array scheme, moving the load of y ahead of the immediate load requires saving the four fields of the first operation, copying the corresponding fields from the second slot into the first slot, and overwriting the fields in the second slot with the saved values for the immediate load. The array of pointers requires the same three-step approach, except that only the pointer values must be changed. Thus, the compiler saves the pointer to the immediate load, copies the pointer to the load of y into the first slot in the array, and overwrites the second slot in the array with the saved pointer to the immediate load. For the linked list, the operations are similar, except that the code must save enough pointer state to let it traverse the list.

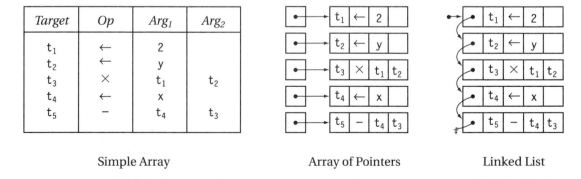

Target	Op	Arg_1	Arg_2
t_1	←	2	
t_2	←	y	
t_3	×	t_1	t_2
t_4	←	x	
t_5	−	t_4	t_3

Simple Array   Array of Pointers   Linked List

FIGURE 5.6   Implementations of Three-Address Code

Now, consider what happens in the front end when it generates the initial round of IR. With the simple array form and the array of pointers, the compiler must select a size for the array—in effect, the number of quadruples that it expects in a block. As it generates the quadruples, it fills in the array. If the array is too large, it wastes space. If it is too small, the compiler must reallocate it to obtain a larger array and copy the contents of the "too small" array into the new, larger array. The linked list, however, avoids these problems. Expanding the list just requires allocating a new quadruple and setting the appropriate pointer in the list.

In a multipass compiler, it may make sense to use distinct implementations to represent the IR at different points in the compilation process. In the front end, where the focus is on generating the IR, a linked list might both simplify the implementation and reduce the overall cost. In an instruction scheduler, with its focus on rearranging the operations, either of the array implementations might make more sense.

Notice that some information is missing from Figure 5.6. For example, no labels are shown, because labels are a property of the block rather than any individual quadruple. Storing a list of labels with the block saves space in each quadruple; it also makes explicit the property that labels occur only on the first operation in a basic block. With labels attached to a block, the compiler can ignore them when reordering operations inside the block, avoiding one more complication.

5.5 STATIC SINGLE-ASSIGNMENT FORM

The *static single-assignment form* (SSA) of a program adds information about both control flow and data flow to the program text. SSA form encodes information about definitions and uses in the name space of the code. Each distinct name is defined by a single operation in the code—hence the name, static single assignment. To reconcile this single-assignment discipline with the effects of control flow, SSA form inserts special operations, called ϕ-functions, at points where control-flow paths meet.

A program is in SSA form when it meets two constraints: (1) each definition has a distinct name; and (2) each use refers to a single definition. To transform an IR program to SSA form, the compiler inserts ϕ-functions at points where different control-flow paths merge and it renames variables to make the single-assignment property hold.

To clarify the impact of these rules, consider the small loop shown on the left side of Figure 5.7. The right column shows the same code in SSA form. Variable names include subscripts to create a distinct name for each definition.

```
                                        x₀ ← ···
                                        y₀ ← ···
                                        if (x₀ ≥ 100) goto next
    x ← ···                    loop:   x₁ ← φ(x₀,x₂)
    y ← ···                            y₁ ← φ(y₀,y₂)
    while(x < 100)                     x₂ ← x₁ + 1
        x ← x + 1                      y₂ ← y₁ + x₂
        y ← y + x                      if (x₂ < 100) goto loop
                              next:x₃ ← φ(x₀,x₂)
                                        y₃ ← φ(y₀,y₂)

        Original Code                      Its SSA Form
```

FIGURE 5.7   A Small Loop in SSA Form

ϕ-functions have been inserted at points where multiple distinct values can reach the start of a block. Finally, the while construct has been rewritten with two distinct tests, to reflect the fact that the initial test refers to x_0 while the end-of-loop test refers to x_2.

A ϕ-function behaves in an unusual way. It defines its target SSA name with the value of its argument that corresponds to the edge along which control entered the block. Thus, when control flows into the loop from above, the ϕ-functions at the top of the loop body copy the values of x_0 and y_0 into x_1 and y_1, respectively. When control flows into the loop from the test at the loop's bottom, the ϕ-functions select their other arguments, x_2 and y_2.

On entry to a basic block, all of its ϕ-functions execute concurrently, before any other statement. Thus, they all read the value of the appropriate argument, then they all define their target SSA names. Defining their behavior in this way allows the algorithms that manipulate SSA form to ignore the ordering of ϕ-functions at the top of a block—an important simplification. It can complicate the process of translating SSA form back into executable code, as we shall see in Section 9.3.4.

SSA form was designed for use in code optimization. The placement of ϕ-functions in SSA form provides the compiler with information about the flow of values; it can use this information to improve the quality of the code that it generates. The name space eliminates any issues related to the lifetime of a value. Since each value is defined in exactly one instruction, it is available along any path that proceeds from that instruction. These two properties simplify and improve many optimization techniques.

The example exposes some oddities of SSA form that bear explanation. Consider the ϕ-function that defines x_1. Its first argument, x_0, is defined in the

BUILDING SSA

Static single-assignment form is the only IR we describe that does not have an obvious construction algorithm. Section 9.3 presents the algorithm in detail. However, a sketch of the construction process will clarify some of the issues. Assume that the input program is already in ILOC form. To convert it to an equivalent linear form of SSA, the compiler must first insert ϕ-functions and then rename the ILOC virtual registers.

The simplest way to insert ϕ-functions adds one for each ILOC virtual register at the start of each basic block that has more than one predecessor in the control-flow graph. This inserts many unneeded ϕ-functions; most of the complexity in the full algorithm is aimed at reducing the number of extraneous ones.

To rename the ILOC virtual registers, the compiler can process the blocks, in a depth-first order. For each virtual register, it keeps a counter. When the compiler encounters a definition of r_i, it increments the counter for r_i, say to k, and rewrites the definition with the name r_{i_k}. As the compiler traverses the block, it rewrites each use of r_i to reflect r_i's current counter. That is, it rewrites r_i with r_{i_k} until it encounters another definition of r_i. (That definition bumps the counter to k + 1.) At the end of a block, it looks down each control-flow edge and rewrites the appropriate ϕ-function parameter for r_i in each block that has multiple predecessors.

After renaming, the code conforms to the two rules of SSA form. Each definition creates a unique name. Each use refers to a single definition. Several better SSA construction algorithms exist; they insert fewer ϕ-functions than this simple approach.

block that precedes the loop. Its second argument, x_2, is defined later in the block containing the ϕ-function. Thus, when the ϕ first executes, one of its arguments has never been defined. In many programming-language contexts, this would cause problems. Since the ϕ-function reads only one argument, and that argument corresponds to the most recently taken edge in the CFG, it can never read the undefined variable.

To use SSA form in a three-address IR, the compiler writer must include a mechanism for representing arbitrarily large operations. Consider the block at the end of a case statement.

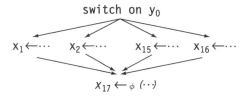

The ϕ-function for x_{17} must have an argument for each case. A ϕ-operation has one argument for each entering control-flow path; thus, it does not fit into the fixed-arity, three-address scheme.

In a simple array representation for three-address code, the compiler writer must either use multiple slots for the ϕ-operation or use a side data structure to hold the ϕ-operations' arguments. In the other two schemes shown in Figure 5.6, the compiler can insert tuples of varying size. For example, the tuples for load and load immediate might have space for just two names, while the tuple for a ϕ-operation might allow for an arbitrary number of names.

5.6   ## MAPPING VALUES TO NAMES

The choice of a specific IR and a level of abstraction helps determine what operations the compiler can manipulate and optimize. For example, a source-level AST makes it easy to find all the references to an array x. At the same time, it hides the details of the address calculations required to access an element of x. In contrast, a low-level, linear IR such as ILOC exposes the details of the address calculation, at the cost of obscuring the fact that a specific reference relates to x. These effects are well known.

The choice of a discipline for assigning internal names to the values that are computed during execution has similar effects. Careful attention to the way that names are generated, manipulated, and used can expose valuable opportunities for optimization. Ignoring this issue can obscure these same opportunities. To make this discussion concrete, consider the short block shown in Figure 5.8(a).

Each operand of an expression is a value, as is the result of evaluating the expression. As written, the block has the name space {a, b, c, d}. This choice of names maps multiple values to a single name. At the start of the block, we can presume that each of b, c, and d has been defined. The use of b in the first statement refers to a different value than the use of b in the third statement—unless c = d. The reuse of the name b in statements two and three conveys no information to the compiler; in fact, it might mislead a casual observer into thinking that this code sets the values of a and c to the same value.

Looking at the second and fourth statements, however, the block clearly sets b and d to the same value. As with statements one and three, the expressions on the right-hand side of the assignment are textually identical. In statements two and four, they use the same values. In statements one and three, they do not.

The IR form of the program often contains more detail than the source version. This detail is generated by the translation from a parsed input program into the IR. Our four-line example might be translated in any number of ways. Two are shown in Figure 5.8(b) and (c). Figure 5.8(b) uses names that follow the names in the source, while (c) assigns a new name to each value in the computation.

The ways in which the compiler generates names can determine what opportunities for optimization it can find. Figure 5.8(b) uses fewer registers. It preserves the confusion over which computations must produce the same result. Figure 5.8(c) uses more registers, but it has the property that textually identical expressions produce the same result. With this naming discipline, the code makes it obvious that a and c receive different values, while b and d receive the same value.

(a) Source Code	(b) Using Source Names	(c) Using Value Names
	$t_1 \leftarrow b$	$t_1 \leftarrow b$
	$t_2 \leftarrow c$	$t_2 \leftarrow c$
	$t_3 \leftarrow t_1 + t_2$	$t_3 \leftarrow t_1 + t_2$
	$a \leftarrow t_3$	$a \leftarrow t_3$
	$t_4 \leftarrow d$	$t_4 \leftarrow d$
	$t_1 \leftarrow t_3 - t_4$	$t_5 \leftarrow t_3 - t_4$
	$b \leftarrow t_1$	$b \leftarrow t_5$
$a \leftarrow b + c$	$t_2 \leftarrow t_1 + t_2$	$t_6 \leftarrow t_5 + t_2$
$b \leftarrow a - d$	$c \leftarrow t_2$	$c \leftarrow t_6$
$c \leftarrow b + c$	$t_4 \leftarrow t_3 - t_4$	$t_5 \leftarrow t_3 - t_4$
$d \leftarrow a - d$	$d \leftarrow t_4$	$d \leftarrow t_5$

FIGURE 5.8 Naming Leads to Different Translations

5.6.1 Naming Temporary Values

In translating source code into an IR, a compiler must invent names for many of the intermediate results in the computation. The choice of name spaces has a surprisingly strong impact on the behavior of the compiler. The strategy for mapping names to values determines, to a large extent, which computations can be analyzed and optimized.

Consider again our earlier example of an array reference, A[i,j]. These two IR fragments represent the same computation at very different levels of abstraction.

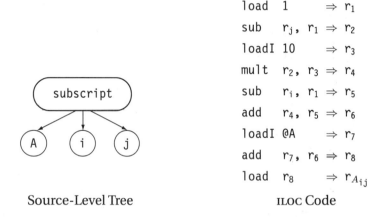

	ILOC Code
load	$1 \Rightarrow r_1$
sub	$r_j, r_1 \Rightarrow r_2$
loadI	$10 \Rightarrow r_3$
mult	$r_2, r_3 \Rightarrow r_4$
sub	$r_i, r_1 \Rightarrow r_5$
add	$r_4, r_5 \Rightarrow r_6$
loadI	$@A \Rightarrow r_7$
add	$r_7, r_6 \Rightarrow r_8$
load	$r_8 \Rightarrow r_{A_{ij}}$

Source-Level Tree   ILOC Code

The low-level IR exposes more details to the compiler. These details can be inferred from the AST, and code can be generated. In a straightforward translation from the AST, each reference to A[i,j] will produce the same code in the executable, independent of context.

In the low-level IR, each intermediate result has its own name. Using distinct names exposes those results to analysis and transformation. In practice, most of the improvement that compilers can achieve in optimization arises from capitalizing on context. To make that improvement possible, the IR must expose the context. Naming can hide context, as when it reuses one name for many distinct values. It can also expose context, as when it creates a correspondence between names and values. This issue is not specifically a property of linear codes; the compiler could use a lower-level AST that exposed the entire address computation.

Naming is a critical part of SSA form. SSA form imposes a strict discipline that generates a name for every value computed by the code, be it a program variable or a transitory intermediate value. This uniform treatment exposes many details to the scrutiny of analysis and improvement. It encodes

THE IMPACT OF NAMING

In the late 1980s, we built an optimizing compiler for FORTRAN. We tried several different naming schemes in the front end. The first version generated a new temporary register for each computation by bumping a next register counter. This produced large name spaces, for example, 985 names for Forsythe, Malcolm, and Moler's implementation of the singular value decomposition (SVD), which was 210 lines of FORTRAN. The name space seemed large for the program size. It caused speed and space problems in the register allocator, where the size of the name space governs the size of many data structures. (Today, we have better data structures and faster machines with more memory.)

The second version used a simple allocate/free protocol to conserve names. The front end allocated temporaries on demand and freed them when the immediate uses were finished. This produced smaller name spaces; for example, SVD used roughly 60 names. This sped up allocation. For example, it reduced the time to solve one critical data-flow problem, finding live variables, by 60 percent for SVD.

Unfortunately, associating multiple expressions with a single temporary name obscured the flow of data and degraded the quality of optimization. The decline in code quality overshadowed any compile-time benefits.

Further experimentation led to a short set of rules that yielded strong optimization while mitigating growth in the name space.

1. Each textual expression received a unique name, determined by entering the operator and operands into a hash table. This ensured that each occurrence of an expression, for example, $r_{17} + r_{21}$, targets the same register.

2. In $\langle op \rangle$ r_i, r_j $\Rightarrow$ r_k, k is chosen so that $i,j < k$.

3. Register copy operations (i2i r_i $\Rightarrow$ r_j in ILOC) are allowed to have $i > j$ when j corresponds to a scalar program variable. The virtual register corresponding to such a variable is set only by move operations. Expressions evaluate into their "natural" register and then are moved to a variable.

(Continued)

THE IMPACT OF NAMING, *Continued*

4. Whenever a store to memory occurs (store r_i ⇒ r_j in ILOC), it is immediately followed by a copy from r_1 into the variable's virtual register. (Rule 1 implies that loads from that location always target the same register. This rule ensures that a variable's register is updated whenever its memory location is updated.)

This name-space scheme used about 90 names for SVD, but exposed all the optimizations found with the first name-space scheme. The compiler used these rules until we adopted SSA form, which has its own naming discipline.

information about where each value was generated. It provides a "permanent" name for the value, even if the corresponding program variable gets redefined. Using the SSA name space can improve the results of analysis and optimization.

5.6.2 Memory Models

Just as the mechanism for naming temporary values affects the information that can be represented in an IR version of a program, so, too, does the compiler's method of choosing storage locations for each value. The compiler must determine, for each value computed in the code, where that value will reside. For the code to execute, the compiler must assign a specific location, such as register r_{13} or 16 bytes from the label L0089. Before the final stages of code generation, however, the compiler may use symbolic addresses that encode a level in the memory hierarchy, for example, registers or memory, but not a specific location within that level.

Consider the ILOC examples used throughout this book. A symbolic memory address is denoted by prefixing it with the character @. Thus, @x is the offset of x from the start of the storage area containing it. Since r_{arp} holds the activation record pointer, an operation that uses @x and r_{arp} to compute an address depends, implicitly, on the decision to store the variable x in the memory reserved for the current procedure's activation record.

In general, compilers work from one of two memory models.

1. *Register-to-Register Model*   Under this model, the compiler keeps values in registers aggressively, ignoring any limitations imposed by the size of

the machine's physical register set. Any value that can legally be kept in a register for most of its lifetime is kept in a register. Values are stored to memory only when the semantics of the program require it—for example, at a procedure call, any local variable whose address is passed as a parameter to the called procedure must be stored back to memory. A value that cannot be kept in a register for most of its lifetime is stored in memory. The compiler generates code to store its value each time it is computed and to load its value at each use.

2. *Memory-to-Memory Model*   Under this model, the compiler assumes that all values are kept in memory locations. Values move from memory to a register just before they are used. Values move from a register to memory just after they are defined. The number of registers named in the IR version of the code can be small compared to the register-to-register model. In this model, the designer may find it worthwhile to include memory-to-memory operations, such as a memory-to-memory add, in the IR.

The choice of memory model is mostly orthogonal to the choice of IR. The compiler writer can build a memory-to-memory AST or a memory-to-memory version of ILOC just as easily as register-to-register versions of either of these IRs. (Stack-machine code and code for an accumulator machine might be exceptions; they contain their own unique memory models.)

The choice of memory model has an impact on the rest of the compiler. With a register-to-register model, the compiler typically uses more registers than the target machine provides. Thus, the register allocator must map the set of virtual registers used in the IR program onto the physical registers provided by the target machine. This often requires insertion of extra load, store, and copy operations, making the code slower and larger. With a memory-to-memory model, however, the IR version of the code typically uses fewer registers than a modern processor provides. Here, the register allocator looks for memory-based values that it can hold in registers for longer periods of time. In this model, the allocator makes the code faster and smaller by removing loads and stores.

Compilers for RISC machines tend to use the register-to-register model for two reasons. First, the register-to-register model more closely reflects the programming models of RISC architectures. RISC machines do not have a full complement of memory-to-memory operations; instead, they implicitly assume that values can be kept in registers. Second, the register-to-register model allows the compiler to encode directly in the IR some of the subtle facts that it derives. The fact that a value is kept in a register means that the compiler,

THE HIERARCHY OF MEMORY OPERATIONS IN ILOC 9X

The ILOC used in this book is abstracted from an IR named ILOC 9X that was used in a research compiler project at Rice University. ILOC 9X includes a hierarchy of memory operations that the compiler uses to encode knowledge about values. At the bottom of the hierarchy, the compiler has little or no knowledge about the value; at the top of the hierarchy, it knows the actual value. These operations are as follows:

Operation	Meaning
immediate load	loads a known constant value into a register.
nonvarying load	loads a value that does not change during execution. The compiler does not know the value, but can prove that it is not defined by a program operation.
scalar load & store	operate on a scalar value, not an array element, a structure element, or a pointer-based value.
general load & store	operate on a value that may be an array element, a structure element, or a pointer-based value. This is the general-case operation.

By using this hierarchy, the front end can encode knowledge about the target value directly into the ILOC 9X code. As other passes discover additional information, they can rewrite operations to change a value from using a general-purpose load to a more restricted form. If the compiler discovers that some value is a known constant, it can replace a general load or a scalar load of that value with an immediate load. If an analysis of definitions and uses discovers that some location cannot be defined by any executable store operation, loads of that value can be rewritten to use a nonvarying load.

Optimizations can capitalize on the knowledge encoded in this fashion. For example, a comparison between the result of a nonvarying load and a constant must itself be invariant—a fact that might be difficult or impossible to prove with a scalar load or a general load.

at some earlier point, had proof that keeping it in a register is safe.[2] Unless it encodes that fact in the IR, the compiler will need to prove it, again and again.

5.7 SYMBOL TABLES

As part of translation, a compiler derives information about the various entities that the program being translated manipulates. It must discover and store many distinct kinds of information. It encounters a wide variety of names— variables, defined constants, procedures, functions, labels, structures, and files. As discussed in the previous section, the compiler also generates many names. For a variable, it needs a data type, its storage class, the name and lexical level of its declaring procedure, and a base address and offset in memory. For an array, the compiler also needs the number of dimensions and the upper and lower bounds for each dimension. For records or structures, it needs a list of the fields, along with the relevant information for each field. For functions and procedures, it needs the number of parameters and their types, as well as the types of any returned values; a more sophisticated translation might record information about what variables a procedure can reference or modify.

The compiler must either record this information in the IR or rederive it on demand. For the sake of efficiency, most compilers record facts rather than recompute them.[3] These facts can be recorded directly in the IR. For example, a compiler that builds an AST might record information about variables as annotations (or attributes) of the node representing each variable's declaration. The advantage of this approach is that it uses a single representation for the code being compiled. It provides a uniform access method and a single implementation. The disadvantage of this approach is that the single access method may be inefficient—navigating the AST to find the appropriate declaration has its own costs. To eliminate this inefficiency, the compiler can thread

---

2. If the compiler can prove that only one name provides access to a value, it can keep that value in a register. If multiple names might exist, the compiler must behave conservatively and keep the value in memory. For example, a local variable x can be kept in a register, unless it can be referenced in another scope. In a language that supports nested scopes, like Pascal or Ada, this reference can occur in a nested procedure. In C, this can occur if the program takes x's address, &x, and accesses the value through that address. In Algol or PL/I, the program can pass x as a call-by-reference parameter to another procedure.

3. The one common exception to this rule occurs when the IR is written to external storage. Such I/O activity is expensive relative to computation, and the compiler makes a complete pass over the IR when it reads the information. Some kinds of information cost less to recompute than to write to external media and read back.

the IR so that each reference has a link back to the corresponding declaration. This adds space to the IR and overhead to the IR builder.

The alternative, as we saw in Chapter 4, is to create a central repository for these facts and provide efficient access to it. This central repository, called a symbol table, becomes an integral part of the compiler's IR. The symbol table localizes information derived from potentially distant parts of the source code. It makes such information easily and efficiently available, and it simplifies the design and implementation of any code that must refer to information about variables derived earlier in compilation. It avoids the expense of searching the IR to find the portion that represents a variable's declaration; using a symbol table often eliminates the need to represent the declarations directly in the IR. (An exception occurs in source-to-source translation. The compiler may build a symbol table for efficiency and preserve the declaration syntax in the IR so that it can produce an output program that closely resembles the input program.) It eliminates the overhead of making each reference contain a pointer to the declaration. It replaces both of these with a computed mapping from the textual name to the stored information. Thus, in some sense, the symbol table is simply an efficiency hack.

At many places in this text, we refer to "the symbol table." As we shall see in Section 5.7.4, the compiler may include several distinct, specialized symbol tables. A careful implementation might use the same access methods for all these tables.

Symbol-table implementation requires attention to detail. Because nearly every aspect of translation refers to the symbol table, efficiency of access is critical. Because the compiler cannot predict, before translation, the number of names that it will encounter, expanding the symbol table must be both graceful and efficient. This section provides a high-level treatment of the issues that arise in designing a symbol table. It presents the compiler-specific aspects of symbol-table design and use. For deeper implementation details and design alternatives, see Section B.4 in Appendix B.

5.7.1 Hash Tables

A key issue in symbol-table design is efficiency. The compiler will access the table frequently. Because hash tables provide constant-time expected-case lookups, they are the method of choice for implementing symbol tables. Hash tables are conceptually elegant. They use a *hash function*, h, to map names to small integers, and use the small integer to index the table. With a hashed symbol table, the compiler stores all the information that it derives about the name n in the table in slot $h(n)$. Figure 5.9 shows a simple ten-slot hash table. It is a vector of records, each record holding the compiler-generated description of a single name. The names a, b, and c have already been inserted. The name d is being inserted, at $h(d) = 2$.

The primary reason to use hash tables is to provide a constant-time expected-case lookup keyed by a textual name. To achieve this, h must be inexpensive to compute. Given an appropriate function h, accessing the record for n requires computing $h(n)$ and indexing into the table at $h(n)$. If h maps two or more symbols to the same small integer, a "collision" occurs. (In Figure 5.9, this would occur if $h(d) = 3$.) The implementation must handle this situation gracefully, preserving both the information and the lookup time. In this section, we assume that h is a perfect hash function—that is, it never produces a collision. Furthermore, we assume that the compiler knows, in advance, how large to make the table. Section B.4 describes hash-table implementation in more detail, including hash functions, collision handling, and schemes for expanding a hash table.

Hash tables are sometimes used as an efficient representation for sparse graphs. Given two nodes, x and y, an entry for the key xy indicates that an edge exists from x to y. (This requires a hash function that generates a good distribution from a pair of small integers; both the multiplicative and universal hash functions described in Section B.4 in Appendix B work well.) A well-implemented hash table can provide fast insertion and a fast test for the presence of a specific edge. Additional information is required to answer questions such as "what nodes are adjacent to x?"

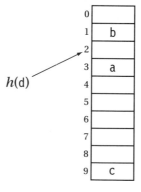

FIGURE 5.9   Hash Table Implementation—The Concept

AN ALTERNATIVE TO HASHING

Hashing is the method most widely used to organize a compiler's symbol table. Multiset discrimination is an interesting alternative that eliminates any possibility of worst-case behavior. The critical insight behind multiset discrimination is that the index can be constructed offline in the scanner.

To use multiset discrimination for a symbol table, the compiler writer must take a different approach to scanning. Instead of processing the input incrementally, the compiler scans the entire program to find the complete set of identifiers. As it discovers each identifier, it creates a tuple ⟨*name,position*⟩, where *name* is the text of the identifier and *position* is its ordinal position in the list of all tokens. It enters all the tuples into a large set.

The next step sorts the set lexicographically. In effect, this creates a set of subsets, one per identifier. Each of these subsets holds the tuples for all the occurrences of its identifier. Since each tuple refers to a specific token, through its *position* value, the compiler can use the sorted set to rewrite the token stream. It makes a linear scan over the set, processing each subset in order. The compiler allocates a symbol-table index for the entire subset, then rewrites the tokens to include that index. This augments the identifier tokens with their symbol-table indexes. If the compiler needs a textual lookup function, the resulting table is ordered alphabetically for a binary search.

The price for using this technique is an extra pass over the token stream, along with the cost of the lexicographic sort. The advantages, from a complexity perspective, are that it avoids any possibility of hashing's worst-case behavior and that it makes the initial size of the symbol table obvious, even before parsing. This technique can be used to replace a hash table in almost any application in which an offline solution will work.

5.7.2 Building a Symbol Table

The symbol table defines two interface routines for the rest of the compiler.

1. *LookUp(name)* returns the record stored in the table at $h(name)$ if one exists. Otherwise, it returns a value indicating that *name* was not found.

2. *Insert(name,record)* stores the information in *record* in the table at $h(name)$. It may expand the table to accommodate the record for *name*.

The compiler can use separate functions for *LookUp* and *Insert*, or they can be combined by passing *LookUp* a flag that specifies whether or not to insert the name. This ensures, for example, that a *LookUp* of an undeclared variable will fail—a property useful for detecting a violation of the declare-before-use rule in syntax-directed translation schemes or for supporting nested lexical scopes.

This simple interface fits directly into the ad hoc syntax-directed translation schemes described in Chapter 4. In processing declaration syntax, the compiler builds up a set of attributes for each variable. When the parser recognizes a production that declares some variable, it can enter the name and attributes into the symbol table using *Insert*. If a variable name can appear in only one declaration, the parser can call *LookUp* first to detect a repeated use of the name. When the parser encounters a variable name outside the declaration syntax, it uses *LookUp* to obtain the appropriate information from the symbol table. *LookUp* fails on any undeclared name. The compiler writer, of course, may need to add functions to initialize the table, to store it to and retrieve it from external media, and to finalize it. For a language with a single name space, this interface suffices.

5.7.3 Handling Nested Scopes

Few programming languages provide only a single unified name space. Typically, a language allows a program to declare names at multiple levels. Each of these levels has a *scope*, or a region in the program's text where the name can be used. Each of these levels has a *lifetime*, or a period in the program's execution where the name has a value.

If the source language allows scopes to be nested one inside another, then the front end needs a mechanism to translate a reference, such as x, to the proper scope and lifetime. The primary mechanism that compilers use to perform this translation is a scoped symbol table.

For the purposes of this discussion, assume that a program can create an arbitrary number of scopes nested one within another. We will defer an in-depth discussion of lexical scoping until Section 6.3.1; however, most programmers have enough experience with the concept for this discussion. Figure 5.10 shows a C program that creates five distinct scopes. We will label the scopes with numbers that indicate the nesting relationships among them. The level *0* scope is the outermost scope, while the level *3* scope is the innermost one.

```
static int w;        /* level 0 */
int x;

void example(int a, int b) {
  int c;             /* level 1 */
  {
    int b, z;        /* level 2a */
    ...
  }
  {
    int a, x;        /* level 2b */
    ...
    {
      int c, x; /* level 3 */
      b = a + b + c + w;
    }
  }
}
```

Level	Names
0	w, x, example
1	a, b, c
2a	b, z
2b	a, x
3	c, x

FIGURE 5.10   Simple Lexical Scoping Example in C

The table on the right side of the figure shows the names declared in each scope. The declaration of b at level *2a* hides the level *1* declaration from any code inside the block that creates level *2a*. Inside level *2b*, a reference to b again refers to the level *1* parameter. In a similar way, the declarations of a and x in level *2b* hide their earlier declarations (at level *1* and level *0*, respectively).

This context creates the naming environment in which the assignment statement executes. Subscripting names to show their level, we find that the assignment refers to

$$b_1 = a_{2b} + b_1 + c_3 + w_0$$

Notice that the assignment cannot use the names declared in level *2a* because that block closes before level *2b* opens.

To compile a program that contains nested scopes, the compiler must map each variable reference to its specific declaration. This process, called *name resolution*, maps each reference to the lexical level at which it is declared. The mechanism that compilers use to accomplish this name resolution is a lexically scoped symbol table. The remainder of this section describes the design and implementation of lexically scoped symbol tables. The corresponding run-time mechanisms, which translate the lexical level of a reference to an address, are described in Section 6.5.2. Scoped symbol tables also have direct application in code optimization. For example, the superlocal value-numbering algorithm presented in Section 8.5.1 relies on a scoped hash table for efficiency.

The Concept

To manage nested scopes, the parser must change, slightly, its approach to symbol-table management. Each time the parser enters a new lexical scope, it can create a new symbol table for that scope. As it encounters declarations in the scope, it enters the information into the current table. *Insert* operates on the current symbol table. When it encounters a variable reference, *LookUp* must first check the table for the current scope. If the current table does not hold a declaration for the name, it checks the table for the surrounding scope. By working its way through the symbol tables for successively lower lexical levels, it either finds the most recent declaration for the name, or fails in the outermost scope—indicating that the variable has no declaration visible in the current scope.

Figure 5.11 shows the symbol table built in this fashion for our example program, at the point where the parser has reached the assignment statement. When the compiler invokes the modified *LookUp* function for the name b, it

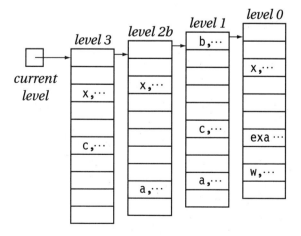

FIGURE 5.11   Simple "Sheaf-of-Tables" Implementation

will fail in level *3*, fail in level *2*, and find the name in level *1*. This corresponds exactly to our understanding of the program—the most recent declaration for b is as a parameter to example, in level *1*. Since the first block at level *2*, block *2a*, has already closed, its symbol table is not on the search chain. The level where the symbol is found, *1* in this case, forms the first part of an address for b. If the symbol-table record includes a storage offset for each variable, then the pair *<level, offset>* specifies where to find b in memory—at *offset* from the start of storage for the *level* scope. We call this pair b's static coordinate.

The Details

To handle this scheme, two additional calls are required. The compiler needs a call that initializes a new symbol table for a scope and one that finalizes the table for a scope.

1. *InitializeScope()* increments the current level and creates a new symbol table for that level. It links the new table to the previous level's table and updates the current level pointer used by *LookUp* and *Insert*.

2. *FinalizeScope()* changes the current-level pointer so that it points to the table for the scope surrounding the current level and then decrements the current level. If the compiler needs to preserve the level-by-level tables for later use, *FinalizeScope* can either leave the table intact in memory or write the table to external media and reclaim its space.

To account for lexical scoping, the parser calls *InitializeScope* each time it enters a new lexical scope and *FinalizeScope* each time it exits a lexical scope.

With this interface, the program in Figure 5.10 would produce the following sequence of calls:

1. *InitializeScope*	10. *Insert(b)*	19. *LookUp(b)*
2. *Insert(w)*	11. *Insert(z)*	20. *LookUp(a)*
3. *Insert(x)*	12. *FinalizeScope*	21. *LookUp(b)*
4. *Insert(example)*	13. *InitializeScope*	22. *LookUp(c)*
5. *InitializeScope*	14. *Insert(a)*	23. *LookUp(w)*
6. *Insert(a)*	15. *Insert(x)*	24. *FinalizeScope*
7. *Insert(b)*	16. *InitializeScope*	25. *FinalizeScope*
8. *Insert(c)*	17. *Insert(c)*	26. *FinalizeScope*
9. *InitializeScope*	18. *Insert(x)*	

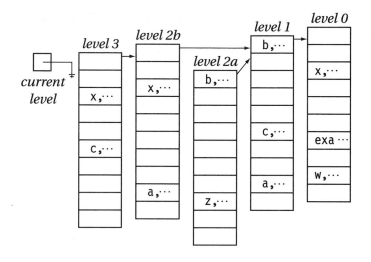

FIGURE 5.12   Final Table for the Example

As it enters each scope, the compiler calls *InitializeScope*. It adds each name to the table using *Insert*. When it leaves a given scope, it calls *FinalizeScope* to discard the declarations for that scope. For the assignment statement, it looks up each of the names, as encountered. (The order of the *LookUp* calls will vary, depending on how the assignment statement is traversed.)

If *FinalizeScope* retains the symbol tables for finalized levels in memory, the net result of these calls will be the symbol table shown in Figure 5.12. The current level pointer is set to an invalid value. The tables for all levels are left in memory and linked together to reflect lexical nesting. The compiler can provide subsequent passes of the compiler with access to the relevant symbol-table information by storing a pointer to the appropriate table in the IR at the start of each new level. Alternatively, identifiers in the IR can point directly to their symbol-table entries.

5.7.4   The Many Uses for Symbol Tables

The preceding discussion focused on a central symbol table, albeit one that might be composed of several tables. In reality, compilers build multiple symbol tables that they use for different purposes.

Structure Table

The textual strings used to name fields in a structure or record exist in a distinct name space from the variables and procedures. The name size might occur in several different structures in a single program. In many programming languages, such as C or Ada, using size as a field in a structure does not preclude its use as a variable or function name.

For each field in a structure, the compiler needs to record its type, its size, and its offset inside the record. It gleans this information from the declarations, using the same mechanisms that it uses for processing variable declarations. It must also determine the overall size for the structure, usually computed as the sum of the field sizes, plus any overhead space required by the run-time system.

There are several approaches for managing the name space of field names.

1. *Separate Tables*   The compiler can maintain a separate symbol table for each record definition. This is the cleanest idea, conceptually. If the overhead for using multiple tables is small, as in most object-oriented implementations, then using a separate table and associating it with the symbol table entry for the structure's name makes sense.

2. *Selector Table*   The compiler can maintain a separate table for field names. To avoid clashes between fields with identical names in different structures, it must use qualified names—concatenate either the name of the structure or something that uniquely maps to the structure, such as the structure name's symbol-table index, to the field name. In this approach, the compiler must somehow link together the individual fields associated with each structure.

3. *Unified Table*   The compiler can store field names in its principal symbol table by using qualified names. This decreases the number of tables, but it means that the principal symbol table must support all of the fields required for variables and functions, as well as all the fields needed for each field-selector in a structure. Of the three options, this is probably the least attractive.

The separate table approach has the advantage that any scoping issues—such as reclaiming the symbol table associated with a structure—fit naturally into the scope management framework for the principal symbol table. When the structure can be seen, its internal symbol table is accessible through the corresponding structure record.

In the latter two schemes, the compiler writer will need to pay careful attention to scoping issues. For example, if the current scope declares a structure fee and an external scope already has defined fee, then the scoping mechanism must correctly map fee into the structure (and its corresponding field entries). This may also introduce complications into the creation of qualified names. If the code contains two definitions of fee, each with a field named size, then fee.size is not a unique key for either field entry. This problem can be solved by associating a unique integer, generated from a global counter, with each structure name.

Linked Tables for Name Resolution in an Object-Oriented Language

In an object-oriented language, the name scoping rules are governed by the structure of the data as much as by the structure of the code. This creates a more complicated set of rules; it also leads to a more complicated set of symbol tables. Java, for example, needs tables for the code being compiled, for any external classes that are both known and referenced in the code, and for the inheritance hierarchy above the class containing the code.

A simple implementation attaches a symbol table to each class, with two nesting hierarchies—one for lexical scoping inside individual methods and the other following the inheritance hierarchy for each class. Since a single class can serve as superclass to several subclasses, this latter hierarchy is more complicated than the simple sheaf-of-tables drawing suggests. However, it is easily managed.

To resolve a name fee when compiling a method m in class C, the compiler first consults the lexically scoped symbol table for m. If it does not find fee in this table, it then searches the scopes for the various classes in the inheritance hierarchy, starting with C and proceeding up the chain of superclasses from C. If this lookup fails to find fee, the search then checks the global symbol table for a class or symbol table of that name. The global table must contain information on both the current package and any packages that have been imported.

Thus, the compiler needs a lexically scoped table for each method, built while it compiles the methods. It needs a symbol table for each class, with links upward through the inheritance hierarchy. It needs links to the other classes in its package and to a symbol table for package-level variables. It needs access to the symbol tables for each imported class. The lookup process is more complex, because it must follow these links in the correct order and examine only names that are visible. However, the basic mechanisms required to implement and manipulate the tables are already familiar.

.

5.8   SUMMARY AND PERSPECTIVE

The choice of intermediate representations has a major impact on the design, implementation, speed, and effectiveness of a compiler. None of the intermediate forms described in this chapter are, definitively, the right answer for all compilers or all tasks in a given compiler. The designer must consider the overall goals of a compiler project when selecting an intermediate form, designing its implementation, and adding auxiliary data structures such as symbol and label tables.

Contemporary compiler systems use all manner of intermediate representations, ranging from parse trees and abstract syntax trees (often used in source-to-source systems) through lower-than-machine-level linear codes (used, for example, in the Gnu compiler systems). Many compilers use multiple IRs—building a second or third one to perform a particular analysis or transformation, then modifying the original, and definitive, one to reflect the result.

CHAPTER NOTES

The literature on intermediate representations and experience with them is sparse. This is somewhat surprising because of the major impact that decisions about IRs have on the structure and behavior of a compiler. The classic IR forms have been described in a number of textbooks [166, 30, 8, 140]. Newer forms like SSA [104, 267, 47] are described in the literature on analysis and optimization. Muchnick provides a modern treatment of the subject and highlights the use of multiple levels of IR in a single compiler [262].

The idea of using a hash function to recognize textually identical operations dates back to Ershov [131]. Its specific application in Lisp systems seems to appear in the early 1970s [116, 159]; by 1980, it was common enough that McCarthy mentions it without citation [252].

Cai and Paige described multiset discrimination as an alternative to hashing [58]. Their intent was to provide an efficient lookup mechanism with guaranteed constant time behavior. The work on shrinking the size of $\mathcal{R}^n$'s AST was done by David Schwartz and Scott Warren.

In practice, the design and implementation of an IR has an inordinately large impact on the eventual characteristics of the completed compiler. Large, complex IRs seem to shape systems in their own image. For example, the large ASTs used in early 1980s programming environments like $\mathcal{R}^n$ limited the size of programs that could be analyzed. The RTL form used in LCC has a low level of abstraction. Accordingly, the compiler does a fine job of managing details such as those needed for code generation, but has few, if any, transformations that require sourcelike knowledge, such as loop blocking to improve memory hierarchy behavior.

CHAPTER 6

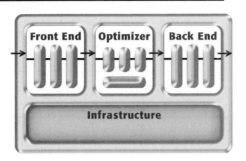

The Procedure Abstraction

INTRODUCTION

The procedure is one of the central abstractions that underlie most modern programming languages. Procedures create a controlled execution environment. Each procedure has its own private named storage. Statements executed inside the procedure can access the private, or local, variables in that private storage. A procedure executes when it is invoked, or called, by another procedure (or the operating system). The called procedure, or callee, may return a value to its caller, in which case the procedure is termed a *function*. This interface between procedures lets programmers develop and test parts of a program in isolation; the separation between procedures provides some insulation against problems in other procedures.

Procedures are the basic unit of work for many compilers. Few systems require that an entire program be presented for compilation at one time. Instead, the compiler can process arbitrary collections of procedures. This feature, known as *separate compilation*, makes it feasible to construct and maintain large programs. Imagine maintaining a one-million-line program without separate compilation. Any change to the source code would require a complete recompilation; the programmer would need to wait while one million lines of code compiled before testing a single-line change.

A WORD ABOUT TIME

This chapter deals with both compile-time and run-time mechanisms. The distinction between events that occur at compile time and those that occur at run time can be confusing. The compiler generates all the code that executes at run time. As part of the compilation process, the compiler analyzes the source code and builds data structures that encode the results of the analysis. (Recall the discussion of lexically scoped symbol tables in Section 5.7.3.) The compiler determines much of the storage layout that the program will use at run time. It then generates the code needed to create that layout, to maintain it during execution, and to access both data objects and code in memory. When the compiled code runs, it accesses data objects and calls procedures or methods. All of the code is generated at compile time; all of the accesses occur at run time.

Procedures play an important role in the way that programmers develop software and that compilers translate programs. Three critical abstractions that procedures provide allow the construction of nontrivial programs.

1. *Control Abstraction*   A procedure provides the programmer with a simple control abstraction; each language has a standard mechanism to invoke a procedure and map a set of arguments, or parameters, from the caller's name space to the callee's name space. The language's standard return mechanism allows the procedure to return control to the caller, continuing execution at the point immediately after the call. This mechanism, referred to as the *calling sequence* or *calling convention*, makes separate compilation possible; the compiler can generate code to invoke an arbitrary procedure without having available the code that implements the called procedure.

2. *Name Space*   Each procedure creates a new protected name space; the programmer can declare names, such as variables and labels. Inside the procedure, those declarations take precedence over any other declarations for the same names that the compiler has seen. Inside the procedure, parameters can be referenced by their local names, rather than their external names. Because the procedure has an isolated,

protected name space, it can function correctly when called from different contexts.

Calling the procedure instantiates its name space. The calling sequence reserves enough space to hold the objects declared in the procedure's name space. The allocation of this space is both automatic and efficient—a consequence of calling the procedure.

3. *External Interface*   Procedures define the critical interfaces among the parts of large software systems. The rules for name scoping, addressability, and orderly preservation of the run-time environment create a context in which the programmer can safely invoke code written by other individuals. This allows the development and use of libraries, for example, for graphical user interfaces, for scientific computation, and for access to system services. The system uses this same interface to start execution of the user's code. After establishing the appropriate run-time environment, the system code invokes a designated entry point, such as main.

The procedure is, in many ways, the fundamental programming abstraction that underlies Algol-like languages. It is an elaborate facade created collaboratively by the compiler and the underlying hardware, with assistance from the operating system. Procedures create named variables and map them to virtual addresses; the operating system maps virtual addresses to physical addresses. Procedures establish rules for visibility of names and addressability; the hardware typically provides several variants of load and store operations. Procedures let us decompose large software systems into components; linkers and loaders knit these together into an executable program that the hardware can execute by advancing its program counter and following branches.

A large part of the compiler's task is putting in place the code needed to realize the various pieces of the procedure abstraction. The compiler must dictate the layout of memory and encode that layout in the generated program. Since it may compile the different components of the program at different times, without knowing their relationships to one another, this memory layout and all the conventions that it induces must be standardized and uniformly applied. The compiler must also use the various interfaces provided by the operating system, to handle input and output, manage memory, and communicate with other processes.

This chapter focuses on the procedure as an abstraction and the mechanisms that the compiler uses to establish its control abstraction, name space, and interface to the outside world.

6.2 CONTROL ABSTRACTION

In Algol-like languages, procedures have a simple and clear call/return discipline. On exit from a procedure, control returns to the point in the calling procedure that follows its invocation. If a procedure invokes other procedures, they return control in the same way. Figure 6.1 shows a Pascal program with several nested procedures. The *call graph* and *execution history* to its right summarize what happens when it executes.

The call graph shows the set of potential calls among the procedures. The program can call Fee twice: once from Foe and the second time from Fum. The execution history shows that, in fact, this happens when the program runs. Each of these calls creates a distinct instance, or *activation*, of Fee. By the time that Fum is called, the first instance of Fee is no longer active. It was created by the call from Foe (event 3) and returned control back to Foe (event 4). In Pascal, no mechanism allows control to return to that activation of Fee; once control returns (event 4), the activation ceases to exist. Thus, when Fum calls Fee (event 6), it creates a new activation of Fee. This second activation ceases to exist after control returns to Fum (event 7).

When the program executes the assignment x := 1 in the first invocation of Fee, the active procedures are Fee, Foe, Fie, and Main. These all lie on a path in the call graph from Main to Fee. Similarly, when it executes the second invocation of Fee, the active procedures (Fee, Fum, Foe, Fie, and Main) lie on a path from Main to Fee. At any point during execution, the procedure activations instantiate some rooted path through the call graph. Pascal's call and return mechanism ensures this.

When the compiler implements call and return, it must arrange to preserve enough information to allow the calls and returns to operate correctly. Thus, when Foe calls Fum, the calling mechanism must preserve the information needed to let control return to Foe. Fum may diverge, or not return, due to a run-time error, an infinite loop, or a call to another procedure that does not return. Still, the call mechanism must preserve enough information to allow execution to resume in Foe when, and if, Fum returns.

This simple call and return behavior can be modelled with a stack. As Fie calls Foe, it pushes the address for a return onto the stack. When Foe returns, it pops the address off the stack and jumps to that address. If all procedures follow this discipline, popping a return address off the stack exposes the next appropriate return address.

The stack mechanism handles recursion as well. The call mechanism, in effect, unrolls the cyclic path through the call graph and creates a distinct activation for each call to a procedure. As long as the recursion terminates, this

```
program Main(input, output);
    var x,y,z: integer;
    procedure Fee;
        var x: integer;
        begin { Fee }
            x := 1;
            y := x * 2 + 1
        end;

    procedure Fie;
        var y: real;
        procedure Foe;
            var z: real;
                procedure Fum;
                    var y: real;
                    begin { Fum }
                        x := 1.25 * z;
                        Fee;
                        writeln('x = ',x)
                    end;
            begin { Foe }
                z := 1;
                Fee;
                Fum
            end;
        begin { Fie }
            Foe;
            writeln('x = ',x)
        end;
    begin { Main }
        x := 0;
        Fie
    end.
```

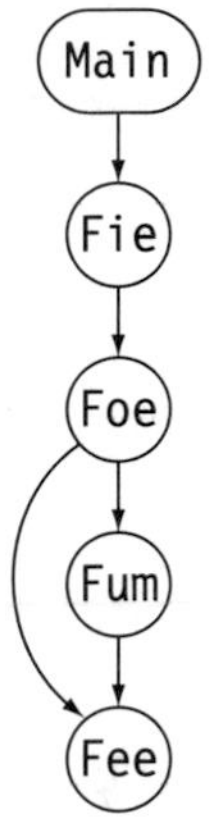

Call Graph

1. Main calls Fie
2. Fie calls Foe
3. Foe calls Fee
4. Fee returns to Foe
5. Foe calls Fum
6. Fum calls Fee
7. Fee returns to Fum
8. Fum returns to Foe
9. Foe returns to Fie
10. Fie returns to Main

Execution History

FIGURE 6.1   Nonrecursive Pascal Program

path will be finite and the stack of return addresses will correctly capture the program's behavior.

To make this concrete, consider the recursive factorial computation shown in Figure 6.2. When invoked to compute (fact 5), it generates a series of recursive calls: (fact 5) calls (fact 4) calls (fact 3) calls (fact 2) calls (fact 1).

```
(define (fact k)
  (cond
    [(<= k 1) 1]
    [else (* (fact (sub1 k)) k)]
  ))
```

FIGURE 6.2   Recursive Factorial Program in Scheme

At this point, the cond statement executes the clause for (<= k 1), terminating the recursion. The recursion unwinds in the reverse order, with the call to (fact 1) returning the value 1 to (fact 2). It, in turn, returns the value 2 to (fact 3), which returns 6 to (fact 4). Finally, (fact 4) returns 24 to (fact 5), which multiplies 24 times 5 to return the answer 120. The recursive program exhibits last-in, first-out behavior, so the stack mechanism correctly tracks all of the return addresses.

More Complex Control Flow

Some programming languages, such as Scheme, allow a procedure to return a procedure and its run-time context (often called a *closure*). When the closure is invoked, the procedure executes in the run-time context from which it was returned. A simple stack is inadequate to implement this control abstraction. Instead, the control information must be saved in some more general structure, such as a linked list, for which returning does not imply deallocation (see Section 6.3.2). Similar problems arise if the language allows references to local variables that outlast a procedure's activation.

6.3   NAME SPACES

In most procedural languages, a complete program will contain multiple name spaces. Each name space, called a *scope*, maps a set of names to a set of values and procedures over a set of statements in the program. This range might be the whole program, some collection of procedures, a single procedure, or a small set of statements. Inside a scope, the programmer can create names that are inaccessible outside the scope. The scope may inherit some names from other scopes. Creating a name, fee, inside a scope can obscure definitions of fee in surrounding scopes—in effect, making them inaccessible inside the scope.

Taken together, the scoping rules give the programmer control over the ways that the program can access information.

6.3.1 Name Spaces of Algol-like Languages

Most traditional programming languages inherit many of the conventions and rules that were defined for Algol 60. This is particularly true of the rules that govern the visibility of names. This section explores the notion of naming that prevails in Algol-like languages, with particular emphasis on the hierarchical scoping rules that apply in such languages.

Nested Lexical Scopes

Most Algol-like languages allow the programmer to nest scopes inside one another. Many object-oriented languages use lexical scoping as one mechanism for name resolution; for example, the scope defined by a method often lies inside the scope of the class containing the method. Scopes of any superclasses nest outside the defining class. The object's instance variables lie in the scope of the class. In procedural languages, scopes can arise when blocks are nested inside each other, as in C or C++, or when procedures are nested inside other procedures, as in Pascal.

Pascal popularized nested procedures. Each procedure defines a new scope, and the programmer can declare new variables and procedures in each scope. It uses the most common scoping discipline, called *lexical scoping*. The general principle behind lexical scoping is simple:

> *In a given scope, each name refers to its lexically closest declaration.*

Thus, if s is used in the current scope, it refers to the s declared in the current scope, if one exists. If not, it refers to the declaration of s that occurs in the closest enclosing scope. The outermost scope contains global variables.

To make lexical scoping concrete, consider the Pascal program shown in Figure 6.3. It contains five distinct scopes, one corresponding to the program Main and one for each of the procedures Fee, Fie, Foe, and Fum. Each procedure declares some set of variables drawn from the set of names x, y, and z. The figure shows each name with a subscript that indicates its level number. Names declared in a procedure always have a level that is one more than the level of the procedure name. Thus, if Main has level 0, as shown, names declared directly in Main, such as x, y, z, Fee, and Fie all have level 1.

Scope	x	y	z
Main	$\langle 1,0 \rangle$	$\langle 1,4 \rangle$	$\langle 1,8 \rangle$
Fee	$\langle 2,0 \rangle$	$\langle 1,4 \rangle$	$\langle 1,8 \rangle$
Fie	$\langle 1,0 \rangle$	$\langle 2,0 \rangle$	$\langle 1,8 \rangle$
Foe	$\langle 1,0 \rangle$	$\langle 2,0 \rangle$	$\langle 3,0 \rangle$
Fum	$\langle 1,0 \rangle$	$\langle 4,0 \rangle$	$\langle 3,0 \rangle$

Static Coordinates

```
program Main₀(input, output);
  var x₁,y₁,z₁: integer;
  procedure Fee_subr 1;
    var x₂: integer;
    begin { Fee }
      x₂ := 1;
      y₁ := x₂ * 2 + 1
    end;

  procedure Fie₁;
    var y₂: real;
    procedure Foe₂;
      var z₃: real;
        procedure Fum₃
          var y₄: real;
          begin { Fum }
            x₁ := 1.25 * z₃;
            Fee₁;
            writeln('x = ',x₁)
          end;
      begin { Foe }
        z₃ := 1;
        Fee₁;
        Fum₃
      end;
    begin { Fie }
      Foe₂;
      writeln('x = ',x₁)
    end;
  begin { Main }
    x₁ := 0;
    Fie₁
  end.
```

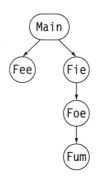

Nesting Relationships

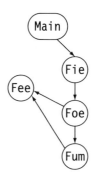

Calling Relationships

FIGURE 6.3   Nested Lexical Scopes in Pascal

To represent names in a lexically scoped language, the compiler can use the *static coordinate* for each name. The static coordinate is a pair $\langle l,o \rangle$, where l is the lexical nesting level from the symbol table and o is the offset of its memory location in the data area for the scope. To obtain l, the front end uses a lexically scoped symbol table, as described in Section 5.7.3. The offset, o, should be stored with the name and its level in the symbol table. (Offsets can be assigned when declarations are processed during context-sensitive analysis.) The table on the right side of Figure 6.3 shows the static coordinate for each variable name in each procedure.

The second part of name translation occurs during code generation. The compiler must use the static coordinate to locate the value at run time. Given a coordinate $\langle l,o \rangle$, the code generator must emit code that translates l into the run-time address of the appropriate data area. Then, it can use the offset o to compute the address for the variable corresponding to $\langle l,o \rangle$. Section 6.5.2 describes two different ways to accomplish this task.

Scoping Rules in Various Languages

Programming languages have many different scoping rules. The compiler writer must understand the specific rules of a source language and must adapt the general translation schemes to work with these specific rules. Figure 6.4 depicts the name scoping rules of several languages.

FORTRAN, the oldest of these languages, creates two scopes: a global scope that holds procedure names and common-block names, and a series of local scopes—one per procedure. A common block consists of a name and a list of variables; these common-block elements are the only global variables. (FORTRAN allows different descriptions of a common block in different files. This forces the compiler to translate common-block references into offsets from the start of the block in order to ensure consistent treatment.) Inside a procedure, the programmer can declare local variables. Local names override common-block-element names if they conflict. By default, a procedure's local variables have a lifetime that matches an invocation of that procedure. The programmer can force a procedure-local variable to have a lifetime that matches the program's lifetime by mentioning it in a save statement. This makes the local variable a *static* variable—its value is preserved across calls to the procedure. All global variables are static—their values are always preserved.

C has more complex rules. It creates a global scope to hold all procedure names, as well as the names of global variables. Each procedure has its own local scope for variables, parameters, and labels. Procedures cannot nest inside one another (as they can in Pascal), but a procedure can contain a block (set off with left and right braces) that creates a separate local scope. Blocks can be

FORTRAN 77 Name Space

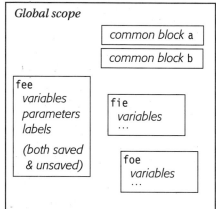

C Name Space

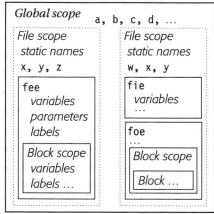

Scheme Name Space

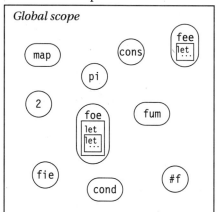

Java Name Space

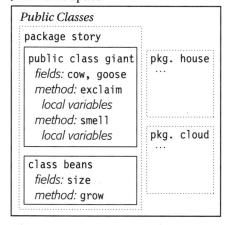

FIGURE 6.4   Name Spaces in Several Languages

nested. Programmers often use a block-level scope to create temporary storage for code generated by a preprocessor macro or to create a local variable whose scope is the body of a loop.

C introduces another level of scoping, a file-wide scope, that includes all of the procedures in a single file (or compilation unit). Names in the file-level scope are declared outside any procedure, using the static attribute. Without the static attribute, these names would be global variables. These names are visible to any procedure in the file, but not outside the file. Both variables and procedures can be declared static.

DYNAMIC SCOPING

The alternative to lexical scoping is called dynamic scoping. The distinction between lexical and dynamic scoping only matters when a procedure refers to a variable that is declared outside the procedure's own scope, sometimes called a *free variable*.

With lexical scoping, the rule is simple and consistent: a free variable is bound to the declaration for its name that is lexically closest to the use. That is, if the compiler starts in the scope containing the use, and checks successive surrounding scopes, the variable is bound to the first declaration that it finds. The declaration always comes from a scope that surrounds the reference.

With dynamic scoping, the rule is equally simple: a free variable is bound to the variable by that name that was most recently created at run time. Thus, when execution encounters a free variable, it binds that free variable to the last created instance of that name. Early implementations created a stack of names, on which every created name was pushed. To bind a free variable, the run-time system searched the name stack from its top downward until a variable with the right name was found. Later implementations are more efficient.

While many early Lisp systems used dynamic scoping, it appears that lexical scoping has become the technique of choice. Dynamic scoping is easy to implement in an interpreter and somewhat harder to implement efficiently in a compiler. It can create bugs that are difficult to detect and hard to understand. Dynamic scoping still appears in some languages; for example, Common Lisp still allows the programmer to force dynamic scoping for variables.

Scheme has a simple set of scoping rules. Almost all objects in Scheme reside in a single global space. Objects can be data or executable expressions. System-provided functions, such as cons, live alongside user-written code and data items. Code, which consists of an executable expression, can create private objects by using a let expression. Nesting lets inside one another can create nested lexical scopes of arbitrary depth.

Java has a limited global name space; the only global names are those of classes declared "public." Each class resides in a package. A package can contain multiple classes. A class can contain both fields (data items) and methods (code). Fields and methods in a public class can be declared public; this makes them accessible to methods in classes in other packages. Fields and methods in a class are accessible to methods in all other classes in the same package, unless a field or method is explicitly declared "private." Classes can nest inside other classes.

If the Java class gi ant declares a field cow, that declaration screates a field cow in every instance of gi ant. As the program creates new gi ants, each of them has its own, individual cow. The class gi ant may need some fields held in common, with one instance, for the entire class. To declare these *class variables*, the programmer declares a *static* field.[1]

6.3.2 Activation Records

The creation of a new separate name space is a critical part of the procedure abstraction. Inside a procedure, the programmer can declare named variables that are not accessible outside the procedure. These named variables may be initialized to known values. In Algol-like languages, local variables have lifetimes that match the procedures that declare them. Thus, they require storage during the lifetime of the invocation, and their values are of interest only while the invocation that created them is active. If multiple invocations of a procedure are active at the same time, each needs its own private copy of the local variables.

To accommodate this behavior, the compiler arranges to set aside a region of memory for each activation of a procedure. We call this block an *activation record* (AR). Under most circumstances, an AR for q is created at run time when some procedure calls q, and it is freed when control returns from q. The AR for q includes all the storage needed for q's local variables, along with any other data needed to maintain q's state. Typically, the AR also holds the return address for this invocation of the procedure. Conveniently, this state information has the same lifetime as the local variables.

The AR for q connects the running code for q to the rest of the program. When p calls q, the code sequence that implements the call must both preserve p's environment and create a new environment for q. Thus, that code creates an AR for q and stores in it the information needed for q to execute and for the return sequence to reconstruct p's environment. (Some of this knowledge is embedded directly in the code for p and q, as well.) Figure 6.5 shows how the contents of an AR might be laid out. The entire AR is addressed through an *activation record pointer* (ARP), with various fields found at positive and negative offsets from the ARP.

---

1. The use of the term *static* may appear odd, until you consider the fact that a class variable exists from the time a class is loaded until execution stops. Thus, a static variable retains its value from the first time it is mentioned until the end of execution.

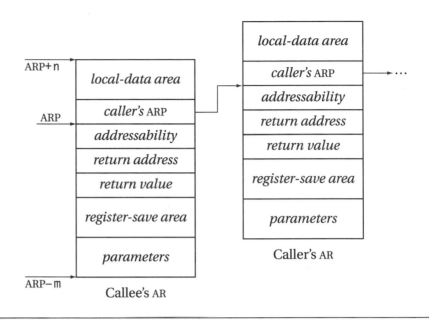

FIGURE 6.5   Typical Activation Records

The parameter area holds space for parameters passed from the caller to the callee. The register save area contains space for the callee to hold values that it must preserve in the calling sequence. The return-value slot provides space that is used to communicate data from the callee back to the caller, if needed, while the return-address slot holds the run-time address where execution should resume when the callee terminates. The slot labelled "addressability" is used by the mechanism that lets the callee access variables in its surrounding lexical scopes (not necessarily the caller). The slot at the callee's ARP holds the caller's ARP, needed to restore its environment when the callee terminates. Finally, the local data area holds space for variables that are local to the callee. For efficiency, parts of the AR may be held in dedicated registers.

Local Storage

A procedure's AR holds its local data and state information. A separate AR is needed for each invocation of the procedure. All access to a procedure's AR uses its ARP as a starting point. Because procedures typically access their AR frequently, most compilers dedicate a hardware register to hold the ARP of the current procedure. In ILOC, we refer to this dedicated register as r_{arp}.

The ARP points to a designated location in the AR. The central part of the AR has a static layout; all the fields have known fixed lengths. This ensures that the code can access those items at fixed offsets from the ARP. The ends of the AR are reserved for storage areas whose sizes may change from one invocation to another. One end typically holds the parameter storage, while the other holds the local data area.

Reserving Space for Local Data Each local data item may need space in the AR. The compiler should assign each such item an appropriately sized area and record the current lexical level and its offset from the ARP in the symbol table. This pair, the lexical level and offset, become the item's static coordinate. Then, the variable can be accessed using an operation like loadAO, with r_{arp} and the offset as its arguments to provide efficient access to local variables.

The compiler cannot know the sizes of some local variables at compile time. The program might read the size of an array from external media or determine it from work done in an earlier phase of the computation.[2] For such variables, the compiler can leave space in the local data area for a pointer to the actual data or to a descriptor for an array (as we shall see in Section 7.5.3). It then arranges to allocate the actual storage elsewhere, at run time. In this case, the static coordinate leads the compiler to the pointer's location, and the actual access either uses the pointer directly or uses the pointer to calculate an appropriate address in the variable-length data area.

Initializing Variables If the source language allows the program to specify an initial value for a variable, the compiler must arrange for that initialization to occur. If the variable is allocated statically—that is, it has a lifetime that is independent of any procedure—and the initial value is known at compile time, the data can be inserted directly into the appropriate locations by the loader. (Static variables are usually stored outside all ARs. Having one instance of such a variable provides the needed semantics—a single value preserved across all the calls. Using a separate static data area—either one per procedure or one for the entire program—lets the compiler use the initialization features commonly found in loaders.)

Local variables, on the other hand, must be initialized at run time. Because a procedure may be invoked multiple times, the only feasible way to set initial

---

2. For example, the later passes of a compiler can often use simpler data structures because they can determine the size of the code being compiled. The front end must have data structures that expand gracefully. The front end can record the appropriate sizes for those structures so that the optimizer and back end can allocate them to appropriate sizes.

values is to generate instructions that store the necessary values to the appropriate locations. In effect, these initializations are assignments that execute before the procedure's first statement, each time it is invoked.

Space for Saved Register Values When p calls q, one of them must save the register values that p needs. It may be necessary to save all the register values; on the other hand, a subset may suffice. On return to p, these saved values must be restored. Since each activation of p stores a distinct set of values, space to hold the register values is set aside in the AR. If the callee saves a register, its value is stored in the callee's register save area. Similarly, if the caller saves a register, its value is stored in the caller's register save area. For a caller p, only one call inside p can be active at a time. Thus, a single register save area in p's AR suffices for all the calls that p can make.

Allocating Activation Records

As part of executing a call from p to q, the executing code must allocate an AR for q and ensure that the various fields in it are filled with the appropriate values. If all the fields shown in Figure 6.5 are actually stored in memory, then the AR must be available to the caller, p, so that it can store the actual parameters, return address, caller's ARP, and addressability information. This forces allocation of q's AR into p, where the size of its local data area may not be known. On the other hand, if these values are passed in registers, actual allocation of the AR can be performed in the callee, q. This lets q allocate the AR, including any space required for the local data area. After allocation, it may store into its AR some of the values passed in registers.

The compiler writer has several options for allocating activation records. This choice affects both the cost of procedure calls and the cost of implementing advanced language features, such as building a closure. It also affects the total amount of memory needed for activation records.

Stack Allocation of Activation Records In many cases, the contents of an AR are only of interest during the lifetime of the procedure whose activation causes the AR's creation. In short, most variables cannot outlive the procedure that creates them, and most procedure activations cannot outlive their callers. With these restrictions, calls and returns are balanced; they follow a last-in, first-out (LIFO) discipline. A call from p to q eventually returns, and any returns that occur between the call from p to q and the return from q to p must result from calls made (either directly or indirectly) by q. In this case, the activation records

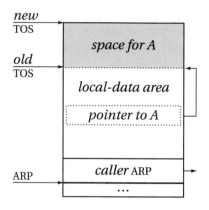

FIGURE 6.6   Stack Allocation of a Dynamically Sized Array

also follow the LIFO ordering; thus, they can be allocated on a stack. Pascal, C, and Java are typically implemented with stack-allocated ARs.

Keeping activation records on a stack has several advantages. Allocation and deallocation are inexpensive; each requires one arithmetic operation on the value that marks the stack's top. The caller can begin the process of setting up the callee's AR. It can allocate all the space up to the local data area. The callee can then extend the AR to include the local data area by incrementing the top-of-stack (TOS) pointer. It can use the same mechanism to extend the current AR incrementally to hold variable-size objects, as shown in Figure 6.6. Here, the callee has copied the TOS pointer into the local data area slot for *A* and then incremented the TOS pointer by the size of *A*. Finally, with stack-allocated ARs, a debugger can walk the stack from its top to its base to produce a snapshot of the currently active procedures.

Heap Allocation of Activation Records   If a procedure can outlive its caller, the stack discipline for allocating ARs breaks down. Similarly, if a procedure can return an object, such as a closure, that includes, explicitly or implicitly, references to its local variables, stack allocation is inappropriate because it will leave behind dangling pointers. In these situations, ARs can be kept in heap storage. Implementations of Scheme and ML typically use heap-allocated ARs. This lets the code dismantle and free an AR when it is no longer needed. In a garbage-collected system, the collector can reclaim this space (see Section 6.7).

A modern memory allocator can keep the cost of heap allocation low (see Section 6.7.2). With heap-allocated ARs, variable-size objects can be allocated as separate heap objects. This complicates deallocation in a system with explicit deallocation; with implicit deallocation, the garbage collector will reclaim the space for these variable-size objects when they become unreachable. To trace through the execution path, the debugger must trace back along the chain of caller ARPs from the current AR.

Static Allocation of Activation Records   If a procedure q calls no other procedures, then q can never have multiple active invocations. We call q a *leaf procedure* since it terminates a path through a graph of the possible procedure calls. The compiler can statically allocate activation records for leaf procedures. This eliminates the run-time cost of AR allocation. If the calling convention requires the caller to save its own registers, then q's AR needs no register save area.

If the language has a Pascal-like call and return mechanism, the compiler can do better than allocating a static AR for each leaf procedure. At any point during execution, only one leaf procedure can be active. (To have two such procedures active, the first one would need to call another procedure, so it would not be a leaf.) Thus, the compiler can allocate a single static AR for use by all of the leaf procedures. The static AR must be large enough to accommodate any of the program's leaf procedures. The static variables declared in any of the leaf procedures can be laid out together in that single AR. Using a single static AR for leaf procedures uses less space than allocating a separate static AR for each leaf procedure.

Of course, any programming language that forbids recursion can allocate all ARs statically. FORTRAN 77 has this property. Creating a statically allocated data area for each procedure, however, can increase the total memory requirements of a program. Unless some execution path has every procedure active, the all-static solution uses more space for ARs than a stack-based scheme would. As one alternative, the compiler might compute the maximum amount of space required by any chain of calls; it could then overlay the ARs on that space. In practice, this produces the same costs and behavior as stack allocation of the ARs.

Coalescing Activation Records   If the compiler discovers a set of procedures that are always invoked in a fixed sequence, it may be able to combine their activation records. For example, if a call from p to q always results in calls to r and s, the compiler may find it profitable to allocate the ARs for q, r, and s at the same time. Combining ARs can save on the costs of allocation; the benefits will vary directly with allocation costs. In practice, this optimization is limited by separate compilation and the use of function-valued parameters. Both limit the compiler's ability to determine the calling relationships that actually occur at run time.

6.3.3 Name Spaces of Object-Oriented Languages

Much has been written about object-oriented design, object-oriented programming, and object-oriented languages. Languages such as Smalltalk, C++, Self, and Java have been developed to support object-oriented programming. Extensions have been written for many other languages to provide them with features that support object-oriented programming. Unfortunately, the term *object-oriented* has been given so many different meanings and implementations that it has come to signify a wide range of language features and facilities.

Fundamentally, object orientation is a reorganization of the program's name space from a procedure-oriented scheme to a data-oriented scheme. This section describes the features of object-oriented languages from the perspective of the resulting program's name space. It relates the name spaces created by object-oriented languages to those found in Algol-like languages.

In a procedural language, scoping effects occur with transitions in the code—entering a procedure or block and leaving a procedure or block. In an object-oriented language, scoping rules and naming are organized around the data in the program, rather than the code. Traditionally, those data items that govern the naming rules are called *objects*. Some object-oriented languages require that every data item be an object; in others, objects and code can contain data items that function in ways similar to variables in Algol-like languages.

From the compiler writer's perspective, object-oriented languages differ from procedural languages in that they need some additional compile-time and run-time support. To understand these additional mechanisms, we must first explore the object abstraction and then relate it to the procedure abstraction.

Objects and Classes

At the heart of object-oriented programming lies the notion of an object. An object is an abstraction that has one or more internal members. These members can be data items, code that manipulates those data items, or other objects. As a software-engineering strategy, objects are used to enforce a discipline of abstraction and data hiding and to control access to the information stored in the object's members.

Graphically, we might represent an object as an array or structure of members, with the provision that a member can be a data item, an executable procedure, or another object.

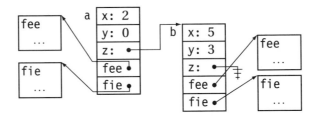

This diagram shows two objects, named a and b. The objects have the same layout; each has five members. The first two members, x and y, hold numbers. The third member, z, holds an object. The last two members, fee and fie hold executable functions. To allow a uniform handling of members, we have shown object members and code members implemented with pointers.

The preceding picture highlights an implementation problem with this simple model for objects—it wastes space with distinct copies of the code to implement fee and fie. If the code members are implemented with pointers, both a and b could use the same copies of fee and fie.

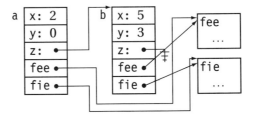

Specifying this kind of code reuse by manipulating pointers in the source language would be tedious. To support code reuse, most object-oriented languages introduce the notion of a *class*. A class is an abstraction that groups together similar objects. All the objects in a class have the same layout. All the objects in a class use the same code members. All the objects in a class have their own distinct data and object members. All member functions are specified with the class. Individual objects are created, or instantiated, by reference to the class.

By requiring that every object be a member of some class, the implementation can optimize space use by storing the code members for the class in an object that represents the class. This adds a member to every object that holds the object's class. It adds a layer of indirection to each code-member reference. Graphically, this might be depicted as

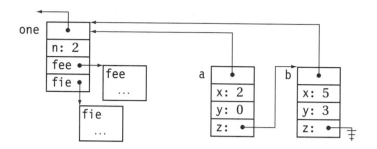

Here, one is the class of both a and b. It holds the code for fee and fie, which are used by both a and b. The representations of a and b have changed, since the representations of fee and fie have moved to one. Furthermore, the object records of a and b now include a pointer to one. Class one has its own private variable, n.

Terminology

The picture of this implementation has become complex enough that we need to introduce terminology to refer to the various parts.

1. *Instance* An instance is the thing that we think of as an object. An instance is an object that belongs to some class. We will assume, for regularity, that every object is an instance of some class.

2. *Object Record* The concrete representation of an instance is its object record. The object record contains all its members (or pointers to them).

3. *Instance Variable* An object's data members are called *instance variables*. In our diagram, a's instance variable x has the value 2. In Java, instance variables are called *fields*. Class one has an instance variable as well, n.

4. *Method* Each code member, or procedure, held in common by the objects of some class is a *method*. Methods are full-fledged procedures. They can have parameters, local variables, and return values.

   The distinction between a method in an object-oriented language and a procedure in Pascal lies in the mechanism for naming it. A method can be named only with respect to an object. Thus, the programmer cannot invoke fee in Java, but must instead write a.fee, where a is an instance of some class that implements fee.

5. *Receiver* Methods are invoked relative to some object. In practice, the implementation adds an implicit parameter to the method that carries a pointer to the appropriate object record. Inside the method, the receiver is accessible using a designated name, such as `this` or `self`.

   In our Java call to `a.fee`, a becomes the receiver inside `fee` and is accessible through the name `this`.

6. *Class* A class is an object that describes the properties of other objects. In particular, a class definition specifies both the instance variables and the methods for each object in the class. The methods become instance variables of the class.

7. *Class Variables* Each class can have instance variables, which are often called class variables. They provide a form of persistent storage visible to any method in the class, independent of the current receiver.

   Because of this similarity in behavior and use to static variables in an Algol-like language, both Java and C++ declare these variables as `static` variables in the class definition. Thus, a local variable of a class becomes an instance variable, while a `static` variable of a class becomes a class variable. In the diagram, the instance variable `n` of class `one` is a class variable.

Inheritance

Most object-oriented languages include the concept of *inheritance*. Inheritance imposes an ancestor relation on classes—each class has one or more parent classes, often called *superclasses*. If β is α's superclass, then α is a *subclass* of β and β's methods work on an object of class α, as long as they are visible in it.

(On the other hand, α's methods are not expected to work on an object of class β, because α's method can access the additional state that an object of class α has. When applied to an object of class β, that state is missing. If the call did occur, the results would likely be catastrophic—when the method tried to access the missing state, some sort of run-time error would occur.)

Inheritance allows the programmer to reuse code by putting common methods in a superclass and using distinct subclasses for methods that must behave differently. Of course, inheritance requires that a subclass have all of the instance variables specified by its superclass—a clear requirement if the superclass methods must work with subclass objects. Additionally, the mechanism for resolving a method name to an executable procedure must

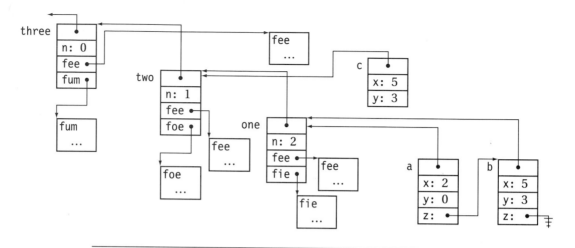

FIGURE 6.7   Finding a Method in the Superclass Hierarchy

extend upward along the chain of superclasses in a natural way. The typical rule works by analogy to a lexically scoped symbol table; if the method is not found in the object's own class, its superclasses are searched, in order by inheritance. The first implementation found is used by the call.

Figure 6.7 shows an example. As before, a and b are members of class one. Now, one has superclass two, and two has superclass three. All of one, two, and three implement the method fee. In addition, each of them implements another method: fie for one, foe for two, and fum for three. The picture shows a third object, c, that is an instance of two. It has instance variables x and y, but objects of class two lack a z.[3]

Mapping Names to Methods

In an object-oriented language, functions must be invoked relative to a specific object, which becomes the receiver. Consider again the structure from Figure 6.7. If the program invokes one.fee, it should find the method defined in class one. An invocation of c.fee should find the fee defined in class two. Finally, an invocation of b.fum should find the implementation in class three.

Conceptually, method lookup behaves as if it performs a search for each procedure call. The search for a method begins in the receiver's class. If that

---

3. The diagram takes one pictorial liberty; it uses the same slot in the object record as a class pointer for the objects (a, b, and c) and as the superclass pointer in the classes (one, two, and three). In a real implementation, the superclass pointer would be a separate field in the object record of each class. The class pointer for a class would point, undoubtedly, to the class class.

fails, the search moves up to the receiver's superclass. This process repeats, moving up the superclass chain until either it locates the method or it fails by exhausting the chain of superclasses. Thus, the search either returns the first implementation found, or it reports failure.

One consequence of this scheme is that the previously suggested misapplication of a method cannot occur. The mechanics of method lookup ensure that an object of class α can never be the receiver for a method of one of α's subclasses. Method lookup proceeds up the superclass chain, not down it. This provides a guarantee reminiscent of a strongly typed language—a method only executes with a receiver for which it is defined.

As the diagram suggests, implementing inheritance requires careful generation of the run-time data structures to support locating and invoking methods—a process often called *dispatching*. Function calls cannot, in general, be handled as in an Algol-like language. Consider what happens inside a method fee declared for class one. If the method for fee calls fie, another method that one implements, can the compiler generate code that calls fie directly? If one has no subclasses, then a direct call to fie must produce the correct behavior.

If, however, one has one or more subclasses, then a call to fie must be handled by indirection through the class hierarchy. If the receiver of fie is an element of some subclass of one and that subclass implements its own fie, then the indirect call will use the object's class pointer, which leads to the appropriate implementation of fie. A direct call, compiled into one's implementation of fee, would invoke the wrong fie.

To make dispatching more efficient, the implementation can place a complete method table in each class, as shown in Figure 6.8. If the class structure can be wholly determined at compile time, then the method tables can be static. Building the tables is easy. The compiler simply treats the inheritance hierarchy as an ordered collection of scopes (one symbol table per class, linked from subclass to superclass, as mentioned in Section 5.7.4). Looking up each method name in this scoped table will resolve it to the implementation that should appear in the class's method table.

If the class structure can change, or it cannot be known at compile time, then the implementation can either use a full lookup in the class hierarchy or it can use complete method tables and include a mechanism to update them when needed. The former strategy produces a run-time representation similar to that shown in Figure 6.7. Dispatching involves tracing up the class hierarchy to the appropriate level and invoking the method found there. The latter strategy uses a run-time representation like the one shown in Figure 6.8. When the class structure changes, for example, by replacing the definition of some class with a new one, the run-time system must rebuild the tables for all affected classes.

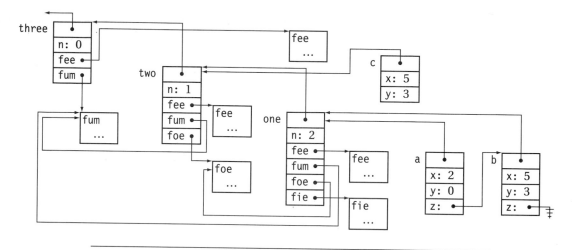

FIGURE 6.8   Class Hierarchy Example with Complete Method Tables in Each Class

Rules for Name Visibility

From the perspective of an executing method, the primary difference between an object-oriented language and an Algol-like language lies in the set of variables that a method can access. In an Algol-like language, such as Pascal, the scoping rules are procedure-centered. Each procedure can access its own parameters and variables, those of surrounding lexical scopes, and any global names. In an object-oriented language, the access rules are object-centered.

When the program invokes a method one.fee, what can that method access? First, fee has access to any names declared locally inside the method, including any parameters it is passed. The code for fee may include lexically nested scopes, which behave in the same way that they would in an Algol-like language. (This implies that a call to a method creates an activation record.) Second, fee can access any of one's instance variables that it knows. (If fee is a superclass method, it may not see all of one's instance variables.) Third, it has access to the class variables of the class that defined fee and any superclasses of that class. Finally, if the language supports a global name scope, it has access to global variables.

To make this concrete, go back to Figure 6.7. Invoking foe with receiver b allows foe to access the values of x and y in b's object record, but not z, since foe is declared in class two and two declares only x and y. Foe can access all of the class variables in two, as well as those in three (and any other superclasses up the chain). It cannot access the class variables of one, because it has no access to the implementation of any of its subclasses.

In contrast, invoking fee with receiver b allows fee access to all of b's instance variables, since the class that declares fee is one. Fee also has access to the class variables of one, two, and three.

Because the set of names that are visible inside a method depends heavily on the class structure of the language, parameter passing assumes a larger role in object-oriented programs than in a classic Algol-like language. Inside a method, the code can invoke another method only if it has the appropriate receiver object; typically, those objects must either be global variables or parameters.

6.4 COMMUNICATING VALUES BETWEEN PROCEDURES

The central notion underlying the concept of a procedure is abstraction. The programmer abstracts common operations relative to a small set of names, or *formal parameters*, and encapsulates those operations in a procedure. To use the procedure, the programmer invokes it with an appropriate *binding* of values, or *actual parameters*, to those formal parameters. The called procedure executes, using the formal parameter names to access the values passed as actual parameters. It can also return a result.

6.4.1 Passing Parameters

Parameter binding maps the actual parameters at a call site to the formal parameters of the called procedure. It lets the programmer write a procedure without knowledge of the contexts in which the procedure will execute. It lets the program invoke the procedure from many distinct contexts without knowledge of the procedure's internal operation. Parameter binding is critical to our ability to write abstract, modular code.

Most modern programming languages use one of two conventions for mapping actual parameters at a call site to the formal parameters declared inside the called procedure, namely, *call-by-value* binding and *call-by-reference* binding. While these techniques differ in their behavior, the distinction between them is best explained by understanding their implementation.

Call by Value

Consider the following procedure, written in C, and several call sites that invoke it:

```
int fee(int x, int y) {        c = fee(2,3);
  x = 2 * x;                    a = 2;
  y = x + y;                    b = 3;
  return y;                     c = fee(a,b);
}                               a = 2;
                                b = 3;
                                c = fee(a,a);
```

With call by value, as in C, the caller copies the value of an actual parameter into the appropriate location for the corresponding formal parameter—either a register or a parameter slot in the callee's AR. Only one name refers to that value—the name of the formal parameter. Its value is an initial condition, determined by evaluating the actual parameter at the time of the call. If the callee changes its value, that change is visible inside the callee, but not in the caller.

The three invocations produce the following results when invoked using call-by-value parameter binding:

Call by	a		b		Return
Value	in	out	in	out	Value
fee(2,3)	–	–	–	–	7
fee(a,b)	2	2	3	3	7
fee(a,a)	2	2	3	3	6

With call by value, the binding is simple and intuitive.

One variation on call by value is call by value and result. In the value-result scheme, the values of formal parameters are copied back into the actual parameters as part of the process of returning control from the callee to the caller. Ada includes value-result parameters. The value-result mechanism also satisfies the rules in the FORTRAN 77 language definition.

Call by Reference

With call-by-reference parameter passing, the caller stores a pointer in the AR slot for each parameter. If the actual parameter is a variable, it stores the variable's address in memory. If the actual parameter is an expression, the caller evaluates the expression, stores the result in its own AR, and then stores a pointer to that result in the appropriate parameter slot in the callee's AR.

CALL-BY-NAME PARAMETER BINDING

Algol introduced another parameter-binding mechanism, *call by name*. In call-by-name binding, a reference to a formal parameter behaves exactly as if the actual parameter had been textually substituted in its place, with appropriate renaming. This simple rule can lead to complex behavior. Consider the following artificial example in Algol 60:

```
begin comment Simple array example;
  procedure zero(Arr,i,j,u1,u2);
    integer Arr;
    integer i,j,u1,u2;
    begin;
      for i := 1 step 1 until u1 do
        for j := 1 step 1 until u2 do
          Arr := 0;
    end;
  integer array Work[1:100,1:200];
  integer p, q, x, y, z;
  x := 100;
  y := 200;
  zero(Work[p,q],p,q,x,y);
end
```

The call to zero assigns zero to every element of the array Work. To see this, rewrite zero with the text of the actual parameters.

While call-by-name binding was easy to define, it was difficult to implement and to understand. In general, the compiler must produce, for each formal parameter, a function that evaluates the actual parameter to return a pointer. These functions are called *thunks*. Generating competent thunks was complex; evaluating a thunk for each parameter access was expensive. In the end, these disadvantages overcame any advantages that call-by-name parameter binding offered.

Constants should be treated as expressions to avoid any possibility of the callee changing the value of a constant. Some languages forbid passing expressions as actual parameters to call-by-reference formal parameters.

Inside the called procedure, each reference to a call-by-reference formal parameter involves an extra level of indirection. Call by reference differs from call by value in two critical ways. First, any redefinition of a reference formal parameter is reflected in the corresponding actual parameter. Second, any reference formal parameter might be bound to a variable that is accessible by another name inside the called procedure. When this happens, we say that the names are *aliases*, since they refer to the same storage location. Aliasing can create counterintuitive behavior.

Consider the earlier example, rewritten in FORTRAN 77, which uses call-by-reference parameter binding.

```
integer function fee(x,y)          c = fee(2,3)
   integer x, y                    a = 2
   x = 2 * x                       b = 3
   y = x + y                       c = fee(a,b)
   fee = y                         a = 2
end                                b = 3
                                   c = fee(a,a)
```

With call-by-reference parameter binding, the example produces different results. We assume that the FORTRAN compiler handles aliased parameters in the intuitive way, even though the FORTRAN 77 standard states that the final call, fee(a,a), is not "standard conforming."

| Call by | a | | b | | Return |
Reference	in	out	in	out	Value
fee(2,3)	–	–	–	–	7
fee(a,b)	2	4	3	7	7
fee(a,a)	2	8	3	3	8

Notice that the second call redefines both a and b; the behavior of call by reference is intended to communicate changes made in the called procedure to the calling environment. The third call makes x and y aliases for each other in fee. The first statement redefines a to have the value 4. The next statement references a's value twice, adds the value of a to itself, and redefines a to have the value 8. This causes fee to return the value 8, rather than 6.

In both call by value and call by reference, the space requirements for representing parameters are small. Since the representation of each parameter must be copied into the AR of the called procedure on each call, this has an impact on the cost of the call. Passing a large object by value entails copying the entire object. Some languages allow the implementation to pass arrays and structures by reference. Others include provisions that let the programmer specify that passing a particular parameter by reference is acceptable; for example the const attribute in C assures the compiler that a parameter with the attribute is not modified.

6.4.2 Returning Values

To return a value from a function, as opposed to changing the value of one of its actual parameters, the compiler must set aside space for the returned value. Because the return value, by definition, is used after the called procedure terminates, it needs storage outside the called procedure's AR. If the compiler writer can ensure that the return value is of small fixed size, then it can store the value either in the caller's AR or in a designated register.

All of our pictures of the AR have included a slot for a returned value. To use this slot, the caller allocates space for the returned value in its own AR, and stores a pointer to that space in the return slot of its own AR. The callee can load the pointer from the caller's return-value slot (using the copy of the caller's ARP that it has in the callee's AR). It can use the pointer to access the storage set aside in the caller's AR for the returned value. As long as both caller and callee agree about the size of the returned value, this works.

If the caller cannot know the size of the returned value, the callee may need to allocate space for it, presumably on the heap. In this case, the callee allocates the space, stores the returned value there, and stores the pointer in the return-value slot of the caller's AR. On return, the caller can access the return value using the pointer that it finds in its return-value slot.

If both the caller and callee know that the return value is small—the size of the return-value slot or less—then they can eliminate the indirection. For a small return value, the callee can store the value directly into the return value slot of the caller's AR. The caller can then use the value directly from its AR. This improvement requires, of course, that both the caller and callee recognize this case and handle it the same way.

(This is an excellent example of the kind of improvement that can cause incompatibility between different compilers for the same language on the same machine. Imagine two compilers, one that implemented this improvement and another that did not. An executable that contained code compiled with each compiler might well fail with a cryptic run-time error caused by dereferencing a return value as if it were a pointer. The possibility of this kind of disastrous failure usually stops compiler writers from making even minor changes to the linkage convention.)

6.5 ESTABLISHING ADDRESSABILITY

As part of the linkage convention, the compiler must ensure that each procedure can generate an address for each variable that it needs to reference. In an Algol-like language, a procedure can refer to global variables, local variables, and any variable declared in a surrounding lexical scope. In general, the address calculation consists of two portions: finding the address of the chunk of memory for the scope containing the value, called a *data area*, and finding the offset within that data area.

6.5.1 Trivial Base Addresses

For many variables, the compiler can emit code that generates the base address in one or two instructions. The easiest case is a local variable of the current procedure. If the variable is stored in the procedure's AR, the compiler can use the ARP as its base address. While the exact sequence of operations will depend on the addressing modes that the IR can represent, a number of options are possible. These include using a single "register + immediate offset" operation (like loadAI), using an "address + offset" operation (like loadAO) if the offset is too large for an immediate field, or using a three-operation sequence (loadAI, add, load). In any of these scenarios, the address calculation should be fast.

(Sometimes, a local variable is not stored at a constant offset from the procedure's ARP. The value might reside in a register, in which case loads and stores are not needed. If the variable has an unpredictable or changing size, the compiler will store it in an area reserved for variable-size objects, either at the end of the AR or in the heap. In this case, the compiler can reserve space in the AR for a pointer to the variable's actual location. It then needs to generate one additional indirection to access the variable.)

Access to global and static variables is handled similarly, except that the compiler may need to load the base address into a register. It can emit an immediate load of a symbolic, assembly-level label for the base address. It must use consistent rules to generate such labels. Typically, it adds a prefix, a suffix, or both to a source-code name, using characters that are illegal in the source language. The assembler and loader will replace the symbolic label with the correct run-time value.

For example, a global variable fee might lead to the label &fee., assuming that neither ampersand (&) nor period (.) can appear in a source-language name. The compiler would emit the appropriate assembly-language pseudo-operation to reserve space for fee and attach the label to that pseudo-operation. To get fee's run-time address into a register, it would emit an operation such as `loadI &fee. ⇒ r`$_i$. The next operation can then use r_i to access the memory location for `fee`.

The compiler need not know where `fee` is stored. It uses a relocatable label to ensure that the appropriate run-time address is written into the instruction stream. The immediate load operation ensures that r_i will contain the appropriate address. The assembler, linker, and loader resolve the symbol `&fee.` to a run-time address.

Global variables may be labelled individually or in larger groups. In FORTRAN, for example, the language collects global variables into common blocks. A typical FORTRAN compiler establishes one label for each common block. It assigns an offset to each variable in each common block and generates `load` and `store` operations relative to the common block's label. If the data area is larger than the offset allowed in a "register + offset" operation, it may be advantageous to have multiple labels for parts of the data area.

Similarly, the compiler may combine all the static variables in a single scope into one data area. This reduces the likelihood of an unexpected naming conflict; such conflicts are discovered during linking or loading and can be confusing to the programmer. To avoid such conflicts, the compiler can base the label on a globally visible name associated with the scope. This strategy can also decrease the number of base addresses used by any procedure, reducing demand for registers. Using too many registers to hold base addresses may adversely affect overall run-time performance.

6.5.2 Local Variables of Other Procedures

In a lexically scoped language, the compiler must provide a mechanism to map static coordinates to hardware addresses for the corresponding variables. To accomplish this, the compiler must put in place data structures that let it compute the addresses of the ARs of the lexical scopes that surround the current procedure.

For example, assume that `fee`, at lexical level m, references variable a declared in `fee`'s lexical ancestor `fie`, at level n. The parser converts this reference into a static coordinate $\langle n,o \rangle$, where o is a's offset in the AR for `fie`. The compiler can compute the number of lexical levels between `fee` and `fie` as $m-n$. (The coordinate $\langle m-n,o \rangle$ is called a *static-distance coordinate*. It specifies the lexical distance between `fee`'s AR and `fie`'s AR, as well as a's offset from `fie`'s ARP.)

To convert $\langle n,o \rangle$ into a run-time address, the compiler needs a mechanism for tracking lexical ancestry among activation records. It must emit the code required to keep this information current at run time. Then, at each reference to a local variable of another scope, the compiler must emit code that uses this run-time data structure to compute the desired address.

Several mechanisms have been used to solve this problem. We will examine two, namely, access links and a global display.

Access Links

With access links, the compiler ensures that each AR contains a pointer to the AR of its immediate lexical ancestor. The code uses this pointer, called an *access link* or a *static link*, to access nonlocal variables. The access links form a chain that includes all the lexical ancestors of the current procedure, as shown in Figure 6.9. Thus, any local variable of another procedure that is visible to the current procedure is stored in an AR on the chain of access links.

To access a variable $\langle n,o \rangle$ from a level m procedure, the compiler emits code that walks the chain of links to find the level n ARP. Then, it emits a

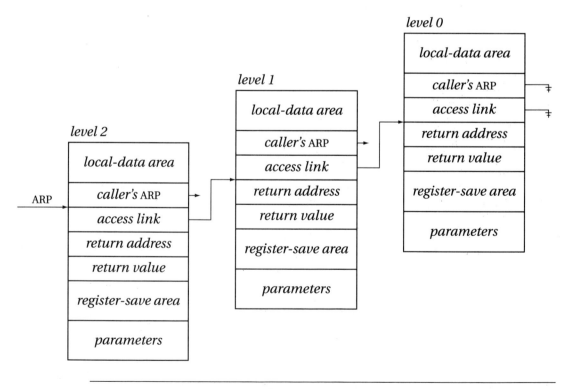

FIGURE 6.9   Using Access Links

load using the level n ARP and o. To make this concrete, consider the program represented by Figure 6.9. Assume that m is 2 and that the access link is stored at an offset of -4 from the ARP. The following table shows the ILOC code that a compiler might generate for three different static coordinates. The left column gives the static coordinate; the right one shows the corresponding ILOC code. Each sequence leaves the result in r_2.

$\langle 2,24 \rangle$	loadAI r_{arp},24	$\Rightarrow r_2$
$\langle 1,12 \rangle$	loadAI r_{arp},-4	$\Rightarrow r_1$
	loadAI r_1,12	$\Rightarrow r_2$
$\langle 0,16 \rangle$	loadAI r_{arp},-4	$\Rightarrow r_1$
	loadAI r_1,-4	$\Rightarrow r_1$
	loadAI r_1,16	$\Rightarrow r_2$

Since the compiler has the static coordinate for each reference, it can compute the static distance $(m-n)$. The distance tells it how many chain-following loads to generate, so the compiler can emit the correct sequence for each non-local reference. The cost of the address calculation is proportional to the static difference. If programs exhibit shallow lexical nesting, the difference in cost between accessing two variables at different levels will be fairly small.

To maintain access links, the compiler must add code to each procedure call that finds the appropriate ARP and stores it as the callee's access link. For a caller at level m and a callee at level n, three cases arise. If $n = m + 1$, the callee is nested inside the caller, and the callee can use the caller's ARP as its access link. If $n = m$, the callee's access link is the same as the caller's access link. Finally, if $n < m$, the callee's access link is the level $n-1$ access link for the caller. (If n is zero, the access link is null.) The compiler can generate a sequence of $m-n+1$ loads to find this ARP and store that pointer as the callee's access link.

Global Display

In this scheme, the compiler allocates a single global array, called the *display*, to hold the ARPs of the most recent activations of a procedure at each lexical level. All references to local variables of other procedures become indirect references through the display. To access a variable $\langle n,o \rangle$, the compiler uses the ARP from element n of the display. It uses o as the offset and generates the appropriate load operation. Figure 6.10 shows this situation.

Returning to the static coordinates used in the discussion of access links, the following table shows code that the compiler might emit for a display-based implementation. Assume that the current procedure is at lexical level 2, and that the label _disp gives the address of the display.

$\langle 2,24 \rangle$	loadAI	$r_{arp},24$	$\Rightarrow r_2$
$\langle 1,12 \rangle$	loadI	_disp	$\Rightarrow r_1$
	loadAI	$r_1,4$	$\Rightarrow r_1$
	loadAI	$r_1,12$	$\Rightarrow r_2$
$\langle 0,16 \rangle$	loadI	_disp	$\Rightarrow r_1$
	loadAI	$r_1,16$	$\Rightarrow r_2$

With a display, the cost of nonlocal access is fixed. With access links, the compiler generates a series of $m-n$ loads; with a display, it uses $n \times l$ as offset into the display, where l is the length of a pointer (4 in the example). Local access is still cheaper than nonlocal access, but with a display, the penalty for nonlocal access is constant, rather than variable.

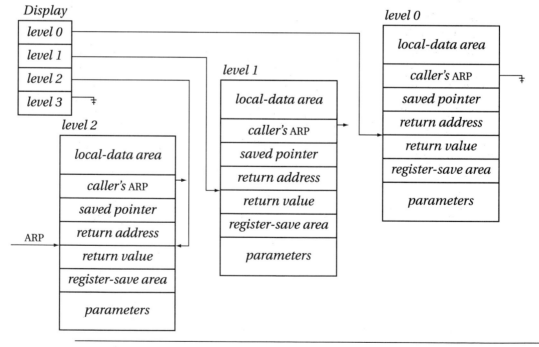

FIGURE 6.10   Using a Global Display

Of course, the compiler must insert code where needed to maintain the display. Thus, when procedure p at level n calls some procedure q at level $n+1$, p's ARP becomes the display entry for level n. (While p is executing, that entry is unused.) The simplest way to keep the display current is to have p update the level n entry when control enters p and to restore it on exit from p. On entry, p can copy the level n display entry to the reserved addressability slot in its AR and store its own ARP in the level n slot of the display.

Of course, many of these display updates can be avoided. The only procedures that can use the ARP stored by a procedure p are procedures q that p calls (directly or indirectly), where q is nested inside p's scope. Thus, any p that does not call a procedure nested inside itself need not update the display. This eliminates all updates in leaf procedures, as well as many other updates.

Choosing between Them

The compiler can implement only one of these techniques. Both have strengths and weaknesses.

1. Each adds overhead. The cost of display maintenance is constant—a load and store on call and return. The cost of access-link maintenance varies, but the common case of a level n procedure calling a level $n+1$ procedure is cheap.

2. References through a display have constant cost. If nonlocal accesses occur often enough to be a concern, the display pointer may end up occupying its own register. In the same scenario, however, it is likely that the display will stay in cache, decreasing the actual cost of indirection through the display.

3. References through the access-link chain incur a variable cost. Since the start of the chain is stored at the ARP, no register is required to point to the chain. Since the compiler has little control over how the ARs map to the cache, traversing the chain may incur cache misses.

In practice, the cost difference between these two schemes depends on the ratio of nonlocal references to procedure calls and returns.

There are, however, cases in which the choice is clear. For example, if ARs can outlive the invocations that create them, access links still work, while a global display does not. This makes access links the common choice for languages that treat procedures as first-class objects.

6.6 STANDARDIZED LINKAGES

The procedure linkage is a contract between the compiler, the operating system, and the target machine that clearly divides responsibility for naming, allocation of resources, addressability, and protection. The procedure linkage ensures interoperability of procedures between the user's code, as translated by the compiler, and code from other sources, including system libraries, application libraries, and code written in other programming languages. Typically, all of the compilers for a given combination of target machine and operating system use the same procedure linkage, to the extent possible.

The linkage convention serves to isolate each procedure from the different environments found at call sites that invoke it. Assume that procedure p has an integer parameter x. Different calls to p may bind x to a local variable stored in the calling procedure's stack frame, to a global variable, to an element of some static array, and to the result of evaluating an integer expression such as $y + 2$. Because the procedure linkage specifies how to evaluate and store the value passed to x in the calling procedure, and how to access x in the called procedure, the compiler can generate code for the body of the called procedure that ignores the differences between the run-time environments at the different calls to p. As long as all the procedures obey the linkage convention, the details will mesh to create the seamless transfer of values promised by the source-language specification.

The linkage convention is, of necessity, machine-dependent. For example, the linkage convention implicitly depends on information such as the number of registers available on the target machine, and the mechanisms for executing a call and a return.

Figure 6.11 shows how the pieces of a standard procedure linkage fit together. Each procedure has a *prologue sequence* and an *epilogue sequence*. Each call site includes both a *precall sequence* and a *postreturn sequence*.

Precall   The precall sequence begins the process of constructing the callee's environment. It evaluates the actual parameters, determines the return address, and, if necessary, the address of space reserved to hold a return value. If a call-by-reference parameter is currently allocated to a register, the precall sequence needs to store it into the caller's AR so that it can pass that location's address to the callee.

Many of the values shown in the diagrams of the AR can be passed to the callee in registers. The return address, an address for the return value, and the caller's ARP are obvious candidates. The first k actual parameters can be passed in registers as well—a typical value for k might be 4. If the

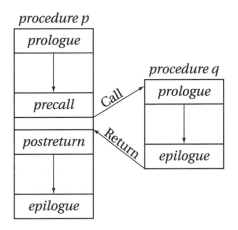

FIGURE 6.11   A Standard Procedure Linkage

call has more than k parameters, the remaining actual parameters must be stored in either the callee's AR or the caller's AR.

Postreturn   The postreturn sequence undoes the actions of the precall sequence. It must restore any call-by-reference and call-by-value-result parameters that need to be returned to registers. It restores any caller-saved registers from the register save area. It may need to deallocate all or part of the callee's AR.

Prologue   The prologue sequence for a procedure completes the task of constructing the callee's run-time environment. It may create space in the callee's AR to store some of the values passed by the caller in registers. It must create space for local variables and initialize them, as necessary. If the callee references a procedure-specific static data area, it may need to load the label for that data area into a register.

Epilogue   The epilogue sequence for a procedure begins the process of dismantling the callee's environment and reconstructing the caller's environment. It may participate in deallocating the callee's AR. If the procedure returns a value, the epilogue may be responsible for storing the value into the address specified by the caller. (Alternatively, the code generated for a return statement may perform this task.) Finally, it restores the caller's ARP and jumps to the return address.

This is a general framework for building the linkage convention. Many of the tasks can be shifted between caller and callee. In general, moving work into the prologue and epilogue sequences produces more compact code. The precall and postreturn sequences are generated for each procedure call, while the prologue and epilogue occur once per procedure. If procedures are called, on average, more than once, then there are fewer prologue and epilogue sequences than precall and postreturn sequences.

Saving Registers

At some point in the call sequence, any register values that the caller expects to survive across the call must be saved into memory. The caller can perform this task; since the caller knows precisely which values are live across the call, it might preserve fewer registers than the callee. This convention is named *caller saves*. The callee can perform this task; since the callee knows precisely which registers it will use, it may let some values remain untouched in their registers. This convention is named *callee saves*.

Each convention has arguments in its favor. The procedure that saves and restores registers can potentially use knowledge of its own behavior to avoid some of the saves and restores. For any specific division of labor, we can construct programs for which it works well and programs for which does not. Many modern systems take a middle ground and designate half the register set for caller-saves treatment and the other half for callee-saves treatment. In practice, this seems to work well. It encourages the compiler to put long-lived values in callee-saves registers, where they will be stored only if the callee actually needs the register. It encourages the compiler to put short-lived values in caller-saves registers, where it may avoid saving them at a call.

Allocating the Activation Record

In the most general case, both the caller and the callee need access to the callee's AR. Unfortunately, the caller cannot know, in general, how large to make the callee's AR (unless the compiler and linker can contrive to have the linker paste the appropriate values into each call site).

With stack-allocated ARs, a middle ground is possible. Since allocation consists of incrementing the stack-top pointer, the caller can begin the creation of the callee's AR by bumping the stack top and storing values into the appropriate places. When control passes to the callee, it can extend the partially built AR by further incrementing the stack top to create space for local data. In this scheme, the postreturn sequence can reset the stack-top pointer, performing the entire deallocation in one step.

With heap-allocated ARs, it may not be possible to extend the callee's AR incrementally. In this situation, the caller can pass almost all of the val-

MORE ABOUT TIME

In a typical system, the linkage convention is negotiated between the compiler implementors and the operating-system implementors at an early stage of the system's development. Thus, issues such as the distinction between caller-saves and callee-saves registers are decided at design time. When the compiler runs, it must emit procedure prologue and epilogue sequences for each procedure, along with precall and postreturn sequences for each call site. This code executes at run time. Thus, the compiler cannot know the return address that it should store into a callee's AR. (Neither can it know, in general, the address of that AR.) It can, however, include a mechanism that will generate the return address at link time (using a relocatable assembly language label) or at run time (using some offset from the program counter) and store it into the appropriate location in the callee's AR.

Similarly, in a system that uses a display to provide addressability for local variables of other procedures, the compiler cannot know the run-time addresses of the display or the AR. Nonetheless, it emits code to maintain the display. The mechanism that achieves this requires two pieces of information: the lexical nesting level of the current procedure and the address of the global display. The former is known at compile time; the latter can be determined at link time by using a relocatable assembly language label. Thus, the prologue can simply store the current display entry for the procedure's level into its AR (using a `loadAO` from the display address) and store it into the AR (using a `storeAO` relative to the ARP).

ues needed for the AR in registers; the prologue sequence can allocate an appropriate-size AR and store values into it as needed. The one major complication in this scheme arises when a procedure has an excess number of formal parameters. All of our diagrams show the actual parameters stored in the callee's AR; with heap-allocated ARs, it may be impossible for the caller to save actual parameter values there. In this situation, the compiler writer may choose to have the caller store excess actual parameters in its own AR. This eliminates any need for the caller to access the callee's AR and lets the callee assume complete responsibility for allocating and deallocating its own AR. Of course, parameters stored in the caller's AR may be slightly more expensive to access, since the caller's ARP may not always be in a register when control is in the callee.

Managing Displays and Access Links

Either mechanism for managing nonlocal access requires some work in the calling sequence. Using a display, the prologue sequence updates the display record for its own level and the epilogue sequence restores it. If the procedure never calls a more deeply nested procedure, it can skip this step. Using access links, the precall sequence must locate the appropriate first access link for the callee. The amount of work varies with the difference in lexical level between caller and callee. As long as the called procedure is known at compile time, either scheme is reasonably efficient. If the callee is unknown (if it is, for example, a function-valued parameter), the compiler may need to emit special-case code to perform the appropriate steps.

6.7 MANAGING MEMORY

Another issue that the compiler writer must face in implementing procedures is memory management. In most modern systems, each program executes in its own logical address space. The layout, organization, and management of this address space requires cooperation between the compiler and the operating system to provide an efficient implementation that falls within the rules and restrictions imposed by the source language and the target machine.

6.7.1 Memory Layout

The compiler, the operating system, and the target machine cooperate to ensure that multiple programs can execute safely on an interleaved (time-sliced) basis. Many of the decisions about how to lay out, manipulate, and manage a program's address space lie outside the purview of the compiler writer. However, the decisions have a strong impact on the code that must be generated and the performance achieved by that code. Thus, the compiler writer must have a broad understanding of these issues.

Placing Run-Time Data Structures

At run time, a compiled program consists of executable code and several distinct categories of data. The compiled code is often of fixed size. Some of the data areas are also fixed in size; for example, the data areas for global and

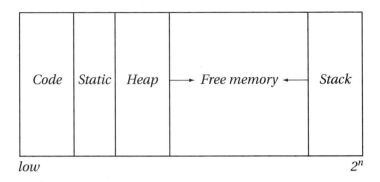

FIGURE 6.12 Logical Address-Space Layout

static variables in languages like FORTRAN and C neither grow nor shrink during execution. Other data areas have sizes that change throughout execution; for example, the area that holds ARs for active procedures expands and shrinks as the program executes.

Figure 6.12 shows a typical layout for the address space used by a single compiled program. Fixed size executable code sits at the low end of the address space; the adjacent region, labelled *Static* in the diagram, holds static and global data areas, along with certain kinds of compiler-generated data. (Depending on the program and source language, the compiler may also need to store constants, jump tables for switch statements, method tables, and information to support garbage collection and debugging.) The remainder of the address space is devoted to data areas that expand and contract; if the language allows stack allocation of ARs, the compiler needs to leave space for both the heap and the stack. To allow the best utilization of the space, they should be placed at opposite ends of the open space and allowed to grow toward each other. The heap grows toward higher addresses; the stack grows toward lower addresses.

From the compiler's perspective, the logical address space is the whole picture. However, modern computer systems typically execute many programs in an interleaved fashion. The operating system maps several different logical address spaces into the single address space supported by the target machine. Figure 6.13 shows this larger picture. Each program is isolated in its own logical address space; each can behave as if it has its own machine.

A single logical address space can be spread across disjoint segments (or pages) of the physical address space; thus, the addresses 100,000 and 200,000 in the program's logical address space need not be 100,000 bytes apart in physical memory. In fact, the physical address associated with the logical address 100,000 may be larger than the physical address associated with the logical address 200,000. The mapping from logical addresses to physical addresses is

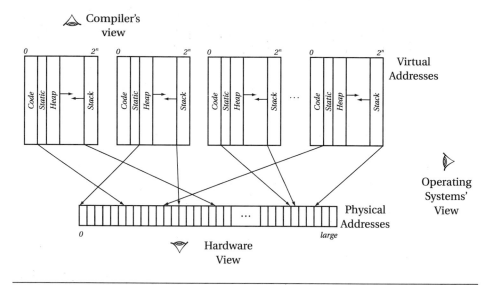

FIGURE 6.13 Different Views of the Address Space

maintained cooperatively by the hardware and the operating system. It is, in almost all respects, beyond the compiler's purview.

Impact of Memory Model on Code Shape

The compiler writer must decide whether to keep values in registers aggressively or to keep them in memory. This decision has a major impact on the code that the compiler emits for individual statements.

With a memory-to-memory model, the compiler works within the limited set of registers on the target machine. The code that it emits uses real register names. The compiler ensures, on a statement-by-statement basis, that demand for registers does not exceed the set of registers available on the target machine. Under these circumstances, register allocation becomes an optimization that improves the code, rather than a transformation that is necessary for correctness.

With a register-to-register model, the compiler assumes that it has a set of virtual registers, rather than the real register set of the target machine. The virtual register set has unlimited size. The compiler associates a virtual register with each value that can legally reside in a register;[4] such a value is stored to memory only when it is passed as a call-by-reference parameter, when it is

---

4. In general, a value can be kept in a register if it can be accessed using only a single name. We call such a value an *unambiguous value*.

passed as a return value, or when the register allocator spills it (see Chapter 13). With a register-to-register memory model, the register allocator must be run to reduce demand for registers and to map the virtual register names to target-machine register names.

Alignment and Padding

Target machines have specific requirements on where data items can be stored. A typical set of restrictions might specify that 32-bit integers and 32-bit floating-point numbers begin on word (32-bit) boundaries, that 64-bit floating-point data begin on doubleword (64-bit) boundaries, and that string data begin on halfword (16-bit) boundaries. We call these *alignment rules*.

Some machines have a specific instruction to implement procedure calls; it might save registers or store the return address. Such support can add further alignment restrictions; for example, the instruction might dictate some portions of the AR format and add an alignment rule for the start of each AR. The DEC VAX computers have a particularly elaborate call instruction; it automatically stores registers and other portions of the processor state.[5]

To comply with the target machine's alignment rules, the compiler may need to waste some space. To assign locations in a data area, the compiler should order the variables into groups, from those with the most restrictive alignment rules to those with the least. (For example, doubleword alignment is more restrictive than full-word alignment.) Typically, the assembler has a directive to ensure that the loader begins a data area on a given alignment, such as a doubleword boundary. Starting at such a boundary, the compiler can assign all the variables in the most restricted category, followed by the next most restricted class, and so on, until all variables have been assigned offsets. Since alignment rules almost always specify a power of two, the end of each category will naturally fit the restriction for the next category.

Relative Offsets and Cache Performance

The widespread use of cache memories in modern computer systems has subtle implications for the layout of variables in memory. If two values are used in proximity in the code, the compiler would like to ensure that they can reside in the cache at the same time. This can be accomplished in two ways.

---

5. For each procedure, the compiler determines what registers and state bits must be saved. It encodes this information into a bit mask that is stored before the procedure's prologue. A procedure-call instruction retrieves the mask and interprets it, saving the specified registers and state bits.

A PRIMER ON CACHE MEMORIES

One way that machine architects try to bridge the gap between processor speed and memory speed is through the use of *cache memories*. A cache is a small, fast memory placed between the processor and main memory. The cache is divided into a series of equal-sized *frames*. Each frame has an address field, called its *tag*, that holds a main-memory address.

The hardware automatically maps memory locations to cache frames. The simplest mapping, used in a direct-mapped cache, computes the cache address as the main memory address modulo the size of the cache. This partitions the memory into a linear set of blocks, each the size of a cache frame. A *line* is a memory block that maps to a frame. At any point in time, each cache frame holds a copy of the data from one of its blocks. Its tag field holds the address in memory where that data normally resides.

On each read access to memory, the hardware checks to see if the requested word is already in its cache frame. If so, the requested bytes are returned to the processor. If not, the block currently in the frame is evicted and the requested block is brought into the cache.

Some caches use more complex mappings. A set-associative cache uses multiple frames for each cache line, typically two or four frames per line. A fully associative cache can place any block in any frame. Both these schemes use an associative search over the tags to determine if a block is in the cache. Associative schemes use a policy to determine which block to evict; common schemes are random replacement and least-recently-used (LRU) replacement.

In practice, the effective memory speed is determined by memory bandwidth, cache block length, the ratio of cache speed to memory speed, and the percentage of accesses that hit in the cache. From the compiler's perspective, the first three are fixed. Compiler-based efforts to improve memory performance focus on increasing the hit ratio.

Some architectures provide instructions that allow a program to give the cache hints as to when specific blocks should be brought into memory (*prefetched*) and when they are no longer needed (*flushed*).

In the best situation, the two values would share a single cache block, which guarantees that the values are fetched from memory to the cache together. If they cannot share a cache block, the compiler would like to ensure that the two variables map to different cache lines. The compiler can achieve this by controlling the distance between their addresses.

If we consider just two variables, controlling the distance between them seems manageable. When all the active variables are considered, however, the problem of optimal arrangement for a cache is NP-complete. Most variables have interactions with many other variables; this creates a web of relationships that the compiler may not be able to satisfy concurrently. If we consider a loop that uses several large arrays, the problem of arranging mutual non-interference becomes even worse. If the compiler can discover the relationship between the various array references in the loop, it can add padding between the arrays to increase the likelihood that the references hit different cache lines and, thus, do not interfere with each other.

As we saw previously, the mapping of the program's logical address space to the hardware's physical address space need not preserve the distance between specific variables. Carrying this thought to its logical conclusion, the reader should ask how the compiler can ensure anything about relative offsets that are larger than the size of a virtual-memory page. The processor's physical cache may use either virtual addresses or physical addresses in its tag fields. A virtually addressed cache preserves the spacing between values that the compiler creates; with such a cache, the compiler may be able to plan noninterference between large objects. With a physically addressed cache, the distance between two locations in different pages is determined by the page mapping (unless cache size $\leq$ page size). Thus, the compiler's decisions about memory layout have little, if any, effect, except within a single page. In this situation, the compiler should focus on getting objects that are referenced together into the same page and, if possible, the same cache block.

6.7.2   Algorithms to Manage the Heap

Many programming languages deal with objects that are dynamically created and destroyed. The compiler cannot usually determine the size or lifetime of such objects. To handle such objects, the compiler and the operating system create a pool of dynamically allocatable storage that is commonly called the *run-time heap*, or just the heap. Many issues arise in creating and managing the heap; some of these are exposed to the source-language programmer, while others are only visible to the authors of system software.

This section briefly explores some of the algorithms used to manage heaps. It considers the case of an explicitly managed heap, in which the programmer must allocate and free space. The next section explores algorithms that perform implicit deallocation.

We assume a simple interface to the heap, namely, a routine allocate(size) and a routine free(address). The allocate routine takes an integer argument size and returns the address of a block of space in the heap that contains at least size bytes. The free routine takes the address of a block of previously allocated space in the heap and returns it to the pool of free space.

The critical issues that arise in designing algorithms for explicitly managing the heap are the speeds of both allocate and free and the extent to which the pool of free space becomes fragmented into small blocks. We first consider a simple allocation model, *first-fit allocation*.

First-Fit Allocation

The goal of a first-fit allocator is to allocate and free space in the heap quickly. The first-fit scheme emphasizes speed over memory utilization. Every block in the heap has a hidden field that holds its size, as bookkeeping overhead. In general, the size field is located in the word preceding the address returned by allocate. Blocks available for allocation reside on a list called the *free list*. In addition to the mandatory size field, each block on the free list has a pointer to the next block on the free list (or null for the last block) and a pointer to the block itself in the last word of the block.

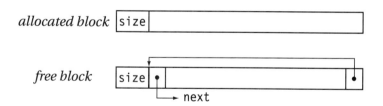

The initial condition for the heap is a single large block placed on the free list, with the last word containing a pointer to the block's start and a null next field.

A call allocate(k) causes the following sequence of events. The allocate routine walks the free list until it discovers a block with size greater than or equal to k plus one word for the size field. Assume it finds an appropriate block, b_i. It removes b_i from the free list. If b_i is larger than necessary, allocate creates a new free block from the excess space at the end of b_i and places that block on the free list. The allocate routine returns a pointer to the second word of b_i.

If allocate fails to find a large enough block, it tries to extend the heap. If it succeeds in extending the heap, it returns a block of appropriate size from this newly allocated portion of the heap. If extending the heap fails, allocate reports failure (typically by returning a null pointer).

To deallocate a block, the program calls free with the address of the block, b_j. The simplest implementation of free adds b_j to the head of the free list and returns. This produces a fast free routine. Unfortunately, it leads to an allocator that, over time, fragments memory into small blocks.

To overcome this flaw, the allocator can use the pointer at the end of a freed block to coalesce adjacent free blocks. The free routine loads the word preceding b_j's size field, which is the end-of-block pointer for the block that immediately precedes b_j in memory. If that word contains a valid pointer, and it points to a matching block header (one whose address plus size field points to the start of b_j), then both b_j and its predecessor are free. The free routine can combine them by increasing the predecessor's size field and storing the appropriate pointer in the last word of b_j. Coalescing the new block onto its predecessor avoids updating the free list.

To make this scheme work, allocate and free must maintain the end-of-block pointers. Each time that free processes a block, it must update the end-of-block pointer with the address of the head of the block. The allocate routine must invalidate either the next pointer or the end-of-block pointer to prevent free from coalescing a freed block with an allocated block in which those fields have not been overwritten.

The free routine can also try to combine b_j with its successor b_k in memory. It can use b_j's size field to locate the start of b_k. It can use b_k's size field and end-of-block pointer to determine if b_k is free. If b_k is free, then free can combine the two blocks, removing b_k from the free list and adding b_j to the free list. To make this free-list update efficient, the free list needs to be doubly linked. Of course, the pointers are stored in unallocated blocks, so the space overhead is irrelevant. Extra time required to update the doubly linked free list is minimal.

As described, the coalescing scheme depends on the fact that the relationship between the final pointer and the size field in a free block are absent in an allocated block. While it is extremely unlikely that the allocator will identify an allocated block as free, this can happen. To ensure against this unlikely event, the implementor can make the end-of-block pointer a field that exists in both allocated and free blocks. On allocation, the pointer is set to contain an address outside the heap, such as zero. On freeing, the pointer is set to the block's own address. The cost of this added assurance is an extra field in each allocated block and an extra store for each allocation.

Many variations on first-fit allocation have been tried. They trade off the cost of allocate, the cost of free, the amount of fragmentation produced by

ARENA-BASED ALLOCATION

Inside the compiler itself, the compiler writer may find it profitable to use a specialized allocator. Compilers have phase-oriented activity. This lends itself well to an arena-based allocation scheme.

With an arena-based allocator, the program creates an arena at the beginning of an activity. It uses the arena to hold allocated objects that are related in their use. Calls to allocate objects in the arena are satisfied in a stacklike fashion; an allocation involves incrementing a pointer to the arena's high-water mark and returning a pointer to the newly allocated block. No call is used to deallocate individual objects; they are freed when the arena that contains them is deallocated.

The arena-based allocator is a compromise between traditional allocators and garbage-collecting allocators. With an arena-based allocator, the calls to allocate can be made lightweight (as in the modern allocator). No freeing calls are needed; the program frees the entire arena in a single call when it finishes the activity for which the arena was created.

a long series of allocations, and the amount of space wasted by returning blocks larger than requested.

Multipool Allocators

Modern allocators use a simple technique derived from first-fit allocation but simplified by a couple of observations about the behavior of programs. As memory sizes grew in the early 1980s, it became reasonable to waste some space if doing so led to faster allocation. At the same time, studies of program behavior suggested that real programs allocate memory frequently in a few common sizes and infrequently in large or unusual sizes.

Modern allocators use separate memory pools for several common sizes. Typically, selected sizes are powers of 2, starting with a small block size (such as 16 bytes) and running up to the size of a virtual-memory page (typically 4096 or 8192 bytes). Each pool has only one size of block, so allocate can return the first block on the appropriate free list, and free can simply add the block to the head of the appropriate free list. For requests larger than a page, a separate first-fit allocator is used. Allocators based on these ideas are fast. They work particularly well for heap allocation of activation records.

These changes simplify both allocate and free. The allocate routine must check for an empty free list and increase the appropriate pool by a page if it is empty. The free routine simply inserts the block at the head of the free list for its size. A careful implementation could determine the size of a freed block by checking its address against the memory segments allocated for each pool. Alternative schemes include using a size field as before, and, if the allocator places all the storage on a page into a single pool, storing the size of the blocks in a page in the first word of the page.

Debugging Help

Programs written with explicit allocation and deallocation are notoriously difficult to debug. It appears that programmers have difficulty deciding when to free heap-allocated objects. If the allocator can quickly distinguish between an allocated object and a free object, then the heap-management software can provide the programmer with some help in debugging.

For example, to coalesce adjacent free blocks, the allocator needs a pointer from the end of a block back to its head. If an allocated block has that pointer set to an invalid value, then the deallocation routine can check that field and report a run-time error when the program attempts to deallocate a free block or an illegal address—a pointer to anything other than the start of an allocated block.

For a modest additional overhead, the heap-management software can provide additional help. By linking together allocated blocks, the allocator can create an environment for memory-allocation debugging tools. A snapshot tool can walk the list of allocated blocks. Tagging blocks by the call site that created them lets the tool expose memory leaks. Timestamping them allows the tool to provide the programmer with detailed information about memory use. Tools of this sort can provide invaluable help in locating blocks that are never deallocated.

6.7.3 Implicit Deallocation

Many programming languages allow an implementation to deallocate memory objects automatically when they are no longer in use. This requires some care in the implementation of both the allocator and the compiled code. To perform implicit deallocation, or *garbage collection*, the compiler and run-time system must include a mechanism for determining when an object is no longer of interest, or dead, and a mechanism for reclaiming and recycling the dead space.

The work associated with garbage collection can be performed incrementally, for individual statements, or it can be performed as a batch-oriented task that runs on demand, when the free-space pool is exhausted. *Reference counting* is a classic way to perform incremental garbage collection. *Mark-sweep collection* is a classic approach to performing batch-oriented collection.

Reference Counting

This technique adds a counter to each heap-allocated object. The counter tracks the number of outstanding pointers that refer to the object. When the allocator creates the object, it sets the reference count to one. Each assignment to a pointer variable adjusts two reference counts. It decrements the reference count of the pointer's preassignment value and increments the reference count of the pointer's postassignment value. When an object's reference count drops to zero, no pointer exists that can reach the object, so the system can safely free the object. Freeing an object may, in turn, discard pointers to other objects. This must decrement the reference counts of those objects. Thus, discarding the last pointer to an abstract syntax tree should free the entire tree. When the root node's reference count drops to zero, it is freed and its descendant's reference counts are decremented. This, in turn, should free the descendants, decrementing the counts of their children. This continues until the entire AST has been freed.

The presence of pointers in allocated objects creates problems for reference-counting schemes, as follows:

1. The running code needs a mechanism to distinguish pointers from other data. It may either store extra information in the header field for each object or limit the range of pointers to less than a full word and use the remaining bits to "tag" the pointer. Batch collectors face the same problem and use the same solutions.

2. The amount of work done for a single decrement can grow quite large. If external constraints require bounded deallocation times, the run-time system can adopt a more complex protocol that limits the number of objects deallocated for each pointer assignment. By keeping a queue of objects that must be freed and limiting the number handled on each reference-count adjustment, the system can distribute the work of freeing objects over a larger set of operations. This amortizes the cost of freeing over the set of all assignments to heap-allocated objects and bounds the work done per assignment.

3. The program might form cyclic graphs with pointers. The reference counts for a cyclic data structure cannot be decremented to zero.

When the last external pointer is discarded, the cycle becomes both unreachable and nonrecyclable. To ensure that such objects are freed, the programmer must break the cycle before discarding the last pointer to the cycle. (The alternative—performing reachability analysis on the pointers at run time—would make reference counting prohibitively expensive.) Many categories of heap-allocated objects, such as variable-length strings and activation records, cannot be involved in such cycles.

Reference counting incurs additional cost on every pointer assignment. The amount of work done for a specific assignment can be bounded; in any well-designed scheme, the total cost can be limited to some constant factor times the number of pointer assignments executed plus the number of objects allocated. Proponents of reference counting argue that these overheads are small enough and that the pattern of reuse in reference-counting systems produces good program locality. Opponents of reference counting argue that real programs do more pointer assignments than allocations, so that garbage collection achieves equivalent functionality with less total work.

Batch Collectors

Batch collectors consider deallocation only when the free-space pool has been exhausted. When the allocator fails to find needed space, it invokes the batch collector. The collector pauses the program's execution, examines the pool of allocated memory to discover unused objects, and reclaims their space. When the collector terminates, the free-space pool is nonempty.[6] The allocator can finish its original task and return a newly allocated object to the caller. (As with reference counting, schemes exist that perform collection incrementally to amortize the cost over longer periods of execution.)

Logically, batch collectors proceed in two phases. The first phase discovers the set of objects that can be reached from pointers stored in program variables and compiler-generated temporaries. The collector conservatively assumes that any object reachable in this manner is live and that the remainder are dead. The second phase deallocates and recycles dead objects. Two commonly used techniques are *mark-sweep* collectors and *copying* collectors. They differ in their implementation of the second phase of collection—recycling.

---

6. Unless all space has been used. In that case, the allocator tries to obtain additional space from the operating system, which it uses as a free-space pool. If no additional space is available, the allocation fails.

Clear all marks
Worklist ← { pointer values from activation records & registers }

while (Worklist ≠ ∅)
    remove p from the Worklist
    if (p→object is unmarked)
        mark p→object
        add pointers from p→object to Worklist

FIGURE 6.14   A Simple Marking Algorithm

Identifying Live Data

Collecting allocators discover live objects by using a marking algorithm. The collector needs a bit for each object in the heap, called a *mark bit*. This bit can be stored in the object's header, alongside tag information used to record pointer locations or object size. Alternatively, the collector can create a dense bit map for the heap when needed. The initial step clears all the mark bits and builds a worklist that contains all the pointers stored in registers and in activation records that correspond to current or pending procedures. The second phase of the algorithm walks forward from these pointers and marks every object that is reachable from this set of visible pointers.

Figure 6.14 presents a high-level sketch of a marking algorithm. It is a simple fixed-point computation that halts because the heap is finite and the marks prevent a pointer contained in the heap from entering the *Worklist* more than once. The cost of marking is, in the worst case, proportional to the number of pointers contained in program variables and temporaries plus the size of the heap.

The marking algorithm can be either precise or conservative. The difference lies in how the algorithm determines that a specific data value is a pointer in the final line of the *while* loop.

- In a precise collector, the compiler and run-time system know the type and layout of each object. This information can be recorded in object headers, or it can be known implicitly from the type system. Either way, with precise knowledge, only real pointers are followed in the marking phase.

- In a conservative marking phase, the compiler and run-time system may be unsure about the type and layout of some, if not all, objects. Thus, when an object is marked, the system considers each field that may be a possible pointer. If its value might be a pointer, it is treated as a pointer. Any value that does not represent a word-aligned address might be excluded, as might values that fall outside the known boundaries of the heap.

Conservative collectors have limitations. They fail to reclaim some objects that a precise collector would find. If the program can hide a pointer so that the marking phase does not find it, the collector can incorrectly free an allocated object. Nonetheless, conservative collectors have been successfully retrofitted into implementations for languages such as C that do not normally support garbage collection.

When the marking algorithm halts, any unmarked object must be unreachable from the program. Thus, the second phase of the collector can treat that object as dead. Some objects marked as live may also be dead. However, the collector lets them survive because it cannot prove them dead. As the second phase traverses the heap to collect the garbage, it can reset the mark fields to "unmarked." This lets the collector avoid the initial traversal of the heap in the marking phase.

Mark-Sweep Collectors

The *mark-sweep* collectors reclaim and recycle objects by making a linear pass over the heap. The collector adds each unmarked object to the free list (or one of the free lists), where the allocator will find it and reuse it. With a single free list, the same collection of techniques used to coalesce blocks in the first-fit allocator applies. If compaction is desirable, it can be implemented by incrementally shuffling live objects downward during the sweep, or with a postsweep compaction pass.

Copying Collectors

The copying collectors divide memory into two pools, an *old* pool and a *new* pool. The allocator always operates from the old pool. The simplest type of copying collector is called *stop and copy*. When an allocation fails, a stop and copy collector copies all the live data from the old pool into the new pool and swaps the identities of the old and new pools. The act of copying live data compacts it; after collection, all the free space is in a single contiguous block. Collection can be done in two passes, like mark-sweep, or it can be done incrementally, as live data is discovered. An incremental scheme can mark objects in the old pool as it copies them to avoid copying the same object multiple times.

An important family of copying collectors are the *generational collectors*. These collectors capitalize on the observation that an object that survives one collection is more likely to survive subsequent collections. To capitalize on this observation, generational collectors derive their "new" and "old" pools by repartitioning the free space so that successive collections examine only newly allocated objects. Generational schemes vary in how often they declare a new generation, freezing the surviving objects and exempting them from the next collection, and whether or not they periodically re-examine the older generations.

Comparing the Techniques

Garbage collection frees the programmer from worrying about when to release memory and from tracking down the inevitable storage leaks that result from attempting to manage allocation and deallocation explicitly. The individual schemes have their strengths and weaknesses. In practice, the benefits of implicit deallocation outweigh the disadvantages of either scheme for most applications.

Reference counting distributes the cost of deallocation more evenly across program execution than does batch collection. However, it increases the cost of every assignment that involves a heap-allocated value—even if the program never runs out of free space. In contrast, batch collectors incur no cost until the allocator fails to find needed space. At that point, however, the program incurs the full cost of collection. Thus, any allocation can provoke a collection.

Mark-sweep collectors examine the entire heap, while copying collectors only examine the live data. Copying collectors actually move every live object, while mark-sweep collectors leave them in place. The tradeoff between these costs will vary with the application's behavior and with the actual costs of various memory references.

Reference-counting implementations and conservative batch collectors have problems recognizing cyclic structures, because they cannot distinguish between references from within the cycle and those from without. The mark-sweep collectors start from an external set of pointers, so they discover that a dead cyclic structure is unreachable. The copying collectors, starting from the same set of pointers, simply fail to copy the objects involved in the cycle.

Copying collectors compact memory as a natural part of the process. The collector can either update all the stored pointers, or it can require use of an indirection table for each object access. A precise mark-sweep collector can compact memory, too. The collector would move objects from one end of memory into free space at the other end. Again, the collector can either rewrite the existing pointers or mandate use of an indirection table.

In general, a good implementor can make both mark-sweep and copying work well enough that they are acceptable for most applications. In applications that cannot tolerate unpredictable overhead, such as real-time controllers, the collector must incrementalize the process, in a fashion similar to the amortized reference-counting scheme. Such collectors are called *real-time collectors*.

6.8 SUMMARY AND PERSPECTIVE

The primary rationale for moving beyond assembly language is to provide a more abstract programming model and, thus, raise both programmer productivity and the understandability of programs. Each abstraction added to a programming language requires a translation technique to the target machine's instruction set before it can be used. This chapter has explored the techniques commonly used to translate some of these abstractions.

Procedural programming was invented early in the history of programming. Some of the first procedures were debugging routines written for early computers; the availability of these prewritten routines allowed programmers to understand the run-time state of an errant program. Without such routines, tasks that we now take for granted, such as examining the contents of a variable or asking for a trace of the call stack, required the programmer to enter long machine-language sequences without error.

The introduction of lexical scoping in languages like Algol 60 influenced language design for decades. Most modern programming languages carry forward some of the Algol philosophy toward naming and addressability. Techniques developed in the 1960s and 1970s, such as access links and displays, reduced the run-time cost of this abstraction. These techniques are still used today.

Object-oriented languages take the scoping concepts of Algol-like languages and reorient them in data-directed ways. The compiler for an object-oriented language applies compile-time and run-time structures invented for lexical scoping to implement the naming discipline imposed by the inheritance hierarchy of a specific program.

Modern languages have added some new twists. By making procedures first-class objects, languages like Scheme have created new control-flow paradigms. These require variations on traditional implementation techniques—for example, heap allocation of activation records. Similarly, the growing acceptance of implicit deallocation requires occasional conservative treatment of a pointer. If the compiler can exercise a little more care and free the programmer from ever deallocating storage again, that appears to be a good tradeoff. (Generations of experience suggest that programmers are not effective at freeing all the storage that they allocate. They also free objects to which they retain pointers.)

As new programming paradigms come into vogue, they will introduce new abstractions that require careful thought and implementation. By studying the successful techniques of the past and understanding the constraints and costs involved in real implementations, compiler writers will develop strategies that decrease the run-time penalty for using higher levels of abstraction.

CHAPTER NOTES

Much of the material in this chapter comes from the accumulated experience of the compiler-construction community. The best way to learn more about the name-space structures of various languages is to consult the language definitions themselves. These documents are a necessary part of a compiler writer's library.

Procedures appeared in the earliest high-level languages—that is, languages that were more abstract than assembly language. FORTRAN [26] and Algol 60 [265] both had procedures with most of the features found in modern languages. Object-oriented languages appeared in the late 1960s with SIM-ULA 67 [269] followed closely by Smalltalk 72 [223].

Lexical scoping was introduced in Algol 60 and has persisted to the present day. The early Algol compilers introduced most of the support mechanisms described in this chapter, including activation records, access links, and parameter-passing techniques. Much of the material from Sections 6.3 through 6.6 was present in these early systems [282]. Optimizations quickly appeared, like folding storage for a block-level scope into the containing procedure's activation record. Early IBM 370 linkage conventions recognized the difference between leaf procedures and others; they avoided allocating a register save area for leaf routines. Murtagh took a more complete and systematic approach to coalescing activation records [264].

The classic reference on memory layouts and the economics of memory-allocation schemes is Knuth's *Art of Computer Programming* [220, Section 2.5]. Modern allocators, based on a pool of common sizes, appeared in the early 1980s.

Reference counting dates to the early 1960s and has been used in many systems [90, 117]. Cohen and, later, Wilson provide broad surveys of the literature on garbage collection [87, 332]. Conservative collectors were introduced by Boehm and Weiser [44, 112, 42]. Copying collectors appeared in response to virtual memory systems [137, 74]; they led, somewhat naturally, to the generational collectors in widespread use today [238, 324]. Hanson introduced the notion of arena-based allocation [171].

CHAPTER 7

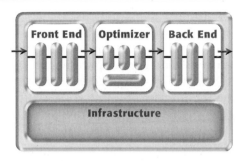

Code Shape

7.1 INTRODUCTION

In practice, a compiler can implement some source-language constructs on a given target machine in many ways. These variations use different operations and different approaches. Some of these implementations are faster than others; some use less memory; some use fewer registers; some might consume less power during execution. We consider these differences to be matters of *code shape*.

Code shape has a strong impact both on the behavior of the compiled code and on the ability of the optimizer and back end to improve it. Consider, for example, the way that a C compiler might implement a switch statement that switched on a single-byte character value. The compiler might use a cascaded series of if-then-else statements to implement the switch statement. Depending on the layout of the tests, this could produce different results. If the first test is for zero, the second for one, and so on, then this approach devolves to linear search over a field of 256 keys. If characters are uniformly distributed, the character searches will require an average of 128 tests and branches per character—an expensive way to implement a case statement. If, instead, the tests perform a binary search, the average case would involve eight tests and branches—a more palatable number. To trade data space for speed, the

307

compiler can construct a table of 256 labels and interpret the character by loading the corresponding table entry and jumping to it—with a constant overhead per character.

All of these are legal implementations of the switch statement. Deciding which implementation makes sense for a particular switch statement depends on many factors. In particular, the number of individual cases and their relative frequencies of execution are important, as is detailed knowledge of the cost structure for branching on the target machine. Even when the compiler cannot determine the information that it needs to make the best choice, it must make a choice. The differences among the possible implementations, and the compiler's choice, are matters of code shape.

As another example, consider the simple expression x + y + z, where x, y, and z are integers. Figure 7.1 shows several ways of implementing the expression. In source-code form, we may think of the operation as a ternary add, shown on the left. However, mapping this idealized operation into a sequence of binary additions exposes the impact of evaluation order. The three versions on the right show three possible evaluation orders, both as three-address code and as abstract syntax trees. (We assume that each variable is in an appropriately named register and that the source language does not specify the evaluation order for such an expression.) Because integer addition is both commutative and associative, all three orders are equivalent; the compiler must choose one to implement.

Left associativity would produce the first binary tree. This tree seems "natural" in that left associativity corresponds to our left-to-right reading style. Consider what happens if we replace y with the literal constant 2 and z with 3. Of course, x + 2 + 3 is equivalent to x + 5. The compiler should detect the computation of 2 + 3, evaluate it, and fold the result directly into the code. In the left-associative form, however, 2 + 3 never occurs. The order x + z + y hides it, as well. The right-associative version exposes the

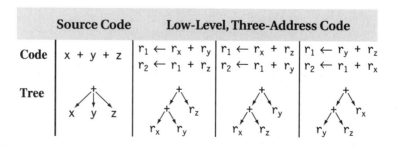

FIGURE 7.1   Alternate Code Shapes for x + y + z

opportunity for improvement. For each prospective tree, however, there is an assignment of variables and constants to x, y, and z that does not expose the constant expression for optimization.

As with the switch statement, the best shape for this expression cannot be known without information about the context in which it appears. If, for example, the expression x + y has been computed recently and neither the value of x nor the value of y has changed, then using the leftmost shape would let the compiler replace the first operation, $r_1 \leftarrow r_x + r_y$, with a reference to the previously computed value. In this situation, the best choice among the three evaluation orders might depend on context from the surrounding code.

This chapter explores the code-shape issues that arise in implementing many common source-language constructs. It focuses on the code that should be generated for specific constructs, while largely ignoring the algorithms required to pick specific assembly-language instructions. The issues of instruction selection, register allocation, and instruction scheduling are treated separately, in later chapters.

7.2 ASSIGNING STORAGE LOCATIONS

A procedure may compute many values. Some of them have names in the source code; in an Algol-like language, the programmer provides a name for each variable. Other values have no explicit names—for example, the value i - 3 in the expression A[i - 3, j + 2]. Named values have defined lifetimes. They may be modified by other procedures. They may be visible in the debugger. These facts limit where the compiler can place them and how long it must preserve them. In contrast, the compiler has more freedom in how it treats unnamed values, such as i - 3. It must handle them in ways that are consistent with the meaning of the program, but it has great leeway in determining where these values reside and how long they are retained.

The compiler's decisions about both named and unnamed values have a strong impact on the final code that it produces. In particular, decisions about unnamed values determine the set of values exposed to analysis and transformation in the optimizer. In choosing a storage location for each value, the compiler must observe the rules of both the source language and the target-machine's memory hierarchy. In general, it can place a scalar value in a register or in memory. The available memory may be divided into distinct subregions, or data areas, as discussed in Chapter 6.

7.2.1 Laying Out Data Areas

To assign variables in an Algol-like language to storage classes, the compiler might apply rules similar to the following ones:

> *if x is declared locally in procedure p, and*
> > *its value is <u>not</u> preserved across distinct invocations of p*
> > > *then assign it to procedure-local storage*
>
> > *if its value is preserved across invocations of p*
> > > *then assign it to procedure-static storage*
>
> *if x is declared as globally visible*
> > *then assign it to global storage*
>
> *if x is allocated under program control*
> > *then assign it to the run-time heap*

Object-oriented languages follow rules that are different, but no more complex.

Each of these data areas has its own constraints. The compiler can place procedure-local storage inside the procedure's activation record, precisely because the lifetime of a procedure-local variable matches the lifetime of an invocation of that procedure. Since the code already needs the ARP in a register, this leads to efficient access with operations like loadAO and loadAI. Frequent access to the AR will likely keep it in cache.

Static and global data areas are stored outside the AR of any procedure, because their lifetimes extend, potentially, to the program's entire execution. This may require an extra loadI to get the run-time address of some relocatable symbol (an assembly-language label) into a register for use as a base address.

Values stored in the heap have lifetimes that the compiler cannot easily predict. A value can be placed in the heap by two distinct mechanisms. The programmer can explicitly allocate storage from the heap; the compiler should not override that decision. The compiler can place a value on the heap when it detects that the value might outlive the procedure that creates it. In either case, a value in the heap is represented by a full address, rather than an offset.

7.2.2 Keeping a Value in a Register

In addition to assigning each value a data area and location, the compiler must determine whether or not it can safely keep the value in a register. If the value can safely reside in a register, and a register is available for the value's entire lifetime, that value may not need space in memory. Many compilers assign a *virtual register* to each value that can legally reside in a register and rely on the register allocator to map the virtual registers to the target-machine's physical registers.

If the compiler uses virtual registers, then it assigns each value either a virtual register or a memory location, but not both. When the allocator decides that it cannot keep some virtual register in the register set, it assigns that value space in the memory area reserved for spilling registers. The allocator inserts a load at each use of the value to move it into a temporary register and a store after each definition to update the value in its home in memory. If the allocator keeps a static value in a register, it must load the value before its first use in the procedure and store it back to memory before leaving the procedure (both at the exit of a procedure and at a call site).

To determine whether or not a value can be kept in a register, the compiler must know the number of distinct names by which the code can access it. For example, a local variable can be kept in a register as long as its address is never taken, its value is never used in a nested procedure, and it is not passed as a call-by-reference parameter to another procedure. Each of these actions creates a second path for accessing the variable. Consider the following code fragment in C:

```
void fee() {
  int a, *b;
    ...
  b = &a;
    ...
}
```

The assignment b = &a creates a second name by which the code can access a. The compiler must assign a storage location to a; otherwise, it cannot meaningfully apply the address operator to a. However, it cannot even keep a's value in a register between consecutive references to a unless it can prove that the intervening code cannot assign to *b. Similarly, it cannot keep the value of *b in a register between references unless it can prove that the intervening code cannot assign to a.

In general, the code between two references can contain other pointer-based assignments or calls to procedures that might contain pointer-based assignments. Also, multiple paths through the procedure can assign b different addresses. Taken together, these complications make the analysis needed to keep either a or *b in a register difficult. In practice, many compilers give up and leave a in memory.

A value that can be kept in a register is sometimes called an *unambiguous value*; a variable that can have more than one name is called an *ambiguous value*. Ambiguity arises in several ways. Values stored in pointer-based variables are often ambiguous. Interactions between call-by-reference formal parameters and name-scoping rules can make the formal parameters ambiguous. Many compilers treat array-element values as ambiguous values because the compiler cannot tell if two references, such as A[i,j] and A[m,n], can ever refer to the same location. The compiler can perform analyses to disambiguate some of these cases. Unfortunately, analysis cannot resolve all ambiguities. Thus, the compiler must be prepared to handle ambiguous values cautiously and correctly.

The compiler must treat any value as ambiguous unless it can prove that the value is unambiguous. Ambiguous values are kept in memory rather than in registers; they are loaded and stored as necessary. Careful reasoning about the language can help the compiler. For example, in C, any local variable whose address is never taken is unambiguous. Similarly, the ANSI C standard requires that references through pointer variables be type-consistent; thus an assignment to *b can only change the value of a location for which b is a legal pointer. Unfortunately, the standard exempts character pointers from this restriction, so an assignment to a character pointer can change a value of *any* type.

ANSI C includes two keywords that affect the compiler's ability to analyze the contents of potentially ambiguous values. The restrict keyword lets the programmer declare that a pointer is unambiguous. It is often used when a procedure passes an address directly at a call site. The volatile keyword lets the programmer declare that the contents of a variable may change arbitrarily and without notice. It is used for hardware device registers and for variables that might be modified by interrupt service routines or other threads of control in an application.

7.2.3 Machine Idiosyncrasies

For any processor, the compiler writer will find a collection of machine-specific rules that it must obey.

An architecture may partition the register set into distinct classes. The classes may be disjoint; a common scheme has separate register files for "floating-point" and "general-purpose" registers. The classes may overlap, as often happens with "floating-point" and "double-precision floating-point."

Within a class, additional constraints may occur, as with architectures where double-precision, floating-point values must occupy a pair of adjacent registers. Other common register classes include condition-code registers, predicate registers, branch-target registers, and segment registers.

The architecture may partition a single register class into multiple disjoint register files. Such a machine groups a set of functional units around a register set. Each functional unit has fast access to its nearby registers and limited access to registers in the other register sets. This strategy lets the architect use more functional units. It puts the burden for placing operations and data together on the compiler.

Target-specific issues arise for memory-resident values, as well. Many architectures restrict the starting address of a value based on its perceived type. Thus, integer and single-precision floating-point data might be required to start on a word boundary (an address that is an integral multiple of the word size), while character data might begin at any even address. Doubleword and quadword boundaries occur, as well.

The details of storage assignment can directly affect performance. As memory hierarchies become deeper and more complex, issues of locality and reuse have a larger impact on running time. The compiler can, by changing the layout of code and data in memory and by reordering accesses, increase both locality and reuse.

7.3 ARITHMETIC OPERATORS

Modern processors provide broad support for evaluating expressions. A typical RISC machine has a full complement of three-address operations, including arithmetic, logical shift, and boolean operations. The three-address form lets the compiler name the result of any operation and preserve it for later reuse. It also eliminates one of the major complications of two-address instructions—destructive operations.

To generate code for a trivial expression, such as x + y, the compiler first emits code to ensure that the values of x and y are in known registers, say r_x and r_y. If x is stored in memory at some offset, @x, in the current activation record, the resulting code might be

```
loadI  @x        ⇒ r₁
loadAO rarp, r₁  ⇒ rx
```

If, however, the value of x is already in a register, the compiler can simply use that register's name in place of r_x. The compiler follows a similar chain of decisions to ensure that y is in a register. Finally, it emits an instruction to perform the addition, such as

$$\text{add } r_x, \; r_y \; \Rightarrow \; r_t$$

If the expression is represented by a tree, this scheme fits naturally into a postorder walk of the tree. The code in Figure 7.2(a) does this by embedding

```
expr(node) {
  int result, t1, t2;
  switch(type(node)) {
    case ×,÷,+,−:
      t1 ← expr(LeftChild(node));
      t2 ← expr(RightChild(node));
      result ← NextRegister();
      emit(op(node), t1, t2, result);
      break;

    case IDENT:
      t1 ← base(node);
      t2 ← offset(node);
      result ← NextRegister();
      emit(loadAO, t1, t2, result);
      break;

    case NUM:
      result ← NextRegister();
      emit(loadI, val(node), none,
             result);
      break;
  }
  return result;
}
```

(a) Tree-walk Code Generator

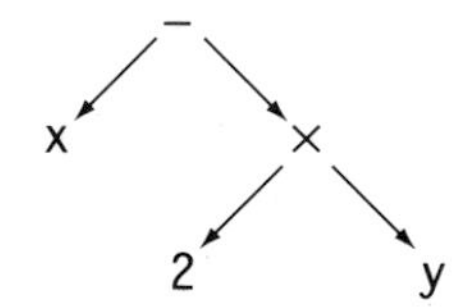

(b) Abstract Syntax Tree for
x − 2 × y

loadI	@x	$\Rightarrow r_1$
loadAO	r_{arp}, r_1	$\Rightarrow r_2$
loadI	2	$\Rightarrow r_3$
loadI	@y	$\Rightarrow r_4$
loadAO	r_{arp}, r_4	$\Rightarrow r_5$
mult	r_3, r_5	$\Rightarrow r_6$
sub	r_2, r_6	$\Rightarrow r_7$

(c) Naive Code

FIGURE 7.2 Simple Tree-Walk for Expressions

the code-generating actions into a recursive tree-walk routine. It relies on two routines, *base* and *offset*, to hide some of the complexity. The *base* routine returns the name of a register holding the base address for an identifier; if needed, it emits code to get that address into a register. The *offset* routine has a similar function; it returns the name of a register holding the identifier's offset relative to the address returned by *base*.

The same code handles +, -, ×, and ÷. From a code-generation perspective, these operators are interchangeable (ignoring commutativity). Invoking the routine *expr* from Figure 7.2(a) on the AST for x - 2 × y shown in part (b) of the figure produces the results shown in part (c) of the figure. The example assumes that neither x nor y is already in a register and that both are stored in the current AR.

Notice the similarity between this tree-walk approach to code generation and the ad hoc syntax-directed translation scheme shown in Figure 4.14. The tree-walk algorithm makes more details explicit, including the handling of terminals and the evaluation of left subtrees before right. The syntax-directed translation scheme abstracts away the first issue. It has no control over the order of evaluation, since the parser dictates the order of application for the individual actions. Still, the two schemes produce roughly equivalent code.

7.3.1 Reducing Demand for Registers

Many issues affect the quality of the generated code. For example, the choice of storage locations has a direct impact, even for this simple expression. If y were in a global data area, the sequence of instructions needed to get y into a register might require an additional loadI to obtain the base address and a register to hold that value. Alternatively, if y were in a register, the two instructions used to load it into r_5 could be omitted, and the compiler would use the name of the register holding y in the mult instruction. Keeping the value in a register avoids both the memory access and any address calculation. If both x and y were in registers, the seven-instruction sequence would be shortened to a three-instruction sequence (two, if the target machine supports an immediate multiply instruction).

Code-shape decisions encoded into the tree-walk code generator have an effect, too. The naive code in the figure uses eight registers, including r_{arp}. It is tempting to assume that the register allocator, when it runs late in compilation, can reduce the number of registers to a minimum. For example, the register allocator could rewrite the expression as

```
loadI    @x          ⇒ r₁
loadAO   r_arp, r₁  ⇒ r₁
loadI    2           ⇒ r₂
loadI    @y          ⇒ r₃
loadAO   r_arp, r₃  ⇒ r₃
mult     r₂, r₃     ⇒ r₂
sub      r₁, r₂     ⇒ r₂
```

This drops register use from eight registers to four, including r_{arp}. It leaves the result in r_2 so that both x, in r_1, and y, in r_3, are available for later use.

However, loading x before computing $2 \times y$ still wastes a register—an artifact of the decision in the tree-walk code generator to evaluate the left child before the right child. Using the opposite order would produce the sequence shown on the left side in the following code. The register allocator could rewrite this to use only two registers (plus r_{arp}), as shown on the right side.

```
loadI    @y          ⇒ r₁          loadI    @y          ⇒ r₁
loadAO   r_arp, r₁  ⇒ r₂          loadAO   r_arp, r₁  ⇒ r₁
loadI    2           ⇒ r₃          loadI    2           ⇒ r₂
mult     r₃, r₂     ⇒ r₄          mult     r₂, r₁     ⇒ r₁
loadI    @x          ⇒ r₅          loadI    @x          ⇒ r₂
loadAO   r_arp, r₅  ⇒ r₆          loadAO   r_arp, r₂  ⇒ r₂
sub      r₆, r₄     ⇒ r₇          sub      r₂, r₁     ⇒ r₁
```

        Evaluating 2 × y First   After Register Allocation

The allocator cannot fit all of x, y, and x + 2 × y into two registers. As written, the code preserves x and not y. While careful optimization might convert the three-register code into the two-register code by moving the sequence that loads x later in the computation, it may be easier and more direct to generate the sequence that produces better code after optimization and register allocation.

Of course, evaluating the right child first is not a general solution. For the expression 2 × y + x, the appropriate rule is "left child first." Some expressions, such as x + (5 + y) × 7 defy a static rule. The best evaluation order for limiting register use is 5 + y, then multiplying by 7, and finally adding x—in effect, alternating between right and left children.

GENERATING LOAD ADDRESS-IMMEDIATE

A careful reader might notice that the code in Figure 7.2 never generates ILOC's load address-immediate instruction, loadAI. Instead, it generates a load immediate (loadI), followed by a load address-offset (loadAO):

```
loadI   @x     ⇒ r₁
loadAO  rₐᵣₚ,r₁ ⇒ r₂              instead of    loadAI rₐᵣₚ, @x ⇒ r₂
```

Throughout the book, we have assumed that it is preferable to generate this two-operation sequence, rather than the single operation. Three factors suggest this course.

1. The longer code sequence gives an explicit name to @x. If @x is reused in contexts other than a loadAO instruction, the explicit name is useful.

2. The offset @x may be too large for the immediate field of a loadAI operation. If it will not fit, the compiler must either generate the sequence that uses loadI or store the label in memory and use a full-fledged load to retrieve it.

3. The two-instruction sequence leads to a clean functional decomposition in the code generator, shown in Figure 7.2. The logic required to fold the constant into the subsequent loadAO is an optimization.

Subsequent optimization can easily convert the two-instruction sequence into a single loadAI if the constant offset is not reused. For example, some register allocators can perform this conversion automatically if the intermediate register is needed for some other value (see Chapter 13).

If the compiler needs to generate the loadAI directly, two approaches make sense. The compiler writer can pull the case logic contained in *base* and *offset* up into the case for *IDENT* in Figure 7.2. This accomplishes the objective, at the cost of uglier and less modular code. Alternatively, the compiler writer can have *emit* maintain a small instruction buffer and perform local peephole optimization on instructions as they

(Continued)

GENERATING LOAD ADDRESS-IMMEDIATE, *Continued*

---

are generated (see Section 11.4.1). Keeping the buffer small makes this practical. If the compiler follows the "more-demanding-subtree-first" rule, the offset will be generated immediately before the loadAO instruction. Recognizing a loadI that feeds into a loadAO is easy in the peephole paradigm.

To choose the best evaluation order for subtrees of an expression tree, the compiler needs information about the details of each subtree. To minimize register use, the compiler should first evaluate the more demanding subtree—the subtree that needs the most registers. The code must preserve the first value computed across the evaluation of the second subtree; thus, handling the less demanding subtree first increases the demand for registers in the more demanding subtree by one register. This requires an initial pass over the code to gather information, followed by a pass that emits the actual code.

A single pass, such as the ad hoc syntax-directed translation scheme, can either discover the more demanding subtree or emit code. It cannot do both. This general principle, analysis followed by translation or transformation, applies in code generation and global optimization. As Floyd observed in 1961, the compiler can produce better code if we let it examine the code before forcing it to make final decisions about how to implement the code.

7.3.2 Accessing Parameter Values

The tree-walk code generator implicitly assumes that a single access method works for all identifiers. Names that represent formal parameters may need different treatment. A call-by-value parameter passed in the AR can be handled as if it were a local variable. A call-by-reference parameter passed in the AR requires one additional indirection. Thus, for the call-by-reference parameter x, the compiler might generate

$$
\begin{array}{lll}
\text{loadI} & \text{@x} & \Rightarrow r_1 \\
\text{loadAO} & r_{arp}, r_1 & \Rightarrow r_2 \\
\text{load} & r_2 & \Rightarrow r_3
\end{array}
$$

to obtain x's value. The first two operations move the memory address of the parameter's value into r_2. The final operation moves the value itself into r_3.

Many linkage conventions pass the first few parameters in registers. As written, the code in Figure 7.2 cannot handle a value that is permanently kept in a register. The necessary extension, however, is easy to implement.

For call-by-value parameters, the *IDENT* case must check if the value is already in a register. If so, it assigns the register number to *result* or copies the value into a new virtual register. Otherwise, it uses the standard mechanisms to load the value from memory.

For a call-by-reference parameter whose address is passed in a register, the compiler needs to emit only the single operation that loads the value from memory. The value, however, must reside in memory across each assignment unless the compiler can prove that it is unambiguous.

7.3.3   Function Calls in an Expression

So far, we have assumed that all the operands in an expression are variables, constants, and temporary values produced by other subexpressions. Function calls also occur as operands in expressions. To evaluate a function call, the compiler simply generates the calling sequence needed to invoke the function (see Sections 6.6 and 7.9) and emits the code necessary to move the returned value to a register. The linkage convention limits the impact on the calling procedure of executing the function.

The presence of a function call may restrict the compiler's ability to change an expression's evaluation order. The function may have side effects that modify the values of variables used in the expression. The compiler must respect the implied evaluation order of the source expression, at least with respect to the call. Without knowledge about the possible side effects of a call, the compiler cannot move references across the call. The compiler must assume the worst case—that the function both modifies and uses every variable that it can access. The desire to improve on worst-case assumptions, such as this one, has motivated much of the work in interprocedural analysis (see Section 9.4.2).

7.3.4   Other Arithmetic Operators

To handle other arithmetic operations, we can extend our simple model. The basic scheme remains the same: get the operands into registers, perform the operation, and store the result, if necessary. The precedence encoded in the expression grammar ensures the intended order. Unary operators, such as unary minus, evaluate their sole subtree and then perform the specified operation. (Pointer dereferences behave in the same way.) Some operators require complex code sequences for their implementation (for example, exponentiation, trigonometric functions, and reduction operators). These may be expanded directly inline, or they may be handled with a function call to a library routine supplied by the compiler or the operating system.

7.3.5 Mixed-Type Expressions

One complication allowed by many programming languages is an operation with operands of different types. (Here, we are concerned primarily with base types in the source language, rather than programmer-defined types.) As described in Section 4.2, the compiler must recognize this situation and insert the conversion code required by each operator's conversion table. Typically, this involves converting one or both operands to a more general type and performing the operation in that more general type. The operation that consumes the result value may need to convert it to yet another type.

Some machines provide instructions to perform these conversions directly; others expect the compiler to generate complex, machine-dependent code. In either case, the compiler writer may want to provide conversion operators in the IR. Such an operator encapsulates all the details of the conversion, including any control flow, and lets the compiler subject it to uniform optimization. Thus, code motion can pull an invariant conversion out of a loop without concern for the loop's internal control flow.

Typically, the programming-language definition specifies a formula for each conversion. For example, to convert `integer` to `complex` in FORTRAN 77, the compiler first converts the `integer` to a `real`. It uses the resulting number as the real part of the complex number and sets the imaginary part to a `real` zero.

For user-defined types, the compiler will not have a conversion table that defines each specific case. However, the source language still defines the meaning of the expression. The compiler's task is to implement that meaning; if a conversion is illegal, then it should be prevented. As seen in Chapter 4, many illegal conversions can be detected and prevented at compile time. When a compile-time check is either impossible or inconclusive, the compiler should generate a run-time check that tests for illegal cases. When the code attempts an illegal conversion, the check should raise a run-time error.

7.3.6 Assignment as an Operator

Most Algol-like languages implement assignment with the following simple rules:

1. Evaluate the right-hand side of the assignment.

2. Evaluate the left-hand side of the assignment.

3. Move the value from the right-hand side into the location specified by the left-hand side's value.

Thus, in a statement like $x \leftarrow y$, the two expressions x and y are evaluated differently. Since y appears to the right of the assignment operator, it is evaluated to produce a value; if y is an integer variable, that value is an integer. Since x is to the left of the assignment operator, it is evaluated to produce a location; if x is an integer variable, that value is the location of an integer. This might be an address in memory, or it might be a register. To distinguish between these modes of evaluation, we sometimes refer to the result of evaluation on the right-hand side of an assignment as as an *rvalue* and the result of evaluation on the left-hand side of an assignment as an *lvalue*.

An assignment can involve an lvalue that specifies a location with a different type than the rvalue. Depending on the types, either a conversion may be needed or a type error may occur. For conversion, the typical source-language rule has the compiler evaluate the rvalue to its natural type—the type it would generate without the context of the assignment. That result is then converted to the type of the location named by the lvalue, and stored in the appropriate location.

7.3.7 Commutativity, Associativity, and Number Systems

The compiler can often take advantage of algebraic properties of the various operators. Addition and multiplication are commutative and associative, as are the boolean operators. Thus, if the compiler sees a code fragment that computes $x + y$ and then computes $y + x$, with no intervening assignments to either x or y, it should recognize that they compute the same value. Similarly, if it sees the expressions $x + y + z$ and $w + x + y$, it should recognize that $x + y$ is a common subexpression. If it evaluates both expressions in strict left-to-right order, it will never recognize the common subexpression, since it will compute the second expression as $w + x$ and then $w + x + y$.

The compiler should use commutativity and associativity to improve the quality of code that it generates. Reordering expressions can expose additional opportunities for many transformations. However, a brief warning is in order.

> *Due to limitations in precision, floating-point numbers on a computer represent only a subset of the real numbers, and floating-point operations do not preserve associativity. As a result, compilers should not reorder floating-point computations unless the language definition specifically allows it.*

Consider the following example. We can assign floating-point values to x, y, and z such that x, y < z, z - x = z, and z - y = z, but z - (x + y) $\neq$ z. In that case, the result depends on the order of evaluation. Computing as (z - x) - y produces a result identical to z, while evaluating x + y first and subtracting that quantity from z produces a result that is distinct from z.

This problem arises from the approximate nature of floating-point numbers; the mantissa is small relative to the range of the exponent. To add two numbers, the hardware must normalize them; if the difference in exponents is larger than the precision of the mantissa, the smaller number will be truncated to zero. The compiler cannot easily work its way around this issue. Thus, it should heed the warning and avoid reordering float-point computations.

7.4 BOOLEAN AND RELATIONAL OPERATORS

Most programming languages operate on a richer set of values than numbers. Usually, this includes the results of boolean and relational operators, both of which produce boolean values. Because most programming languages have relational operators that produce boolean results, we treat the boolean and relational operators together. A common use for boolean and relational expressions is to alter the program's control flow. Much of the power of modern programming languages derives from the ability to compute and test such values.

To introduce boolean values, language designers add productions to the standard expression grammar, as shown in Figure 7.3. (We have used the symbols ¬ for not, ∧ for and, and ∨ for or to avoid any confusion with the corresponding ILOC operations.) The compiler writer must, in turn, decide how to represent these values and how to compute them. For arithmetic expressions, such design decisions are largely dictated by the target architecture, which provides number formats and instructions to perform basic arithmetic.

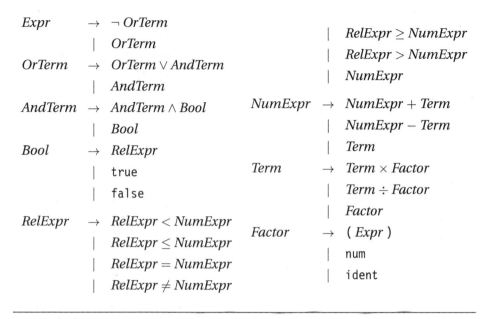

$$
\begin{array}{rcl}
\textit{Expr} & \rightarrow & \neg\ \textit{OrTerm} \\
& | & \textit{OrTerm} \\
\textit{OrTerm} & \rightarrow & \textit{OrTerm} \lor \textit{AndTerm} \\
& | & \textit{AndTerm} \\
\textit{AndTerm} & \rightarrow & \textit{AndTerm} \land \textit{Bool} \\
& | & \textit{Bool} \\
\textit{Bool} & \rightarrow & \textit{RelExpr} \\
& | & \texttt{true} \\
& | & \texttt{false} \\
\textit{RelExpr} & \rightarrow & \textit{RelExpr} < \textit{NumExpr} \\
& | & \textit{RelExpr} \leq \textit{NumExpr} \\
& | & \textit{RelExpr} = \textit{NumExpr} \\
& | & \textit{RelExpr} \neq \textit{NumExpr}
\end{array}
\qquad
\begin{array}{rcl}
& | & \textit{RelExpr} \geq \textit{NumExpr} \\
& | & \textit{RelExpr} > \textit{NumExpr} \\
& | & \textit{NumExpr} \\
\textit{NumExpr} & \rightarrow & \textit{NumExpr} + \textit{Term} \\
& | & \textit{NumExpr} - \textit{Term} \\
& | & \textit{Term} \\
\textit{Term} & \rightarrow & \textit{Term} \times \textit{Factor} \\
& | & \textit{Term} \div \textit{Factor} \\
& | & \textit{Factor} \\
\textit{Factor} & \rightarrow & (\ \textit{Expr}\ ) \\
& | & \texttt{num} \\
& | & \texttt{ident}
\end{array}
$$

FIGURE 7.3 Adding Booleans and Relationals to the Expression Grammar

Fortunately, processor architects appear to have reached a widespread agreement about how to support arithmetic. Similarly, most architectures provide a rich set of boolean operations. However, support for relational operators varies widely from one architecture to another. The compiler writer must use an evaluation strategy that matches the needs of the language to the available instruction set.

7.4.1   Representations

Traditionally, two representations have been proposed for boolean values: a numerical encoding and a positional encoding. The former assigns specific values to true and false and manipulates them using the target machine's arithmetic and logical operations. The latter approach encodes the value of the expression as a position in the executable code. It uses comparisons and conditional branches to evaluate the expression; the different control-flow paths represent the result of evaluation. Each approach works well for some examples, but not for others.

Numerical Encoding

When the program stores the result of a boolean or relational operation into a variable, the compiler must ensure that the value has a concrete representation. The compiler writer must assign numerical values to true and false that work with the hardware operations such as and, or, and not. Typical values are zero for false and either one or a word of ones ($\neg$false) for true.

For example, if b, c, and d are all in registers, the compiler might produce the following code for the expression $b \vee c \wedge \neg d$:

$$
\begin{array}{lll}
\text{not } r_d & \Rightarrow r_1 \\
\text{and } r_c, r_1 & \Rightarrow r_2 \\
\text{or } \ r_b, r_2 & \Rightarrow r_3
\end{array}
$$

For a comparison, like $x < y$, the compiler must generate code that compares x and y and assigns the appropriate value to the result. If the target machine supports a comparison operation that returns a boolean, the code is trivial:

$$
\text{cmp\_LT } r_x, \ r_y \ \Rightarrow r_1
$$

If, on the other hand, the comparison defines a condition code that must be read with a conditional branch, the resulting code is longer and more involved. [1] This style of comparison leads to a messier implementation for $x < y$.

$$
\begin{array}{llll}
& \text{comp} & r_x, \ r_y & \Rightarrow cc_1 \\
& \text{cbr\_LT } cc_1 & & \rightarrow L_1, L_2 \\
L_1: & \text{loadI} & \text{true} & \Rightarrow r_2 \\
& \text{jumpI} & & \rightarrow L_3 \\
L_2: & \text{loadI} & \text{false} & \Rightarrow r_2 \\
& \text{jumpI} & & \rightarrow L_3 \\
L_3: & \text{nop} & &
\end{array}
$$

Implementing $x < y$ with condition-code operations requires more operations than using a comparison that returns a boolean.

---

1. ILOC is flexible on this point. It includes comparisons that return booleans, such as cmp_LT shown in the example. It includes a comparison that returns a condition code, comp, and a set of conditional branch operators, such as cbr_LT, that interpret a condition code (see Section A.5.1, "Alternate Branch Syntax.")

```
           comp    r_a, r_b  ⇒ cc_1    // a < b
           cbr_LT  cc_1       → L_1,L_2
L_1: loadI  true      ⇒ r_1
     jumpI            → L_3
L_2: loadI  false     ⇒ r_1
     jumpI            → L_3

L_3: comp   r_c, r_d  ⇒ cc_2    // c < d
     cbr_LT cc_2       → L_4,L_5
L_4: loadI  true      ⇒ r_2
     jumpI            → L_6
L_5: loadI  false     ⇒ r_2
     jumpI            → L_6

L_6: comp   r_e, r_f  ⇒ cc_3    // e < f
     cbr_LT cc_3       → L_7,L_8
L_7: loadI  true      ⇒ r_3
     jumpI            → L_9
L_8: loadI  false     ⇒ r_3
     jumpI            → L_9

L_9: and    r_2,r_3   ⇒ r_4
     or     r_1,r_4   ⇒ r_5
```

FIGURE 7.4   Naive Encoding for $a < b \lor c < d \land e < f$

Positional Encoding

In the previous example, the code at L_1 creates the value true and the code at L_2 creates the value false. At each of those points, the value is both fixed and known. In some cases, the code need not produce a concrete value for the expression's result. Instead, the compiler can encode the value in a position—a location in the code, such as L_1.

Figure 7.4 shows the code that a tree-walk code generator might emit for the expression $a < b \lor c < d \land e < f$. This code evaluates the three subexpressions, $a < b$, $c < d$, and $e < f$, and uses boolean operations to combine the resulting

```
            comp    rₐ, r_b ⇒ cc₁
            cbr_LT  cc₁     → L₃,L₁
    L₁: comp    r_c, r_d ⇒ cc₂
            cbr_LT  cc₂     → L₂,L₄
    L₂: comp    r_e, r_f ⇒ cc₃
            cbr_LT  cc₃     → L₃,L₄
    L₃: loadI   true    ⇒ r₅
            jumpI           → L₅
    L₄: loadI   false   ⇒ r₅
            jumpI           → L₅
    L₅: nop
```

FIGURE 7.5   Positional Encoding with short-circuit evaluation for $a < b \vee c < d \wedge e < f$

values. Unfortunately, this produces a sequence of operations in which every path takes eleven operations, including three branches and three jumps.

Some of the complexity of this code arises from the decision to represent the subexpressions with true and false. Using a positional encoding with short-circuit evaluation can lead to a much simpler sequence of operations, as shown in Figure 7.5. This version of the code produces a value only for the final expression and leaves the value in r_5. The subexpression values are encoded as positions in the code.

Positional encoding avoids assigning an actual value to the expression until an operation requires a value. For example, assigning the result to a variable forces the code to provide a concrete value. Positional encoding represents the expression's value implicitly in the control-flow path taken through the code. This often leads to more compact code that executes fewer operations. This is particularly noticeable with an instruction set that uses condition codes, as previously shown.

Positional encoding makes sense if an expression's result is never stored. When the code uses the result of an expression to determine control flow, positional encoding often avoids extraneous operations. For example, in the code fragment

$$\text{if } (x < y)$$
$$\text{then } statement_1$$
$$\text{else } statement_2$$

the sole use for $x < y$ is to determine whether *statement*$_1$ or *statement*$_2$ executes. Producing an explicit value for $x < y$ serves no purpose, unless it makes the control flow more efficient.

On a machine where the compiler must produce the value using a comparison and a branch, the compiler can simply place the code for *statement*$_1$ and *statement*$_2$ in the locations where it would assign true and false, respectively. This use of positional encoding leads to simpler, faster code than using numerical encoding.

```
        comp    r_x, r_y  ⇒ cc_1    // x < y
        cbr_LT  cc_1       → L_1,L_2
L_1:  code for statement_1
        jumpI             → L_6
L_2:  code for statement_2
        jumpI             → L_6
L_6:  nop
```

Here, the code to evaluate $x < y$ has been combined with the code to select between *statement*$_1$ and *statement*$_2$. The code represents the result of $x < y$ as a position, either L_1 or L_2.

Short-Circuit Evaluation

In many cases, the value of a subexpression determines the value of the entire expression. For example, in $a < b \lor c < d \land e < f$, if $a < b$, the value of the remainder of the expression does not matter. Similarly, if both $a \geq b$ and $c \geq d$, the value of $e < f$ does not matter. The code in Figure 7.5 uses these facts. If $a < b$, the code branches directly to the sequence of statements that produces the value true for the expression.

This way of improving evaluation of boolean and relational expressions is called *short-circuit evaluation*. In short-circuit evaluation, the code evaluates only as much of the expression as is required to determine the final value, and no more. Short-circuit evaluation relies on two boolean identities:

$$\forall\ x,\ \text{false} \land x = \text{false}$$
$$\forall\ x,\ \ \text{true} \lor x = \text{true}$$

Short-circuit evaluation can reduce the cost of evaluating expressions by taking into account the run-time values of the operands in the expressions.

Some programming languages, like C, require the compiler to use short-circuit evaluation. For example, the expression

$$(x \;!= 0 \;\&\& \; y / x > 0.001)$$

in C relies on short-circuit evaluation for safety. If x is zero, y / x is not defined. Clearly, the programmer intends to avoid the hardware exception triggered by division by zero. The language definition specifies that this code will never perform the division if x has the value zero.

7.4.2 Hardware Support for Relational Operations

Specific, low-level details in the target machine's instruction set strongly influence the choice of a representation for relational values. In particular, the compiler writer must pay attention to the handling of condition codes, compare operations, and conditional move operations, as they have a major impact on the relative costs of the various representations. We will consider four schemes for supporting relational expressions: straight condition codes, condition codes augmented with a conditional move operation, boolean-valued comparisons, and predicated operations. Each scheme is an idealized version of a real implementation.

Figure 7.6 shows two source-level constructs and their implementations under each of these schemes. The upper half of the figure shows an if-then-else that controls a pair of simple assignment statements. The bottom half shows assignment of a boolean value.

Straight Condition Codes

In this scheme, the comparison operation sets a condition-code register. The only instruction that interprets the condition code is a conditional branch, with variants that branch on each of the six relations ($<, \leq, =, \geq, >$, and $\neq$). These instructions may exist for operands of several types.

The compiler must use conditional branches to interpret the value of a condition code. If the sole use of the result is to determine control flow, as in Figure 7.6(a), then the conditional branch that the compiler uses to read the condition code can often implement the source-level control-flow construct, as well. If the result is used in a boolean operation, or it is preserved in a variable, as in (b), the code must convert it into a concrete representation

Source Code	if (x < y)
	      then a ← c + d
	      else a ← e + f	

ILOC Code	comp r_x, r_y ⇒ cc_1
	cbr_LT cc_1 → L_1, L_2
	L_1: add r_c, r_d ⇒ r_a
	     jumpI → L_{out}
	L_2: add r_e, r_f ⇒ r_a
	     jumpI → L_{out}
	L_{out}: nop
	Straight Condition Codes
		cmp_LT r_x, r_y ⇒ r_1
		cbr r_1 → L_1, L_2
		L_1: add r_c, r_d ⇒ r_a
		     jumpI → L_{out}
		L_2: add r_e, r_f ⇒ r_a
		     jumpI → L_{out}
		L_{out}: nop
		Boolean Compare

	comp r_x, r_y ⇒ cc_1 add r_c, r_d ⇒ r_1 add r_e, r_f ⇒ r_2 i2i_LT cc_1, r_1, r_2 ⇒ r_a **Conditional Move**	cmp_LT r_x, r_y ⇒ r_1 not r_1 ⇒ r_2 (r_1)? add r_c, r_d ⇒ r_a (r_2)? add r_e, r_f ⇒ r_a **Predicated Execution**

(a)

Source Code	x ← a < b ∧ c < d	

ILOC Code	comp r_a, r_b ⇒ cc_1
	cbr_LT cc_1 → L_1, L_2
	L_1: comp r_c, r_d ⇒ cc_2
	     cbr_LT cc_2 → L_3, L_2
	L_2: loadI false ⇒ r_x
	     jumpI → L_4
	L_3: loadI true ⇒ r_x
	     jumpI → L_4
	L_4: nop
	Straight Condition Codes
		cmp_LT r_a, r_b ⇒ r_1
		cmp_LT r_c, r_d ⇒ r_2
		and r_1, r_2 ⇒ r_x
		
		Boolean Compare

	comp r_a, r_b ⇒ cc_1 i2i_LT cc_1, r_T, r_F ⇒ r_1 comp r_c, r_d ⇒ cc_2 i2i_LT cc_2, r_T, r_F ⇒ r_2 and r_1, r_2 ⇒ r_x **Conditional Move**	cmp_LT r_a, r_b ⇒ r_1 cmp_LT r_c, r_d ⇒ r_2 and r_1, r_2 ⇒ r_x **Predicated Execution**

(b)

FIGURE 7.6   Implementing Boolean and Relational Operators

SHORT-CIRCUIT EVALUATION AS AN OPTIMIZATION

Short-circuit evaluation arose from a positional encoding of the values of boolean and relational expressions. On processors that use condition codes to record the result of a comparison and use conditional branches to interpret the condition code, short circuiting makes sense.

As processors include features like conditional move, boolean-valued comparisons, and predicated execution, the advantages of short-circuit evaluation will likely fade. With branch latencies growing, the cost of the conditional branches required for short circuiting grows too. When the branch costs exceed the savings from avoiding evaluation, short circuiting will no longer be an improvement. Instead, full evaluation will be faster.

When the language requires short-circuit evaluation, as does C, the compiler may need to perform some analysis to determine when it is safe to substitute full evaluation for short-circuit evaluation. Thus, future C compilers may include analysis and transformation to replace short circuiting with full evaluation, just as compilers in the past have performed analysis and transformation to replace full evaluation with short-circuit evaluation.

of a boolean. The two loadI operations in (b) do this. Either way, the code has at least one conditional branch per relational operator.

The strength of condition codes comes from another feature that processors usually implement alongside condition codes. Typically, arithmetic operations on these processors set a condition code to reflect their computed results. If the compiler can arrange to have the arithmetic operations that must be performed set a condition code appropriately, then the comparison operation can be omitted. Thus, advocates of this architectural style argue that it allows a more efficient encoding of the program—the code may execute fewer instructions than it would with a comparator that puts a boolean value in a general-purpose register.

Conditional Move

This scheme adds a conditional move instruction to the straight condition-code model. In ILOC, a conditional move looks like:

$$\text{i2i\_LT } cc_i, r_j, r_k \Rightarrow r_m$$

If the condition code cc_i matches LT, then the value of r_j is copied to r_m. Otherwise, the value of r_k is copied to r_m.

Conditional move retains the principal advantage of using condition codes —avoiding a comparison when an earlier operation has already set the condition code. As shown in Figure 7.6(a), it lets the compiler encode simple conditional operations with branches. Here, the compiler speculatively evaluates the two additions. It uses conditional move for the final assignment. This is safe as long as neither addition can raise an exception.

If the compiler has values for true and false in registers, say r_T for true and r_F for false, then it can use conditional move to convert the condition code into a boolean. Figure 7.6(b) uses this strategy. It compares a and b and creates the boolean result in r_1. It computes the boolean for $c < d$ into r_2. It computes the final result as the logical and of r_1 and r_2.

The conditional move instruction can be expected to execute in a single cycle. To the extent that it allows the compiler to avoid branches, conditional move should lead to faster code.

Boolean-Valued Comparisons

This scheme avoids condition codes entirely. The comparison operation returns a boolean value in either a general-purpose register or a dedicated boolean register. The conditional branch takes that result as an argument that determines its behavior.

Boolean-valued comparisons do not help in Figure 7.6a. The code is equivalent to the straight condition-code scheme. It requires comparisons, branches, and jumps to evaluate the if-then-else construct.

The strength of this model shows in Figure 7.6(b). Like conditional move, it can evaluate a relational operator without a branch, as shown in the example in (b). However, it does not need to convert the result of the comparisons to boolean values. The uniform representation of boolean and relational values leads to more concise, more efficient code for this example.

A weakness of this model is that it requires explicit comparisons. Whereas the condition-code models can sometimes avoid the comparison by arranging to have condition codes set by arithmetic operations, the boolean-valued comparison model always requires an explicit comparison.

Predicated Execution

Architectures that support predicated execution make some (or all) operations take a boolean-valued operand that determines whether or not the operation takes effect. This technique, called *predicated execution*, lets the compiler avoid conditional branches in many situations. In ILOC, we write a predicated instruction by including a predicate expression before the instruction. To remind the reader of the predicate's purpose, we enclose it in parentheses and follow it with a question mark. For example,

$$(r_{17})? \text{ add } r_a, r_b \Rightarrow r_c$$

indicates an add operation $(r_a + r_b)$ that executes if and only if r_{17} contains the value true.

The example in Figure 7.6(a) shows the strength of predicated execution. The code is simple and concise. It generates two predicates, r_1 and r_2. It uses them to control the code in the then and else parts of the source construct. Predication leads to the same code as the boolean-compare scheme for the example in Figure 7.6(b).

The processor can use predication to avoid executing the operation, or it can execute the operation and use the predicate to avoid assigning the result. As long as the idled instruction does not raise an exception, the differences between these two approaches are irrelevant to our discussion. Our examples show the operations required to produce both the predicate and its complement. To avoid this, a processor could provide comparisons that define two registers, one with the boolean value and the other with its complement.

7.4.3 Choosing a Representation

The compiler writer has some latitude in deciding when to use each of these representations. That decision depends on hardware support for comparisons, the costs of branching (particularly a mispredicted conditional branch), the desirability of short-circuit evaluation, and how the result is used by the surrounding code.

Comparing the four implementations in Figure 7.6 shows the differences between the schemes. Consider the if-then-else construct in (a). All four schemes produce execution paths of the same length—four operations. If branches disrupt execution, the branching schemes (on the top) may take longer to execute. The nonbranching schemes (on the bottom) avoid such disruption; they also produce more compact code.

The boolean assignment in (b) shows the difference between an implicit result for comparison and an explicit one. The condition-code schemes (on the left) require more code than the boolean-compare schemes (on the right). The assignment necessitates a concrete representation that can be stored into r_x. Producing that representation directly results in clean, concise code. In a short-circuit evaluation, predication would produce better code than the boolean comparison.

7.5 STORING AND ACCESSING ARRAYS

So far, we have assumed that variables stored in memory contain scalar values. Many programs need arrays or similar structures. The code required to locate and reference an element of an array is surprisingly complex. This section shows several schemes for laying out arrays in memory and describes the code that each scheme produces for an array reference.

7.5.1 Referencing a Vector Element

The simplest form of an array has a single dimension; we call a one-dimensional array a *vector*. Vectors are typically stored in contiguous memory, so that the ith element immediately precedes the $i+1^{st}$ element. Thus, a vector $V[3\ldots10]$ generates the following memory layout, where the number below a cell indicates its index in the vector:

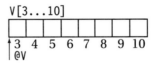

When the compiler encounters a reference, like $V[6]$, it must use the index into the vector, along with facts available from the declaration of V, to generate an offset for $V[6]$. The actual address is then computed as the sum of the offset and a pointer to the start of V, which we write as @V.

As an example, assume that V has been declared as $V[low...high]$, where *low* and *high* are the vector's lower and upper bounds. To translate the reference $V[i]$, the compiler needs both a pointer to the start of storage for V and the offset of element i within V. The offset is simply $(i - low) \times w$, where w is the length of a single element of V. Thus, if *low* is 3, i is 6, and w is 4, the offset is $(6 - 3) \times 4 = 12$. Assuming that r_i holds the value of i, the following code fragment computes the address of V[i] into r_4 and loads its value into r_V:

```
loadI @V      ⇒ r@V  // get V's address
subI  r_i, 3  ⇒ r_1  // (offset - lower bound)
multI r_1, 4  ⇒ r_2  // × element length, 4
add   r@V,r_2 ⇒ r_3  // address of V[i]
load  r_3     ⇒ r_V  // value of V[i]
```

Notice that the textually simple reference V[i] introduces three arithmetic operations. This sequence can be simplified and improved. Using a lower bound of zero eliminates the subtraction. If w is a power of two, the multiply can be replaced with an arithmetic shift; many base types in real programming languages have this property. Adding the address and offset seems unavoidable; perhaps this explains why most processors include an addressing mode that takes a base address and an offset and accesses the location at base address + offset. In ILOC, we write this as loadAO.

```
loadI   @V      ⇒ r@V  // get V's address
subI    r_i, 3  ⇒ r_1  // (offset - lower bound)
lshiftI r_1, 2  ⇒ r_2  // × element length, 4
loadAO  r@V,r_2 ⇒ r_V  // value of V[i]
```

If the compiler knows the lower bound of V, it can fold the subtraction of that value into @V. Rather than using @V as the base address for V, it can use $@V_0 = @V - low \times w$. We call $@V_0$ the *false zero* of V.

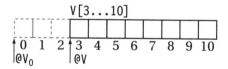

Using $@V_0$ and assuming that i is in r_i, the code for accessing V[i] becomes

```
loadI   @V_0      ⇒ r@V_0  // adjusted address for V
lshiftI r_i, 2    ⇒ r_1    // × element length, 4
loadAO  r@V_0, r_1 ⇒ r_V    // value of V[i]
```

This version of the code is shorter and, presumably, faster. In a hand-coded assembly program, this final sequence would be preferred. In the compiler, the longer sequence may produce better results, by exposing details such as the multiply and the add to optimization. Low-level improvements, such as converting the multiply into a shift and rewriting the add-load sequence with loadAO can be done late in compilation.

If the compiler does not have an array's bounds available, it might calculate the array's false zero at run time and reuse that value in each reference to the array. For example, it can compute the false zero on entry to a procedure that references elements of the array multiple times. An alternative strategy, employed in languages like C, forces the use of zero as a lower bound. This makes $@V_0 = @V$ and simplifies all array-address calculations. However, attention to detail in the compiler can achieve the same results without restricting the programmer's choice of a lower bound.

7.5.2 Array Storage Layout

Accessing an element of a multidimensional array requires more work. Before discussing the code sequences that the compiler must generate, we must consider how the compiler will map array indexes to memory locations. Most implementations use one of three schemes: *row-major order*, *column-major order*, or *indirection vectors*. The source-language definition usually specifies one of these mappings.

The code required to access an array element depends on the way that the array is mapped to memory. Consider the array A[1...2,1...4]. Conceptually, it looks like

$$
A \quad
\begin{array}{|c|c|c|c|}
\hline
1,1 & 1,2 & 1,3 & 1,4 \\
\hline
2,1 & 2,2 & 2,3 & 2,4 \\
\hline
\end{array}
$$

In linear algebra, the *row* of a two-dimensional matrix is its first dimension, and the *column* is its second dimension. In row-major order, the elements of A are mapped onto consecutive memory locations so that adjacent elements of a single row occupy consecutive memory locations. This produces the following layout:

$$
\begin{array}{|c|c|c|c|c|c|c|c|}
\hline
1,1 & 1,2 & 1,3 & 1,4 & 2,1 & 2,2 & 2,3 & 2,4 \\
\hline
\end{array}
$$

The following loop nest shows the effect of row-major order on memory access patterns:

```
for i ← 1 to 2
    for j ← 1 to 4
        A[i,j] ← A[i,j] + 1
```

In row-major order, the assignment statement steps through memory in sequential order, beginning with A[1,1], A[1,2], A[1,3], and on through A[2,4]. This sequential access works well with most memory hierarchies. Moving the i loop inside the j loop produces an access sequence that jumps between rows, accessing A[1,1], A[2,1], A[1,2], ..., A[2,4]. For a small array like A, this is not a problem. For arrays that are larger than the cache, the lack of sequential access could produce poor performance in the memory hierarchy. As a general rule, row-major order produces sequential access when the rightmost subscript, j in this example, varies fastest.

The obvious alternative to row-major order is column-major order. It keeps the columns of A in contiguous locations, producing the following layout:

| 1,1 | 2,1 | 1,2 | 2,2 | 1,3 | 2,3 | 1,4 | 2,4 |

Column-major order produces sequential access when the leftmost subscript varies fastest. In our doubly nested loop, having the i loop in the outer position produces nonsequential access, while moving the i loop to the inner position would produce sequential access.

A third alternative, not quite as obvious, has been used in several languages. This scheme uses indirection vectors to reduce all multidimensional arrays to a set of vectors. For our array A, this would produce

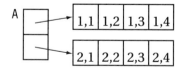

Each row has its own contiguous storage. Within a row, elements are addressed as in a vector. To allow systematic addressing of the row vectors, the compiler allocates a vector of pointers and initializes it appropriately. A similar scheme can create column-major indirection vectors.

This scheme appears simple, but it introduces two kinds of complexity. First, it requires more storage than the simpler row-major or column-major

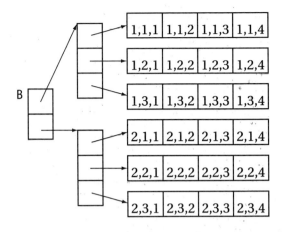

FIGURE 7.7   Indirection Vectors in Row-Major Order for B[1...2,1...3,1...4]

layouts. Each array element has a storage location, as for the other two layouts; additionally, the inner dimensions require indirection vectors. The number of entries in the vectors can grow quadratically in the array's dimension. Figure 7.7 shows the layout for a more complex array, B[1...2,1...3,1...4]. Second, a fair amount of initialization code is required to set up all the pointers for the array's inner dimensions.

Each of these schemes has been used in a popular programming language. For languages that store arrays in contiguous storage, row-major order has been the typical choice; the one notable exception is FORTRAN, which uses column-major order. Both BCPL and Java support indirection vectors.

7.5.3 Referencing an Array Element

Programs that use arrays usually contain references to individual array elements. As with vectors, the compiler must translate an array reference into a starting address for the array's storage and an offset where the element is located relative to the starting address.

This section describes the address calculations for arrays stored as a contiguous block in row-major order and as a set of indirection vectors. The calculations for column-major order follow the same basic scheme as those for row-major order, with the order of dimensions reversed. We leave those equations for the reader to derive.

Row-Major Order

In row-major order, the address calculation must find the start of the row and then generate an offset within the row as if it were a vector. Extending the notation that we used to describe the bounds of a vector, we add subscripts to *low* and *high* that specify a dimension. Thus, low_1 refers to the lower bound of the first dimension, and $high_2$ refers to the upper bound of the second dimension. In our example A[1...2,1...4], low_1 is 1 and $high_2$ is 4.

To access element A[i,j], the compiler must emit code that computes the address of row i and follow that with the offset for element j, which we know from Section 7.5.1 will be $(j - low_2) \times w$. Each row contains 4 elements, computed as $high_2 - low_2 + 1$, where $high_2$ is the highest-numbered column and low_2 is the lowest-numbered column—the upper and lower bounds for the second dimension of A. To simplify the exposition, let $len_k = high_k - low_k + 1$, the length of the kth dimension. Since rows are laid out consecutively, row i begins at $(i - low_1) \times len_2 \times w$ from the start of A. This suggests the address computation

$$@A + (i - low_1) \times len_2 \times w + (j - low_2) \times w$$

Substituting actual values for i, j, low_1, $high_2$, low_2, and w, we find that A[2,3] lies at offset

$$(2 - 1) \times (4 - 1 + 1) \times 4 \; + \; (3 - 1) \times 4 \; = \; 24$$

from A[1,1] (assuming that @A points at A[1,1], at offset 0). Looking at A in memory, we find that the address of A[1,1] + 24 is, in fact, the address of A[2,3].

0	4	8	12	16	20	24	28
1,1	1,2	1,3	1,4	2,1	2,2	2,3	2,4

@A   A[2,3]

In the vector case, we were able to simplify the calculation when upper and lower bounds were known at compile time. Applying the same algebra to create a false zero in the two-dimensional case produces

$$@A + (i \times len_2 \times w) - (low_1 \times len_2 \times w) + (j \times w) - (low_2 \times w), \text{ or}$$

$$@A + (i \times len_2 \times w) + (j \times w) - (low_1 \times len_2 \times w + low_2 \times w)$$

The last term, $(low_1 \times len_2 \times w + low_2 \times w)$, is independent of i and j, so it can be factored directly into the base address

$$@A_0 = @A - (low_1 \times len_2 \times w + low_2 \times w) = @A - 20$$

Now, the array reference is simply

$$@A_0 + i \times len_2 \times w + j \times w$$

Finally, we can refactor and move the w outside, saving an extraneous multiply:

$$@A_0 + (i \times len_2 + j) \times w$$

For the address of A[2,3], this evaluates to

$$@A_0 + (2 \times 4 + 3) \times 4 = @A_0 + 44$$

Since $@A_0$ is just $@A - 20$, this is equivalent to $@A - 20 + 44 = @A + 24$, the same location found with the original version of the array address polynomial.

If we assume that i and j are in r_i and r_j, and that len_2 is a constant, this form of the polynomial leads to the following code sequence:

```
loadI    @A₀        ⇒ r@A₀    // adjusted base for A
multI    rᵢ, len₂   ⇒ r₁      // i × len₂
add      r₁, rⱼ     ⇒ r₂      // + j
multI    r₂, 4      ⇒ r₃      // × element length, 4
loadAO   r@A₀, r₃   ⇒ rₐ      // value of A[i,j]
```

In this form, we have reduced the computation to two multiplications and two additions (one in the loadAO). The second multiply can be rewritten as a shift.

If the compiler does not have access to the array bounds, it must either compute the false zero at run time or use the more complex polynomial that includes the subtractions that adjust for lower bounds. The former option can be profitable if the elements of the array are accessed multiple times in a procedure; computing the false zero on entry to the procedure lets the code use the less expensive address computation. The more complex computation makes sense only if the array is accessed infrequently.

The ideas behind the address computation for arrays with two dimensions generalize to arrays of higher dimension. The address polynomial for an array stored in column-major order can be derived in a similar fashion. The optimizations that we applied to reduce the cost of address computations apply equally well to the addressing polynomials for these other kinds of arrays.

Indirection Vectors

Using indirection vectors simplifies the code generated to access an individual element. Since the outermost dimension is stored as a set of vectors, the final step looks like the vector access described in Section 7.5.1. For B[i,j,k], the final step computes an offset from k, the outermost dimension's lower bound, and the length of an element for B. The preliminary steps derive the starting address for this vector by following the appropriate pointers through the indirection-vector structure.

Thus, to access element B[i,j,k] in the array B shown in Figure 7.7, the compiler uses B, i, and the length of a pointer, to find the vector for the subarray B[i,*,*]. Next, it uses that result, along with j and the length of a pointer to find the vector for the subarray B[i,j,*]. Finally, it uses the vector-address computation for index k, and element length w to find the address of B[i,j,k] in this vector.

If the current values for i, j, and k exist in registers r_i, r_j, and r_k, respectively, and @B$_0$ is the zero-adjusted address of the first dimension, then B[i,j,k] can be referenced as follows:

```
loadI   @B₀        ⇒ r@B₀   // false zero of B
multI   rᵢ,4       ⇒ r₁     // pointer is 4 bytes
loadAO  r@B₀,r₁    ⇒ r₂     // get @B[i,*,*]

multI   rⱼ,4       ⇒ r₃     // pointer is 4 bytes
loadAO  r₂,r₃      ⇒ r₄     // get @B[i,j,*]

multI   rₖ,4       ⇒ r₅     // pointer is 4 bytes
loadAO  r₄,r₅      ⇒ rB     // value of B[i,j,k]
```

This code assumes that the pointers in the indirection structure have already been adjusted to account for nonzero lower bounds. If the pointers have not been adjusted, then the values in r_j and r_k must be decremented by the corresponding lower bounds. The multiplies can be replaced by shifts in this example.

Using indirection vectors, the reference requires just two instructions per dimension. This property made the indirection-vector implementation of arrays efficient on systems in which memory access is fast relative to arithmetic —for example, on most computer systems prior to 1985. Several compilers used indirection vectors to manage the cost of address arithmetic. As the cost of memory accesses has increased relative to arithmetic, this scheme has lost its advantage. If systems again appear with memory latencies that are small relative to the time needed to perform arithmetic, indirection vectors may again emerge as a practical way to decrease access costs.

For cache-based machines, locality is critical to performance. When arrays grow to be much larger than the cache, storage order affects locality. Row-major and column-major storage schemes produce good locality for some array-based operations. There is little reason to believe that indirection vectors produce good spatial locality. It seems more likely that this scheme generates a reference stream that appears random to the memory system.

Accessing Array-Valued Parameters

When an array is passed as a parameter, most implementations pass it by reference. Even in languages that use call by value for all other parameters, arrays are usually passed by reference. Consider the mechanism required to pass an array by value. The calling procedure would need to copy each array element's value into the activation record of the called procedure. Passing the array as a reference parameter can greatly reduce the cost of each call.

If the compiler is to generate array references in the called procedure, it needs information about the dimensions of the array that is bound to the parameter. In FORTRAN, for example, the programmer is required to declare the array using either constants or other formal parameters to specify its dimensions. Thus, FORTRAN gives the programmer responsibility for passing to the called procedure the information that it needs to address correctly a parameter array.

Other languages leave the task of collecting, organizing, and passing the necessary information to the compiler. This approach is necessary if the array's size cannot be statically determined because it is allocated at run time. Even when the size can be statically determined, this approach is useful because it abstracts away details that would otherwise clutter the code. In these circumstances, the compiler builds a descriptor that contains both a pointer to the start of the array and the necessary information about each dimension. The descriptor has a known size, even when the array's size cannot be known at compile time. Thus, the compiler can allocate space for the descriptor in the AR of the called procedure. The value passed in the array's parameter slot is a pointer to this descriptor, which is called a *dope vector*.

When the compiler generates a reference to an array that has been passed as a parameter, it must extract the information from the dope vector. It generates the same address polynomial that it would use for a reference to a local array, loading values out of the dope vector as needed. The compiler must decide, as a matter of policy, which form of the addressing polynomial it will use. With the naive address polynomial, the dope vector must contain a pointer to the start of the array, the lower bound of each dimension, and the sizes of all but one of the dimensions. With the address polynomial based on the false zero, the lower-bound information is unnecessary. As long as the compiler always uses the same form of the polynomial, it can generate code to build dope vectors as part of the prologue for each procedure call.

A given procedure may be invoked from many call sites, each passing a different array. The PL/I procedure main in Figure 7.8 contains two statements that call fee. The first passes array x, while the second passes y. Inside fee, the actual parameter (x or y) is bound to the formal parameter A. To allow the code for fee to reference the appropriate location, it needs a dope vector for A. The

```
program main;
  begin;
    declare x(1:100,1:10,2:50),
        y(1:10,1:10,15:35) float;
    ...
    call fee(x)
    call fee(y);
  end main;
```

At the First Call

$A \longrightarrow$

$@x_0$
100
10
49

```
procedure fee(A)
  declare A(*,*,*) float;
  begin;
    declare x float;
      declare i, j, k fixed binary;
      ...
    x = A(i,j,k);
      ...
  end fee;
```

At the Second Call

$A \longrightarrow$

$@y_0$
10
10
21

FIGURE 7.8 Dope Vectors

respective dope vectors, which contain the false zero and the lengths of each dimension of the array passed at the corresponding call site, are shown on the right-hand side of the figure.

Notice that the cost of accessing an array-valued parameter is higher than the cost of accessing an array declared locally. At best, the dope vector introduces additional memory references to access the relevant entries. At worst, it prevents the compiler from performing optimizations that rely on complete knowledge of an array's declaration.

7.5.4 Range Checking

Most programming-language definitions assume, either explicitly or implicitly, that a program refers only to array elements within the defined bounds of an array. A program that references an out-of-bounds element is, by definition, not well formed. Some languages (for example, Java and Ada) require that out-of-bounds accesses be detected and reported. In other languages, many compilers have included mechanisms to detect and report out-of-bounds array accesses.

The simplest implementation of *range checking*, as this is called, inserts a test before each array reference. The test verifies that each index value falls in the valid range for the dimension in which it is used. In an array-intensive program, the overhead of such checks can be significant. Many improvements on this simple scheme are possible. The least expensive alternative is to prove, in the compiler, that a given reference cannot generate an out-of-bounds reference.

If the compiler intends to insert range checks for array-valued parameters, it may need to include additional information in the dope vectors. For example, if the compiler uses the address polynomial based on the array's false zero, it has length information for each dimension, but not upper and lower bound information. It might perform an imprecise test by checking the offset against the array's overall length. However, to perform a precise test, it must include the upper and lower bounds for each dimension in the dope vector and test against them.

When the compiler generates run-time code for range checking, it inserts many copies of the code to report an out-of-range subscript. Typically, this involves a branch to a run-time error routine. During a normal execution, these branches are almost never taken (particularly if the error handler stops execution). If the target machine lets the compiler predict the likely direction of a branch, these exception branches should be predicted as not taken. The compiler may also want to annotate its IR with the fact that these branches lead to an abnormal termination. This allows subsequent phases of the compiler to differentiate between the "normal" execution path and the "error" path; the compiler may be able to use this knowledge to produce better code along the normal path.

7.6 CHARACTER STRINGS

The operations that programming languages provide for character data are different from those provided for numerical data. The level of programming-language support for character strings ranges from C's, where most manipulation takes the form of calls to library routines, to PL/I's, where assignment of individual characters, forming arbitrary substrings of character strings, and even concatenation of strings occur as first-class operators in the language. To present the issues that arise in string implementation, this section discusses the implementation of string assignment, string concatenation, and computing a string's length.

String operations can be costly. Older CISC architectures, such as the IBM S/370 and the DEC VAX, provide extensive support for string manipulation. Modern RISC machines rely more heavily on the compiler to code these complex operations using a set of simpler operations. The basic operation, copying bytes from one location to another, arises in many different contexts.

7.6.1 String Representations

The compiler writer must choose a representation for strings; the details of that representation have a strong impact on the cost of string operations.

To see this point, consider the following two representations of a string b. The one on the left is traditional in C implementations. It uses a simple vector of characters, with a designated character ('\0') serving as a terminator. The glyph b̸ represents a blank. The representation on the right stores the length of the string (8) alongside its contents. Many language implementations have used this approach.

Null Termination   Explicit Length Field

If the length field takes more space than the null terminator, then storing the length will marginally increase the size of the string in memory. (Our examples assume the length is 4 bytes; in practice, it might be smaller.) However, storing the length simplifies several operations on strings. If a language allows varying-length strings to be stored inside a string allocated with some fixed length, the implementor might also store the allocated length with the string. The compiler can use the allocated length for run-time bounds checking on assignment and concatenation.

7.6.2 String Assignment

String assignment is conceptually simple. In C, an assignment from the third character of b to the second character of a can be written as shown on the left.

a[1] = b[2];

```
loadI    @b      ⇒ r@b
cloadAI  r@b,2  ⇒ r₂
loadI    @a      ⇒ r@a
cstoreAI r₂     ⇒ r@a,1
```

On a machine with character-sized memory operations (cload and cstore), this translates into the simple code shown on the right. (Recall that the first character in a is a[0] because C uses zero as the lower bound of all arrays.)

If, however, the underlying hardware does not support character-oriented memory operations, the compiler must generate more complex code. Assuming that both a and b begin on word boundaries, that a character occupies 1 byte, and that a word is 4 bytes, the compiler might emit the following code:

```
loadI    @b                  ⇒ r@b  // address of b
load     r@b                 ⇒ r₁   // get 1st word
andI     r₁,0x0000FF00      ⇒ r₂   // mask away others
lshiftI  r₂,8                ⇒ r₃   // move it over 1 byte
loadI    @a                  ⇒ r@a  // address of a
load     r@a                 ⇒ r₄   // get 1st word
and      r₄,0xFF00FFFF      ⇒ r₅   // mask away 2nd char
or       r₃,r₅               ⇒ r₆   // put in new 2nd char
store    r₆                  ⇒ r@a  // put it back in a
```

This code loads the word that contains b[2], extracts the character, shifts it into position, masks it into the proper position in the word that contains a[1], and stores the result back into place. (The added complexity of this code sequence may explain why character-oriented load and store operations are becoming common again.)

The code is similar for longer strings. PL/I has a string assignment operator. The programmer can write a statement such as a = b; where a and b have been declared as character strings. Assume that the compiler uses the explicit length representation. The following simple loop will move the characters on a machine with byte-oriented load and store operations:

```
                loadI    @b        ⇒ r@b
                loadAI   r@b,−4  ⇒ r1       // get b's length
                loadI    @a        ⇒ r@a
                loadAI   r@a,−4  ⇒ r2       // get a's length
                cmp_LT   r2,r1   ⇒ r3       // will b fit in a?
                cbr      r3        → Lsov,L1  // raise overflow
a = b;     L1: loadI    0         ⇒ r4       // counter
                cmp_LT   r4,r1   ⇒ r5       // more to copy?
                cbr      r5        → L2,L3
           L2: cloadAO  r@b,r4  ⇒ r6       // get char from b
                cstoreAO r6        ⇒ r@a,r4  // put it in a
                addI     r4,1    ⇒ r4       // increment offset
                cmp_LT   r4,r1   ⇒ r7       // more to copy?
                cbr      r7        → L2,L3
           L3: nop                          // next statement
```

Notice that this code tests the lengths of a and b to avoid overrunning a. The label L_{sov} represents a run-time error handler for string-overflow conditions.

In a language with null-terminated strings, the code changes somewhat. Consider the simple C loop for copying the string at b into the string at a.

```
                                    loadI   @b      ⇒ r_@b   // get pointers
                                    loadI   @a      ⇒ r_@a

                                    loadI   NULL    ⇒ r_1    // terminator
      do {
        *a++ = *b++;           L_1: cload   r_@b    ⇒ r_2    // get next char
      } while (*b != '\0')          cstore  r_2     ⇒ r_@a   // store it

                                    addI    r_@b,1  ⇒ r_@b   // bump pointers

                                    addI    r_@a,1  ⇒ r_@a

                                    cmp_NE  r_1,r_2 ⇒ r_4

                                    cbr     r_4     → L_1,L_2

                               L_2: nop                      // next statement
```

If the target machine supports autoincrement on load and store operations, the two adds in the loop can be performed in the cload and cstore operations, which reduces the loop to four operations. (Recall that C was designed for the PDP/11, which supported auto-post-increment.) Without autoincrement, the compiler would generate better code by using cloadAO and cstoreAO with a common offset. That would require only one add operation inside the loop. (Note that the code changes the value of $r_{@a}$ and $r_{@b}$.)

Without byte-oriented memory operations, the code becomes more complex. The compiler could replace the load, store, add portion of the loop body with the scheme for masking single characters in the body of the loop shown earlier. The result is a functional, but ugly, loop that requires many more instructions to copy b into a.

The alternative is to adopt a somewhat more complex scheme that makes word-length load and store operations an advantage rather than a burden. The compiler can use a word-oriented loop, followed by a post-loop clean-up operation that handles any leftover characters at the end of the string. This is shown in Figure 7.9.

The code required to set up the loop is more complex, because it must compute the length of the substring that can be moved with word operations ($\lceil length(b) \div 4 \rceil$). The loop body contains five instructions. It uses just one-quarter of the iterations used by the character-oriented loop.

After the word-oriented loop terminates, a character-oriented loop handles the remaining one, two, or three characters. Of course, if the compiler knows the length of the strings (and they are reasonably short), it can completely avoid generating the loop and, instead, emit the right sequence

```
        loadI    @b              ⇒ r_@b
        loadAI   r_@b,-4         ⇒ r_1      // get b's length
        loadI    @a              ⇒ r_@a
        loadAI   r_@a,-4         ⇒ r_2      // get a's length
        cmp_LT   r_2,r_1         ⇒ r_3      // will b fit in a?
        cbr      r_3             → L_sov,L_1 // to error routine
L_1:    andI     r_1,0xFFFFFFFC  ⇒ r_4      // rounded length(b)
        loadI    0               ⇒ r_5      // offset in string
        cmp_LT   r_5,r_4         ⇒ r_7      // more for the loop?
        cbr      r_7             → L_2,L_3
L_2:    loadAO   r_@b,r_5        ⇒ r_8      // get word from b
        storeAO  r_8             ⇒ r_@a,r_5 // put it into a
        addI     r_5,4           ⇒ r_5      // increment offset
        cmp_LT   r_5,r_4         ⇒ r_9      // more for the loop?
        cbr      r_9             → L_2,L_3
L_3:    cmp_LT   r_5,r_1         ⇒ r_10     // done yet?
        cbr      r_10            → L_4,L_5
L_4:    cloadAO  r_@a,r_5        ⇒ r_11     // get next char
        cstoreAO r_11            ⇒ r_@b,r_5 // put next char
        addI     r_5,1           ⇒ r_5      // bump offset
        cmp_LT   r_5,r_1         ⇒ r_12     // done yet?
        cbr      r_12            → L_4,L_5
L_5:    nop                                 // next statement
```

FIGURE 7.9   String Assignment (a = b) Using Whole-Word Operations

of loads and stores. This avoids the overhead of the loop, but can produce a larger program.

More complex cases exist. These include strings, or substrings, that are not word aligned and assignments whose source and destination overlap. In general, the character-by-character loops work correctly in these cases. The more efficient word-by-word loops require additional work, such as preloops to reach word boundaries and small amounts of additional space to buffer characters and compensate for different alignments in the source and destination. In practice, many compilers call a carefully optimized library routine to implement the nontrivial cases.

7.6.3 String Concatenation

Concatenation is simply a shorthand for a sequence of one or more assignments. It comes in two basic forms: appending string b to string a, and creating a new string that contains a followed immediately by b.

The former case is a length computation followed by an assignment. The compiler emits code to determine the length of a. Space permitting, it then performs an assignment of b to the space that immediately follows the contents of a. (If sufficient space is not available, the code raises an error at run time.) The latter case requires copying each character in a and each character in b. The compiler treats the concatenation as a pair of assignments and generates code as shown in the previous section.

In either case, the compiler should ensure that enough space is allocated to hold the result. In practice, either the compiler or the run-time system must know the allocated length of each string. If the compiler knows those lengths, it can perform the check during code generation and avoid emitting code for a run-time check. In cases in which the compiler cannot know the lengths of a and b, it must generate code to compute the lengths at run time and to perform the appropriate test and branch.

7.6.4 String Length

Programs that manipulate strings often need to compute the length of a character string. In C programs, the function strlen in the standard library takes a string as its argument and returns the string's length, expressed as an integer. In PL/I, the built-in function length performs the same function. The two string representations described previously lead to radically different costs for the length computation.

1. *Null-Terminated String* The length computation must start at the beginning of the string and examine each character, in order, until it reaches the null character. The code is similar to the C character-copying loop. It requires time proportional to the length of the string.

2. *Explicit Length Field*   The length computation is a memory reference. In ILOC, this becomes a loadI of the string's starting address into a register, followed by a loadAI to obtain the length. The cost is constant and small.

The tradeoff between these representations is simple. Null-termination saves a small amount of space, but requires more code and more time for the length computation. An explicit length field costs one more word per string, but makes the length computation take constant time.

A classic example of a string optimization problem is finding the length that would result from the concatenation of two strings, a and b. In a language with string operators, this might be written as length(a + b) where + signifies concatenation. This expression has two obvious implementations: construct the concatenated string and compute its length (strlen(strcat(a,b)) in C), and sum the lengths of a and b (strlen(a) + strlen(b) in C). The latter solution, of course, is desired. With an explicit length field, the operation can be optimized to use two loads and an add.

7.7   STRUCTURE REFERENCES

The other kind of complex data structure that occurs in most programming languages is a structure, or some variation on it. In C, a structure aggregates individually named elements, often of different types. A list implementation, in C, might, for example, use the following structure to create lists of integers:

```
struct node {
  int value;
  struct node *next;
}
NilNode = {0, (struct node*) 0};
struct node *NIL = &NilNode;
```

Each node contains a single integer and a pointer to another node. NilNode is a node with value 0 and next set to an illegal value (0).

Working with structures in C requires the use of *pointer values*. For example, the declaration of NIL creates a value of type *pointer to* node and initializes it so that it points to NilNode (using the address-of operator &). The use of pointers introduces two distinct problems for the compiler: *anonymous values* and *structure layout*.

7.7.1   Loading and Storing Anonymous Values

A C program creates an instance of a structure in one of two ways. It can declare a structure instance; in the preceding example NilNode is declared as an instance of node. Alternatively, the code can dynamically allocate a structure instance. For a variable fee declared as a *pointer to* node, the allocation would look like:

```
fee = (node *) malloc(sizeof(node));
```

The only access to this new node is through the pointer fee. Thus, we think of it as an anonymous value, since it has no permanent name.

Because the only name for an anonymous value is a pointer, the compiler cannot easily determine if two pointer references specify the same memory location. Consider the code fragment

```
1   p1 = (node *) malloc(sizeof(node));
2   p2 = (node *) malloc(sizeof(node));
3   if (...)
4      then p3 = p1;
5      else p3 = p2;
6   p1->value = ...;
7   p3->value = ...;
8   ...    = p1->value;
```

The first two lines create anonymous nodes. Line 6 writes the node reachable through p1 and line 7 writes through p3. Because of the two paths through the if-then-else, p3 can refer to either the node allocated in line 1 or in line 2. Finally, line 8 references p1->value.

To implement the sequence of assignments in lines 6 through 8, the compiler should keep the value that is reused in a register. Unfortunately, it cannot easily determine whether line 8 refers to the value generated in line 6 or the value generated in line 7. To know which node is referenced in line 8, the compiler must know the value of the conditional expression evaluated in line 3. While it may be possible in certain specific instances (for example, 1 > 2), it is undecidable in the general case. Unless it has deep knowledge about the value of the conditional expression, the compiler must emit conservative code for the three assignments. It must load the value used in line 8 from memory, even though it had the value in a register quite recently.

This uncertainty about references to anonymous objects prevents the compiler from keeping values used in pointer-based references in registers. It can make statements involving pointer-based references less efficient than corresponding computations on unambiguous local variables. Analyzing pointer values and using the results of that analysis to disambiguate references —that is, to rewrite references in ways that let the compiler keep some values in registers—is a major source of potential optimization for pointer-intensive programs. Unfortunately, the analysis required to disambiguate pointer references can be expensive because it may require that the compiler examine the entire program.

A similar effect occurs for code that makes intensive use of arrays. Unless the compiler performs an in-depth analysis of the array subscripts, it may not be able to determine whether two array references overlap. When the compiler cannot distinguish between two references, such as a[i,j,k] and a[i,j,l], it must treat both references conservatively. The problem of disambiguating array references, while challenging, is easier than disambiguating pointer references.

7.7.2 Understanding Structure Layouts

When it emits code for structure references, the compiler needs to know both the starting address of the structure instance and the offset and length of each structure element. To maintain this information, the compiler typically builds a separate table of structure layouts. This compile-time table must include the textual name for each structure element, its offset within the structure, and its source-language data type. For the list example, the compiler might build the following structures:

Structure Layout Table

Name	Length	1ˢᵗ Element
node	4	0 ●
...	...	2 ●

Element Table

Name	Length	Offset	Type	Next
node.value	4	0	int	●
node.next	4	4	node *	●
...	...	...	...	...

Entries in the element table use fully qualified names. This avoids conflicts due to reuse of a name in several distinct structures. (Few languages insist that programs use distinct element names in different structures.)

With this information, the compiler can easily generate code for structure references. For a pointer p1 declared as a node *, the reference p1->next might translate into the ILOC sequence

```
loadI  4        ⇒ r₁   // offset of next
loadAO rₚ₁,r₁ ⇒ r₂    // value of p1->next
```

Here, the compiler finds the offset of next by following the table from the node entry in the structure table to the chain of entries for node in the element table. Walking that chain, it finds the entry for node.next and its offset, 4.

In laying out a structure and assigning offsets to its elements, the compiler must obey the alignment rules of the target architecture. This may force it to leave unused space in the structure. The compiler confronts this problem when it lays out the structure declared on the left:

```
struct example {
    int fee;
    double fie;
    int foe;
    double fum;
} e1;
```

0	4	8	12	16	20	24	28
fee	···		fie	foe	···		fum

Elements in Declaration Order

0	4	8	12	16	20
fie		fum		fee	foe

Elements Ordered for Alignment

The top-right drawing shows the structure layout if the compiler is constrained to place the elements in declaration order. Because fie and fum must be doubleword aligned, the compiler must insert padding after fee and foe. If the compiler could order the elements in memory arbitrarily, it could use the layout shown on the bottom and avoid the need for padding. This is a language-design issue: the language definition specifies whether or not the layout of a structure is exposed to the user.

7.7.3 Arrays of Structures

Many programming languages allow the user to declare an array of structures. If the user is allowed to take the address of a structure-valued element of an array, then the compiler must lay out the data in memory as multiple copies of the structure layout. If the programmer cannot take the address of a structure-valued element of an array, the compiler might lay out the structure as if it were a structure composed of elements that are, themselves, arrays. Depending on how the surrounding code accesses the data, these two strategies may have strikingly different performance on a system with cache memory.

To address an array of structures laid out as multiple copies of the structure, the compiler uses the array-address polynomials described in Section 7.5. The overall length of the structure, including any needed padding, becomes the element size w in the address polynomial. The polynomial generates the address of the start of the structure instance. To obtain the value of a specific element, the element's offset is added to the instance's address.

If the compiler has laid out the structure with elements that are arrays, it must compute the starting location of the element array using the offset-table information and the array dimension. This address can then be used as the starting point for an address calculation using the appropriate array-address polynomial.

7.7.4 Unions and Run-Time Tags

Unions and variants present one extra complication. To emit code for a reference to an element of a union, the compiler must resolve the reference to a specific offset. The union can encompass multiple structure definitions. If multiple structure definitions use the same name, the compiler needs some way to resolve the name to its intended position in the run-time object.

This problem has a linguistic solution. The programming language can force the programmer to make the reference unambiguous. Consider the following declarations in C:

```
struct n1 {                union two {
  int kind;                  struct {
  int value;                   int kind;
} i1;                          int value;
struct n2 {                  } inode;
  int kind;                  struct {
  float value;                 int kind;
} f1;                          float value;
union one {                  } fnode;
  struct n1 inode;         } u2;
  struct n2 fnode;
} u1;                       u1.inode.value = 1;
                            u2.fnode.value = 2.0;
```

Both unions, one and two, can hold a "node" with either an integer value or a floating-point value. To distinguish between them, the programmer must write a fully qualified name, as shown in the two assignments at the end of the example.

Notice that n1 and n2 exist as structure declarations in their own right. The programmer can allocate and manipulate an n1 or an n2. In contrast, the definition of two creates and uses two anonymous structures that have meaning only in the context of two. To decrease the burden of writing these fully qualified names, it is tempting to move the responsibility for discriminating between variants into the type system. However, it is hard, in practice, to ensure that every reference to an element in a union resolves to a single type.

As an alternative, some systems have relied on run-time discrimination. Here, each variant in the union has a field that distinguishes it from all other variants. The compiler can emit code to check the value of that field—essentially a case statement based on the distinguishing field's value—and ensure that each object is handled correctly. The language may require that the programmer include this "tag" field and its values in the declaration; alternatively, the compiler could generate and insert the tags automatically. In such a system, the compiler has a strong motivation to perform type checking—removing the type-case code is a significant savings in run time and code space.

Of course, to the extent that the variants are identical, the language can allow less qualified uses of them. Many languages recognize this and treat variants with identical initial components in a special way. The program can refer to those initial components by qualifying them to a particular variant.

7.8 CONTROL-FLOW CONSTRUCTS

A basic block is just a maximal-length sequence of straight-line, unpredicated code. Any statement that does not affect control flow can appear inside a block. Any control-flow transfer ends the block, as does a labelled statement since it can be the target of a branch. As the compiler generates code, it can build up basic blocks by simply aggregating consecutive, unlabelled, non-control-flow operations. (We assume that a labelled statement is not labelled gratuitously—that is, every labelled statement is the target of some branch.) The representation of a basic block need not be complex. For example, if the compiler has an assembly-like representation held in a simple linear array, then a block can be described by a pair, $\langle first, last \rangle$, that holds the indexes of the instruction that begins the block and the instruction that ends the block. (If the block indexes are stored in ascending numerical order, an array of *firsts* will suffice.)

To tie a set of blocks together so that they form a procedure, the compiler must insert code that implements the control-flow operations of the source program. To capture the relationships among blocks, many compilers build a control-flow graph (CFG, see Sections 5.3.2 and 9.2.1) and use it for analysis, optimization, and code generation. In the CFG, nodes represent basic blocks and edges represent possible transfers of control between blocks. Typically, the CFG is a derivative representation that contains references to a more detailed representation of each block.

The code to implement control-flow constructs resides in the basic blocks—at or near the end of each block. (In ILOC, there is no fall-through case on a branch, so every block ends with a branch or a jump. If the IR models delay slots, then the control-flow operation may not be the last operation in the block.) While many different syntactic conventions have been used to express control flow, the number of underlying concepts is small. This section examines many of the control-flow constructs found in modern programming languages.

7.8.1 Conditional Execution

Most programming languages provide some version of the if-then-else construct. Given the source text

```
if expr
    then statement₁
    else statement₂
statement₃
```

the compiler must generate code that evaluates *expr* and branches to one of *statement*₁ or *statement*₂ based on the value of *expr*. The ILOC code that implements *statement*₁ and *statement*₂ must end with a jump to *statement*₃. As we saw in Section 7.4, the compiler has many options for implementing if-then-else constructs.

The discussion in Section 7.4 focused on evaluating the controlling expression. It showed how the underlying instruction set influenced the strategies for handling both the controlling expression and, in some cases, the controlled statements.

Programmers can place arbitrarily large code fragments inside the then and else parts. The size of these code fragments has an impact on the compiler's strategy for implementing the if-then-else construct. With trivial then and else parts, as shown in Figure 7.6, the primary consideration for the compiler is matching the expression evaluation to the underlying hardware. As the then and else parts grow, the importance of efficient execution inside the then and else parts begins to outweigh the cost of executing the controlling expression.

For example, on a machine that supports predicated execution, using predicates for large blocks in the then and else parts can waste execution cycles. Since the processor must issue each predicated instruction to one of its functional units, each operation with a false predicate has an opportunity cost—it ties up an issue slot. With large blocks of code under both the then and else parts, the cost of unexecuted instructions may outweigh the overhead of using a conditional branch.

Figure 7.10 illustrates this tradeoff. It assumes that both the then and else parts contain ten independent ILOC operations and that the target machine can issue two operations per cycle.

The left side shows code that might be generated using predication; it assumes that the value of the controlling expression is in r_1. The code issues two instructions per cycle. One of them executes in each cycle. All of the then part's operations are issued to Unit 1, while the else part's operations are issued

Using Predicates		Using Branches	
Unit 1	**Unit 2**	**Unit 1**	**Unit 2**
comparison $\Rightarrow r_1$		*compare & branch*	
(r_1) op$_1$	$(\neg r_1)$ op$_{11}$	L_1: op$_1$	op$_2$
(r_1) op$_2$	$(\neg r_1)$ op$_{12}$	op$_3$	op$_4$
(r_1) op$_3$	$(\neg r_1)$ op$_{13}$	op$_5$	op$_6$
(r_1) op$_4$	$(\neg r_1)$ op$_{14}$	op$_7$	op$_8$
(r_1) op$_5$	$(\neg r_1)$ op$_{15}$	op$_9$	op$_{10}$
(r_1) op$_6$	$(\neg r_1)$ op$_{16}$	jumpI $\rightarrow$ L$_3$	
(r_1) op$_7$	$(\neg r_1)$ op$_{17}$	L_2: op$_{11}$	op$_{12}$
(r_1) op$_8$	$(\neg r_1)$ op$_{18}$	op$_{13}$	op$_{14}$
(r_1) op$_9$	$(\neg r_1)$ op$_{19}$	op$_{15}$	op$_{16}$
(r_1) op$_{10}$	$(\neg r_1)$ op$_{20}$	op$_{17}$	op$_{18}$
		op$_{19}$	op$_{20}$
		jumpI $\rightarrow$ L$_3$	
		L_3: nop	

FIGURE 7.10   Predication versus Branching

BRANCH PREDICTION BY USERS

One urban compiler legend concerns branch prediction. FORTRAN has an arithmetic if statement that takes one of three branches, based on whether the controlling expression evaluates to a negative number, to zero, or to a positive number. One early compiler allowed the user to supply a weight for each label that reflected the relative probability of taking that branch. The compiler then used the weights to order the branches in a way that minimized total expected delay from branching.

After the compiler had been in the field for a year, the story goes, a maintainer discovered that the branch weights were being used in the reverse order—maximizing the expected delay. No one had complained. The story is usually told as a fable about the value of programmers' opinions about the behavior of code they have written. (Of course, no one reported the improvement, if any, from using the branch weights in the correct order.)

to Unit 2. The code avoids all branching. If each operation takes a single cycle, it takes ten cycles to execute the controlled statements, independent of which branch is taken.

The right side shows code that might be generated using branches; it assumes that control flows to L_1 for the then part or to L_2 for the else part. Because the instructions are independent, the code issues two instructions per cycle. Following the then path takes five cycles to execute the operations for the taken path, plus the cost of the terminal jump. The cost for the else part is identical.

The predicated version avoids the initial branch required in the unpredicated code (to either L_1 or L_2 in the figure), as well as the terminal jumps (to L_3). The branching version incurs the overhead of a branch and a jump, but may execute faster. Each path contains a conditional branch, five cycles of operations, and the terminal jump. (Some of the operations may be used to fill delay slots on the jumps.) The difference lies in the effective issue rate— the branching version issues roughly half the instructions of the predicated version. As the code fragments in the then and else parts grow larger, this difference becomes larger.

Choosing between branching and predication to implement an if-then-else requires some care. Several issues should be considered, as follows:

1. *Expected frequency of execution for each part*   If one side of the conditional is expected to execute significantly more often, techniques that

speed execution of that path may produce faster code. This bias may take the form of predicting a branch, of executing some instructions speculatively, or of reordering the logic.

2. *Uneven amounts of code* If one path through the construct contains many more instructions than the other, this may weigh against predication or for a combination of predication and branching.

3. *Control flow inside the construct* If either path through the construct contains nontrivial control flow, such as another if-then-else, a loop, a case statement, or a procedure call, predication may not be the most efficient choice. In particular, nested if constructs create more complex predicate expressions and lower the percentage of issued instructions that are actually executed.

To make the best decision, the compiler must consider all these factors, as well as the surrounding context. These factors may be difficult to assess early in compilation; for example, optimization may change them in significant ways.

7.8.2 Loops and Iteration

Most programming languages include loop constructs to perform iteration. The first FORTRAN compiler introduced the do loop to perform iteration. Today, loops are found in many forms. For the most part, they have a similar structure.

Consider the C for loop as an example. Figure 7.11 shows how the compiler might lay out the code. The for loop has three controlling expressions: e_1, which provides for initialization; e_2, which evaluates to a boolean and governs execution of the loop; and e_3, which executes at the end of each iteration and, potentially, updates the values used in e_2. We will use this figure as the basic schema to explain the implementation of several kinds of loops.

If the loop body consists of a single basic block—that is, it contains no other control flow—then the loop that results from this schema has an initial branch plus one branch per iteration. The compiler might hide the latency of this branch in one of two ways. If the architecture allows the compiler to predict whether or not the branch is taken, the compiler should predict the branch in step four as being taken (to start the next iteration). If the architecture allows the compiler to move instructions into the delay slot(s) of the branch, the compiler should attempt to fill the delay slot(s) with instruction(s) from the loop body.

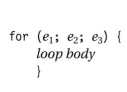

for $(e_1; e_2; e_3)$ {
    loop body
    }

Example for Loop

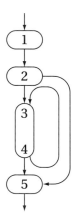

Step	Purpose
1	Evaluate e_1
2	Test $e_2 \Rightarrow r_i$ cbr $r_i \rightarrow 3,5$
3	*loop body*
4	Evaluate e_3 Test $e_2 \Rightarrow r_j$ cbr $r_j \rightarrow 3,5$
5	Code after loop

Loop Schema

FIGURE 7.11   Code Layout in a C for Loop

For Loops

To map a for loop into code, the compiler follows the schema in Figure 7.11. The following example makes the five steps concrete by showing the ILOC code that results from a specific loop. Steps 1 and 2 produce a single basic block, as shown in the following code:

for (i=1; i<=100; i++) {
    loop body
}
next statement

```
        loadI   1       ⇒ rᵢ    // Step 1
        loadI   100     ⇒ r₁    // Step 2
        cmp_GT  rᵢ,r₁   ⇒ r₂
        cbr     r₂       → L₂,L₁
L₁: loop body                   // Step 3
        addI    rᵢ,1    ⇒ rᵢ    // Step 4
        cmp_LE  rᵢ,r₁   ⇒ r₃
        cbr     r₃       → L₁,L₂
L₂: next statement              // Step 5
```

In this case, step 1 is preceded by a loadI to move the constant 1 into a register for use in step 4. If the loop body (step 3) either consists of a single basic block or it ends with a single basic block, then the update and test in step 4 can be optimized with that block. This may allow the compiler to improve the code—for example, it might use operations from the end of step 3 to fill delay slots in the branch from step 4.

The compiler can also shape the loop so that it has only one copy of the test—the one in step 2. In this form, step 4 evaluates e_3 and then jumps to step 2. This form of the loop is one operation smaller than the two-test form. (The cmp_GT disappears and the cbr becomes a jump.) However, it creates a two-block loop for even the simplest loops, and it lengthens the path through the loop by at least one operation. When code size is a serious consideration, then consistent use of this more compact loop form might be worthwhile. As long as the loop-ending jump is an immediate jump, the hardware can take steps to minimize any disruption that it might cause.

The canonical loop shape from Figure 7.11 also sets the stage for later optimization. For example, if e_1 and e_2 contain only known constants, as in the example, the compiler can fold the value from step 1 into the test in step 2 and either eliminate the compare and branch (if control enters the loop) or eliminate the loop body (if control never enters the loop). In the single-test loop, the compiler cannot do this. Instead, the compiler finds two paths leading to the test—one from step 1 and one from step 4. The value used in the test, r_i, has a varying value along the edge from step 4, so the test's outcome is not predictable.

FORTRAN's DO Loop

In FORTRAN, the iterative loop is a do loop. It resembles the C for loop, but has a more restricted form.

```
                                loadI   1        ⇒ rⱼ      // j ← 1

                                loadI   1        ⇒ rᵢ      // Step 1

                                loadI   100      ⇒ r₁      // Step 2

                                cmp_GT  rᵢ,r₁    ⇒ r₂

                                cbr     r₂       → L₂,L₁

    j = 1
    do 10 i = 1, 100       L₁: loop body                  // Step 3
        loop body
        j = j + 2              addI    rⱼ,2     ⇒ rⱼ      // j ← j + 2

10      continue               addI    rᵢ,1     ⇒ rᵢ      // Step 4

    next statement             cmp_LE  rᵢ,r₁    ⇒ r₃

                               cbr     r₃       → L₁,L₂

                          L₂: next statement              // Step 5
```

The comments map portions of the ILOC code back to the schema in Figure 7.11.

The definition of FORTRAN, like that of many languages, has some interesting quirks. One such peculiarity relates to do loops and their index variables. The number of iterations of a loop is fixed before execution enters the loop. If the program changes the index variable's value, that change does not affect the number of iterations that execute. For example, the following loop should execute 100 iterations, even though the loop increments i.

```
                                            loadI   1       ⇒ rᵢ     // Step 1
                                            loadI   1       ⇒ r₁     // Shadow

                                            loadI   100     ⇒ r₂     // Step 2
                                            cmp_GT  r₁,r₂   ⇒ r₃
        do 10 i = 1, 100                    cbr     r₃      → L₂,L₁
            loop body
            i = i + 2               L₁:  loop body              // Step 3
10          continue                        addI    rᵢ,2    ⇒ rᵢ    // i ← i + 2
        next statement
                                            addI    rᵢ,1    ⇒ rᵢ    // Step 4
                                            addI    r₁,1    ⇒ r₁    // Shadow
                                            cmp_LE  r₁,r₂   ⇒ r₄
                                            cbr     r₄      → L₁,L₂

                                   L₂:  next statement           // Step 5
```

To ensure the correct behavior, the compiler may need to generate a hidden induction variable, called a *shadow index variable*, to control the iteration. In this example, the shadow index variable is r_2.

Unless the compiler can determine that the loop body does not modify the induction variable, the compiler must generate a shadow variable. If the loop contains a call to another procedure and passes the induction variable as a call-by-reference parameter, the compiler must assume that the called procedure modifies the induction variable, unless the compiler can prove otherwise.

Interprocedural analysis—that is, analyzing the whole program—routinely pays off in this situation. Programmers pass loop index variables like i as a parameter so that the program can include the index's value in output that it generates. Interprocedural analysis can easily recognize when passing a loop index variable does not change its value. This lets the compiler eliminate the shadow variable.

While Loops

A while loop can also be implemented with the loop schema in Figure 7.11. Unlike the C for loop or the FORTRAN do loop, a while loop has no initialization. Thus, the code is even more compact.

```
                                cmp_LT  rx,ry  ⇒ r1    // Step 2
                                cbr     r1     → L1,L2
while (x < y) {
    loop body               L1: loop body             // Step 3
}
                                cmp_LT  rx,ry  ⇒ r2    // Step 4
next statement
                                cbr     r2     → L1,L2

                            L2: next statement         // Step 5
```

Replicating the test in step 4 creates the possibility of a loop with a single basic block. The same benefits that accrue to a for loop from this structure also occur for a while loop.

Until Loops

An until loop iterates as long as the controlling expression is false. It checks the controlling expression after each iteration. Thus, it always enters the loop and performs at least one iteration. This produces a particularly simple loop structure, since it avoids steps 1 and 2 in the schema.

```
                            L1: loop body             // Step 3
{
    loop body                   cmp_LT  rx,ry  ⇒ r2    // Step 4
} until (x < y)
                                cbr     r2     → L2,L1
next statement
                            L2: next statement         // Step 5
```

C does not have an until loop. Its do construct is similar to an until loop, except that the sense of the condition is reversed. It iterates as long as the condition evaluates to true, where the until iterates as long as the condition is false.

Expressing Iteration as Tail Recursion

In Lisp-like languages, iteration is often implemented (by programmers) using a stylized form of recursion. If the last action executed by a function is a call, that call is known as a *tail call*. If the tail call is a self-recursion, the call is known as a *tail recursion*. For example, to find the last element of a list in Scheme, the programmer might write the following simple function:

```
(define (last alon)
  (cond
    ((empty? alon) empty)
    ((empty? (cdr alon)) (car alon))
    (else (last (cdr alon)))))
```

The tail-recursive call can be optimized into a jump back to the top of the procedure plus some assignments to create the effects of parameter binding. Thus, the code can avoid most of the overhead entailed in a procedure call. It need not create a new AR, evaluate arguments, save and restore registers, or adjust a display or access link. Most of the precall sequence disappears; all of the postreturn sequence disappears. Additionally, it avoids executing all the returns (and epilogue sequences) that would have executed in a standard implementation for the call. The resulting code can rival a for loop in efficiency.

7.8.3 Case Statements

Many programming languages include some variant of a *case* statement. FORTRAN had its computed goto. Algol-W introduced the *case* statement in its modern form. BCPL and C have a switch construct. PL/I has a generalized construct that maps well onto a nested set of if-then-else statements. As the introduction to this chapter hinted, implementing a *case* statement efficiently is complex.

Consider C's switch statement. The implementation strategy should be to (1) evaluate the controlling expression; (2) branch to the selected case; and (3) execute the code for that case. Steps 1 and 3 are well understood; they follow from discussions elsewhere in this chapter. The cases often end with a break statement that transfers control to the statement following the switch statement.

The complicated part of implementing a *case* statement is emitting efficient code to locate the designated case.

Linear Search

The simplest way to locate the appropriate case is to treat the *case* statement as the specification for a nested set of if-then-else statements. For example, the switch statement on the left could be translated into the nest of if statements on the right.

```
switch (b×c+d)              t₁ ← b×c+d
{                           if (t₁ = 0)
  case 0:  block₀;             then block₀
           break;          else if (t₁ = 1)
  case 1:  block₁;             then block₁
           break;          else if (t₁ = 2)
  ...                          then block₂
  case 9:  block₉;          ...
           break;          else if (t₁ = 9)
  default: block₁₀;            then block₉
           break;             else block₁₀
}
```

This translation preserves the meaning of the switch statement, but makes the cost of reaching individual cases dependent on the order in which they are written. In essence, this code uses linear search to discover the desired case. Still, when the number of cases is small, this strategy can be efficient.

Binary Search

As the number of cases rises, the efficiency of linear search becomes a problem. The classic answers to efficient search apply in this situation. If the compiler can impose an order on the case labels, it can use binary search to obtain a logarithmic search rather than a linear one.

The idea is simple. The compiler builds a compact ordered table of case labels, along with their corresponding branch labels. It uses binary search to discover a matching case label, or the absence of a match. Finally, it either branches to the corresponding label or to the default case.

For the preceding switch statement, the following jump table and search routine might be used:

Value Label

Value	Label
0	LB_0
1	LB_1
2	LB_2
3	LB_3
4	LB_4
5	LB_5
6	LB_6
7	LB_7
8	LB_8
9	LB_9

```
t₁ ← b × c + d
down ← 0
up ← 10
while (down + 1 < up)
{
   middle ← (up + down + 1) ÷ 2
   if (Value[middle]    t₁)
      then down ← middle
      else up ← middle
}
if (Value[down]= t₁)
   then jump to Label[down]
   else jump to LB_default
```

In this scheme, the code fragments for each block are independent. Block *i* begins with a label, LB_i, and ends with a jump to the statement following the case statement. The default case is in block $LB_{default}$.

The binary search discovers the appropriate case label, if it exists, in $\log_2(n)$ iterations, where *n* is the number of cases. If the label does not exist, it discovers that fact and jumps to the block for the default case.

Since the compiler inserts the search code, it should choose the operations carefully. The computation of middle requires two adds and a shift. The if-then-else will take more time. The address computation on the load is simple—a shift and an address + offset load. With either conditional move or predicated execution (Section 7.4.2), the compiler can update up and down in two operations. Without them, the update takes a branch, a copy, and a jump.

Directly Computing the Address

If the case labels form a compact set, the compiler can do better than binary search. In the example, the switch statement has labels for every integer from zero to nine. In this situation, the compiler can build a vector that contains the block labels, LB_i, and find the appropriate label by performing a simple address calculation.

For the example, the label can be found by computing t_1 as before, and using t_1 as an index into the table. In this scenario, the code to implement the case statement might be

```
t₁ ← b × c + d
if (0 > t₁ or t₁ > 9)
    then jump to LB_default
    else
        t₂ ← memory(@Table + t₁ × 4)
        jump to t₂
```

assuming that the representation of a label is 4 bytes long.

For a dense set of labels, this scheme generates efficient code. The cost is both small and constant. If a few holes exist in the label set, the compiler can fill those slots with the label for the default case. If no default case exists, the appropriate action depends on the language. In C, for example, the code should branch to the first statement after the switch, so the compiler can place that label in each hole in the table.

Choosing among the Approaches

The compiler must select an appropriate implementation scheme for each case statement. The decision depends on the number of cases and the properties of the set of case labels. For a handful of cases, the nested if-then-else scheme may work well. For a larger set of cases whose values do not form a compact set, binary search is a reasonable alternative. (However, a programmer who steps through the assembly code in a debugger might be surprised to find a while loop embedded in the case statement!) When the set is compact, a direct computation using a jump table is probably the best alternative.

For a sufficiently large set of cases, the compiler might adopt a hybrid strategy, combining two or more schemes. The pseudo-code for addressing the preceding jump table actually implements a hybrid scheme. It checks for a value outside the range 0 to 9 using a simple conditional and either jumps to $LB_{default}$ or uses the table to jump to the appropriate label. This makes

LB$_{default}$ the case for any value outside the range—a potentially huge set—and uses the jump table for the dense set of cases in the range.

If the compiler writer includes a jump-table implementation, it should make the set of potential targets of the jump visible in the IR form of the program, if possible. In ILOC, the compiler could generate the appropriate set of tbl pseudo-operations. The absence of such hints will force later analysis passes to add spurious edges to the control-flow graphs that they build. These inaccuracies in the CFG can lead to a loss of precision in the information that the analysis produces.

7.8.4 Break Statements

Several languages implement variations on a break or exit statement. The break statement is a structured way to exit a control-flow construct. In a loop, break transfers control to the first statement following the loop. For nested loops, a break typically exits the innermost loop. Some languages, such as Ada and Java, allow an optional label on a break statement. This causes the break statement to exit from the enclosing construct specified by that label. In a nested loop, a labelled break allows the program to exit several loops at once. C also uses break in its switch statement, to transfer control to the statement that follows the switch statement.

These actions have simple implementations. Each loop and case statement should end with a label for the statement that follows the loop. A break would be implemented as an immediate jump to that label. Some languages include a skip or continue statement that jumps to the next iteration of a loop. It can be implemented as an immediate jump to the code that reevaluates the controlling expression and tests its value. Alternatively, the compiler can simply insert a copy of the evaluation, test, and branch at the point where the skip occurs.

7.9 PROCEDURE CALLS

Implementing procedure calls is, for the most part, straightforward. As shown in Figure 7.12, a procedure call consists of precall and postreturn sequences in the caller, and a prologue and an epilogue in the callee. A single procedure can contain multiple call sites, each with its own precall and postreturn sequences. Under most circumstances, it will contain one prologue sequence

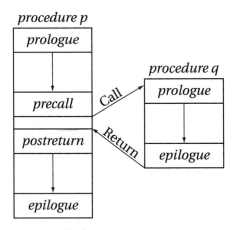

FIGURE 7.12   A Standard Procedure Linkage

and one epilogue sequence.[2] Many of the details involved in these sequences are described in Section 6.6. This section focuses on issues that affect the compiler's ability to generate efficient, compact, and consistent code for procedure calls.

As a general rule, moving operations from the precall and postreturn sequences into the prologue and epilogue sequences should reduce the overall size of the final code. If the call from p to q shown in Figure 7.12 is the only call to q in the entire program, then moving an operation from the precall sequence in p to the prologue in q (or from the postreturn sequence in p to the epilogue in q) has no impact on code size. If, however, other calls to q exist and the compiler moves an operation from the caller to the callee (at all the call sites), it should reduce the overall code size by replacing multiple copies of an operation with a single one. As the number of calls to a single procedure rises, the savings grow. We assume that most procedures are called from several locations; if not, both the programmer and the compiler should consider including the procedure inline at the point of its only invocation.

7.9.1   Evaluating Actual Parameters

In building the precall sequence, the compiler must emit code to evaluate the actual parameters, or arguments to the call. It treats parameters as expressions.

---

2. If the language allows multiple entry points to a procedure, as do FORTRAN and PL/I, then the procedure may contain multiple prologue sequences.

For call-by-value parameters, the precall sequence evaluates the actual parameter and stores the resulting value in a location designated for that parameter—either in a register or in the callee's AR. For call-by-reference parameters, the precall sequence computes an address for each actual parameter and stores it in a location designated for that parameter. If the parameter resides in a register in the caller, or if it is an expression, the compiler may need to create a location for the parameter's value so that it has an address to pass to the callee.

If the source language specifies an order of evaluation for the actual parameters, the compiler must, of course, follow that order. Otherwise, it should use a consistent order—either left to right or right to left. The evaluation order matters for parameters that might have side effects. For example, a program that used two routines push and pop to manipulate a stack would produce different results for the sequence push(pop() − pop()) under left-to-right and right-to-left evaluation.

Procedures may have several implicit arguments. These include the procedure's ARP, the caller's ARP, the return address, and any information needed to establish addressability. In object-oriented languages, the receiver's address is an implicit parameter. Some of these arguments are passed in registers; typically, the ARP and return address reside in registers. Many architectures have an operation like jsr $label_1 \Rightarrow r_i$ that transfers control to $label_1$ and places the address of the next operation (following the jsr) in r_i. Other implicit arguments, such as the caller's ARP, typically reside in memory.

7.9.2 Procedure-Valued Parameters

When a call site passes a procedure as a parameter, that value requires special treatment. If p calls q, passing procedure r as an argument, it must pass to q more information than r's starting address. In particular, if the compiled code uses access links to find nonlocal variables, the callee needs r's lexical level so that a subsequent call to r can find the correct access link for r's level. The compiler can construct an ⟨*address,level*⟩ pair and pass it (or its address) in place of the procedure-valued parameter. When the compiler constructs the precall sequence for a procedure-valued parameter, it must insert the extra code to fetch the lexical level and adjust the access link accordingly.

7.9.3 Saving and Restoring Registers

Under any calling convention, one or both of the procedures involved in a procedure call must preserve register values. Often, linkage conventions use a combination of caller-saves and callee-saves registers. As both the cost of memory operations and the number of registers have risen, the cost of saving and restoring registers at call sites has increased, to the point where it merits careful attention.

In choosing a strategy to save and restore registers, the compiler writer must consider both efficiency and code size. Some features of the target machine impact this choice. Features that spill a portion of the register set can reduce code size. Examples include register windows on the SPARC machines, the multiregister load and store operations on the PowerPC processors, and the high-level call operation on the VAX. Each offers the compiler a compact way to save and restore some portion of the register set. In using these features, however, the compiler writer must take speed into account as well. For example, on some PowerPC models, a sequence of store operations runs faster than the equivalent store-multiple operation.

While larger register sets can increase the number of registers that the code saves and restores, in general, using these additional registers improves the speed of the resulting code. With fewer registers, the compiler would be forced to generate loads and stores throughout the code; with more registers, many of these spills occur only at a call site. (The larger register set should reduce the total number of spills in the code.) The concentration of saves and restores at call sites presents the compiler with opportunities to handle them in better ways than it might if they were spread across an entire procedure.

> *Using multiregister memory operations*　When saving and restoring adjacent registers, the compiler can often use a multiregister memory operation. Many architectures support doubleword and quadword load and store operations. This can reduce code size; it may also improve execution speed. Generalized load multiple and store multiple operations can have the same effects.

> *Using a library routine*　As the number of register save and restore operations rises, the size of the precall and postreturn sequences becomes an issue. The compiler writer can replace the sequence of individual memory operations with a call to a compiler-supplied save or restore routine. Done across all calls, this can produce a significant savings in code size. Since the save and restore routines are known only to the compiler, it can use a minimal call sequence to keep the run-time cost low.

> The save and restore routines can take an argument that specifies which registers must be preserved. It may be worthwhile to generate optimized versions for common cases, such as preserving all the caller-saves or callee-saves registers.

Combining responsibilities   To further reduce overhead, the compiler might combine the work for caller-saves and callee-saves registers. In this scheme, the caller passes a value to the callee that specifies which registers it must save. The callee adds the registers it must save to the value and calls the appropriate compiler-provided save routine.[3] The epilogue passes the same value to the restore routine so that it can restore the needed registers. This approach limits the overhead to one call to save registers and one to restore them. It separates responsibility (caller saves versus callee saves) from the cost to call the routine.

The compiler writer must pay close attention to the code-size and run-time speed implications of the various options. The code should use the fastest operations for saves and restores. This requires a close look at the costs of single-register and multiregister operations on the target architecture. Using library routines to perform saves and restores can save space; careful implementation of those library routines may mitigate the added cost of invoking them.

7.9.4 Optimizations for Leaf Procedures

The compiler can easily recognize leaf routines by the fact that they call no other procedure. The prologue and epilogue sequences for leaf procedures can be tailored to eliminate operations whose sole purpose is to set up for subsequent calls. Examples include storing the return address and updating a display; both of these are unnecessary in a leaf procedure. (If the register holding the return address or an access link is needed, the register allocator will spill it.)

The compiler might also be able to simplify the register-save behavior. In particular, for a small leaf procedure that needs relatively few registers, the compiler can target those values to caller-saves registers and avoid saving its callee-saves registers. With the previously suggested library save and restore approach, further optimization is possible; the leaf procedure can modify the caller's specification for caller-saves registers if it knows that their values will pass through the leaf procedure unmodified. In this scheme, the leaf procedure explicitly saves the registers that it needs. This may reduce the total number of saves and restores performed at the call—a routine that needed just four registers might save them explicitly with inline code and avoid calling the

---

3. In this scheme, the natural place to store all the saved registers is in the callee's AR. The save and restore routines can use the callee's AR to access the register-save area.

save and restore routines altogether. (This scheme might completely avoid the saves and restores specified by the caller.)

7.10 IMPLEMENTING OBJECT-ORIENTED LANGUAGES

As we saw in Chapter 6, the major difference between an object-oriented language and an Algol-like language lies in the mechanisms for mapping names to run-time objects. The major hurdle in implementing an object-oriented language is linking together the run-time structures that the program traverses to find methods, data members, and other objects.

Consider the problem from the perspective of generating code for an individual method. Since the method can access any member of any object that becomes its receiver, the compiler must establish an offset for each member that applies uniformly to every receiver—to every object that can find the current method. The compiler constructs these offsets as it processes the declarations for a class—objects themselves contain no code. The following subsections explore some of the alternatives.

7.10.1 Single Class, No Inheritance

The simplest case arises when the class structure is known at compile time and involves no inheritance. Assume that we have a class giant with methods fee, fie, foe, and fum, and data members x and y, which are both numbers. To simplify programming with giants, the class maintains a class variable, n, that records the number of giants already created. To allow for object creation, every class implements the method new, which is located at offset zero in its method table. The compiler must lay out object records for each instance of class giant, along with an object record for the class giant (an instance of class class).

The object record for an instance of giant is just a vector of length three. The first slot in the vector holds its class pointer, which has the address of the concrete representation of the class giant. The next two slots hold the data members, x and y. Each object of class giant has a similar object record, created by giant's method new.

The class record for giant itself must contain space for all its class variables, just n in this case, and for all its methods. Conceptually, the class record contains two members: a table of the entry-point addresses for all the methods, and a slot for n. Since the method table is referred to only by address, it can actually be allocated inline as part of the class record. If the compiler always puts the method table at a fixed offset in the class record, the code can find it easily and inexpensively—for example, with a loadAO using the class pointer and the appropriate offset. For giant then, the compiler might assign the following offsets in the record table:

	new	fee	fie	foe	fum	n
offset	0	4	8	12	16	20

After the code has created two instances of giant, called fred and joe, the run-time structures associated with giant should look like this:

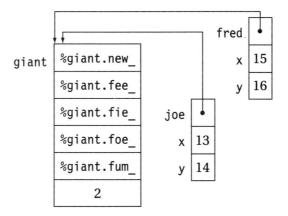

The method table in giant's class record consists of pointers to the code for each method. Rather than depict this explicitly in the diagram, we have shown a mangled form of each method's name. Compilers often compute such assembly-level labels from procedure names by adding characters that the programmer cannot use in the source language. The diagram uses fully qualified names, to which it adds a percent sign (%) as a prefix and an underscore (_) as a suffix. This creates an easily computed, consistent label.

The values of data members are stored at the appropriate offsets. To distinguish them, we have set joe.x to 13, joe.y to 14, fred.x to 15, and fred.y to 16. Since two instances of giant exist, giant.n contains the value 2. If the program includes code to initialize data members, the compiler must include that code in the method for new.

To clarify matters, consider the code that the compiler generates for giant's new method. It must allocate space for a new object record, initialize each data member to an appropriate value, increment giant.n and return a pointer to the newly created object record. Since new is a full-fledged procedure, it also needs to implement the linkage convention; it may need to preserve some register values, to create an activation record, and to restore the environment before it returns. (If new is simple enough, it may be able to keep all of its state in registers reserved for linkage.) The compiler labels the entry point to new with its mangled label, %giant.new_. In any method, the compiler adds the receiver's designated name as an implicit first parameter, assumed to be this unless another name is explicitly specified.

When the compiler sees a construct involving a giant, the code that it generates is similar to the code that would be used in an Algol-like language. For example, a statement such as jane ← giant.new that instantiates a giant would use a name-mangled label to obtain the address of giant's class record and generate a procedure call to the address stored at that address.[4]

Similarly, an expression that invoked joe's method for fum would generate a call to %giant.fum_ with joe as its receiver. In any context where joe.fum can legally appear, joe must map to a known location—one whose address can be computed. That location either begins joe's object record or contains a pointer to joe's object record. (The difference must be clear from the type information in the calling context.) The compiler generates code to load the address at offset zero in joe's object record; this points to the start of the class record for giant. It generates code to load the word at offset 16 in the class record, where it finds the address of %giant.fum_. Finally, it generates a procedure call to that address, passing joe's address implicitly to the parameter this. Other parameters are handled using the standard techniques for the procedure linkage.

To create other classes, the compiler follows the same steps. It assigns offsets in the object record for an instance and in the class record. It compiles the methods using those offsets and indirect references through the appropriate object records. It uses name mangling to create a distinct label for each procedure and for the class record. It uses static initialization with the appropriate labels to fill in the method table.

7.10.2 Single Inheritance

Inheritance complicates the implementation of an object-oriented language in several ways. The class record for each class needs a couple of extra members. The mechanism for finding and invoking a method must locate methods accessible because of inheritance. Finally, for those methods to work, the

---

4. If the compiler cannot statically allocate giant's class record, it may need one more layer of indirection. The compiler can create a static global variable for giant and have the code that creates giant's class record store the appropriate address into that global location.

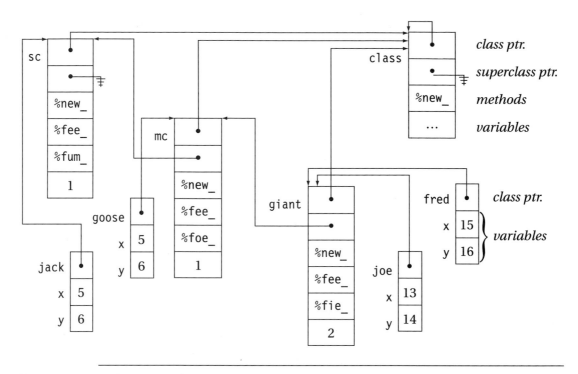

FIGURE 7.13   Implementing Inheritance

object record for each instance must include all of the instance variables speci-fied by each of the superclasses. The extra members in class and object records are trivial to add; the extra methods require more work.

With inheritance, the programmer might implement class giant in a differ-ent way. Figure 7.13 shows one such implementation. Because of inheritance, the object records for a class now have a class pointer; it is the first member of the class's object record. The second member of any class's object record is its superclass pointer. The superclass pointer reveals that giant is a subclass of mc, which is a subclass of sc. Examining the diagram shows that every class implements new. All the classes except class implement fee. Giant inherits foe from mc and fum from sc.

If the class structure is fixed and known, the compiler can simplify the implementation of method dispatch by including a complete method table in each class. In this scheme, any method can be invoked using the receiver's class pointer and the offset for the method in the class's method table. This avoids extra indirections through the inheritance hierarchy. If the class structure can change at run time, the compiler might still arrange to use complete method tables. To achieve this, it must provide a mechanism for building the method tables at run time. This mechanism is used at the start of execution to build the initial tables. It is reinvoked when the class structure changes (for example, when the class loader brings in new classes in Java). To make this more efficient, the compiler writer should avoid recalculating method tables in portions of the class hierarchy that have not changed.

If the compiler cannot arrange to use complete method tables, then the code may need to perform a lookup through the class hierarchy as part of every method dispatch. For example, if the language allows creation of a new class at run time, then dynamic dispatch may be needed. In this case, the compiler must implement method lookup by searching the method tables for each class, in ancestral order. This may drastically increase the cost of each invocation.

To perform dynamic method lookup, the compiler must map each method name to a search key. This mapping can be simple—using the method name or a hash index for the method name as the key. It can be complex—the compiler might assign each distinct method name an integer from some compact set using a link-time mechanism. In either case, the compiler must generate tables that can be searched at run time to find the method instance implemented by the most recent ancestor of the receiver's class.

To improve method lookup in this environment, the run-time system can implement a method cache—a software analog of the hardware data caches found on many modern processors. The method cache has a small number of entries, say 1,000. A cache entry consists of a key, a class, and a method pointer. The key is a pair that contains a class and a method search key. A method lookup first checks the cache for an entry with the method's search key and the receiver's class. If the entry exists, the lookup returns the cached method pointer. If the entry does not exist, the lookup performs the full-fledged search, starting with the receiver's class and working up the superclass chain, until it finds the method search key. At this point, it creates a new cache entry for the result of the current search and returns the method pointer.

Of course, creating a new entry may force the eviction of some other cache entry. Standard cache replacement policies, such as least-recently used or round robin, can be used to select the entry for replacement. Larger caches retain more information but require more memory and may take longer to search. At any operation that changes the class structure, the method cache can be cleared to prevent lookup from finding an incorrect result.

Laying Out Object Records

The implementation of inheritance affects the way that the compiler must lay out object records. For inheritance to work, an object must work correctly as the receiver for a method defined in its own class or any superclass. This dictates the order in which its data members occur. If `fred` is the receiver for a method of class `mc`, the method can know only about the instance variables that `fred` inherits from `mc` and `mc`'s ancestors. For those inherited methods to work, however, those instance variables must have the same offsets in an instance of `giant` that they have in an instance of `mc`. Otherwise, the method from `mc` will reference the wrong values when invoked with `fred` or `joe` as its receiver.

This suggests, in general, that the various members be laid out in inheritance order. The first instance variables found in the object record of an object `jim` of class `giant` are from the definition of `sc`, followed by those from `mc`, followed by those from `giant`. This leads to the following layout:

class pointer	sc data members	mc data members	giant data members

Now, an instance variable has the same offset in every class where it exists up its superclass chain.[5]

This same notion also carries through to the layout of method tables. In a system that uses a complete method table in each class, having a consistent mapping from method names to offsets up the hierarchy chain is critical. A method present in any class, such as `new`, always has the same offset. The simple way to ensure this is to follow the same discipline for method-table offsets as previously described for data members. Methods defined in the current class are at the end of the method table, preceded by methods from the immediate superclass, and so on up the inheritance chain. However, when a class declares a new implementation for a method defined by one of its superclasses, the method pointer for that implementation must be stored at the same offset as the previous implementation of that method.

Multiple Inheritance

To provide programmers with more flexibility in sharing both methods and data, some object-oriented languages allow a class to inherit directly from multiple superclasses. These languages usually relax the requirement for inclusion found in single inheritance hierarchies—a class may inherit some, but not all, methods from a superclass. This requires a linguistic mechanism for specifying precisely which members are inherited from each superclass.

---

5. One corollary of this observation, not reflected in the diagrams, is that the object record for each class must include any instance variables specified in the declaration of class `class`.

Multiple inheritance further complicates the problem of laying out object records. If class c inherits from a and b, but a and b are unrelated in the inheritance hierarchy, then the compiler must devise a single object record that operates correctly with the methods from both classes. This requires additional support to adjust the environment in a way that allows a single method implementation to work for instances of class b and instances of class c.

Assume that class c implements fee, inherits fie from a, and inherits foe and fum from b. The object layout for single inheritance will work for two of the three classes—for example, a and c.

class pointer	a data members	b data members	c data members

Our layout rule puts one superclass first, a in this case, and the actual class last, c in this case. When a method from a is invoked with this object record, it finds all of a's instance variables at their expected offsets. Since the method was compiled with the class definition for a, rather than b or c, it cannot access any of the instance variables that exist because of inheritance from b or directly from the definition of class c. Thus, the method will function correctly.

Similarly, when a method compiled as part of c is invoked with this object record as its receiver, it will find all of the instance variables in their expected positions. Since c's specification includes the specification of its inheritance, the compiler knows where every instance variable resides in the object record.

The problem arises with an invocation of one of b's methods. The instance variables in the object record because of inheritance from b are in the wrong place; they are offset from the start of the object record by the cumulative length of a's instance variables. To compensate for this, and to let a method compiled with b function correctly, the compiler must insert code to adjust the receiver pointer so that it points into the middle of the object record—to the appropriate point relative to b's instance variables.

To adjust the offset, the compiler has two choices. It can record the constant adjustment in the object record and use a linkage convention that always adds an offset to the receiver pointer this. This adds a load and an addition to each call—a small penalty. Alternatively, it can create a so-called *trampoline function* for each method from class b—a function that increments this by the required amount and then invokes the actual method from b. On return, it decrements the receiver pointer, if needed (that is, if the receiver is passed by reference). This adds a procedure call to the chain—a larger penalty than the load and addition. The class record for c using trampoline functions is shown in Figure 7.14.

Two facts make trampoline functions worth considering. First, they incur a penalty only on calls to methods inherited from b. Calls involving

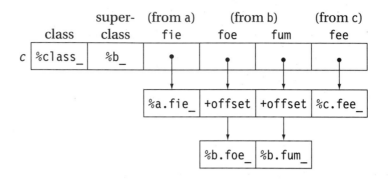

FIGURE 7.14   Multiple Inheritance with Trampoline Functions

methods from *a* and from *c* incur no penalty. Second, the trampoline function may optimize better than the load-and-add strategy. Optimization for object-oriented languages usually includes a significant amount of inline substitution. Since the trampoline function is class-specific, the offset can appear as a literal constant. This eliminates the memory reference; with inline substitution, the overhead reduces to a load immediate and an addition, which occur only for calls to *b*. Taken over all the invocations of methods visible in *c*, the trampoline function may produce faster code.

As a final adjustment, the compiler may also need to insert a duplicate copy of the class pointer. This way, a method compiled with *b* finds the class pointer immediately in front of its *b* instance variables. This class pointer should point to *c*, so that any method in *b* that is hidden by a definition in *c* resolves to the right method pointer.

Handling Casts

Because the compiler must place both code and data members at their designated offsets, this transformation creates object records for a class that intersperse methods and instance variables. This poses no problem for correctness, as the compiler knows the correct offsets for each reference. If *c* inherits from *b*, which inherits from *a*, the object record for class *c* looks like:

class pointer	superclass pointer	*a* methods	*a* data	*b* methods	*b* data	*c* methods	*c* data

where the methods for a class are immediately followed by the class variables for that class.

7.11 SUMMARY AND PERSPECTIVE

One of the more subtle tasks that confronts the compiler writer is selecting a pattern of target-machine operations to implement each source-language construct. Multiple implementation strategies are possible for almost any source-language statement. The specific choices made at compiler-design time have a strong impact on the code that the compiler generates.

In a compiler that is not intended for production use—a debugging compiler or a student compiler—the compiler writer might select easy to implement translations for each strategy that produce simple, compact code. In an optimizing compiler, the compiler writer should focus on translations that expose as much information as possible to the later phases of the compiler—low-level optimization, instruction scheduling, and register allocation. These two different perspectives lead to different shapes for loops, to different disciplines for naming temporary variables, and, possibly, to different evaluation orders for expressions.

The classic example of this distinction might be the case statement. In a debugging compiler, the implementation as a cascaded series of if-then-else constructs is fine. In an optimizing compiler, the inefficiency of myriad tests and branches makes a more complex implementation scheme worthwhile. The effort to improve the case statement must be made when the IR is originally generated; few, if any, optimizers will convert a cascaded series of conditionals into a binary search or a direct jump table.

CHAPTER NOTES

The material contained in this chapter falls, roughly, into two categories: generating code for expressions and handling control-flow constructs. Expression evaluation is well explored in the literature. Discussions of how to handle control flow are rarer; much of the material on control flow in this chapter derives from folklore, experience, and careful reading of the output of compilers.

Floyd presented the first multipass algorithm for generating code from expression trees [143]. He points out that both redundancy elimination and algebraic reassociation have the potential to improve the results of his algorithm. Sethi and Ullman [301] proposed a two-pass algorithm that is optimal for a simple machine model; Proebsting and Fischer extended this work to account for small memory latencies [278]. Aho and Johnson [5] introduced dynamic programming to find least-cost implementations.

The predominance of array calculations in scientific programs led to work on array-addressing expressions and to optimizations (like strength reduction, Section 10.3.3) that improve them. The computations described in Section 7.5.3 follow Scarborough and Kolsky [297].

Harrison used string manipulation as a motivating example for the pervasive use of inline substitution and specialization [174]. The example mentioned at the end of Section 7.6.4 comes from that paper.

Mueller and Whalley describe the impact of different loop shapes on performance [263]. Bernstein provides a detailed discussion of the options that arise in generating code for *case* statements [38]. Calling conventions are best described in processor-specific and operating-system-specific manuals.

CHAPTER 8

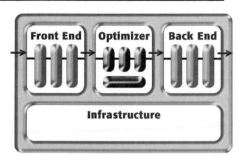

Introduction to Code Optimization

8.1 INTRODUCTION

The goal of the compiler's middle section, or optimizer, is to transform the IR program created by the front end into an IR program that computes the same results in a better way. Here, "better" can take on many meanings. It usually implies faster code, but it might imply more compact code. The programmer might want the optimizer to produce code that consumes less power when it runs or costs less to run under some model for resource accounting. All of these goals fall into the realm of optimization.

Opportunities for optimization arise from many sources. To make this discussion concrete, consider the inefficiencies that can arise in implementing source-language abstractions. Because the front end translates source code into IR without performing extensive analysis of the surrounding context, if any, it will typically generate IR that handles the most general case of a construct. The optimizer can determine some of the context by performing additional analysis; unfortunately, some context cannot be known at compile time.

Consider what happens when the compiler must generate code for an array reference, such as A[i,j]. Without specific knowledge about A, i, and j and the surrounding context, the compiler must generate the full expression for addressing a two-dimensional array. As we saw in Chapter 7, this computation would be

$$address\text{(A)}$$
$$+ (i - low_1\text{(A)}) \times (high_2\text{(A)} - low_2\text{(A)} + 1) \times size$$
$$+ (j - low_2\text{(A)}) \times size$$

where *address* is the run-time address of the first element of the array, low_i(A) and $high_i$(A) are the lower and upper bounds, respectively, of A's i^{th} dimension, and *size* is the size of an element of A. This computation is expensive. The compiler's ability to improve this code depends directly on its analysis of the code and the surrounding context.

If A is declared locally, with known bounds and a known type, then, as discussed in Section 7.5, the compiler can usually perform large parts of this address computation at compile time and simply use the result at run time. For example, the term

$$(high_2\text{(A)} - low_2\text{(A)} + 1) \times size$$

can be computed at compile time and treated as a constant at run time (using a loadI, for example). Other parts of the computation can be improved, as well (see Section 7.5).

If the compiler can recognize that the reference A[i,j] occurs inside a loop nest where i and j change in an orderly well-understood way, it may replace some of the integer multiplications in the computation with additions—a transformation called *operator strength reduction*. Strength reduction replaces the sequence $i \cdot k, (i+1) \cdot k, (i+2) \cdot k, \ldots$, with a sequence i'_0, i'_1, i'_2, where $i'_0 = i \cdot k$, and $i'_m = i'_{m-1} + k$, for $m > 0$. When the program executes, it performs more additions and fewer multiplications. If multiplication costs more than addition, the new sequence is an improvement.

Sometimes, the compiler cannot discover facts that would allow it to improve the code. If the value of j is read from an external source, such as a file or the keyboard, then the compiler cannot improve the code that computes the address of A[i,j]. In such circumstances, the compiler must generate code that will handle any legal case. It might also generate code that detects illegal cases, such as $j > high_2$(A).

This simple example demonstrates both one motivation for optimization and the basic operation of a code optimizer.

The goal of code optimization is to discover, at compile time, information about the run-time behavior of the program and to use that information to improve the code generated by the compiler.

Improvement can take many forms. The previous examples all focused on the most common goal of optimization: speeding up the execution of the compiled code. For some applications, however, the size of the compiled code is important. Examples include code that will be committed to read-only memory, where size is an economic constraint, or code that will be transmitted over a limited-bandwidth communications channel before it executes, where size has a direct impact on time to completion. Optimization, for these applications, should produce code that occupies less space. In some situations, the user wants to optimize for other criteria, such as register use, memory use, power consumption, or response to real-time events.

Historically, optimizing compilers have focused primarily on the run-time speed of the compiled code. Most of our discussion of optimization will deal with speed. This emphasis on speed often comes at the expense of space—larger code size from replicated operations. This is a classic tradeoff in algorithm design—time versus space. Because of the rising importance of code space and data space in embedded and interactive computing, we will focus some of the discussion on techniques that either reduce the space requirements of the program or, at least, do not increase them significantly.

Optimization is a large and detailed subject. This chapter, and the two that follow, provide a brief introduction to the subject. This chapter lays the groundwork. Other books explore it in greater depth and detail [262, 260, 19]. The next section examines a routine from LINPACK, a well-known library that provides efficient implementations of many algorithms in numerical linear algebra. It uses that routine to explore some of the concepts needed for an in-depth study of the problems and techniques of code improvement. The remainder of the chapter takes a classic problem in code optimization, finding and eliminating redundant expressions, and uses it to illustrate both the opportunities and the challenges of optimization.

The following two chapters delve more deeply into the problems of analysis and transformation of programs. Chapter 9 presents an overview of static analysis. It describes some of the analysis problems that an optimizing compiler must solve and presents practical techniques that have been used to solve them. Chapter 10 lays out a taxonomy for optimizations on a uniprocessor machine and populates the taxonomy with an example transformation in each category.

8.2 BACKGROUND

Until the early 1980s, many compiler writers considered optimization as a feature that should be added to the compiler only after its other parts were working well. This led to a distinction between *debugging compilers* and *optimizing compilers*. A debugging compiler emphasized quick compilation at the expense of code quality. These compilers did not significantly rearrange the code, so a strong correspondence remained between the source code and the executable code. This simplified the task of mapping a run-time error to a specific line of source code; hence, the term *debugging* compiler. In contrast, an optimizing compiler focuses on improving the running time of the executable code at the expense of compile time. Spending more time in compilation often produces better code. Because the optimizer often moves operations around, the mapping from source code to executable code is less transparent, and debugging is, accordingly, harder.

As RISC processors have moved into the marketplace (and as RISC implementation techniques were applied to CISC architectures), more of the burden for improving run-time performance has fallen on compilers. To increase performance, processor architects have turned to features that require more support from the compiler. These include delay slots on branches, nonblocking memory operations, increased use of pipelines, and increased numbers of functional units. Processors have become much more performance sensitive to both high-level issues of program layout and structure and to low-level details of scheduling and resource allocation. As the performance gap created by optimization has grown, the expectations for code quality have grown, to the point where optimization has become an expected part of modern compilers.

The routine inclusion of an optimizer, in turn, changes the environment in which both the front end and the back end operate. Optimization further insulates the front end from performance concerns. To an extent, this simplifies the task of IR generation in the front end. At the same time, optimization changes the code that the back end processes. Modern optimizers assume that the back end will handle resource allocation; thus, they typically target an idealized machine that has an unlimited supply of registers, memory, and functional units. This, in turn, has placed more pressure on the techniques used in the compiler's back end.

If compilers are to shoulder their share of responsibility for run-time performance, they must include optimizers. As we shall see, the tools of optimization also play a large role in the compiler's back end. For these reasons, it is important to introduce optimization and explore some of the issues that it raises before discussing the techniques used in a compiler's back end.

```
          subroutine dmxpy (n1, y, n2, ldm, x, m)
          double precision y(*), x(*), m(ldm,*)
            ...
          jmin = j+16
          do 60 j = jmin, n2, 16
            do 50 i = 1, n1
              y(i) = ((((((((((((((( (y(i))
     $                + x(j-15)*m(i,j-15)) + x(j-14)*m(i,j-14))
     $                + x(j-13)*m(i,j-13)) + x(j-12)*m(i,j-12))
     $                + x(j-11)*m(i,j-11)) + x(j-10)*m(i,j-10))
     $                + x(j- 9)*m(i,j- 9)) + x(j- 8)*m(i,j- 8))
     $                + x(j- 7)*m(i,j- 7)) + x(j- 6)*m(i,j- 6))
     $                + x(j- 5)*m(i,j- 5)) + x(j- 4)*m(i,j- 4))
     $                + x(j- 3)*m(i,j- 3)) + x(j- 2)*m(i,j- 2))
     $                + x(j- 1)*m(i,j- 1)) + x(j) *m(i,j))
50        continue 60 continue
            ...
          end
```

FIGURE 8.1   Excerpt from dmxpy in LINPACK

8.2.1 An Example from LINPACK

To understand some of the issues that arise in optimizing real programs, consider the code fragment shown in Figure 8.1, which comes from the FORTRAN version of the routine dmxpy in the LINPACK numerical library. The nest wraps two loops around a single long assignment that forms the core of a routine that computes y + x × m, for vectors x and y and matrix m. It is instructive to consider the code from two different perspectives: first, the transformations that the author hand-applied in an attempt to improve performance, and second, the challenges that the compiler faces in translating this loop nest to run efficiently on a specific processor.

Before the author hand-transformed the code, the loop nest performed a simpler version of the same computation, namely, the following:

```
     do 60 j = 1, n2
       do 50 i = 1, n1
         y(i) = y(i) + x(j) * m(i,j)
50     continue
60 continue
```

To improve performance, the outer loop has been been *unrolled*. The statement in the original loop body is y(i) = y(i) + x(j) * m(i,j). Sixteen copies of the loop body have been created, with different values for j, ranging from j through j-15. The increment in the outer loop has changed from 1 to 16. These 16 loop bodies have been merged into a single statement, eliminating 15 additions (the distinct occurrences of y(i) + ...) and most of the loads and stores of y(i).

Four other versions of the loop nest precede the one shown in Figure 8.1. These other loop nests handle the cases that arise when n2 is not a multiple of 16. Acting in concert, they process up to 15 columns of m, leaving j set to a value for which n2 - j is an integral multiple of 16. The first loop handles a single column of m, corresponding to an odd n2. The other three loop nests handle 2, 4 and 8 columns of m. This guarantees that the final loop nest, shown in Figure 8.1, can process the columns 16 at a time.

Ideally, the compiler should be able to transform the original loop nest into the more efficient version, or into whatever form is most appropriate for a given target machine. However, this requires a combination of techniques that few compilers include. In the case of dmxpy, the programmer rewrote the code to ensure that the shape of the final code would let the compiler generate efficient target-machine code.

8.2.2 Considerations for Optimization

The programmer applied these transformations in the belief that they would make the program run faster. The programmer had to believe that they would preserve the meaning of the program. (After all, if transformations need not preserve meaning, why not replace the entire procedure with a single nop?)

These two issues, safety and profitability, lie at the heart of every optimization. The compiler must have a mechanism to prove that each application of the transformation is safe—that is, it preserves the program's meaning. The compiler must have a reason to believe that applying the transformation is profitable—that is, it improves the program's performance. If either of these is not true—that is, applying the transformation will change the program's meaning or will make its performance worse—the compiler should not apply the transformation.

Safety

How did the programmer know that this transformation was safe? That is, why did the programmer believe that the transformed code produces the same

DEFINING SAFETY

Correctness is the single most important criterion that a compiler must meet—the code that the compiler produces must have the same meaning as the input program. Each time the optimizer applies a transformation, that action must preserve the correctness of the translation.

Typically, *meaning* is defined as the observable behavior of the program. For a batch program, this is the memory state after it halts, along with any output it generates. If the program terminates, the values of all visible variables immediately before it halts should be the same under any translation scheme. For an interactive program, behavior is more complex and difficult to capture.

Plotkin formalized this notion as *observational equivalence*.

> *For two expressions, M and N, we say that M and N are observationally equivalent if and only if, in any context C where both M and N are closed (that is, have no free variables), evaluating C[M] and C[N] either produces identical results or neither terminates* [275].

Thus, two expressions are observationally equivalent if their impact on the visible, external environment is identical.

In practice, compilers use a simpler and looser notion of equivalence than Plotkin's, namely, that if, in their actual program context, two different expressions e and e' produce identical results, then the compiler can substitute e' for e.

This standard is looser than Plotkin's. It deals only with contexts that actually arise in the program; tailoring code to context is the source of many opportunities for optimization. It does not mention what happens when a computation goes awry, or diverges.

In practice, compilers take care not to introduce divergence—the original code would work correctly, but the optimized code tries to divide by zero, or loops indefinitely. The opposite case, where the original code would diverge, but the optimized code does not, is rarely mentioned.

results as the original code? Close examination of the loop nest shows that the only interaction between successive iterations occurs through the elements of y.

■ A value computed as y(i) is not reused until the next iteration of the outer loop. The iterations of the inner loop are independent of one another, because each iteration defines precisely one value and no other iteration references that value. Thus, the iterations can execute in any order. (For example, we can reverse the inner loop and run it from n1 to 1 without changing the results.)

■ The interaction through y is limited in its effect. The ith element of y accumulates the sum of all the ith iterations of the inner loop. This pattern of accumulation is safely reproduced in the unrolled loop.

A large part of the analysis done in optimization goes toward proving the safety of transformations.

Profitability

Why did the programmer think that unrolling the loop would improve performance? That is, why is the transformation profitable? Several different effects of unrolling might speed up the code.

■ The total number of loop iterations is reduced by a factor of 16. This reduces the overhead operations due to loop control: adds, compares, jumps, and branches. If the loop executes thousands of times, these savings become significant.

This argument might suggest unrolling by an even larger factor. Finite resource limits probably dictated the choice of 16. For example, the inner loop uses the same 16 values of x for all the iterations of the inner loop. Many processors have only 32 registers that can hold a floating-point number. Unrolling by 32, the next power of 2, would ensure that these "loop-invariant" values of x could not be kept in registers. This would add memory operations to the inner loop that would probably undo any savings from unrolling.

■ The array address computations contain duplicated work. Consider the use of y(i). The original code computed y(i)'s address once per multiplication of x and m; the transformed code computes it once per 16 multiplications. The unrolled code does $\frac{1}{16}$ as much work to address y(i). The 16 references to m, and to a lesser extent x, should include common portions that the loop can compute once and reuse, as well.

- The unrolled inner loop performs 16 multiplies and 16 adds, ignoring address calculations, for 17 loads and 1 store, assuming that the x values stay in registers. The original loop performed 1 multiply and 1 add for 2 loads and 1 store. The transformed loop is less likely to be memory bound.[1] It has enough independent arithmetic to overlap the operations and hide some of their latencies.

Unrolling can help with other, machine-dependent effects. It increases the amount of code in the inner loop; this may let the instruction scheduler hide latencies better. If the end-of-loop branch has a long latency, unrolling may let the compiler fill all the delay slots of that branch. On some processors, unused delay slots must be filled with nops. In this case, unrolling can decrease the total number of nops fetched; this reduces total memory traffic and, perhaps, the power used to execute the program.

Risk

If transformations intended to improve performance make it harder for the compiler to generate good code for the program, those potential problems should be considered as profitability issues. The hand transformations performed on dmxpy create new challenges for a compiler, including the following:

- *Demand for registers:* The original loop needed only a handful of registers to hold its active values. Only x(j), some part of the address calculations for x, y, and m, and the loop index variables need registers across loop iterations, while y(i) and m(i,j) need registers briefly. In contrast, the transformed loop has 16 elements of x to keep in registers across the loop, along with the 16 values of m and y(i) that need registers briefly.

- *Form of address calculation:* The original loop dealt with 3 addresses, one each for y, x, and m. Because the transformed loop references many more distinct locations in each iteration, the compiler must shape the address calculations carefully to avoid repeated calculations and excessive demand for registers. In the worst case, the code might use independent calculations for all 16 elements of x, all 16 elements of m, and the 1 element of y.

---

1. To determine whether the loop is actually memory bound would require detailed knowledge about the target processor, including the latencies for its various operations and the number and kinds of operations it can issue in a single cycle.

If the compiler shapes the address calculations appropriately, it can use a single pointer for m and a single pointer for x, each with 16 constant-valued offsets. It can rewrite the loop to use that pointer in the end-of-loop test, obviating the need for another register and eliminating another update. Planning and optimization make the difference between these two cases.

Other problems, of a machine-specific nature, arise as well. For example, scheduling the 17 loads and 1 store, the 16 multiplies, the 16 adds, plus the address calculations and loop-overhead operations in each iteration requires some care. The compiler may need to issue some of the load operations in a previous iteration so that it can schedule the initial floating-point operations in a timely fashion.

8.2.3 Opportunities for Optimization

As we have seen, the task of optimizing a simple loop can involve complex considerations. In general, optimizing compilers capitalize on opportunities that arise from several distinct sources.

1. *Reducing the overhead of abstraction* As we saw for the array-address calculation at the beginning of the chapter, the data structures and types introduced by programming languages require run-time support. Optimizers use analysis and transformation to reduce this overhead.

2. *Taking advantage of special cases* Often, the compiler can use knowledge about the context in which an operation executes to specialize that operation. As an example, a C++ compiler can sometimes determine that a call to a virtual function always uses the same implementation. In that case, it can remap the call and reduce the cost of each invocation.

3. *Matching processor resources* If the resource requirements of a program differ from those provided by the processor, the compiler may transform the program to align its needs more closely with the processor's capabilities. The transformations applied to dmxpy have this effect; they decrease the number of memory accesses per floating-point operation.

These are broad areas, described in sweeping generality. As we discuss specific analysis and transformation techniques, in Chapters 9 and 10, we will fill in these areas with more detailed examples.

8.3 | REDUNDANT EXPRESSIONS

As a concrete example, consider the problem of finding and eliminating redundant expressions inside a basic block. A basic block is a maximal-length segment of straight-line, unpredicated code. To keep the problem simple, our algorithms will ignore anything that happens either before or after the block. An expression $x + y$ is redundant inside a block if it has already been computed in the block, and no intervening operation redefines x or y. If the compiler finds a redundant expression, it can save that value at the first computation and replace any subsequent evaluations with references to the saved value.

We can approach this problem at the source level, as shown in Figure 8.2. The original code, in (a), computes $2 \times y$ twice. The code in (b) shows it rewritten to avoid the duplicated operation. The rewritten code has more statements but fewer operations. When the compiler translates it into target-machine code, the lower operation count will, generally, produce faster code. Programmers will protest that they do not write code that contains redundant expressions like these. Preprocessors and other tools that generate source code are more likely to create them than is a careful programmer. Such expressions also arise, in vast quantity, as details like address calculations are elaborated during the translation from source code to a lower-level IR. The compiler can apply these techniques for redundancy elimination on lower-level IRs, as well.

For the compiler to detect and eliminate redundancies automatically, it needs algorithms that find the redundancies and algorithms that rewrite the code without the redundancies. We will explore two different approaches to this problem: building a DAG and computing value numbers.

$$m \leftarrow 2 \times y \times z$$
$$n \leftarrow 3 \times y \times z$$
$$o \leftarrow 2 \times y - z$$

(a) Original Code

$$t_0 \leftarrow 2 \times y$$
$$m \leftarrow t_0 \times z$$
$$n \leftarrow 3 \times y \times z$$
$$o \leftarrow t_0 - z$$

(b) Rewritten Code

FIGURE 8.2 Redundant Expressions at the Source Level

8.3.1 Building a Directed Acyclic Graph

One way to represent redundant computation explicitly is with a directed acyclic graph (DAG). In an AST, each node has at most one parent. Thus, the AST for the example code in Figure 8.2(a) might be as follows:

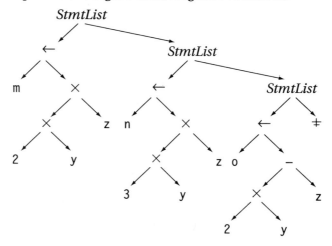

In contrast, the DAG represents each distinct expression once. In a DAG a node can have multiple parents. Each parent represents a distinct reference to the value represented by the node; any node with multiple parents *must* be a redundant expression. A DAG built from the previous AST would look like:

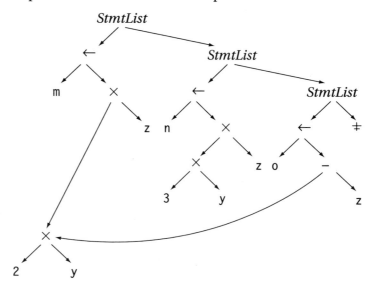

The DAG exposes the fact that the subexpression 2 × y occurs twice in the source code. The node representing 2 × y has two parents: the multiplication in the first assignment and the subtraction in the third assignment. The compiler can generate code that takes advantage of this fact (similar to Figure 8.2(b)). The key to using DAGs as a tool for redundancy elimination is to locate these identical expressions systematically and efficiently.

The easiest way to accomplish this is to modify the routines that the compiler uses to construct its AST. If this constructor uses hashing to detect identical subtrees, it will build DAGs that contain one subtree for each distinct expression. This would produce the desired sharing of 2 × y. It would also discover that all the instances of y have identical values, as do all the instances of z. Thus, the actual DAG would be more complex than the preceding one, as shown in the following DAG.

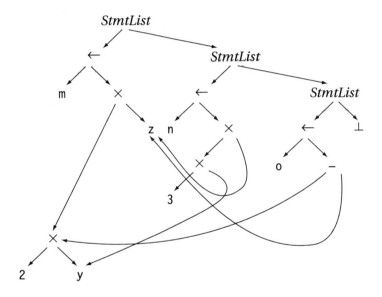

This DAG uses even fewer nodes to represent the same three statements. The parse tree has 24 nodes, the first DAG has 21 nodes, and this final DAG has 18 nodes. (If the goal is to shrink the AST, this idea works.)

In this case, both instances of 2 × y have the same value. However, that is coincidence rather than careful planning. The hash-based constructor uses a textual notion of equality, so y equals y, independent of its value. The constructor ensures that two operations share a representation if they have the same operator and their operands have the same representation. Consider what would happen if we changed the left-hand side of the second assignment from n to y. The textual mechanism used to match y against y has no way to determine that an intervening assignment changes y's value. Thus, the DAG for this modified example still shares the representation of 2 × y, even though the two occurrences might have different values. If our goal is to identify subexpressions that must compute the same value, then we need a mechanism to account for the impact of assignments.

To make the hash-based DAG constructor reflect assignments, we can track the different versions of each variable. The mechanism is simple: associate a counter with each variable and, at each assignment, increment the counter for the variable that is redefined. In the hash-based constructor, append the counter to every variable name before hashing. With these changes, the hash-based constructor will build a DAG in which two expressions have the same representation if and only if they are textually identical *and* none of the variables used in the expression is redefined between the two occurrences of the expression. (This counter scheme is formalized in SSA form, an IR described in Sections 5.5 and 9.3).

Pointer Assignments

Assigning a new value to y has a limited effect that the subscripting scheme models well. Pointer assignments have more wide-reaching effects. An assignment, such as *p = 0; in C, must increment the subscript of every variable that it could possibly modify. If the compiler has detailed knowledge about the value of the pointer, it may be able to limit this effect and increment a small set of subscripts. If, however, the compiler has little or no knowledge about where p might point, it must increment the subscript of every variable that the pointer assignment might modify—potentially, every variable in the entire program.

This sounds drastic, but it shows the real impact of an ambiguous pointer operation on the set of facts that the compiler can derive. If the source language allows arbitrary pointer arithmetic, this includes every variable stored in memory. Without arbitrary pointer arithmetic, the compiler can limit it to those variables that can be reached by a pointer, sometimes approximated as the set of variables whose address is taken in the program. One major motivation for performing pointer analysis is to shrink the size of these sets.

In a compiler that uses a treelike representation for code, embedding the DAG-building machinery directly into the tree constructors has advantages. It produces smaller IR programs, with concomitant benefits for compilation. It makes the representation of redundancy explicit: any operation with multiple parents must be redundant. Finally, it ensures a complete and thorough application of the ideas. As other parts of the compiler manipulate the IR,

THE IMPORTANCE OF ORDER

The specific order in which expressions are written has an impact on the ability of optimization algorithms to analyze and transform them. Consider the sequence of assignments used to illustrate DAG construction.

$$m \leftarrow 2 \times y \times z$$
$$n \leftarrow 3 \times y \times z$$
$$o \leftarrow 2 \times y - z$$

The hash-based DAG-construction algorithm discovers that $2 \times y$ is repeated in the first and third statements. It fails to notice that $y \times z$ occurs twice, in the first and second statements. Treating multiplication as left-associative hides the repetition of $y \times z$. Treating multiplication as right-associative exposes $y \times z$, but hides $2 \times y$.

In general, using commutativity, associativity, and distributivity to reorder expressions can change the results of optimization. Consider, for example, the expression $3 \times a \times 5$. Any representation that uses binary $\times$ has only two possible groupings:

$(3 \times a) \times 5$ and

$3 \times (a \times 5)$.

Neither ordering groups the two constants together. Thus, the expression 3×5, which the compiler can evaluate at compile time, is never considered.

Because there are a prohibitively large number of ways to reorder a large expression, compilers use heuristic techniques to search for better expression orderings. For example, the IBM FORTRAN H Compiler generated all of its array-address computations in an order that tended to improve other optimizations. Other compilers have sorted the operands of commutative operations into an order that corresponds to the loop nesting level at which they are defined. Because so many solutions are possible, this is a problem for which the compiler writer must experiment with different ideas to determine what is appropriate for a specific language, compiler, and coding style.

for example, rewriting $2 \times x \times y$ as $x \times y + x \times y$, the hashing constructors would ensure that the resulting IR reflected directly any common subexpressions.

8.3.2 Value Numbering

The notion of encoding redundancies into tree nodes does not fit into a compiler that uses a linear IR. For a linear IR, the compiler writer might want a technique that analyzes the linear IR and rewrites it to eliminate redundancies. The classic technique for accomplishing this is called *value numbering*. The idea is simple. The algorithm assigns a distinct number to each value computed at run time, with the property that two expressions, e_i and e_j have the same value number if and only if e_i and e_j are provably equal for all possible operands of the expressions.

Value numbering relies on the same insight that underlies DAG construction: the compiler can use a hash table to identify expressions that produce the same value. The operational definition for "redundant" changes slightly; two expressions are considered redundant if they have the same operator and their operands have the same value numbers. To map variables, constants, and computed values to their value numbers, the compiler uses a hash table. For a variable or a constant, the compiler can use its scanned text as its hash key. For an expression containing an operator, it can construct a hash key from the operator and the value numbers of its operands; identical hash keys must produce identical run-time values.

As new values are computed, they receive new value numbers. Because the hash keys use the value numbers of the operands, rather than their names, the algorithm handles unambiguous assignments in a natural way. In the sequence

$$x \leftarrow a + d$$
$$y \leftarrow a$$
$$z \leftarrow y + d$$

y gets the same value number as a, so $y + d$ gets the same value number as $a + d$. Ambiguous assignments, typically ones involving pointers or array elements, still may have disastrous effects that must be modelled by invalidating the value numbers of all variables that a pointer might touch.

Figure 8.3 shows the basic value-numbering algorithm, assuming simple expressions of the form *result$_e$ ←operand$_1$ op$_e$ operand$_2$* as input. It starts with

for each expression e in the block of the form
  result$_e$ ← operand$_1$ op$_e$ operand$_2$

1. *get the value numbers for operand$_1$ and operand$_2$*

2. *construct a hash key from the operator and*
   the value numbers for operand$_1$ and operand$_2$

3. *if the hash key is already present in the table then*
     replace expression e with a copy operation and
     record the value number for result$_e$
   else
     insert the hash key into the table
     assign the hash key a new value number and
     record that value number for result$_e$

FIGURE 8.3   Value Numbering a Single Block

an empty value table. To obtain the value number for an operand, it looks up the operand in the value table. If an entry exists, it uses the value number already assigned to that entry. If no entry exists, it creates one and assigns it a new value number. Once it has value numbers for all the operands, it constructs a hash key for the entire expression and uses that key to look it up in the value table. If an entry exists, then expression *e* is redundant. If no entry exists, the expression is not redundant, so the algorithm enters it in the table with its new value number. It also records the value number in the entry for *result$_e$*, the name defined by the expression. Extending the algorithm to expressions of arbitrary arity is straightforward.

To see how the algorithm works, consider the following example. Column (a) shows a short basic block before value numbering.

(a) Original Code	(b) Value Numbered Code	(c) Rewritten Code
a ← b + c	$a^3 \leftarrow b^1 + c^2$	a ← b + c
b ← a − d	$b^5 \leftarrow a^3 - d^4$	b ← a − d
c ← b + c	$c^6 \leftarrow b^5 + c^2$	c ← b + c
d ← a − d	$d^5 \leftarrow a^3 - d^4$	d ← b

Column (b) shows the value numbers that the algorithm assigns to each name. Initially, with an empty value table, b and c get new value numbers. Using the value numbers for b (namely 1) and c (namely 2) along with the operator "+," the value-numbering algorithm creates for the first expression a textual string "1 + 2" to use as the hash key, or input, to a hash function. Using the output of the hash function as an index, the value-numbering algorithm looks for the hash key in the value table. The lookup fails, so the algorithm creates an entry for the hash key and assigns it value number 3. To ensure that subsequent references to a discover its correct value number, the algorithm also creates an entry for a and assigns it value number 3. Repeating this process for each operation, in sequential order, produces the set of value numbers shown as superscripts in the figure.

The value numbers reveal, correctly, that the two occurrences of b + c produce different values, due to the intervening redefinition of b. On the other hand, the two occurrences of a − d produce the same value, since they have the same input value numbers and the same operator. The algorithm discovers this and records it by assigning b and d the same value number, 5. Armed with this fact, the compiler can rewrite the code as shown in column (c). Subsequent passes in the compiler may eliminate the copy d ← b. (We could add a mechanism to the value-numbering algorithm that aggressively replaces future references to d with b. This would make the copy operation unnecessary. As a matter of software engineering, we prefer to insert the copy and assume that a later compiler pass will eliminate it.)

Extending the Algorithm

The value-numbering algorithm is a natural place to perform several other local optimizations. Commutative operations that differ only in the order of their operands should receive the same value numbers. To handle this, the compiler can order the operands of each commutative operator using some convenient scheme—such as sorting them by value number. Similarly, if the algorithm knows that all the operands of some operation are constants and it has their values, it can perform the operation at compile time and fold the answer directly into the code. To handle this, the compiler writer needs to include a notation in the value table that denotes a constant value. When it finds a constant-valued expression, the compiler should evaluate the operation, assign the result a value number, and replace any subsequent uses with a reference to the constant value.

We can also extend the value-numbering algorithm to discover operations that have no effect because they apply some algebraic identity. For example, x + 0 should receive the same value number as x. To handle algebraic identities, the algorithm needs special-case code to detect each identity. A series of tests, one per identity, can easily become long enough that it produces an unacceptable slowdown in the value-numbering process. Instead, the tests should be organized as a tree that first switches on the operator. Since each operator has only a few identities, this keeps the overhead of checking for identities small. The following table shows some of the identities that can be handled in this way:

for each operation e in the block of the form
$$result_e \leftarrow operand_1 \; op_e \; operand_2$$

1. *get the value numbers for $operand_1$ and $operand_2$*

2. *if all the operands to op_e are constant*
   evaluate it and replace later uses with references

3. *if the operation is an identity*
   replace it with a copy operation

4. *if op_e is commutative*
   sort the operands by their value numbers

5. *construct a hash key from the operator and*
   the value numbers for $operand_1$ and $operand_2$

6. *if the hash key is already present in the table then*
   replace operation e with a copy operation and
   record the value number found for $result_e$
   else
       insert the hash key into the table
       assign the hash key a new value number and
       record that value number for $result_e$

FIGURE 8.4   Value Numbering with Extensions

Algebraic Identities for Value Numbering			
$a + 0 = a$	$a - 0 = a$	$a - a = 0$	$2 \times a = a + a$
$a \times 1 = a$	$a \times 0 = 0$	$a \div 1 = a$	$a \div a = 1, a \neq 0$
$a^1 = a$	$a^2 = a \times a$	$a \gg 0 = a$	$a \ll 0 = a$
$a \text{ AND } a = a$	$a \text{ OR } a = a$	$\text{MAX}(a,a) = a$	$\text{MIN}(a,a) = a$

A clever implementor will discover other identities, including some that are type specific. Computing exclusive-or on two values with the same value number should produce a zero of the appropriate type. Also, numbers in IEEE floating-point format have some special cases introduced by the explicit representations of ∞ and NaN (<u>N</u>ot <u>a</u> <u>N</u>umber); for example, $\infty - \infty = \text{NaN}$, $\infty - \text{NaN} = \text{NaN}$, and $\infty \div \text{NaN} = \text{NaN}$.

Figure 8.4 shows the algorithm with these extensions. Step 2 evaluates and folds constant-valued operations. Step 3 checks for operations that it can eliminate because they implement algebraic identities. Step 4 reorders the operands of commutative operations. Steps 1, 5, and 6 are carried over from the original algorithm. Even with these extensions, the cost per IR operation remains extremely low. Each step has an efficient implementation.

The Role of Naming

The choice of names for variables and values can limit the effectiveness of value numbering. Consider what happens when the algorithm is applied to the following short block:

$a \leftarrow x + y$	$a^3 \leftarrow x^1 + y^2$	$a \leftarrow x + y$
$b \leftarrow x + y$	$b^3 \leftarrow x^1 + y^2$	$b \leftarrow a$
$a \leftarrow 17$	$a^4 \leftarrow 17^4$	$a \leftarrow 17$
$c \leftarrow x + y$	$c^3 \leftarrow x^1 + y^2$	$c \leftarrow x + y$
Original Code	Value Numbered Code	Rewritten Code

The algorithm processes the first operation and assigns it the value number 3. When it encounters the second operation, it discovers that a table entry already exists for the hash key "1 + 2" (from $x + y$), so it creates an entry for b and assigns it the value number already assigned the key, which is 3. The operation is replaced with $b \leftarrow a$.

Next, the algorithm processes the third operation. This assigns the value number 4 to both the constant 17 and a. Finally, the algorithm processes the final operation. It discovers that the expression is redundant, with value number 3. However, the recorded instance of that value, in a, no longer exists because the third operation overwrote it. The algorithm cannot eliminate this instance of $x + y$ because it has lost track of where that value resides.

We can cure this problem in two distinct ways. The algorithm can build and maintain a mapping from value numbers to names. Each assignment must update the mapping. Alternatively, the compiler can rewrite code in a way that gives each assignment a distinct name. Adding a subscript to each name for uniqueness is sufficient. (Like the version numbers for assignment in the DAG construction, this scheme approximates one property of SSA form.) Under this new naming discipline, the example block becomes

$$a_0 \leftarrow x_0 + y_0$$
$$b_0 \leftarrow x_0 + y_0$$
$$a_1 \leftarrow 17$$
$$c_0 \leftarrow x_0 + y_0$$

With these new names, the code defines each value exactly once. Thus, no value is ever redefined and lost, or *killed*. When we apply the algorithm to this block, it produces the desired result. Operations two and four are proved redundant; each can be replaced with a copy operation from a_0. The new naming scheme, however, lets us do better than that. Because each value number has a unique name, we can omit the copy operations $b_0 \leftarrow a_0$ and $c_0 \leftarrow a_0$.

This improvement in optimization has a corresponding cost. Before we can execute the code, we must reconcile the new name space with the old meaning of the program. In particular, the compiler may need to insert some operations to reconcile names at points where control-flow paths merge. If two paths enter a block, and the most recent definition of a along one path is a_{13} and it is a_{17} along the other path, the compiler may need to create a new name, say a_{23} to represent the merger of a_{13} and a_{17}, and insert copy operations at the end of each predecessor block—$a_{23} \leftarrow a_{17}$ in one and $a_{23} \leftarrow a_{13}$ in the other. We will see an algorithm for performing this kind of copy insertion in Section 9.3.

8.3.3 Lessons from Redundancy Elimination

DAG construction and value numbering share some characteristics that are typical of most compiler-based techniques for code improvement. Both methods must address two problems.

Discovering opportunities The first step in both techniques is to examine each expression in the block and determine whether or not an equivalent expression has already been seen. DAG construction creates an abstract name for each operation that consists of the operator ($+$, $\times$, and so on) and the names of its operands. It uses this abstract name as a key into a hash table. If an entry already exists for this name, then the expression is redundant. Value numbering uses a similar mechanism, but one that differs in a critical way. The DAG construction considers two operands identical if they have the same name, that is, the same spelling. The value-numbering algorithm considers two operands identical if they have the same value number. This lets it track a value through a copy operation, as in the sequence $x \leftarrow a + d$, $y \leftarrow a$, and $z \leftarrow y + d$. The hash-based constructor uses a lexical notion of identity that cannot detect that $a + d$ and $y + d$ must compute the same value.

Transforming the code Once the compiler has proved that an expression is redundant, it must modify the IR to capitalize on this fact. In the DAG construction, the compiler encodes this fact directly in the structure of the DAG. Since the goal is to ensure a single node for each instance of the redundant expression, it records the redundancy in the hash table by recording the appropriate node's name. When a subsequent operation refers to the operation, it will find the single instance. Value numbering operates by rewriting the operations. When it finds a redundant operation, it replaces the operation with a copy operation.

This two-part structure occurs in many optimizations. These techniques have a portion that analyzes the code to find opportunities where a transformation can be safely applied and a portion that modifies the IR to perform the transformation. The next section provides background for discussing both analysis and transformation. Section 8.5 takes the value-numbering technique and extends it to operate over regions larger than a basic block. Section 8.6 looks at redundancy elimination for a whole procedure. Rather than extending value numbering again, we will use an algorithm that computes *available expressions*, a classic problem in data-flow analysis, and uses the results to rewrite the code. This approach finds a different set of improvements than value numbering.

8.4 SCOPE OF OPTIMIZATION

The two techniques described in the previous section both operate on basic blocks. As we saw, both techniques gather information about the context that precedes a statement and use that knowledge in an attempt to improve the program. Many optimizations improve the code by deriving contextual knowledge and using it to improve or specialize the code. Thus, the amount of context that a technique considers plays an important role in describing it, implementing it, and understanding it. In general, both analyses and transformations fall into one of five categories, or scopes: local, superlocal, regional, global, or whole program.

8.4.1 Local Methods

These methods confine their attention to basic blocks. Local methods are usually the simplest to analyze and understand. Figure 8.5 shows a code fragment that contains seven basic blocks, *A, B, C, D, E, F,* and *G.* Each ends with a jump or a branch.

Inside a basic block, two important properties hold. First, statements are executed sequentially. Second, if any statement executes, the entire block executes.[2] These two properties let the compiler prove, with relatively simple analyses, facts that may be stronger than those provable for larger scopes. Thus, local methods sometimes make improvements that simply cannot be obtained for larger scopes. However, local methods are limited to improvements that involve operations that all occur in the same block.

8.4.2 Superlocal Methods

These methods operate over *extended basic blocks* (EBBs). An EBB β is a set of blocks $\beta_1, \beta_2, \ldots, \beta_n$ where β_1 may have multiple predecessors and every other β_i, $2 \leq i \leq n$ has a unique predecessor in the EBB. The blocks, $\beta_i \in \beta$, form a tree that can be entered only at its root, β_1. β can have multiple exits—a branch or jump at the end of some β_i that targets a block not in β.

The example in Figure 8.5 has three maximal-size EBBs: $\{A,B,C,D,E\}$, $\{F\}$, and $\{G\}$. The first contains three distinct paths, $\{A,B\}$, $\{A,C,D\}$, and $\{A,C,E\}$. The last two are trivial EBBs that consist of a single block each. However, since both F and G have multiple predecessors, they cannot be included in the EBBs of their predecessors.

Inside an EBB, the compiler can use facts discovered in earlier blocks to improve the code in later blocks. Superlocal methods can treat the individual paths through an EBB as if they were in a single block. In the example, a superlocal method might use facts discovered in A to improve B, C, D, and/or E. In value numbering, the compiler can use the results of processing A as a starting point for B and/or C. It can use the results of processing A and C as a starting point for D and/or E. These additional facts can expose additional opportunities for transformation and improvement; larger contexts often lead to larger sets of opportunities.

8.4.3 Regional Methods

These methods operate over scopes larger than a single EBB but smaller than a full procedure. In the example, the compiler might find an advantage to

---

2. A run-time exception can interrupt the execution of a block. Typically, an exception causes a transfer of control to an exception handler. The handler may cure the problem and return control to the block and reexecute the operation that caused the exception. Alternately, it may terminate execution. In the former case, the compiler needs to understand which operations can cause exceptions and what side effects the exception handler may have. The latter case is transparent to the optimizer, since execution ends abnormally.

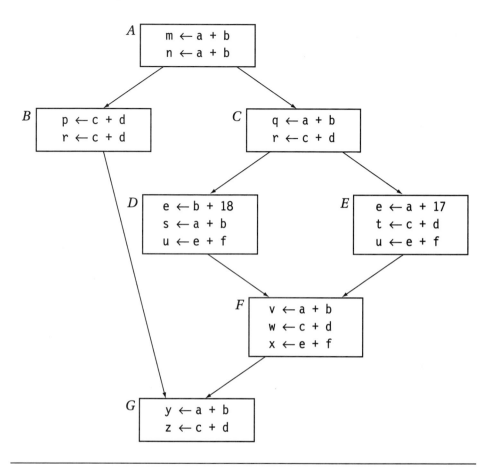

FIGURE 8.5   Example Code Fragment

considering all seven blocks in a single region, such as {A,B,C,D,E,F,G}, or in a hierarchically nested set of regions, such as {A,B,{C,D,E,F},G}. This would allow it to use facts from C, D, and E when it considered F, for example.

Regional methods focus on a smaller scope than the full procedure. In some cases, this produces sharper analysis that enables a transformation. Inside a loop nest, for example, the compiler may be able to prove that a heavily used pointer is invariant (single-valued), even though it is modified elsewhere in the procedure. Such knowledge may enable optimizations such as keeping the value referenced by the pointer in a register.

The compiler can choose regions in many different ways. A region might be defined by some source-code control structure, such as a loop nest; alternatively, it may be a subset of the control-flow graph defined by some graph-theoretic property, such as a dominator relation (see Section 8.5.2).

Loop-based methods follow a simple plan—focus the effort of optimization on those regions that are likely to execute most frequently. Loop bodies execute, on average, much more often than the code that surrounds them, so it makes sense to focus on loops. Other commonly used regions include subtrees of the dominator tree and cycles in the static single-assignment graph (see Sections 9.3 and 10.3).

Regional methods differ from superlocal methods in that they deal with merge points in the CFG. At a merge point, a regional method must have a strategy for combining the distinct sets of facts that hold true on each path that enters the merge point. Regional methods differ from global methods in that they consider only subranges of a procedure. This focus on a limited region can be either a strength or a limitation.

8.4.4 Global Methods

These methods, also called *intraprocedural* methods, examine an entire procedure. The motivation for global methods is simple: decisions that are locally optimal may have bad consequences in some larger context. The procedure provides a natural boundary for both analysis and transformation. Procedures are abstractions that encapsulate and insulate run-time environments. At the same time, they serve as boundaries for separate compilation in many systems.

Global transformations almost always need global analysis. Data-flow analysis evolved to meet this challenge. Thus, global techniques usually involve some kind of intraprocedural analysis to gather facts, followed by the application of those facts to determine the safety and profitability of specific transformations. Global methods discover opportunities for improvement that local methods cannot.

8.4.5 Whole-Program Methods

These methods, also called *interprocedural methods*, consider the entire program as their scope. Just as moving from a local scope to a global scope exposes new opportunities, so moving from single procedures to the entire program can expose new opportunities. It also raises new challenges. In looking at whole programs, the compiler encounters complications and limitations from name-scoping rules and parameter binding that do not exist inside a single procedure.

We classify any transformation that involves more than one procedure as an interprocedural transformation. In some cases, these techniques analyze the entire program; in other cases the compiler may examine just a subset of the source code. Two classic examples of interprocedural optimizations are inline substitution, which replaces a procedure call with a copy of the body of the called procedure, and interprocedural constant propagation, which propagates and folds information about constants throughout the entire program.

8.5 VALUE NUMBERING OVER REGIONS LARGER THAN BASIC BLOCKS

Redundancies can occur among expressions in different basic blocks. Neither of the techniques presented in Section 8.3 discovers these cases; both techniques confine their attention to a single block. This section presents two methods that extend value numbering to larger regions—first to extended basic blocks and then to even larger regions. For value numbering, moving to larger scopes allows the transformation to remove more redundant expressions. In general, this leads to faster code.

8.5.1 Superlocal Value Numbering

To improve the results of value numbering, the compiler can extend its scope from a single basic block to an EBB. To apply the algorithm, the compiler should value number each path through the EBB. In the code fragment from Figure 8.5, it must value number $\{A,B\}$, $\{A,C,D\}$, and $\{A,C,E\}$. Consider $\{A,C,D\}$. The compiler uses local value numbering on A, then uses the resulting hash table as an initial state for value numbering C. Finally, it can use the resulting table to begin processing D. In effect, it treats $\{A,C,D\}$ as if it were a single block. This approach can find redundancies and constant-valued expressions that the local algorithm misses.

To apply the algorithm to a second path, say $\{A,C,E\}$, the compiler could begin again with A, then proceed to C, then proceed to E. Handling each path in the EBB separately, it could achieve the desired result. However, the cost of value numbering would rise unreasonably due to the redundant processing of blocks like A that are prefixes of more than one EBB. In a superlocal algorithm, we want the optimization benefits that come from examining increased context for as small an increase in compile time as possible. To accomplish this, EBB-based algorithms often capitalize on the tree structure of the EBB.

To make value numbering over EBBs efficient, the compiler must reuse the results of blocks that occur on multiple paths through the EBB. Whether it

INTRAPROCEDURAL VERSUS INTERPROCEDURAL

Few terms in compilation create as much confusion as the word *global*. Global analysis and optimization operate on a procedurewide scope. The modern English connotation, however, suggests an all-encompassing scope.

Interest in analysis and optimization across procedure boundaries, beginning with IBM's PL/I optimizing compiler and growing throughout the 1980s, led to heavy use of the terms *intraprocedural*, for single-procedure techniques, and *interprocedural*, for techniques that look at two or more procedures. Since these words are so close in spelling and pronunciation, they are easy to confuse and awkward to use.

Perkin-Elmer Corporation tried to remedy this confusion when it introduced its "universal" optimizing compiler; the system performed extensive inlining followed by aggressive optimization on the resulting code. This term did not stick. We prefer the term *whole program* and use it whenever possible. It conveys the right distinction and reminds the reader and listener that "global" is not "universal."

processes the blocks depth first or breadth first, it needs a way to undo the effects of processing a block. After $\{A,C,D\}$, it must recreate the state for the end of $\{A,C\}$ so that it can reuse that state to process E. Among the many ways that the compiler can accomplish this are:

- It can record the state of the table at each block boundary and restore that state when needed. This might increase the space requirements of the algorithm, but it lets the algorithm process each block once.

- It can unwind the effects of a block by walking the block backward and, at each operation, undoing the work of the forward pass. Some problems arise with lost information—if an operation generated a new value number for x in the forward pass, what was x's previous value number? This approach requires that the forward pass record some additional information.

- It can implement the value table using the mechanisms developed for lexically scoped hash tables (see Section 5.7.3). As it enters a block, it creates a new scope. To retract the block's effects, it deletes that block's scope.

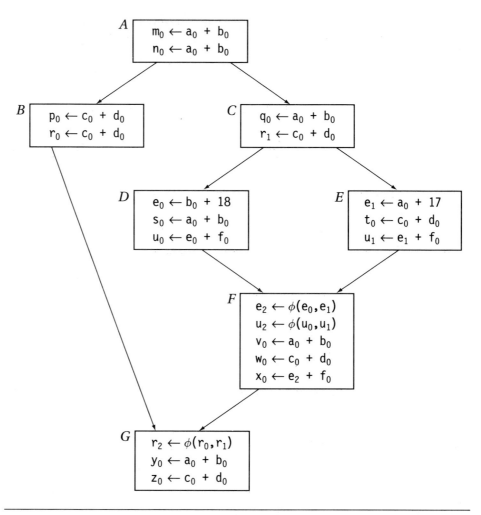

FIGURE 8.6   Example in SSA Form

All three schemes work. The scoped value table offers the lowest cost, particularly if we reuse the mechanisms developed to manage scoped symbol tables. Because the compiler can estimate the size of the table required for each scope, it can avoid the complications that arise in symbol table implementation from the need to expand the table when it becomes full. (In an ILOC code fragment, the maximum number of names is three times the number of ILOC operations.)

With the scoped value table, one complication remains. If a name is defined in several blocks, the effect of a definition in one block may be recorded in the scope associated with another block. In this case, retracting the table and deleting the scope associated with a block may not remove all the facts related to the block. The value-numbering algorithm may need to repair entries in other scopes whose value numbers have been superseded.[3]

To avoid this complication, the compiler can perform superlocal value numbering on a representation where each name is defined exactly once. This naming discipline simplifies value numbering by ensuring that the definitions in a block are recorded in the scope of the value table associated with that block. As discussed in Section 8.3.2, it can also make value numbering more effective.

We have already seen an IR that has this property—SSA form (see Section 5.5). SSA form has two important properties. Each name is defined by exactly one operation, and each use of a value refers to exactly one definition. The former property is precisely what we need to make the scoped value-table version of superlocal value numbering work efficiently. Figure 8.6 shows our ongoing example in SSA form.

In the example, the superlocal algorithm would first process all the paths through the EBB {A,B,C,D,E}, then the EBB {F}, and, finally, the EBB {G}. (In fact, since the algorithm does not rely on any context from before each EBB's header, the algorithm can process these EBBs in any order.) In detail, the actions might occur in the following order:

1.	*Create a scope for A.*		12.	*Value number E.*
2.	*Value number A.*		13.	*Delete E's scope.*
3.	*Create a scope for B.*		14.	*Delete C's scope.*
4.	*Value number B.*		15.	*Delete A's scope.*
5.	*Delete B's scope.*		16.	*Create a scope for F.*
6.	*Create a scope for C.*		17.	*Value number F.*
7.	*Value number C.*		18.	*Delete F's scope.*
8.	*Create a scope for D.*		19.	*Create a scope for G.*
9.	*Value number D.*		20.	*Value number G.*
10.	*Delete D's scope.*		21.	*Delete G's scope.*
11.	*Create a scope for E.*			

---

3. The "sheaf of tables" implementation shown in Section 5.7.3 avoids this problem, but the space-efficient techniques presented in Section B.4.5 in Appendix B combine the storage for definitions in distinct blocks.

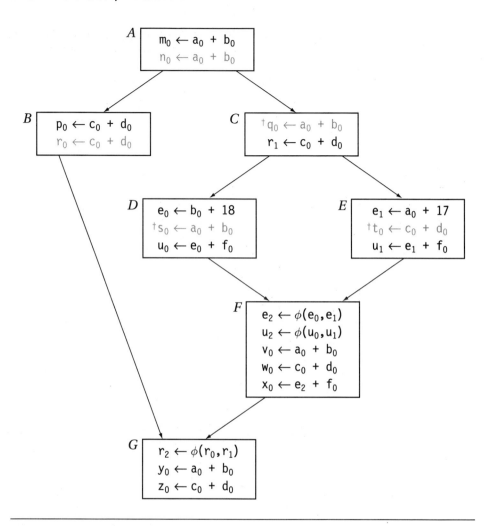

Figure 8.7 Result of Superlocal Value Numbering

For each basic block, the superlocal algorithm creates a scope, applies local value numbering, recurses on any successors in the current EBB, and then deletes the scope. By using a lightweight mechanism for handling scopes, the compiler writer can keep the cost of the superlocal algorithm close to that of the local algorithm.

In terms of effectiveness, the superlocal algorithm removes more redundant computations than the local algorithm. In Figure 8.7, the computations that the algorithm removes are shown in gray, rather than black. The operations marked with a † would be missed by local value numbering because they rely on values computed in a predecessor block. The algorithm does quite well, within an EBB. It misses some opportunities, however. Because F and G form their own EBBs, the computations of $a_0 + b_0$ in those blocks are not treated as redundant, even though they clearly are. Similarly, the algorithm does not recognize $c_0 + d_0$ in blocks F and G as redundant.

Finally, the computation of $e_2 + f_0$ in F exposes a different problem. The computation is redundant; any path that reaches block F computes $e + f$ and neither e nor f is redefined before the evaluation in F. However, those computations compute different values, so they must have different value numbers. To recognize this redundancy requires a different notion of equivalence, as we will see in Section 8.6.

Despite these shortcomings, the superlocal algorithm deserves consideration. It catches more redundancies than the local algorithm for a minimal added cost. With an efficient implementation of the scoped hash table, the overhead of handling EBBs can be kept small.

Not all local techniques extend cleanly to EBBs. Value numbering works well because it replaces redundant computations with equivalent values, in place. Techniques that insert new operations or move existing ones can be more complex. This problem arises, for example, in superlocal instruction scheduling. Moving an operation from block b_j into a predecessor b_i can necessitate changes in other successors of b_i. Moving an operation from b_i to b_j may necessitate inserting a copy of the operation into b_i's other successors.

8.5.2 Dominator-Based Value Numbering

The superlocal value-numbering algorithm misses some opportunities because it must discard the entire value table when it reaches a block that has multiple predecessors in the CFG. The next step in expanding the scope of value numbering should be a technique that can address the redundancies in blocks F and G in Figure 8.6—operations are redundant because they were computed in an earlier EBB. To achieve this, we need a method that propagates its knowledge across join points in the CFG—in the example, from D and E into F, and from B and F into G.

The superlocal method does not extend directly to regions that include join points. To value number F, it cannot use the table from D, which represents the EBB $\{A,C,D\}$, because control can enter F from E as well. Of course, it cannot use the table from E, which represents $\{A,C,E\}$, either, because it fails to account for the path from D to F. The algorithm could try to merge the value tables for D and E. The merge operation would need to unify the value numbers assigned along disjoint paths. For example, the computations of $e + f$ in D and E receive different value numbers. Equally important, the algorithm would

RESOURCE CONSTRAINTS AND PROFITABILITY

Value numbering is, perhaps, the cleanest example of a technique for which increasing the scope leads directly to better results. The goal of value numbering is to discover redundant expressions and remove their redundant evaluations. Moving to larger scopes, as shown in Section 8.5, lets the algorithm discover and remove more redundant expressions. The question remains, does this lead to faster code? Machine-dependent effects can lead to situations in which removing a redundancy produces slower code.

For example, replacing a redundant evaluation with a reference can extend the lifetime of the value produced by the first evaluation. This can increase the demand for registers and, in the worst case, cause the register allocator to introduce additional stores and loads to handle the demand. Of course, the replacement might also decrease demand for registers—for example, if both operands are the last uses of a value.

This effect is subtle. It depends, in particular, on how often each of the operations executes—both the ones removed from the program and those added to it. Calculating the productivity of a specific replacement involves many low-level details, including the impact of all the other replacements. The difficulty of predicting this impact has caused compiler writers, in general, to ignore such effects and assume the transformation is profitable. This practice goes back to the first FORTRAN compiler, where Backus instructed his team to assume, during optimization, that enough registers would be available and to defer the problem of mapping the computation onto registers to a later pass [25].

need to check for values computed along one path but not the other. A use of b + 18 in F would find a redundant computation along the path entering F from D but not along the path entering F from E. Thus, b + 18 is not redundant. The complications that arise in extending the value-numbering algorithm to handle merge points are discouraging.

There is, however, a table that the algorithm can use for F. Both paths that reach F have a common prefix, $\{A,C\}$. A is the sole entry to this code fragment. Every path from A to F passes through A and C. Thus, the compiler knows that every operation in A and every operation in C must execute before the first operation in F. The algorithm can use the table produced by processing C as the initial state for processing F.

What about assignments in D and E? By using SSA form, the compiler can sidestep the problem of a value being redefined between C and F. Since each name is defined by exactly one operation, the operations in D and E can add information to the value table, but they cannot invalidate it. If an operation in F refers to a value created in D or E, the name for that value cannot be in the table for C. In fact, SSA form guarantees the compiler that any reference in F to a value created in D or E will use the name defined by a ϕ-function at the top of F. (Notice what happened to the definitions of e and the subsequent use in F. Compare Figure 8.5 with Figure 8.6.)

Using C's table to initialize the value-numbering step for F allows the compiler to eliminate the computations of $a_0 + b_0$ and $c_0 + d_0$. It does not let the compiler discover that $e_2 + f_0$ has been computed along every path that reaches F, since the value was computed between C and F.

Using the same principle, the algorithm can use A's table when it processes G. This lets it eliminate the evaluation of $a_0 + b_0$ in G, since the original computation lies in A. It cannot, however, eliminate the computation of $c_0 + d_0$, since the earlier computations are in B and C.

Dominators

The value-numbering algorithm needs a way to find the most recent common ancestor along all paths that reach a block. Inspecting the CFG for the example, we see that the following relationships hold:

For block	A	B	C	D	E	F	G
Use table from	—	A	A	C	C	C	A

In each case, the relationship selects the closest predecessor that lies on every path from A to the node. Since A has no predecessors, it has no such node. This relationship is one form of the *dominator* relationship.

In a CFG, if node x appears on every path from the graph's entry to y, then we say that x *dominates* y, denoted $x \gg y$. By definition, $x \gg x$. If $x \gg y$ and $x \neq y$, then x *strictly dominates* y, denoted $x \gg y$. The full set of dominators for y is denoted $\text{DOM}(y)$. $\text{DOM}(F)$ is just $\{A, C, F\}$. The *immediate dominator* of y is the strict dominator of y that is closest to y. It is denoted $\text{IDOM}(y)$.

The example shows that a node can have multiple dominators. Nodes A and C lie on every path from A to F, so $A \gg F$, $C \gg F$, and $F \geq F$. The following table shows the full set of dominators for the example:

Block	A	B	C	D	E	F	G
≫	—	{A}	{A}	{A, C}	{A, C}	{A, C}	{A}
DOM	{A}	{A, B}	{A, C}	{A, C, D}	{A, C, E}	{A, C, F}	{A, G}
DOM	—	A	A	C	C	C	A

The final line in the table shows IDOM for each block. How do these sets relate to the regional value-numbering algorithm?

For a block b, each block in DOM$(b) - \{b\}$ must execute on every path that reaches b. Thus, in value numbering b, the compiler knows that every block in DOM$(b) - \{b\}$ has executed before b. It can use the value table of any block in DOM$(b) - \{b\}$ to initialize the value table for b. Which of those blocks is best?

IDOM(b) is the block in DOM$(b) - \{b\}$ with the largest DOM set—that is, if $i = $ IDOM(b), then DOM(i) contains j (as well as DOM(j)), for every other $j \in \{$DOM$(b) - \{b\}\}$. The compiler should use i's table to initialize b's value table because i occurs on every path leading to b and i's value table contains more information than the table for any other node in DOM$(b) - \{b\}$.

To apply this insight, the optimizer can apply the local value-numbering method to each block. For a block b, it should use the scoped value table that applies at the end of block IDOM(b). This fits into the same basic framework of extending and retracting scopes that we used in superlocal value numbering. The computation of DOM and IDOM is left to Section 9.3.1.

Using IDom for Value Numbering

We can visualize the IDOM relationship by building the *dominator tree* for the control-flow graph. In the tree, a node's parent is its immediate dominator. For the ongoing example, the dominator tree looks like:

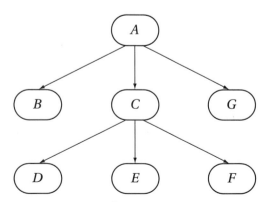

For a given node, such as D, IDOM(D) is its parent in the dominator tree, while its DOM set contains itself, along with all of its ancestors in the tree. Thus, IDOM(D) is C and DOM(D) is { D,C,A}.

The dominator-based value-numbering algorithm traverses the dominator tree in preorder. This ensures that the appropriate tables have been constructed prior to visiting a block. This can produce a counterintuitive traversal order; for example, the algorithm could visit G before F. Since the only facts that the algorithm can use while visiting G are those discovered while processing A, the relative ordering of F and G is not only unspecified, it is also irrelevant.

8.6 GLOBAL REDUNDANCY ELIMINATION

Value numbering analyzes the use of values in a program, identifies expressions that have the same value, and rewrites the code to remove redundant computations. Its focus is on values, rather than names. Its scope can be extended, in a straightforward way, to include large parts of a CFG. Neither superlocal value numbering nor dominator-based value numbering can propagate information along the back edge of a cycle. Thus, they miss the opportunity to discover some redundant operations.

The superlocal and dominator-based value-numbering algorithms perform both analysis and transformation in a single pass over a region in the CFG. Because they cannot propagate information around a cycle in the CFG, they can rewrite the code as they discover opportunities.

An algorithm that processes an entire cycle can, potentially, find more redundant operations. However, it must process the entire cycle before it can propagate information to the block at the head of the cycle. Thus, it cannot rewrite the header block until it has analyzed the entire cycle. It cannot rewrite the second block until it has analyzed and rewritten the first block, and so on. To solve this problem, most global optimization algorithms separate analysis from transformation. For redundancy elimination, this involves a phase that identifies all the expressions that must be redundant, followed by a phase that rewrites all the code to eliminate the extraneous evaluations.

The classic method for discovering redundant expressions uses *data-flow analysis* to compute the set of expressions that are *available* on entry to each block. The term *available* is defined as follows:

- An expression e is *defined* at point p in the CFG if its value is computed at p. We call p a *definition site* for e.

- An expression *e* is *killed* at point *p* in the CFG if one or more of its operands is defined at *p*. We call *p* a *kill site* for *e*.

- An expression *e* is *available* at point *p* in the CFG if every path leading to *p* contains a prior definition of *e*, and *e* is not killed between that definition and *p*.

Knowing that an expression *e* is available at *p* does not, on its own, make the code run faster. The compiler must rewrite the code to capitalize on this knowledge. The simplest rewriting scheme creates a new temporary variable to hold *e*'s value, inserts code as needed to copy earlier evaluations of *e* into that temporary variable, and replaces the redundant evaluations with a copy from the temporary variable.

Our treatment of global redundancy elimination divides along these lines. First, we show an algorithm for computing the set of expressions that are available on entry to each block. Next, we describe a simple mechanism to rewrite the code and replace the redundant expressions. The final subsection compares the results of global redundancy elimination against the various value-numbering algorithms.

The Role of Names

At its heart, global redundancy elimination relies on a syntactic notion of redundancy. It finds repeated evaluations of e + f because they use the names e and f. Thus, it operates on the program's original name space, rather than the SSA name space. It avoids the need for versioned names by tracking where variables are killed. Thus, in the sequence

$$x \leftarrow e + f$$
$$e \leftarrow 5$$
$$y \leftarrow e + f$$

it recognizes that the second occurrence of e + f is not redundant because the redefinition of e kills the expression e + f.

To represent the set of potentially redundant expressions, the compiler needs a distinct name for each such expression. The compiler can easily construct such names. Drawing on one of the critical ideas behind value numbering, it can build a map from expressions to names using a hash table. In a linear pass over the CFG, it can construct a hash key from each operator and the names of its operands and assign that key a distinct number. To ensure a compact name space, the compiler should derive the numbers by simply incrementing a counter. The set of expression names can be no smaller than the set of variable names plus constants. It can be no larger than the number of expressions in the CFG.

8.6.1 Computing Available Expressions

The first step in global redundancy elimination is to compute the set of expressions that are available at various points in the program. The result of this computation is, for each block n, a set AVAIL(n) that contains the names of all expressions that are available on entry to block n. The computation is formalized as a series of simultaneous equations that involve sets associated with the individual blocks in the CFG. As in classic algebra, the equations involve some sets that are known and others that are unknown. The compiler solves the equations using one of several well-known algorithms. Its goal is to find the most precise values that it can for each originally unknown set.

To compute AVAIL sets, the equations require two sets per block whose values are determined solely by the operations in the block. The first set, DEEXPR(n), contains the set of downward exposed expressions in n. That is, $e \in$ DEEXPR(n) if and only if n evaluates e and none of e's operands is defined between the last evaluation of e in the block and the block's end. If $e \in$ DEEXPR(n), then e is available at the exit of n. The second set, EXPRKILL(n), contains all those expressions that are "killed" by a definition in n. An expression is killed if one or more of its operands are redefined in the block. If e is available on entry to n ($e \in$ AVAIL(n)) and $e \notin$ EXPRKILL(n), then e is available at the end of n.

Given the DEEXPR and EXPRKILL sets for all the blocks, the compiler can compute the AVAIL sets by solving the following system of equations:

$$\text{AVAIL}(n_0) = \emptyset$$

$$\text{AVAIL}(n) = \bigcap_{m \in pred(n)} (\text{DEEXPR}(m) \cup (\text{AVAIL}(m) \cap \overline{\text{EXPRKILL}(m)}))$$

Here, n_0 is the entry node to the CFG. For each block, n, the equation finds the set of expressions that is available on each CFG edge entering n. For each edge, $\langle m,n \rangle$, it computes the set of expressions available along that edge as the union of DEEXPR(m) and (AVAIL(m) $\cap \overline{\text{EXPRKILL}(m)}$). The former term contains those expressions defined in m that survive to the end of m. The latter term contains expressions that are available on entry to m and are not killed in m. The intersection ensures that expressions in AVAIL(n) are available on all edges that enter n.

$$\text{VARKILL} \leftarrow \emptyset$$
$$\text{DEEXPR}(n) \leftarrow \emptyset$$

for $i = k$ to 1
    assume operation o_i is "$x \leftarrow y$ op z"
    if ($y \notin \text{VARKILL}$) and ($z \notin \text{VARKILL}$)
      then add "$y + z$" to $\text{DEEXPR}(n)$
    $\text{VARKILL} \leftarrow \text{VARKILL} \cup \{x\}$

$$\text{EXPRKILL}(n) \leftarrow \emptyset$$

for each expression e in the procedure
    for each variable $v \in e$
      if $v \in \text{VARKILL}$
        then $\text{EXPRKILL}(n) \leftarrow \text{EXPRKILL}(n) \cup \{e\}$

FIGURE 8.8   Computing Local Information for AVAIL

Computing the Local Sets

Before it can compute AVAIL sets, the compiler needs to produce the DEEXPR and EXPRKILL sets for each block. Computing DEEXPR is straightforward. Computing EXPRKILL is more complex. Figure 8.8 shows an algorithm for computing these sets for a basic block n.

It initializes the sets VARKILL and DEEXPR(n). Then, in a pass from the bottom of the block to its top, it fills in these sets. For each operation, $x \leftarrow y$ op z, it checks y and z for membership in VARKILL. If neither is in VARKILL, then y op z is downward exposed and belongs in DEEXPR(n). Since the operation defines x, the algorithm adds x to VARKILL.

The second part of the algorithm computes EXPRKILL(n) from the VARKILL set. This computation is straightforward. For each expression e computed in the procedure, it checks to see if n kills any of e's operands. If so, it adds e to EXPRKILL(n).

To speed up this computation, the compiler might precompute a map $M(v)$ from a variable v to the set of expressions that include it. Then, it can construct EXPRKILL(n) by iterating over variables v in VARKILL and adding $M(v)$ to EXPRKILL(n).

Computing AVAIL

The equations for AVAIL specify the contents of AVAIL(n) as a function of the DEEXPR, EXPRKILL, and AVAIL sets of n's predecessors in the CFG. We can use a simple iterative algorithm, like the one in Figure 8.9, to solve for AVAIL. The

$$\text{for } i = 0 \text{ to } k$$
$$\quad \text{Compute } \text{DEExpr}(b_i) \text{ and } \text{ExprKill}(b_i) \text{ as in Figure 8.8}$$
$$\quad \text{Avail}(b_i) \leftarrow \emptyset$$
$$\text{Changed} \leftarrow \text{true}$$
$$\text{while } (\text{Changed})$$
$$\quad \text{Changed} \leftarrow \text{false}$$
$$\quad \text{for } i = 0 \text{ to } k$$
$$\quad\quad \text{OldValue} \leftarrow \text{Avail}(b_i)$$
$$\quad\quad \text{Avail}(b_i) = \bigcap_{p \in pred(b_i)} (\text{DEExpr}(p) \cup (\text{Avail}(p) \cap \overline{\text{ExprKill}(p)}))$$
$$\quad\quad \text{if } \text{Avail}(b_i) \neq \text{OldValue then}$$
$$\quad\quad\quad \text{Changed} \leftarrow \text{true}$$

FIGURE 8.9   A Simple Iterative Algorithm for Available Expressions

algorithm assumes that the blocks in the CFG have been named b_0 through b_k.

The initialization step computes DEExpr and ExprKill sets for each block and sets all the Avail sets to $\emptyset$. The iteration step repeatedly computes new Avail sets for each block. It halts when the Avail sets stop changing. As we shall see in Section 9.2, the structure of the Avail equation, combined with properties of the underlying problem and the iterative algorithm, ensure that the algorithm will reach a fixed point and halt.

Available expressions is a *global data-flow analysis problem*. Many such problems are described in the literature on code optimization. Compilers solve these problems to find places in the code where it is safe to apply a related transformation. The algorithms for solving such equations are called *global data-flow algorithms*. Many such algorithms have been proposed. Iterative algorithms, like the one shown in Figure 8.9, have the advantages of robustness and simplicity. (This algorithm is another example of a fixed-point algorithm.)

8.6.2 Replacing Redundant Computations

Once the compiler has derived Avail sets for each block in the CFG, it can use the knowledge encoded in those sets to transform the code. (Knowledge, alone, does not make the code run faster.) The rewriting phase of redundancy elimination must replace any redundant expressions with copy operations of the values preserved at earlier evaluations, and it must insert the code to preserve those earlier results. Our algorithm will replace the actual redundant evaluation with a copy operation. Rather than focus on eliminating the copies, we assume that subsequent passes of the compiler will eliminate most, if not all, of those copy operations. This simplifies the rewriting phase and allows the compiler to bring its strongest tools for copy elimination to bear on the result of this rewriting step.

To simplify the process, we use two passes. The first pass identifies places where an available expression can be reused and rewrites those operations with a copy from a new compiler-generated temporary variable. The second pass traverses the code and inserts the copy operations needed to define the compiler-generated temporaries that the first pass inserted. This approach only generates a temporary in response to an actual replacement and only inserts copies for those temporaries.

(As an alternative, the compiler could preserve every value in an appropriate temporary register. Each time the code computed a given expression, the compiler could insert a copy operation to save its value. This approach generates many spurious copy operations. While those extra copies can be removed by a good dead-code eliminator, it is better to avoid inserting them.)

In the first pass, the compiler can perform local value numbering on each block and initialize the value table for block n with the expressions in AVAIL(n). If local value numbering finds an evaluation of e in the block, where $e \in$ AVAIL(n), it rewrites the expression with a copy operation from a newly generated name, $temp_i$, where i is the index of e in the name space—e's unique integer identifier. Whenever it performs such a replacement, the compiler records the fact in a boolean array USED by setting USED(i) to *true*. The copy operation replaces the redundant computation, just like the other copies inserted by local value numbering.

In the second pass, the compiler inserts copies for each expression recorded in the USED array. For each block n, if $e \in$ DEEXPR(n) and the entry for e in USED is *true*, it must insert a copy after the last definition of e in n that moves the value of e into $temp_i$. While this sounds complicated, a single linear pass over the code can insert all the required copy operations.

This approach to copy insertion adds copies only to preserve expressions that are involved in redundant evaluations. Still, it can, and does, insert unneeded copies. If USED(e) is *true*, the rewriting phase preserves every remaining evaluation of e. Potentially, this preserves some evaluations of e that can never reach a use of the corresponding temporary variable. A clever compiler writer can engineer rewriting strategies that insert fewer copies, but the additional work in rewriting must trade off against savings elsewhere. The extra copies inserted by this simple technique are useless—that is, their values are never used. Dead-code elimination will remove them efficiently and naturally.

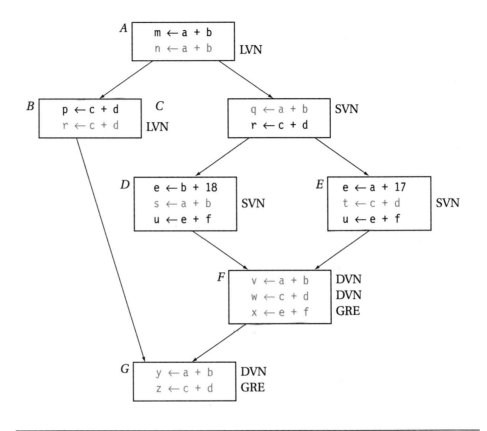

8.6.3 Putting It Together

Combining these two phases—analysis to compute AVAIL followed by rewriting that uses AVAIL to initialize local value numbering—produces a method for removing redundant expressions from an entire procedure, represented by its CFG. The resulting algorithm discovers a different set of redundant operations than any of the value-numbering algorithms.

Figure 8.10 shows the ongoing example, in its original name space (rather than in SSA form). Expressions that can be removed as redundant are shown in gray. The labels to their right show the first algorithm in the sequence that can discover and remove the redundancy. The labels can be decoded as follows:

Label	Algorithm	Section
LVN	Local value numbering	8.3.2
SVN	Superlocal value numbering	8.5.1
DVN	Dominator-based value numbering	8.5.2
GRE	Global redundancy elimination	8.6

The first three algorithms, LVN, SVN, and DVN, form a strict hierarchy. DVN discovers everything found by SVN and LVN. Similarly, SVN finds every redundancy that LVN finds. GRE, on the other hand, uses a different approach and finds a somewhat different set of improvements. For example, only GRE can discover that the evaluation of e $+$ f in F can reuse the values computed in D and E.

The three value-numbering algorithms recognize identical values, so that they can discover that a $+$ b and c $+$ d produce the same value if a $=$ c and b $=$ d (or a $=$ d and b $=$ c). This same focus on value identity lets the value-numbering algorithms recognize that x $+$ 0 is identical to x, or that 2 $\times$ y is equivalent y $+$ y. Because GRE relies on textual identity, it cannot, in general, discover such identities. However, since it uses LVN to perform replacement, it will discover replacements based on local value identity.

8.7 ADVANCED TOPICS

It is often assumed that optimizing over larger scopes produces better code than optimizing over smaller scopes. For value numbering, we saw that increasing the context available to the algorithm allows it to find more opportunities for improvement. Global redundancy elimination, on the other hand, discovers a distinct and different set of improvements. It can find some opportunities that no value-numbering approach finds. It cannot discover some opportunities that even local value numbering finds.

Sometimes, however, increasing the context available to an optimization does not improve the result. Local and superlocal methods work on constrained problems that are simpler than the general problems seen in global or interprocedural problems. In the smaller scopes, the compiler can often prove stronger facts than in larger scopes. In the larger scopes, analysis is harder because the control-flow interactions and name-space manipulations add complexity. Larger scopes expose more opportunities for optimization; unfortunately, they often admit only weaker analysis.

Expanding the scope of analysis and transformation from a single block (or an EBB) to a larger region that includes join points in the CFG introduces uncertainty about the flow of control. In a single basic block, the compiler knows that only one path can execute. The paths through an EBB exclude join points, so the compiler knows what blocks in the EBB always precede a given block. Regional and global methods include join points; the code for these blocks must function correctly as part of multiple paths through the code. Some of these paths may be infeasible—that is, they can never execute. If the compiler can discover infeasible paths, it can ignore them during analysis. If it cannot (and this is the general case), it must assume that they might execute. The assumption that all paths through the CFG are feasible makes analysis less precise and limits the compiler's ability to transform the code.

Expanding the scope of analysis and transformation from a single procedure to include multiple procedures introduces further complications. Whole program, or interprocedural, methods must model the ways that the name space changes at procedure calls. Values become inaccessible; values are renamed; values cease to exist. When a procedure is called from several distinct procedures, each with its own distinct context, the code for the called procedure must work correctly in each of those contexts, with each corresponding name space. These effects do not occur in most single-procedure analysis problems.

Increasing a transformation's scope also increases its potential to have a widespread impact on resource allocation. For example, many transformations increase the demand for registers, sometimes called *register pressure*. If the transformation creates too much register pressure, the allocator may insert enough spill code to negate the original improvement. Thus, moving to a larger scope of optimization is an act of faith in the strength of the new method *and* in the ability of the rest of the compiler to handle the resulting code. It usually pays off. Sometimes, however, smaller scopes of optimization win.

Sometimes, compilers replicate code to increase the context available for optimization and to create new opportunities for optimization. This section describes two approaches to replication: cloning blocks within a procedure and substituting an entire procedure in place of a call to it. These techniques provide a counterpoint to the main story of this chapter—that we can modify algorithms to handle larger and more complex regions. Instead, these approaches modify the code to create larger regions with simple control flow.

8.7.1 Cloning to Increase Context

The various value-numbering algorithms demonstrate that moving to larger scopes, with increased context, can expose additional opportunities for

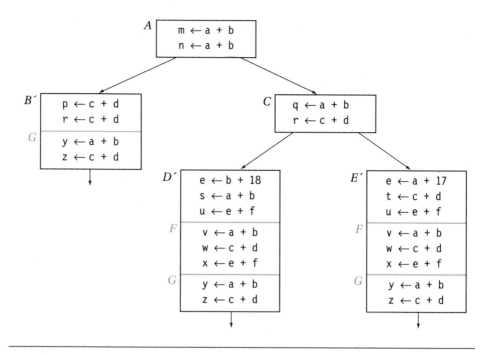

FIGURE 8.11 Example after Cloning

---

improvement. Still, even the dominator-based technique fails to detect some possible replacements. In the ongoing example, the evaluations of e + f in block *F* and c + d in block *G* are clearly redundant—each expression is evaluated along every path from the entry point. However, none of the value-numbering techniques can discover them or replace them.[4]

Both of these expressions occur in blocks that have multiple predecessors in the CFG. In general, these merge points in the CFG cause a loss of information during optimization. To address this problem, compilers sometimes clone basic blocks to eliminate merge points.

To clone a block, the compiler appends a copy of the block to the end of each predecessor block. Figure 8.11 shows the result of cloning blocks *F* and *G* in our continuing example. This creates three new blocks, *B′*, *D′*, and *E′*. The figure shows the original block boundaries in gray. It includes an outbound edge from each copy of *G* (in *B′*, *D′*, and *E′*) to remind us that the compiler must connect each copy to each of the original successors of the original block *G*.

---

4. Global redundancy elimination has its own weaknesses. In the sequence x ← a + d, y ← a, and z ← y + d, it cannot detect that x and z receive the same value.

Cloning blocks in this manner improves the results of optimization in three principal ways.

1. *It creates longer blocks.* Longer blocks let local optimization handle more context. In the case of value numbering, the superlocal and dominator versions are as strong as the local version. For some techniques, however, this is not the case. For instruction scheduling, for example, superlocal and dominator versions are weaker than the local method. In that case, cloning, followed by local optimization, can produce better code.

2. *It eliminates branches.* Combining two blocks eliminates a branch between them. Branches take time to execute. They also disrupt some of the performance-critical mechanisms in the processor, such as instruction fetching and many of the pipelined functions. The net effect of removing branches is to shorten execution time—by eliminating operations and by making hardware mechanisms for predicting behavior more effective.

3. *It creates points where optimization can occur.* When cloning eliminates a merge point, it can create new points in the program where the compiler can derive more precise knowledge about the run-time context. For example, in block D', the variable x gets the value b + 18 + f, and in E', x gets the value a + 17 + f. No point in the original code had either of these properties.

Of course, cloning has its costs, too. After cloning, the example has 24 arithmetic operations rather than the original 17. The larger code may run more quickly because it avoids some end-of-block jumps. It might run more slowly if its size causes additional instruction-cache misses. It may also allow more effective optimization; for example, the local value-numbering algorithm can now recognize that the two occurrences of x ← e + f are redundant. In applications in which the user is more concerned about code space than speed, cloning may not be productive.

8.7.2 Inline Substitution

Procedure calls present a significant barrier to optimization. Calling another procedure has direct costs; the program must execute all the operations in the calling sequence. In some cases, the calling sequence is more general than necessary. Calling another procedure has indirect costs; unless the compiler has precise information about what the callee does, it must assume that the callee behaves adversely—modifying every value that it can access. In many cases, the compiler cannot obtain that information, and code quality in the calling procedure suffers as a result.

Similar effects happen in the callee. As it translates a procedure, the compiler makes assumptions about the run-time environment that the code will inherit from its callers. In the absence of precise information, the compiler must ensure that the callee operates correctly in any legal environment. With better information, it can often generate more efficient, less general code.

Some of the inefficiency arises from lack of information. If the compiler can analyze the whole program before compiling any of its parts, it can address this problem. The rest of the inefficiency is an inherent part of procedural programming. A procedure can be invoked from many distinct call sites, each with a distinct set of run-time conditions. As long as the compiler must build a single executable that works for all call sites, the resulting code must sacrifice efficiency, in some calling contexts, for generality.

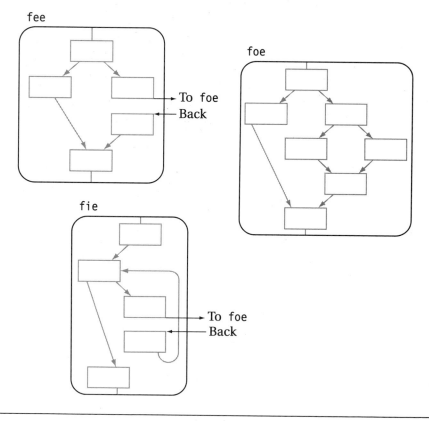

FIGURE 8.12   Before Inline Substitution

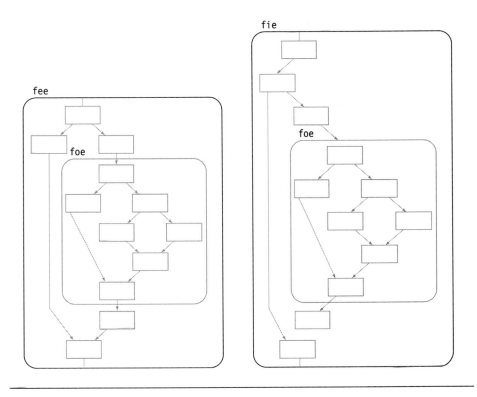

FIGURE 8.13   After Inline Substitution

To combat these inefficiencies, compilers can perform *inline substitution* or *inlining*. This transformation replaces a call site with the body of the callee, with appropriate renaming and copying to simulate the effects of parameter binding at the original call site. Figure 8.12 depicts a code fragment that has two callers, fee and fie. They both invoke foe. Substituting the body of foe for the calls to foe creates the situation shown in Figure 8.13. Each of fee and fie has a private copy of the code in foe. The compiler can tailor these private copies of foe with the code that now surrounds them. The result should be better code for the two new procedures than was possible with the three original procedures, at the expense of greater code space.

The potential improvements come from several sources.

1. *More effective optimization* Eliminating the call exposes code in both the caller and the callee to the same analyses and transformations. The compiler can derive more precise information and apply that knowledge over a larger part of the program—the combined procedures.

2. *Eliminating operations* Inlining the body of foe eliminates most of the operations in the calling sequence. This includes saving and restoring registers, establishing addressability, and performing the jumps or branches to transfer control. Some variable accesses may become simpler (for example, array values accessed through a dope vector).

Of course, inline substitution succeeds in improving the code only to the extent that the optimizer and code generator can capitalize on these opportunities. The potential pitfalls include problems from increased code size and increased demand for registers.

(Inline substitution eliminates the save/restore behavior in the calling sequence, which breaks up the flow of values across the call site. This "splitting" action changes the register-allocation problem. If the call occurs in a region where demand for registers is high, inlining can make matters worse and induce additional register spills. Due to some of the quirks of register spilling, demand at the call site can induce spills in other parts of the program.)

8.8 SUMMARY AND PERSPECTIVE

The optimizer in a modern compiler contains a collection of techniques that try to improve the performance of the compiled code. Most optimization tries to speed up the executable code. For some applications, other measures, such as code size or power consumption, are important. This chapter has examined redundancy elimination in depth and used it to explore some of the issues that arise in an optimizer.

Optimizations improve the performance of programs by tailoring general translation schemes to the specific details of the code at hand. The transformations in an optimizer try to remove the overhead introduced in support of source-language abstractions, including data structures, control structures, and error checking. They try to recognize special cases that have efficient implementations and rewrite the code to realize those savings. They try to match the resource needs of the program against the actual resources available on the processor, including functional units, the finite storage at each level in the memory hierarchy (registers, cache, translation lookaside buffers, and memory), the various bandwidths for moving data, and instruction-level parallelism.

Before the optimizer can apply any transformation, it must determine that the proposed rewrite of the code is safe—that it preserves the code's original meaning. Typically, this requires that the optimizer analyze the code. In the value-numbering methods, the process of constructing a hash key and performing the lookup ensures that an operation that "hits" in the value table must duplicate an operation encountered earlier in the block or in a preceding block. In global redundancy elimination, the optimizer computes available expressions to discover which expressions must be available on entry to each block—and can, therefore, be replaced with copy operations.

Once it has determined that applying a transformation is safe, the optimizer must decide whether or not it improves the code. For the forms of redundancy elimination described in this chapter, the compiler assumes, without deep analysis, that they improve the code. This assumption has three critical components, as follows: (1) a copy is at least as cheap as performing the original operation; (2) most of the copies that redundancy elimination adds are later eliminated; and (3) redundancy elimination does not increase demand for registers enough to overcome its benefits. If all these assumptions hold, and if the code contains redundant expressions, then redundancy elimination, in any of its forms, improves the code.

This chapter introduced many of the terms and issues that arise in optimization. The interested reader is referred to the chapters on data-flow analysis (Chapter 9) and scalar optimization (Chapter 10) for more material on the subject.

CHAPTER NOTES

The example in Section 8.2 comes from the basic linear algebra subroutines that appear in the LINPACK library [123]. The discussion hints that loop unrolling has other effects. Kennedy showed that the compiler can use unrolling to eliminate register-to-register copies in a loop [202]; Cooper and Waterman showed that unrolling can change power consumption on some processors [102].

The opportunity for improving code through finding and eliminating redundancies was recognized quite early. Ershov achieved some of these effects in a system in the 1950s [131]. Floyd mentioned the potential for improvement, as well as the impact that using commutativity might have [143].

Local value numbering is usually credited to Balke in the late 1960s [15, 86]. The extension to EBBs is natural and has, undoubtedly, been done in many compilers. The specific algorithms for superlocal and dominator-based value numbering that we present are due to Simpson [306, 50]. (See the notes in Chapter 9 about dominators.)

Cocke described the use of available expressions to perform global common-subexpression elimination [82]. That paper clearly decomposes the optimization into an analysis problem followed by a transformation. Subsequent work has refined and improved the notion of redundancy elimination based on availability. See, for example, the description of lazy code motion in Section 10.3.2.

Code replication is an old idea [15]. Block cloning has been used to improve scheduling [190] and redundancy elimination [41]. Inline substitution has been widely used and studied [111, 290, 93].

CHAPTER 9

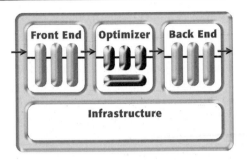

Data-Flow Analysis

9.1 INTRODUCTION

As we saw in Chapter 8, optimization is the process of analyzing a program and transforming it in ways that improve its run-time behavior. Before the compiler can change the code, it must locate points in the program where changing the code is likely to improve it, *and* the compiler must prove that changing the code at those points is safe. Both tasks require a deeper understanding of the code than the compiler's front end typically derives. To gather the information needed to locate opportunities and to justify optimizations, compilers use some form of static analysis.

In general, static analysis involves reasoning, at compile time, about what happens at run time, including how values flow at run time and what values variables can take on at run time. In simple cases, this can produce precise results—the compiler can know exactly what will happen when the code executes. If it can derive precise information, the compiler might replace the run-time evaluation of an expression or function with an immediate load of the result. On the other hand, if the code reads values from any external source, involves even modest amounts of control flow, or encounters any ambiguous memory references (from pointers, array references, or call-by-reference parameters), then analyzing the code becomes much harder and the results of the analysis are less precise.

In Chapter 8, we developed a series of techniques to find and eliminate redundancies—operations that must produce the same result. In some cases, the compiler knew the value of the result and could simply replace the computation with its value. In other cases, the compiler could not know the value, but could still improve the code by eliminating redundant operations. All these methods were driven by static analysis.

The local and superlocal value-numbering algorithms derive reasonably precise information about the flow of values in straight-line code (Sections 8.3.2 and 8.5.1). They examine the operations, in order, and record their potential effects. A large part of the precision of these methods comes directly from the fact that these algorithms handle only limited kinds of control flow. This same fact limits the regions over which they operate.

The dominator-based value-numbering algorithm (DVN) analyzes and improves larger regions of code (Section 8.5.2). Control flow is a limiting factor in the analysis. When DVN processes a block with multiple predecessors, it must discard any information about blocks that lie between the current block and its immediate dominator. For the same reason, DVN can never recognize a redundancy that is carried around the back edge that closes a loop.

Global common-subexpression elimination based on available expressions takes a different approach (Section 8.6). It performs data-flow analysis and uses the resulting knowledge to replace redundant evaluations with references to earlier computations. It handles arbitrary control flow but is more limited in the kinds of redundancies that it can detect. The set-based analysis of available expressions cannot track values through assignments. It does not lend itself to recognizing and simplifying algebraic identities.

As we have seen, the compiler can perform static analyses over different scopes. Local value numbering performs local analysis. The computation of EXPRKILL sets in available expressions is also local. Many specialized analyses are performed on loop nests. The best-known static analysis techniques are global techniques that operate on an entire procedure. Larger scopes are possible: interprocedural analysis techniques derive information about the impact that executing a procedure call has on the run-time environment of the calling procedure. Some problems require interprocedural analysis: for example, any reasonably sophisticated analysis of pointer values must look across procedure boundaries.

This chapter explores the most common form of static analysis—data-flow analysis—in more detail. Compilers use data-flow analysis to drive optimization and code generation. Section 9.2 presents a more detailed treatment of the iterative algorithm for solving data-flow problems. Along the way, it introduces additional data-flow problems that compilers have used to find safe and profitable opportunities for transformations. Section 9.3 discusses static single-assignment form, or SSA form, in greater detail. The SSA form of a program encodes both control flow and data flow in a simple, intuitive way. It serves as the base on which many modern transformations and code-generation algorithms build. The advanced topics section examines issues in data-flow analysis that arise from unstructured control flow, from the use of pointers and arrays, and from the modular decomposition of programs.

9.2 ITERATIVE DATA-FLOW ANALYSIS

In Chapter 8, we saw that moving from a regional algorithm for redundancy elimination to a global algorithm required the use of a global analysis phase. The compiler had to compute an AVAIL set for each block in the control-flow graph (CFG) before it could transform any of the blocks. The safety of the transformation depended on the accuracy of the AVAIL sets, and those sets relied on facts that the analyzer could derive only by looking at the entire procedure.

Computing available expressions is a form of *data-flow analysis*—that is, compile-time reasoning about the run-time flow of values. Data-flow analysis consists of solving a set of equations, posed over a graphical representation of the code, to discover facts about what can occur when a program runs. In an optimizing compiler, the primary uses for data-flow analysis are to locate opportunities for optimization—places where the compiler can apply some transformation—and to prove that applying a transformation at some point in the code is safe.

Data-flow analysis has also been used to help programmers better understand their programs. Analysis to locate data-flow anomalies suggests situations that are likely the result of logical flaws in a program. Examples include use of an undefined variable and definition of a variable that is never used. The appearance of either condition suggests a problem with the program's logic.

9.2.1 Live Variables

As a second detailed example of a data-flow analysis problem, consider finding *live variables*. A variable v is *live* at point p if and only if there is a path from p to a use of v along which v is not redefined. Compilers use live-variable information in a number of ways.

STATIC VERSUS DYNAMIC ANALYSIS

The notion of static analysis leads directly to the question, what about dynamic analysis? By definition static analysis tries to estimate, at compile time, what will happen at run time. In many situations, the compiler cannot tell what will happen, even though the answer might be obvious with knowledge of one or more run-time values.

Consider, for example, the C fragment

```
x = y * z + 12;
* p = 0;
q = y * z + 13;
```

It contains a redundant expression $(y * z)$ if and only if p does not contain the address of either y or z. At compile time, the value of p and the address of y and z may be unknowable. At run time, they are known and can be tested. Testing these values at run time would allow the code to avoid recomputing $y * z$, where compile-time analysis might be unable to answer the question.

However, the cost of testing whether p = &y or p = &z or neither and acting on the result is likely to exceed the cost of recomputing $y * z$. For dynamic analysis to make sense, it must be a priori profitable—that is, the savings must exceed the cost of performing the analysis. This happens in some cases; in most cases, it does not. In contrast, the cost of static analysis can be amortized over multiple runs of the executable code, so it is more attractive, in general.

- Live-variable information plays a critical role in global register allocation (see Section 13.5). The register allocator need not keep values in registers unless they are live; when a value makes the transition from being live to being not live, the allocator can reuse its register for another purpose.

- Live-variable information is used to improve the SSA construction; a value does not need a ϕ-function in any block where it is not live. Using liveliness information in this way can significantly reduce the number of ϕ-functions that the compiler must insert when building the SSA form of a program.

- The compiler can use live information to detect references to uninitialized variables. If some variable v is live on entry to the procedure, then a path exists from the entry n_0 to a use of v along which v is not assigned a value. If v is a local variable, this path represents a way to reference v when it has not been assigned a value.

- Finally, live-variable information can be used directly to drive transformations. For example, a value that is no longer live need not be stored back to memory (a transformation called *useless-store elimination*).

Liveness is a property of variables, either source-level variables or compiler-generated temporary names, where availability is a property of expressions. Thus, the domain of live analysis is different than that of available expressions.

Equations for Live Variables

To compute live-variable information, the compiler can annotate each node n in a CFG with a set, LIVEOUT(n), that contains the name of every variable that is live on exit from n. These sets are defined by the following equations:

$$\text{LIVEOUT}(n_f) = \emptyset$$

$$\text{LIVEOUT}(n) = \bigcup_{m \in succ(n)} \text{UEVAR}(m) \cup (\text{LIVEOUT}(m) \cap \overline{\text{VARKILL}(m)})$$

Here, UEVAR(m) contains the upward-exposed variables in m—those variables that are used in m before any redefinition in m. VARKILL(m) contains all the variables that are defined in m, and n_f is the exit node of the CFG, and the overline on a set such as VARKILL indicates its logical complement.

The equation encodes the definition in an intuitive way. LIVEOUT(n) is just the union of those variables that are live on input to some block m that follows n. The definition requires that a value be live on some path, not on all paths. Thus, the contributions of the successors of n in the CFG are unioned together to form LIVEOUT(n). The contribution of a specific successor m of n is:

$$\text{UEVAR}(m) \cup (\text{LIVEOUT}(m) \cap \overline{\text{VARKILL}(m)}).$$

A variable, v, is live on entry to m under one of two conditions. It can be referenced in m before it is redefined in m, in which case $v \in \text{UEVAR}(m)$. It can be live on exit from m and pass unscathed through m because m does not redefine it, in which case $v \in \text{LIVEOUT}(m) \cap \overline{\text{VARKILL}(m)}$. Combining these two sets, with $\cup$, gives the necessary contribution of m to $\text{LIVEOUT}(n)$. To compute $\text{LIVEOUT}(n)$, the analyzer combines the contributions of all n's successors.

To compute LIVEOUT sets, the compiler can use a three-step algorithm.

1. Build a CFG. This involves traversing the IR version of the code, discovering basic blocks, and instantiating nodes and edges to represent the blocks and the transitions among them. Figure 9.1 shows this algorithm.

2. Gather the initial information for each block. Typically, the analyzer must traverse the block and perform some simple computations. For LIVEOUT, this involves computing UEVAR and VARKILL in a backward walk over each block. This computation appears in the left column of Figure 9.2.

3. Use an iterative fixed-point algorithm to propagate information around the CFG. At each node, the algorithm evaluates the data-flow equation. It halts when the information stops changing. The right column of Figure 9.2 shows one such algorithm.

Each step requires a deeper explanation.

Differences Between AVAIL and LIVEOUT

Comparing the equations for AVAIL and LIVEOUT reveals some fundamental differences between the two problems. The AVAIL set for a block depends on its predecessors in the CFG, while the LIVEOUT set for a block depends on its CFG successors. We call available expressions a *forward* problem because information flows forward along the CFG edges. Similarly, live variables is a *backward* problem because information flows backward along the CFG edges.

The equations for AVAIL combine the contributions of different paths using intersection. Thus, an expression is available on entry to n if and only if it is available along *all paths* leading to n. The computation of LIVEOUT sets combines the contributions of different paths using union. Thus, any variable that is live along *any path* leading from block n is live on exit from n. Data-flow problems are sometimes characterized as *any path* problems or *all paths* problems.

```
                                            for i ← 1 to next - 1
                                              j ← Leader[i] + 1
                                              while (j ≤ n and op_j ∉ Leader)
                                                j ← j + 1
                                              j ← j - 1
                                              Last[i] ← j

                                              if op_j is "cbr r_k→l_1,l_2" then
                   next ← 1                      add edge from j to node for l_1
                   Leader[next++] ← 1            add edge from j to node for l_2

                   for i ← 1 to n             else if op_j is "jumpI→l_1" then
                     if op_i has a label l_i then  add edge from j to node for l_1
                       Leader[next++] ← i
                       create a CFG node for l_i  else if op_j is "jump→r_1" then
                                                add edges from j to all other nodes

                   Finding Leaders              Finding Last & Adding Edges
```

FIGURE 9.1   Building a Control-Flow Graph

Building the Control-Flow Graph

At its simplest, the CFG identifies the beginning and the end of each basic block and connects the resulting blocks with edges that describe the possible transfers of control among blocks. Initially, let's assume that the CFG builder receives, as input, a simple, linear IR that represents a procedure in a classic, Algol-like language. At the end of this section, we briefly explore some of the complications that can arise in CFG construction.

To begin, the compiler must find the beginning and the end of each basic block. In a linear IR, the initial operation of a block is sometimes called a *leader*. An operation is a leader if it is the first operation in the procedure, *or* if it has a label that is, potentially, the target of some branch. The compiler can identify all the leaders in a single pass over the IR, shown on the left-hand side of Figure 9.1. It iterates over the operations in the program, in order, finds the labelled statements, and records them as leaders.[1]

The second pass finds every operation that ends a block. It assumes that every block ends with a branch or a jump and that branches specify labels for both outcomes—a "branch taken" label and a "branch not taken" label. This simplifies the handling of blocks and allows the compiler's back end to

---

1. If the code contains labels that are not used as branch targets, this may unnecessarily split blocks. A more complex algorithm would only add branch and jump targets to the leader set. If the code contains any ambiguous jumps—that is, a jump to an address in a register—then it must include all labelled statements as leaders anyway.

choose which path will be the "fall through" case of a branch. (For the moment, assume branches have no delay slots.)

To find the end of each block, the algorithm iterates through the blocks, in order of their appearance in the *Leader* array. It walks forward through the IR until it finds the leader of the following block. The operation immediately before that leader ends the current block. The algorithm records that operation's index in Last[i], so that the pair ⟨Leader[i],Last[i]⟩ describes block i. It adds the needed edges to the CFG.

As we assumed in Chapter 5, the CFG should have a unique entry node n_0 and a unique exit node n_f. The underlying code should have this shape. If it does not, a simple postpass over the graph can create n_0 and n_f.

Complications in CFG Construction

Features of the IR, the target architecture, and even the source language can complicate this process. For example, an ambiguous jump—ILOC's jump operation—may force the compiler to add an edge from the jump to every labelled block in the procedure. This can add edges to the CFG that never occur at run time, degrade the quality of the data-flow information that the compiler derives, and reduce the effectiveness of optimization. In general, the compiler writer should avoid creating ambiguous jumps when the targets can be known, even if this requires extra analysis during IR generation. The ILOC examples in this book avoid using the jump-to-register operation, jump, in favor of the immediate jump, jumpI.

The compiler writer can improve this situation, to some extent, by including features in the IR that record potential jump targets. ILOC includes the tbl pseudo-operation to let the compiler record the potential targets of an ambiguous jump. Anytime that the compiler generates a jump, it should follow the branch with a set of tbl operations that record the possible targets for the branch. When it builds the CFG, the compiler can use these hints to limit the number of spurious edges. Any jump followed by a set of tbls gets an edge to each block named in those tbl operations. Any jump that has no tbls generates an edge to each labelled block.

In the later stages of compilation, the compiler may need to build a CFG from target-machine code. At this point, the target architecture can complicate the process. The algorithm in Figure 9.1 assumes that all leaders, except the first, are labelled. If the target machine has fall-through branches, the algorithm must be extended to recognize unlabelled statements that receive control on a fall-through path. If the code has been scheduled and it models branch-delay slots, the problem becomes harder. A labelled statement that sits in a branch delay slot is a member of two distinct blocks. The compiler can cure this by replication—creating a new (unlabelled) copy of the operations in the delay slots.

Delay slots also complicate finding the end of a block. If a branch or jump can occur in a branch delay slot, the CFG builder must walk forward from the leader to find the block-ending branch—the first branch it encounters. Branches in the delay slot of a block-ending branch can, themselves, be pending on entry to the target block. They can split the target block and force creation of new blocks and new edges. The analysis required to create a CFG in these circumstances is much more complex.

Some languages, such as Pascal and Algol, allow jumps to labels outside the current procedure. This transfer can be modelled in the current procedure with a branch to a CFG node created to represent the target. The complication arises on the other end of the branch, where a transfer from an unknown source can reach a block. For this reason, nonlocal gotos are usually restricted to lexically nested procedures, where the compiler can see the CFGs for all related procedures at once. In that situation, it can insert the needed edge and model the effects correctly.

Gathering Initial Information

For LiveOut, the analyzer must compute the UEVar and VarKill sets for each block. A single pass can compute both. For each block, the analyzer initializes these sets to $\emptyset$. Next, it walks the block, in order from top to bottom, and updates both UEVar and VarKill to reflect the impact of each operation. The left side of Figure 9.2 shows the details of this computation.

for i ← 1 to number of operations
  assume op_i is "x ← y op z"
    if i ∈ **Leader** *then*
      b ← block number for i
      UEVar(b) ← $\emptyset$
      VarKill(b) ← $\emptyset$
    if y ∉ VarKill(b) *then*
      UEVar(b) ← UEVar(b) ∪ {y}
    if z ∉ VarKill(b) *then*
      UEVar(b) ← UEVar(b) ∪ {z}
    VarKill(b) ← VarKill(b) ∪ {x}

  Gathering Initial Information

N ← number of blocks − 1
for i ← 0 to N
  LiveOut(i) ← $\emptyset$
changed ← true
while (changed)
  changed ← false
  for i ← 0 to N
    recompute LiveOut(i)
    if LiveOut(i) *changed then*
      changed ← true

  Solving the Equations

FIGURE 9.2   Iterative Live Analysis

This process is simpler than the corresponding part of the AVAIL computation because LIVEOUT uses VARKILL rather than EXPRKILL. Computing EXPRKILL from VARKILL adds significantly to the cost of local analysis in the AVAIL computation (see Figure 8.8 for comparison).

Consider the code fragment shown in Figure 9.3. It consists of a single loop that contains a nested if-then-else construct. Many of the details in the code have been abstracted away. To compute LIVEOUT sets for the example, the compiler would first construct the CFG and compute the UEVAR and $\overline{\text{VARKILL}}$ sets for each block. By inspection, we can see that it would generate the following sets:

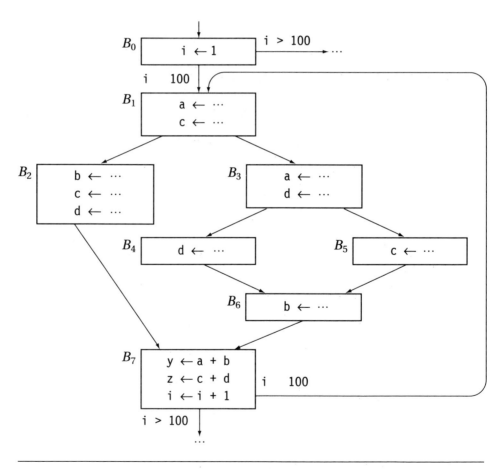

FIGURE 9.3   Example LIVEOUT Computation

	B_0	B_1	B_2	B_3	B_4	B_5	B_6	B_7
UEVar	$\emptyset$	$\emptyset$	$\emptyset$	$\emptyset$	$\emptyset$	$\emptyset$	$\emptyset$	$\{a,b,c,d,i\}$
VarKill	$\{a,b,c,d,y,z\}$	$\{b,d,i,y,z\}$	$\{a,i,y,z\}$	$\{b,c,i,y,z\}$	$\{a,b,c,i,y,z\}$	$\{a,b,d,i,y,z\}$	$\{a,c,d,i,y,z\}$	$\{a,b,c,d\}$

Because we have elided the right-hand sides of most opeartions, the UEVar sets are unusally sparse. With all the details, the UEVar sets for most blocks would be nonempty.

Solving the Equations for LiveOut

To solve for the values of the LiveOut sets, the compiler writer can adapt the iterative algorithm from Figure 8.9. The Avail-specific code can be replaced with equivalent code for LiveOut; the resulting iterative algorithm computes a fixed-point, as did the earlier algorithm.

The right side of Figure 9.2 shows one iterative scheme for solving the LiveOut equations. It initializes all of the LiveOut sets to $\emptyset$. Next, it computes the LiveOut set for each block, in order from B_0 to B_7. It repeatedly computes the LiveOut sets until they stop changing. This produces the following values in the LiveOut sets. The first row shows initial values.

Iteration	LiveOut(n)							
	B_0	B_1	B_2	B_3	B_4	B_5	B_6	B_7
0	$\emptyset$	$\emptyset$	$\emptyset$	$\emptyset$	$\emptyset$	$\emptyset$	$\emptyset$	$\emptyset$
1	$\emptyset$	$\emptyset$	$\{a,b,c,d,i\}$	$\emptyset$	$\emptyset$	$\emptyset$	$\{a,b,c,d,i\}$	$\emptyset$
2	$\emptyset$	$\{a,i\}$	$\{a,b,c,d,i\}$	$\emptyset$	$\{a,c,d,i\}$	$\{a,c,d,i\}$	$\{a,b,c,d,i\}$	$\{i\}$
3	$\{i\}$	$\{a,i\}$	$\{a,b,c,d,i\}$	$\{a,c,d,i\}$	$\{a,c,d,i\}$	$\{a,c,d,i\}$	$\{a,b,c,d,i\}$	$\{i\}$
4	$\{i\}$	$\{a,c,i\}$	$\{a,b,c,d,i\}$	$\{a,c,d,i\}$	$\{a,c,d,i\}$	$\{a,c,d,i\}$	$\{a,b,c,d,i\}$	$\{i\}$
5	$\{i\}$	$\{a,c,i\}$	$\{a,b,c,d,i\}$	$\{a,c,d,i\}$	$\{a,c,d,i\}$	$\{a,c,d,i\}$	$\{a,b,c,d,i\}$	$\{i\}$

Iteration 1 produces empty LIVEOUT sets for every block except B_7's predecessors. (Only B_7 has a nonempty UEVAR set.) Computing

$$\text{UEVAR}(B_7) \cup (\text{LIVEOUT}(B_7) \cap \overline{\text{VARKILL}(B_7)})$$

produces the set $\{a,b,c,d,i\}$. Both LIVEOUT(B_2) and LIVEOUT(B_6) have this value at the end of iteration 1. Iteration 2 fills in more of LIVEOUT sets. From B_2, LIVEOUT(B_1) gets $\{a,i\}$. Both B_4 and B_5 get $\{a,c,d,i\}$ from B_6. Finally, LIVEOUT(B_7) gets $\{i\}$ from B_1; the computation uses the most recent value for LIVEOUT(B_1).

Iteration 3 propagates $\{i\}$ into LIVEOUT(B_0). LIVEOUT(B_3) gets $\{a,c,d,i\}$. The edge $\langle B_3, B_4 \rangle$ contributes $\{a,c,i\}$, while the edge $\langle B_3, B_5 \rangle$ adds $\{a,d,i\}$. Thus, LIVEOUT(B_3) is identical to LIVEOUT(B_4) and LIVEOUT(B_5), but B_4 and B_5 each pass on only a subset of their own LIVEOUT sets.

Iteration 4 adds $\{c\}$ to LIVEOUT(B_1), from the edge $\langle B_1, B_3 \rangle$. Finally, iteration 5 recomputes all the LIVEOUT sets without changing any of them, so the analyzer exits the `while` loop and halts.

9.2.2 Properties of the Iterative LIVEOUT Solver

Data-flow analysis similar to the LIVEOUT computation form the analytical backbone of scalar optimizing compilers. Many techniques have been developed to solve data-flow problems. We focus on the iterative algorithm because of its speed, its robust behavior, and the fact that it has a well-understood, underlying theory. This section sketches answers to three critical questions about the iterative solver for LIVEOUT:

1. Does the analysis terminate?

2. What answer does the analysis compute?

3. How fast is the analysis?

The compiler writer should consider each of these questions in designing analysis passes.

Termination

Iterative live-variable analysis halts because the sets grow monotonically throughout the computation. The algorithm initializes each LIVEOUT set to $\emptyset$.

Careful reasoning about the *while* loop shows that the LiveOut sets can become larger but can never shrink. The size of any LiveOut set is bounded by the number of variables, $|V|$. In the example from Figure 9.3, V is $\{a,b,c,d,i,y,z\}$ and every LiveOut set is either V or a proper subset of V.

Because $|V|$ is bounded, the sequence of LiveOut sets that the algorithm can compute is bounded. Thus, the iteration must eventually halt. When it halts, the solver has found a fixed point for this particular instance of the LiveOut computation.

Correctness

Recall the definition of a live variable: A variable v is *live* at point p if and only if there is a path from p to a use of v along which v is not redefined. Liveness is defined in terms of paths in the graph. A path must exist from p to a use of v that contains no definitions of v—we call this a v-clear path.

LiveOut(n) contains v if and only if v is live at the end of block n. To form LiveOut(n), the algorithm computes the contribution to LiveOut(n) of each successor of n in the CFG. It combines these contributions using union because $v \in \text{LiveOut}(n)$ if v is live on *any* path leaving n. How does this local computation over individual edges relate to the property (liveness) defined over all paths?

The LiveOut sets computed by the iterative algorithm form a fixed-point solution to the equations. The theory of iterative data-flow analysis, which is beyond the scope of this text, assures us that a fixed point exists for these particular equations and that the fixed point is unique [199]. The all-paths solution of the definition is also a fixed point for the equations, called the *meet-over-all-paths solution*. The uniqueness of the fixed point guarantees us that the sets computed by the iterative algorithm are identical to the meet-over-all-paths solution called for by the definition.

Efficiency

The fixed-point solution to the LiveOut equations for a specific procedure is independent of the order in which the solver computes the individual sets—a consequence of uniqueness. Thus, the compiler writer is free to choose an order that improves the analyzer's running time.

A *reverse postorder* (RPO) traversal of the graph is particularly effective for the iterative algorithm. A postorder traversal visits as many of a node's children as possible, in a consistent order, before visiting the node. (In a cyclic graph,

$N \leftarrow$ *number of blocks* -1
for $i \leftarrow 0$ *to* N
    LIVEOUT(i) $\leftarrow \emptyset$
changed $\leftarrow$ *true*
while (changed)
    changed $\leftarrow$ *false*
    for $i \leftarrow 1$ *to* N
    $j \leftarrow$ *Reverse Preorder[i]*
    LIVEOUT(j) $= \bigwedge\limits_{k \in succ(j)} f_{\langle j, k \rangle}$ (LIVEOUT(k))
        if LIVEOUT(j) *has changed then*
            changed $\leftarrow$ *true*

FIGURE 9.4   Round-Robin, PostOrder Solver for LIVEOUT

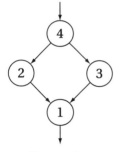

Postorder

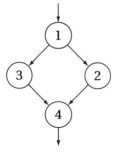

Reverse Postorder

a node's child may also be its ancestor.) An RPO traversal is the opposite—it visits as many of a node's predecessors as possible before visiting the node itself. A node's RPO number is simply $n + 1$ minus its postorder number, where n is the number of nodes in the graph.

For a forward problem, such as AVAIL, the iterative algorithm should use an RPO computed on the CFG. For a backward data-flow problem, such as LIVEOUT, the algorithm should use an RPO computed on the reverse CFG. (The reverse CFG is just the CFG with its edges reversed, so that n_f is its entry node and n_0 is its exit node.) The RPO of the reverse CFG is equivalent to reverse preorder on the original CFG.

If the iterative algorithm uses the appropriate RPO traversal, it can often avoid the need to initialize some of the sets. For example, in live analysis, it suffices to initialize LIVEOUT(n_f) to $\emptyset$. In a reverse postorder traversal of the CFG, the solver will compute the LIVEOUT set of every node, except n_f, before the computation at any of its reverse preorder successors tries to use the set's value.

To see the impact of ordering, consider the impact of an RPO traversal on the example LIVEOUT computation from Figure 9.3. One RPO numbering for the reverse CFG is

Block	B_0	B_1	B_2	B_3	B_4	B_5	B_6	B_7
RPO Number	8	7	2	6	4	5	3	1

Visiting the nodes in this order produces the following iterations:

	LiveOut(n)							
Iteration	B_0	B_1	B_2	B_3	B_4	B_5	B_6	B_7
0	$\emptyset$	$\emptyset$	$\emptyset$	$\emptyset$	$\emptyset$	$\emptyset$	$\emptyset$	$\emptyset$
1	$\{i\}$	$\{a,c,i\}$	$\{a,b,c,d,i\}$	$\{a,c,d,i\}$	$\{a,c,d,i\}$	$\{a,c,d,i\}$	$\{a,b,c,d,i\}$	$\emptyset$
2	$\{i\}$	$\{a,c,i\}$	$\{a,b,c,d,i\}$	$\{a,c,d,i\}$	$\{a,c,d,i\}$	$\{a,c,d,i\}$	$\{a,b,c,d,i\}$	$\{i\}$
3	$\{i\}$	$\{a,c,i\}$	$\{a,b,c,d,i\}$	$\{a,c,d,i\}$	$\{a,c,d,i\}$	$\{a,c,d,i\}$	$\{a,b,c,d,i\}$	$\{i\}$

The algorithm halts in three iterations, rather than the five iterations required with a traversal ordered strictly by block number. Comparing this table against the earlier computation, we can see why. On the first iteration, the algorithm computed correct LiveOut sets for all nodes except B_7. It took a second iteration for B_7 because of the back edge—the edge from B_7 to B_1. The third iteration is needed to recognize that the algorithm has reached its fixed point.

9.2.3 Limitations on Data-Flow Analysis

There are limits to what a compiler can learn from data-flow analysis. In some cases, the limits arise from the assumptions underlying the analysis. In other cases, the limits arise from features of the language being analyzed. To make informed decisions, the compiler writer must understand what data-flow analysis can do and what it cannot do.

When it computes the LiveOut set for a node n in the CFG, the iterative algorithm uses the sets LiveOut, UEVar, and VarKill for all of n's successors in the CFG. This implicitly assumes that execution can reach all of those successors; in practice, one or more of them may not be reachable. Consider the code fragment shown in Figure 9.5 along with its CFG.

The assignment to x in B_0 is live because of the use of x in B_1 The assignment to x in B_2 kills that value. If B_1 never executes, then x's value from B_0 is not live past the comparison with y, and x $\notin$ LiveOut(B_0). If the compiler can prove that the test (y $<$ x) is always false, then control will never transfer to block B_1 and the assignment to z will never execute. If the call to f has no side effects,

```
x ← f(17)
if (y < x) then
    z ← x + 3
    x ← 0
```

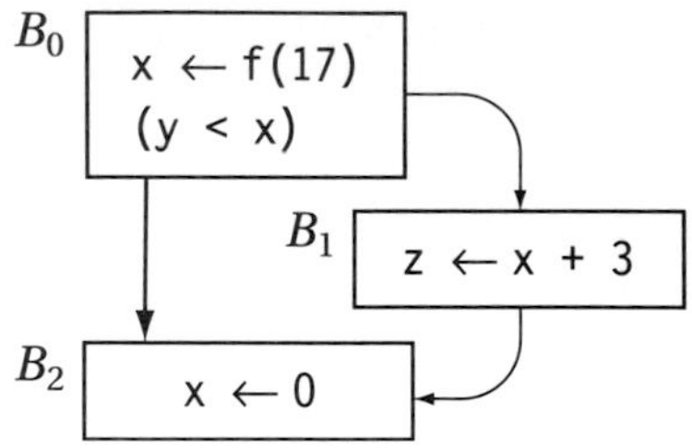

FIGURE 9.5   Control Flow Limits the Precision of Data-Flow Analysis

the entire statement is useless and need not be executed. Since the test's result is known, the compiler can completely eliminate both blocks B_0 and B_1.

The equations for LiveOut, however, take the union over all successors of the block. Thus, the analyzer computes LiveOut(B_0) as

$$\text{UEVar}(B_1) \cup (\text{LiveOut}(B_1) \cap \overline{\text{VarKill}(B_1)}) \; \bigcup$$

$$\text{UEVar}(B_2) \cup (\text{LiveOut}(B_2) \cap \overline{\text{VarKill}(B_2)})$$

All data-flow analysis techniques assume that all paths through the CFG can actually be taken. Thus, the information that they compute summarizes the possible data-flow events, assuming that each path can be taken. This limits the precision of the resulting information; we say that the information is precise "up to symbolic execution." With this assumption, x is live on exit from B_0 and both B_0 and B_1 must be preserved.

Another way that imprecision creeps into the results of data-flow analysis comes from the treatment of arrays, pointers, and procedure calls. An array reference, such as A[i,j,k], refers to a single element of A. However, without analysis that reveals the values of i, j, and k, the compiler cannot tell which element is being accessed. For this reason, compilers have traditionally lumped together all references to an array A. Thus, a use of A[x,y,z] counts as a use of A, and a definition of A[c,d,e] counts as a definition of A.

Some care must be taken, however, to avoid making too strong an inference. The compiler, knowing that its information on arrays is imprecise, must interpret that information conservatively. Thus, if the goal of the analysis is to determine where a value is no longer live (that is, the value must have been killed), a definition of A[i,j,k] does not kill the value of A. If the goal is to recognize where a value *might* not survive, then a definition of A[i,j,k] *might* redefine any element of A.

Naming Sets in Data-Flow Equations

In writing the data-flow equations for classic problems, we have renamed many of the sets that contain local information. The original papers used more intuitive set names. Unfortunately, those names clash with each other across problems. For example, available expressions, live variables, reaching definitions, and very busy expressions all use some notion of a Kill set. These four problems, however, are defined over three distinct domains: expressions (Avail and VeryBust), definition points (Reaches), and variables (LiveOut). Thus, using Kill or Killed leads to confusion across problems.

The names that we have adopted encode both the domain and a hint as to the set's meaning. Thus, VarKill(n) contains the set of variables killed in block n, while ExprKill(n) contains the set of expressions killed in the same block. Similarly, UEVar(n) contains the set of upward-exposed variables in block n, while UEExpr(n) contains the set of upward-exposed expressions. While these names are somewhat awkward, they make explicit the distinction between the notion of kill used in available expressions (ExprKill) and the one used in reaching definitions (DefKill).

Pointers add another level of imprecision to the results of static analysis. Explicit arithmetic on pointers makes matters worse. Without an analysis that specifically tracks the values of pointers, the compiler must interpret an assignment to a pointer-based variable as a potential definition for every variable that the pointer might reach. Type safety can limit the set of objects potentially defined by an assignment through a pointer; a pointer to t can only be used to modify objects of type t. Without analysis of pointer values or a guarantee of type safety, assignment to a pointer-based variable can force the analyzer to assume that every variable has been modified. In practice, this often prevents the compiler from keeping the value of a pointer-based variable in a register across any pointer-based assignment. Unless the compiler can specifically prove that the pointer used in the assignment cannot point to the memory location corresponding to the value in the register, this is the only safe course.

In practice, the complexity of pointer analysis keeps many compilers from using registers to hold the values of pointer-based variables. Usually, some variables can be exempted from this treatment—such as a local variable whose address has never been explicitly taken. The alternative is to perform data-flow analysis aimed at disambiguating pointer-based references—reducing the set of possible variables that a pointer might reference at each point in the code.

Procedure calls provide a final source of imprecision. To model the data flow in the current procedure accurately, the compiler must understand, in detail, what the called procedure does to each variable that is accessible to both of them. The called procedure may, in turn, call other procedures. They will, of course, have their own potential impact.

Unless the compiler has accurate information that summarizes the effects of all the procedures in a program, it must estimate their worst-case behavior. While the specific assumptions vary from problem to problem, the general assumption is that the called procedure will both reference and modify every variable that it can address and that call-by-reference parameters create ambiguous references. Since few procedures actually behave in this fashion, this kind of assumption usually overestimates the impact of a procedure call. This introduces further imprecision into the results of data-flow analysis.

9.2.4 Other Data-Flow Problems

Compilers use data-flow analyses to prove the safety of applying transformations in particular situations. Thus, many distinct data-flow problems have been proposed, each to drive a particular optimization.

Available Expressions

Chapter 8 introduced the problem of discovering the set of expressions available at each point in the code. Available expressions is formulated as a forward data-flow problem computed over the domain of expressions computed in a program. The resulting AVAIL sets are used to drive global common-subexpression elimination.

Reaching Definitions

In some cases, the compiler needs to know where an operand was defined. If multiple paths in the CFG lead to the operation, then multiple definitions may provide the value of the operand. To find the set of definitions that reach a block, the compiler can compute *reaching definitions*. The domain of REACHES is the set of definition points in the procedure. A definition d of some variable v

reaches operation i if and only if i reads the value of v and there exists a v-clear path from d to l.

The compiler annotates each node n in the CFG with a set $\text{REACHES}(n)$, computed as a forward data-flow problem:

$$\text{REACHES}(n_0) = \emptyset$$

$$\text{REACHES}(n) \ = \ \bigcup_{m \,\in\, preds(n)} (\text{DEDEF}(m) \cup (\text{REACHES}(m) \cap \overline{\text{DEFKILL}(m)}))$$

$\text{DEDEF}(m)$ is the set of downward-exposed definitions in m—that is, those definitions in m for which the defined name is not subsequently redefined in m. $\text{DEFKILL}(m)$ contains *all* the definition points that are obscured by a definition of the same name in m—that is, $d \in \text{DEFKILL}(m)$ if d defines some name v and m contains a definition that also defines v. Thus $\overline{\text{DEFKILL}(m)}$ consists of the definition points that are not obscured in m.

DEDEF and DEFKILL are both defined over the set of definition points, but computing each of them requires a mapping from names (variables and compiler-generated temporaries) to definition points. Thus, gathering the initial information for reaching definitions is more complex than it is for live variables.

Very Busy Expressions

An expression e is considered *very busy* on exit from block n if e is evaluated and used along every path that leaves n, and evaluating e at the end of n would produce the same result as the first evaluation of e along each path leaving n. Very busy analysis is a backward data-flow problem over the domain of expressions.

$$\text{VERYBUST}(n_f) = \emptyset$$

$$\text{VERYBUST}(n) \ = \ \bigcap_{m \,\in\, succ(n)} (\text{UEEXPR}(m) \cup (\text{VERYBUST}(m) - \overline{\text{EXPRKILL}(m)}))$$

Here $\text{UEEXPR}(m)$ is the set of upward-exposed expressions—those used in m before they are killed. $\text{EXPRKILL}(m)$ is the set of expressions defined in m; it is the same set that appears in the equations for available expressions.

IMPLEMENTING DATA-FLOW FRAMEWORKS

The equations for many global data-flow problems show a striking similarity. For example, available expressions, live variables, reaching definitions, and very busy expressions all have propagation functions of the form

$$f(x) = c_1 \, op_1 \, (x \, op_2 \, c_2)$$

where c_1 and c_2 are constants determined by the actual code and op_1 and op_2 are standard set operations such as $\cup$, $\cap$, and $-$. This similarity shows up in the proofs that these problems have rapid iterative data-flow frameworks. It should also show up in their implementations.

The compiler writer can easily abstract away the details in which these problems differ and implement a single, parameterized analyzer. The analyzer needs functions to compute c_1 and c_2, implementations of the operators, and an indication of the problem's direction. In return, it produces the desired data-flow information.

This implementation strategy encourages code reuse. It hides the low-level details of the solver. At the same time, it creates a situation in which the compiler writer can profitably invest effort on optimizing the implementation. For example, a scheme that allows the framework to implement $f(x) = a \, op_1 \, (x \, op_2 \, b)$ as a single function may outperform an implementation that uses $f_1(x) = a \, op_1 x$ and $f_2(x) = x \, op_2 \, b$ and computes $f(x)$ as $f_1(f_2(x))$. This scheme lets all the client transformations benefit from optimizing set representations and operator implementations.

The compiler can use the results of this analysis to locate opportunities for *code hoisting*. If e is very busy at p, then the compiler can insert an evaluation of e at p and eliminate the first evaluation along each path that leaves p. This transformation shortens no path, but reduces the number of operations in the overall program. Thus, it reduces code space.

Constant Propagation

If the compiler can prove that some variable v always has the value c at point p in the code, then it can replace a use of v at p with c. This replacement lets the compiler specialize the code at p based on the value c. For example, if the compiler knows a loop's upper bound, it can often eliminate the comparison and branch needed to test for the case where the loop is never entered. To prove that v has value c at some point p, the compiler can perform global constant propagation.

The domain for this problem is the set of pairs $\langle v_i, c_i \rangle$, where v_i is a variable and c_i is either a constant or the special value $\perp$ that indicates an unknown value. The analysis annotates each node n in the CFG with a set CONSTANTS(n) that contains all the variable–value pairs that the compiler can prove to hold on entry to n. The CONSTANTS sets are defined as

$$\text{CONSTANTS}(n) \;=\; \bigwedge_{p \,\in\, preds(n)} F_p(\text{CONSTANTS}(p))$$

where $\wedge$ performs a pairwise meet on two sets of pairs, and $F_p(x)$ is a block-specific function that models the effects of p on a set of known constants x. Each of these requires a little more explanation. The initial value for each CONSTANTS set is $\emptyset$.

The meet operation compares two pairs $\langle v, c_1 \rangle$ and $\langle v, c_2 \rangle$ and produces a result as follows: if $c_1 = c_2$, then $\langle v, c_1 \rangle \wedge \langle v, c_2 \rangle$ is $\langle v, c_1 \rangle$; and if $c_1 \neq c_2$, then $\langle v, c_1 \rangle \wedge \langle v, c_2 \rangle$ is $\langle v, \perp \rangle$. (Notice that these rules produce $\langle v, \perp \rangle$ if either c_1 or c_2 is $\perp$.) Thus, if on one path entering n, v has the value 3 and on the other path v has the value 5, the compiler cannot assert any value for v on entry to n, so the analysis uses the value $\perp$ to indicate an unknown value. If both paths show v with the same value, say 13, $\wedge$ produces the pair $\langle v, 13 \rangle$.

The other critical part of the equation is the block-specific function F_p. In the other data-flow frameworks that we have seen, the block-specific effects are modelled with a small number of set operations. Given CONSTANTS(p), the algorithm computes the set that holds at the end of p by modelling each operation in the block as follows:

$\text{x} \leftarrow \text{y}$ *if* CONSTANTS(p) $= \{\langle \text{x}, c_1 \rangle, \langle \text{y}, c_2 \rangle, \ldots\}$ *then*

$\qquad$ CONSTANTS(p) $= (\text{CONSTANTS}(p) - \{\langle \text{x}, c_1 \rangle\}) \cup \{\langle \text{x}, c_2 \rangle\}$

$\text{x} \leftarrow \text{y } op \text{ z}$ *if* CONSTANTS(p) $= \{\langle \text{x}, c_1 \rangle, \langle \text{y}, c_2 \rangle, \langle \text{z}, c_3 \rangle \ldots\}$ *then*

$\qquad$ CONSTANTS(p) $= (\text{CONSTANTS}(p) - \{\langle \text{x}, c_1 \rangle\}) \cup \{\langle \text{x}, c_2 \ op \ c_3 \rangle\}$

where subtraction represents removal of an item from the set. Modelling each operation in the block, in order, produces the set of constants that hold at the end of the block. This, in turn, is used in the $\wedge$ operation that computes the CONSTANTS set for p's successor.

The compiler writer can extend the model to include special cases. If one operand in an operation is unknown and the other is known to be the zero or the identity element for the operator, the model can determine the resulting value. Many operators have zero or identity elements that the model can check.

The domain of CONSTANTS is large but finite. Because the value for a specific variable in a specific block's CONSTANTS set can only change twice (from unspecified to c_1 to $\perp$), the iterative algorithm runs quickly on instances of this problem, in practice.

The compiler can use the information in the CONSTANTS sets directly to improve the code. Operations whose arguments are all constants can be evaluated at compile time; any references to the resulting value can be converted to use a literal value. Constant values in tests may eliminate branches. Constant values in complex computations can create opportunities for simplification. Folding constants in place of references is one of the more profitable transformations that the compiler can apply. (See Sections 10.3.3 and 10.4.1 for simpler, stronger algorithms.)

9.3 STATIC SINGLE-ASSIGNMENT FORM

Over time, many different data-flow problems have been formulated. If each transformation uses its own idiosyncratic analysis, the amount of time and effort spent implementing, debugging, and maintaining the analysis passes can grow unreasonably large. To limit the number of analyses that the compiler writer must implement and that the compiler must run, it is desirable to use a single analysis to perform multiple transformations.

One strategy for implementing this "universal" analysis involves building a variant form of the program that encodes both data flow and control flow directly into the IR. Static single-assignment form (SSA), introduced in Sections 5.5 and 8.5.1, has this property. It can serve as the basis for a large set of transformations. From a single implementation that translates the code into SSA form, a compiler can perform many of the classic scalar optimizations.

Consider the various uses of the variable x in the code fragment shown on the left side of Figure 9.6. The gray lines show which definitions can reach each use of x. The right side of the figure shows the same fragment, rewritten to convert x to SSA form. Definitions of x have been renamed, with subscripts, to ensure that each definition has a unique SSA name. For simplicity, we have left the references to other variables unchanged.

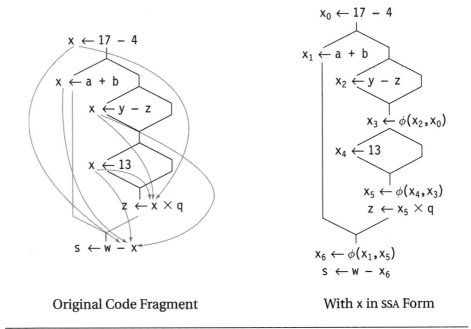

Original Code Fragment	With x in SSA Form

FIGURE 9.6   SSA: Encoding Control Flow into Data Flow

The SSA form of the code includes new assignments (to x_3, x_5, and x_6) that reconcile the distinct SSA names for x with the uses of x (in the assignments to s and z). These assignments ensure that, along each edge in the CFG, the current value of x has been assigned a unique name, independent of which path brought control to the edge. The right side of these assignments contains a special function, a ϕ-function, that combines the values from distinct edges.

A ϕ-function takes as arguments the SSA names for the values associated with each edge that enters the block. When control enters a block, all the ϕ-functions in the block execute, concurrently. They evaluate to the argument that corresponds to the edge along which control entered the block. Notationally, we write the arguments left-to-right to correspond to the edges left-to-right. On the printed page, this is easy. In an implementation, it requires some bookkeeping.

The SSA construction inserts a ϕ-function after each point in the CFG where multiple paths converge—each join point. At join points, distinct SSA names must be reconciled to a single name. After the entire procedure has been converted to SSA form, two rules hold: (1) each definition in the procedure creates a unique name, and (2) each use refers to a single definition. To transform a procedure into SSA form, the compiler must insert the appropriate ϕ-functions for each variable into the code, and it must rename variables with subscripts to make the two rules hold. This simple, two-step plan produces the basic SSA construction algorithm.

9.3.1 A Simple Method for Building SSA Form

To construct the SSA form of a program, the compiler must insert ϕ-functions at join points in the CFG, and it must rename variables and temporary values to conform with the rules that govern the SSA name space. The algorithm follows this outline.

1. *Inserting ϕ-functions*   At the start of each block that has multiple predecessors, insert a ϕ-function, such as y ← ϕ(y, y), for every name y that the code either defines or uses in the current procedure. The ϕ-function should have one argument for each predecessor block in the CFG. This rule inserts a ϕ-function in every case where one is needed. It also inserts many extraneous ϕ-functions.

   The algorithm can insert the ϕ-functions in arbitrary order. The definition of ϕ-functions requires that all the ϕ-functions at the top of a block execute concurrently—that is, they all read their input parameters simultaneously, then write their output values simultaneously. This lets the algorithm avoid many minor details that an ordering might introduce.

2. *Renaming*   After ϕ-functions have been inserted, the compiler can compute reaching definitions (see Section 9.2.4). Because the inserted ϕ-functions are definitions, they ensure that only one definition reaches any use. Next, it can rename each use—both variables and temporaries—to reflect the definition that reaches it. The compiler must sort out the definitions that reach each ϕ-function and make the names correspond to the paths along which they reach the block containing the ϕ-function. This requires some bookkeeping but is conceptually straightforward.

This algorithm constructs a correct SSA form for the program. Each variable is defined exactly once, and each reference uses the name of a distinct definition. However, the resulting SSA form has, potentially, many more ϕ-functions than are needed. The extra ϕ-functions are problematic. They decrease the precision of some kinds of analysis when performed over SSA form. They occupy space, so the compiler wastes memory representing ϕ-functions that are either redundant (that is, $x_j \leftarrow \phi(x_i, x_i)$) or are not live. They increase the cost of any algorithm that uses the resulting SSA form, since it must traverse all the extraneous ϕ-functions.

We call this version of SSA "*maximal SSA form*." To build SSA form with fewer ϕ-functions requires more work; in particular, the compiler must analyze the code to determine where potentially distinct values converge in the CFG. This computation relies on the notion of dominance that we first encountered in Section 8.5.2.

The next three subsections present, in detail, an algorithm to build *semipruned SSA form*—a version with fewer ϕ-functions. Section 9.3.2 presents a fast algorithm to compute the dominance information needed to guide the insertion of ϕ-functions. Section 9.3.3 gives an algorithm to insert ϕ-functions, and Section 9.3.4 shows how to rewrite variable names to complete the construction of SSA form. Section 9.3.5 discusses the difficulties that can arise in converting the code back into an executable form.

9.3.2 Dominance

The primary problem with maximal SSA form is that it contains too many ϕ-functions. To reduce their number, the compiler must determine more carefully where they are required. The key to doing this efficiently and effectively is dominance information. This section develops a data-flow framework that computes dominance and introduces the notion of a *dominance frontier*. The next section uses dominance frontiers to improve ϕ-function placement.

Computing Dominators

Dominance is one of the oldest ideas in compilation. In a CFG, node *i dominates* node *j* if every path from the entry node to *j* passes through *i*. Many methods have been proposed for computing dominance. In practice, a simple data-flow approach can perform as well as the more complex algorithms.

To formulate the dominance calculation as a data-flow problem, we have the compiler annotate each node with a DOM set. Formally, $i \in$ DOM (j) if and only if i dominates j. By definition, a node dominates itself, so $i \in$ DOM(i). The data-flow equations for the DOM computation are simple:

$$\text{DOM}(n) = \{n\} \cup \left(\bigcap_{m \in preds(n)} \text{DOM}(m) \right)$$

with the initial conditions that $\text{DOM}(n_0) = \{n_0\}$, and $\forall n \neq n_0$, $\text{DOM}(n) = N$, where N is the set of nodes in the CFG. From an implementation perspective, it may be more efficient to leave the sets, other than $\text{DOM}(n_0)$, initially empty and implement the intersection operator so that it omits empty sets.

This formulation is intuitive. $\text{DOM}(n)$ is simply the intersection of the DOM sets of n's predecessors, plus n itself. The intersection finds the common ancestors of n's predecessors. Any node $m \neq n$ that is not in the intersection cannot lie on every path from n_0 to n.

These equations for DOM can be solved with the iterative algorithm. It will quickly discover the unique fixed-point solution for an instance of the problem.

An Example Consider the CFG from Figure 9.3. It is captured, in summary form, in the upper left corner of Figure 9.7. The node labels form an RPO num-

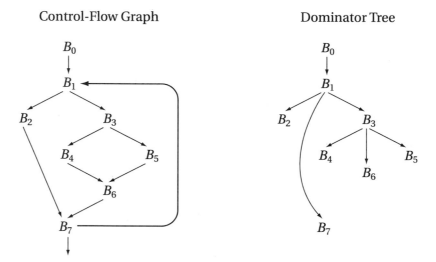

Control-Flow Graph   Dominator Tree

Progress of the Iterative Solution for DOM

Itera-tion	DOM(n)							
	0	**1**	**2**	**3**	**4**	**5**	**6**	**7**
—	{0}	N	N	N	N	N	N	N
1	{0}	{0,1}	{0,1,2}	{0,1,3}	{0,1,3,4}	{0,1,3,5}	{0,1,3,6}	{0,1,7}
2	{0}	{0,1}	{0,1,2}	{0,1,3}	{0,1,3,4}	{0,1,3,5}	{0,1,3,6}	{0,1,7}

FIGURE 9.7   Dominance for the LIVEOUT Example

bering, computed by a traversal that visits right children before left children. Using the iterative algorithm and taking the nodes in this order produces the results shown in the table at the bottom of the figure.

The graph's simple structure lets the algorithm find the correct DOM sets in a single pass, labelled iteration 1. The back edge (an edge that runs from a higher-numbered node to a lower-numbered node, $\langle B_7, B_1 \rangle$ in this case) adds nothing to DOM (B_1) because DOM (B_1) is initialized to N. The algorithm needs a second pass to recognize that the sets no longer change.

The tree shown in the upper right portion of Figure 9.7 is the example's *dominator tree*. (Recall that we used this data structure in dominator-based value numbering in Section 8.5.2.) In the dominator tree, a node n is the child of its immediate dominator, IDOM(n). In the example, B_4, B_5, and B_6 are all children of B_3, even though control reaches B_6 through one of B_4 or B_5.

Improving the Method's Efficiency

The iterative framework for dominators is both simple and intuitive. A straight-forward implementation, however, is relatively inefficient because of the sparsity of the DOM sets. We can improve the efficiency of the iterative dominance computation by noticing that the algorithm only needs to store IDOM for each node. It can compute all of the other information from the IDOMS.

The IDOM relationship encodes both the graph's dominator tree and the DOM sets for each of its nodes. In Figure 9.7, IDOM(6) is 3, IDOM(3) is 1, and IDOM(1) is 0. The DOM set for 6 is $\{0, 1, 3, 6\}$, exactly the nodes lying on the path from 6 to 0 in the dominator tree. If we represent a node's inclusion in its own DOM set implicitly, then we can recreate DOM(n) by walking the dominator tree from IDOM(n) to the root.

To use IDOM as a proxy for the DOM sets, we need a fast method for computing the intersection of two DOM sets, using only the IDOM information. When we walk the dominator tree to recreate a DOM set, we encounter the nodes in DOM(n) in a consistent order. Think of this set as a list. The intersection of two DOM sets, in this order, will be their common prefix. We can compute that intersection by starting at the end of each list and moving backward through the lists until we find a common node. The rests of the lists must be identical, and the first common node can represent the DOM set produced by the intersection.

One complication arises. In computing DOM(i) $\cap$ DOM(j), the algorithm needs to know, at each point, whether to walk further up from i, from j, or from both. If we name the nodes with their RPO numbers, then the intersection routine can simply compare the numbers. Figure 9.8 shows the algorithm. It

```
intersect(i, j)
    finger1 ← i
    finger2 ← j
    while (finger1 ≠ finger2)
        while (finger1 > finger2)
            finger1 = IDOM(finger1)
        while (finger2 > finger1)
            finger2 = IDOM(finger2)
    return finger1
```

FIGURE 9.8   Intersecting DOM Sets by Proxy

uses two pointers to trace paths upward through the tree. When they agree, they both point to the node representing the result of the intersection.

Thus, $IDOM(n)$ is the key to finding $DOM(n)$ efficiently. Given the IDOM of each node, we can derive $DOM(n)$ by starting with n and walking the chain of immediate dominators back to n_0. This approach saves space. The IDOM sets all contain exactly one item, so each node has a singleton set. It avoids the cost of allocating and initializing a separate DOM set for each node. It minimizes data movement—the intersection operator walks upward from the two nodes whose DOM sets are being combined until it finds their nearest common dominator. The result of the operation is the name of that node. The rest of the set can be obtained by walking upward from that first common ancestor. It is efficient; intersection takes time proportional to the size of the input sets, rather than the size of the graph. The result is an implementation that is both simple and fast.

A Harder Example   Figure 9.9 shows an example in which the dominance information is harder to compute. It requires four iterations. The right side of the figure shows the contents of the IDOM array at each stage of the algorithm. The notation u indicates an uninitialized set. We have omitted the fourth iteration, in which the IDOM values do not change.

Dominance Frontiers

The key to placing ϕ-functions lies in understanding which variables need a ϕ-function at each join point. To solve this problem efficiently and effectively, the compiler can turn the question around. It can determine, for each definition point, the set of join points that need a ϕ-function for the value created by the definition. Dominance plays a critical role in this computation.

		IDOM(n)		
n	Initial Values	After 1st Iteration	After 2nd Iteration	After 3rd Iteration
B_6	6	6	6	6
B_5	u	6	6	6
B_4	u	6	6	6
B_3	u	4	4	6
B_2	u	4	6	6
B_1	u	6	6	6

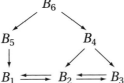

FIGURE 9.9   A Graph with a More Complex Shape

Consider a definition in node n of the CFG. That value could potentially reach every node m where $n \in \text{DOM}(m)$ without need for a ϕ-function, since every path that reaches m passes through n. The only way that the value does not reach m is if another definition of the same name intervenes—that is, it occurs in some node p between n and m. In this case, the definition in n does not force the presence of a ϕ-function; instead, the redefinition in p does.

A definition in node n forces a ϕ-function in join nodes that lie just outside the region of the CFG that n dominates. More formally, a definition in node n forces a corresponding ϕ-function in any join node m where (1) n dominates a predecessor of m ($q \in preds(m)$ and $n \in \text{DOM}(q)$), and (2) n does not strictly dominate m, that is, $m \notin \text{DOM}(n) - \{n\}$. (Adding this notion of "strict dominance" allows a ϕ-function at the start of a single-block loop. In that case, $n = m$, and $m \notin \text{DOM}(n) - \{n\}$.) We call the collection of nodes m that have this property with respect to n the *dominance frontier* of n, denoted DF(n).

Informally, DF(n) contains the first nodes reachable from n that n does not dominate, on each CFG path leaving n. In the example from Figure 9.7, B_3 dominates B_4, B_5, and B_6 but does not dominate B_7. On every path leaving B_3, B_7 is the first node that B_3 does not dominate. Thus, DF(B_3) = $\{B_7\}$.

To compute dominance frontiers, consider the following observations. First, nodes in a dominance frontier must be join points in the graph. Second, the predecessors of any join point, j, must have j in their respective dominance-frontier sets unless the predecessor dominates j. This is a direct result of the previous definition of dominance frontiers. Finally, the dominators of j's predecessors must themselves have j in their dominance-frontier sets, unless they also dominate j.

for all nodes, n
DF(n) ← φ
for all nodes, n
   if n has multiple predecessors then
      for each predecessors p of n
        runner ← p
        while runner ≠ IDom[n]
          DF(runner) ← DF(runner) ∪ {n}
        runner ← IDom(runner)

FIGURE 9.10   Computing Dominance Frontiers

These observations lead to a simple algorithm. First, we identify each join point, j; any node with more than one incoming edge is a join point. We then examine each CFG predecessor, p, of j and walk up the dominator tree starting at p. We stop the walk when we reach j's immediate dominator —j is in the dominance frontier of each of the nodes in the walk, except for j's immediate dominator. Intuitively, all the rest of j's dominators are shared by j's predecessors as well. Since they dominate j, they will not have j in their dominance frontiers.

Figure 9.10 shows the algorithm. A small amount of bookkeeping is needed to ensure that any j is added to a node's dominance frontier only once.

Example   To compute the full set of dominance frontiers for the graph in Figure 9.7, we need both the CFG and the IDom set for each node in the graph. From the dominator tree that we built earlier, shown on the upper right side of the figure, we can read both Dom and IDom for each node.

n	0	1	2	3	4	5	6	7
Dom(n)	{0}	{0,1}	{0,1,2}	{0,1,3}	{0,1,3,4}	{0,1,3,5}	{0,1,3,6}	{0,1,7}
IDom(n)	{—}	{0}	{1}	{1}	{3}	{3}	{3}	{1}

To compute dominance frontiers, the analyzer chooses a join point in the CFG and walks upward from each of its CFG predecessors through the dominator tree. The example CFG has three join points:

1. B_6 It walks back from B_5 to B_3, adding B_6 to DF(B_5). It walks back from B_4 to B_3, adding B_6 to DF(B_4).

2. B_7 It walks back from B_2 directly to B_1, adding B_7 to DF(B_2). It walks back from B_6 to B_3 to B_1, adding B_7 to DF(B_6) and DF(B_3).

3. B_1 B_0 has no immediate dominator, so $B_1 \notin$ DF(B_0). Working from B_7, it discovers that B_7's immediate dominator is B_1. Thus, it adds B_1 to DF(B_7) and to no other set.

Accumulating these results, we obtain the following dominance frontiers:

n	0	1	2	3	4	5	6	7
DF(n)	$\emptyset$	$\emptyset$	$\{7\}$	$\{7\}$	$\{6\}$	$\{6\}$	$\{7\}$	$\{1\}$

9.3.3 Placing ϕ-Functions

The naive algorithm placed a ϕ-function for every variable at the start of every join node. With dominance frontiers, the compiler can determine more precisely where ϕ-functions might be needed. The basic idea is simple. A definition of x in block b forces a ϕ-function at every join node in DF*(b)*. Since that ϕ-function is a new definition of x, it may force the insertion of additional ϕ-functions.

The compiler can further narrow the set of ϕ-functions that it inserts. A variable that is used exclusively within a single block can never have a live ϕ-function. To apply this observation, the compiler can compute the set of names that are live across multiple blocks—a set that we will call the *global names*. It can insert ϕ-functions for those names and ignore any name that is never live across multiple blocks. (This restriction distinguishes semipruned SSA form from other varieties of SSA form.)

The compiler can find the global names cheaply. In each block, it looks for names with upward-exposed uses—the UEVAR set from the live variables calculation. Any name that appears in one or more LIVEOUT sets must be in the UEVAR set of some block. Taking the union of all the UEVAR sets gives the compiler the set of names that are live on entry to one or more blocks and, hence, live in multiple blocks.

The algorithm, shown on the left side of Figure 9.11, is derived from the computation shown for LIVEOUT analysis. It constructs a single set, *Globals*, where the LIVEOUT computation must compute a distinct set for each block. As it builds the *Globals* set, it also constructs, for each name, a list of all blocks

Globals ← ∅
Initialize all the Blocks sets to ∅
for each block b
    VARKILL ← ∅
      for each operation i in b, in order
        assume that op_i *is* "$x \leftarrow y$ op z"
        if $y \notin$ VARKILL *then*
          Globals ← *Globals* ∪ {y}
        if $z \notin$ VARKILL *then*
          Globals ← *Globals* ∪ {z}
        VARKILL ← VARKILL ∪ {x}
        Blocks(x) ← *Blocks(x)* ∪ {b}

        Finding Global Names

for each name $x \in$ *Globals*
   WorkList ← *Blocks(x)*
   for each block $b \in$ *WorkList*
      for each block d in DF*(b)*
        insert a ϕ-*function for x in d*
        WorkList ← *WorkList* ∪ {d}

      Inserting ϕ-Functions

FIGURE 9.11   Inserting ϕ-Functions

that contain a definition of that name. These block lists serve as an initial worklist for the ϕ-insertion algorithm.

The algorithm for inserting ϕ-functions is shown on the right side of Figure 9.11. For each global name x, it initializes *WorkList* with *Blocks(x)*. For each block b on the *WorkList*, it inserts ϕ-functions at the head of every block d in b's dominance frontier. Since all the ϕ-functions in a block execute concurrently, by definition, the algorithm can insert them at the head of d in any order. After adding a ϕ-function for x to d, the algorithm adds d to the *WorkList* to reflect the new assignment to x in d.

To improve efficiency, the compiler should avoid two kinds of duplication. First, the algorithm should avoid placing any block on the worklist more than once per global name. It can keep a checklist of blocks that have already been processed. Since the algorithm must reset the checklist for each global name, the implementation should use a sparse set or a similar structure (see Section B.2.3).

Second, a given block can be in the dominance frontier of multiple nodes that appear on the *WorkList*. To avoid inserting duplicate ϕ-functions for a variable(i) into a block, the compiler can maintain a checklist of blocks that already contain ϕ-functions for i. This takes a single sparse set, reinitialized along with *WorkList*. The alternative is searching inside the block for an existing ϕ-function; the checklist is probably faster.

Example

The first step in applying this algorithm to the running example, shown in Figures 9.3 and 9.7, is to compute the *Globals* and *Blocks* sets. *Globals* is $\{a,b,c,d,i\}$. The *Blocks* sets are

Names	a	b	c	d	i	y	z
Blocks	$\{1,3\}$	$\{2,6\}$	$\{1,2,5\}$	$\{2,3,4\}$	$\{0,7\}$	$\{7\}$	$\{7\}$

Notice that the algorithm creates *Blocks* sets for y and z, even though they are not in *Globals*. Separating the computation of *Globals* from that of *Blocks* would avoid instantiating these extra sets, at the cost of another pass over the code.

The algorithm also needs the dominance frontiers for the CFG, which we calculated as

n	0	1	2	3	4	5	6	7
DF(n)	$\emptyset$	$\emptyset$	$\{7\}$	$\{7\}$	$\{6\}$	$\{6\}$	$\{7\}$	$\{1\}$

With this information, the analyzer can apply the algorithm on the right side of Figure 9.11.

Consider the work that it does for the variable a. Since a has definitions in $Blocks(a) = \{B_1,B_3\}$, the algorithm must insert a ϕ-function in every node in $DF(B_1) = \emptyset$ and $DF(B_3) = \{B_7\}$. Adding the ϕ-function to B_7 also adds B_7 to the worklist. (The ϕ-function in B_7 is, itself, a definition of a.) The algorithm inserts a ϕ-function in each block in $DF(B_7) = \{B_1\}$. Since B_1 has already been on the worklist, the algorithm neither inserts a duplicate ϕ-function nor adds $DF(B_1)$ to the worklist. This completes its work for a. It follows the same process for each name in *Globals*, to produce the following insertions:

Global Names	a	b	c	d	i
Blocks with ϕ-*functions*	$\{7,1\}$	$\{7,1\}$	$\{7,6,1\}$	$\{7,6,1\}$	$\{1\}$

The resulting code appears in Figure 9.12.

Limiting the algorithm to global names lets it avoid inserting dead ϕ-functions for x and y in block B_1. (B_1 is $\mathrm{DF}(B_7)$ and B_7 contains definitions of both x and y.) However, the distinction between local names and global names is not sufficient to avoid all dead ϕ-functions. The ϕ-functions for a and c in B_1 are dead because both names are redefined before their values are used. To avoid inserting these ϕ-functions, the compiler must construct LIVEOUT sets and add a test based on liveness to the inner loop of the ϕ-insertion algorithm.

9.3.4 Renaming

In the description of maximal SSA form, we stated that renaming variables was conceptually straightforward. The details, however, require some explanation.

In the final SSA form, each global name has a single base name, and individual definitions of that base name are distinguished by the addition of a numerical subscript. For a name that corresponds to a source-language variable, say x, the algorithm uses x as the base name. Thus, the first definition of x that the renaming algorithm encounters will be named x_0 and the second will be x_1. For a compiler-generated temporary, the algorithm must generate a distinct name.

The algorithm renames both definitions and uses in a preorder walk over the dominator tree. In each block, it first renames the values defined by ϕ-functions at the head of the block, then it visits each operation in the block, in order. It rewrites the operands with current SSA names, then it creates a new SSA name for the result of the operation. This latter act makes the new name current. After all the operations in the block have been rewritten, the algorithm rewrites the appropriate ϕ-function parameters in each CFG successor of the block, using the current SSA names. Finally, it recurs on any children of the block in the dominator tree. When it returns from those recursive calls, it restores the set of current SSA names to the state that existed before the current block was visited.

To manage this process, the compiler uses a counter and a stack for each global name. A name's stack holds the name's most recent subscript—its current SSA name. At each definition, the algorithm generates a new subscript for the targeted name by pushing the value of its current counter onto the stack and incrementing the counter. The value on top of the stack is the new SSA name. As the final step in processing a block, the algorithm pops all the names generated in that block off their respective stacks. This restores the set of names that held in the block's immediate dominator, for use, if necessary, on the block's siblings in the dominator tree.

The stack and the counter serve distinct and separate purposes. As control in the algorithm moves up and down the dominator tree, the stack is managed

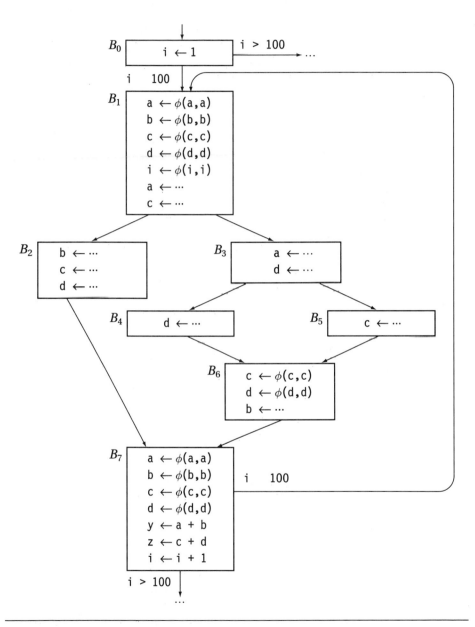

FIGURE 9.12 Example with ϕ-Functions

THE DIFFERENT FLAVORS OF SSA FORM

Several distinct flavors of SSA form have been proposed in the literature. The flavors differ in their criteria for inserting ϕ-functions. For a given program, they can produce different sets of ϕ-functions.

Minimal SSA inserts a ϕ-function at any join point where two distinct definitions for the same original name meet. This is the minimal number consistent with the definition of SSA. Some of those ϕ-functions, however, may be dead; the definition says nothing about the values being live when they meet.

Pruned SSA adds a liveness test to the ϕ-insertion algorithm to ensure that it only adds live ϕ-functions. The construction must compute LIVEOUT sets, so the cost of building pruned SSAs is higher than that of building a minimal SSA.

Semipruned SSA is a compromise between minimal SSAs and pruned SSAs. Before inserting ϕ-functions, the algorithm eliminates any names that are not live across a block boundary. This can shrink the name space and reduce the number of ϕ-functions without the overhead of computing LIVEOUT sets. This is the algorithm given in Figure 9.11

Of course, the number of ϕ-functions depends on the specific program being converted into SSA form. For some programs, the reductions obtained by semipruned SSAs and pruned SSAs are significant. Shrinking the SSA form can lead to faster compilation, since passes that use SSA form then operate on programs that contain fewer operations—fewer ϕ-functions.

to simulate the lifetime of the most recent definition in the current block. The counter, on the other hand, grows monotonically to ensure that each successive ⟨*name,subscript*⟩ pair maps to a distinct definition.

Figure 9.13 summarizes the algorithm. It initializes the stacks and counters, then calls *Rename* on the root of the dominator tree—the entry node of the CFG. *Rename* rewrites the block and recurs on successors in the dominator tree. To finish with the block, *Rename* pops any names that were pushed onto stacks while processing the block. The function *NewName* manipulates the counters and stacks to create new incarnations as needed.

for each global name i
  counter[i] ← 0
  stack[i] ← ∅
Rename(n₀)

Rename(b)
  for each ϕ-function in b, "x ← ϕ(···)"
    rename x as NewName(x)
  for each operation "x ← y op z" in b

    rewrite y as top(stack[y])
    rewrite z as top(stack[z])
    rewrite x as NewName(x)

  for each successor in the CFG
    fill in ϕ-function parameters

  for each successor s in the dominator tree
    Rename(s)

  for each operation "x ← y op z" in b
    and each ϕ-function "x ← ϕ(···)"
    pop(stack[x])

NewName(n)
  i ← counter[n]
  counter[n] ← counter[n] + 1
  push nᵢ onto stack[n]
  return nᵢ

FIGURE 9.13   Renaming after ϕ-Insertion

One final detail remains. At the end of block b, *Rename* must rewrite ϕ-function parameters in each of b's CFG successors. The compiler must assign an ordinal parameter slot in those ϕ-functions for b. When we draw the SSA form, we always assume a left-to-right order that matches the left-to-right order in which the edges are drawn. Internally, the compiler can number the edges and parameter slots in any consistent fashion that produces the desired result. This requires cooperation between the code that builds the SSA form and the code that builds the CFG. (For example, if the CFG implementation uses a list of edges leaving each block, the order of that list can determine the mapping.)

Example

To finish the continuing example, let's apply the renaming algorithm to Figure 9.12. Assume that a_0, b_0, c_0, and d_0 are defined on entry to B_0. Figure 9.14 shows the states of the counters and stacks for global names at various points during the process. A picture labelled "Before B_i" shows the counters and stacks when *Rename* is called with block B_i. A picture labelled "End of B_i" shows the state after processing the block but before *Rename* has popped B_i's names from the various stacks. The figure shows the state at the end of each block; it includes the entry states for B_0, B_3, and B_7 for clarity.

	a	b	c	d	i
Counters	1	1	1	1	0
Stacks	a_0	b_0	c_0	d_0	

Before B_0

	a	b	c	d	i
Counters	1	1	1	1	1
Stacks	a_0	b_0	c_0	d_0	i_0

End of B_0

	a	b	c	d	i
Counters	3	2	3	2	2
Stacks	a_0	b_0	c_0	d_0	i_0
	a_1	b_1	c_1	d_1	i_1
	a_2		c_2		

End of B_1

	a	b	c	d	i
Counters	3	3	4	3	2
Stacks	a_0	b_0	c_0	d_0	i_0
	a_1	b_1	c_1	d_1	i_1
	a_2	b_2	c_2	d_2	
			c_3		

End of B_2

	a	b	c	d	i
Counters	3	3	4	3	2
Stacks	a_0	b_0	c_0	d_0	i_0
	a_1	b_1	c_1	d_1	i_1
	a_2		c_2		

Before B_3

	a	b	c	d	i
Counters	4	3	4	4	2
Stacks	a_0	b_0	c_0	d_0	i_0
	a_1	b_1	c_1	d_1	i_1
	a_2		c_2	d_3	
	a_3				

End of B_3

	a	b	c	d	i
Counters	4	3	4	5	2
Stacks	a_0	b_0	c_0	d_0	i_0
	a_1	b_1	c_1	d_1	i_1
	a_2		c_2	d_3	
	a_3			d_4	

End of B_4

	a	b	c	d	i
Counters	4	3	5	5	2
Stacks	a_0	b_0	c_0	d_0	i_0
	a_1	b_1	c_1	d_1	i_1
	a_2		c_2	d_3	
	a_3		c_4		

End of B_5

FIGURE 9.14 States in the Renaming Example (*Continued*)

	a	b	c	d	i
Counters	4	4	6	6	2
Stacks	a_0	b_0	c_0	d_0	i_0
	a_1	b_1	c_1	d_1	i_1
	a_2	b_3	c_2	d_3	
	a_3		c_5	d_5	

End of B_6

	a	b	c	d	i
Counters	4	4	6	6	2
Stacks	a_0	b_0	c_0	d_0	i_0
	a_1	b_1	c_1	d_1	i_1
	a_2		c_2		

Before B_7

	a	b	c	d	i
Counters	5	5	7	7	3
Stacks	a_0	b_0	c_0	d_0	i_0
	a_1	b_1	c_1	d_1	i_1
	a_2	b_4	c_2	d_6	i_2
	a_4		c_6		

End of B_7

FIGURE 9.14   States in the Renaming Example, *Continued*

The algorithm makes a preorder walk over the dominator tree visiting the nodes in ascending order, B_0 to B_7. As it proceeds through the blocks, it takes the following actions:

1. B_0 This block contains only one operation. *Rename* rewrites i with i_0, increments the counter, and pushes i_0 onto the stack for i. Next, it rewrites the first parameter of each ϕ-function with the appropriate names from the current state, a_0, b_0, c_0, d_0, and i_0. It then recurs on B_0's child in the dominator tree, B_1. After that, it pops the stack for i and returns.

2. B_1 On entering B_1, *Rename* rewrites the ϕ-function targets with new names, a_1, b_1, c_1, d_1, and i_1. Next, it rewrites the definitions of a and c as a_2 and c_2. Neither of B_1's CFG successors have ϕ-functions. Next, it

recurs on B_1's dominator-tree children, B_2 and B_3. It pops the stacks and returns.

3. B_2 This block has no ϕ-functions to rewrite. Next, *Rename* rewrites the three operations, creating b_2, c_3, and d_2. It then rewrites ϕ-function parameters in B_7, which is B_2's CFG successor, replacing the first parameter of each ϕ-function with the appropriate name that holds at the end of B_2: a_2, b_2, c_3, and d_2. Finally, it pops the stacks and returns.

4. B_3 Next, *Rename* recurs on B_3. Look at the picture labelled "Before B_3." It has the stacks from "End of B_1" and the counters from "End of B_2." It rewrites the two assignments with a_3 and d_3. Neither CFG successor has ϕ-functions to process. *Rename* recurs on B_3's dominator-tree children, B_4, B_5, and B_6. It then pops the stacks and returns.

5. B_4 This block has one operation. *Rename* rewrites d as d_4. Next, it rewrites the first parameter of each ϕ-function in B_6 with the corresponding current name, c_2 and d_4. It pops the stack for d and returns.

6. B_5 This block also has one operation. *Rename* rewrites c as c_4, and then rewrites the second parameter of each ϕ-function in B_6. These become c_4 and d_3. It pops the stack for c and returns.

7. B_6 *Rename* rewrites the ϕ-function targets as c_5 and d_5. It rewrites the assignment to b as b_3. Next, it rewrites the second parameter for each ϕ-function in B_7 with the current SSA names (a_3, b_3, c_5, and d_5). Since B_6 has no dominator-tree children, *Rename* returns upward, to B_3, where it returns to B_2. It recurs downward on B_2's final dominator-tree child, B_7. It then pops the stacks and returns.

8. B_7 First, *Rename* rewrites the ϕ-function targets, creating a_4, b_4, c_6, and d_6. It rewrites the uses of global names in the next two assignments, but not their targets, since neither y nor z is a global name. In the last assignment, it rewrites the use with i_1, then creates a new name, i_2, for the definition.

   Only one of B_7's CFG successors is shown, B_1. *Rename* rewrites the second parameter of each ϕ-function in B_1 with its current SSA name (a_4, b_4, c_6, d_6, and i_2). *Rename* pops the stacks, returns to B_1, to B_0, and halts.

Figure 9.15 shows the code after *Rename* halts.

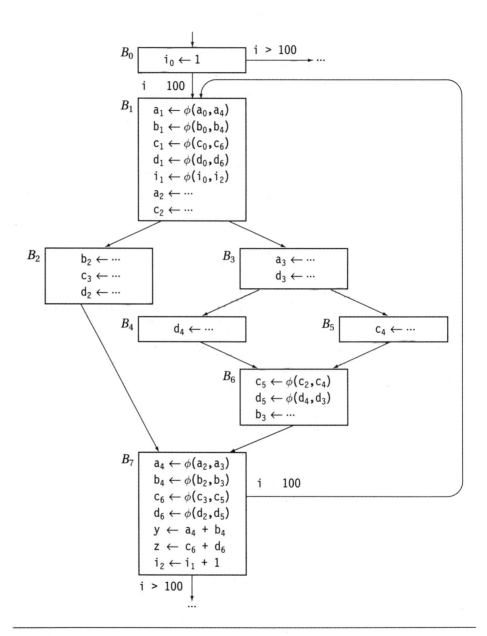

FIGURE 9.15 Example after Renaming

A Final Improvement

A clever implementation of *NewName* can reduce the time and the space expended on stack manipulation. The primary use of the stacks is to reset the name space on exit from a block. If a block redefines the same base name several times, *NewName* needs only to keep the most recent name. This happened with a and c in block B_1 of the example. *NewName* may overwrite the same stack slot multiple times within a single block.

This makes the maximum stack sizes predictable; no stack can be larger than the depth of the dominator tree. It lowers the overall space requirements, avoids the need for overflow tests on each push, and decreases the number of push and pop operations. It requires another mechanism for determining which stacks to pop on exit from a block. *NewName* can thread together the stack entries for a block. *Rename* can use the thread to pop the appropriate stacks.

9.3.5 Reconstructing Executable Code from SSA Form

Because processors do not implement ϕ-functions, the compiler must translate SSA form back into executable code. Looking at the examples, it is tempting to believe that the compiler can simply drop the subscripts from names and delete the ϕ-functions. If the compiler simply builds SSA form and converts it back into executable code, this approach will work. However, transformations that rely on the SSA name space may cause this simple renaming process to produce incorrect code.

In local value numbering (LVN), we saw that using the SSA name space could allow the transformation to discover and eliminate more redundancies.

Original Name Space		SSA Name Space	
Before LVN	**After LVN**	**Before LVN**	**After LVN**
$a \leftarrow x + y$	$a \leftarrow x + y$	$a_0 \leftarrow x_0 + y_0$	$a_0 \leftarrow x_0 + y_0$
$b \leftarrow x + y$	$b \leftarrow a$	$b_0 \leftarrow x_0 + y_0$	$b_0 \leftarrow a_0$
$a \leftarrow 17$	$a \leftarrow 17$	$a_1 \leftarrow 17$	$a_1 \leftarrow 17$
$c \leftarrow x + y$	$c \leftarrow x + y$	$c_0 \leftarrow x_0 + y_0$	$c_0 \leftarrow a_0$

The code on the left shows a four-operation block and the results that LVN produces when it uses a name space drawn from the source code. The code on the right shows the same example using the SSA name space. Because the SSA name space gives a_0 a distinct name from a_1, LVN can replace the evaluation of $x_0 + y_0$ in the final operation with a reference to a_0.

Notice, however, that dropping the subscripts on variable names produces incorrect code, since it assigns c the value 17. More aggressive transformations, such as code motion and copy folding, can rewrite the SSA form in ways that introduce more subtle problems.

To avoid such problems, the compiler can keep the SSA name space intact and replace each ϕ-function with a set of copy operations—one along each incoming edge. For a ϕ-function $x_{14} \leftarrow \phi(x_{12},x_{13})$, the compiler should insert $x_{14} \leftarrow x_{12}$ along the edge carrying the value x_{12} and the copy $x_{14} \leftarrow x_{13}$ along the edge carrying the value x_{13}. Figure 9.16 shows the running example after ϕ-functions have been replaced with copy operations. The four ϕ-functions that were in B_7 have been replaced with a set of four copies in each of B_2 and B_6. Similarly, the two ϕ-functions in B_6 induce a pair of copies in B_4 and B_5. In both these cases, the compiler can insert the copies into the predecessor blocks.

The ϕ-functions in B_1 reveal a more complicated situation. Because its predecessor blocks have multiple successors, the compiler cannot insert the copy operations at the end of its predecessors. Inserting the copies directly into the predecessors will cause them to execute on the exit paths from the loop (labelled $i > 100$). Without detailed knowledge of the code that can be reached along those exit paths, we cannot tell whether or not inserting these copies would produce incorrect behavior. In general, however, it can produce incorrect behavior. Neither can the compiler insert the copies at the top of B_1; the copies must use the names by which the values are known in the predecessor blocks.

To solve this problem, the compiler can split the edges from B_0 to B_1 and from B_7 to B_1, and insert a block in midedge to hold the copies, as shown in Figure 9.16. An edge whose source has multiple successors and whose destination has multiple predecessors is called a *critical edge*. Blocks B_8 and B_9 were inserted to break the critical edges. After copy insertion, the example appears to have many superfluous copies. Fortunately, the compiler can remove most, if not all, of these copies with subsequent optimizations, such as copy folding (see Section 13.5.6).

Splitting critical edges creates a location for the necessary copy operations and cures most of the problems that arise during copy insertion. However, two more subtle problems can arise. The first, which we call the *lost-copy problem*, arises from a combination of aggressive program transformations and critical edges. The second, which we call the *swap problem*, arises from an interaction of some aggressive program transformations and the detailed definition of SSA form.

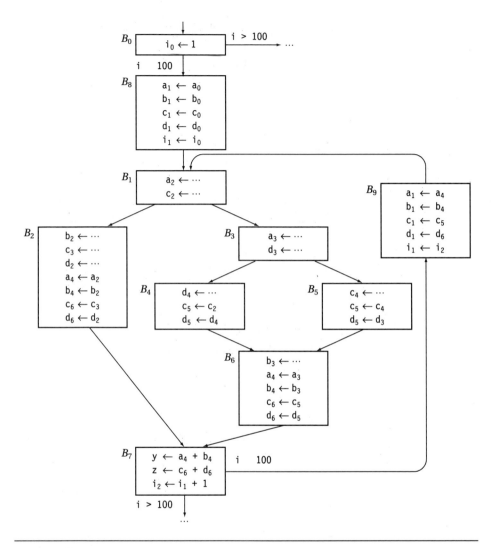

FIGURE 9.16   Example after Copy Insertion

The Lost-Copy Problem

Many SSA-based algorithms require that critical edges be split. Sometimes, however, the compiler cannot, or should not, split critical edges. For example, if the critical edge is the back edge of a heavily executed loop, adding a block with one or more copy operations and a jump may have an adverse impact

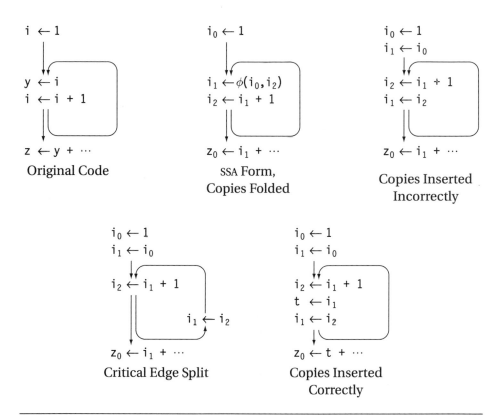

FIGURE 9.17   An Example of the Lost-Copy Problem

on execution speed. Similarly, adding blocks and edges in the late stages of compilation can interfere with nonlocal scheduling, register allocation, and optimizations such as code placement.

The lost-copy problem arises from the combination of copy folding and critical edges that cannot be split. Figure 9.17 shows an example. The top left panel shows the original code—a simple loop. In the next panel, the compiler has converted the loop into SSA form and folded the copy from i to y, replacing the sole use of y with a reference to i_1. The top right panel shows the code produced by straightforward copy insertion into the ϕ-function's predecessor blocks. This changes the value used in the assignment to z_0 after the loop. The original code assigned it the second to last value of i, while the transformed code assigns it the last value of i. The lower left panel shows that splitting the critical edge—the loop's back edge—produces correct behavior. However, it adds a jump to every iteration of the loop.

This problem arose from the combination of an unsplit critical edge and copy folding's manipulation of the name space. Copy folding eliminated the assignment $y \leftarrow i$ by folding i_1 into the reference to y in the block following the loop. This extended i_1's lifetime. Then, the copy-insertion algorithm replaced the ϕ-function at the top of the loop body with a copy operation in each of that block's predecessors. This inserts the copy $i_1 \leftarrow i_2$ at the bottom of the block—at a point where i_1 is still live.

To avoid the lost-copy problem, the compiler must detect when it tries to insert a copy whose target is still live. When this happens, it must copy the value to a temporary name and rewrite subsequent uses of the overwritten name with the new temporary. This rewriting step can be done with a step modelled on the SSA renaming algorithm. The bottom right panel in Figure 9.17 shows the code produced by this approach.

The Swap Problem

The same property of ϕ-functions that lets the insertion algorithm introduce them in any order gives rise to the swap problem. When a block executes, all its ϕ-functions are assumed to execute concurrently before any other statement in the block. All the ϕ-functions in the block read their appropriate input parameters at the same time. Then, they redefine their target values, all at the same time.

Figure 9.18 shows a simple example of the swap problem. The left side shows the original code, a simple loop that swaps the values of x and y. The center shows the code converted to SSA form and subjected to aggressive

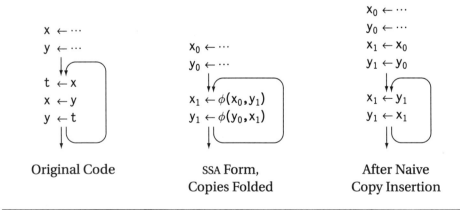

Original Code   SSA Form, Copies Folded   After Naive Copy Insertion

Figure 9.18   An Example of the Swap Problem

copy folding. In this form, with the rules for evaluating ϕ-functions, the code retains its original meaning. When the loop body executes, the ϕ-function parameters are read before any of the ϕ-function targets are defined. On the first iteration, it reads x_0 and y_0 before defining x_1 and y_1. On subsequent iterations, it reads x_1 and y_1 before redefining them both. The right side shows the same code, after performing the naive copy-insertion algorithm. Because the copies execute sequentially, rather than concurrently, both x_1 and y_1 incorrectly receive the same value.

At first glance, it might appear that splitting the back edge—a critical edge—helps. However, this simply places the same two copies, in the same order, in another block. To fix this problem, the compiler can copy each of the values into a temporary, to mimic the defined behavior of the ϕ-functions. This produces a sequence of four assignments, $t \leftarrow y_1$, $s \leftarrow x_1$, $x_1 \leftarrow t$, and $y_1 \leftarrow s$ in the block that forms the loop's body. Unfortunately, it doubles the number of operations in the loop, so it is not a good solution to the problem. Instead, the compiler should minimize the number of copies it inserts.

In fact, the swap problem does not require a cyclic set of copies; all it takes is a set of ϕ-functions that have, as inputs, variables defined as outputs of other ϕ-functions in the same block. In the acyclic case, in which ϕ-functions reference the results of other ϕ-functions in the same block, the compiler can avoid the problem by carefully ordering the inserted copies.

To solve this problem, in general, the compiler can detect cases in which ϕ-functions reference the targets of other ϕ-functions in the same block. For each cycle of references, it must insert a copy to a temporary that breaks the cycle. Then, it can schedule the copies to respect the dependences implied by the ϕ-functions.

9.4 ADVANCED TOPICS

This chapter has focused on iterative data-flow analysis and the construction of SSA form, which directly and efficiently embodies many of the data-flow relationships in a procedure. One property of the flow graph is critical for other, noniterative data-flow algorithms; whether or not the graph is *reducible*. Section 9.4.1 discusses flow-graph reducibility.

So far in the chapter, the examples have all come from global (intraprocedural) data-flow analysis. Section 9.4.2 introduces some of the problems that arise in extending the scope of data-flow analysis from a procedure to the whole program. It presents a brief overview of several analysis problems that have scopes larger than a single procedure.

9.4.1 Structural Data-Flow Algorithms and Reducibility

Section 9.2.2 presents the iterative algorithm because it works, in general, on any set of well-formed equations on any graph. Other data-flow analysis algorithms exist; many of these work by deriving a simple model of the control-flow structure of the code being analyzed and using that model to solve the equations. Often, that model is built by finding a sequence of transformations to the graph that reduce its complexity—by combining nodes or edges in carefully defined ways. This graph-reduction process lies at the heart of almost every data-flow algorithm *except* the iterative algorithm.

Noniterative data-flow algorithms work, in general, by applying a series of transformations to a flow graph, each of which selects a subgraph and replaces it by a single node to represent the subgraph. This creates a series of derived graphs in which each graph differs from its predecessor in the series by the effect of a single transformation step. As it transforms the graph, the analyzer computes data-flow sets for the new representer nodes in each successive derived graph. These sets summarize the replaced subgraph's effects. The transformations reduce well-behaved graphs to a single node. The algorithm then reverses the process, going from the final derived graph, with its single node, back to the original flow graph. As it expands the graph back to its original form, the analyzer computes the final data-flow sets for each node.

In essence, the reduction phase gathers information from the entire graph and consolidates it, while the expansion phase propagates the effects in the consolidated set back out to the nodes of the original graph. Any graph for which such a reduction phase succeeds is deemed *reducible*. If the graph cannot be reduced to a single node, it is *irreducible*.

Figure 9.19 shows a pair of transformations that can be used to test reducibility and to build a structural data-flow algorithm. T_1 removes a self-loop, an edge that runs from a node back to itself. The figure shows T_1 applied to b, denoted $T_1(b)$. T_2 folds a node b that has exactly one predecessor a back into a; it removes the edge $\langle a, b \rangle$, and makes a the source of any edges that originally

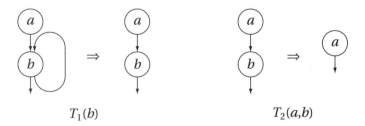

$T_1(b)$ $T_2(a,b)$

FIGURE 9.19   Transformations T_1 and T_2

left b. If this leaves multiple edges from a to some node n, it consolidates those edges. The figure shows T_2 applied to a and b, denoted $T_2(a, b)$. Any graph that can be reduced to a single node by repeated application of T_1 and T_2 is deemed "reducible."

To understand how this works, consider the CFG from our continuing example. Figure 9.20 shows one sequence of applications of T_1 and T_2 that reduces it to a single-node graph. It applies T_2 until no more opportunities exist: $T_2(B_1, B_2)$, $T_2(B_3, B_4)$, $T_2(B_3, B_5)$, $T_2(B_3, B_6)$, $T_2(B_1, B_3)$, and $T_2(B_1, B_7)$. Next, it uses $T_1(B_1)$ to remove the loop, followed by $T_2(B_0, B_1)$ to complete the reduction. Since this sequence reduces the graph to a single node, the original graph is reducible.

Other application orders also reduce the graph. For example, starting with $T_2(B_1, B_3)$ leads to a different series of transformations. T_1 and T_2 have the finite Church-Rosser property, which ensures that the final result is independent of the order of application and that the sequence terminates. Thus, the analyzer can apply T_1 and T_2 opportunistically—finding places in the graph where one of them applies and using it.

The bottom half of Figure 9.20 shows one attempt at reducing the graph from Figure 9.9. The analyzer uses $T_2(B_6, B_5)$ followed by $T_2(B_6, B_4)$. At that point, however, no remaining node or pair of nodes is a candidate for either T_1 or T_2. Thus, the analyzer cannot reduce the graph any further. (No other order will work either.) The graph is not reducible to a single node; it is *irreducible*.

The failure of T_1 and T_2 to reduce this graph arises from a fundamental property of the graph. The graph is irreducible because it contains a loop, or cycle, that has edges that enter it at different nodes. In terms of the source language, the program that generated the graph has a loop with multiple entries. We can see this in the graph; consider the cycle formed by B_1 and B_2. It has edges entering it from all of B_3, B_4, and B_5. Similarly, the cycle formed by B_2 and B_3 has edges that enter it from both B_1 and B_2.

Irreducibility poses a serious problem for algorithms built on transformations like T_1 and T_2. If the reduction sequence cannot complete, producing a single-node graph, then the method must either report failure, modify the graph by splitting one or more nodes, or use an iterative approach to solve the system on the reduced graph. In general, the methods based on structurally reducing the flow graph are limited to reducible graphs.[2] The iterative algorithm, in contrast, works correctly on an irreducible graph.

To transform an irreducible graph to a reducible graph, the analyzer can split one or more nodes. The simplest split for the example graph clones the

---

2. Throughout the text, we have focused on iterative fixed-point algorithms. We emphasize iterative data-flow analysis because it is robust across different problems and different graphs. Because it is a fixed-point algorithm, it also provides a nice continuity, all the way back to the subset construction in Chapter 2.

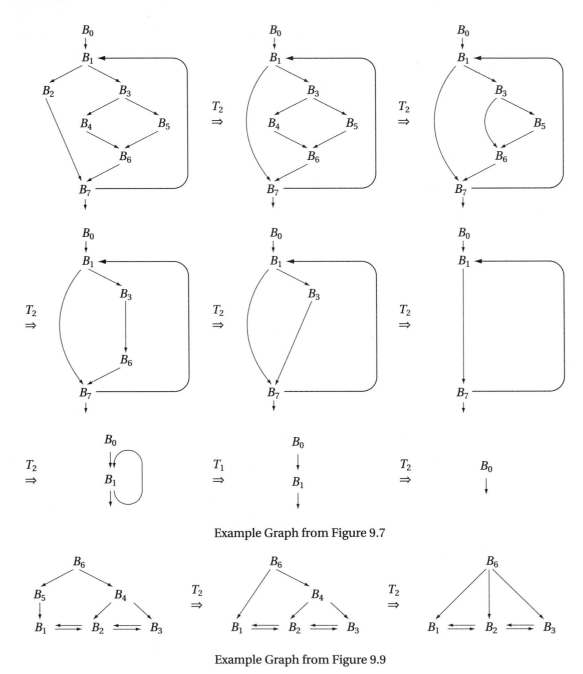

Example Graph from Figure 9.7

Example Graph from Figure 9.9

FIGURE 9.20   Reduction Sequences for Example Graphs

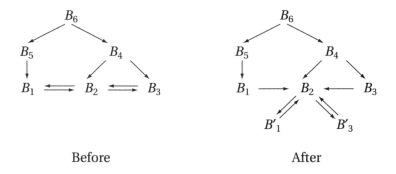

Before   After

FIGURE 9.21   Node Splitting

blocks needed to retarget the edges $\langle B_2, B_1 \rangle$ and $\langle B_2, B_3 \rangle$. This creates a loop with only one entry, through B_2. On the paths that originally entered the loop through B_1 or B_3, those blocks execute as prologues to the loop. This creates a reducible graph, as shown in Figure 9.21. B_1 and B_3 each have a unique predecessor. B_2 has five predecessors, but forms the sole entry to a complex loop formed from B_2, B_1', and B_3'. Since B_1' and B_3' each have a unique predecessor, this loop has a unique entry point and is, itself, reducible. Node splitting produced a reducible graph, at the cost of cloning two nodes.

Both folklore and published studies suggest that irreducible graphs rarely arise in global data-flow analysis. The rise of structured programming in the 1970s made programmers much less likely to use arbitrary transfers of control, like the goto statement found in many programming languages. Structured loop constructs, such as do, for, while, and until loops, cannot produce irreducible graphs. However, transferring control out of a loop (for example, C's break statement) creates a CFG that is irreducible to a backward analysis. (Since the loop has multiple exits, the reverse CFG has multiple entries.) Similarly, irreducible graphs may arise more often in interprocedural analysis from mutually recursive subroutines. For example, the call graph of a hand-coded, recursive-descent parser is likely to have irreducible subgraphs. Fortunately, an iterative analyzer can handle irreducible graphs correctly and efficiently.

9.4.2   Interprocedural Analysis

Procedure calls introduce imprecision into global data-flow analysis. When the compiler encounters a procedure call, and it does not have detailed information about the behavior of the called procedure, it must assume that the call has worst-case effects. For example, the called procedure might modify any value that it can access: global variables, call-by-reference parameters, and names from surrounding lexical scopes.

In practice, procedures usually behave better than these worst-case assumptions would imply. To avoid losing knowledge at each call site, the compiler can analyze the entire program and record information that summarizes the behavior of the various calls. Such analyses are often formulated as interprocedural data-flow analysis problems. These data-flow problems resemble their global counterparts. Instead of a control-flow graph, interprocedural problems usually involve a *call graph*, in which nodes represent procedures and edges represent procedure calls, or a graph derived from the call graph. If p calls q multiple times, each call produces a distinct edge in the call graph.

Control-Flow Analysis

The first problem that the compiler must address in interprocedural analysis is the construction of a call graph. In the simplest case, in which every procedure call invokes a known procedure with its name specified as a literal constant, this problem is straightforward. Once the programmer uses a procedure-valued variable, or passes a procedure as a parameter, however, the problem grows more complex.

If the source language only allows the programmer to pass procedures as arguments into procedures, then the problem can be solved by building an approximate call graph and propagating the names of passed procedures around the approximate graph, adding edges as it goes. If procedures can be returned from a call—that is, the programmer can write a procedure-valued function—then more complex analysis is required. Finally, object-oriented programming can further obscure the call graph by making the interpretation of names depend on run-time type information, collected with class-hierarchy analysis.

Summary Problems

To summarize the side effects of procedure calls, the compiler can compute sets containing the variables that might be modified or referenced during a call. The compiler can use these "summary" sets to replace the worst-case assumptions used for call sites in global data-flow analysis. The classic interprocedural summary problem is the *may modify* problem, which annotates each call site with a set containing the names of all variables that might be modified by executing the call.

May modify is one of the simplest interprocedural data-flow problems, but it illustrates many of the problems that can arise. The problem is specified with a set of equations

$$\text{MOD}(p) = \text{LOCALMOD}(p) \cup \left(\bigcup_{e=(p,q)} unbind_e(\text{MOD}(q)) \right)$$

where $e = (p,q)$ is an edge from p to q in the call graph, and $unbind_e$ (q) is a function that maps names in q into names in p according to the bindings at the call site corresponding to e. LOCALMOD contains variables modified locally in p. It is computed as the set of names defined in p, minus those that are strictly local to p. To compute the set of names that might be modified by a specific call from p to q, the compiler takes the *unbind* of $\text{MOD}(q)$ and factors into the result any aliases that hold on entry to q. An analogous formulation can find *may reference* sets, which hold the sets of names that might be referenced as a result of executing a call.

MOD information can significantly improve the results of global analysis. For example, the worst-case assumptions at a call site force global constant propagation to lose knowledge of values that involve parameters and global variables. Simple MOD analysis shows which facts it may safely retain.

Interprocedural Constant Propagation

Interprocedural constant propagation tracks known constant values of global variables and parameters as they propagate across the call graph. The problem is conceptually similar to global constant propagation, but it has an additional layer of complication. Interprocedural constant propagation must propagate values across edges in the call graph, and it must understand the bindings that can occur at each call (including returned values). Additionally, it must model the transmission of values through a procedure p's body—from entering p to each call site inside p to any values that p returns. Thus, the intraprocedural component of this problem is more complex than in the summary problems because it can be a function of what the analysis has already discovered, rather than an invariant set.

Several compilers have used *jump functions* to model the intraprocedural effects. The compiler constructs an explicit model that maps known constants at procedure entry (or return from a call) to constant values at other calls and returns. The data-flow equations include specific invocations of the jump functions; the analyzer invokes them as needed during the propagation phase. Jump-function implementations range from simple static approximations that do not change during analysis, through small, parameterized models, to performing complete global constant propagation. In practice, simple models seem to capture most of the effects, at least as measured by improvement in the code.

Pointer Analysis

Ambiguous memory references interfere with an optimizer's ability to improve the code. One major source of ambiguity is the use of pointer-based values. The goal of pointer analysis is to determine, for each pointer in the code, the set of memory locations to which it may refer. Without such analysis, the compiler must assume that each pointer can refer to any addressable value, including any space allocated on the run-time heap, any variable whose address is explicitly taken, and any variable passed as a call-by-reference parameter.

One common form of pointer analysis computes POINTSTO sets. These sets contain ⟨*name, object list*⟩ pairs, where the *object list* specifies a set of memory locations that *name* might access. The goal of analysis is to shrink the object lists. For example, the compiler cannot keep an ambiguous value in a register. However, if analysis shows that a pointer refers to precisely one object, and that no other pointers to the object are used in some region in the code, then the compiler can promote the object into a register in that region.

Many techniques for computing POINTSTO sets have been proposed. The techniques vary in how they approximate behavior inside a procedure; *flow-insensitive* methods ignore control flow inside a procedure, while *flow-sensitive* methods account for internal control flow. Some techniques track context through the program by associating a partial call-graph path with each fact. The optimizer can compare paths to determine if two facts can hold simultaneously. Because flow sensitivity and context sensitivity both increase the cost of the analysis, researchers have tried to quantify the benefits that accrue from each. In some applications, flow-insensitive, context-insensitive information appears to suffice. For others, the added precision of more complex analysis helps.

A limited form of ambiguity arises with the use of call-by-reference formal parameters. While this situation can be modelled with the more general POINTSTO formulations, it can also be handled as a complex kind of summary information. This approach computes a set of *alias pairs* for each procedure. If ⟨x,y⟩ ∈ ALIAS(p), then on some path entering p, x and y may refer to the same location.

Inlining as an Alternative

As an alternative to interprocedural analysis, the compiler can perform inline substitution (see Section 8.7.2). Inline expansion of a call site converts the interprocedural problem into a global problem. This approach is attractive because it lets the compiler writer bring the best intraprocedural methods to bear on the problem. However, inlining has potential problems that include code growth, compile time, and the difficulty of generating good code for much larger programs. (In particular, the name space of the postinlining code may be radically larger than that of the original program. This may cause space problems for global analysis and spilling problems for global register allocation.)

Inlining has the potential to radically improve code in situations in which it can make the compiler's knowledge more precise. For example, in object-oriented code, inlining can often reduce the set of object types (classes) that are possible at a given call site. This can eliminate the need for dynamic dispatch and replace it with simple intraprocedural control flow. This eliminates one of the largest sources of overhead in the implementation of object-oriented languages. This is particularly advantageous for procedures (methods) that have small bodies—limiting the potential for negative effects.

Recompilation

Once the compiler uses knowledge about one procedure to optimize another, the correctness of the resulting code depends on the state of both procedures. A subsequent change to the source code of one procedure might change facts that the compiler used to justify the safety of optimizations in other procedures; when this happens, the compiler must recompile the code where it applied the invalidated optimization. Thus, systems that use interprocedural analysis or optimization must pay strict attention to this issue. To resolve this issue, the compiler must either perform a recompilation analysis to track changes in the interprocedural data-flow sets and determine where those changes mandate recompilation or adopt a structure that allows the compiler to avoid the issue.

In general, recompilation analysis requires that the compiler track changes in the results of interprocedural analysis and identify when those changes can invalidate an optimization. For each kind of interprocedural analysis that the compiler performs, it also performs a shadow analysis that detects when recompilation should occur. This increases the amount of analysis, but reduces the amount of compilation.

The alternative approach is to reoptimize the entire program for each compilation. These systems, sometimes called *link-time optimizers*, defer parts of optimization and code generation until the entire program is present. Since the results are only recorded in the executable, and that executable is discarded on the next compilation, this strategy sidesteps the recompilation problem. This approach increases the number of times each component of the executable is analyzed and optimized, but it avoids the complexity of tracking recompilation dependences.

9.5 SUMMARY AND PERSPECTIVE

Most optimization tailors general-case code to the specific context that occurs in the compiled code. The compiler's ability to tailor code is often limited by its knowledge of the program's range of run-time behaviors.

Data-flow analysis allows the compiler to model the run-time behavior of a program at compile time and to draw important, specific knowledge out of the models. Many data-flow problems have been proposed; this chapter presented several of them. Many of those problems have properties that lead to efficient analyses. In particular, problems that can be expressed in a rapid iterative framework have efficient solutions using simple iterative solvers.

Static single assignment form is an intermediate form that encodes both data-flow information and control-dependence information into the name space of the program. Working with SSA form often simplifies both analysis and transformation. Many modern transformations rely on the SSA form of the code.

CHAPTER NOTES

Credit for the first data-flow analysis is usually given to Vyssotsky at Bell Labs in the early 1960s [325]. Earlier work, in the original FORTRAN compiler, included the construction of a control-flow graph and a Markov-style analysis over the CFG to estimate execution frequencies [25]. This analyzer, built by Lois Haibt, might be considered a data-flow analyzer.

Using tbl operations to record hints for ambiguous jumps has worked well in the Massively Scalar Compiler Project at Rice. Almost all transfers of control are encoded using the immediate forms; in the few cases for which a jump to register is needed, the front end generates a concise set of tbls.

Waterman describes the problems that delay slots can cause for CFG construction [95]. Related problems arise in the construction of interprocedural call graphs. Ryder [295], Callahan et al. [60], and Hall and Kennedy [170] explored these problems in the relatively simple setting of FORTRAN programs. Shivers attacked the problem in Scheme [305].

Iterative data-flow analysis has been well explored. Among the seminal papers on this topic in the compilation literature are Kildall's 1973 paper [212], work by Hecht and Ullman [177], and two papers by Kam and Ullman [199, 200]. The treatment in this chapter follows Kam's work.

This chapter focuses on iterative data-flow analysis. Many other algorithms for solving data-flow problems have been proposed [207]. Kennedy's path-listing algorithm precomputes an order for visiting the nodes [205]. The interested reader should explore the structural techniques, including interval analysis [16, 17, 56], T_1-T_2 analysis [323, 176], the Graham-Wegman algorithm [163, 164], balanced-tree, path-compression [318, 319], graph-grammars [208], and the partitioned-variable technique [342].

Dominance has a long history in the literature. Prosser introduced dominance in 1959 but gave no algorithm to compute dominators [280]. Lowry and Medlock describe the algorithm used in their compiler [243]; it takes at least $O(N^2)$ time, where N is the number of statements in the procedure. Several authors developed faster algorithms based on removing nodes from the CFG [9, 3, 281]. Tarjan proposed an $O(N \log N + E)$ algorithm based on depth-first search and union-find [317]. Lengauer and Tarjan improved this time bound [235], as did others [172, 22, 55]. The data-flow formulation for dominators is taken from Allen [13, 16]. The fast data structures for iterative dominance are from an as yet unpublished paper by Cooper, Harvey, and Kennedy. The algorithm in Figure 9.10 is from Ferrante, Ottenstein, and Warren [138].

The SSA construction is based on the seminal work by Cytron et al. [104]. It, in turn, builds on work by Shapiro and Saint [303], by Reif [284, 320], and by Ferrante, Ottenstein, and Warren [138]. The algorithm in Section 9.3.3 builds semipruned SSA form [46]. The details of the renaming algorithm and the algorithm for reconstructing executable code are described by Briggs et al. [47]. The complications introduced by critical edges have long been recognized in the literature of optimization [293, 124, 119, 121, 215]; it should not be surprising that they also arise in the translation from SSA back into executable code.

The IBM PL/I optimizing compiler was one of the earliest systems to perform interprocedural data-flow analysis [313]. A large body of literature has emerged on side-effect problems [31, 29, 96, 97] and on interprocedural constant propagation [62, 105, 329]. Burke and Torczon [57] formulated an analysis that determines which modules in a large program must be recompiled in response to a change in a program's interprocedural information. Pointer analysis is inherently interprocedural; a growing body of literature describes that problem [330, 187, 72, 228, 75, 115, 129, 333, 302, 180, 106, 181]. Ayers, Gottlieb and Schooler described a practical system that analyzed and optimized a subset of the entire program [24].

CHAPTER 10

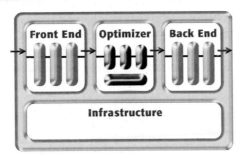

Front End Optimizer Back End

Infrastructure

Scalar Optimizations

10.1 INTRODUCTION

Code optimization in a compiler consists of analyses and transformations intended to improve the quality of the code that the compiler produces. Data-flow analysis, discussed in detail in Chapter 9, enables the compiler to discover opportunities for transformation and to prove the safety of applying the transformations. However, analysis is just the prelude to transformation: the compiler improves the code's performance by rewriting it.

Data-flow analysis serves as a unifying conceptual framework for the classic problems in static analysis. Problems are posed as data-flow frameworks. Instances of these problems, exhibited by programs, are solved using some general-purpose solver. The results are produced as sets of facts that annotate some form of the code. Sometimes, the insights of analysis can be directly encoded into the IR form of the code, as with SSA form.

Unfortunately, no unifying framework exists for optimizations—which combine a specific analysis with the rewriting necessary to achieve a desired improvement. Optimizations consume and produce the compiler's IR; they might be viewed as complex rewriting engines. Some optimizations are specified as detailed algorithms; for example, dominator-based value numbering builds up a collection of facts from low-level details (Section 8.5.2). Others are specified by high-level descriptions; for example, global redundancy elimination operates from a set of data-flow equations (Section 8.6), and inline substitution is usually described as replacing a call site with the text of the called procedure with appropriate substitution of actual parameters for formal parameters (Section 8.7.2). The techniques used to describe and implement transformations vary widely.

The optimizer in a modern compiler is typically structured as a series of filters. Each filter, or pass, takes as its input the IR form of the code. Each pass produces as its output a rewritten version of the IR form of the code. This structure has evolved for several practical reasons. It breaks the implementation into smaller pieces, avoiding some of the complexity that arises in large, monolithic programs. It allows independent implementation and testing of the passes, which simplifies development, testing, and maintenance. It allows the compiler to provide different levels of optimization by activating a different set of passes for each level. Some passes execute once; others may execute several times in the sequence.

One of the critical issues in the design of an optimizer, then, is selecting a set of passes to implement and an order in which to run them. The selection of passes determines what specific inefficiencies in the IR program are discovered and how the code is improved to reduce or eliminate the inefficiencies. The order of execution determines how the passes interact.

For example, in the appropriate context ($r_2 \geq 0$ and $r_5 = 4$), the optimizer might rewrite `mult` $r_2,r_5 \Rightarrow r_{17}$ as `lshiftI` $r_2,2 \Rightarrow r_{17}$. This improves the code by reducing demand for registers and replacing a potentially expensive operation, `mult`, with a cheaper operation, `lshiftI`. In most cases, this is profitable. If, however, the next pass relies on commutativity to rearrange expressions, then replacing a multiply with a shift forecloses an opportunity (multiply is commutative; shift is not). To the extent that it makes later passes less effective, it may hurt overall code quality. Deferring the replacement of multiplies by shifts may avoid this problem; the context needed to prove safety and profitability for this rewrite is likely to survive the intervening passes.

Sometimes, the optimizer should repeat a pass multiple times. For example, eliminating dead, or useless, code benefits the compiler in several ways. It shrinks the IR program, so later passes have less code to process. It eliminates some definitions and uses, so it may make the results of data-flow analysis sharper. Finally, it improves the resulting code—its actual purpose—by removing operations whose execution cannot be noticed. Because of the first two effects, dead-code elimination is often run early in compilation. For the final effect, it should run late in the compilation. Some passes are known to make code useless, so dead-code elimination might also be run after such

OPTIMIZATION AS SOFTWARE ENGINEERING

Having a separate optimizer can simplify the design and implementation of a compiler. The optimizer simplifies the front end; it can generate general-purpose code and ignore special cases. The optimizer simplifies the back end; it can focus on mapping the IR version of the program to the target machine. Without an optimizer, both the front end and back end must be concerned with finding opportunities for improvement and exploiting them.

In a pass-structured optimizer, each pass contains a transformation and the analysis required to support it. In principle, each task that the optimizer performs can be implemented once. This provides a single point of control and lets the compiler writer implement complex functions once, rather than many times. For example, deleting an operation from the IR can be complicated. If the deleted operation leaves a basic block empty, except for the block-ending branch or jump, then the transformation should also delete the block and reconnect the block's predecessors to its successors, as appropriate. Keeping this functionality in one place simplifies implementation, understanding, and maintenance.

From a software engineering perspective, the pass structure, with a clear separation of concerns, makes sense. It lets each pass focus on a single task. It provides a clear separation of concerns—value numbering ignores register pressure and the register allocator ignores common subexpressions. It lets the compiler writer test passes independently and thoroughly, and it simplifies fault isolation.

passes. Thus, compilers often run dead-code elimination several times during a compilation.

This chapter presents a selected set of transformations. The material is organized around a taxonomy of transformations, presented in Section 10.2. Section 10.3 presents example optimizations for those parts of the taxonomy that are not well covered in other chapters. The advanced topics section briefly discusses four subjects: combining optimizations for better results, operator strength reduction, optimizing for objective functions other than speed, and choosing an optimization sequence.

10.2 A TAXONOMY FOR TRANSFORMATIONS

The first hurdle in building an optimizer is conceptual. The literature on optimization describes hundreds of distinct algorithms for improving IR programs. The compiler writer must select a subset of these transformations to apply. Reading the original papers provides little help in the decision process, since most of the authors recommend using their own transformations.

To organize the space of optimizations, we use a simple taxonomy that categorizes transformations by the effect that they have on the code. The taxonomy is, of necessity, approximate. For example, some transformations have more than one effect. At a high level, we divide the transformations into two categories: machine-independent transformations and machine-dependent transformations.

Machine-independent transformations are those that largely ignore the details of the target machine. In many cases, the profitability of a transformation actually depends on detailed machine-dependent issues, but the implementation of the transformation ignores them.

For example, when local value numbering finds a redundant computation, it replaces it with a reference. This eliminates a computation, but it may increase the demand for registers. If the increased demand forces the register allocator to spill some value to memory, the cost of the memory operations probably exceeds the savings from eliminating the operation. However, value numbering deliberately ignores this effect because it cannot accurately determine whether a value must be spilled.

Machine-dependent transformations are those that explicitly consider details of the target machine. Many of these transformations fall into the realm of code generation, in which the compiler maps the IR form of the code onto the target machine. However, some machine-dependent transformations fall in the realm of the optimizer. (Most are beyond the scope of this chapter, however.) Examples include transformations that rearrange the code to improve its behavior with regard to cache memory or that attempt to expose instruction-level parallelism.

While the distinction between these two categories is somewhat artificial, it has long been used as a first cut at classifying transformations.

10.2.1 Machine-Independent Transformations

In truth, there are a limited number of machine-independent ways that the compiler can improve the program. We will concern ourselves with five effects, shown in Figure 10.1. They are

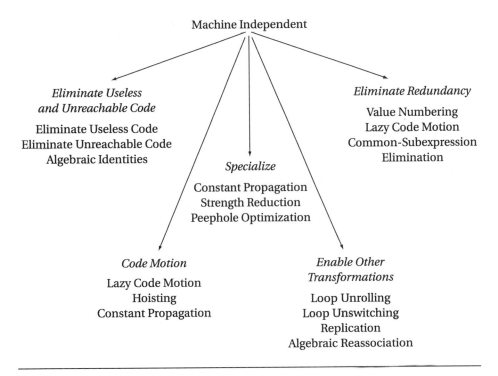

FIGURE 10.1   Machine-Independent Transformations

- *Eliminate useless and unreachable code:* If the compiler can prove that an operation is either useless or unreachable, it can eliminate the operation. Methods include useless-code elimination and unreachable-code elimination (Section 10.3.1), simplification of algebraic identities (part of local value numbering in Section 8.3.2), and sparse conditional constant propagation (Section 10.4.1), which discovers and removes some kinds of unreachable code.

- *Move an operation to a place where it executes less frequently:* If the compiler can find a place where an operation will execute less frequently and produce the same answer, it can move the operation there. Methods include lazy code motion (Section 10.3.2) and constant propagation (Sections 9.2.4, 10.3.3, and 10.4.1), which moves a computation from run time to compile time.

- *Specialize a computation:* If the compiler can understand the specific context in which an operation will execute, it can often specialize the code to that context. Methods include operator strength reduction (Section 10.4.2), constant propagation (Sections 9.2.4, 10.3.3, and 10.4.1), and peephole optimization (Section 11.4.1).

- *Enable other transformations:* If the compiler can rearrange the code in a way that exposes more opportunities for other transformations, it can improve the overall effectiveness of optimization. Methods include inline substitution (Section 8.7.2), cloning (Sections 8.7.1 and 12.4.2), and algebraic reassociation (Section 10.3.4).

- *Eliminate a redundant computation:* If the compiler can prove that a computation is redundant, it can replace the computation with a reference to the previously computed value. Methods include local value numbering (Section 8.3.2), superlocal value numbering (Section 8.5.1), dominator-based value numbering (Section 8.5.2), and global common-subexpression elimination (Section 8.6).

We have already seen optimizations in each of these categories. Section 10.3 fills in the machine-independent part of the taxonomy more fully by presenting additional optimizations in each category, except redundancy elimination, an area already explored to a reasonable depth in Chapter 8.

Some techniques fit into several categories. Lazy code motion achieves both code motion and redundancy elimination. Constant propagation achieves a type of code motion—moving operations from run time to compile time—and specialization. In at least one form (see Section 10.4.1), it identifies and eliminates certain kinds of unreachable code.

10.2.2 Machine-Dependent Transformations

In machine-dependent transformations, the effects that the compiler can exploit are more limited. It can

- *Take advantage of special hardware features:* Often, processor architects include features that they believe will help program execution. Such features include specialized operations—like a load operation that bypasses the cache hierarchy, a branch operation that tells the branch-prediction hardware not to track its results, or an advisory prefetch operation. If the compiler can make effective use of these features, they will, indeed, speed program execution. Recognizing opportunities to use these features often takes additional work. The compiler writer might add new transformations to the optimizer or use a more complex instruction selection process. Some of this work falls into the realm of instruction selection, described in depth in Chapter 11.

■ *Manage or hide latency:* In some cases, the compiler can arrange the final code in a way that hides the latency of some operations. For example, memory operations can have latencies in the tens or hundreds of cycles. If the target machine supports either a prefetch operation or a nonblocking load, the compiler may find a schedule that issues a memory operation far enough in advance of its use to hide the latency. Rearranging the iteration order of a loop or a set of nested loops, or changing the packing of values into memory, can improve run-time cache locality and help manage latency by reducing the number of memory operations that miss in the cache. Instruction scheduling, described in detail in Chapter 12, addresses some of these problems. The compiler writer may, however, need to add transformations that directly address these issues.

■ *Manage bounded machine resources:* Another source of complexity in compilation comes from the fact that the target machine has bounded resources—registers, functional units, cache memory, and main memory. The compiler must map the needs of the computation onto the bounded resources that the machine provides, and when the computation needs more resources than are available, the compiler must rewrite the code in a way that reduces its resource needs. For example, register allocation maps a computation's values to the target machine's register set; Chapter 13 describes this problem in detail.

Figure 10.2 shows the machine-dependent portion of the taxonomy. Because an example of each of these effects is the subject of a separate chapter, we omit them from this chapter.

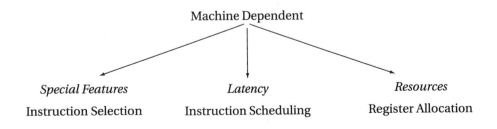

FIGURE 10.2   Machine-Dependent Transformations

10.3 EXAMPLE OPTIMIZATIONS

This section describes additional optimizations in four of the five categories that we identified as machine-independent transformations. Each is intended to improve performance on a scalar uniprocessor machine. The selection of optimizations is illustrative, rather than exhaustive. However, each transformation is a good example of how to achieve the specific effect associated with its category of machine-independent transformations.

10.3.1 Eliminating Useless and Unreachable Code

Sometimes, a program contains computations that have no externally visible effect. If the compiler can determine that a given operation has this property, it can remove the operation from the program. In general, programmers do not intentionally create such code. However, it arises in most programs as the direct result of optimization in the compiler and often from macro expansion in the compiler's front end.

Two distinct effects can make an operation eligible for removal. The operation can be *dead* or *useless*—that is, no operation uses its result, or any use of its result cannot be detected externally. The operation can be *unreachable*—that is, no valid control-flow path contains the operation. If a computation falls into either category, it can be eliminated.

Removing useless or unreachable code yields a smaller IR program, which leads to a smaller executable program and to faster compilation. It may also increase the compiler's ability to improve the code. For example, unreachable code may have effects that show up in the results of static analysis and prevent the application of some transformations. In this case, removing the unreachable block may change the analysis results and allow further transformations (see, for example, sparse conditional constant propagation in Section 10.4.1).

Some forms of redundancy elimination also remove useless code. For example, local value numbering applies algebraic identities to simplify the code. Examples include $x + 0 \Rightarrow x$, $y \times 1 \Rightarrow y$, and $\max(z,z) \Rightarrow z$. Each of these eliminates a useless operation—by definition, an operation that, when removed, makes no difference in the program's externally visible behavior.

The algorithms in this section modify the control-flow graph (CFG). Thus, they distinguish branches (cbr) from jumps (jump). Close attention to this distinction will help the reader understand the algorithms.

Eliminating Useless Code

The classic algorithms for eliminating useless code operate in a manner similar to mark-sweep garbage collectors (see Section 6.7.3). Like mark-sweep collectors, they perform two passes over the code. The first pass begins by clearing all the mark fields and marking "critical" operations. An operation is *critical* if it sets return values for the procedure,[1] it is an input/output statement, or it affects the value in a storage location that may be accessible from outside the procedure. Examples of critical operations include code in the procedure's entry and exit blocks and calls to other procedures. Next, it traces the operands of critical operations back to their definitions and marks those operations as useful. This process continues, in a simple worklist iterative scheme, until no more operations can be marked as useful. The second pass walks the code and removes any operation not marked as useful.

Figure 10.3 makes these ideas concrete. The algorithm, which we call *Dead*, assumes that the code is in SSA form. This simplifies the process because each use refers to a single definition. *Dead* consists of two passes. The first, called *MarkPass*, discovers the set of useful operations. The second, called *SweepPass*, removes useless operations. *MarkPass* relies on reverse dominance frontiers, defined later in this section.

The treatment of operations other than branches or jumps is straightforward. The marking phase determines whether an operation is useful. The sweep phase removes operations that have not been marked as useful.

The treatment of control-flow operations is more complex. Every jump is considered useful. Branches are considered useful only if the execution of a useful operation depends on their presence. As the marking phase discovers useful operations, it also marks the appropriate branches as useful. To map from a marked operation to the branches that it makes useful, the algorithm relies on the notion of *control dependence*.

The definition of control dependence relies on postdominance. In a CFG, node j postdominates node i if every path from i to the CFG's exit node passes through i. Using postdominance, we can define control dependence as follows: in a CFG, node j is control-dependent on node i if and only if

1. There exists a nonnull path from i to j such that j postdominates every node on the path after i. Once execution begins on this path, it must flow through j to reach the CFG's exit (from the definition of postdominance), and

---

1. This can happen in any of several ways, including an assignment to a call-by-reference parameter, assignment through an unknown pointer, or an actual return statement.

```
         Dead( )                          MarkPass( )
           MarkPass( )                      WorkList ← ∅
           SweepPass( )
                                          for each operation i
                                            clear i's mark
                                            if i is critical then
                                              mark operation i
                                              WorkList ← WorkList ∪ {i}

         SweepPass( )                     while (WorkList ≠ ∅)
           for each operation i             remove i from WorkList
             if i is unmarked then            (assume i is x ← y op z)
               if i is a branch then
                 rewrite i with a jump       if def(y) is not marked then
                   to i's nearest marked        mark def(y)
                   postdominator                WorkList ← WorkList ∪ {def(y)}
               if i is not a jump then        if def(z) is not marked then
                 delete i                       mark def(z)
                                                WorkList ← WorkList ∪ {def(z)}

                                            for each block b ∈ RDF(block(i))
                                              let j be the branch that ends b
                                              if j is unmarked then
                                                mark j
                                                WorkList ← WorkList ∪ {j}
```

FIGURE 10.3 Useless Code Elimination

2. j does not strictly postdominate i. Another edge leaves i and control may flow along a path to a node not on the path to j. There must be a path beginning with this edge that leads to the CFG's exit without passing through j.

In other words, two or more edges leave block i. One edge leads to j, and one or more of the other edges do not. Thus, the decision made at the branch ending block i can determine whether or not j executes. If an operation in j is useful, then the branch ending i is also useful.

This notion of control dependence is captured precisely by the *reverse dominance frontier* of j, denoted RDF(j). Reverse dominance frontiers are simply dominance frontiers computed on the reverse CFG. When *MarkPass* marks an operation as useful, it visits every block in the reverse dominance frontier of the block containing this useful operation and marks its block-ending branch as useful. As it marks these branches, it adds them to the worklist.

SweepPass replaces any unmarked branch with a jump to its first postdominator that contains a marked operation. If the branch is unmarked, then its successors, down to its immediate postdominator, contain no useful operations. (Otherwise, when those operations were marked, the branch would have been marked.) A similar argument applies if the immediate postdominator contains no marked operations. To find the nearest useful postdominator, the algorithm can walk up the postdominator tree until it finds a block that contains a useful operation. Since, by definition, the exit block is useful, this search must terminate.

After *Dead* runs, the code contains no useless computations. It may contain empty blocks, which can be removed by the next algorithm.

Eliminating Useless Control Flow

Optimization can change the IR form of the program so that it has useless control flow. If the compiler includes optimizations that can produce useless control flow as a side effect, the compiler should include a pass that simplifies the CFG by eliminating useless control flow. This section presents a simple algorithm called *Clean* that handles this task.

Clean uses four transformations on the CFG, shown in Figure 10.4. They are applied in the following order:

1. *Folding a Redundant Branch*   If *Clean* finds a block that ends in a branch, and both sides of the branch target the same block, it should replace the branch with a jump to the target block. This situation arises as the result of other simplifications. For example, B_i might have had two successors, each with a jump to B_j. If another transformation removed all the computations from those blocks, then removing the empty blocks might produce the initial graph shown in Part (1) of Figure 10.4.

2. *Removing an Empty Block*   If *Clean* finds a block that contains only a jump, it can merge the block into its successor. This situation arises when other passes remove all of the operations from a block B_i. Consider the initial graph in Part (2) of Figure 10.4. Since B_i has only one successor, B_j, the transformation retargets the edges that enter B_i to B_j and deletes B_i from B_j's set of predecessors. This simplifies the graph. It should also speed up execution. In the original graph, the paths through B_i needed two control-flow operations to reach B_j. In the transformed graph, those paths use one operation to reach B_j.

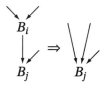

(1) Folding a Redundant Branch   (2) Removing an Empty Block

(3) Combining Blocks   (4) Hoisting a Branch

FIGURE 10.4   Transformations Used in Clean

3. *Combining Blocks*   If *Clean* finds a block B_i that ends in a jump to B_j and B_j has only one predecessor, it can combine the two blocks. This situation can arise in several ways. Another transformation might eliminate other edges that entered B_j, or B_i and B_j might be the result of folding a redundant branch (described previously). In either case, the two blocks can be combined into a single block. This eliminates the jump at the end of B_i.

4. *Hoisting a Branch*   If *Clean* finds a block B_i that ends with a jump to an empty block B_j and B_j ends with a branch, *Clean* can replace the block-ending jump in B_i with a copy of the branch from B_j. In effect, this hoists the branch into B_i. This situation arises when other passes eliminate the operations in B_j, leaving a jump to a branch. The transformed code achieves the same effect with just a branch. This adds an edge to the CFG. Notice that B_i cannot be empty, or else empty block removal would have eliminated it. Similarly, B_i cannot be B_j's sole predecessor, or else *Clean* would have combined the two blocks. (After hoisting, B_j still has at least one predecessor.)

Some bookkeeping is required to implement these transformations. Some of the modifications are trivial. To fold a redundant branch in a program represented with ILOC and a graphical CFG, *Clean* simply overwrites the block-ending branch with a jump and adjusts the successor and predecessor lists of the blocks. Others are more difficult. Merging two blocks may involve allocating space for the merged block, copying the operations into the new block, adjusting the predecessor and successor lists of the new block and its neighbors in the CFG, and discarding the two original blocks.

Clean applies these four transformations in a systematic fashion. It traverses the graph in postorder, so that B_i's successors are simplified before B_i, unless the successor lies along a back edge with respect to the postorder numbering. In that case, *Clean* will visit the predecessor before the successor. This is unavoidable in a cyclic graph. Simplifying successors before predecessors reduces the number of times that the implementation must move some edges.

In some situations, more than one of the transformations may apply. Careful analysis of the various cases leads to the order shown in Figure 10.5. The algorithm uses a series of *if* statements rather than an *if-then-else* to let it apply multiple transformations in a single visit to a block.

If the CFG contains back edges, then a pass of *Clean* may create additional opportunities—namely, unprocessed successors along the back edges. These, in turn, may create other opportunities. For this reason, *Clean* repeats the transformation sequence iteratively until the CFG stops changing. It must

```
OnePass( )
    for each block i, in postorder
        if i ends in a conditional branch then
            if both targets are identical then
                replace the branch with a jump

        if i ends in a jump to j then
            if i is empty then
                replace transfers to i with transfers to j

            if j has only one predecessor then
                coalesce i and j

            if j is empty and ends in a conditional branch then
                overwrite i's jump with a copy of j's branch


Clean( )
    while the CFG keeps changing
        compute postorder
        OnePass( )
```

FIGURE 10.5   The Algorithm for *Clean*

compute a new postorder numbering between calls to *OnePass* because each pass changes the underlying graph. Figure 10.5 shows pseudo-code for *Clean*.

Clean does not handle all the cases that can arise. For example, it cannot, by itself, eliminate an empty loop. Consider the CFG shown in Figure 10.6(a). Assume that block B_2 is empty. None of *Clean*'s transformations can eliminate B_2. The branch that ends B_2 is not redundant. B_2 does not end with a jump, so *Clean* cannot combine it with B_3. Its predecessor ends with a branch rather than a jump, so *Clean* can neither combine B_2 with B_1 nor fold its branch into B_1.

However, cooperation between *Clean* and *Dead* can eliminate the empty loop. *Dead* used control dependence to mark useful branches. If B_1 and B_3 contain useful operations, but B_2 does not, then the marking pass in *Dead* will not mark the branch ending B_2 as useful because $B_2 \notin \text{RDF}(B_3)$. Because the branch is useless, the code that computes the branch condition is also useless. Thus, *Dead* eliminates all of the operations in B_2 and converts the branch that ends it into a jump to its closest useful postdominator, B_3. This eliminates the original loop and produces the CFG shown in Figure 10.6(b).

In this form, *Clean* folds B_2 into B_1, as shown in Figure 10.6(c). This also makes the branch at the end of B_1 redundant. *Clean* rewrites it with a jump, producing the CFG shown in Figure 10.6(d). At this point, if B_1 is B_3's sole remaining predecessor, *Clean* coalesces the two blocks into a single one.

This cooperation is simpler and more effective than adding another transformation to *Clean* that handles empty loops. Such a transformation might recognize a branch from B_i to itself and, for an empty B_i, rewrite it with a jump to the branch's other target. The problem lies in determining when B_i is truly empty. If B_i contains no operations other than the branch, then the code that computes the branch condition must lie outside the loop. Thus, the

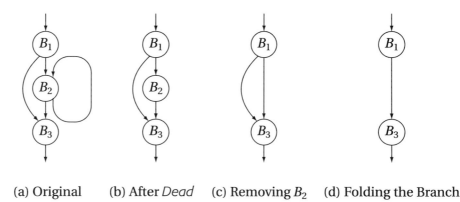

(a) Original   (b) After *Dead*   (c) Removing B_2 (d) Folding the Branch

FIGURE 10.6   Removing an Empty Loop

transformation is safe only if the self-loop never executes. Reasoning about the number of executions of the self-loop requires knowledge about the run-time value of the comparison, a task that is, in general, beyond a compiler's ability. If the block contains operations, but only operations that control the branch, then the transformation would need to recognize the situation with pattern matching. In either case, this new transformation would be more complex than the four included in *Clean*. Relying on the combination of *Dead* and *Clean* achieves the appropriate result in a simpler, more modular fashion.

Eliminating Unreachable Code

Sometimes the CFG contains code that is unreachable. The compiler should find unreachable blocks and remove them. A block can be unreachable for two distinct reasons: there may be no path through the CFG that leads to the block, or the paths that reach the block may not be executable—for example, guarded by a condition that always evaluates to false.

The former case is easy to handle. The compiler can perform a simple mark-sweep-style reachability analysis on the CFG. Starting with the entry, it marks every reachable node in the CFG. If all branches and jumps are unambiguous, then all unmarked blocks can be deleted. With ambiguous branches or jumps, the compiler must preserve any block whose address can reach such a branch or jump.[2] This analysis is simple and inexpensive. It can be done during traversals of the CFG for other purposes or during CFG construction itself.

Handling the second case is harder. It requires the compiler to reason about the values of expressions that control branches. Section 10.4.1 presents an algorithm that finds some blocks that are unreachable because the paths leading to them are not executable.

10.3.2 Code Motion

Moving a computation to a point where it executes less frequently than it executed in its original position should reduce the total operation count of the running program. The first transformation presented in this section, *lazy code motion*, uses code motion to speed up execution. Because loops tend to execute many more times than the code that surrounds them, much of the work in

---

2. If the source language includes the ability to perform arithmetic on pointers or labels, every block must be preserved. Otherwise, the compiler should be able to limit the preserved set to those blocks whose labels are referenced.

this area has focused on moving loop-invariant expressions out of loops. Lazy code motion performs loop-invariant code motion. It extends the notions originally formulated in the available expressions problem to include operations that are redundant along some, but not all, paths. It inserts code to make them redundant on all paths and removes the newly redundant expression.

Some compilers, however, optimize for other criteria. If the compiler is concerned about the size of the executable code, it may consider code motion to reduce the number of copies of a specific operation. The second transformation presented in this section, *hoisting*, uses code motion to reduce duplication of instructions. It discovers cases in which inserting an operation makes several copies of the same operation redundant without changing the values computed by the program.

Lazy Code Motion

Lazy code motion (LCM) uses data-flow analysis to discover both operations that are candidates for code motion and locations where it can place those operations. The algorithm operates on the IR form of the program and its CFG, rather than SSA form. The algorithm consists of six sets of data-flow equations and a simple strategy for interpreting the results as directions for modifying the code.

LCM combines code motion with elimination of redundant and partially redundant computations. Redundancy was introduced in Chapter 8. A computation is partially redundant at point p if it occurs on some, but not all, paths that reach p. Figure 10.7 shows two ways that an expression can be partially redundant. In the first example, a ← b × c occurs on one path leading to the merge point but not on the other. To make the second computation redundant, LCM inserts an evaluation of a ← b × c on the other path. In the second example, a ← b × c is redundant along the loop's back edge but not along the edge entering the loop. Inserting an evaluation of a ← b × c before the loop makes the occurrence inside the loop redundant. By making the loop-invariant computation redundant and eliminating it, LCM moves it out of the loop.

To accomplish this, the optimizer solves a series of data-flow problems. It computes information about *availability*, a forward data-flow problem familiar from Section 8.6, and about *anticipability*, a related notion solved as a backward data-flow problem. The next step uses the results of these analyses to compute an *earliest placement*; this annotates each edge with a set describing the expressions for which this edge is a legal placement and no earlier placement in the graph is possible. The algorithm then looks for possible *later placements*—situations in which moving an expression forward in the

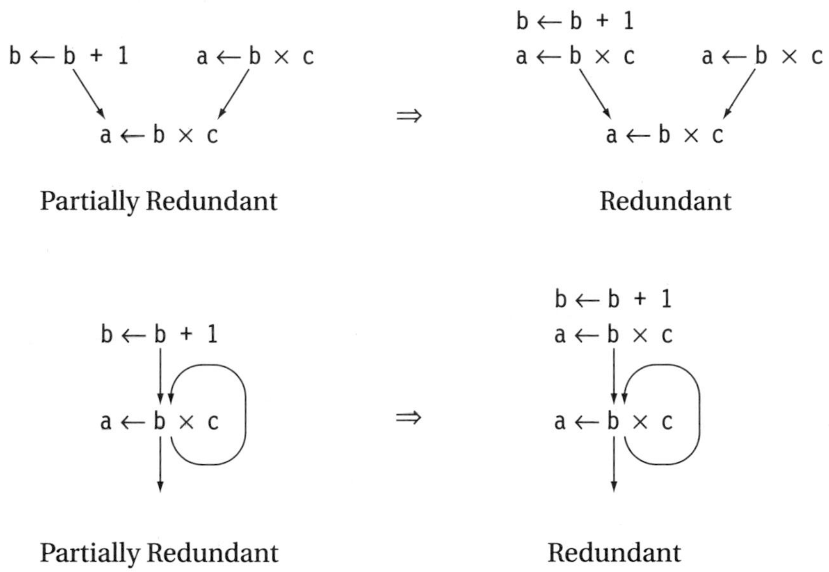

FIGURE 10.7 Converting Partial Redundancies into Redundancies

CFG or later in execution from its earliest placement achieves the same effect as the earliest placement. Finally, it computes an *insertion set* for each edge that specifies which expressions to insert along that edge and a *deletion set* for each node that contains the expressions to remove from the corresponding block. A simple follow-on pass interprets the insertion and deletion sets and rewrites the IR.

Background The first step in solving the data-flow equations is to compute local predicates for each block. LCM uses three kinds of local information.

1. DEEXPR(b) is the set of expressions e in block b that are downward exposed. If $e \in$ DEEXPR(b), evaluating e at the end of block b produces the same value as evaluating it in its original position.

2. UEEXPR(b) is the set of upward-exposed expressions e in block b. If $e \in$ UEEXPR(b), evaluating e at the entry to block b produces the same value as evaluating it in its original position.

3. EXPRKILL(b) is the set of expressions e that are killed in block b. If $e \in$ EXPRKILL(b), then b contains a redefinition of one or more operands

of e. As a consequence, evaluating e at the entry to b may produce a different value than evaluating it at the end of b.

We have used all these sets in other data-flow problems.

The equations for LCM rely on several implicit assumptions about the shape of the code. They assume that textually identical expressions always define the same name, which suggests an unlimited set of names—one name for each textually distinct expression. (This is rule one from the register-naming rules described in Section 5.6.1.) Since every definition of r_k comes from the expression $r_i + r_j$ and no other expression defines r_k, the optimizer does not need to find each definition of $r_i + r_j$ and copy the result into a temporary location for later reuse. Instead, it can simply use r_k.

LCM moves expressions, not assignments. Requiring that textually identical expressions define the same virtual register implies that program variables are set by register-to-register copy operations. The code in Figure 10.8 has this property. By dividing the name space into variables and expressions, we can limit the domain of LCM to expressions. In that example, the variables are r_2, r_4, and r_8, each of which is defined by a copy operation. All the other names, r_1, r_3, r_5, r_6, r_7, r_{20}, and r_{21}, represent expressions. The following table shows the local information for the blocks in the example:

	B_1	B_2	B_3
DEEXPR	$\{r_1, r_3, r_5\}$	$\{r_7, r_{20}, r_{21}\}$	$\cdots$
UEEXPR	$\{r_1, r_3\}$	$\{r_6, r_{20}, r_{21}\}$	$\cdots$
EXPRKILL	$\{r_5, r_6, r_7\}$	$\{r_5, r_6, r_7\}$	$\cdots$

Available Expressions   The first step in LCM computes available expressions.

$$\text{AVAILIN}(n) = \bigcap_{m \in preds(n)} \text{AVAILOUT}(m), \quad n \neq n_0$$

$$\text{AVAILOUT}(m) = \text{DEEXPR}(m) \cup (\text{AVAILIN}(m) \cap \overline{\text{EXPRKILL}(m)})$$

The form of the equations differs slightly from the one shown in Section 8.6. In this form, the equations compute a distinct set for each block's entry, AVAILIN, and its exit, AVAILOUT. The AVAIL sets in Section 8.6 are identical to the AVAILIN sets here. The AVAILOUT sets represent the contribution of a block to its successors' AVAILIN sets. The solver must initialize AVAILIN(n_0) to $\emptyset$ and the remaining AVAILIN and AVAILOUT sets to contain the set of all expressions in the procedure.

For the example in Figure 10.8, the equations for availability produce the following results:

	B_1	B_2	B_3
AVAILIN	$\emptyset$	$\{r_1, r_3\}$	$\{r_1, r_3\}$
AVAILOUT	$\{r_1, r_3, r_5\}$	$\{r_1, r_3, r_7, r_{20}, r_{21}\}$	$\cdots$

In global redundancy elimination, we interpreted $x \in$ AVAILIN(b) to mean that, along every path from n_0 to b, x is computed and none of its operands is redefined between the point where x is computed and b. An alternative view, useful in understanding LCM, is that $x \in$ AVAILIN(b) if and only if the compiler could place an evaluation of x at the entry to b and obtain the result produced by the most recent evaluation on any control-flow path from n_0 to b. In this light, the AVAILIN sets tell the compiler how far forward in the CFG it can move the evaluation of x, ignoring any uses of x.

Anticipable Expressions Availability provides LCM with information about moving evaluations forward in the CFG. LCM also needs information about moving

```
B₁: loadI   1        ⇒ r₁
    i2i     r₁       ⇒ r₂
    loadAI  r₀,@m    ⇒ r₃
    i2i     r₃       ⇒ r₄
    cmp_LT  r₂,r₄    ⇒ r₅
    cbr     r₅        → B₂,B₃
B₂: mult    r₁₇,r₁₈  ⇒ r₂₀
    add     r₁₉,r₂₀  ⇒ r₂₁
    i2i     r₂₁      ⇒ r₈
    addI    r₂,1     ⇒ r₆
    i2i     r₆       ⇒ r₂
    cmp_GT  r₂,r₄    ⇒ r₇
    cbr     r₇        → B₃,B₂
B₃: ...
```

$$\left\{ \begin{array}{c} r_1, r_3, r_5, r_6, \\ r_7, r_{20}, r_{21} \end{array} \right\}$$

Set of Expressions

A Simple Loop

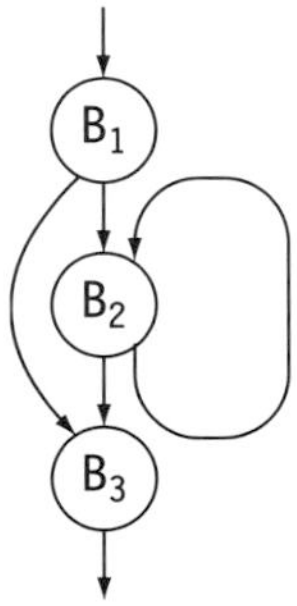

Its CFG

FIGURE 10.8 Example for Lazy Code Motion

evaluations backward in the CFG. To obtain this, it computes information about *anticipable expressions*, namely, expressions that can be evaluated earlier in the CFG than their current block.

The UEEXPR sets capture this notion locally. If $e \in$ UEEXPR(b), then b contains at least one evaluation of e and that evaluation uses operands that are defined before entry to b. Thus, $e \in$ UEEXPR(b) implies that an evaluation of e at the entry to b must produce the same value as the first evaluation of e in b, so the compiler can safely move that first evaluation to block b's entry.

The second set of data-flow equations for LCM extends the notion of anticipability across multiple blocks. It is a backward data-flow problem.

$$\text{ANTOUT}(n) = \bigcap_{m \in succ(n)} \text{ANTIN}(m), \quad n \neq n_f$$

$$\text{ANTIN}(m) = \text{UEEXPR}(m) \cup (\text{ANTOUT}(m) \cap \overline{\text{EXPRKILL}(m)})$$

LCM must initialize the ANTOUT set for n_f to $\emptyset$ and the remaining ANTIN and ANTOUT sets to contain the set of all expressions in the procedure.

ANTIN and ANTOUT provide the compiler with information about the backward motion of expressions in ANTOUT(b). If $x \in$ ANTOUT(b), then the compiler can place an evaluation of x at the end of block b and produce the same value as the next evaluation on any path leaving b.

For the ongoing example, the equations for anticipability produce the following results:

	B_1	B_2	B_3
ANTIN	$\{r_1, r_3\}$	$\{r_{20}, r_{21}\}$	$\emptyset$
ANTOUT	$\emptyset$	$\emptyset$	$\emptyset$

Earliest Placement Given availability, which encodes information about forward movement in the CFG, and anticipability, which encodes information about backward movement in the CFG, the compiler can compute an *earliest placement* for each expression. To keep the equations simple, it is easier to place computations on edges in the CFG rather than in the nodes. This lets the equations compute a placement without having to choose a block. The compiler can defer until later the decision to place the operation at the end of the edge's source, at the start of its destination, or in a new block in midedge. (See the discussion of critical edges in Section 9.3.5.)

For an edge $\langle i, j \rangle$ in the CFG, an expression e is in EARLIEST(i, j) if and only if the computation can legally move to $\langle i, j \rangle$ and cannot move to any earlier edge in the CFG. The equation for EARLIEST reflects this condition:

$$\textsc{Earliest}(i,j) = \textsc{AntIn}(j) \cap \overline{\textsc{AvailOut}(i)} \cap (\textsc{ExprKill}(i) \cup \overline{\textsc{AntOut}(i)})$$

These conditions all have simple explanations. For e to be legal on edge $\langle i,j \rangle$ and not be movable further up in the CFG, the following three conditions must hold:

1. $e \in \textsc{AntIn}(j)$ proves that the compiler can move e to the head of j.

2. $e \notin \textsc{AvailOut}(i)$ proves that no previous computation of e is available on exit from i. If $e \in \textsc{AvailOut}(i)$, then a computation of e on $\langle i,j \rangle$ would be redundant.

3. $e \in (\textsc{ExprKill}(i) \cup \overline{\textsc{AntOut}(i)})$ proves that e cannot move upward, through i, to an earlier edge. If $e \in \textsc{ExprKill}(i)$, then e would produce a different result at the head of block i, so it cannot move through i. If $e \in \overline{\textsc{AntOut}(i)}$, then e cannot move into block i.

Since LCM cannot move an expression earlier than n_0, LCM should ignore the final term, $(\textsc{ExprKill}(i) \cup \overline{\textsc{AntOut}(i)})$ for $i = n_0$. This simplification marginally reduces the cost of computing EARLIEST.

Computing EARLIEST requires no iteration; it relies solely on previously computed values. EARLIEST is used, in turn, in the computation of the LATER sets. Because the LATER computation iterates, it may be faster to precompute the EARLIEST sets for each edge. Alternatively, the compiler writer can forward substitute the right-hand side of the definition of EARLIEST (i, j) directly into the next set of equations.

For the continuing example, the EARLIEST computation produces the following sets:

	$\langle B_1, B_2 \rangle$	$\langle B_1, B_3 \rangle$	$\langle B_2, B_2 \rangle$	$\langle B_2, B_3 \rangle$
EARLIEST	$\{r_{20}, r_{21}\}$	$\emptyset$	$\emptyset$	$\emptyset$

Later Placement The final data-flow problem in LCM determines whether an earliest placement can be moved forward (or later) in the CFG, while achieving the same effect.

$$\textsc{LaterIn}(j) = \bigcap_{i \in pred(j)} \textsc{Later}(i,j), \quad j \neq n_0$$

$$\text{LATER}(i,j) = \text{EARLIEST}(i,j) \cup \text{LATERIN}(i) \cap \overline{\text{UEEXPR}(i)}, \quad i \in pred(j)$$

The solver must initialize $\text{LATERIN}(n_0)$ to $\emptyset$.

An expression $e \in \text{LATERIN}(k)$ if and only if every path that reaches k includes an edge $\langle p, q \rangle$ such that $e \in \text{EARLIEST}(p, q)$, and the path from q to k neither redefines e's operand nor contains an evaluation of e (that earlier placement would anticipate). The EARLIEST term in the equation for LATER ensures that $\text{LATER}(i,j)$ includes $\text{EARLIEST}(i,j)$. The rest of that equation puts e into $\text{LATER}(i,j)$ if e can be moved forward from i ($e \in \text{LATERIN}(i)$) and a placement at the entry to i does not anticipate a use in i ($e \notin \text{UEEXPR}(i)$).

Once the equations have been solved, $e \in \text{LATERIN}(i)$ implies that the compiler could move the evaluation of e forward through i without losing any benefit—that is, there is no evaluation of e in i that an earlier evaluation would anticipate, and $e \in \text{LATER}(i,j)$ implies that the compiler could move an evaluation of e in i forward to j.

For the ongoing example, these equations produce the following sets:

	B_1	B_2	B_3
LATERIN	$\emptyset$	$\emptyset$	$\emptyset$

	$\langle B_1, B_2 \rangle$	$\langle B_1, B_3 \rangle$	$\langle B_2, B_2 \rangle$	$\langle B_2, B_3 \rangle$
LATER	$\{r_{20}, r_{21}\}$	$\emptyset$	$\emptyset$	$\emptyset$

Rewriting the Code   The final step in performing lazy code motion is to rewrite the code so that it capitalizes on the knowledge derived from the data-flow computations. To simplify the process, LCM computes two additional sets, INSERT and DELETE.

The INSERT set specifies, for each edge, the computations that LCM should insert on that edge.

$$\text{INSERT}(i,j) = \text{LATER}(i,j) \cap \overline{\text{LATERIN}(j)}$$

If i has only one successor, LCM can insert the computations at the end of i. If j has only one predecessor, it can insert the computations at the entry of j.

If neither condition applies, the edge $\langle i, j \rangle$ is a critical edge and the compiler should split $\langle i, j \rangle$ by inserting a block in the middle of the edge to hold the computations specified in INSERT(i, j).

The DELETE set specifies for a block which computations LCM should delete from the block.

$$\text{DELETE}(i) = \text{UEEXPR}(i) \cap \overline{\text{LATERIN}(i)}, \quad i \neq n_0$$

DELETE(n_0) is empty, of course, since no block precedes it. If $e \in \text{DELETE}(i)$, then the first computation of e in i is redundant after all the insertions have been made. Any subsequent evaluation of e in i that has upward-exposed uses—that is, the operands are not defined between the start of i and the evaluation—can also be deleted. Because all evaluations of e define the same name, the compiler need not rewrite subsequent references to the deleted evaluation. Those references will simply refer to earlier evaluations of e that LCM has proven to produce the same result.

For our example, the INSERT and DELETE sets are simple.

	$\langle B_1, B_2 \rangle$	$\langle B_1, B_3 \rangle$	$\langle B_2, B_2 \rangle$	$\langle B_2, B_3 \rangle$
INSERT	$\{r_{20}, r_{21}\}$	$\emptyset$	$\emptyset$	$\emptyset$

	B_1	B_2	B_3
DELETE	$\emptyset$	$\{r_{20}, r_{21}\}$	$\emptyset$

Interpreting the INSERT and DELETE sets rewrites the code as shown in Figure 10.9. LCM deletes the expressions that define r_{20} and r_{21} from B_2 and inserts them on the edge from B_1 to B_2.

Since B_1 has two successors and B_2 has two predecessors, $\langle B_1, B_2 \rangle$ is a critical edge. Thus, LCM must split the edge, creating a new block B_{2a} to hold the inserted computation of r_{20}. Splitting $\langle B_1, B_2 \rangle$ adds an extra jump to the code. Subsequent work in code generation will almost certainly implement the jump in B_{2a} as a fall-through, eliminating any cost associated with it.

Notice that LCM leaves the copy defining r_8 in B_2. LCM moves expressions, not assignments. (Recall that r_8 is a variable, not an expression.) If the copy is unnecessary, the register allocator will discover that fact and coalesce it away.

```
B₁:  loadI   1         ⇒ r₁
     loadAI  r₀,@m      ⇒ r₂
     cmp_LT  r₁,r₂      ⇒ r₃
     cbr     r₃         → B₂ₐ,B₃
B₂ₐ: mult    r₁₇,r₁₈    ⇒ r₂₀
     add     r₁₉,r₂₀    ⇒ r₂₁
     jump               → B₂
B₂:  i2i     r₂₁        ⇒ r₈
     addI    r₁,1       ⇒ r₄
     i2i     r₄         ⇒ r₁
     cmp_GT  r₁,r₂      ⇒ r₅
     cbr     r₅         → B₃,B₂
B₃:  ...
```

The Transformed Code

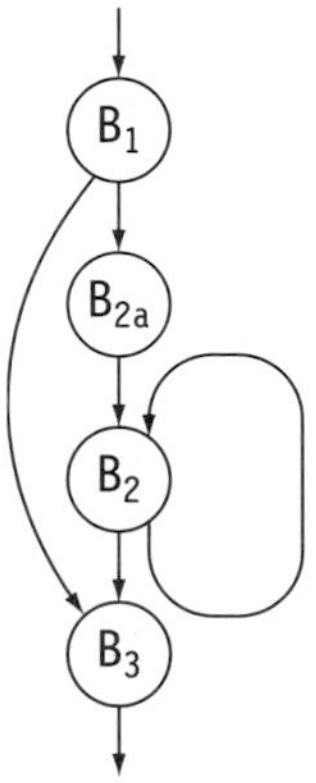

Its CFG

FIGURE 10.9   Example after Lazy Code Motion

Hoisting

The compiler can also use code motion to shrink the size of the compiled code. Section 9.2.4 introduced the notion of very busy expressions. The compiler can use the results of computing VERYBUSY sets to perform *code hoisting*.

The idea is simple. An expression $e \in$ VERYBUSY(b), for some block b, if and only if e is evaluated along every path leaving b and evaluating e at the end of b would produce the same result as the next evaluation of e along every path leaving b. (That is, none of e's operands is redefined between the end of b and the next evaluation of e along every path leaving b.) To shrink the code, the compiler can insert an evaluation of e at the end of b and replace the first occurrence of e on each path leaving b with a reference.

To replace those expressions directly, the compiler would need to locate them. It could insert e, then solve another data-flow problem, proving that the path from b to some evaluation of e is e-clear. Alternatively, it could traverse each of the paths leaving b to find the first block where e is defined—by looking in the block's UEEXPR set. Each of these approaches seems complicated.

A simpler approach has the compiler visit each block b and insert an evaluation of e at the end of b, for every expression $e \in \text{VERYBUSY}(b)$. If the compiler uses a uniform discipline for naming, as suggested in the discussion of LCM, then each evaluation will define the appropriate name. Subsequent application of LCM or redundancy elimination will then remove the newly redundant expressions.

10.3.3 Specialization

In most compilers, the shape of the IR program is determined by the front end, before any detailed analysis of the code. Of necessity, this produces general code that works in any context that the running program might encounter. With analysis, however, the compiler can often learn enough to narrow the contexts in which the code must operate. This creates the opportunity for the compiler to specialize the sequence of operations in ways that capitalize on its knowledge of the context in which the code will execute.

As an example, consider constant propagation. Constant propagation tries to discover specific values taken on by the arguments to an operation. For an operation such as $x \leftarrow y \times z$, if the compiler discovers that y always has the value 4 and z is nonnegative, it can replace the multiply with a shift operation, which is often less expensive. If it also discovers that z has the value 17, it can replace the operation with an immediate load of 68. These operations form a hierarchy. The multiply is general; it works for any values of y and z (although it may raise an exception for some of them). The shift is less general: it produces the correct result if and only if y has the value 4 and z is nonnegative. Of course if either y or z is zero, x is also zero. The load immediate is least general: it works only when the operands have the property that the value of $y \times z$ is known.

Other examples of specialization include *peephole optimization* and *tail-recursion elimination*. Peephole optimization slides a small "window" (the peephole) over the code and looks for simplifications within the window. It originated as an efficient way to perform some final local optimization, after code generation (see Section 11.4.1).

Tail-recursion elimination recognizes when the final operation performed in a procedure is a self-recursive call. It replaces the call with a jump to the procedure's first instruction allowing reuse of the activation record and avoiding the expense of the full procedure linkage convention. This important case arises in programs that use recursion to traverse data structures or to perform iterative calculations. The next section presents a detailed example of specialization—an SSA-based algorithm for constant propagation.

Constant Propagation

Using SSA form, we can reformulate constant propagation in a much more intuitive way than the equations in Section 9.2.4. The algorithm, called *sparse simple constant propagation* (SSCP), is shown in Figure 10.10.

SSCP consists of an initialization phase and a propagation phase. The initialization phase iterates over the SSA names. For each SSA name n, it examines the operation that defines n and sets *Value(n)* according to a simple set of rules. If n is defined by a ϕ-function, SSCP sets *Value(n)* to $\top$. If n's value is a known constant c, SSCP sets *Value(n)* to c. If n's value cannot be known—for example, it is defined by reading a value from external media—SSCP sets *Value(n)* to $\bot$. Finally, if n's value is not known, SSCP sets *Value(n)* to $\top$. If *Value(n)* is not $\top$, the algorithm adds n to the worklist.

The propagation phase is straightforward. It removes an SSA name n from the worklist. The algorithm examines each operation o that uses n, where o defines some SSA name m. If *Value(m)* has already reached $\bot$, then no further evaluation is needed. Otherwise, it models the evaluation of o by interpreting the operation over the lattice values of its operands. If the result is lower than *Value(m)*, it lowers *Value(m)* accordingly and adds m to the worklist. The algorithm halts when the worklist is empty.

Interpreting an operation over lattice values requires some care. For a ϕ-function, the result is simply the meet of the lattice values of all the ϕ-function's arguments—even if one or more arguments have the value $\top$. For other kinds of operations, the compiler must apply operator-specific knowledge. If any operand has the lattice value $\top$, the evaluation returns $\top$. If none of the operands has the value $\top$, the model should produce an appropriate value. For the operation $x \leftarrow y \times z$, with $Value(y) = 3$ and $Value(z) = 17$, the model should produce the value 51. If $Value(y) = \bot$, the model should produce zero for $Value(z) = 0$ and $\bot$ for any other lattice value. SSCP needs similar interpretations for each value-producing operation in the IR.

Complexity The propagation phase of SSCP is a classic fixed-point scheme. The arguments for termination and complexity follow from the length of descending chains through the lattice that it uses to represent values, shown in Figure 10.10. The *Value* associated with any SSA name can have one of three initial values—$\top$, some constant c_i other than $\top$ or $\bot$, and $\bot$. The propagation phase can only lower its value. For a given SSA name, this can happen at most twice—from $\top$ to c_i to $\bot$. SSCP adds an SSA name to the worklist only when its value changes, so each SSA name appears on the worklist at most twice. SSCP evaluates an operation when one of its operands is removed from the worklist. Thus, the total number of evaluations is at most twice the number of uses in the program.

Worklist ← ∅

for each SSA name n
  initialize Value(n) by rules
    specified in the text
    if Value(n) ≠ ⊤ then
      Worklist ← Worklist ∪ {n}

while (Worklist ≠ ∅)
  remove some n from Worklist
  for each operation o that uses n
    let m be the SSA name that o defines
    if Value(m) ≠ ⊥ then
      t ← result of modelling m using meet rule
      if t ≠ Value(m) then
        Value(m) ← t
        Worklist ← Worklist ∪ {m}

$$\top \wedge x = x \qquad \forall x$$
$$c_i \wedge c_j = c_i \quad \text{if } c_i = c_j$$
$$c_i \wedge c_j = \bot \quad \text{if } c_i \neq c_j,$$
$$c_i \neq \top, c_j \neq \top$$
$$\bot \wedge x = \bot \qquad \forall x$$

Meet Rule

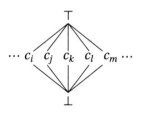

The Lattice

FIGURE 10.10   Sparse Simple Constant Propagation

Coverage SSCP discovers all of the constants found by the data-flow framework in Section 9.2.4. Because it initializes unknown values to ⊤, rather than ⊥, it can propagate some values into cycles in the graph—loops in the CFG. Algorithms that begin with the value ⊤, rather than ⊥, are often called *optimistic* algorithms. The intuition behind this term is that initialization to ⊤ allows the algorithm to propagate information into a cyclic region, optimistically assuming that the value along the back edge will confirm this initial propagation. An initialization to ⊥, called *pessimistic*, disallows that possibility.

To see this, consider the SSA fragment in Figure 10.11. If the algorithm pessimistically initializes x_1 and x_2 to ⊥, it will not propagate the value 17 into the loop. When it evaluates the ϕ-function for x_1, it computes $17 \wedge \bot$ to yield ⊥. With x_1 set to ⊥, x_2 also gets set to ⊥, even if i_{12} has a known value, such as 0.

If, on the other hand, the algorithm optimistically initializes unknown values to ⊤, it can propagate the value of x_0 into the loop. When it computes a value for x_1, it evaluates $17 \wedge \top$ and assigns the result, 17, to x_1. Since x_1's value has changed, the algorithm places x_1 on the worklist. The algorithm then reevaluates the definition of x_2. If, for example, i_{12} has the value 0, then this assigns x_2 the value 17 and adds x_2 to the worklist. When it reevaluates the ϕ-function, it computes $17 \wedge 17$ and proves that x_1 is 17.

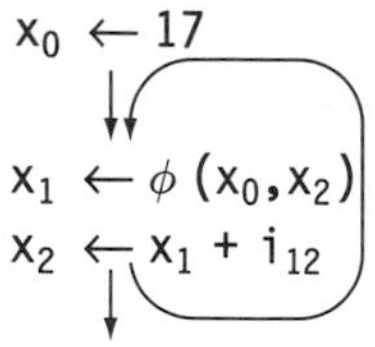

$$x_0 \leftarrow 17$$

$$x_1 \leftarrow \phi(x_0, x_2)$$

$$x_2 \leftarrow x_1 + i_{12}$$

Time	Lattice Values					
Step	Pessimistic			Optimistic		
	x_0	x_1	x_2	x_0	x_1	x_2
0	17	$\perp$	$\perp$	17	$\top$	$\top$
1	17	$\perp$	$\perp$	17	17	$17 \wedge i_{12}$

FIGURE 10.11   Optimistic Constant Example

Consider what would happen if i_{12} has the value 2, instead. Then, when SSCP evaluates $x_1 + i_{12}$, it assigns x_2 the value 19. Now, x_1 gets the value $17 \wedge 19$, or $\perp$. This, in turn, propagates back to x_2, producing the same final result as the pessimistic algorithm.

10.3.4   Enabling Other Transformations

Often, an optimizer includes passes whose primary purpose is to create or expose opportunities for other transformations. In some cases, a transformation changes the shape of the code to make it more amenable to optimization. In other cases, the transformation creates a point in the code where specific conditions hold that make another transformation safe. By directly creating the necessary code shape, these enabling transformations reduce the sensitivity of the optimizer to the shape of the input code.

Several enabling transformations are described in other parts of the book. Block cloning (Section 8.7.1) replicates individual blocks to eliminate branches and to create situations in which the compiler can derive more precise knowledge of the context that a block inherits from its CFG predecessors. For example, Section 12.4.2 describes how block cloning can improve the results of instruction scheduling. Inline substitution (Section 8.7.2) merges two procedures to eliminate the overhead of a procedure call and to create a larger context for specialization. This section presents three simple enabling transformations: *loop unrolling, loop unswitching,* and *renaming*.

Loop Unrolling

Loop unrolling is one of the oldest enabling transformations. To unroll a loop, the compiler replicates the loop's body and adjusts the logic that controls the number of iterations performed. Consider the simple loop shown in Figure 10.12(a).

If the compiler replaces the loop's body with four copies of itself, unrolling the loop by a factor of four, it can execute the same useful work with one-quarter the number of comparisons and branches. If the compiler knows the value of n, say 100, and the unrolling factor evenly divides n, then the unrolled loop has the simple form shown in Figure 10.12(b).

```
do i = 1 to n by 1
   a(i) = a(i) + b(i)
   end
```

(a) Original Loop

```
do i = 1 to 100 by 4
   a(i)   = a(i) + b(i)
   a(i+1) = a(i+1) + b(i+1)
   a(i+2) = a(i+2) + b(i+2)
   a(i+3) = a(i+3) + b(i+3)
   end
```

(b) Unrolled by 4, n = 100

```
i = 1
do while (i+3 ≤ n)
   a(i)   = a(i) + b(i)
   a(i+1) = a(i+1) + b(i+1)
   a(i+2) = a(i+2) + b(i+2)
   a(i+3) = a(i+3) + b(i+3)
   i = i + 4
   end
do while (i ≤ n)
   a(i) = a(i) + b(i)
   i = i + 1
   end
```

(c) Unrolled by 4, Arbitrary n

```
i = 1
if (mod(n,2) > 0) then
   a(i) = a(i) + b(i)
   i = i + 1
if (mod(n,4) > 1) then
   a(i)   = a(i) + b(i)
   a(i+1) = a(i+1) + b(i+1)
   i = i + 2
do j = i to n by 4
   a(j)   = a(j) + b(j)
   a(j+1) = a(j+1) + b(j+1)
   a(j+2) = a(j+2) + b(j+2)
   a(j+3) = a(j+3) + b(j+3)
   end
```

(d) Unrolled by 4, Arbitrary n

FIGURE 10.12   Unrolling a Simple Loop

When the loop bounds are unknown, unrolling requires some additional logic to support values of n for which $mod(n,4) \neq 0$. The version of the loop in Figure 10.12(c) shows a simple way to handle these cases. The version in Figure 10.12(d) achieves the same result with a little more code. In return for a more complex loop body, the version in Figure 10.12(d) may allow some improvements for the two iterations handled by the middle case.

The excerpt from dmxpy in the LINPACK library, shown in Section 8.2.1, uses the scheme from Figure 10.12(d). The full code includes the cases for one, two, four, eight, and sixteen iterations. In each case, the unrolled loop contains another loop, so the amount of work in the inner loop justifies the extensive unrolling of the outer loop.

Loop unrolling reduces the total number of operations executed by the program. It also increases the program's size. (If the loop body grows too large for the instruction cache, the resulting cache misses can overcome any benefit from lower loop overhead.) However, the primary justification for unrolling loops is to create a better code shape for other optimizations.

Unrolling has two key effects that can create opportunities for other transformations. It increases the number of operations in the loop body. For short loops and long branch latencies, this can produce a better schedule. In particular, it may give the scheduler more independent operations that it can execute at the same time. It may give the scheduler enough operations to fill branch delay slots. It can allow the scheduler to move consecutive memory accesses together. This improves locality and opens up the possibility of using memory operations that process more data at once.

As a final note, if the loop computes a value in one iteration that is used in a later iteration—a *loop-carried data dependence*—and if copy operations are needed to preserve the value for later use, unrolling can eliminate the copy operations. For multiple cycles of copies, unrolling by the least common multiple of the various cycle lengths will eliminate all the copies.

Loop Unswitching

Loop unswitching hoists loop-invariant control-flow operations out of a loop. If the predicate in an if-then-else construct is loop invariant, then the compiler can rewrite the loop by pulling the if-then-else out of the loop and generating a tailored copy of the loop inside each half of the new if-then-else. Figure 10.13 shows this transformation for a short loop.

Unswitching is an enabling transformation; it allows the compiler to tailor loop bodies in ways that are otherwise hard to achieve. After unswitching, the remaining loops contain less control flow. They execute fewer branches and

```
                                        if (x > y) then
    do i = 1 to n                           do i = 1 to n
       if (x > y)                               a(i) = b(i) * x
           then a(i) = b(i) * x         else
           else a(i) = b(i) * y             do i = 1 to n
                                               a(i) = b(i) * y
```

Original Loop   Unswitched Version

FIGURE 10.13   Unswitching a Short Loop

other operations to support those branches. This can lead to better scheduling, better register allocation, and faster execution. If the original loop contained loop-invariant code that was inside the if-then-else, then LCM could not move it out of the loop. After unswitching, LCM easily finds and removes such redundancies.

Unswitching also has a simple, direct effect that can improve a program—it moves the branching logic that governs the loop-invariant conditional out of the loop. Moving control flow out of loops is difficult. Techniques based on data-flow analysis, like LCM, have problems moving such constructs because the transformation modifies the CFG on which the analysis relies. Techniques based on value numbering can recognize some cases where the predicates controlling if-then-else constructs are identical, but they will not try to remove the construct from a loop.

Renaming

Most of the transformations presented in this chapter involve rewriting or reordering the operations in a program. Having the right code shape can expose opportunities for optimization. Similarly, having the right set of names can expose opportunities for optimization.

In local value numbering, for example, we saw the following example:

$$a \leftarrow x + y \qquad\qquad a_0 \leftarrow x_0 + y_0$$
$$b \leftarrow x + y \qquad\qquad b_0 \leftarrow x_0 + y_0$$
$$a \leftarrow 17 \qquad\qquad a_1 \leftarrow 17$$
$$c \leftarrow x + y \qquad\qquad c_0 \leftarrow x_0 + y_0$$

Original Code   SSA Form

In the original code, local value numbering can recognize that all three computations of $x + y$ produce the same result. However, it cannot replace the final occurrence of $x + y$ because the intervening assignment to a has destroyed the copy of $x + y$ that it recognizes.

Converting the code to SSA form produces a name space like the one shown on the right. With an SSA name space, $x_0 + y_0$ remains available at the final operation, so local value numbering can replace the evaluation with a reference to a_0. (The alternative is to alter the local value-numbering algorithm so that it recognizes b as another copy of $x + y$. Renaming is the simpler and more general solution.)

In general, careful use of names can expose additional opportunities for optimization by making more facts visible to analysis and by avoiding some of the side effects that come with reuse of storage. For data-flow-based optimizations, like LCM, the analysis relies on lexical identity—redundant operations must have the same operation and their operands must have the same names.[3] A scheme that encodes some value identity, perhaps derived from value numbering, into the name space can expose more redundancies to LCM and let it eliminate them.

In instruction scheduling, names create the dependences that limit the scheduler's ability to rearrange operations. If the reuse of a name reflects the actual flow of values, these dependences are a critical part of correctness. If the reuse of a name occurs because the register allocator has placed two distinct values in the same register for efficiency, these dependences can unnecessarily restrict scheduling—leading, in some cases, to less efficient code.

Renaming is a subtle issue. The SSA construction renames all the values in the program according to a particular discipline. The resulting name space helps in many optimizations. The naming conventions described in the discussion of lazy code motion, and in the sidebar, The Impact of Naming (see Chapter 5), simplify the implementation of many transformations by creating a one-to-one mapping between the name used for a value and the textual form of the operation that computed the value. Compiler writers have long recognized that moving operations around in the control-flow graph (and, in fact, changing the CFG itself) can be beneficial. In the same way, they should recognize that the compiler need not be bound by the name space introduced by the programmer or by the translation from a source language to a specific IR. Renaming values to a name space appropriate to the task at hand can improve the effectiveness of many optimizations.

---

3. LCM does not use SSA names because those names obscure lexical identity. Recreating that lexical identity incurs extra cost; as a result, an SSA-based LCM will run more slowly than the version described in Section 10.3.2.

10.3.5 Redundancy Elimination

Chapter 8 uses redundancy elimination as its primary example to explore the different scopes of optimization. It describes local value numbering, super-local value numbering, and dominator-based value numbering—all based on a bottom-up, detail-oriented approach that uses hashing to recognize values that must be equivalent. It shows the use of available expressions to perform global common-subexpression elimination as a way of introducing global analysis and transformation and makes the point that global optimization typically requires a separation between analysis and transformation.

Earlier in this chapter, LCM appears as an example of code motion. It extends the data-flow approach pioneered with available expressions to a framework that unifies code motion and redundancy elimination. Hoisting eliminates identical operations to reduce code size; this reduction does not, typically, decrease the number of operations that the program executes.

10.4 ADVANCED TOPICS

Most of the examples in this chapter have been chosen to illustrate a specific effect that the compiler can use to speed up the executable code. Sometimes, performing two optimizations together can produce results that cannot be obtained with any combination of applying them separately. The next subsection shows one such example—combining constant propagation with unreachable code elimination. Section 10.4.2 presents a second, more complex example of specialization: operator strength reduction with linear function test replacement. The algorithm that we present, *OSR*, is simpler than previous algorithms because it relies on properties of SSA form. Section 10.4.3 briefly describes some of the other objective functions that compilers consider. Finally, Section 10.4.4 discusses some of the issues that arise in choosing a specific application order for the optimizer's set of transformations.

10.4.1 Combining Optimizations

Sometimes, formulating two distinct optimizations together and solving them jointly can produce results that cannot be obtained by any combination of the optimizations run separately. As an example, consider the sparse simple constant propagation algorithm described in Section 10.3.3. It assigns a lattice

THE SSA GRAPH

In some algorithms, viewing the SSA form of the code as a graph simplifies either the discussion or the implementation. The algorithm for strength reduction interprets the SSA form of the code as a graph.

In SSA form, each name has a unique definition, so that a name specifies a particular operation in the code that computed its value. Each use of a name occurs in a specific operation, so the use can be interpreted as a chain from the use to its definition. Thus, a simple lookup table that maps names to the operations that define them creates a chain from each use to the corresponding definition. Mapping a definition to the operations that use it is slightly more complex. However, this map can easily be constructed during the renaming phase of the SSA construction.

We draw SSA graphs with edges that run from a use to its corresponding definition. This indicates the relationship implied by the SSA names. The compiler needs to traverse the edges in both directions. Strength reduction moves, primarily, from uses to definitions. The sparse conditional constant propagation algorithm can be viewed as moving from definitions to uses on the SSA graph. The compiler writer can easily add the data structures needed to allow traversal in both directions.

value to the result of each operation in the SSA form of the program. When it halts, it has tagged every definition with a lattice value that is either $\top$, $\bot$, or a constant. A definition can have the value $\top$ only if it relies on an uninitialized variable, indicating a logical problem in the code being analyzed.

Sparse simple constant propagation assigns a lattice value to the operand used by a conditional branch. If the value is $\bot$, then either branch target is reachable. If the value is neither $\bot$ nor $\top$, then the operand must have a known value and the compiler can rewrite the branch with a jump to one of its two targets, simplifying the CFG. Since this removes an edge from the CFG, it may remove the last edge entering the block labelled with the removed branch target, making that block unreachable. In principle, constant propagation can ignore any effects of an unreachable block. Sparse simple constant propagation has no mechanism to take advantage of this knowledge.

We can extend the sparse simple constant propagation algorithm to capitalize on these observations. The resulting algorithm, called *sparse conditional constant propagation* (SCCP), appears in Figure 10.14(a). Figure 10.14(b)

SSAWorkList ← ∅
CFGWorkList ← {n_0}
for each block b
  mark b as unreachable
  for each operation o in b
    Value(o) ← ⊤

while (CFGWorkList ≠ ∅ or
    SSAWorkList ≠ ∅)

  if CFGWorkList ≠ ∅ then
    remove some b from CFGWorkList
    mark b as reachable
    simultaneously model all the
      ϕ-functions in b
    model, in order, each
      operation o in b

  if SSAWorkList ≠ ∅ then
    remove some s = ⟨u,v⟩ from SSAWorkList
    let o be the operation that uses v
    if Value(o) ≠ ⊥ then
      t ← result of modelling o
      if t ≠ Value(o) then
        Value(o) ← t
        for each SSA edge e = ⟨o,x⟩
          if block(x) is reachable
            then add e to SSAWorkList

(a) The Algorithm

$\underline{\text{x} \leftarrow \text{c:}}$ (*for constant* c)
Value(x) ← c

$\underline{\text{x} \leftarrow \phi(\text{y},\text{z}):}$
Value(x) ← *Value(y)* ∧ *Value(z)*

$\underline{\text{x} \leftarrow \text{y op z:}}$
if Value(y) ≠ ⊥ & Value(z) ≠ ⊥
  then Value(x) ← interpretation
      of Value(y) op Value(z)

$\underline{\text{cbr } r_i \rightarrow l_1, l_2:}$
if r_i = ⊥ or r_i = TRUE
  and block l_1 is marked as unreachable
  then add block l_1 to CFGWorkList
if r_i = ⊥ or r_i = FALSE
  and block l_2 is marked as unreachable
  then add block l_2 to CFGWorkList

$\underline{\text{jump} \rightarrow l_1:}$
if block l_1 is marked as unreachable
  then add block l_1 to CFGWorkList

(b) Modelling Rules

FIGURE 10.14   Sparse Conditional Constant Propagation

sketches the modelling rules for the kinds of operations that SCCP must process.

To avoid including the effects of unreachable operations, SCCP handles both initialization and propagation differently than the sparse simple constant algorithm. First, SCCP marks each block with a reachability tag. Initially, each block's tag is set to indicate that the block is unreachable. Second, SCCP must initialize the lattice value for each SSA name to ⊤. The earlier algorithm handles assignments of known constant values during initialization (for example, for $x_i \leftarrow 17$, it can initialize *Value*(x_i) to 17). SCCP does not change the lattice value until it proves that the assignment is reachable. Third, the algorithm needs two worklists for propagation: one for blocks in the CFG and the other for edges in the SSA graph. Initially, the CFG worklist contains only the entry node n_0, while the SSA worklist is empty. The iterative propagation runs until it exhausts both worklists (a classic, albeit complex, fixed-point calculation).

To process a block b from the CFG worklist, SCCP first marks b as reachable. Next, it models the effect of all the ϕ-functions in b, taking care to read the lattice values of all the relevant arguments before redefining the lattice values of their outputs. (Recall that all the ϕ-functions in a block execute simultaneously.) Next, SCCP models the execution of each operation in b in a linear pass over the block. Figure 10.14(b) shows a set of typical modelling rules. These evaluations may change the lattice values of the SSA names defined by the operations.

Any time that SCCP changes the lattice value for a name, it must examine the SSA graph edges that connect the operation defining the changed value to subsequent uses. For each such edge, $s = \langle u,v \rangle$, if the block containing v is reachable, SCCP adds the edge s to the SSA worklist. Uses in an unreachable block are evaluated once SCCP discovers that the block is reachable.

The last operation in b must be either a jump or a branch. If it is a jump to a block marked as unreachable, SCCP adds that block to the CFG worklist. If it is a branch, SCCP examines the lattice value of the controlling conditional expression. This indicates that one or both branch targets are reachable. If this selects a target that is not yet marked as reachable, SCCP adds it to the CFG worklist.

After the propagation step, a final pass is required to replace operations that have operands with *Value* tags other than ⊥. It can specialize many of these operations. It should also rewrite branches that have known outcomes with the appropriate jump operations. (This lets later passes remove the code and simplify the control flow, as in Section 10.3.1). SCCP cannot rewrite the code until it knows the final lattice value for each definition, since a *Value* tag that indicates a constant value may later become ⊥.

Subtleties in Evaluating and Rewriting Operations

Some subtle issues arise in modelling individual operations. For example, if the algorithm encounters a multiply operation with operands ⊤ and ⊥, it might conclude that the operation produces ⊥. Doing so, however, is premature. Subsequent analysis might lower the ⊤ to zero, so that the multiply produces a value of zero. If SCCP uses the rule ⊤ × ⊥ → ⊥, it introduces the potential for nonmonotonic behavior—the multiply's value might follow the sequence ⊤, ⊥, 0. This can increase the running time of the algorithm, since the time bound depends on monotonic progress through a shallow lattice. Equally important, it can incorrectly cause other values to reach $\perp$.

To address this, SCCP should use three rules for multiplies that involve $\perp$, as follows: $\top \times \perp \rightarrow \top$, $\alpha \times \perp \rightarrow \perp$ for $\alpha \neq \top$ and $\alpha \neq 0$, and $0 \times \perp \rightarrow 0$. This same effect occurs for any operation for which the value of one argument can completely determine the result. Other examples include a shift by more than the word length, a logical AND with zero, and a logical OR with all ones.

Some rewrites have unforeseen consequences. For example, replacing $4 \times x$, for nonnegative x, with a shift replaces a commutative operation with a noncommutative one. If the compiler subsequently tries to rearrange expressions using commutativity, this early rewrite forecloses an opportunity. This kind of interaction can have noticeable effects on code quality. To choose when the compiler should convert $4 \times x$ into a shift, the compiler writer must consider the order in which optimizations will be applied.

Effectiveness

SCCP finds constants that the sparse simple constant algorithm cannot find. Similarly, it discovers unreachable code that cannot be found by any combination of the algorithms described in Section 10.3.1. It derives its power from combining reachability analysis with the propagation of lattice values. It can eliminate some CFG edges because the lattice values are sufficient to determine which path a branch takes. It can ignore SSA edges that arise from unreachable operations (by initializing those definitions to $\top$) because those operations will be evaluated if the block becomes marked as reachable. The power of SCCP arises from the interplay between these ideas—constant propagation and reachability.

If reachability played no role in determining the lattice values, then the same effects could be achieved by performing constant propagation (and rewriting constant-valued branches as jumps) followed by unreachable-code elimination. If constant propagation played no role in reachability, then the same effects could be achieved by the other order—unreachable-code elimination followed by constant propagation. The power of SCCP to find simplifications beyond those combinations comes precisely from the fact that the two optimizations are interdependent.

10.4.2 Strength Reduction

Strength reduction is a transformation that replaces a repeated series of expensive ("strong") operations with a series of inexpensive ("weak") operations that

```
         loadI   0        ⇒ r_s0
         loadI   1        ⇒ r_i0
         loadI   100      ⇒ r_100
    l_1: phi     r_i0,r_i2 ⇒ r_i1
         phi     r_s0,r_s2 ⇒ r_s1
         subI    r_i1,1    ⇒ r_1
         multI   r_1,4     ⇒ r_2
         addI    r_2,@a    ⇒ r_3
         load    r_3       ⇒ r_4
         add     r_s1,r_4  ⇒ r_s2
         addI    r_i1,1    ⇒ r_i2
         cmp_LE  r_i2,r_100 ⇒ r_5
         cbr     r_5       → l_1,l_2
    l_2: ...
```

Original Code

```
         loadI   0        ⇒ r_s0
         loadI   @a       ⇒ r_t6
         addI    r_t6,396 ⇒ r_lim
    l_1: phi     r_t6,r_t8 ⇒ r_t7
         phi     r_s0,r_s2 ⇒ r_s1
         load    r_t7      ⇒ r_4
         add     r_s1,r_4  ⇒ r_s2
         addI    r_t7,4    ⇒ r_t8
         cmp_LE  r_t8,r_lim ⇒ r_5
         cbr     r_5       → l_1,l_2
    l_2: ...
```

Strength-Reduced Code

FIGURE 10.15   Strength Reduction Example

compute the same values. The classic example replaces integer multiplications based on a loop index with equivalent additions. This particular case arises routinely from the expansion of array and structure addresses in loops. The left side of Figure 10.15 shows the ILOC code that might be generated for the following simple loop:

```
sum ← 0
for i ← 1 to 100
    sum ← sum + a(i)
```

The code is in semipruned SSA form; the purely local values (r_1, r_2, r_3, and r_4) have neither subscripts nor ϕ-functions. Notice how the reference to a(i) expands to four operations—the subI, multI, and addI that compute $(i-1) \times 4 + @a$ and the load that defines r_4.

For each iteration, this sequence of operations computes the address of a(i) from scratch as a function of the loop index variable i. Consider the sequence of values taken on by r_{i_1}, r_1, r_2, and r_3.

$$r_{i_1}: \{\, 1, 2, 3, \dots, 100 \,\}$$
$$r_1: \quad \{\, 0, 1, 2, \dots, 99 \,\}$$
$$r_2: \quad \{\, 0, 4, 8, \dots, 396 \,\}$$
$$r_3: \quad \{\, \texttt{@a}, \texttt{@a+4}, \texttt{@a+8}, \dots, \texttt{@a+396} \,\}$$

The values in r_1, r_2, and r_3 exist solely to compute the address for the `load` operation. If the program computed each value of r_3 from the preceding one, it could eliminate the operations that define r_1 and r_2. Of course, r_3 would then need an initialization and an update. This would make it a nonlocal name, so it would also need a ϕ-function at both 1_1 and 1_2.

The right side of Figure 10.15 shows the code after strength reduction, linear-function test replacement, and dead-code elimination. It computes those values formerly in r_3 directly into r_{t_7} and uses r_{t_7} in the `load` operation. The end-of-loop test, which used r_1 in the original code, has been modified to use r_{t_8}. This makes the computations of r_1, r_2, r_3, r_{i_0}, r_{i_1}, and r_{i_2} all dead. They have been removed to produce the final code. Now, the loop contains just five operations, ignoring ϕ-functions, while the original code contained eight. (In translating from SSA form back to executable code, the ϕ-functions become copy operations that the register allocator can usually remove.)

If the `multI` operation is more expensive than an `addI`, the savings will be larger. Historically, the high cost of multiplication justified strength reduction. However, even if multiplication and addition have equal costs, the strength-reduced form of the loop may be preferred because it creates a better code shape for later transformations and for code generation. In particular, if the target machine has an autoincrement addressing mode, then the `addI` operation in the loop can be folded into the memory operation. This option simply does not exist for the original multiply.

The rest of this section presents a simple algorithm for strength reduction, called *OSR*, followed by a scheme for linear function test replacement that works with *OSR* to move the end-of-loop test from operating on r_{i_2} to using r_{t_8}. *OSR* operates on the SSA graph for the code; Figure 10.16 shows the relationship between the ILOC SSA form for the example and its SSA graph.

Background Strength reduction looks for contexts in which an operation, such as a multiply, executes inside a loop and its operands are (1) a value that does not vary in that loop, called a *region constant*, and (2) a value that varies systematically from iteration to iteration, called an *induction variable*. When it finds this situation, it creates a new induction variable that computes the same sequence of values as the original multiplication in a more efficient

```
        loadI   0         ⇒ r_s0
        loadI   1         ⇒ r_i0
        loadI   100       ⇒ r_100
  l_1: phi     r_i0,r_i2  ⇒ r_i1
       phi     r_s0,r_s2  ⇒ r_s1
       subI    r_i1,1     ⇒ r_1
       multI   r_1,4      ⇒ r_2
       addI    r_2,@a     ⇒ r_3
       load    r_3        ⇒ r_4
       add     r_4,r_s1   ⇒ r_s2
       addI    r_i1,1     ⇒ r_i2
       cmp_LE  r_i2,r_100 ⇒ r_5
       cbr     r_5        → l_1,l_2
  l_2: ...
```

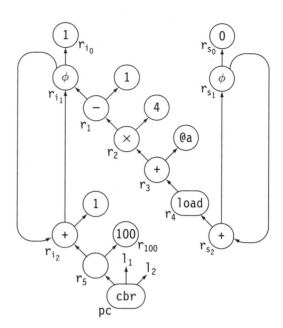

Example in ILOC SSA Form	Corresponding SSA Graph

FIGURE 10.16   Relating SSA in ILOC to the SSA Graph

way. The restrictions on the form of the multiply operation's operands ensure that this new induction variable can be computed using additions, rather than multiplications.

We call an operation that can be reduced in this way a *candidate operation*. To simplify the presentation of *OSR*, we consider only candidate operations that have one of the following forms:

$$x \leftarrow c \times i \qquad x \leftarrow i \times c \qquad x \leftarrow i \pm c \qquad x \leftarrow c + i$$

where c is a region constant and i is an induction variable. The key to finding and reducing candidate operations is efficient identification of region constants and induction variables. An operation is a candidate if and only if it has one of these forms, including the restrictions on operands.

A region constant can either be a literal constant, such as 10, or a loop-invariant value—one not modified inside the loop. With the code in SSA form, the compiler can determine if an argument is loop invariant by checking the location of its sole definition—its definition must dominate the entry to the loop that defines the induction variable. *OSR* can check both of these conditions in constant time. Performing lazy code motion and constant propagation before strength reduction may expose more values as region constants.

Intuitively, an induction variable is a variable whose values in the loop form an arithmetic progression. For the purposes of this algorithm, we can use a much more specific and restricted definition: an induction variable is a strongly connected component (scc) of the SSA graph in which each operation that updates its value is one of (1) an induction variable plus a region constant, (2) an induction variable minus a region constant, (3) a ϕ-function, or (4) a register-to-register copy from another induction variable. While this definition is much less general than conventional definitions, it is sufficient to enable the *OSR* algorithm to find and reduce candidate operations. To identify induction variables, *OSR* finds sccs in the SSA graph and iterates over them to determine if each operation in the scc is of one of these four types.

Because *OSR* defines induction variables in the SSA graph and region constants relative to a loop in the CFG, the test to determine if a value is constant relative to the loop containing a specific induction variable is complicated. Consider an operation o of the form $x \leftarrow i \times c$ where i is an induction variable. For o to be a candidate for strength reduction, c must be a region constant with respect to the outermost loop in which i varies. To test whether c has this property, *OSR* must relate the scc for i in the SSA graph back to a loop in the CFG.

OSR finds the SSA-graph node with the lowest reverse postorder number in the scc defining i. It considers this node to be the header of the scc and records that fact in the header field of each node of the scc. (Any node in the SSA graph that is not part of an induction variable has its header field set to *null*.) In SSA form, the induction variable's header is the ϕ-function at the start of the outermost loop in which it varies. In an operation $x \leftarrow i \times c$ where i is an induction variable, c is a region constant if the CFG block that contains its definition dominates the CFG block that contains i's header. This condition ensures that c is invariant in the outermost loop in which i varies. To perform this test, the SSA construction must produce a map from each SSA node to the CFG block where it originated.

The header field plays a critical role in determining whether or not an operation can be strength reduced. When *OSR* encounters an operation $x \leftarrow y \times z$, it can determine if y is an induction variable by following the SSA graph edge to y's definition and inspecting its header field. A *null* header field indicates that y is not an induction variable. If both y and z have *null* header fields, the operation cannot be strength reduced.

If one of y or z has a non-*null* header field, then *OSR* uses that header field to determine if the other operand is a region constant. Assume y's header is not *null*. To find the CFG block for the entry to the outermost loop where y varies, *OSR* consults the SSA-to-CFG map, indexed by y's header. If the CFG block containing z's definition dominates the CFG block of y's header, then z is a region constant relative to the induction variable y.

The Algorithm   To perform strength reduction, *OSR* must examine each operation and determine if one of its operands is an induction variable and the other is a region constant. If the operation meets these criteria, *OSR* can reduce it by creating a new induction variable that computes the needed values and replacing the operation with a register-to-register copy from this new induction variable. (It should avoid creating duplicate induction variables.)

Based on the preceding discussion, we know that *OSR* can identify induction variables by finding SCCs in the SSA graph. It can discover a region constant by examining the value's definition. If the definition results from an immediate operation, or its CFG block dominates the CFG block of the induction variable's header, then the value is a region constant. The key is putting these ideas together into an efficient algorithm.

OSR uses Tarjan's strongly connected region finder to drive the entire process. As shown in Figure 10.17, *OSR* takes an SSA graph as its argument and repeatedly applies the strongly connected region finder, *DFS*, to it. (This process stops when *DFS* has visited every node in G.)

DFS performs a depth-first search of the SSA graph. It assigns each node a number, corresponding to the order in which it visits the node. It pushes each node onto a stack and labels the node with the lowest depth-first number on a node that can be reached from its children. When it returns from processing the children, if the lowest node reachable from n has n's number, then n is the header of an SCC. *DFS* pops nodes off the stack until it reaches n; all of those nodes are members of the SCC.

DFS removes SCCs from the stack in an order that simplifies the rest of *OSR*. When an SCC is popped from the stack and passed to *Process*, *DFS* has already visited all of its children in the SSA graph. If we interpret the SSA graph so that its edges run from uses to definitions, as shown in the SSA graph in Figure 10.16, then candidate operations are encountered only after their operands have been passed to *Process*. When *Process* encounters an operation that is a candidate for strength reduction, its operands have already been classified. Thus, *Process* can examine operations, identify candidates, and invoke *Replace* to rewrite them in strength-reduced form during the depth-first search.

DFS passes each SCC to *Process*. If the SCC consists of a single node n that has one of the candidate forms ($x \leftarrow c \times i$, $x \leftarrow i \times c$, $x \leftarrow i \pm c$, or $x \leftarrow c + i$), *Process* passes n to *Replace*, along with its induction variable, *iv*, and

```
OSR(G)
  nextNum ← 0

  while there is an unvisited n ∈ G
    DFS(n)

DFS(n)
  n.Num ← nextNum++
  n.Visited ← true
  n.Low ← n.Num
  push(n)

  for each operand o of n
    if o.Visited = false then
      DFS(o)
      n.Low ← min(n.Low,o.Low)

    if o.Num < n.Num and
      o is on the stack
      then n.Low ← min(n.Low,o.Num)

  if n.Low = n.Num then
    SCC ← ∅
    until x = n do
      x ← pop( )
      SCC ← SCC ∪ { x }
    Process(SCC)
```

```
Process(N)
  if N has only one member n
    then if n is a candidate operation
      then Replace(n,iv,rc)
      else n.Header ← null
  else ClassifyIV(N)

ClassifyIV(N)
  IsIV ← true
  for each node n ∈ N
    if n is not a valid update for
      an induction variable
      then IsIV ← false

  if IsIV then
    header ← n ∈ N with the
      lowest RPO number
    for each node n ∈ N
      n.Header ← header
  else
    for each node n ∈ N
      if n is a candidate operation
        then Replace(n,iv,rc)
        else n.Header ← null
```

FIGURE 10.17   Operator Strength Reduction Algorithm

its region constant, *rc*. *Replace* rewrites the code, as described in the following section.[4] If the scc contains multiple nodes, *Process* passes the scc to *ClassifyIV* to determine whether or not it is an induction variable.

ClassifyIV examines each node in the scc to check it against the set of valid updates for an induction variable. If all the updates are valid, the scc is an induction variable, and *Process* sets each node's header field to contain the node in the scc with the lowest reverse postorder number. If the scc is not an induction variable, *ClassifyIV* revisits each node in the scc to test it as a candidate operation, either passing it to *Replace* or setting its header to show that it is not an induction variable.

---

4. The process of identifying *n* as a candidate necessarily identifies one operand as an induction variable, *iv*, and the other as a region constant, *rc*.

Rewriting the Code The remaining piece of *OSR* implements the rewriting step. Both *Process* and *ClassifyIV* call *Replace* to perform the rewrite. Figure 10.18 shows the code for *Replace* and its support functions *Reduce* and *Apply*.

Replace takes three arguments, an SSA-graph node *n*, an induction variable *iv*, and a region constant *rc*. The latter two are operands to *n*. *Replace* calls *Reduce* to rewrite the operation represented by *n*. Next, it replaces *n* with a copy operation from the result produced by *Replace*. It sets *n*'s header field, and returns.

Reduce and *Apply* do most of the work. They use a hash table to avoid inserting duplicate operations. Since *OSR* works on SSA names, a single global hash table suffices. It can be initialized in *OSR* before the first call to *DFS*. *Insert* adds entries to the hash table; *Lookup* queries the table.

The plan for *Reduce* is simple. It takes an opcode and its two operands and either creates a new induction variable to replace the computation or returns the name of an induction variable previously created for the same combination of opcode and operands. It consults the hash table to avoid duplicate work. If the desired induction variable is not in the hash table, it creates the induction

```
Replace(n, iv, rc)
    result ← Reduce(n.op, iv, rc)
    replace n with a copy from result
    n.header ← iv.header

Reduce(op,iv,rc)
    result ← Lookup(op, iv, rc)
    if result is "not found" then
        result ← NewName()
        Insert(op, iv, rc,result)

        newDef ← Clone(iv, result)
        newDef.header ← iv.header

        for each operand o of newDef
            if o.header = iv.header
            then rewrite o with
                    Reduce(op, o, rc)
            else if op is × or
                    newDef.op is φ
                then replace o with
                        Apply(op, o, rc)
    return result
```

```
Apply(op, o1, o2)
    result ← Lookup(op, o1, o2)
    if result is "not found" then
        if o1 is an induction variable
            and o2 is a region constant
        then result ← Reduce(op, o1, o2)

        else if o2 is an induction variable
            and o1 is a region constant
        then result ← Reduce(op, o2, o1)

        else
            result ← NewName()
            Insert(op, o1, o2,result)

            Find block b dominated by the
                definitions of o1 and o2

            Create "op o1, o2 ⇒ result"
                at the end of b and set its
                header to null

    return result
```

FIGURE 10.18   Algorithm for the Rewriting Step

variable in a two-step process. First, it calls *Clone* to copy the definition for *iv*, the induction variable in the operation being reduced. Next, it recurs on the operands of this new definition.

These operands fall into two categories. If the operand is defined inside the scc, it is part of *iv*, so *Reduce* recurs on that operand. This forms the new induction variable by cloning its way around the scc of the original induction variable *iv*. An operand defined outside the scc must be either the initial value of *iv* or a value by which *iv* is incremented. The initial value must be a ϕ-function argument from outside the scc; *Reduce* calls *Apply* on each such argument. *Reduce* can leave an induction-variable increment alone, unless the candidate operation is a multiply. For a multiply, *Reduce* must compute a new increment as the product of the old increment and the original region constant *rc*. It invokes *Apply* to generate this computation.

Apply takes an opcode and two operands, locates an appropriate point in the code, and inserts that operation. It returns the new SSA name for the result of that operation. A few details need further explanation. If this new operation is, itself, a candidate, *Apply* invokes *Reduce* to handle it. Otherwise, *Apply* gets a new name, inserts the operation, and returns the result. (If both *o1* and *o2* are constant, *Apply* can evaluate the operation and insert an immediate load.) It locates an appropriate block for the new operation using dominance information. Intuitively, the new operation must go into a block dominated by the blocks that define its operands. If one operand is a constant, *Apply* can duplicate the constant in the block that defines the other operand. Otherwise, both operands must have definitions that dominate the header block, and one must dominate the other. *Apply* can insert the operation immediately after this later definition.

Back to the Example   Consider what happens when *OSR* encounters the example in Figure 10.16. Assume that it begins with the node labelled r_{s_2} and that it visits left children before right children. It recurs down the chain of operations that define r_4, r_3, r_2, r_1, and r_{i_1}. At r_{i_1}, it recurs on r_{i_2} and then r_{i_0}. It finds the two single-node sccs that contain the literal constant one. Neither is a candidate, so *Process* marks them as non-induction variables by setting their headers to *null*.

The first nontrivial scc that *DFS* discovers contains r_{i_1} and r_{i_2}. All the operations are valid updates for an induction variable, so *ClassifyIV* marks each node as an induction variable by setting its header field to point to the node with the lowest depth-first number in the scc—the node for r_{i_1}.

Now, *DFS* returns to the node for r_1. Its left child is an induction variable and its right child is a region constant, so it invokes *Reduce* to create an induction variable. In this case, r_1 is $r_{i_1} - 1$, so the induction variable has an initial value equal to one less than the initial value of the old induction variable, or zero.

The increment is the same. Figure 10.19 shows the scc that *Reduce* and *Apply* create, under the label "for r_1." Finally, the definition of r_1 is replaced with a copy operation, $r_1 \leftarrow r_{t_1}$. The copy operation is marked as an induction variable.

Next, *DFS* discovers the scc that consists of the node labelled r_2. *Process* discovers that it is a candidate because its left operand (the copy that now defines r_1) is an induction variable and its right operand is a region constant. *Process* invokes *Replace* to create an induction variable that is $r_1 \times 4$. *Reduce* and *Apply* clone the induction variable for r_1, adjust the increment since the operation is a multiply, and add a copy to r_2.

DFS next passes the node for r_3 to *Process*. This creates another induction variable with @a as its initial value and copies its value to r_3.

Process handles the load, followed by the scc that computes the sum. It finds that none of these operations are candidates.

Finally, *OSR* invokes *DFS* on the unvisited node for the cbr. *DFS* visits the comparison, the previously marked induction variable, and the constant 100. No further reductions occur.

The ssa graph in Figure 10.19 shows all of the induction variables created by this process. The induction variables labelled "for r_1" and "for r_2" are dead.

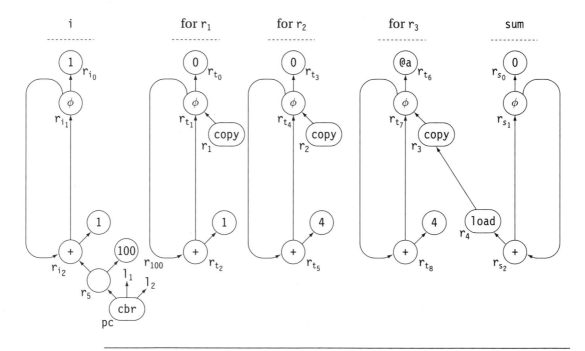

FIGURE 10.19   Transformed ssa Graph for the Example

The induction variable for i would be dead, except that the end-of-loop test still uses it. To eliminate this induction variable, the compiler can apply linear-function test replacement to transfer the test to the induction variable for r_3.

Linear-Function Test Replacement

Strength reduction often eliminates all uses of an induction variable, except for an end-of-loop test. In that case, the compiler may be able to rewrite the end-of-loop test to use another induction variable found in the loop. If the compiler can remove this last use, it can eliminate the original induction variable as dead code. This transformation is called linear-function test replacement (LFTR).

To perform LFTR, the compiler must (1) locate comparisons that rely on otherwise unneeded induction variables, (2) locate an appropriate new induction variable that the comparison could use, (3) compute the correct region constant for the rewritten test, and (4) rewrite the code. Having LFTR cooperate with *OSR* can simplify all of these tasks to produce a fast, effective transformation.

The operations that LFTR targets compare the value of an induction variable against a region constant. *OSR* examines each operation in the program to determine if it is a candidate for strength reduction. It can easily and inexpensively build a list of all the comparison operations that involve induction variables. After *OSR* finishes its work, LFTR should revisit each of these comparisons. If the induction-variable argument of a comparison was strength reduced by *OSR*, LFTR should retarget the comparison to use the new induction variable.

To facilitate this process, *Reduce* can record the mathematical relationship used to derive each new induction variable that it creates. It can insert a special LFTR edge from each node in the original induction variable to the corresponding node in its reduced counterpart and label it with the opcode and region constant of the candidate operation responsible for creating the new induction variable. Figure 10.20 shows these edges added to the SSA graph for the example. The example involved a series of reductions; these create a chain of edges with the appropriate labels. Starting from the original induction variable, we find the labels −1, x4, and +@a.

When LFTR finds a comparison that should be replaced, it can follow the edges from its induction-variable argument to the final induction variable that resulted from a chain of one or more reductions. The comparison should use this induction variable with an appropriate new region constant.

The labels on the edges that LFTR traverses describe the transformation that must be applied to the original region constant to derive the new region constant. In the example, the trail of edges leads from r_{i_2} to r_{t_8} and produces

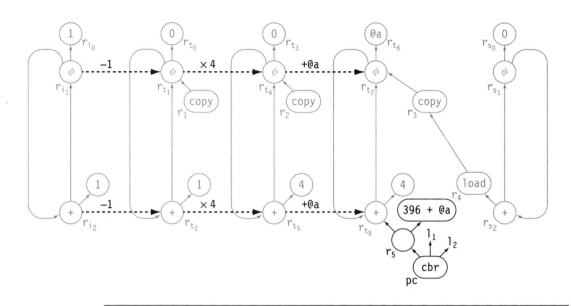

FIGURE 10.20   Example after LFTR

the value $(100 - 1) \times 4 + @a$ for the transformed test. Figure 10.20 shows the edges and the rewritten test.

This version of LFTR is simple, efficient, and effective. It relies on close collaboration with *OSR* to identify comparisons that might be retargeted and to leave behind a record of the reductions that it performed. Using these two data structures, LFTR can find comparisons to retarget, find the appropriate place to retarget them, and find the necessary transformation for the comparison's constant argument.

10.4.3 Other Objectives for Optimization

Generating Smaller Code

In some applications, the size of the compiled code is important. If an application is transmitted across a relatively slow communications link before it executes, then the perceived running time is the sum of the download time plus the running time. This places a premium on code size, since the user waits while the code is transmitted. Similarly, in many embedded applications, the code is stored in a permanent, read-only memory (ROM). Since larger ROMs cost more money, code size becomes an economic issue.

The compiler writer can attack this problem by employing transformations that directly shrink the code.

- *Hoisting* (described in Section 9.2.4) shrinks the code by replacing multiple identical operations with a single, equivalent operation. As long as the expression is very busy at the point of insertion, hoisting does not lengthen any of the execution paths.

- *Sinking* moves common code sequences forward in the CFG to a point where one copy of the sequence suffices. In *cross jumping*, a specialized form of sinking, the compiler examines all the jumps that target the same label. If the same operation precedes each jump to the label, the compiler can move the operation to the label and keep just one copy of it. This eliminates duplication without lengthening execution paths.

- *Procedure abstraction* uses pattern matching techniques to find repeated code sequences and replace them with calls to a single common implementation. If the common code sequence is longer than the sequence required for the call, this saves space. It makes the code slower, since every abstracted code sequence is replaced with a call to the abstracted procedure and a jump back. Procedure abstraction can be applied across the whole program to find common sequences from different procedures.

As another approach, the compiler can avoid using transformations that enlarge the code. For example, loop unrolling typically expands the code. Similarly, LCM may enlarge the code by inserting new operations. By choosing algorithms carefully and avoiding those that cause significant code growth, the compiler writer can build a compiler that always produces compact code.

Avoiding Page Faults and Instruction-Cache Misses

In some environments, the overhead from page faults and instruction-cache misses makes it worthwhile to transform the code in ways that improve the code's memory locality. The compiler can use several distinct but related effects to improve the paging and cache behavior of the instruction stream.

- *Procedure Placement:* If *A* calls *B* frequently, the compiler should ensure that *A* and *B* occupy adjacent locations in memory. If they fit on the same page, this can reduce the program's working set. Placing them in adjacent locations also reduces the likelihood of a conflict in the instruction cache.

- *Block Placement:* If block b_i ends in a branch and the compiler knows that the branch usually transfers control to b_j, then it can place b_i and b_j in contiguous memory. This makes b_j the fall-through case of the branch (and most processors both support and favor the fall-through case). It also increases the effectiveness of any hardware prefetching mechanism in the instruction cache.

- *Fluff Removal:* If the compiler can determine that some code fragments execute rarely—that is, they are the (mostly) untaken targets of branches—then it can move them to distant locations. Such rarely executed code needlessly fills the cache and decreases the density of useful operations brought into the processor. (For exception handlers, it may pay to keep the code on the same page, but move it out of line.)

To implement these transformations effectively, the compiler needs accurate information about how often each path through the code is taken. Typically, gathering this information requires a more complex compilation system that collects execution-profile data and relates that data back to the code. The user compiles an application and runs it on "representative" inputs. The profile data from these runs is then used to optimize the code in a second compilation. An alternative, as old as compilation, is to build a model of the CFG and estimate execution frequencies using reasonable transition probabilities.

10.4.4 Choosing an Optimization Sequence

Choosing a specific set of transformations and an order for applying them is a critical task in the design of an optimizing compiler. For any particular problem, many distinct techniques exist. Each of them catches a different set of cases. Many of them address parts of several problems.

To make this concrete, recall the methods that we have presented for eliminating redundancies. These include three value-numbering techniques (local, superlocal, and dominator-based) and two techniques based on data-flow analysis (global common-subexpression elimination based on available expressions and lazy code motion). The value-numbering techniques find and eliminate redundancies using a value-based notion of redundancy. They differ in the scope of optimization—covering single blocks (local), extended basic blocks (superlocal), and the entire CFG minus back edges (dominator-based). They also perform constant propagation and use algebraic identities to remove some useless operations. The data-flow-based techniques use a lexical notion of redundancy—two operations are equivalent only if they have the same names. Global common-subexpression elimination only removes redundancies, while lazy code motion removes redundancies and partial redundancies and performs code motion.

In designing an optimizing compiler, the compiler writer must decide how to remove redundancies. Choosing among these five methods involves decisions about which cases are important, the relative difficulty of implementing the techniques, and how the compile-time costs compare to the run-time benefits. To complicate matters further, more techniques exist.

Equally difficult, optimizations that address different effects interact with each other. Optimizations can create opportunities for other optimizations, as constant propagation and lazy code motion improve strength reduction by revealing more values as region constants. Symmetrically, optimizations can make other optimizations less effective, as redundancy elimination can complicate register allocation by making values live over longer regions in a program. The effects of two optimizations may overlap. In a compiler that implements sparse conditional constant propagation, the constant-folding capabilities of the value-numbering techniques are less important.

After selecting a set of optimizations, the compiler writer must choose an order in which to apply them. Some constraints on the order are obvious; for example, it is worth running constant propagation and code motion before strength reduction. Others are less obvious; for example, should loop unswitching precede strength reduction or not? Should the constant-propagation pass convert $x \leftarrow y \times 4$, for $y \geq 0$, to a shift operation? The decision may depend on which passes precede constant propagation and which passes follow it. Finally, some optimizations might be run multiple times. Dead-code elimination cleans up after strength reduction. After strength reduction, the compiler might run constant propagation again in an attempt to convert any remaining multiplies to shifts. Alternately, it might use local value numbering to achieve the same effect, reasoning that any global effects have already been caught.

If the compiler writer intends to provide different levels of optimization, this entails designing several compilation sequences, each with its own rationale and its own set of passes. Higher levels of optimization typically add more transformations. They may also repeat some optimizations to capitalize on opportunities created by earlier transformations. See Muchnick [262] for suggested orders in which to perform optimizations.

10.5 SUMMARY AND PERSPECTIVE

The design and implementation of an optimizing compiler is a complex undertaking. This chapter has introduced a conceptual framework for thinking about transformations—the taxonomy of effects. Each category in the taxonomy is represented by several examples—either in this chapter or elsewhere in the book.

The challenge for the compiler writer is to select a set of transformations that work well together to produce good code—code that meets the user's needs. The specific transformations implemented in a compiler determine, to a large extent, the kinds of programs for which it will produce good code.

CHAPTER NOTES

While the algorithms presented in this chapter are modern, many of the basic ideas were well known in the 1960s and 1970s. Dead-code elimination, code motion, strength reduction, and redundancy elimination are all described by Allen in 1969 [12] and in Cocke and Schwartz [86]. A number of survey papers from the 1970s provide overviews of the state of the field [15, 28, 308]. Modern books by Morgan [260] and Muchnick [262] both discuss the design, structure, and implementation of optimizing compilers. Wolfe [335] and Allen and Kennedy [19] focus on dependence-based analysis and transformations.

Dead implements a mark-sweep style of dead-code elimination that was introduced by Kennedy [203, 206]. It is reminiscent of the Schorr-Waite marking algorithm [299]. *Dead* is specifically adapted from the work of Cytron et al. [104, Section 7.1]. *Clean* was developed and implemented in 1992 by Rob Shillner [245].

LCM improves on Morel and Renvoise's classic algorithm for partial redundancy elimination [259]. That original paper inspired many improvements, including [76, 121, 312, 124]. Knoop, Rüthing, and Steffen's lazy code motion [215] improved code placement; the formulation in Section 10.3.2 uses equations from Drechsler and Stadel [125]. Bodik, Gupta, and Soffa combined this approach with replication to find and remove all redundant code [41].

Hoisting appears in the Allen-Cocke catalogue as a technique for reducing code space [15]. The formulation using very busy expressions appears in several places, including Fischer and LeBlanc [140]. Sinking or cross-jumping is described by Wulf et al. [339].

Both peephole optimization and tail-recursion elimination date to the early 1960s. Peephole optimization was first described by McKeeman [253]. Tail-recursion elimination is older; folklore tells that McCarthy described it at the chalkboard during a talk in 1963. Steele's thesis [314] is a classic reference for tail-recursion elimination.

The sparse simple constant algorithm, sscp, is due to Reif and Lewis [285]. Wegman and Zadeck reformulate sscp to use ssa form and present the sccp algorithm given in Section 10.4.1 [328, 329]. Their work clarified the distinction between optimistic and pessimistic algorithms; Click discusses the same issue from a set-building perspective [79].

Loop optimizations have been studied extensively [27, 19]; Kennedy used unrolling to avoid copy operations at the end of a loop [202]. Cytron, Lowreg, and Zadeck present an interesting alternative to unswitching [105]. Wolf and Lam unified the treatment of a set of loop optimizations called the *unimodular* transformations [334]. McKinley et al. give practical insight into the impact of memory optimizations on performance [89, 254].

Combining optimizations, as in sccp, often leads to improvements that cannot be obtained by independent application of the original optimizations. Value numbering combines redundancy elimination, constant propagation, and simplification of algebraic identities [50]. lcm combines elimination of redundancies and partial redundancies with code motion [215]. Click and Cooper [81] combine Alpern's partitioning algorithm [20] with sccp [329]. Many authors have combined register allocation and instruction scheduling [158, 267, 268, 261, 45, 274, 298].

Operator strength reduction has a rich history. One family of strength-reduction algorithms developed out of work by Allen, Cocke, and Kennedy [204, 83, 85, 18, 250]. The *OSR* algorithm is in this family [101]. Another family of algorithms grew out of the data-flow approach to optimization exemplified by the lcm algorithm; a number of sources give techniques in this family [118, 192, 198, 120, 216, 209, 69]. The version of *OSR* in Section 10.3.3 only reduces multiplications. Allen et al. show the reduction sequences for many other operators [18]; extending *OSR* to handle these cases is straightforward.

Shrinking existing code or generating smaller programs has been a persistent theme in the literature. Fabri gives algorithms to reduce data-memory requirements by automatic generation of storage overlays [134]. Marks had the compiler synthesize both a compact, program-specific instruction set and an interpreter for that instruction set [249]. Fraser, Myers, and Wendt used procedure abstraction based on suffix-trees [148]. Recent work has focused on compressing code for transmission over networks [130, 145] and on directly generating small code—either with hardware assistance for decoding [233, 234] or without it [99].

Modern algorithms for code placement begin with Pettis and Hansen [273]. Later work includes work on branch alignment [59, 340] and code layout [88, 73, 156]. These optimizations improve performance by improving the behavior of code memory in a hierarchical memory system. They also eliminate branches and jumps.

CHAPTER 11

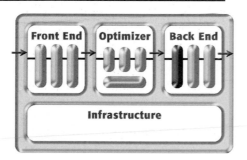

Instruction Selection

As code generation begins, the program exists in IR form. The code generator must convert the IR program into code that can run on the target machine. The compiler must (1) select a sequence of target-machine operations that implement the IR operations—a process called *instruction selection*; (2) choose an order in which the operations should execute—a process called *instruction scheduling*; and (3) decide which values should reside in registers at each point in the program—a process called *register allocation*. In each case, the compiler must rewrite the code to reflect those decisions. Most compilers handle each of these three processes separately. The term *code generation* is often used to refer to instruction selection. This chapter examines the challenges that arise in performing instruction selection. The next two chapters examine instruction scheduling and register allocation.

In designing a code generator, the compiler writer must be concerned with low-level details of the code and their mapping onto the instruction set architecture (ISA) and hardware resources of the target machine. If the IR program already represents some or all of these low-level details, then instruction selection can consider the details and tailor its selections accordingly. If

545

the IR represents programs at a higher level of abstraction, then instruction selection must fill in some or all of the details itself. (Mechanically generating such detail at this late stage in compilation can lead to templatelike code with a low level of customization.) Compilers that perform little or no optimization generate code directly from the IR produced by the front end.

The complexity of instruction selection arises from the fact that there are usually many distinct ways to perform a given computation on a typical target machine. Abstract away, for the moment, the issues of instruction scheduling and register allocation; we will return to them in the next two chapters. If each IR operation had just one implementation on the target machine, the compiler could simply map each such operation to the equivalent sequence of machine operations. In most contexts, however, a target machine may implement each IR construct in many ways.

Consider, for example, copying a value from one general-purpose register, r_i, to another, r_j, on a machine that uses ILOC as its native instruction set. As we shall see, even ILOC has enough complexity to expose many of the problems of code generation. The obvious implementation of $r_i \rightarrow r_j$ uses i2i $r_i \Rightarrow r_j$; such a register-to-register copy is typically one of the least expensive operations that a processor provides. However, other implementations abound. These include, for example, each of the following operations:

addI	$r_i,0 \Rightarrow r_j$		subI	$r_i,0 \Rightarrow r_j$
multI	$r_i,1 \Rightarrow r_j$		divI	$r_i,1 \Rightarrow r_j$
lshiftI	$r_i,0 \Rightarrow r_j$		rshiftI	$r_i,0 \Rightarrow r_j$
orI	$r_i,0 \Rightarrow r_j$		xorI	$r_i,0 \Rightarrow r_j$

There is also an implementation that uses andI with an operand of all ones. If the processor maintains a register whose value is always zero, another set of operations works, using add, sub, lshift, rshift, or, and xor. A larger set of two-operation sequences, including a store followed by a load and a pair of xor operations using a third register, also works. Many other multioperation sequences are possible.

A human programmer would rapidly discount most, if not all, of these alternate sequences. Using i2i is simple, fast, and obvious. An automated process, however, may need to consider all the possibilities and make the appropriate choices. The ability of a specific instruction set to accomplish the same effect in multiple ways increases the complexity of instruction selection. For ILOC, the ISA provides only a few, simple, low-level operations for each particular effect. Even so, it supports myriad ways to implement register-to-register copy.

Real processors are more complex. They may include higher-level operations and multiple addressing modes that the code generator should consider. While these features allow a skilled programmer or a carefully crafted compiler to create more efficient programs, they also increase the number of choices that the instruction selector confronts—they make the space of potential implementations larger.

Each alternate sequence has its own costs. Most machines implement simple operations, such as i2i, add, and lshift, so that they execute in a single cycle. Some operations, like integer multiplication and division, may take longer. The speed of a memory operation depends on many factors, including the detailed current state of the computer's memory system.

In some cases, the actual cost of an operation might depend on context. If, for example, the processor has several functional units, it might be better to perform a register-to-register copy using an operation other than copy that will execute on an underutilized functional unit. If the unit would otherwise be idle, the operation is, effectively, free. Moving it onto the underutilized unit might actually speed up the entire computation. If the code generator must rewrite the copy to a specific operation that executes only on the underutilized unit, this is a selection problem. Otherwise, it is a scheduling problem.

In most cases, the compiler writer wants the back end to produce code that runs quickly. However, other metrics are possible. For example, if the final code will run on a battery-powered device, the compiler might consider the typical power consumption of each operation. (Individual operations may consume different amounts of power.) The costs in a system that tries to optimize for power might be radically different than the costs that a speed metric would use. The costs for power would depend heavily on underlying hardware details and, thus, might change from one implementation of a processor to another. Similarly, if code space is critical, the compiler writer might assign costs based solely on sequence length. Alternatively, the compiler writer might simply exclude all multioperation sequences that achieve the same effect as a single-operation sequence.

To further complicate matters, some ISAs place additional constraints on specific operations. An integer multiply might need to take its operands from a subrange of the registers. A floating-point operation might need its operands in even-numbered registers. A memory operation might only execute on one of the processor's functional units. A floating-point unit might support the sequence $(r_i \times r_j) + r_k$ with a single operation that runs faster than the sequence consisting of separate multiply and add operations would run. Load-multiple and store-multiple operations might require contiguous registers. The memory system might deliver its best bandwidth and latency for double-word or quadword loads, rather than singleword loads. Restrictions like these constrain instruction selection. At the same time, they increase the importance of finding a solution that uses the best operation at each point in the input program.

When the level of abstraction of the IR and the target machine differ significantly, or the underlying computation models differ, instruction selection can play a critical role in bridging that gap. The extent to which instruction selection can map the computations in the IR program efficiently to the target machine will often determine the efficiency of the generated code. For example, consider three scenarios for generating code from an ILOC-like IR.

1. *A simple, scalar RISC machine*   The mapping from IR to assembly is straightforward. The code generator might consider only one or two assembly-language sequences for each IR operation.

2. *A CISC processor*   To make effective use of a CISC's instruction set, the compiler may need to aggregate several IR operations into a single target-machine operation.

3. *A stack machine*   The code generator must translate from the register-to-register computational style of ILOC to a stack-based style with its implicit names and, in some cases, destructive operations.[1]

As the gap in abstraction between the IR and the target ISA grows, so does the need for tools to help build code generators.

While instruction selection can play an important role in determining code quality, the compiler writer must keep in mind the enormous size of the search space that the instruction selector might explore. As we shall see, even moderately sized instruction sets can produce search spaces that contain hundreds of millions of states. Clearly, the compiler cannot afford to explore such spaces in either a careless or an exhaustive way. The techniques that we describe explore the space of alternative code sequences in a disciplined way and either limit their searching or precompute enough information to make a deep search efficient.

11.1.1 Building Retargetable Compilers

Systematic approaches to code generation have made it possible to build *retargetable compilers*. A retargetable compiler typically has support for multiple instruction sets and mechanisms to simplify adding more.

---

1. Moving from a single-address, or stack, IR (like bytecodes) to a three-address machine entails similar problems. The code generator must introduce a new name space. Translating to three-address form may introduce opportunities for reuse of values that would suggest further optimizations, such as local value numbering.

INTERACTIONS OF INSTRUCTION SELECTION WITH SCHEDULING AND ALLOCATION

The three major processes in the back end are instruction selection, instruction scheduling, and register allocation. All three have a direct impact on the quality of the generated code, and they all interact with each other.

Selection directly changes the scheduling process. Selection dictates both the time required for an operation and the functional units on which it can execute. Scheduling might affect instruction selection. If the code generator can implement an IR operation with either of two assembly operations, and those operations use different resources, the code generator might need to understand the final schedule to ensure the best choice.

Selection interacts with register allocation in several ways. If the target machine has a uniform register set, then the instruction selector can assume an unlimited supply of registers and rely on the allocator to insert the loads and stores needed to fit the values into the register set. If, on the other hand, the target machine has rules that restrict register usage, then the selector must pay close attention to specific physical registers. This can complicate selection and predetermine some or all of the allocation decisions. In this case, the code generator may use a coroutine to perform local register allocation during instruction selection.

Keeping selection, scheduling, and allocation separate—to the extent possible—can simplify implementation and debugging of each process. However, since each of these processes can constrain the others, the compiler writer must take care to avoid adding unnecessary constraints.

The goal of retargetable compiler development is to maximize reuse of components in the compiler. Ideally, the front end and optimizer need minimal changes, and much of the back end can be reused, as well. This makes good use of the investment in building, debugging, and maintaining the common parts of the compiler.

The modern approach to portability places most of the responsibility for handling diverse targets on the instruction selector. The compiler uses

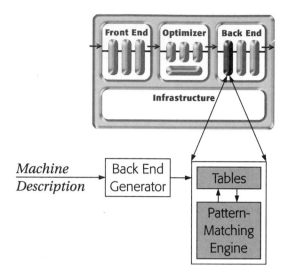

FIGURE 11.1   A Retargetable Back End

a common IR for all targets and, in some cases, all source languages.[2] It optimizes the intermediate form based on a set of assumptions that hold true on most, if not all, target machines. Finally, it uses a back end in which the compiler writer has tried to isolate and extract the target-dependent details.

(Since the scheduler and register allocator operate on the target machine's assembly code, those parts of the compiler need target-dependent information. This information includes operation latencies, register-set sizes, the number and capabilities of the functional units, alignment restrictions, the target machine's calling conventions, and, frequently, other kinds of details. Still, the compiler shares the underlying algorithms and implementation across all platforms.)

The most important key to building retargetable compilers lies in the automatic construction of instruction selectors. Figure 11.1 shows how such a system might work. The instruction selector consists of a pattern-matching engine coupled to a set of tables that encode the needed knowledge about mapping from the IR to the target ISA. The resulting selector consumes the compiler's IR and produces assembly code for the target machine. In such a

---

2. In practice, adding a new language often means adding some new operations to the IR. The goal, however, is to extend the IR, rather than to reinvent it.

system, the compiler writer creates a description of the target machine and runs the back-end generator (sometimes called a *code-generator generator*). The back-end generator, in turn, uses the specification to derive the tables needed by the pattern matcher. Like a parser generator, the back-end generator runs offline, during compiler development. Thus, we can use algorithms to create the tables that require more time than even a long compilation.

While the goal is to isolate all machine-dependent code in the instruction selector, scheduler, and register allocator, the reality almost always falls somewhat short of this ideal. Some machine-dependent details creep, unavoidably, into earlier parts of the compiler. For example, the alignment restrictions of activation records may differ among target machines, changing offsets for values stored in ARs. The compiler may need to represent features such as predicated execution, branch delay slots, and multiword memory operations explicitly if it is to make good use of them. However, to the extent that target-dependent details can be pushed into instruction selection, doing so reduces the number of changes that must be made elsewhere in the compiler, and it simplifies the task of retargeting.

This chapter examines two approaches to automating the construction of instruction selectors. The next section introduces a simple tree-walk algorithm for instruction selection to provide a detailed introduction to the problem. The following two sections present different ways to apply pattern-matching techniques to transform IR sequences to assembly sequences. Both methods are description based. The compiler writer describes the target machine's ISA in a formal notation; a tool then constructs a pattern-matching instruction selector for use at compile time. Both have been used in successful portable compilers.

The first technique uses the theory of tree pattern matching to create a bottom-up rewrite system. It assumes, at least conceptually, that the compiler uses a treelike IR. The compiler writer describes the target machine's ISA using tree patterns that resemble a low-level abstract syntax tree. Each pattern takes the form of a rewrite rule that replaces a subtree with a value and an associated assembly sequence that implements the subtree. A pattern matcher discovers a rewrite sequence for the IR tree that reduces it to a single value; a second pass follows the rewrite sequence and emits the associated code.

The second technique takes a well-understood optimization technique, *peephole optimization*, and adapts it to code generation. Peephole optimizers work from a library of patterns, instances of which are recognized and improved. They work, at least conceptually, on linear IRs. They limit their attention to a small window of operations—the "peephole." This simplifies and speeds up pattern matching. It also limits the set of matches that they can find. Peephole-based instruction selection has been used since the early 1980s. By associating with each IR construct a rule for rewriting it in the target machine's assembly code, the compiler writer can make a peephole optimizer replace the IR program with an assembly program. Adding patterns usually improves code quality. Section 11.4 explores this approach in more detail.

11.2 A SIMPLE TREE-WALK SCHEME

To make the discussion concrete, consider the issues that can arise in generating code for an assignment statement such as $w \leftarrow x - 2 \times y$. It might be represented by an AST, as shown on the left, or by a table of quadruples, as shown on the right.

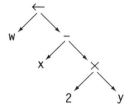

Op	**Arg$_1$**	**Arg$_2$**	**Result**
$\times$	2	y	t_1
$-$	x	t_1	w

Instruction selection must produce an assembly-language program from IR representations like these two. For the sake of discussion, assume that it must generate operations in the ILOC subset shown in Figure 11.2.

In Chapter 7, we saw that a simple tree-walk routine could generate code from the AST for an expression. The code in Figure 7.2 handled the binary operators, $+$, $-$, $\times$, and $\div$ applied to variables and numbers. It generated naive code for the expression and was intended to illustrate an approach that might

Arithmetic Operations		**Memory Operations**	
add	$r_1, r_2 \Rightarrow r_3$	store	$r_1 \quad\quad \Rightarrow r_2$
addI	$r_1, c_2 \Rightarrow r_3$	storeAO	$r_1 \quad\quad \Rightarrow r_2, r_3$
sub	$r_1, r_2 \Rightarrow r_3$	storeAI	$r_1 \quad\quad \Rightarrow r_2, c_3$
subI	$r_1, c_2 \Rightarrow r_3$	loadI	$c_1 \quad\quad \Rightarrow r_3$
rsubI	$r_2, c_1 \Rightarrow r_3$	load	$r_1 \quad\quad \Rightarrow r_3$
mult	$r_1, r_2 \Rightarrow r_3$	loadAO	$r_1, r_2 \Rightarrow r_3$
multI	$r_1, c_2 \Rightarrow r_3$	loadAI	$r_1, c_2 \Rightarrow r_3$

FIGURE 11.2 The ILOC Subset

CODE LAYOUT

Before it begins emitting code, the compiler has the opportunity to lay out the basic blocks in memory. If each branch in the IR has two explicit branch targets, as ILOC does, then the compiler can choose either of a block's logical successors to follow it in memory. With only one explicit branch target, often called a *fall-through branch*, rearranging the blocks requires more work.

Two architectural considerations should guide this decision. On some processors, taking the branch requires more time than falling through to the next operation. On machines with cache memory, blocks that execute together should be located together. Both of these favor the same strategy for layout. If block *a* ends in a branch that targets *b* and *c*, the compiler should place the more frequently taken target after *a* in memory.

Of course, if a block has multiple predecessors in the control-flow graph, only one of them can immediately precede it in memory. The others will require a branch or jump to reach it.

be used to generate either a low-level, linear IR or assembly code for a simple RISC machine.

The simple tree-walk approach generates the same code for every instance of a particular AST node type. While this produces correct code, it never capitalizes on the opportunity to tailor the code to specific circumstances and context. If a compiler performs significant optimization after instruction selection, this may not be a problem. Without subsequent optimization, however, the final code is likely to contain obvious inefficiencies.

Consider, for example, the way that the simple tree-walk routine handles variables and numbers. The code for the relevant cases is

```
case IDENT:                          case NUM:
    t1 ← base(node);                     result ← NextRegister();
    t2 ← offset(node);                   emit (loadI, val(node),
    result ← NextRegister();                 none, result);
    emit (loadAO, t1, t2, result);       break;
    break;
```

For variables, it relies on two routines, *base* and *offset*, to get the base address and offset into registers. It then emits a loadAO operation that adds these two values to produce an effective address and retrieves the contents of the memory location at that address. Because the AST does not differentiate between the storage classes of variables, *base* and *offset* presumably consult the symbol table to obtain the additional information that they need.

Extending this scheme to a more realistic set of cases, including variables that have different-sized representations, call-by-value and call-by-reference parameters, and variables that reside in registers for their entire lifetimes, would require writing explicit code to check each case at each reference. This would make the code for the *IDENT* case much longer (and much slower). It eliminates much of the appealing simplicity of the hand-coded tree-walk scheme.

The code to handle numbers is equally naive. It assumes that a number should be loaded into a register in every case, and that *val* can retrieve the number's value from the symbol table. If the operation that uses the number (its parent in the tree) has an immediate form on the target machine and the constant has a value that fits into the immediate field, the compiler should use the immediate form, since it uses one fewer register. If the number is of a type not supported by an immediate operation, the compiler must arrange to store the value in memory and generate an appropriate memory reference to load the value into a register. This, in turn, may create opportunities for further improvement, such as keeping the constant in a register.

To make this discussion concrete, consider the three multiply operations shown in Figure 11.3. The symbol-table annotations appear below the leaf nodes in the trees. For an identifier, this consists of a name, a label for the base address (or ARP to indicate the current activation record), and an offset from the base address. Below each tree are two code sequences—the code generated by the simple tree-walk evaluator and the code we would like the compiler to generate. In the first case, a × b, the inefficiency comes from the fact that the tree-walk scheme does not generate loadAI operations. More complicated code in the *IDENT* case can cure this problem.

The second case, a × 2 is harder. The code generator could implement the multiply with a multI operation. To recognize this fact, however, the code generator must look beyond the local context. To work this into the tree-walk scheme, the case for × might recognize that one subtree evaluates to a constant. Alternatively, the code that handles the *NUM* node might determine that its parent can be implemented with an immediate operation. Either way, it requires nonlocal context that violates the simple tree-walk paradigm.

The third case, c × d, has another nonlocal problem. Both subtrees of × refer to a variable at offset 4 from its base address. The references have different base addresses. The original tree-walk scheme generates an explicit loadI operation for each constant—@G, 4, @H, and 4. A version amended to use loadAI, as previously mentioned, would either generate separate loadIs for @G and @H

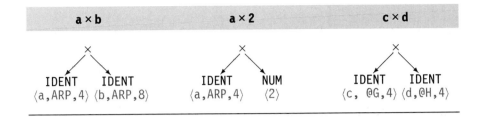

a × b	a × 2	c × d

Generated Code

```
                                                        loadI    @G      ⇒ r5
                                                        loadI    4       ⇒ r6
loadI    4         ⇒ r5       loadI    4        ⇒ r5     loadAO   r5,r6   ⇒ r7
loadAO   rarp,r5  ⇒ r6       loadAO   rarp,r5  ⇒ r6     loadI    @H      ⇒ r8
loadI    8         ⇒ r7       loadI    2        ⇒ r7     loadI    4       ⇒ r9
loadAO   rarp,r7  ⇒ r8       mult     r6,r7    ⇒ r8     loadAO   r8,r9   ⇒ r10
mult     r6,r8    ⇒ r9                                   mult     r7,r10  ⇒ r11
```

Desired Code

```
                                                        loadI    4        ⇒ r5
loadAI   rarp,4  ⇒ r5        loadAI   rarp,4  ⇒ r5      loadAI   r5,@G    ⇒ r6
loadAI   rarp,8  ⇒ r6        multI    r5,2    ⇒ r6      loadAI   r5,@H    ⇒ r7
mult     r5,r6   ⇒ r7                                    mult     r6,r7    ⇒ r8
```

FIGURE 11.3   Variations on Multiply

or it would generate two loadIs for 4. (Of course, the lengths of the values of @G and @H come into play. If they are too long, then the compiler must use the 4s as the immediate operands to the loadAI operations.)

The fundamental problem with this third example lies in the fact that the final code contains a common subexpression that was hidden in the AST. To discover the redundancy and handle it appropriately, the code generator would require code that explicitly checks the base address and offset values of subtrees and generates appropriate sequences for all the cases. Handling one case

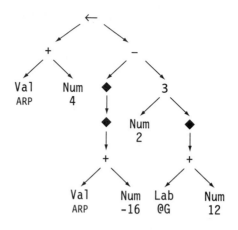

FIGURE 11.4 Low-Level AST for w ←x − 2 × y

in this fashion would be clumsy. Handling all the similar cases that can arise would require a prohibitive amount of additional coding.

A better way of catching this kind of redundancy is to expose the redundant details in the IR and let the optimizer eliminate them. For the example assignment, w ← x − 2 × y, the front end might produce the low-level tree shown in Figure 11.4. This tree has several new kinds of node. A Val node represents a value known to reside in a register, such as the ARP in r_{arp}. A Lab node represents a relocatable symbol, typically an assembly-level label used for either code or data. A ◆ node signifies a level of indirection; its child is an address and it produces the value stored at that address. These new node types require the compiler writer to specify more matching rules. In return, however, additional detail can be optimized, such as the duplicate references to 4 in c × d.

This version of the tree exposes details at a lower level of abstraction than the target ILOC instruction set. Inspecting this tree reveals, for instance, that w is a local variable stored at offset 4 from the ARP, that x is a call-by-reference parameter (note the two ◆ nodes), and that y is stored at offset 12 from label @G. Furthermore, the additions that are implicit in loadAI and storeAI operations appear explicitly in the tree—as a subtree of a ◆ node or as the left child of an ← node.

Exposing more detail in the AST should lead to better code. Increasing the number of target-machine operations that the code generator considers should also lead to better code. Together, however, these factors create a situation in which the code generator can discover many different ways to implement a given subtree. The simple tree-walk scheme had one option for each

OPTIMAL CODE GENERATION

The tree-walk scheme for selecting instructions produces the same code sequence each time it encounters a particular kind of AST node. More realistic schemes consider multiple patterns and use cost models to choose among them. This leads, naturally, to the question, can a compiler make optimal choices?

If each operation has an associated cost, and we ignore the effects of instruction scheduling and register allocation, then optimal instruction selection is possible. The tree-pattern-matching code generators described in Section 11.3 produce locally optimal sequences—that is, each subtree is computed by a minimal-cost sequence.

The difficulty of capturing run-time behavior in a single cost number calls into question the importance of such a claim. The impact of execution order, bounded hardware resources, and context-sensitive behavior in the memory hierarchy all complicate the problem of determining the actual cost of any specific code sequence.

In practice, most modern compilers largely ignore scheduling and allocation during instruction selection and assume that the costs associated with various rewrite rules are accurate. Given these assumptions, the compiler looks for locally optimal sequences—those that minimize the estimated cost for an entire subtree. The compiler then performs scheduling and allocation in one or more postpasses over the code produced by instruction selection.

AST node type. To make effective use of the target machine's instruction set, the code generator should consider as many possibilities as is practical.

This increased complexity does not arise from a particular methodology or a specific matching algorithm; rather, it reflects the actual situation—a given machine might provide many different ways to implement an IR construct. When the code generator considers multiple possible matches for a given subtree, it needs a way to choose among them. If the compiler writer can associate a cost with each pattern, then the matching scheme can select patterns in a way that minimizes the costs. If the costs truly reflect performance, this sort of cost-driven instruction selection should lead to good code.

The compiler writer needs tools that help to manage the complexity of code generation for real machines. Rather than writing code that explicitly navigates the IR and tests the applicability of each operation, the compiler writer should specify rules, and the tools should produce the code required to match those rules with the IR form of the code. The next two sections explore two different approaches to managing the complexity that arises for the instruction set of a modern machine. The next section explores the use of tree-pattern-matching techniques. These systems fold the complexity into the process of constructing the matcher, in the same way that scanners fold their choices into the transition tables of DFAs. The following section examines the use of peephole optimization for instruction selection. The peephole-based systems move the complexity of choice into a uniform scheme for low-level simplification followed by pattern matching to find the appropriate instructions. To keep the cost of matching low, these systems limit their scope to short segments of code—two or three operations at a time.

11.3 | INSTRUCTION SELECTION VIA TREE-PATTERN MATCHING

The compiler writer can use tree-pattern-matching tools to attack the complexity of instruction selection. To transform code generation into tree-pattern-matching, both the IR form of the program and the target machine's instruction set must be expressed as trees. As we have seen, the compiler can use a low-level AST as a detailed model of the code being compiled. It can use similar trees to represent the operations available on the target processor. For example, ILOC's addition operations might be modelled by operation trees that look like:

$$\text{add } r_i, r_j \Rightarrow r_k \qquad\qquad \text{addI } r_i, c_j \Rightarrow r_k$$

By systematically matching operation trees with subtrees of an AST, the compiler can discover all the potential implementations for the subtree.

To work with tree patterns, we need a more convenient notation for describing them. Using a prefix notation, we can write the operation tree for add as $+(r_i, r_j)$ and addI as $+(r_i, c_j)$. The leaves of the operation tree encode information about the storage types of the operands. For example, in $+(r_i, c_j)$, the symbol r denotes an operand in a register and the symbol c denotes a known constant operand. Subscripts are added to ensure uniqueness, just as we did in the rules for an attribute grammar. If we rewrite the AST from Figure 11.4 in prefix form, it becomes

$$\leftarrow (+(\text{Val}_1,\text{Num}_1), -(\blacklozenge(\blacklozenge(+(\text{Val}_2,\text{Num}_2))), \times(\text{Num}_3, \blacklozenge(+(\text{Lab}_1,\text{Num}_4)))))).$$

While the drawing of the tree may be more intuitive, this linear prefix form contains the same information.

Given an AST and a collection of operation trees, the goal is to map the AST to operations by *tiling* the AST with operation trees. A tiling is a collection of ⟨*ast-node,op-tree*⟩ pairs, where *ast-node* is a node in the AST and *op-tree* is an operation tree. The presence of an ⟨*ast-node,op-tree*⟩ pair in the tiling means that the target-machine operation corresponding to *op-tree* could implement *ast-node*. Of course, the choice of an implementation for *ast-node* depends on the implementations of its subtrees. The tiling will specify, for each of *ast-node*'s subtrees, an implementation that connects with *op-tree*.

A tiling *implements* the AST if it implements every operation and each tile "connects" with its neighbors. We say that a tile connects with its neighbors if, for each ⟨*ast-node,op-tree*⟩ pair, *ast-node* is covered by a leaf in another *op-tree* in the tiling, unless *ast-node* is the root of the AST. Where two such trees overlap (at *ast-node*), they must agree on where to store the value corresponding to their common node. If both assume that it is in a register, then the code sequences for the two *op-trees* are compatible. If one assumes that it is in memory and the other that it is in a register, the code sequences are incompatible, since they will not correctly transmit the value produced by the lower tree to the leaf of the upper tree.

Given a tiling that implements an AST, the compiler can easily generate assembly code in a bottom-up walk. Thus, the key to making this approach practical lies in algorithms that quickly find good tilings for an AST. Several efficient techniques have emerged for matching tree patterns against low-level ASTs. All these systems associate costs with the operation trees and produce minimal cost tilings. They differ in the technology used for matching—tree matching, text matching, and bottom-up rewrite systems—and in the generality of their cost models—static fixed costs versus costs that can vary during the matching process.

11.3.1 Rewrite Rules

The compiler writer encodes the relationships between operation trees and subtrees in the AST as a set of *rewrite rules*. The rule set includes one or more rules for every kind of node in the AST. A rewrite rule consists of a production in a tree grammar, a code template, and an associated cost. Figure 11.5 shows a set of rewrite rules for tiling our low-level AST with ILOC operations.

Consider rule 16. It describes a tree that computes the sum of a value located in a Reg and an immediate value in a Num. The left side of the table gives the tree pattern for the rule, $Reg \rightarrow + (Reg_1, Num_2)$. The center column lists its cost, 1. The right column shows an ILOC operation to implement the rule, addI $r_1, n_2 \Rightarrow r_{new}$. The operands in the tree pattern, Reg_1 and Num_2, correspond to the operands r_1 and n_2 in the code template. The compiler must rewrite the field r_{new} in the code template with the name of a register allocated to hold the result of the addition. This register name will, in turn, become a leaf in the subtree that connects to this subtree.

The written, linear form of the tree patterns provides less intuition than the tree representation. In the discussion that follows, we will often use the drawn form to refer to a pattern. For example, the following drawing represents rule 16. Its result, at the + node, is implicitly a Reg.

The tree grammar shown in Figure 11.5 is similar to the grammars that we used to specify the syntax of programming languages. Each rewrite rule, or production, has a nonterminal symbol as its left-hand side. In rule 16, the nonterminal is Reg. Reg represents a collection of subtrees that the tree grammar can generate, in this case using rules 6 through 25. The right-hand side of a rule is a linearized tree pattern. In rule 16, that pattern is $+ (Reg_1, Num_2)$, representing the addition of two values, a Reg and a Num.

The nonterminals in the grammar allow for abstraction. They serve to connect the rules in the grammar. They also encode knowledge about where the corresponding value is stored at run time and what form it takes. For example, Reg represents a value produced by a subtree and stored in a register, while Val represents a value already stored in register. A Val might be a global value, such as the ARP. It might be the result of a computation performed in a disjoint subtree—a common subexpression.

The cost associated with a production should provide the code generator with a realistic estimate of the run-time cost of executing the code in the template. For rule 16, the cost is 1 to reflect the fact that the tree can be implemented with a single operation that requires just one cycle to execute. The code generator uses the costs to choose among the possible alternatives. Some matching techniques restrict the costs to numbers. Others allow costs that vary during matching to reflect the impact of previous choices on the cost of the current alternatives.

	Production	Cost	Code Template
1	Goal $\rightarrow$ Assign	0	
2	Assign $\rightarrow$ $\leftarrow$ (Reg$_1$,Reg$_2$)	1	store r_2 $\Rightarrow r_1$
3	Assign $\rightarrow$ $\leftarrow$ (+ (Reg$_1$,Reg$_2$), Reg$_3$)	1	storeAO r_3 $\Rightarrow r_1,r_2$
4	Assign $\rightarrow$ $\leftarrow$ (+ (Reg$_1$,Num$_2$), Reg$_3$)	1	storeAI r_3 $\Rightarrow r_1,n_2$
5	Assign $\rightarrow$ $\leftarrow$ (+ (Num$_1$,Reg$_2$), Reg$_3$)	1	storeAI r_3 $\Rightarrow r_2,n_1$
6	Reg $\rightarrow$ Lab$_1$	1	loadI l_1 $\Rightarrow r_{new}$
7	Reg $\rightarrow$ Val$_1$	0	
8	Reg $\rightarrow$ Num$_1$	1	loadI n_1 $\Rightarrow r_{new}$
9	Reg $\rightarrow$ $\blacklozenge$ (Reg$_1$)	1	load r_1 $\Rightarrow r_{new}$
10	Reg $\rightarrow$ $\blacklozenge$ (+ (Reg$_1$,Reg$_2$))	1	loadAO r_1,r_2 $\Rightarrow r_{new}$
11	Reg $\rightarrow$ $\blacklozenge$ (+ (Reg$_1$,Num$_2$))	1	loadAI r_1,n_2 $\Rightarrow r_{new}$
12	Reg $\rightarrow$ $\blacklozenge$ (+ (Num$_1$,Reg$_2$))	1	loadAI r_2,n_1 $\Rightarrow r_{new}$
13	Reg $\rightarrow$ $\blacklozenge$ (+ (Reg$_1$,Lab$_2$))	1	loadAI r_1,l_2 $\Rightarrow r_{new}$
14	Reg $\rightarrow$ $\blacklozenge$ (+ (Lab$_1$,Reg$_2$))	1	loadAI r_2,l_1 $\Rightarrow r_{new}$
15	Reg $\rightarrow$ + (Reg$_1$,Reg$_2$)	1	add r_1,r_2 $\Rightarrow r_{new}$
16	Reg $\rightarrow$ + (Reg$_1$,Num$_2$)	1	addI r_1,n_2 $\Rightarrow r_{new}$
17	Reg $\rightarrow$ + (Num$_1$,Reg$_2$)	1	addI r_2,n_1 $\Rightarrow r_{new}$
18	Reg $\rightarrow$ + (Reg$_1$,Lab$_2$)	1	addI r_1,l_2 $\Rightarrow r_{new}$
19	Reg $\rightarrow$ + (Lab$_1$,Reg$_2$)	1	addI r_2,l_1 $\Rightarrow r_{new}$
20	Reg $\rightarrow$ - (Reg$_1$,Reg$_2$)	1	sub r_1,r_2 $\Rightarrow r_{new}$
21	Reg $\rightarrow$ - (Reg$_1$,Num$_2$)	1	subI r_1,n_2 $\Rightarrow r_{new}$
22	Reg $\rightarrow$ - (Num$_1$,Reg$_2$)	1	rsubI r_2,n_1 $\Rightarrow r_{new}$
23	Reg $\rightarrow$ $\times$ (Reg$_1$,Reg$_2$)	1	mult r_1,r_2 $\Rightarrow r_{new}$
24	Reg $\rightarrow$ $\times$ (Reg$_1$,Num$_2$)	1	multI r_1,n_2 $\Rightarrow r_{new}$
25	Reg $\rightarrow$ $\times$ (Num$_1$,Reg$_2$)	1	multI r_2,n_1 $\Rightarrow r_{new}$

FIGURE 11.5 Rewrite Rules for Tiling the Low-Level Tree with ILOC

Tree patterns can capture context in a way that the simple tree-walk code generator cannot. Rules 10 through 14 each match two operators (◆ and +). These rules express the conditions in which the ILOC operators loadA0 and loadAI can be used. The tree-walk code generator matches one operator at a time. Any subtree that matches one of these three rules can be tiled with a combination of other rules. A subtree that matches rule 10 can be tiled with the combination of rule 15 to produce an address and rule 9 to load the value. This flexibility makes the set of rewrite rules ambiguous. The ambiguity reflects the fact that the target machine has several ways to implement this particular subtree.

In Figure 11.5, Reg appears as both a terminal and a nonterminal symbol. This reflects an abbreviation in the example. A complete set of rules would include a set of productions that rewrite Reg with a specific register name, such as $Reg \rightarrow r_0$, $Reg \rightarrow r_1, \ldots$, and $Reg \rightarrow r_k$.

To apply these rules to a tree, we look for a sequence of rewriting steps that reduces the tree to a single symbol. For an AST that represents a complete program, that symbol should be the goal symbol. For an interior node, that symbol typically represents the value produced by evaluating the subtree rooted at the expression. The symbol also must specify where the value exists—typically in a register, in a memory location, or as a known constant value.

Consider, for example, the subtree that represents the reference to y in Figure 11.4, which is shown in the leftmost panel of Figure 11.6. (Recall that y was at offset 12 from the label @G.) The remaining panels show one reduction sequence for that subtree. The first match in the sequence recognizes that the left leaf (a Lab node) matches rule 6. This allows us to rewrite it as a Reg. The rewritten tree now matches the right-hand side of rule 11, ◆ (+ (Reg,Num)), so we can rewrite the entire subtree rooted at ◆ as a Reg. Thus, the rewrite sequence ⟨6,11⟩ reduces the entire subtree to a Reg.

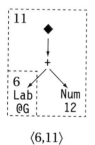

⟨6,11⟩

FIGURE 11.6   A Simple Tree Rewrite Sequence

To summarize such a sequence, we will use a drawing like the one at left. The dashed boxes show the specific right-hand sides that matched the tree, with the rule number recorded in the upper left corner of each box. The list of rule numbers below the drawing indicates the sequence in which the rules were applied. The rewrite sequence replaces the boxed subtree with the final rule's left-hand side.

Notice how the nonterminals ensure that the operation trees connect appropriately at the points where they overlap. Rule 6 rewrites a Lab as a Reg. The left leaf in rule 11 is a Reg. Viewing the patterns as rules in a grammar folds all of the considerations that arise at the boundaries between operation trees into the labelling of nonterminals.

For this trivial subtree, the rules generate many rewrite sequences, reflecting the ambiguity of the grammar. Figure 11.7 shows eight of these sequences. All the rules in our scheme have a cost of one, except for rules 1 and 7. Since none of the rewrite sequences use these rules, their costs are identical to their sequence length. The sequences fall into three categories by cost. The first pair of sequences, $\langle 6,11 \rangle$ and $\langle 8,14 \rangle$, each have cost two. The next four sequences, $\langle 6,8,10 \rangle$, $\langle 8,6,10 \rangle$, $\langle 6,16,9 \rangle$ and $\langle 8,19,9 \rangle$, each have cost three. The final two sequences, $\langle 6,8,15,9 \rangle$ and $\langle 8,6,15,9 \rangle$, each have cost four.

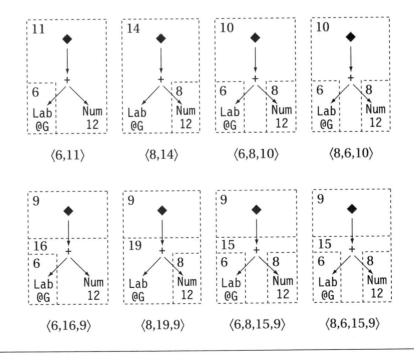

FIGURE 11.7   Potential Matches

```
loadI   @G    ⇒ rᵢ          loadI   12    ⇒ rᵢ              loadI   @G    ⇒ rᵢ
loadAI  rᵢ,12 ⇒ rⱼ          loadAI  rᵢ,@G ⇒ rⱼ              loadI   12    ⇒ rⱼ
                                                            loadAO  rᵢ,rⱼ ⇒ rₖ
        ⟨6,11⟩                      ⟨8,14⟩                         ⟨6,8,10⟩


loadI   12    ⇒ rᵢ          loadI   @G    ⇒ rᵢ          loadI   12    ⇒ rᵢ
loadI   @G    ⇒ rⱼ          addI    rᵢ,12 ⇒ rⱼ          addI    rᵢ,@G ⇒ rⱼ
loadAO  rᵢ,rⱼ ⇒ rₖ          load    rⱼ    ⇒ rₖ          load    rⱼ    ⇒ rₖ
        ⟨8,6,10⟩                    ⟨6,16,9⟩                    ⟨8,19,9⟩


            loadI   @G    ⇒ rᵢ              loadI   12    ⇒ rᵢ
            loadI   12    ⇒ rⱼ              loadI   @G    ⇒ rⱼ
            add     rᵢ,rⱼ ⇒ rₖ              add     rᵢ,rⱼ ⇒ rₖ
            load    rₖ    ⇒ rₗ              load    rₖ    ⇒ rₗ
                   ⟨6,8,15,9⟩                      ⟨8,6,15,9⟩
```

FIGURE 11.8   Code Sequences for the Matches

To produce assembly code, the selector uses the code templates associated with each rule. A rule's code template consists of a sequence of assembly-code operations that implements the subtree generated by the production. For example, rule 15 maps the tree pattern $+(Reg_1, Reg_2)$ to the code template add $r_1, r_2 \Rightarrow r_{new}$. The selector replaces each of r_1 and r_2 with the register name holding the result of the corresponding subtree. It allocates a new virtual register name for r_{new}. A tiling for an AST specifies which rules the code generator should use. The code generator uses the associated templates to generate assembly code in a bottom-up walk. It supplies names, as needed, to tie the storage locations together and emits the instantiated operations corresponding to the walk.

The code generator should choose a tiling that produces the lowest-cost assembly-code sequence. Figure 11.8 shows the code that corresponds to each potential tiling. Arbitrary register names have been substituted as appropriate. Both ⟨6,11⟩ and ⟨8,14⟩ produce the lowest cost—two. They lead to different, but equivalent code sequences. Because they have identical costs, the selector is free to choose between them. The other sequences are, as expected, more costly.

If loadAI only accepts arguments in a limited range, the sequence ⟨8,14⟩ might not work, since the address that eventually replaces @G may be too large for the immediate field in the operation. To handle this kind of restriction, the compiler writer can introduce the notion of an appropriately limited constant into the rewriting grammar. This might take the form of a new terminal symbol that can only represent integers in a given range, such as $0 \leq i < 4096$ for a 12-bit field. With such a distinction, and code that checks each instance of an integer to classify it, the code generator could avoid the sequence $\langle 8,14 \rangle$, unless @G falls in the allowable range for an immediate operand of loadAI.

The cost model drives the code generator to select one of the better sequences. For example, notice that the sequence $\langle 6,8,10 \rangle$ uses two loadI operations, followed by a loadAO. The code generator prefers the lower-cost sequences, each of which avoids one of the loadI operations and issues fewer operations. Similarly, the cost model avoids the four sequences that use an explicit addition—preferring, instead, to perform the addition implicitly in the addressing hardware.

11.3.2 Finding a Tiling

To apply these ideas to code generation, we need an algorithm that can construct a good tiling—that is, a tiling that produces efficient code. Given a set of rules that encode the operator trees and relate them to the structure of an AST, the code generator should discover an efficient tiling for a specific AST. Several efficient techniques for constructing such a tiling exist. They are similar in concept, but differ in detail.

To simplify the algorithm, we make two assumptions about the form of the rewrite rules. First, each operation has, at most, two operands. Extending the algorithm to handle the general case is straightforward, but the details complicate the explanation. Second, a rule's right-hand side contains at most one operation. This simplifies the matching algorithm, at no loss in generality. A simple, mechanical procedure can transform the unrestricted case to this simpler case. For a production $\alpha \rightarrow \mathsf{op}_1(\beta, \mathsf{op}_2(\gamma, \delta))$, rewrite it as $\alpha \rightarrow \mathsf{op}_1(\beta, \alpha')$ and $\alpha' \rightarrow \mathsf{op}_2(\gamma, \delta)$, where α' is a new symbol that only occurs in these two rules. The number of nonterminals and productions that this introduces is bounded by the number of times that any operator appears in the original grammar.

To make this concrete, consider rule 11, Reg $\rightarrow \blacklozenge$ (+ (Reg$_1$,Num$_1$)). The transformation rewrites it as Reg $\rightarrow \blacklozenge$ (R11P2) and R11P2 $\rightarrow$ + (Reg$_1$,Num$_1$), where R11P2 is a new symbol. Notice that the new rule for R11P2 is identical to rule 16 that describes addI. The transformation adds another ambiguity to the grammar. However, tracking and matching the two rules independently lets the pattern matcher consider the cost of each. The pair of rules that replaces rule 11 should have a cost of one, the cost of the original rule. (Each rule might have fractional cost, or one of them might have zero cost.) This reflects the fact

Tile(n)
  Label(n) ← ∅
  if n is a binary node then
    Tile(left(n))
    Tile(right(n))
    for each rule r that matches n's operation
      if left(r) ∈ *Label(left(n)) and right(r)* ∈ *Label(right(n))*
        then Label(n) ← *Label(n)* ∪ *{r}*
  else if n is a unary node then
    Tile(left(n))
    for each rule r that matches n's operation
      if left(r) ∈ *Label(left(n))*
        then Label(n) ← *Label(n)* ∪ *{r}*
  else / n is a leaf */*
    Label(n) ← *{ **all rules that match the operation in** n}*

FIGURE 11.9   Compute *Label* Sets to Tile an AST

that rewriting with rule 16 produces an addI operation, while the rule for R11P2 folds the addition into the address generation of a loadAI operation. The new rule specializes the match by capitalizing on the context, when possible.

The goal of tiling is to label each node in the AST with a set of patterns that the compiler can use to implement it. Since rule numbers correspond directly to right-hand-side patterns, the code generator can use them as a shorthand for the patterns. The compiler can compute sequences of rule numbers, or patterns, for each node in a postorder traversal of the tree. Figure 11.9 sketches an algorithm, *Tile*, that finds tilings for a tree rooted at node *n* in the AST. It annotates each AST node *n* with a set *Label(n)* containing all the rule numbers that can be used to tile the tree rooted at node *n*. It computes the *Label* sets in a postorder traversal to ensure that it labels a node's children before it labels the node.

Consider the inner loop for the case of a binary node. To compute *Label(n)*, it examines each rule *r* that implements the operation specified by *n*. It uses the functions *left* and *right* to traverse both the AST and the tree patterns (or right-hand sides of the rules).[3] Because *Tile* has already labelled *n*'s children, it can use a simple membership test to compare *r*'s children against *n*'s children. If *left(r)* ∈ *Label(left(n))*, then *Tile* has already discovered that it can generate code

---

3. Recall that each rule specifies an operator and at most two children. Thus, for a rule *r*, *left(r)* and *right(r)* have clear meanings.

for n's left subtree in a way that is compatible with using r to implement n. A similar argument holds for the right subtrees of both r and n. If both subtrees match, then r belongs in *Label(n)*.

To speed up this matching process, we can precompute all possible matches, store them in a table, and replace the inner loop for both binary nodes and unary nodes with a table reference indexed by the operator at node n and the label sets of its children. The label sets are bounded. If R is the number of rules, then $|Label(n)| \leq$ R, and there can be no more than 2^R distinct label sets. Fortunately, the structure of the grammar rules out many of those sets. If each rule has one operator and two children, then the lookup table can be indexed by the operator and the label sets of the two children. This leads to a table of size $|operation\ trees| \times |label\ sets|^2$, which can still be huge. For a machine with 200 operations and a grammar with 1,000 label sets, the resulting table has 200,000,000 entries. Fortunately, the tables constructed for this purpose are sparse and can be encoded efficiently. (In fact, finding ways to build and encode these tables efficiently was one of the key advances that made tree-pattern-matching a practical tool for code generation.)

Finding the Low-Cost Matches

The algorithm in Figure 11.9 finds all of the matches in the pattern set. In practice, we want the code generator to find the lowest-cost match. While it could derive the lowest-cost match from the set of all matches, there are more efficient ways to compute it.

In a bottom-up pass over the AST, the code generator can discover the lowest-cost match for each subtree. Bottom-up order ensures that it can compute the cost of each alternative match—the cost of the matched rule plus the costs of the associated subtree matches. In principle, it can discover matches as in Figure 11.9 and retain the lowest-cost ones, rather than all the matches. In practice, the process is slightly more complex.

The cost function depends, inherently, on the target processor; it cannot be derived automatically from the grammar. Instead, it must encode properties of the target machine and reflect the interactions that occur between operations in an assembly program—particularly the flow of values from one operation to another.

A value in the compiled program may have several different forms. The distinctions among these forms matter to the instruction selector because they change the set of target-machine operations that can use the value. On a typical machine, a value may be in a register or in a memory location, or it might be a compile-time constant small enough to fit into some or all of the immediate operations.

When the instruction selector tries to find matches for a particular subtree, it must know the cost of evaluating each of the subtree's operands. If those operands may be in different storage classes—such as registers, memory locations, or immediate constants—the code generator must know the cost of evaluating the operand into each of those storage classes. Thus, it must track the lowest-cost sequences that generate each of these storage classes. As it makes the bottom-up traversal to compute costs, the code generator can easily determine the lowest-cost match for each storage class. This adds a small amount of work to the process, but the increase is bounded by a factor equal to the number of storage classes—a number that depends entirely on the target machine, and not on the number of rewrite rules.

A careful implementation can accumulate these costs while tiling the tree. If, at each match, the code generator retains the lowest-cost matches, it will produce a locally optimal tiling. That is, at each node, no better alternative exists, given the rule set and the cost functions. This bottom-up accumulation of costs implements a dynamic-programming solution to finding the minimal-cost tiling.

If we require that the costs be fixed, the cost computation can be folded into the construction of the pattern matcher. This moves computation from compile time to the construction algorithm and almost always produces a faster code generator. If we allow the costs to vary and account for the context in which a match is made, then the cost comparison must be done at compile time. This may slow down the code generator, but it allows more flexibility in the cost functions, and the cost functions might more accurately reflect run-time behavior.

11.3.3 Tools

This tree-oriented, bottom-up approach to code generation leads to efficient instruction selectors. There are several ways that the compiler writer can implement code generators based on these principles.

1. We can hand code a matcher, similar to *Tile*, that explicitly checks for matching rules as it tiles the tree. A careful implementation can limit the set of rules that must be examined for each node. This avoids the large sparse table and leads to a compact code generator.

2. Since the problem is finite, we can encode it as a finite automaton—a tree-matching automaton—and obtain the low-cost behavior of a DFA.

In this scheme, the look-up table encodes the transition function of the automaton, implicitly incorporating all the required state information. Several different systems have been built that use this approach, often called bottom-up rewriting systems (BURS).

3. The grammar-like form of the rules suggests using parsing techniques. The parsing algorithms must be extended to handle the highly ambiguous grammars that result from machine descriptions and to choose least-cost parses.

4. By linearizing the tree into a prefix string, the problem can be translated to a string-matching problem. Then, the compiler can use algorithms from string-pattern-matching to find the potential matches.

Tools are available that implement each of the last three approaches. The compiler writer produces a description of a target machine's instruction set, and a code-generator generator creates executable code from the description.

The automated tools differ in details. The cost per emitted instruction varies with the technique. Some are faster; some are slower; none is slow enough that it has a major impact on the speed of the resulting compiler. The approaches allow different cost models. Some systems restrict the compiler writer to a fixed cost for each rule; in return, they can perform some or all of the dynamic programming during table generation. Others allow more general cost models that may vary the cost during the matching process; these systems must perform the dynamic programming during code generation. In general, however, all these approaches produce code generators that are both efficient and effective.

11.4 INSTRUCTION SELECTION VIA PEEPHOLE OPTIMIZATION

Another technique for performing the matching operations that lie at the heart of instruction selection builds on a technology developed for late-stage optimization, called *peephole optimization*. To avoid encoding complexity in the code generator, this approach combines systematic local optimization on a low-level IR with a simple scheme for matching the IR to target-machine operations. This section introduces peephole optimization, explores its use as a mechanism for instruction selection, and describes the techniques that have been developed to automate construction of peephole optimizers.

11.4.1 Peephole Optimization

The basic idea behind peephole optimization is simple: the compiler can efficiently discover local improvements by examining short sequences of adjacent operations. As originally proposed, the peephole optimizer ran after all other steps in compilation. It both consumed and produced assembly code. The optimizer had a sliding window, or "peephole," that it moved over the code. At each step, it examined the operations in the window, looking for specific patterns that it could improve. When it recognized a pattern, it would rewrite it with a better instruction sequence. The combination of a limited pattern set and a limited area of focus led to fast processing.

A classic example pattern is a store followed by a load from the same location. The load can be replaced by a copy.

$$
\begin{array}{ll}
\texttt{storeAI } r_1 \quad \Rightarrow r_0,8 \\
\texttt{loadAI } \quad r_{arp},8 \Rightarrow r_{15}
\end{array}
\quad \Rightarrow \quad
\begin{array}{ll}
\texttt{storeAI } r_1 \Rightarrow r_{arp},8 \\
\texttt{i2i} \qquad r_1 \Rightarrow r_{15}
\end{array}
$$

If the peephole optimizer recognized that this rewrite made the store operation dead (that is, the load was the sole use for the value stored in memory), it could also eliminate the store operation. In general, however, recognizing dead stores requires global analysis that is beyond the scope of a peephole optimizer. Other patterns amenable to improvement by peephole optimization include simple algebraic identities, such as

$$
\begin{array}{ll}
\texttt{addI } r_2,0 \Rightarrow r_7 \\
\texttt{mult } r_4,r_7 \Rightarrow r_{10}
\end{array}
\quad \Rightarrow \quad
\texttt{mult } r_4,r_2 \Rightarrow r_{10}
$$

and cases where the target of a branch is, itself, a branch

$$
\begin{array}{ll}
\texttt{jumpI } \rightarrow l_{10} \\
l_{10}: \texttt{jumpI } \rightarrow l_{11}
\end{array}
\quad \Rightarrow \quad
\begin{array}{ll}
\texttt{jumpI } \rightarrow l_{11} \\
l_{10}: \texttt{jumpI } \rightarrow l_{11}
\end{array}
$$

If this eliminates the last branch to l_{10}, the basic block beginning at l_{10} becomes unreachable and can be eliminated. Unfortunately, proving that the operation at l_{10} is unreachable takes more analysis than is typically available during peephole optimization (see Section 10.3.1).

Early peephole optimizers used a limited set of hand-coded patterns. They used exhaustive search to match the patterns but ran quickly because of the small number of patterns and the small window size—typically two or three operations.

TREE PATTERN MATCHING ON QUADS?

The terms used to describe these techniques—*tree pattern matching and peephole optimization*—contain implicit assumptions about the kinds of IR to which they can be applied. BURS theory deals with rewriting operations on trees. This creates the impression that BURS-based code generators require tree-shaped IRs. Similarly, peephole optimizers were first proposed as a final assembly-to-assembly improvement pass. The idea of a moving instruction window strongly suggests a linear, low-level IR for a peephole-based code generator.

Both techniques can be adapted to fit most IRs. A compiler can interpret a low-level linear IR like ILOC as trees. Each operation becomes a tree node; the edges are implied by the reuse of operands. Similarly, if the compiler assigns a name to each node, it can interpret trees as a linear form by performing a postorder treewalk. A clever implementor can adapt the methods presented in this chapter to a wide variety of actual IRs.

Peephole optimization has progressed beyond matching a few patterns. Increasingly complex ISAs led to a more systematic approach. A modern peephole optimizer breaks the process into three distinct tasks: expansion, simplification, and matching. It replaces the pattern-driven optimization of early systems with a systematic application of symbolic interpretation and simplification.

Structurally, this looks like a compiler. The expander recognizes the input code in IR form and builds an internal representation. The simplifier performs some rewriting operations on that IR. The matcher transforms the IR into target-machine code, typically assembly code (ASM). If the input and output languages are the same, this system is a peephole optimizer. With different languages as input and output, the same algorithms can perform instruction selection, as we shall see in Section 11.4.2.

The expander rewrites the assembly code, operation by operation, into a sequence of lower-level IR operations (LLIR) that represents all the direct effects of an operation—at least, all of them that affect program behavior. If the operation add $r_i, r_j \Rightarrow r_k$ sets the condition code, then its LLIR representation must include operations that assign $r_i + r_j$ to r_k and that set the condition code to the appropriate value. Typically, the expander has a simple structure. Operations can be expanded individually, without regard to context. The process uses a template for each ASM operation and substitutes appropriate register names, constants, and labels in the templates.

The simplifier makes a pass over the LLIR, examining the operations in a small window on the LLIR and systematically trying to improve them. The basic mechanisms of simplification are forward substitution, algebraic simplification (for example, $x + 0 \Rightarrow x$), evaluating constant-valued expressions (for example, $2 + 17 \Rightarrow 19$), and eliminating useless effects, such as the creation of unused condition codes. Thus, the simplifier performs limited local optimization on the LLIR in the window. This subjects all the details exposed in the LLIR (address arithmetic, branch targets, and so on) to a uniform level of local optimization.

In the final step, the matcher compares the simplified LLIR against the pattern library, looking for the pattern that best captures all the effects in the LLIR. The final code sequence may produce effects beyond those required by the LLIR sequence; for example, it might create a new, albeit useless, condition-code value. It must, however, preserve the effects needed for correctness. It cannot eliminate a live value, regardless of whether the value is stored in memory, a register, or in an implicitly set location such as the condition code.

Figure 11.10 shows how this approach might work on the example from Section 11.2. It begins, in the upper left, with the quadruples for the low-level AST shown in Figure 11.4. (Recall that the AST computes $w \leftarrow x - 2 \times y$, with w stored at offset 4 in the local AR, x stored as a call-by-reference parameter whose pointer is at offset –16 from the ARP, and y at offset 12 from the label @G.) The expander creates the LLIR shown on the upper right. The simplifier reduces this code to produce the LLIR code in the bottom right. From this LLIR fragment, the matcher constructs the ILOC code in the lower left.

The key to understanding this process lies in the simplifier. Figure 11.11 shows the successive sequences that the peephole optimizer has in its window as it processes the low-level IR for the example. Assume that it has a three-operation window. Sequence 1 shows the window with the first three operations. No simplification is possible. The optimizer rolls the first operation, defining r_{10}, out of the window and brings in the definition of r_{13}. In this window, it can substitute r_{12} forward into the definition of r_{13}. Because this makes r_{12} dead, the optimizer discards the definition of r_{12} and pulls another operation into the bottom of the window to reach sequence 3. Next, it folds r_{13} into the memory reference that defines r_{14}, producing sequence 4.

No simplification is possible on sequence 4, so the optimizer rolls the definition of r_{11} out of the window. It cannot simplify sequence 5, either, so it rolls

r_{10}	$\leftarrow$	2
r_{11}	$\leftarrow$	@G
r_{12}	$\leftarrow$	12
r_{13}	$\leftarrow$	$r_{11} + r_{12}$
r_{14}	$\leftarrow$	$M(r_{13})$

Op	Arg$_1$	Arg$_2$	Result					
×	2	y	t_1	*Expand*	r_{15}	$\leftarrow$	$r_{10} \times r_{14}$
−	x	t_1	w	$\Rightarrow$	r_{16}	$\leftarrow$	−16

r_{17}	$\leftarrow$	$r_{arp} + r_{16}$
r_{18}	$\leftarrow$	$M(r_{17})$
r_{19}	$\leftarrow$	$M(r_{18})$
r_{20}	$\leftarrow$	$r_{19} - r_{15}$
r_{21}	$\leftarrow$	4
r_{22}	$\leftarrow$	$r_{arp} + r_{21}$
$M(r_{22})$	$\leftarrow$	r_{20}

$\Downarrow$ *Simplify*

loadI	2	$\Rightarrow r_{10}$		r_{10}	$\leftarrow$	2
loadI	@G	$\Rightarrow r_{11}$		r_{11}	$\leftarrow$	@G
loadAI	$r_{11},12$	$\Rightarrow r_{14}$		r_{14}	$\leftarrow$	$M(r_{11} + r_{12})$
mult	r_{10},r_{14}	$\Rightarrow r_{15}$	*Match*	r_{15}	$\leftarrow$	$r_{10} \times r_{14}$
loadAI	$r_{arp},-16$	$\Rightarrow r_{18}$	$\Leftarrow$	r_{18}	$\leftarrow$	$M(r_{arp} + -16)$
load	r_{18}	$\Rightarrow r_{19}$		r_{19}	$\leftarrow$	$M(r_{18})$
sub	r_{19},r_{15}	$\Rightarrow r_{20}$		r_{20}	$\leftarrow$	$r_{19} - r_{15}$
storeAI	r_{20}	$\Rightarrow r_{arp},4$		$M(r_{arp} + 4)$	$\leftarrow$	r_{20}

FIGURE 11.10   *Expand, Simplify,* and *Match* Applied to the Example

the definition of r_{14} out of the window, too. It can simplify sequence 6 by forward substituting −16 into the addition that defines r_{17}. That action produces sequence 7. The optimizer continues in this manner, simplifying the code when possible and advancing when it cannot. When it reaches sequence 13, it halts because it cannot further simplify the sequence and it has no additional code to bring into the window.

$$
\begin{array}{|l|}
\hline
r_{10} \leftarrow 2 \\
r_{11} \leftarrow @G \\
r_{12} \leftarrow 12 \\
\hline
\end{array}
$$

Sequence 1

$$
\begin{array}{|l|}
\hline
r_{11} \leftarrow @G \\
r_{12} \leftarrow 12 \\
r_{13} \leftarrow r_{11} + r_{12} \\
\hline
\end{array}
$$

Sequence 2

$$
\begin{array}{|l|}
\hline
r_{11} \leftarrow @G \\
r_{13} \leftarrow r_{11} + 12 \\
r_{14} \leftarrow M(r_{13}) \\
\hline
\end{array}
$$

Sequence 3

$$
\begin{array}{|l|}
\hline
r_{11} \leftarrow @G \\
r_{14} \leftarrow M(r_{11} + 12) \\
r_{15} \leftarrow r_{10} \times r_{14} \\
\hline
\end{array}
$$

Sequence 4

$$
\begin{array}{|l|}
\hline
r_{14} \leftarrow M(r_{11} + 12) \\
r_{15} \leftarrow r_{10} \times r_{14} \\
r_{16} \leftarrow -16 \\
\hline
\end{array}
$$

Sequence 5

$$
\begin{array}{|l|}
\hline
r_{15} \leftarrow r_{10} \times r_{14} \\
r_{16} \leftarrow -16 \\
r_{17} \leftarrow r_{arp} + r_{16} \\
\hline
\end{array}
$$

Sequence 6

$$
\begin{array}{|l|}
\hline
r_{15} \leftarrow r_{10} \times r_{14} \\
r_{17} \leftarrow r_{arp} + -16 \\
r_{18} \leftarrow M(r_{17}) \\
\hline
\end{array}
$$

Sequence 7

$$
\begin{array}{|l|}
\hline
r_{15} \leftarrow r_{10} \times r_{14} \\
r_{18} \leftarrow M(r_{arp} + -16) \\
r_{19} \leftarrow M(r_{18}) \\
\hline
\end{array}
$$

Sequence 8

$$
\begin{array}{|l|}
\hline
r_{18} \leftarrow M(r_{arp} + -16) \\
r_{19} \leftarrow M(r_{18}) \\
r_{20} \leftarrow r_{19} - r_{15} \\
\hline
\end{array}
$$

Sequence 9

$$
\begin{array}{|l|}
\hline
r_{19} \leftarrow M(r_{18}) \\
r_{20} \leftarrow r_{19} - r_{15} \\
r_{21} \leftarrow 4 \\
\hline
\end{array}
$$

Sequence 10

$$
\begin{array}{|l|}
\hline
r_{20} \leftarrow r_{19} - r_{15} \\
r_{21} \leftarrow 4 \\
r_{22} \leftarrow r_{arp} + r_{21} \\
\hline
\end{array}
$$

Sequence 11

$$
\begin{array}{|l|}
\hline
r_{20} \leftarrow r_{19} - r_{15} \\
r_{22} \leftarrow r_{arp} + 4 \\
M(r_{22}) \leftarrow r_{20} \\
\hline
\end{array}
$$

Sequence 12

$$
\begin{array}{|l|}
\hline
r_{20} \leftarrow r_{19} - r_{15} \\
M(r_{arp} + 4) \leftarrow r_{20} \\
\hline
\end{array}
$$

Sequence 13

FIGURE 11.11   Sequences Produced by the Simplifier

Returning to Figure 11.10, compare the simplified code with the original code. The simplified code consists of those operations that roll out the top of the window, plus those left in the window when simplification halts. After simplification, the computation takes eight operations, instead of fourteen. It uses seven registers (other than r_{arp}), instead of thirteen.

Several design issues affect the ability of a peephole optimizer to improve code. The ability to detect when a value is dead plays a critical role in simplification. The handling of control-flow operations determines what happens at block boundaries. The size of the peephole window limits the optimizer's ability to combine related operations. For example, a larger window would let the simplifier fold the constant 2 into the multiply operation. The next three subsections explore these issues.

Dead Values

The ability to recognize useless effects, expressed as dead values, is critical to this process. Recall that a value is dead at some point p in the code if no path exists from p to any use of that value. Unfortunately, determining that a value is dead requires, in general, analysis of the entire name scope in which the value is created. How, then, can the simplifier know that some values are dead when it limits its focus to a small window on the code?

During the expansion process, the optimizer can construct a list of dead variables for each operation. Two observations make this possible. First, the expander can do its work in a backward pass over the code. As it walks each block, processing CFG successors (other than self-successors, of course) before their predecessors, it can build a list of dead variables. Second, most of the dead values that matter are purely local values—that is, they are defined and used entirely inside a single block. These values can be distinguished as a matter of code shape—the compiler can use a separate range of names or register numbers for these values—or the optimizer can settle for the values it can detect.

The classic example of a frequently dead value that needs to be tracked is the condition code. In the description of a real machine, as opposed to ILOC's virtual machine, details such as a condition code arise. Some computers have the arithmetic operations set the condition code; if a block ends by testing a computed value against zero, the comparison can sometimes be avoided by using a previously computed condition code. Naturally, the expander must include these condition-code effects. Unless dead condition codes can be detected and eliminated, however, these irrelevant condition-code assignments may prevent the peephole optimizer from combining operations that it could, otherwise, combine.

For example, consider the computation $r_i \times r_j + r_k$. If both $\times$ and $+$ set the condition code, the two-operation sequence might generate the following LLIR.

$$r_{t1} \leftarrow r_i \times r_j$$
$$cc \leftarrow f_x(r_x, r_g)$$
$$r_{t2} \leftarrow r_{t1} + r_k$$
$$cc \leftarrow f_+ (r_{t1}, r_k)$$

Since the addition follows the multiplication, the first value stored in the condition code is dead.

If the simplifier eliminates the operation that sets the condition code for the multiplication, $cc \leftarrow f_x(r_i, r_j)$, it can combine the remaining three operations into a multiply-add operation, assuming the target machine has such an instruction. If it cannot eliminate $cc \leftarrow f_x(r_i, r_j)$, however, that prevents the matcher from using multiply-add.

Control-Flow Operations

The presence of control-flow operations complicates the simplifier. The easiest way to handle them is to clear the simplifier's window when it reaches a branch, a jump, or a labelled instruction. This keeps the simplifier from moving effects onto paths where they were not present.

The simplifier can achieve better results by examining the context around branches, but it introduces several special cases to the process. If the input language encodes branches with a single target and a fall-through path, then the simplifier should track and eliminate dead labels. If it eliminates the last use of a label and the preceding block has a fall-through exit, then it can remove the label, combine the blocks, and simplify across the old boundary. If the input language encodes branches with two targets, or the preceding block ends with a jump, then a dead label implies an unreachable block that can be completely eliminated. In either case, the simplifier should track the number of uses for each label and eliminate labels that can no longer be referenced. (The expander can count label references, allowing the simplifier to use a simple reference-counting scheme to track the number of remaining references.)

A more aggressive approach might consider the operations on both sides of a branch. Some simplifications may be possible across the branch, combining effects of the operation immediately before the branch with those of the operation at the branch's target. However, the simplifier must account for *all* the paths reaching the labelled operation.

Predicated operations require some of these same considerations. At run time, the predicate values determine which operations actually execute. In effect, the predicates specify a path through a simple CFG, albeit one without explicit labels or branches. The simplifier must recognize these effects and treat them in the same cautious fashion that it uses for labelled operations.

Physical versus Logical Windows

The discussion, so far, has focused on a window containing adjacent operations in the low-level IR. This notion has a nice physical intuition and makes the concept concrete. However, adjacent operations in the low-level IR may not operate on the same values. In fact, as target machines offer more instruction-level parallelism, a compiler's front end and optimizer must generate IR programs that have more independent and interleaved computations to keep the target machine's functional units busy. In this case, the peephole optimizer may find very few opportunities for improving the code.

To improve this situation, the peephole optimizer can use a logical window rather than a physical window. With a logical window, it considers operations that are connected by the flow of values within the code—that is, it considers together operations that define and use the same value. This creates the opportunity to combine and simplify related operations, even if there are other operations between them.

During expansion, the optimizer can link each definition with the next use of its value in the same block. This lets the simplifier put logical pairs together rapidly. When it encounters operation i, it tries to simplify it in conjunction with i's logical successor—the operation in the block that next uses the value defined by i. (Since simplification relies, in large part, on forward substitution, there is little reason to consider the next physical operation, unless it uses i's result.) Using a logical window within a block can make the simplifier more effective, reducing both compilation time required and the number of operations remaining after simplification. In our example, a logical window would let the simplifier fold the constant 2 into the multiplication.

Extending this idea to larger scopes adds some complication. The compiler can attempt to simplify operations that are logically adjacent but too far apart to fit in the peephole window together—either within the same block or in different blocks. This requires a global analysis to determine which uses each definition can reach (that is, reaching definitions from Section 9.2.4). Additionally, the simplifier must recognize that a single definition may reach multiple uses, and a single use might refer to values computed by several distinct definitions. Thus, the simplifier cannot simply combine the defining operation with one user and leave the remaining operations stranded. It must either limit its consideration to simple situations, such as a single definition and a single use, or multiple uses with a single definition, or it must perform some careful analysis to determine whether a combination is both safe and profitable. These complications suggest applying a logical window within a local or superlocal context. Moving the logical window beyond an extended basic block adds significant complications to the simplifier.

11.4.2 Peephole Transformers

The advent of more systematic peephole optimizers, as described in the previous section, created the need for more complete pattern sets for a target machine's assembly language. Because the three-step process translates all operations into LLIR and tries to simplify all the LLIR sequences, the matcher needs the ability to translate arbitrary LLIR sequences back into assembly code for the target machine. Thus, these modern peephole systems have much larger pattern libraries than earlier, partial systems. As computers moved from 16-bit instructions to 32-bit instructions, the explosion in the number of distinct assembly operations made hand-generation of the patterns problematic. To handle this explosion, most modern peephole systems include a tool that automatically generates a matcher from a description of a target machine's instruction set.

The advent of tools to generate the large pattern libraries needed to describe a processor's instruction set has made peephole optimization a competitive technology for instruction selection. One final twist further simplifies the picture. If the front end directly generates the LLIR used in the peephole optimizer, the compiler no longer needs an expander. Similarly, the simplifier need not deal with useless effects. The effects, like setting an extraneous condition code, arose because the expander lacked sufficient context to decide whether or not they were useful. This created the need for the expander to compute lists of dead values and for the simplifier take them into account. If the front end directly generates the LLIR, it can generate the effects it needs and omit those it does not need.

This scheme also reduces the work required to retarget a compiler to another processor. To change processors, the compiler writer must (1) provide an appropriate machine description to the pattern generator so that it can produce a new instruction selector, (2) change the LLIR sequences generated by earlier phases so that they fit the new ISA, and (3) modify the instruction scheduler and register allocator to reflect the characteristics of the new ISA. While this encompasses a significant amount of work, the infrastructure for describing, manipulating, and improving the LLIR sequences remains intact. Put another way, the LLIR sequences for radically different machines must capture their differences; however, the base language in which those

RISC, CISC, AND INSTRUCTION SELECTION

Early proponents of RISC architectures suggested that RISCs would lead to simpler compilers. Early RISC machines, like the IBM 801, had many fewer addressing modes than contemporary CISC machines (like DEC's VAX-11). They featured register-to-register operations, with separate load and store operations for moving data between registers and memory. In contrast, the VAX-11 accommodates both register and memory operands; many operations were supported in both two-address and three-address forms.

The RISC machines did simplify instruction selection. They offered fewer ways to implement a given operation. They had fewer restrictions on register use. However, their load-store architectures increased the importance of register allocation.

In contrast, CISC machines have operations that encapsulate more complex functionality into a single operation. To make effective use of these operations, the instruction selector must recognize larger patterns over larger code fragments. This increases the importance of systematic instruction selection; the automated techniques described in this chapter are more important for CISC machines, but equally applicable to RISC machines.

sequences are written remains the same. This allows the compiler writer to build a set of tools that are useful across many architectures and to produce a machine-specific compiler by generating the appropriate low-level IR for the target ISA and providing an appropriate set of patterns for the peephole optimizer.

The other advantage of this scheme lies in the simplifier. This stripped-down peephole transformer still includes a simplifier. Systematic simplification of code, even when performed in a limited window, provides a significant advantage over a simple hand-coded pass that walks the IR and rewrites it into assembly language. Forward substitution, application of simple algebraic identities, and constant folding can produce shorter, more efficient LLIR sequences. These, in turn, may lead to better code for a target machine.

Several important compiler systems have used this approach. The best known may be the Gnu compiler system, GCC. Its front end generates a low-level IR known as register-transfer language (RTL). The optimization passes manipulate RTL to produce improved RTL. The back end consumes RTL and produces assembly code for the various target computers using a peephole scheme. The simplifier is implemented using systematic symbolic interpretation. The matching step in the peephole optimizer actually interprets the RTL code as trees and uses a simple tree-pattern-matcher built from a description of the target machine. Other systems, such as Davidson's VPO, turn a machine description into a grammar and generate a small parser that processes the RTL in a linear form to perform the matching step.

11.5 ADVANCED TOPICS

Both BURS-based and peephole-based instruction selectors have been designed for compile-time efficiency. Both techniques are limited, however, by the knowledge contained in the patterns that the compiler writer provides. To find the best instruction sequences, the compiler writer might consider using search. The idea is simple. Combinations of instructions sometimes have surprising effects. Because the results are unexpected, they are rarely foreseen by a compiler writer and, therefore, are not included in the specification produced for a target machine.

Two distinct approaches that use exhaustive search to improve instruction selection have appeared in the literature. The first involves a peephole-based system that discovers and optimizes new patterns as it compiles code. The second involves a brute-force search of the space of possible instructions.

11.5.1 Learning Peephole Patterns

A major issue that arises in implementing or using a peephole optimizer is the tradeoff between the time spent specifying the target machine's instruction set and the speed and quality of the resulting optimizer or instruction selector. With a complete pattern set, the cost of both simplification and matching can be kept to a minimum by using an efficient pattern-matching technique. Of course, someone must generate all those patterns. On the other hand, systems that interpret the rules during simplification or matching have a larger overhead per LLIR operation. Such a system can operate with a much smaller set of rules. This makes the system easier to create. However, the resulting simplifier and matcher run more slowly.

One effective way to generate the explicit pattern table needed by a fast, pattern-matching peephole optimizer is to pair it with an optimizer that has a symbolic simplifier. In this scheme, the symbolic simplifier records all the patterns it simplifies. Each time it simplifies a pair of operations, it records the initial pair and the simplified pair.[4] Then, it can record the resulting pattern in the lookup table to produce a fast, pattern-matching optimizer.

By running the symbolic simplifier on a training set of applications, the optimizer can discover most of the patterns it needs. Then, the compiler can use the table as the basis of a fast pattern-matching optimizer. This lets the compiler writer expend computer time during design to speed up routine use of the compiler. It greatly reduces the complexity of the patterns that must be specified.

Increasing the interaction between the two optimizers can further improve code quality. At compile time, the fast pattern matcher will encounter some LLIR pairs that match no pattern in its table. When this occurs, it can invoke the symbolic simplifier to search for an improvement, bringing the power of search to bear only on the LLIR pairs for which it has no preexisting pattern.

To make this approach practical, the symbolic simplifier should record both successes and failures. This allows it to reject previously seen LLIR pairs without the overhead of symbolic interpretation. When it succeeds in improving a pair, it should add the new pattern to the optimizer's pattern table, so that future instances of that pair will be handled by the more efficient mechanism.

This learning approach to generating patterns has several advantages. It applies effort only on previously unseen LLIR pairs. It compensates for holes in the training set's coverage of the target machine. It provides the thoroughness of the more expensive system while preserving most of the speed of the pattern-directed system.

In using this approach, however, the compiler writer must determine when the symbolic optimizer should update the pattern tables and how to accommodate those updates. Allowing an arbitrary compilation to rewrite the pattern table for all users seems unwise; synchronization and security issues are sure to arise. Instead, the compiler writer might opt for periodic updates—storing the newly found patterns away so they can be added to the table as a routine maintenance action.

11.5.2 Generating Instruction Sequences

The learning approach has an inherent bias; it assumes that the low-level patterns should guide the search for an equivalent instruction sequence. Some compilers have taken an exhaustive approach to the same basic problem.

---

4. The symbolic simplifier may need to check a proposed pattern against the machine description to ensure that the simplification is not too general—for example, if it relies on a specific constant value for one operand, the input pattern must encode this restriction.

Instead of trying to synthesize the desired instruction sequence from a low-level model, they adopt a generate and test approach.

The idea is simple. The compiler, or compiler writer, identifies a short sequence of assembly-language instructions that should be improved. The compiler then generates all assembly-language sequences of cost one, substituting the original arguments into the generated sequence. It tests each one to determine if it has the same effect as the target sequence. When it has exhausted all sequences of a given cost, it increments the cost of the sequences and continues. This process continues until (1) it finds an equivalent sequence, (2) it reaches the cost of the original target sequence, or (3) it reaches an externally imposed limit on either cost or compile time.

While this approach is inherently expensive, the mechanism used for testing equivalence has a strong impact on the time required to test each candidate sequence. A formal approach, using a low-level model of machine effects, is clearly needed to screen out subtle mismatches, but a faster test can catch the gross mismatches that occur most often. If the compiler simply generates and executes the candidate sequence, it can compare the results against those obtained from the target sequence. This simple approach, applied to a few well-chosen inputs, should eliminate most of the inapplicable candidate sequences with a low-cost test.

This approach is, obviously, too expensive to use routinely or to use for large code fragments. In some circumstances, however, it merits consideration. If the application writer or the compiler can identify a small, performance-critical section of code, the gains from an outstanding code sequence may justify the cost of exhaustive search. For example, in some embedded applications, the performance-critical code consists of a single inner loop. Using exhaustive search for small code fragments—to improve either speed or space—may be worthwhile.

Similarly, exhaustive search has been applied as part of the process of retargeting a compiler to a new architecture. This application uses exhaustive search to discover particularly efficient implementations for IR sequences that the compiler routinely generates. Since the cost is incurred when the compiler is ported, the compiler writer can justify the use of search by amortizing that cost over the many compilations that are expected to use the new compiler.

11.6 SUMMARY AND PERSPECTIVE

At its heart, instruction selection is a pattern-matching problem. The difficulty of the problem depends on the level of abstraction of the compiler's IR, the complexity of the target machine, and the quality of code desired from the compiler. In some cases, a simple tree-walk approach will produce adequate results. For harder instances of the problem, however, the systematic search conducted by either tree-pattern-matching or peephole optimization can yield better results. Creating a handcrafted tree-walk code generator that achieves the same results would take much more work. While these two approaches differ in almost all their details, they share a common vision—the use of pattern matching to find a good code sequence among the myriad sequences possible for any given IR program.

The tree-pattern matchers discover low-cost tilings by taking the low-cost choice at each decision point. The resulting code implements the computation specified by the IR program. The peephole transformers systematically simplify the IR program and match what remains against a set of patterns for the target machine. Because they lack explicit cost models, no argument can be made for their optimality. They generate code for a computation with the same effects as the IR program, rather than a literal implementation of the IR program. Because of this subtle distinction in the two approaches, we cannot directly compare the claims for their quality. In practice, excellent results have been obtained with each approach.

The practical benefits of these techniques have been demonstrated in real compilers. Both LCC and GCC run on many platforms. The former uses tree-pattern-matching; the latter uses a peephole transformer. The use of automated tools in both systems has made them easy to understand, easy to retarget, and, ultimately, widely accepted in the community.

Equally important, the reader should recognize that both families of automatic pattern matchers can be applied to other problems in compilation. Peephole optimization originated as a technique for improving the final code produced by a compiler. In a similar way, the compiler can apply tree-pattern-matching to recognize and rewrite computations in an AST. BURS technology can provide a particularly efficient way to recognize and improve simple patterns, including the algebraic identities recognized by value numbering.

CHAPTER NOTES

Most early compilers used hand-coded, ad hoc techniques to perform instruction selection [25]. With sufficiently small instruction sets, or large enough compiler teams, this worked. For example, the BLISS-11 compiler generated excellent code for the PDP-11, with its limited repertoire of operations [339]. The small instruction sets of early computers and minicomputers let researchers and compiler writers ignore some of the problems that arise on modern machines.

For example, Sethi and Ullman [301], and, later, Aho and Johnson [5] considered the problem of generating optimal code for expression trees. Aho, Johnson, and Ullman extended their ideas to expression DAGS [6]. Compilers based on this work used ad hoc methods for the control structures and clever algorithms for expression trees.

In the late 1970s, two distinct trends in architecture brought the problem of instruction selection to the forefront of compiler research. The move from 16- to 32-bit architectures precipitated an explosion in the number of operations and address modes that the compiler had to consider. For a compiler to explore even a large fraction of the possibilities, it needed a more formal and powerful approach. At the same time, the nascent Unix operating system began to appear on multiple platforms. This sparked a natural demand for C compilers and increased interest in retargetable compilers [196]. The ability to easily retarget the instruction selector plays a key role in determining the ease of porting a compiler to new architectures. These two trends started a flurry of research on instruction selection that started in the 1970s and continued well into the 1990s [155, 122, 67, 161, 66, 276, 277].

The success of automation in scanning and parsing made specification-driven instruction selection an attractive idea. Glanville and Graham mapped the pattern matching of instruction selection onto table-driven parsing [155, 160, 162]. Ganapathi and Fischer attacked the problem with attribute grammars [151].

Tree-pattern-matching code generators grew out of early work in table-driven code generation [162, 40, 230, 10, 175] and in tree-pattern-matching [182, 71]. Pelegrí Llopart formalized many of these notions in the theory of bottom-up rewrite systems (BURS) [271]. Subsequent authors built on this work to create a variety of implementations, variations, and table-generation algorithms [147, 146, 277]. The *Twig* system combined tree-pattern-matching and dynamic programming [322, 2].

The first peephole optimizer appears to be McKeeman's system [253]. Bagwell [28], Wulf et al. [339], and Lamb [227] describe early peephole systems. The cycle of expand, simplify, and match described in Section 11.4.1 comes from Davidson's work [107,110]. Kessler also worked on deriving peephole optimizers directly from low-level descriptions of target architectures [211]. Fraser and Wendt adapted peephole optimization to perform code generation [149 150]. The machine learning approach described in Section 11.5.1 was described by Davidson and Fraser [108].

Massalin proposed the exhaustive approach described in Section 11.5.2 [251]. It was applied in a limited way in GCC by Granlund and Kenner [165].

CHAPTER 12

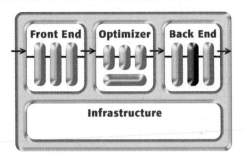

Front End **Optimizer** **Back End**

Infrastructure

Instruction Scheduling

12.1 INTRODUCTION

The order in which operations are presented for execution can have a significant effect on the length of time it takes to execute a sequence of them. Different operations may take different lengths of time. The memory system may take more than one cycle to deliver operands to the register set or to a functional unit. The functional units themselves may take several execution cycles to deliver the results of an operation. If an operation tries to reference a result before it is ready, the processor typically delays the operation's execution until the value is ready—that is, it *stalls*. The alternative, used in some processors, is to assume that the compiler can predict these stalls and reorder operations to avoid them. If no useful operations can be inserted to delay an operation, the compiler must insert one or more nops. In the former case, referencing the result too early degrades performance. In the latter case, the hardware assumes that this problem never happens, so when it does, the computation produces incorrect results. The compiler should try to order the instructions to avoid the first problem. It must avoid the second one.

Many processors can initiate execution of more than one operation in each cycle. The order in which the operations are presented for execution can determine the number of operations started, or *issued*, in a cycle. Consider, for

585

example, a simple processor with one integer functional unit and one floating-point functional unit and a compiled loop that consists of 100 integer operations and 100 floating-point operations. If the compiler orders the operations so that the first 75 operations are integer operations, the floating-point unit will sit idle until the processor finally reaches some work for it. If all the operations are independent (an unrealistic assumption), the best order would be to alternate operations between the two units.

Informally, instruction scheduling is the process whereby a compiler reorders the operations in the compiled code in an attempt to decrease its running time. Conceptually, an instruction scheduler looks like:

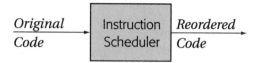

The instruction scheduler takes as input a partially ordered list of instructions; it produces as output a list of instructions constructed from the same set of operations. The scheduler assumes a fixed set of operations; it does not add operations in the way that the register allocator may add spill code. The scheduler assumes a fixed name space; it does not change which values are stored in registers, although it might rename some specific values to eliminate register conflicts. The scheduler expresses its results by changing the sequence of operations.

The primary goals of the instruction scheduler are to preserve the meaning of the code that it receives as input, to minimize execution time by avoiding wasted cycles spent in interlocks and stalls, and to avoid introducing extra register spills due to increased variable lifetimes. Of course, the scheduler should operate efficiently.

If the processor can issue multiple operations in a single cycle, it must have a mechanism to determine how many operations to issue. On a very-long instruction word (VLIW) machine, the processor issues one operation per functional unit in each cycle—all gathered into a single fixed-format instruction. An instruction contains either a useful operation or a nop in each slot. Packed VLIW machines avoid many of these nops by using variable-length instructions; the instruction stream contains information that lets the processor find instruction boundaries during the fetch and decode process.

Superscalar processors determine the number of operations to issue by looking at the next k operations in the instruction stream, where k is fixed and small. (Typically, k is equal to the number of functional units or a bit larger.) The processor examines each operation in order and issues it, if possible. When the processor encounters an operation that cannot be issued because of resource constraints or operand availability, it stops issuing operations and waits for the next cycle. An out-of-order superscalar processor looks at a larger window on the instruction stream. It issues as many operations as possible, looking past operations that cannot issue in the current cycle.

This diversity of mechanisms blurs the distinction between an operation and an instruction. On VLIW and packed VLIW machines, an instruction contains multiple operations. On superscalar machines, we usually refer to a single operation as an instruction and describe these machines as issuing multiple instructions per cycle. Throughout this book, we have used the term *operation* to describe a single opcode and its operands that the compiler expects to execute on a single functional unit. The discussion of scheduling uses that same terminology. The scheduler reorders operations. In deference to tradition, we still refer to this problem as *instruction scheduling*, although it might be more accurately called *operation scheduling*. On a VLIW or packed VLIW architecture, the scheduler packs operations into instructions that execute in a given cycle. On a superscalar architecture, either in-order or out-of-order, the scheduler reorders operations to let the processor issue as many as possible in each cycle.

This chapter examines scheduling and the tools and techniques that compilers use to perform it. The next several subsections provide background information needed to discuss scheduling and understand both the algorithms and their impact.

12.2 THE INSTRUCTION-SCHEDULING PROBLEM

Recall the example given for instruction scheduling in Section 1.5. Figure 12.1 reproduces it. The column labelled "*Start*" shows the cycle in which each operation begins execution. Assume that the processor has a single functional unit; memory operations take three cycles; a mult takes two cycles; and all other operations complete in a single cycle. With these assumptions, the original code, shown on the left, takes twenty cycles.

The scheduled code, shown on the right, is much faster. It separates long-latency operations from operations that reference their results. This separation allows operations that do not depend on these results to execute concurrently with them. The code issues load operations in the first three cycles; the results are available in cycles 4, 5, and 6, respectively. This schedule requires an extra register, r_3, to hold the result of the third concurrently executing load operation, but it allows the processor to perform useful work while waiting for the first arithmetic operand to arrive. The overlap among operations effectively hides the latency of the memory operations. The same idea, applied throughout the block, hides the latency of the mult operation. The reordering reduces the running time to thirteen cycles, a 35 percent improvement.

Start	Original Code				Start	Scheduled Code			
1	loadAI	r_{arp}, @w	$\Rightarrow$	r_1	1	loadAI	r_{arp}, @w	$\Rightarrow$	r_1
4	add	r_1, r_1	$\Rightarrow$	r_1	2	loadAI	r_{arp}, @x	$\Rightarrow$	r_2
5	loadAI	r_{arp}, @x	$\Rightarrow$	r_2	3	loadAI	r_{arp}, @y	$\Rightarrow$	r_3
8	mult	r_1, r_2	$\Rightarrow$	r_1	4	add	r_1, r_1	$\Rightarrow$	r_1
9	loadAI	r_{arp}, @y	$\Rightarrow$	r_2	5	mult	r_1, r_2	$\Rightarrow$	r_1
12	mult	r_1, r_2	$\Rightarrow$	r_1	6	loadAI	r_{arp}, @z	$\Rightarrow$	r_2
13	loadAI	r_{arp}, @z	$\Rightarrow$	r_2	7	mult	r_1, r_3	$\Rightarrow$	r_1
16	mult	r_1, r_2	$\Rightarrow$	r_1	9	mult	r_1, r_2	$\Rightarrow$	r_1
18	storeAI	r_1	$\Rightarrow$	r_{arp},0	11	storeAI	r_1	$\Rightarrow$	r_{arp},0

FIGURE 12.1   Scheduling Example from the Introduction

Not all blocks are amenable to improvement in this fashion. Consider, for example, the following block that computes x^8:

Start				
1	loadAI	r_{arp},@x	$\Rightarrow$	r_1
4	mult	r_1,r_1	$\Rightarrow$	r_1
6	mult	r_1,r_1	$\Rightarrow$	r_1
8	mult	r_1,r_1	$\Rightarrow$	r_1
10	storeAI	r_1	$\Rightarrow$	r_{arp},@x

The three mult operations have long latencies. Unfortunately, each instruction uses the result of the previous instruction. Thus, the scheduler can do nothing to improve this code because it has no independent instructions that can be issued while the mults are executing. Because it lacks independent operations that can execute in parallel, we say that this block has no *instruction-level parallelism* (ILP). Given enough ILP, the scheduler can hide memory latency and functional-unit latency.

All of the examples we have seen so far deal, implicitly, with a target machine that issues a single operation in each cycle. On such a machine, operations and instructions are identical because each instruction contains a single operation. Almost all modern computers have multiple functional units and the ability to issue several operations in each cycle. We will introduce the list-scheduling algorithm for a single-issue machine and point out what must be done to extend the basic algorithm to handle multioperation instructions. We continue to use the term *operation* to refer to a single opcode issued to a specific functional unit and use *instruction* only when referring to the set of all operations that issue in a single cycle. With this view, it would be more precise to call this process *operation scheduling;* however, tradition has precedence, so we continue to call it *instruction scheduling*.

To define scheduling more formally we must define the *dependence graph* $\mathcal{D} = (N, E)$ of a block, sometimes called its *precedence graph*. Each node $n \in N$ is an operation in the input code fragment. There is edge $e = \langle n_1, n_2 \rangle \in E$ if and only if n_2 uses the result of n_1 as an operand. In addition to its edges, each node has two attributes, a *type* and a *delay*. For a node n, the operation corresponding to n must execute on a functional unit of type *type*(n) and it requires *delay*(n) cycles to complete. The example in Figure 12.1 produces the dependence graph shown in Figure 12.2.

Nodes with no predecessors in $\mathcal{D}$, such as a, c, e, and g in the example, are called *leaves* of the graph. Since the leaves depend on no other operations, they can be scheduled as early as possible. Nodes with no successors in $\mathcal{D}$, such as i in the example, are called *roots* of the graph. A dependence graph can have multiple roots. The roots are, in some sense, the most constrained nodes in the graph because they cannot execute until all of their ancestors have executed. With this terminology, it appears that we have drawn $\mathcal{D}$ upside down—at least with relationship to the parse trees and abstract syntax trees used earlier. Placing the leaves at the top of the figure, however, creates a rough correspondence between placement in the drawing and eventual placement in the scheduled code. A leaf is at the top of the tree because it can execute early in the schedule. A root is at the bottom of the tree because it must execute after each of its ancestors.

Given a dependence graph $\mathcal{D}$ for a code fragment, a schedule S maps each node $n \in N$ to a nonnegative integer that denotes the cycle in which it should be issued, assuming that the first operation issues in cycle one. This provides a clear and concise definition of an instruction, namely, the ith instruction is the set of operations $\{n \,|\, S(n) = i\}$. A schedule must meet three constraints.

1. $S(n) \geq 1$, for each $n \in N$. This constraint forbids operations from being issued before execution starts. Any schedule that violates this constraint is not well formed. For the sake of uniformity, the schedule must also have at least one operation n' with $S(n') = 1$.

```
a:   loadAI   r0, 0   ⇒ r1
b:   add      r1, r1  ⇒ r1
c:   loadAI   r0, 8   ⇒ r2
d:   mult     r1, r2  ⇒ r1
e:   loadAI   r0, 16  ⇒ r2
f:   mult     r1, r2  ⇒ r1
g:   loadAI   r0, 24  ⇒ r2
h:   mult     r1, r2  ⇒ r1
i:   storeAI  r1      ⇒ r0,0
```

Example Code   Its Dependence Graph

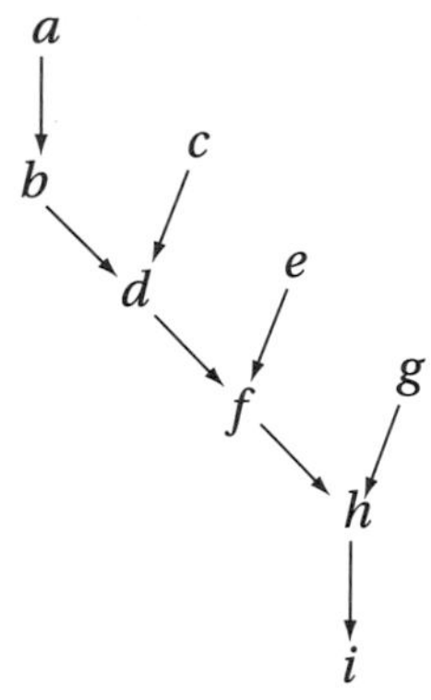

FIGURE 12.2   Dependence Graph for the Example

2. If $\langle n_1, n_2 \rangle \in E$, $S(n_1) + delay(n_1) \leq S(n_2)$. This constraint enforces correctness. An operation cannot be issued until the operations that produce its operands have completed. A schedule that violates this rule changes the flow of data in the code and is likely to produce incorrect results.

3. Each instruction contains no more operations of each type t than the target machine can issue in a cycle. This constraint enforces feasibility, since a schedule that violates it contains instructions that the target machine cannot possibly issue. (On a VLIW machine, the scheduler must fill unused slots in an instruction with nops.)

The compiler should only produce schedules that meet all three constraints.

Given a well-formed schedule that is both correct and feasible, the length of the schedule is simply the cycle number in which the last operation completes, assuming the first instruction issues in cycle one. This can be computed as

$$L(S) = \max_{n \in N}(S(n) + delay(n)).$$

Assuming that *delay* captures all the operational latencies, schedule S should execute in $L(S)$ time. With a notion of schedule length comes the notion of a *time-optimal* schedule. A schedule S_i is time-optimal if $L(S_i) \leq L(S_j)$ for all other schedules S_j that contain the same set of operations.

The dependence graph captures important properties of the schedule. Computing the total delay along the paths through the graph exposes additional detail about the block. Annotating the dependence graph $\mathcal{D}$ for our example with information about cumulative latency yields the following graph.

The path length from a node to the end of the computation is shown as a superscript on the node. The values clearly show that the path *abdfhi* is longest—it is the *critical path* that determines overall execution time for this example.

How, then, should the compiler schedule this computation? An operation can only be scheduled into an instruction when its operands are available. Since *a*, *c*, *e*, and *g* have no predecessors in the graph, they are the initial candidates for scheduling. The fact that *a* lies on the critical path strongly suggests that it be scheduled into the first instruction. Once *a* has been scheduled, the longest latency path remaining in $\mathcal{D}$ is *cdefhi*, suggesting that *c* be scheduled as the second instruction. With the schedule *ac*, *b* and *e* tie for the longest path. However, *b* needs the result of *a*, which will not be available until the fourth cycle. This makes *e* followed by *b* the better choice. Continuing in this fashion leads to the schedule *acebdgfhi*. This matches the schedule shown on the left side of Figure 12.1.

However, the compiler cannot simply rearrange the instructions into the proposed order. Recall that both *c* and *e* define r_2 and *d* uses the value that *c* stores in r_2. The scheduler cannot move *e* before *d* unless it renames the result of *e* to avoid the conflict with *c*'s definition of r_2. This constraint arises not from the flow of data, as with the dependences modelled by edges in $\mathcal{D}$. Instead, it arises from the need to avoid interfering with the dependences modelled in $\mathcal{D}$. These constraints are often called *antidependences*.

The scheduler can produce correct code in at least two different ways. It can discover the antidependences that are present in the input code and respect them in the final schedule, or it can rename values to avoid them. The example contains four antidependences, namely, $e \rightarrow c$, $e \rightarrow d$, $g \rightarrow e$, and $g \rightarrow f$. All of them involve redefinition of r_2. (Constraints exist based on r_1 as well, but each antidependence on r_1 duplicates a dependence based on the flow of values.)

Respecting antidependences changes the set of schedules that the compiler can produce. For example, it cannot move e before c or d. This forces it to produce a schedule such as *acbdefghi*, which requires eighteen cycles. While this schedule is a 10 percent improvement over the unscheduled code (*abcdefghi*), it is not competitive with the 35 percent improvement obtained by renaming to produce *acebdgfhi*, as shown on the right side of Figure 12.1.

As an alternative strategy, the scheduler can systematically rename the values in the block to eliminate antidependences before it schedules the code. This approach frees the scheduler from the constraints imposed by antidependences, but it creates the potential for problems if the scheduled code requires spill code. The act of renaming does not change the number of live variables; it simply changes their names and gives the scheduler freedom to overlap the operations in ways that the antidependences would prevent. Increasing overlap, however, can increase demand for registers and force the register allocator to insert more spill code—adding long-latency operations and forcing another round of scheduling.

The simplest renaming scheme assigns a new name to each value as it is produced. In the ongoing example, this scheme produces the following code. This version of the code has the same pattern of definitions and uses.

a: loadAI $\quad r_0, 0 \quad \Rightarrow r_1$

b: add $\quad\quad r_1, r_1 \Rightarrow r_2$

c: loadAI $\quad r_0, 8 \quad \Rightarrow r_3$

d: mult $\quad\quad r_2, r_3 \Rightarrow r_4$

e: loadAI $\quad r_0, 16 \Rightarrow r_5$

f: mult $\quad\quad r_4, r_5 \Rightarrow r_1$

g: loadAI $\quad r_0, 24 \Rightarrow r_6$

h: mult $\quad\quad r_5, r_6 \Rightarrow r_7$

i: storeAI $r_7 \quad\quad\quad \Rightarrow r_0, 0$

However, the dependence relationships are expressed unambiguously in the code. It contains no antidependences, so naming constraints cannot arise.

12.2.1 Other Measures of Schedule Quality

Schedules can be measured in terms other than time. Two schedules S_i and S_j for the same input code might produce different demand for registers—that is, the maximum number of live values in S_j may be less than in S_i. If the processor requires the scheduler to insert nops for idle functional units, then S_i might have fewer operations than S_j and might fetch fewer instructions as a result. This need not depend solely on schedule length. For example, on a processor with a variable-cycle nop, bunching nops together produces fewer operations and, potentially, fewer instructions. Finally, S_j might require less power than S_i to execute on the target machine because it never uses one of the functional units, fetches fewer instructions, or it causes fewer bit transitions in the processor's, instruction decoder.

12.2.2 What Makes Scheduling Hard?

The fundamental operation in scheduling is gathering operations together into groups based on the cycle in which those operations will begin execution. For each operation, the scheduler must choose an instruction and cycle. For each instruction (and cycle) it must choose a set of operations. In balancing these two viewpoints, it must ensure that an operation issues only when its operands are available. In a given cycle, more than one operation may meet this criterion, so the scheduler must choose among them. Since values are live from their definitions to their last uses, the decisions that the scheduler makes can shorten register lifetimes by moving uses closer to definitions or lengthen them by moving uses farther away from definitions. If too many values become concurrently live, the schedule will be infeasible because it requires too many registers. Balancing all these issues, while searching for a time-optimal schedule, makes scheduling complex.

Local instruction scheduling is NP-complete for all but the most simplistic architectures. Compilers produce approximate solutions to scheduling problems using greedy heuristics. In practice, almost all the scheduling algorithms used in compilers are based on a single family of heuristic techniques, called *list scheduling*. The following section describes list scheduling in detail. Subsequent sections show how to extend the paradigm to larger scopes.

HOW DOES INSTRUCTION SCHEDULING RELATE TO REGISTER ALLOCATION?

The use of specific names can introduce antidependences that limit the scheduler's ability to reorder operations. The scheduler can avoid antidependences by renaming; however, renaming creates a need for the compiler to perform register assignment after scheduling. This is just one example of the complex ways that instruction scheduling and register allocation interact.

The core function of the instruction scheduler is to reorder operations. Since most operations use one or two values and produce a new value, changing their relative order can change the lifetimes of some values. If operation a defines r_1 and b defines r_2, moving b to just before a can have several effects. It lengthens the lifetime of r_2 by one cycle, while shortening the lifetime of r_1. If one of a's operands is a last use, then moving b before a lengthens its lifetime. Symmetrically, if one of b's operands is a last use, the reordering shortens that operand's lifetime.

The net effect of moving b to before a depends on the details of a and b, as well as the surrounding code. If none of the uses involved is a last use, then the swap has no net effect on demand for registers. (Each operation defines a register; swapping them changes the lifetimes of specific registers, but not the aggregate demand for registers.)

In a similar way, register allocation can change the instruction-scheduling problem. The core functions of a register allocator are to rename references and to insert memory operations when demand for registers is larger than the register set. Both these functions affect the ability of the scheduler to produce fast code. When the allocator maps a large virtual name space to the name space of target-machine registers, it can introduce antidependences that constrain the scheduler. Similarly, when the allocator inserts spill code, it adds operations to the code that must, themselves, be scheduled into instructions.

We know, mathematically, that solving these problems together might produce solutions that cannot be obtained by running the scheduler followed by the allocator or the allocator followed by the scheduler. However, both problems are complex enough that we treat them separately. In practice, almost all real-world compilers treat them separately, as well.

12.3   LIST SCHEDULING

List scheduling is a greedy, heuristic approach to scheduling the operations in a basic block. It has been the dominant paradigm for instruction scheduling since the late 1970s, largely because it discovers reasonable schedules and adapts easily to changes in computer architectures. However, list scheduling describes an approach rather than a specific algorithm. Wide variation exists in how it is implemented and how it attempts to prioritize instructions for scheduling. This section explores the basic framework of list scheduling, as well as a couple of variations on the idea.

Classic list scheduling operates over a single basic block. Limiting our consideration to straight-line sequences of code allows us to ignore situations that can complicate scheduling. For example, when the scheduler considers multiple blocks, an operand might depend on more than one previous definition; this can create uncertainty about when the operand is available for use. With several blocks in its scope, the scheduler might move an instruction from one block to another. Such cross-block code motion can force the scheduler to duplicate the instruction—moving it into one successor block may create the need for a copy in each successor block. Similarly, it can cause an instruction to execute on paths where it did not in the original code—moving it into a predecessor block puts it on the path to each of that block's successors. Restricting our consideration to the single-block case avoids these complications.

To apply list scheduling to a block, the scheduler follows a four-step plan.

1. *Rename to avoid antidependences.* To reduce the set of constraints on the scheduler, the compiler renames values. Each definition receives a unique name. This step is not strictly necessary. However, it lets the scheduler find some schedules that the antidependences would have prevented. It also simplifies the scheduler's implementation.

2. *Build a dependence graph, $\mathcal{D}$.* To build the dependence graph, the scheduler walks the block from bottom to top. For each operation, it constructs a node to represent the newly created value. It adds edges from that node to each node that uses the value. Each edge is annotated with the latency of the current operation. (If the scheduler does not perform renaming, $\mathcal{D}$ must represent antidependences as well.)

3. *Assign priorities to each operation.* The scheduler uses these priorities to guide it as it picks from the set of available operations at each step. Many priority schemes have been used in list schedulers. The scheduler may compute several different scores for each node, using one as the

primary ordering and the others to break ties between equally ranked nodes. The most popular priority scheme uses the length of the longest latency-weighted path from the node to a root of $\mathcal{D}$. We will describe other priority schemes later in this section.

4. *Iteratively select an operation and schedule it.* The central data structure of the list-scheduling algorithm is a list of operations that can legally execute in the current cycle, called the *ready list*. Every operation on the ready list has the property that its operands are available. The algorithm starts at the first cycle in the block and picks as many operations to issue in that cycle as possible. It then advances the cycle counter and updates the ready list to reflect both the previously issued operations and the passage of time. It repeats this process until every operation has been scheduled.

Renaming and building $\mathcal{D}$ are straightforward. The priority computations typically involve a traversal of $\mathcal{D}$. The heart of the algorithm, and the key to understanding it, lies in the final step. Figure 12.3 shows the basic framework for this step, assuming that the target machine has a single functional unit.

```
Cycle ← 1
Ready ← leaves of D
Active ← ∅
while (Ready ∪ Active ≠ ∅)
    if Ready ≠ ∅ then
        remove an op from Ready
        S(op) ← Cycle
        add op to Active
    Cycle + +
    for each op ∈ Active
        if S(op) + delay(op) < Cycle then
            remove op from Active
            for each successor s of op in D
                if s is ready
                    then add s to Ready
```

FIGURE 12.3   List-Scheduling Algorithm

The algorithm performs an abstract simulation of the code's execution. It ignores the details of values and operations to focus on the timing constraints imposed by edges in $\mathcal{D}$. To track time, it maintains a simulation clock, in the variable *Cycle*. *Cycle* is initialized to 1, the first operation in the scheduled code, and incremented until every operation in the code has been assigned a time to execute.

The algorithm uses two lists to track operations. The first list, *Ready*, holds any operations that can execute in the current cycle. If an operation is in *Ready*, all of its operands have been computed. Initially, *Ready* contains all the leaves of $\mathcal{D}$, since they depend on no other operations. The second list, *Active*, holds any operations that were issued in an earlier cycle but have not yet completed. At each time step, the scheduler checks *Active* to find operations that have finished. As each operation finishes, the scheduler checks each of its successors s in $\mathcal{D}$ (the operations that use its result) to determine if all of its operands are now available. If they are, it adds s to *Ready*.

At each time step, the algorithm follows a simple discipline. It accounts for any operations completed in the previous cycle, then it schedules an operation for the current cycle. The details of the implementation slightly obscure this structure because the first time step always has an empty *Active* list. The while loop begins in the middle of the first time step. It picks an operation from *Ready* and schedules it. Next, it increments *Cycle* to begin the second time step. It updates *Active* and *Ready* for the beginning of the new cycle, then wraps around to the top of the loop, where it repeats the process of select, increment, and update.

The process terminates when the simulation clock indicates that every operation has executed to completion. At the end, *Cycle* contains the simulated running time of the block. If all operations execute in the time specified by *delay*, and all operands of the leaves of $\mathcal{D}$ are available in the first cycle, this simulated running time should match the actual execution time. A simple postpass can rearrange the operations and insert nops in empty cycles.

An important question at this point is, how good is the schedule that this method generates? The answer depends, in large part, on how the algorithm picks the operation to remove from the *Ready* list in each iteration. Consider the simplest scenario, where the *Ready* list contains at most one item in each iteration. In this restricted case, the algorithm must generate an optimal schedule. Only one operation can execute in the first cycle. (There must be at least one leaf in $\mathcal{D}$, and our restriction ensures that there is exactly one.) At each subsequent cycle, the algorithm has no choices to make—either *Ready* contains an operation and the algorithm schedules it, or *Ready* is empty and the algorithm schedules nothing to issue in that cycle. The difficulty arises when multiple operations are available at some point in the process.

In the ongoing example, $\mathcal{D}$ has four leaves: *a*, *c*, *e*, and *g*. With only one functional unit, the scheduler must select one of the four load operations to execute in the first cycle. This is the role of the priority computation—it assigns each node in $\mathcal{D}$ a set of one or more ranks that the scheduler uses to order the nodes for scheduling. The metric suggested earlier, the longest latency-weighted distance to a root in $\mathcal{D}$, corresponds to always choosing the node on the critical path for the current cycle in the schedule being constructed. (Changing earlier choices might well change the current critical path.) To the limited extent that the impact of a scheduling priority is predictable, this scheme should provide balanced pursuit of the longest paths.

12.3.1 Efficiency Concerns

To pick an operation from the *Ready* list, as described so far, requires a linear scan over *Ready*. This makes the cost of creating and maintaining *Ready* approach $O(n^2)$. Replacing the list with a priority queue can reduce the cost of these manipulations to $O(n \log_2 n)$, for a minor increase in the difficulty of implementation.

A similar approach can reduce the cost of manipulating the *Active* list. When the scheduler adds an operation to *Active*, it can assign it a priority equal to the cycle in which the operation completes. A priority queue that seeks the smallest priority will push all the operations completed in the current cycle to the front, for a small increase in cost over a simple list implementation.

Further improvement is possible in the implementation of `Active`. The scheduler can maintain a set of separate lists, one for each cycle in which an operation can finish. The number of lists required to cover all the operation latencies is *MaxLatency* = $\max_{n \in \mathcal{D}}$ *delay*(*n*). When the compiler schedules operation *n* in *Cycle*, it adds *n* to *WorkList*[(*Cycle* + *delay*(*n*)) mod *MaxLatency*]. When it goes to update the *Ready* queue, all of the operations with successors to consider are found in *WorkList*[*Cycle* mod *MaxLatency*]. This scheme uses a small amount of extra space and a little more time on each insertion into *WorkList*. In return, it avoids the quadratic cost of searching *Active* and replaces it with a linear walk through a smaller *WorkList*.[1]

---

1. The number of operations in the *WorkList*s is identical to the number in *Active*, so the space overhead is just the cost of having multiple *WorkList*s. The extra time comes from introducing the subscript calculations on *WorkList*, including the *mod* calculations.

Caveats

As described, the local list scheduler assumes that all operands of leaves are available on entry to the block. The scheduler must allow for the effects that arise at block boundaries. If the processor has interlocks that stall when an operand is not yet available, the scheduler can rely on those interlocks to ensure that interblock dependences are satisfied. If the processor does not have interlocks, the scheduler must ensure that each predecessor block has enough slack time at the end for all operations to complete. With more contextual knowledge, the scheduler might be able to prioritize leaves in a way that hides that slack time in the successor block.

To extend the algorithm so that it handles instructions that contain multiple operations, we must expand the *while* loop so that it selects an operation for each functional unit. If a given operation can execute on several different functional units, the compiler writer may need to bias the choice of operation by the capabilities of those functional units. If, for example, only one functional unit can execute memory operations, the scheduler must preferentially schedule loads and stores onto that unit. A similar effect happens if the register set is partitioned (see Section 13.6.2); the scheduler may need to place an operation on the unit where its operands reside or in a cycle when the interpartition transfer apparatus is free.

As a final point, memory operations often have uncertain and variable delays due to the behavior of the memory hierarchy. A load operation on a machine with multiple levels of cache memory might have an actual delay ranging from zero cycles to hundreds or thousands of cycles. If the scheduler assumes the worst-case delay, it risks idling the processor for long periods. If it assumes the best-case delay, it will stall the processor on a cache miss. In practice, the compiler can obtain good results by calculating an individual latency for each load based on the amount of instruction-level parallelism available to cover the load's latency. In effect, this schedules the load with regard to the code that surrounds it, rather than the hardware on which it will execute. Once the available instruction-level parallelism is exhausted, the processor will stall until the load completes.

12.3.2 Other Priority Schemes

The complexity of local instruction scheduling forces compilers to use heuristic techniques. In practice, list scheduling produces good schedules— schedules that are near-optimal. However, the behavior of these greedy techniques is rarely robust—small changes in the input may make large differences in the solution.

One algorithmic way of addressing this instability is careful tie breaking. When two or more items have the same rank, the implementation should choose among them based on another priority ranking. (In contrast, implementations of the max function typically exhibit deterministic behavior—they either keep the first value of maximal rank or the last such value. This introduces a systematic bias toward earlier nodes or later nodes in the list.) A good list scheduler uses several different priority rankings to break ties. Among the many priority schemes that have been suggested in the literature are

- A node's rank is the total length of the longest path that contains it. This favors, at each step, the critical path in the original code, ignoring intermediate decisions. This tends toward a depth-first traversal of $\mathcal{D}$.

- A node's rank is the number of immediate successors it has in $\mathcal{D}$. This encourages the scheduler to pursue many distinct paths through the graph—closer to a breadth-first approach. It tends to keep more operations on the *Ready* queue.

- A node's rank is the total number of descendants it has in $\mathcal{D}$. This amplifies the effect of the previous ranking. Nodes that compute critical values for many other nodes are scheduled early.

- A node's rank is higher if it has long latency. This tends to schedule the long-latency nodes early in the block, when more operations remain that might be used to cover their latency.

- A node's rank is higher if it contains the last use of a value. This tends to decrease demand for registers by moving last uses closer to definitions.

Unfortunately, none of these priority schemes dominates the others in terms of overall schedule quality. Each excels on some examples and does poorly on others. Thus, there is little agreement about which rankings to use or in which order to apply them.

12.3.3 Forward versus Backward List Scheduling

An alternate formulation of list scheduling works over the dependence graph in the opposite direction, scheduling from roots to leaves. The first operation scheduled executes in the last cycle of the block, and the last operation scheduled executes first. In this form, the algorithm is called *backward list scheduling*, making the original version *forward list scheduling*.

A standard practice in the compiler community is to try several versions of list scheduling on each block and keep the shortest schedule. Typically, the compiler tries both forward and backward list scheduling; it may try more than one priority scheme in each direction. Like many tricks born of experience, this one encodes several important insights.

First, list scheduling accounts for a small portion of the compiler's execution time. The compiler can afford to try several schemes if it produces better code. Notice that the scheduler can reuse most of the preparatory work—renaming, building $\mathcal{D}$, and some of the computed priorities. Thus, the cost of using multiple schemes amounts to repeating the iterative portion of the scheduler a few times.

Second, practice suggests that neither forward scheduling nor backward scheduling always wins. The difference between forward and backward list scheduling lies in the order in which operations are considered. If the schedule depends critically on the careful ordering of some small set of operations, the two directions may produce noticeably different results. If the critical operations occur near the leaves, forward scheduling seems more likely to consider them together, while backward scheduling must work its way through the remainder of the block to reach them. Symmetrically, if the critical operations occur near the roots, backward scheduling may examine them together, while forward scheduling sees them in an order dictated by decisions made starting at the other end of the block.

To make this latter point more concrete, consider the example shown in Figure 12.4. It shows the dependence graph for a basic block found in the SPEC benchmark program go. The compiler added dependences from the store operations to the block-ending branch to ensure that the memory operations complete before the next block begins execution. (Violating this assumption could produce an incorrect value from a subsequent load operation.) Superscripts on nodes in the dependence graph give the latency from the node to the branch; subscripts differentiate among similar operations. The example assumes operation latencies that appear in the table below the dependence graph.

This example demonstrates the difference between forward and backward list scheduling. It came to our attention in a study of list scheduling; the compiler was targeting an ILOC machine with two integer functional units and one unit to perform memory operations. The five store operations take most of the time in the block. The schedule that minimizes execution time must begin executing stores as early as possible.

Forward list scheduling, using latency to roots for priority, executes the operations in priority order, except for the comparison. It schedules the five

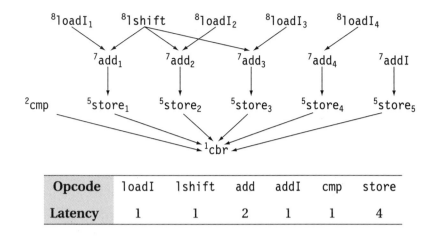

Opcode	loadI	lshift	add	addI	cmp	store
Latency	1	1	2	1	1	4

FIGURE 12.4   Dependence Graph for a Block from go

operations with rank eight, then the five operations with rank seven. It begins on the operations with rank five, and slides the cmp in alongside the stores, since the cmp is a leaf. If ties are broken arbitrarily by taking left-to-right order, this produces the schedule shown on the left side of Figure 12.5. Notice that the memory operations begin in cycle five, producing a schedule that issues the branch in cycle thirteen.

Using the same priorities with backward list scheduling, the compiler first places the branch in the last slot of the block. The cmp precedes it by $delay(\text{cmp}) = 1$ cycle. The next operation scheduled is store_1 (by the left-to-right tie-breaking rule). It is assigned the issue slot on the memory unit that is $delay(\text{store}) = 4$ cycles earlier. The scheduler fills in successively earlier slots on the memory unit with the other store operations, in order. It begins filling in the integer operations, as they become ready. The first is add_1, two cycles before store_1. When the algorithm terminates, it has produced the schedule shown on the right side of Figure 12.5.

The schedule produced by the backward scheduler takes one fewer cycle than the one produced by the forward scheduler. It places the addI earlier in the block, allowing store_5 to issue in cycle four—one cycle earlier than the first memory operation in the forward schedule. By considering the problem in a different order, using the same underlying priorities and tie breakers, the backward algorithm achieves a different result.

Why does this happen? The forward scheduler must place all the rank-eight operations in the schedule before any rank-seven operations. Even though the addI operation is a leaf, its lower rank causes the forward scheduler to defer handling it. By the time the scheduler runs out of rank-eight operations,

	Forward Schedule				Backward Schedule		
	Integer	**Integer**	**Memory**		**Integer**	**Integer**	**Memory**
1	$loadI_1$	lshift	—	1	$loadI_4$	—	—
2	$loadI_2$	$loadI_3$	—	2	addI	lshift	—
3	$loadI_4$	add_1	—	3	add_4	$loadI_3$	—
4	add_2	add_3	—	4	add_3	$loadI_2$	$store_5$
5	add_4	addI	$store_1$	5	add_2	$loadI_1$	$store_4$
6	cmp	—	$store_2$	6	add_1	—	$store_3$
7	—	—	$store_3$	7	—	—	$store_2$
8	—	—	$store_4$	8	—	—	$store_1$
9	—	—	$store_5$	9	—	—	—
10	—	—	—	10	—	—	—
11	—	—	—	11	cmp	—	—
12	—	—	—	12	cbr	—	—
13	cbr	—	—				

FIGURE 12.5 Schedules for the Block from go

other rank-seven operations are available. In contrast, the backward scheduler places the addI before three of the rank-eight operations—a result that the forward scheduler could not consider.

The list scheduling algorithm uses a greedy heuristic to construct a reasonable solution to the problem, but the ranking function does not encode complete knowledge of the problem. To construct a ranking that encodes complete knowledge, the compiler would need to consider all possible schedules—making the ranking process itself NP-complete. Thus, an optimal ranking function is impractical, unless P = NP.

12.3.4 Why Use List Scheduling?

List scheduling has been the dominant algorithm for instruction scheduling for many years. The technique, in its forward and backward forms, uses a greedy heuristic approach to assign each operation to a specific instruction in a specific issue slot. In practice, it produces excellent results for single blocks.

WHAT ABOUT OUT-OF-ORDER EXECUTION?

Some processors include hardware support for executing instructions out of order (OOO). We refer to such processors as *dynamically scheduled* machines. This feature is not new; for example, it appeared on the IBM 360/91. To support OOO execution, a dynamically scheduled processor looks ahead in the instruction stream for operations that can execute before they would in a statically scheduled processor. To do this, the dynamically scheduled processor builds and maintains a portion of the dependence graph at run time. It uses this piece of the dependence graph to discover when each instruction can execute and issues each instruction at the first legal opportunity.

When can an out-of-order processor improve on the static schedule? If run-time circumstances are better than the assumptions made by the scheduler, then the OOO hardware might issue an operation earlier than its position in the static schedule. This can happen at a block boundary, if an operand is available before its worst-case time. Because it knows actual run-time addresses, an OOO processor can also disambiguate some load-store dependences that the scheduler cannot.

OOO execution does not eliminate the need for instruction scheduling. Because the lookahead window is finite, bad schedules can defy improvement. For example, a lookahead window of fifty instructions will not let the processor execute a string of one hundred integer instructions followed by one hundred floating-point instructions in interleaved <integer, floating-point> pairs. It may, however, interleave shorter strings, say of length thirty. OOO execution helps the compiler by improving good, but nonoptimal, schedules.

A related processor feature is dynamic register renaming. This scheme provides the processor with more physical registers than the ISA allows the compiler to name. The processor can break antidependences that occur within its lookahead window by using additional physical registers that are hidden from the compiler to implement two references connected by an antidependence.

List scheduling is efficient. It removes an operation from the *Ready* queue once. It examines each operation for addition to the *Ready* queue once for each edge that enters its node in $\mathcal{D}$. If an operation has m operands, the scheduler visits its node m times. Each visit looks at each of its m operands, so the amount of work involved in placing it on the ready queue is $\mathbf{O}(m^2)$. However, for most operations, m is one or two, so this quadratic cost is trivial.

List scheduling forms the basis for most algorithms that perform scheduling over regions larger than a single block. Thus, understanding its strengths and its weaknesses is important. Any improvement made to local list scheduling has the potential to improve the regional scheduling algorithms, as well.

12.4 ADVANCED TOPICS

Architectural developments in the 1990s increased the importance of instruction scheduling. The widespread use of processors with multiple functional units, increased pipelining, and growing memory latencies combined to make realized performance ever more dependent on execution order. This led to development of more aggressive approaches to scheduling. The first subsection presents three approaches to regional scheduling. The second subsection looks at reshaping the code to improve scheduling.

12.4.1 Regional Scheduling

As with value numbering, moving from single basic blocks to larger scopes can improve the quality of code that the compiler generates. For instruction scheduling, many different approaches have been proposed for regions larger than a block but smaller than a whole procedure. This section outlines three approaches that derive from list scheduling.

Scheduling Extended Basic Blocks

Using the list-scheduling algorithm over extended basic blocks (EBBs) lets the scheduler consider a longer sequence of operations than it can see in a single block. Paths through the EBB form straightline segments of code that the scheduler can treat as if they were single blocks. However, these paths have interim exits between their first and last operation, and several paths may share a common prefix. When an EBB scheduler moves an operation across a block boundary, it must ensure correct behavior along the other paths involved in that interblock transition.

Consider the simple code fragment shown in Figure 12.6. It has one large EBB, $\{B_1, B_2, B_3, B_4\}$, and two trivial EBBs, $\{B_5\}$ and $\{B_6\}$. The large EBB has two

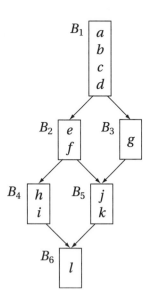

FIGURE 12.6   Extended Basic Block Scheduling Example

paths, $\{B_1, B_2, B_4\}$ and $\{B_1, B_3\}$. They share B_1 as a common prefix. Since the compiler can generate only one schedule for B_1, it must find a schedule that satisfies both paths.

The conflict represented by B_1 can exhibit itself in two ways. The scheduler might move an operation from B_1, for example c, past the branch at the end of B_1 into B_2. In this case, c would no longer be on the path from the entry of B_1 to the entry of B_3, so the scheduler would need to insert a copy of c into B_3 to maintain correctness along the path $\{B_1, B_3\}$. Alternately, the scheduler might move an operation from B_2, for example f, up into B_1. This puts f on the path from the entry of B_1 to the entry of B_3, where it did not previously execute.

Moving f into B_1 can create two problems. It lengthens the path $\{B_1, B_3\}$, with the possibility of slowing down execution along that path. It may change the correctness of that path. To avoid the latter problem, the compiler must rename values to honor the antidependences in the original code. This renaming may, in turn, force the compiler to insert copy operations along some of the edges in the control-flow graph. (The problems that can arise are similar to those that occur in translating SSA form into executable code. See the discussion in Section 9.3.)

The compiler has several alternatives for managing these interblock conflicts. To handle the problems that arise from downward motion, it can insert *compensation code* into blocks that are along exits from the path. Any time that it moves an operation from block B_i into one of B_i's successors, it must consider creating a copy of the instruction in every other immediate successor of B_i. If the value defined by the moved instruction is live in the successor, the instruction is necessary. To handle the problems arising from upward motion, the scheduler can prohibit moving an operation from its original block into a predecessor block. This avoids lengthening other paths that leave the predecessor block.

(A third choice exists. The compiler might clone blocks, based on the surrounding context. See Section 8.7.1. In the example, B_5 could be cloned to provide two implementations, B_5' and B_5'', with the edge from B_2 connected to B_5' and the edge from B_3 connected to B_5''. This would create longer EBBs containing the new blocks. This kind of transformation is beyond the scope of the current discussion.)

To schedule a path through an EBB, the compiler performs renaming, if necessary, over the region. Next, it builds a single dependence graph for the entire path, ignoring any exits from the path. It computes the priority metrics needed to select among ready operations and to break ties. Finally, it applies the iterative scheduling scheme, as for a single block. Each time it assigns an operation to a specific instruction in a specific cycle of the schedule, it must insert any compensation code required by that choice.

The compiler typically schedules each block once. Thus, in our example, the compiler might schedule the path $\{B_1, B_2, B_4\}$ first, because it is the longest path. The next path is $\{B_1, B_3\}$, but B_1 already has a fixed schedule. Thus, the compiler can schedule B_3 with B_1 as a prefix. Finally, it can schedule B_5 and B_6 (in either order). If the compiler has reason to believe that one path through an EBB executes more often than another, it should give preference to that path and schedule it first so that it remains intact for scheduling.

Trace Scheduling

Trace scheduling uses information about actual run-time behavior of the program to select regions for scheduling. It uses profile information gathered by running an instrumented version of the program to determine which blocks execute most frequently. From this information, it constructs a trace, or path, through the control-flow graph, that represents the most frequently executed path.

Given a trace, the scheduler applies the list-scheduling algorithm to the entire trace, in the same way that EBB scheduling applies it to a path through an EBB. With an arbitrary trace, one additional complication arises—the trace may have interim entry points as well as interim exits. If the scheduler moves an operation upward across an interim entry—a join point in the CFG—it needs to copy those operations into the nontrace paths that enter the join point.

To schedule the entire procedure, the trace scheduler constructs a trace and schedules it. It then removes the blocks in the trace from consideration, and selects the next most frequently executed trace. This trace is scheduled, with the requirement that it respect any constraints imposed by previously scheduled code. The process continues, picking a trace, scheduling it, and removing it from consideration, until all the blocks have been scheduled.

EBB scheduling can be considered a degenerate case of trace scheduling in which the individual paths through the EBB are just traces selected with some static approximation to profiling data.

Scheduling Loops

Because loops play a critical role in most computationally intensive tasks, they have received a great deal of attention in the literature on compilation. EBB scheduling can handle a portion of a loop body,[2] but it cannot address latencies that "wrap around" from the bottom of the loop back to the top. Trace scheduling can address these wrap-around problems, but it does so by creating multiple copies of any block that appears more than once in the trace. These shortcomings have led to several techniques that directly address the problem of generating an excellent schedule for the body of an innermost loop.

Specialized loop-scheduling techniques make sense only when the default scheduler is unable to produce compact and efficient code for the loop. If the loop, after scheduling, has a body that contains no stalls, interlocks, or nops, then a specialized loop scheduler is unlikely to improve its performance. Similarly, if the body of the loop is long enough that the end-of-block effects are a tiny fraction of its running time, a specialized scheduler is unlikely to help.

Still, many small, computationally intensive loops benefit from loop scheduling. Typically, these loops have too few operations relative to the length of their critical paths to keep the underlying hardware busy. The key to scheduling these loops is to execute multiple iterations of the loop concurrently. With three iterations executing, for example, a given cycle might issue operations from the start of the ith iteration, from the middle of the $i-1^{st}$ iteration, and from the end of the $i-2^{nd}$ iteration. To create such a schedule, the scheduler creates a fixed-length loop body called a *kernel* and uses modulo arithmetic to schedule into it. In effect, this folds the execution of a single iteration over the kernel. These loops are often called *pipelined loops*.

For a pipelined loop to execute correctly, the code must first execute a *prologue* section that fills up the pipeline. If the kernel executes operations

---

2. If the loop contains only one block, it does not need an *extended* basic block. If it contains any internal control flow except for break-style jumps to the loop bottom, an EBB cannot include all of its blocks.

from three iterations of the original loop, then each kernel iteration processes roughly one-third of each active iteration of the original loop. To start execution, the prologue must perform enough work to prepare for the last third of iteration 1, the second third of iteration 2, and the first third of iteration 3. After the kernel loop completes, a corresponding *epilogue* is needed to complete the final iterations—emptying the pipeline. The need for separate prologue and epilogue sections increases code size. While the specific increase is a function of the loop and the number of iterations that the kernel executes concurrently, it is not unusual for the prologue and epilogue to double the amount of code required for the loop.

An example will make these ideas more concrete. Consider the following loop, written in C:

```
for (i=1; i < 200; i++)
    z[i] = x[i] * y[i];
```

Figure 12.7 shows the code that a compiler might generate for this loop, after optimization. In this case, both operator strength reduction and linear

Cycle	Functional Unit 0			Comments
−4	loadI	@x	$\Rightarrow r_{@x}$	Set up the loop
−3	loadI	@y	$\Rightarrow r_{@y}$	with initial loads
−2	loadI	@z	$\Rightarrow r_{@z}$	
−1	addI	$r_{@x},792$	$\Rightarrow r_{ub}$	
1	L_1: loadAO	$r_{arp},r_{@x}$	$\Rightarrow r_x$	Get x[i] & y[i]
2	loadAO	$r_{arp},r_{@y}$	$\Rightarrow r_y$	
3	addI	$r_{@x},\ 4$	$\Rightarrow r_{@x}$	Bump the pointers
4	addI	$r_{@y},\ 4$	$\Rightarrow r_{@y}$	in shadow of loads
5	mult	r_x,r_y	$\Rightarrow r_z$	The real work
6	cmp_LT	$r_{@x},r_{ub}$	$\Rightarrow r_{cc}$	Shadow of mult
7	storeAO	r_z	$\Rightarrow r_{arp},r_{@z}$	Save the result
8	addI	$r_{@z},\ 4$	$\Rightarrow r_{@z}$	Bump z's pointer
9	cbr	r_{cc}	$\rightarrow L_1,L_2$	Loop-closing branch
	L_2: ...			

FIGURE 12.7 Example Loop Scheduled for One Functional Unit

function test replacement have been applied (see Section 10.3.3). The code in the figure has been scheduled for a machine with a single functional unit. The scheduler has assumed that loads and stores take three cycles, multiplies takes two cycles, and all other operations take one cycle. The first column shows cycle counts, normalized to the first operation in the loop (at label L_1).

The preloop code initializes a pointer for each array and computes an upper bound for the range of $r_{@x}$ into r_{ub} that the end-of-loop test uses in cycle six. The loop body loads x and y, performs the multiply, and stores the result into z. The scheduler has filled all of the issue slots in the shadow of long-latency operations with other operations. During the load latencies, the schedule updates $r_{@x}$ and $r_{@y}$. It performs the comparison in the multiply's shadow. It fills the slots after the store with the update of $r_{@z}$ and the branch. This produces a tight schedule for a one-functional-unit machine.

Consider what happens if we run this code on a superscalar processor with two functional units and the same latencies. Assume that loads and stores must execute on unit zero, that functional units stall until an operation's operands are ready, and that the processor cannot issue operations to a stalled unit. Figure 12.8 shows the execution of the loop's first iteration. The mult in cycle 3 stalls because neither r_x nor r_y is ready. It stalls in cycle 4 waiting for r_y, begins executing again in cycle 5, and produces r_z at the end of cycle 6. This forces the storeA0 to stall until the start of cycle 7. Assuming that the hardware can tell that $r_{@z}$ contains an address that is distinct from $r_{@x}$ and $r_{@y}$, the processor can issue the first loadA0 for the second iteration in cycle 7. If not, then the processor will stall until the store completes.

Cycle	Functional Unit 0			Functional Unit 1		
−2		loadI	@x $\Rightarrow r_{@x}$	loadI	@y	$\Rightarrow r_{@y}$
−1		loadI	@z $\Rightarrow r_{@z}$	addI	$r_{@x}$,792	$\Rightarrow r_{ub}$
1	L_1:	loadA0	$r_{arp},r_{@x} \Rightarrow r_x$	no operation issued		
2		loadA0	$r_{arp},r_{@y} \Rightarrow r_y$	addI	$r_{@x}$, 4	$\Rightarrow r_{@x}$
3		addI	$r_{@y}$, 4 $\Rightarrow r_{@y}$	mult	r_x,r_y	$\Rightarrow r_z$
4		cmp_LT	$r_{@x},r_{ub} \Rightarrow r_{cc}$	stall on r_y		
5		storeA0	r_z $\Rightarrow r_{arp},r_{@z}$	addI	$r_{@z}$, 4	$\Rightarrow r_{@z}$
6		stall on r_z		cbr	r_{cc}	$\rightarrow L_1,L_2$
7		...start of next iteration ...				

FIGURE 12.8 Executing on a Two-Unit Superscalar Processor

Moving to two functional units improved the execution time. It cut the preloop time in half, to two cycles. It reduced the time for the loop body by one third, to six cycles. The critical path executes as quickly as we can expect; the multiply issues before r_y is available and executes as soon as possible. The store proceeds as soon as r_z is available. Some issue slots are wasted (unit 0 in cycle 6 and unit 1 in cycles 1 and 4).

Reordering the linear code can change the execution schedule. For example, moving the update of $r_{@x}$ in front of the load from $r_{@y}$ allows the processor to issue the updates of $r_{@x}$ and $r_{@y}$ in the same cycles as the loads from those registers. This lets some of the operations issue earlier in the schedule, but it does nothing to speed up the critical path. The net result is the same—a six-cycle loop.

Pipelining the code can reduce the time needed for each iteration. Figure 12.9 shows the same loop after the compiler has pipelined it. Here, the scheduler has folded the loop in half so that its kernel executes two iterations concurrently. The loop prologue (cycles −4 to −1) executes setup code, as before, along with the first half of iteration 1. The kernel executes the second half of iteration i and the first half of iteration $i+1$. When the kernel terminates, the epilogue (cycles +1 to +3) performs the second half of the final iteration.

Cycle		Functional Unit 0			Functional Unit 1		
−4		loadI	@x	$\Rightarrow r_{@x}$	loadI	@y	$\Rightarrow r_{@y}$
−3		loadAO	$r_{arp}, r_{@x}$	$\Rightarrow r_{x'}$	addI	$r_{@x}$, 4	$\Rightarrow r_{@x}$
−2		loadAO	$r_{arp}, r_{@y}$	$\Rightarrow r_y$	addI	$r_{@y}$, 4	$\Rightarrow r_{@y}$
−1		loadI	@z	$\Rightarrow r_{@z}$	addI	$r_{@x}$,788	$\Rightarrow r_{ub}$
1	L_1:	loadAO	$r_{arp}, r_{@x}$	$\Rightarrow r_x$	addI	$r_{@x}$, 4	$\Rightarrow r_{@x}$
2		loadAO	$r_{arp}, r_{@y}$	$\Rightarrow r_y$	mult	$r_{x'}, r_y$	$\Rightarrow r_z$
3		cmp_LT	$r_{@x}, r_{ub}$	$\Rightarrow r_{cc}$	addI	$r_{@y}$, 4	$\Rightarrow r_{@y}$
4		storeAO	r_z	$\Rightarrow r_{arp}, r_{@z}$	i2i	r_x	$\Rightarrow r_{x'}$
5		cbr	r_{cc}	$\rightarrow L_1, L_2$	addI	$r_{@z}$, 4	$\Rightarrow r_{@z}$
+1	L_2:	mult	$r_{x'}, r_y$	$\Rightarrow r_z$	no operation issued		
+2		storeAO	r_z	$\Rightarrow r_{arp}, r_{@z}$	no operation issued		
+3		stall on r_y			no operation issued		

FIGURE 12.9 Example Loop after Pipeline Scheduling

To understand the flow of values in the pipelined loop, consider the execution shown in Figure 12.10. It shows the order in which the operations would execute if the pipelined loop executed for four iterations of the source loop. The arrows show the flow of values along the loop's critical path—the two loads, the multiply, and the store.

- The first source-loop iteration begins in the pipelined loop's prologue and completes in the first kernel iteration. These flows are shown with thin gray lines.

- The second source-loop iteration begins in the pipelined loop's first kernel iteration and completes in the second kernel iteration. Its flows are shown with bold lines.

- The third source-loop iteration begins in the pipelined loop's second kernel iteration and completes in the third kernel iteration. Its flows are shown in standard weight lines.

- The final source-loop iteration begins in the pipelined loop's third (and last) kernel iteration. The loop's epilogue code completes the final iteration by performing the multiply and the store. These flows are shown with dotted lines.

The final store operation stalls waiting for the result of the multiply. The epilogue also contains some idle issue slots. If the scheduler has more context surrounding the loop, it may be able to improve the scheduling of the epilogue by hoisting operations from the basic block that follows the epilogue. Ideally, it should fill the idle issue slots and insert another set of operations between the multiply and the store operation.

Review

In essence, the pipeline scheduler folded the loop in half to reduce the number of cycles spent per iteration. The kernel executes one fewer time than the original loop. Both the prologue and the epilogue perform one half of an iteration. The pipelined loop uses two fewer cycles per iteration by overlapping the multiply and store from iteration i with the loads from iteration $i + 1$.

In general, the algorithms for producing pipelined loops require analysis techniques that are beyond the scope of this chapter. The curious reader should consult a textbook on advanced optimization techniques for details.

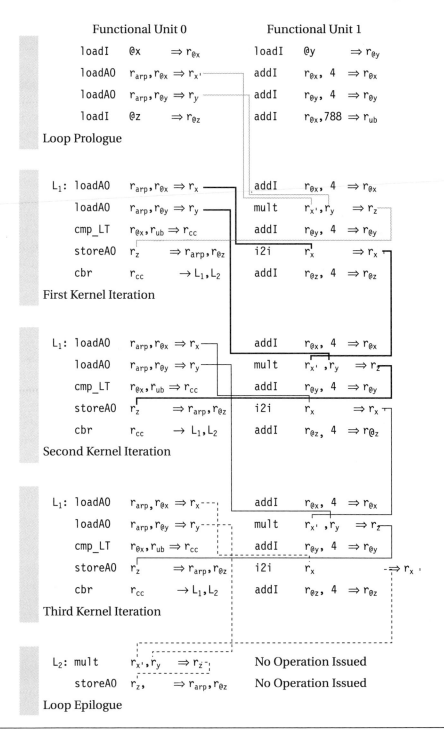

FIGURE 12.10 Flow of Values in the Pipelined Loop

12.4.2 Cloning for Context

In the example from Figure 12.6, the two paths through the EBB (B_1, B_2, B_3, B_4) both contain B_1. The compiler must choose to schedule one path first—either (B_1, B_2, B_4) or (B_1, B_3). The effect is to split the other path in half; if the compiler schedules (B_1, B_2, B_4) first, it must schedule B_3 with respect to the already scheduled B_1. The two other EBBs in the example consist of single blocks—(B_5) and (B_6). Thus, half of the blocks are scheduled as singleton blocks, and any benefits derived from EBB scheduling occur primarily on the path (B_1, B_2, B_4). Every other path through the fragment encounters code that has been scheduled locally.

If the compiler has chosen correctly, and B_1, B_2, B_4 is the most executed path, then splitting (B_1, B_3) is appropriate. If, instead, another path, such as (B_1, B_3, B_5, B_6), executes much more frequently, then the benefits of EBB scheduling have been wasted. Trace scheduling might capture and schedule this path. However, trace scheduling also shows a bias toward the first path scheduled.

To increase the number of multiblock paths that can be scheduled, the compiler can clone basic blocks to recapture context. Cloning may increase performance by creating contexts in which the scheduler has more opportunities to improve the code. It can also decrease the performance penalty when the compiler's choice of an execution path is wrong. With cloning, the compiler replicates blocks that have multiple predecessors to create larger EBBs.

Figure 12.11 shows the result of performing this kind of cloning on the example from Figure 12.6. Block B_5 has been cloned to create separate instances for the path from B_2 and the path from B_3. Similarly, B_6 has been cloned twice, to create an instance for each path entering it.

After cloning, the entire graph forms a single EBB. If the compiler chooses (B_1, B_2, B_4) as the hot path, it will schedule (B_1, B_2, B_4, B_6) first. This leaves two other paths to schedule. It can schedule the path (B_5, B_6'), using the scheduled (B_1, B_2) as context. It can schedule (B_3, B_5', B_6''), using the scheduled (B_1) as context.

Contrast this result with the simple EBB scheduler, which scheduled B_3 with respect to B_1 and both B_5 and B_6 without prior context. Because B_5 and B_6 have multiple predecessors and inconsistent context, the EBB scheduler cannot do better than local scheduling. Creating the extra copies of B_5 and B_6 that give the scheduler extra contexts costs a second copy of statements j and k and two extra copies of statement l. In practice, the compiler can combine the pairs B_4 and B_6, B_5 and B_6', and B_5' and B_6''. This eliminates the end-of-block jump in the first block in each pair.

Of course, the compiler writer must place some limits on this style of cloning to avoid excessive code growth and to avoid unwinding loops. A typical

MEASURING RUN-TIME PERFORMANCE

The primary goal of instruction scheduling is to improve the running time of the generated code. Discussions of performance use many different metrics; the two most common are

Instructions per second The metric commonly used to advertise computers and to compare system performance is the number of instructions executed in a second. This can be measured as instructions issued per second or instructions retired per second.

Time to complete a fixed task This metric uses one or more programs whose behavior is known and compares the time required to complete these fixed tasks. This approach, called *benchmarking*, provides information about overall system performance, both hardware and software, on a particular workload.

No single metric contains enough information to allow evaluation of the quality of code generated by the compiler's back end. For example, if the measure is instructions per second, does the compiler get extra credit for leaving extraneous (but independent) instructions in code? The simple timing metric provides no information about what is achievable for a given program. Thus, it allows one compiler to do better than another but fails to show the distance between the generated code and what is optimal for that code on the target machine.

Numbers that the compiler writer might want to measure include the percentage of executed instructions whose results are actually used and the percentage of cycles spent in stalls and interlocks. The former gives insight into some aspects of predicated execution, while the latter directly measures some aspects of schedule quality.

implementation might clone blocks within an innermost loop, stopping when it reaches a loop-closing edge or back edge. This creates a situation in which the only multiple-entry block in the loop is the first one. All other paths have only single-entry blocks.

A second issue that merits consideration arises in tail-recursive programs. Recall, from Section 7.8.2, that a program is tail recursive if its last action is a recursive self-invocation. When the compiler detects a tail call, it can convert the call to a jump back to the procedure's entry. From the scheduler's point of view, cloning may improve the situation.

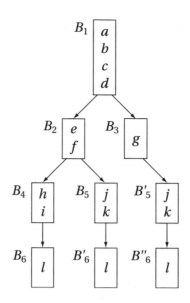

FIGURE 12.11 Cloning to Increase Scheduling Context

The left side of Figure 12.12 shows an abstracted control-flow graph for a tail-recursive routine, after the tail call has been converted to iteration. Block B_1 is entered along two paths, the path from the procedure entry and the path from B_2. This forces the scheduler to use worst-case assumptions about what precedes B_1. By cloning B_1, as shown on the right, the compiler can make control enter $B_{1'}$ along only one edge. This may improve the results of regional

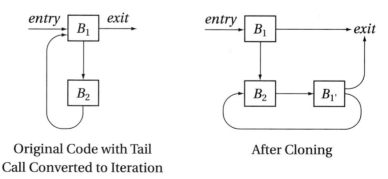

Original Code with Tail
Call Converted to Iteration

After Cloning

FIGURE 12.12 Cloning a Tail Call

scheduling with either an EBB scheduler or a loop scheduler. To further simplify the situation, the compiler might coalesce $B_{1'}$ onto the end of B_2, creating a single-block loop body. The resulting loop can be scheduled with either a local scheduler or a loop scheduler, as appropriate.

12.5 SUMMARY AND PERSPECTIVE

To obtain reasonable performance on a modern processor, the compiler must schedule operations carefully. Almost all modern compilers use some form of list scheduling. The algorithm is easily adapted and parameterized by changing priority schemes, tie-breaking rules, and even the direction of scheduling. List scheduling is robust, in the sense that it produces good results across a wide variety of codes. In practice, it often finds a time-optimal schedule.

Variations on list scheduling that operate over larger regions have been developed in response to real problems. Techniques that schedule extended basic blocks and loops are, in essence, responses to the increase in both the number of pipelines that the compiler must consider and their individual latencies. As machines have become more complex, schedulers have needed more scheduling context to discover enough instruction-level parallelism to keep the machines busy. Software pipelining provides a way of increasing the number of operations issued per cycle and decreasing total time for executing a loop. Trace scheduling was developed for VLIW architectures, for which the compiler needed to keep many functional units busy.

CHAPTER NOTES

Scheduling problems arise in many domains, ranging from construction, through industrial production, through service delivery, to getting payloads onto the space shuttle. A rich literature has grown up about scheduling, including many specialized variants of the problem. Instruction scheduling has been studied as a distinct problem since the 1960s.

Algorithms that guarantee optimal schedules exist for simple situations. For example, on a machine with one functional unit and uniform operation latencies, the Sethi-Ullman labelling algorithm creates an optimal schedule for an expression tree [301]. It can be adapted to produce good code for expression DAGs. Fischer and Proebsting built on the labelling algorithm to derive an algorithm that produces optimal or near optimal results for small memory latencies [278]. Unfortunately, it has trouble when latencies rise or the number of functional units grows.

Much of the literature on instruction scheduling deals with variants on the list-scheduling algorithm described in this chapter. Landskov et al. is often cited as the definitive work on list scheduling [229], but the algorithm goes back, at least, to Heller in 1961 [178]. Other papers that build on list scheduling include Bernstein and Rodeh [37], Gibbons and Muchnick [154], and Hennessy and Gross [179]. Krishnamurthy et al. provide a high-level survey of the literature for pipelined processors [224, 311]. Kerns, Lo, and Eggers developed balanced scheduling as a way to adapt list scheduling to uncertain memory latencies [210, 240].

Many authors have described regional scheduling algorithms. The first automated regional technique was Fisher's trace-scheduling algorithm [141, 142]. It has been used in several commercial systems [128, 242] and numerous research systems [310]. Hwu et al. proposed *superblock* scheduling as an alternative [190]; inside a loop, it clones blocks to avoid join points, in a fashion similar to that shown in Figure 12.11. Click proposed a global scheduling algorithm based on the use of a global value graph [80]. Several authors have proposed techniques to make use of specific hardware features [310, 292]. Other approaches that use replication to improve scheduling include Ebcioğlu and Nakatani [127] and Gupta and Soffa [167]. Sweany and Beaty proposed choosing paths based on dominance information [316]; others have looked at various aspects of that approach [315, 189, 98].

Software pipelining has been explored extensively. Rau and Glaeser introduced the idea in 1981 [283]. Lam presented an algorithm for software pipelining that included a hierarchical scheme for handling control flow inside a loop [226]. Aiken and Nicolau presented a similar approach, called *perfect pipelining* [11] at the same meeting.

The example for backward versus forward scheduling in Figure 12.4 was brought to our attention by Philip Schielke [298]. It is from the SPEC benchmark program go. It captures, concisely, an effect that has caused many compiler writers to include both forward and backward schedulers in their compilers' back ends.

CHAPTER 13

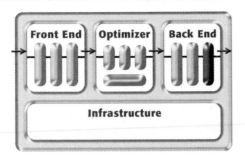

Front End | Optimizer | Back End

Infrastructure

Register Allocation

13.1 INTRODUCTION

Registers are the fastest locations in the memory hierarchy. Often, they are the only memory locations that most operations can access directly. The proximity of registers to the functional units makes good use of registers a critical factor in run-time performance. In compiled code, responsibility for making good use of the target machine's register set lies with the register allocator.

The register allocator determines, at each point in the program, which values will reside in registers and which register will hold each of those values. If the allocator cannot keep a value in a register throughout its lifetime, the value must be stored in memory for some or all of its lifetime. The allocator might relegate a value to memory because the code contains more live values than the target machine's register set can hold. Alternately, the value might be kept in memory between uses because the allocator cannot prove that it can safely reside in a register.

Conceptually, the register allocator takes as its input a program that uses some arbitrary number of registers. It produces as its output an equivalent program that fits into the register set of the target machine.

When the allocator cannot keep some value in a register, it must store the value to memory and load it again when it is next needed. This process is called *spilling* the value to memory.

Typically, the register allocator's goal is to make effective use of the register set provided by the target machine. This includes minimizing the number of load and store operations that execute to perform spilling. However, other goals are possible. For example, in a memory-constrained environment, the user might want the allocator to minimize the memory impact of allocation—both data memory that holds spilled values and code memory that holds spill operations.

A bad decision in the register allocator causes some value to be spilled that might otherwise reside in a register. The cost of this extra spill code rises with memory latency. Thus, the growing disparity between memory speed and processor speed in the 1990s has increased the impact of register allocation on the performance of compiled code.

The next section reviews some of the background issues that create the environment in which register allocators operate. Subsequent sections explore algorithms for register allocation and assignment in both local scopes and global scopes.

13.2 BACKGROUND ISSUES

The register allocator takes code that is almost completely compiled as input—the code has been scanned, parsed, checked, analyzed, optimized, rewritten as target-machine code, and (perhaps) scheduled. The allocator must fit that code into the register set of the target machine by inserting operations that move values between registers and memory. Many decisions made in earlier phases of the compiler affect the allocator's task, as do properties of the target machine's instruction set. This section explores several factors that play a role in shaping the role of the register allocator.

13.2.1 Memory versus Registers

The compiler writer's choice of a memory model (see Section 5.6.2) defines many details of the problem that the allocator must address. In a register-to-register model, earlier phases in the compiler directly encode their knowledge about ambiguity of memory references into the shape of the IR program —by making all unambiguous values reside in virtual registers. Values that are memory based in the IR program are assumed to be ambiguous (see Section 7.2), so the allocator leaves them in memory.

In a memory-to-memory model, the allocator does not have this code shape hint. The IR program keeps all values in memory, and it moves them in and out of registers as they are used and defined. The allocator must determine which values can safely be kept in registers because they are unambiguous. It must then determine whether keeping them in registers is profitable. In this model, the code that the allocator receives as input typically uses fewer registers and executes more memory operations than the equivalent register-to-register code. To obtain good performance, the allocator needs to promote as many of the memory-based values into registers as it can.

Thus, the choice of memory model fundamentally determines the allocator's task. In both scenarios, the allocator's goal is to reduce the number of loads and stores that the final code executes to move values back and forth between registers and memory. In a register-to-register model, allocation is a necessary part of the process that produces legal code; it ensures that the final code fits into the target machine's register set. The allocator inserts load and store operations to move some register-based values into memory—presumably in regions where demand for registers exceeds supply. The allocator tries to minimize the impact of the load and store operations that it inserts.

In contrast, the allocator in a compiler that uses a memory-to-memory model is an optimization that improves the performance of a legal program. The allocator decides to keep some memory-based values in registers, which makes some of the loads and stores in the program unnecessary. The allocator tries to remove as many loads and stores as possible, since this can significantly improve the final code's performance.

Thus, lack of knowledge—limitations in the compiler's analysis—may keep the compiler from allocating a variable to a register. It can also occur when a single code sequence inherits different environments along different paths. These limitations on what the compiler may know tend to favor the register-to-register model. The register-to-register model provides a mechanism for other parts of the compiler to encode knowledge about ambiguity and uniqueness. This knowledge might come from analysis; it might come from understanding the translation of a complex construct; or it might even be derived from the source text in the parser.

13.2.2 Allocation versus Assignment

In a modern compiler, the register allocator solves two distinct problems—register allocation and register assignment—that have sometimes been handled separately in the past. These problems are related but distinct.

1. *Allocation* Register allocation maps an unlimited set of names to the specific set of registers provided by the target machine. In a register-to-register model, register allocation maps virtual registers to a new set of names that models the physical register set and spills values that do not fit in the register set. In a memory-to-memory model, it maps some subset of the memory locations to a set of names that models the physical register set. Allocation ensures that the code will fit the target machine's register set at each instruction.

2. *Assignment* Register assignment maps an allocated name set to the physical registers of the target machine. Register assignment assumes that allocation has been performed, so the code will fit into the set of physical registers provided by the target machine. Thus, at each instruction in the generated code, no more than k values are designated as residing in registers, where k is the number of physical registers. Assignment produces the actual register names required by the executable code.

Register allocation is, in almost any realistic formulation, NP-complete. For a single basic block, with one size of data value, optimal allocation can be done in polynomial time, as long as the cost of storing values back to memory is uniform. Almost any additional complexity in the problem makes it NP-complete. For example, adding a second size of data item, such as a register pair that holds a double-precision floating-point number, makes the problem NP-complete. Alternately, adding a realistic memory model, or the fact that some values need not be stored back to memory, makes the problem NP-complete. Extending the scope of allocation to include control flow and multiple blocks also makes the problem NP-complete. In practice, one or more of these issues arise in compiling for any real system. In many cases, all of them do.

Register assignment, in many cases, can be solved in polynomial time. Given a feasible allocation for a basic block—that is, one in which the demand for physical registers at each instruction does not exceed the number of physical registers—an assignment can be produced in linear time using an analog of interval-graph coloring. The related problem for an entire procedure can be solved in polynomial time—that is, if, at each instruction, the demand for physical registers does not exceed the number of physical registers, then the compiler can construct an assignment in polynomial time.

The distinction between allocation and assignment is both subtle and important. In seeking to improve a register allocator's performance, the compiler writer must understand whether the weakness lies in allocation or assignment and direct effort to the appropriate part of the algorithm.

13.2.3 Register Classes

The physical registers provided by most processors do not form a homogenous pool of interchangeable resources. Most processors have distinct classes of registers for different kinds of values.

For example, most modern computers have both *general-purpose registers* and *floating-point registers*. The former hold integer values and memory addresses, while the latter hold floating-point values. This dichotomy is not new; the early IBM 360 machines had sixteen general-purpose registers and four floating-point registers. Modern processors may add more classes. For example, the IBM/Motorola PowerPC has a separate register class for condition codes, and the Intel IA-64 has additional classes for predicate registers and branch-target registers. The compiler must place each value in a register of the appropriate class.

If the interactions between two register classes are limited, the compiler may be able to allocate registers for them independently. This breaks the problem into smaller, independent components, reduces the size of the data structures, and may produce faster compile times. When two register classes overlap, however, then both classes must be modelled in a single allocation problem. The common architectural practice of keeping double-precision floating-point numbers in pairs of single-precision registers is a good example of this issue. The classes of double-precision values and single-precision values both map to the same underlying set of hardware registers. The compiler cannot allocate one of these classes without considering the other, so it must solve the joint allocation problem.

Even if the different register classes are physically and logically separate, they interact through operations that refer to registers in multiple classes. For example, for many architectures, the decision to spill a floating-point register requires the insertion of an address calculation and some memory operations; these actions use general-purpose registers and change the allocation problem for that class of registers. Thus, the compiler can make independent allocation decisions for the different classes, but those decisions can have consequences that affect allocation in other register classes. Spilling a predicate register or a condition-code register has similar effects. Thus, general-purpose registers should be allocated after the other register classes.

13.3 LOCAL REGISTER ALLOCATION AND ASSIGNMENT

As an introduction to register allocation, consider the problems that arise in producing a good allocation for a single basic block. In optimization, methods that handle a single basic block are termed *local* methods, so these algorithms are local register-allocation techniques. The allocator takes as input a single basic block that incorporates a register-to-register memory model.

To simplify the discussion, we assume that the program starts and ends with the block; it inherits no values from blocks that executed earlier and leaves behind no values for blocks that execute later. Our input program will use only a single class of general-purpose registers. Our target machine will support a single set of k general-purpose registers.

The code shape encodes information about which values can legally reside in a register for nontrivial amounts of time. Any value that can legally reside in a register is kept in a register. The code uses as many register names as needed to encode this information, so it may name more registers than the target machine has. For this reason, we call these preallocation registers *virtual registers*. For a given block, the number of virtual registers that it uses is *MaxVR*.

The basic block consists of a series of N three-address operations $o_1, o_2, o_3, \ldots, o_N$. Each operation, o_i, has the form $op_i\ vr_{i_1}, vr_{i_2} \Rightarrow vr_{i_3}$. The notation vr denotes the fact that these are virtual registers, rather than physical registers. From a high-level view, the goal of local register allocation is to create an equivalent block in which each reference to a virtual register is replaced with a reference to a specific physical register. If $MaxVR > k$, the allocator may need to insert loads and stores to fit the code into the set of k physical registers. An alternative statement of this property is that the output code can have no more than k values in registers at any point in the block.

We will explore two approaches to this problem. The first approach counts the number of references to a value in the block and uses these frequency counts to determine which values will reside in registers. Because it relies on externally derived information—the frequency counts—to make its decisions, we consider this a top-down approach. The second approach relies on detailed, low-level knowledge of the code to make its decisions. It walks over the block and determines, at each operation, whether or not a spill is needed. Because it synthesizes and combines many low-level facts to drive its decision-making process, we consider this a bottom-up approach.

13.3.1 Top-Down Local Register Allocation

The top-down local allocator works from a simple principle: the most heavily used values should reside in registers. To implement this heuristic, it counts the number of occurrences of each virtual register in the block and uses these frequency counts as priorities to allocate virtual registers to physical registers.

If there are more virtual registers than physical registers, the allocator must reserve several physical registers for use in computations that involve values allocated to memory. The allocator must have enough registers to address and load two operands, to perform the operation, and to store the result. The precise number of registers needed depends on the target architecture; on a typical RISC machine, the number might be two to four registers. We will refer to this machine-specific number as *feasible*.

To perform top-down local allocation, the compiler can apply the following simple algorithm:

1. *Compute a priority for each virtual register*. In a linear pass over the operations in the block, the allocator can tally the number of times each virtual register appears. A virtual register's count becomes its priority.

2. *Sort the virtual registers into priority order*. If blocks are reasonably small, it can use a bucket sort, since the scores must fall within a small range, between zero and a small multiple of the block length.

3. *Assign registers in priority order*. The first $k - feasible$ virtual registers are assigned physical registers.

4. *Rewrite the code*. In a second walk over the code, the allocator can rewrite the code. References to virtual registers with assigned physical registers are rewritten with the physical register names. Any reference to a virtual register with no physical register is replaced with a reference to a reserved temporary register; a load or store operation is inserted, as appropriate.

The strength of this approach is that it keeps heavily used virtual registers in physical registers. Its primary weakness lies in the approach to allocation—it dedicates a physical register to a virtual register for the entire basic block. Thus, a value that is heavily used in the first half of the block and unused in the second half of the block occupies its physical register through the second half, even though it is no longer of use. The next section presents a technique that addresses this problem. It takes a fundamentally different approach to allocation—a bottom-up, incremental approach.

13.3.2 Bottom-Up Local Register Allocation

The key idea behind the bottom-up local allocator is to focus on the transitions that occur as each operation executes. It begins with all the registers unoccupied. For each operation, the allocator needs to ensure that its operands are in registers before it executes. It must also allocate a register for the operation's result. Figure 13.1 shows its basic structure along with three support routines that it uses.

The bottom-up allocator iterates over the operations in the block, making allocation decisions on demand. There are, however, some subtleties. By considering vr_{i_1} and vr_{i_2} in order, the allocator avoids using two physical registers

```
/* code for the allocator */
for each operation, i, in order from 1
    to N where i has the form
        op vr_i1 vr_i2 ⇒ vr_i3
    r_x ← ensure(vr_i1, class(vr_i1))
    r_y ← ensure(vr_i2, class(vr_i2))
    if vr_i1 is not needed after i
        then free(r_x,class(r_x))
    if vr_i2 is not needed after i
        then free(r_y,class(r_y))
    r_z ←allocate(vr_i3, class(vr_i3))
    rewrite i as op_i r_x,r_y ⇒ r_z
    if vr_i1 is needed after i
        then class.Next[r_x] ← dist(vr_i1)
    if vr_i2 is needed after i
        then class.Next[r_y] ← dist(vr_i2)
    class.Next[r_z] ← dist(vr_i3)

free(i,class)
    if (class.Free[i] ≠ true) then
        push(i,class)
        class.Name[i] ← −1
        class.Next[i] ← ∞
        class.Free[i] ← true
```

```
ensure(vr,class)
    if (vr is already in class)
        then result ← vr's physical register

    else
        result ← allocate(vr,class)
        emit code to move vr into result
    return result


allocate(vr,class)
    if (class.StackTop ≥ 0)
        then i ← pop(class)
    else
        i ← j that maximizes class.Next[j]
        store contents of j
    class.Name[i] ← vr
    class.Next[i] ← −1
    class.Free[i] ← false

    return i
```

FIGURE 13.1   The Bottom-Up, Local Register Allocator

for an operation with a repeated operand, such as add $r_y,r_y \Rightarrow r_z$. Similarly, trying to free r_x and r_y before allocating r_z avoids spilling a register to hold the result when the operation actually frees a register. Most of the complications are hidden in the routines *Ensure, Allocate*, and *Free*.

The routine *Ensure* is conceptually simple. It takes two arguments, a virtual register, *vr*, holding the desired value, and a representation for the appropriate register class, *class*. If *vr* already occupies a physical register, *Ensure*'s job is done. Otherwise, it allocates a physical register for *vr* and emits code to move *vr*'s value into that physical register. In either case, it returns the physical register.

Allocate and *Free* expose the details of the allocation problem. To understand them, we need a concrete representation for a register class, shown in the C code on the left side of Figure 13.2. A class has Size physical registers, each of which is represented by a virtual register name (Name); an integer that indicates the distance to its next use (Next); and a flag indicating whether or not that physical register is currently in use (Free). The code on the right side of the figure initializes the class structure, using -1 as an out-of-range name and ∞ as the maximum possible distance. To make *Allocate* and *Free* efficient, the class also needs a list of free registers—the Stack in Class. Routines *push* and *pop* manipulate the Stack.

With this level of detail, the code for both *Allocate* and *Free* is straightforward. Each class maintains a stack of free physical registers. *Allocate* returns a physical register from the free list of *class*, if one exists. Otherwise, it selects the value stored in *class* that is used farthest in the future, stores it, and reallocates the physical register for *vr*. Allocate sets the *Next* field to -1, ensuring that this register will not be chosen for the other operand in the current operation. The main loop of the allocator will reset the *Next* field to its appropriate value after it finishes with the current operation. *Free* pushes the register onto the stack and resets its fields in the *class* structure.

```
struct Class {
    int Size;
    int Name[Size];
    int Next[Size];
    int Free[Size];
    int Stack[Size];
    int StackTop;
}
```

initialize(class,size)
  class.Size ← size

  >class.StackTop ← −1
  for i ← 0 to size − 1
    class.Name[i] ← −1
    class.Next[i] ← ∞
    class.Free[i] ← true
    push(i,class)

FIGURE 13.2   Representing a Register Class in C

The function *dist(vr)* returns the index in the block of the next reference to *vr*. The compiler can annotate each reference in the block with the appropriate value for *dist* by making a single backward pass over the block.

The net effect of this bottom-up technique is straightforward. Initially, it assumes that the physical registers are unoccupied and places them on a free list. For the first few operations, it satisfies demand from the free list. When the allocator needs another register and discovers that the free list is empty, it must spill a value from a register to memory. It picks the value whose next use is farthest in the future. As long as the cost of spilling a value is the same for all registers, this choice frees up the register for the longest period of time. In some sense, it maximizes the benefit obtained for the cost of the spill.

In practice, this algorithm produces excellent local allocations. Indeed, several authors have argued that it produces optimal allocations. However, complications arise in practice. At any point in the allocation, some values in registers may need to be stored on a spill, while others may not. For example, if the register contains a known constant value, the store is superfluous since the allocator can recreate the value without a copy in memory. Similarly, a value that was created by a load from memory need not be stored. A value that need not be stored is called *clean*, while a value that needs a store is called *dirty*.

To choose an optimal local allocation, the allocator must take into account the difference in cost between spilling clean values and spilling dirty values. Consider, for example, allocation on a two-register machine, where the values x_1 and x_2 are already in the registers. Assume that x_1 is clean and x_2 is dirty. If the reference string for the remainder of the block is x_3 x_1 x_2, the allocator must spill one of x_1 or x_2. Since x_2's next use lies farthest in the future, the bottom-up local algorithm would spill it, producing the sequence of memory operations shown on the left.

store x_2	
load x_3	load x_3 (overwriting x_1)
load x_2	load x_1
Spill Dirty Value	Spill Clean Value

If, instead, the allocator spills x_1, it produces the sequence of memory operations shown on the right—one fewer memory operation. This scenario suggests that the allocator should preferentially spill clean values over dirty values. The answer is not that simple.

Consider another reference string, x_3 x_1 x_3 x_1 x_2, with the same initial conditions. Consistently spilling the clean value produces the sequence of four memory operations on the left.

```
        load  x₃
        load  x₁                          store  x₂
        load  x₃                          load   x₃
        load  x₁                          load   x₂
     Spill Clean Value                  Spill Dirty Value
```

In contrast, consistently spilling the dirty value produces the sequence on the right, which requires one fewer memory operation. Taking into account the distinction between clean values and dirty values makes the local allocation problem NP-hard. Still, in practice, versions of the bottom-up local allocator produce good local allocations; they tend to be better than those produced by the top-down allocator previously described.

The bottom-up local allocator differs from the top-down local one in the way that it handles individual values. The top-down allocator devotes a physical register to a virtual register for an entire block. The bottom-up allocator assigns a physical register to a virtual register for the distance between two consecutive references to the virtual register. It reconsiders that decision at each invocation of *Allocate*—that is, each time that it needs another register. Thus, the bottom-up algorithm can, and does, produce allocations in which a single virtual register is kept in different physical registers at different points in its lifetime. Similar behavior can be retrofitted into the top-down allocator.

13.4 MOVING BEYOND SINGLE BLOCKS

We have seen how to build good allocators for single blocks. Working top down, we arrived at the frequency-count allocator. Working bottom up, we arrived at the bottom-up local allocator. We could use lessons learned in the bottom-up local algorithm to improve the frequency-count allocator. However, local allocation does not capture the reuse of values across multiple blocks. This happens regularly in practice. Thus, the next step is to extend the scope of allocation beyond single basic blocks.

Unfortunately, moving from a single block to multiple blocks adds many complications. For example, our local allocators assumed implicitly that values do not flow between blocks. The primary reason for moving to a larger scope for allocation is to account for the flow of values between blocks and to generate allocations that handle such flows efficiently. The allocator must correctly handle values computed in previous blocks, and it must preserve values for use in following blocks. To accomplish this, the allocator needs a more sophisticated way of handling "values" than the local allocators use.

13.4.1 Liveness and Live Ranges

Regional and global allocators try to assign values to registers in a way that coordinates their use across multiple blocks. These allocators work from a new name space that reflects the actual patterns of definitions and uses for each value. Rather than allocating variables or values to registers, they allocate *live ranges*. A single live range consists of a set of definitions and uses that are related to each other because their values flow together. That is, a live range contains a set of definitions and a set of uses. This set is self-contained in the sense that every definition that can reach a use is in the same live range as the use and every use that a definition can reach is in the same live range as the definition.

The term *live range* relies, implicitly, on the notion of *liveness*, as explained in the discussion of the live variables problem in Section 9.2.1. Recall that a variable v is *live* at point p if it has been defined along a path from the procedure's entry to p and there exists a path from p to a use of v along which v is not redefined. Anywhere that v is live, its value must be preserved because subsequent execution might use v. Remember, v can be either a source-program variable or a compiler-generated temporary name.

The set of live ranges is distinct from the set of variables and the set of values. Every value computed in the code is part of some live range, even if it has no name in the original source code. Thus, the intermediate results produced by address computations have live ranges, just the same as programmer-named variables, array elements, and addresses loaded for use as branch targets. A specific programmer-named variable may have many distinct live ranges. A register allocator that uses live ranges can place those distinct live ranges in different registers. Thus, a source-language variable might reside in different registers at two distinct points in the executing program.

To make these ideas concrete, consider the problem of finding live ranges in a single basic block. Figure 13.3 shows the block from Figure 1.3. We have added an initial operation to define r_{arp}. The table on the right side shows the distinct live ranges in the block. In straight line code, we can represent a live range as an interval. Notice that each operation defines a value and, thus, starts a live range. Consider r_{arp}. It is defined in operation 1. Every other reference to r_{arp} is a use. Thus, the block uses just one value for r_{arp}. The interval $[1, 11]$ represents this live range.

In contrast, r_w has several live ranges. Operation 2 defines it; operation 7 uses the value from operation 2. Operations 7, 8, 9, and 10 each define a new

				Defines	
				Register	**Interval**
1	loadI	$\cdots$	$\Rightarrow r_{arp}$	r_{arp}	[1,11]
2	loadAI	r_{arp}, 0	$\Rightarrow r_w$	r_w	[2,7]
3	loadI	2	$\Rightarrow r_2$	r_w	[7,8]
4	loadAI	r_{arp}, @x	$\Rightarrow r_x$	r_w	[8,9]
5	loadAI	r_{arp}, @y	$\Rightarrow r_y$	r_w	[9,10]
6	loadAI	r_{arp}, @z	$\Rightarrow r_z$	r_w	[10,11]
7	mult	r_w, r_2	$\Rightarrow r_w$	r_2	[3,7]
8	mult	r_w, r_x	$\Rightarrow r_w$	r_x	[4,8]
9	mult	r_w, r_y	$\Rightarrow r_w$	r_y	[5,9]
10	mult	r_w, r_z	$\Rightarrow r_w$	r_z	[6,10]
11	storeAI	r_w	$\Rightarrow r_{arp}$, 0		

FIGURE 13.3   Live Ranges in a Basic Block

value for r_w; in each case, the following operation uses the value. Thus, the register named r_w in the figure corresponds to five distinct live ranges: [2, 7], [7, 8], [8, 9], [9, 10], and [10, 11]. A register allocator need not keep these distinct live ranges in the same physical register. Instead, it can treat each live range in the block as an independent value for allocation and assignment.

To find live ranges in regions larger than a single block, the compiler must perform live-variable analysis to discover the sets of values that are live on exit from every block. It can annotate each block b with a set LiveOut(b) derived from the analysis and a set LiveIn(b) that contains the set of variables live on entry to b. LiveIn(b) is just UEVar(b) $\cup$ (LiveOut (b) $\cap \overline{\text{VarKill}(b)}$).

At any point in the code, values that are not live need no register. Similarly, the only values that need registers at point p are those values that are live at p, or some subset of those values. Local register allocators, when implemented in real compilers, use LiveOut sets to determine when a value must be preserved in memory beyond its last use in a block. Global allocators use analogous information to discover live ranges and to guide the allocation process.

13.4.2 Complications at Block Boundaries

A compiler that uses local register allocation might compute LiveIn and LiveOut sets for each block as a necessary prelude to provide the local allocator with information about the status of values at the block's entry and

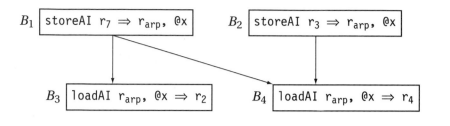

FIGURE 13.4 Problems with Multiple Blocks

exit. The presence of these sets can simplify the task of making the allocations for individual blocks behave appropriately when control flows from one block to another. For example, a value in LIVEOUT(b) must be stored to memory after its last definition in b to ensure that the value will be in the expected location when it is loaded in a subsequent block. In contrast, if the value is not in LIVEOUT(b), it need not be stored, except as a spill for later use inside b.

Some of the effects introduced by considering multiple blocks complicate either assignment or allocation or both. Figure 13.4 illustrates some of the complications that arise in global assignment. Consider the transition that occurs along the edge from block B_1 to block B_3.

B_1 has the value of program variable x in r_7. B_3 wants it in r_2. When it processes B_1, the local allocator has no knowledge of the context created by the other blocks, so it must store x back to x's location in memory (at offset @x from the ARP in r_{arp}). Similarly, when the allocator processes B_3, it has no knowledge about the behavior of B_1, so it must load x from memory. Of course, if it knew the results of allocation on B_1, it could assign x to r_7 and make the load unnecessary. In the absence of this knowledge, it must generate the load. The references to x in B_2 and B_4 further complicate the problem. Any attempt to coordinate x's assignment across blocks must consider both those blocks since B_4 is a successor of B_1, and any change in B_4's treatment of x has an impact on its other predecessor, B_2.

Similar effects arise with allocation. What if x were not referenced in B_2? Even if we could coordinate assignment globally, to ensure that x was always in r_7 when it was used, the allocator would need to insert a load of x at the end of B_2 to let B_4 avoid the initial load of x. Of course, if B_2 had other successors, they might not reference x and might need another value in r_7.

These effects at block boundaries can become complex. They do not fit into a local allocator because they deal with phenomena that are entirely outside a local allocator's scope. If the allocator manages to insert a few extra instructions that iron out the differences, it may choose to insert them in the wrong block—for example, in a block that forms the body of an inner loop rather than in that loop's header block. The local models assume that all instructions execute with the same frequency; stretching the models to handle larger regions invalidates that assumption, too. The difference between a good allocation and a poor one may be a few instructions in the most heavily executed block in the code.

A second issue, both more subtle and more problematic, arises when we try to stretch the local-allocation paradigms beyond single blocks. Consider using the bottom-up local algorithm on block B_1. With only one block, the notion of the "furthest" next reference is clear. The local algorithm has a unique distance to each next reference. With multiple successor blocks, the allocator must take into account references along all the paths leaving B_1. For the last reference to some value y in B_1, the next reference is either the first reference to y in B_3 or the first reference to y in B_4. These two references are unlikely to be in the same position relative to the end of B_1. Alternately, B_3 might not contain a reference to y, while B_4 does contain one. Even if both blocks use y, and the references are equidistant in the input code, local spilling in one block might make them different in unpredictable ways. As the basic metric that underlies the bottom-up local method becomes multivalued, the algorithm's effects become harder to understand and to justify.

All of these problems suggest that a different approach is needed to move beyond local allocation to regional or global allocation. Indeed, the successful global allocation algorithms bear little resemblance to the local ones.

13.5 GLOBAL REGISTER ALLOCATION AND ASSIGNMENT

The register allocator's goal is to minimize the execution time required by the instructions it must insert. The allocator cannot guarantee an optimal solution to this problem. From the perspective of execution time, the difference between two different allocations for the same basic code lies in the number of loads, stores, and copy operations inserted by the allocator and their placement in the code. Since different blocks execute different numbers of times, the placement of spills has a strong impact on the amount of time spent executing spill code. Since block-execution frequencies can vary from run to run, the notion of a best allocation is somewhat tenuous—it must be conditioned to a particular set of execution frequencies.

Global allocation differs from local allocation in two fundamental ways.

1. The structure of a live range can be more complex than in the local allocator. In a single block, a live range is just an interval in a linear

string of operations. Finding live ranges is more complex in a global allocator. A global live range is the web of definitions and uses found by taking the closure of two relationships. For each use in the live range, it includes every definition that can reach that use. For each definition in the live range, it includes every use that definition can reach.

2. Distinct references to the same variable may execute different numbers of times. In a single block, if any operation executes, all the operations execute (unless an exception occurs), so the cost of spilling is uniform. In a larger scope, each reference may be in a different block, so the cost of spilling depends on where the references are located. When it must spill, the global allocator should consider the spill cost of each live range that is a candidate to be spilled.

Any global allocator must address both these issues. This makes global allocation substantially more complex than local allocation.

To address the issue of complex live ranges, a global allocator explicitly creates a name space in which each distinct live range has a distinct name. Then, the allocator maps a live range onto either a physical register or a memory location. To accomplish this, the global allocator first constructs live ranges and renames all the virtual register references in the code to reflect the new name space constructed of the live ranges. To address the issue of execution frequencies, the allocator can annotate each reference or each basic block with an estimated execution frequency. The estimates may come from static analysis or from profile data gathered during actual executions of the program. The estimated execution frequencies are used in the allocator to guide decisions about allocation and spilling.

Finally, global allocators must make decisions about allocation and assignment. They must decide which live ranges will reside in registers. They must decide whether two live ranges can share a single register. They must assign a specific physical register to each live range that is allocated one.

Many global allocators use a graph-coloring paradigm. They build a graph to model the conflicts between live ranges and find an appropriate coloring for the graph. Coloring is used to model register assignment; it lets the allocator know when two values cannot share a register. Different coloring allocators handle allocation (or spilling) in different ways. We will look at top-down allocators that use high-level information to make allocation decisions and at bottom-up allocators that use low-level information to make those decisions. Before examining these two approaches, however, we explore some of the subproblems that the allocators have in common: discovering live ranges, estimating spill costs, and building an interference graph.

GRAPH COLORING

Many global register allocators use *graph coloring* as a paradigm to model the underlying allocation problem. For an arbitrary graph G, a coloring of G assigns a color to each node in G so that no pair of adjacent nodes have the same color. A coloring that uses k colors is termed a k-coloring, and the smallest such k for a given graph is called the graph's *chromatic number*. Consider the following graphs:

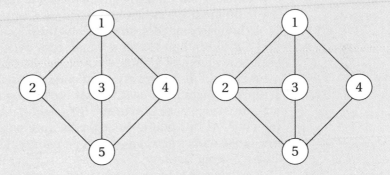

The graph on the left is 2-colorable. For example, assigning *blue* to nodes 1 and 5, and *red* to nodes 2, 3, and 4 produces the desired result. Adding an edge between 2 and 3, as shown on the right, makes the graph 3-colorable, but not 2-colorable. (Assign *blue* to nodes 1 and 5, *red* to nodes 2 and 4, and *white* to node 3.)

For a given graph, the problem of finding its chromatic number is NP-complete. Similarly, the problem of determining if a graph is k-colorable, for some fixed k, is NP-complete. Algorithms that use graph coloring as a paradigm to allocate resources use approximate methods to find colorings that fit the set of available resources.

13.5.1 Discovering Global Live Ranges

To construct live ranges, the compiler must discover the relationships that exist among different definitions and uses. The allocator must derive a name space that groups together into a single name all the definitions that reach a single use and all the uses that a single definition can reach. This suggests an approach in which the compiler assigns each definition a distinct name and merges definition names together that reach a common use.

The SSA form of the code provides a natural starting point for this construction. Recall that in SSA form, each name is defined once, and each use refers to only a single definition. The ϕ-functions inserted to reconcile these two rules record the fact that distinct definitions on different paths in the control-flow graph reach a single reference. Two or more definitions that flow into a ϕ-function belong to the same live range because the ϕ-function creates a name representing all the values. Any operation that references the result of the ϕ-function uses one of these values; which value depends on how control flow reached the ϕ-function. Because all the definitions can be referenced by the same use, they must reside in the same register. Thus, ϕ-functions are the key to building live ranges for code in SSA form.

To build live ranges from SSA form, the allocator uses the disjoint-set union-find algorithm and makes a single pass over the code. The allocator treats each SSA name, or definition, as a set in the algorithm. It examines each ϕ-function in the program, and unions together the sets associated with each ϕ-function parameter and the set for the ϕ-function target. After all the ϕ-functions have been processed, the resulting sets represent the live ranges in the code. At this point, the allocator can either rewrite the code to use the live-range names or it can create and maintain a mapping between SSA names and live-range names.

The left side of Figure 13.5 shows a code fragment in semipruned SSA form that involves source-code variables, a, b, c, and d. To find the live ranges, the

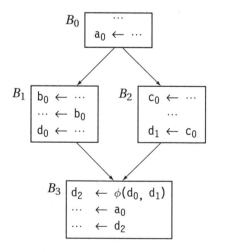

Code Fragment in Pruned SSA Form

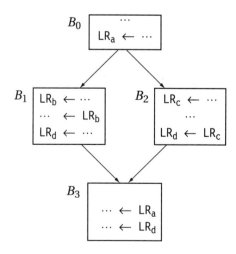

Rewritten in Terms of Live Ranges

FIGURE 13.5   Discovering Live Ranges

allocator assigns each SSA name a set containing its name. It unions together the sets associated with names used in the ϕ-function, $\{d_0\} \cup \{d_1\} \cup \{d_2\}$. This gives a final set of four live ranges: LR_a containing $\{a_0\}$, LR_b containing $\{b_0\}$, LR_c containing $\{c_0\}$, and LR_d containing $\{d_0, d_1, d_2\}$. The right side of the figure shows the code with the names rewritten in terms of these live ranges.

In Section 9.3.5, we saw that transformations applied to the SSA form can introduce complications into this rewriting process. If the allocator simply builds SSA form and uses it to find live ranges, then the rewriting process can simply replace SSA names with live-range names. On the other hand, if the allocator uses SSA form that has been transformed, the rewrite process must deal with the complications described in Section 9.3.5. Since most compilers will perform allocation after instruction selection and, possibly, instruction scheduling, the code that the allocator consumes will not be in SSA form. This forces the allocator to build SSA form for the code and ensures that the rewriting process is straightforward.

13.5.2 Estimating Global Spill Costs

To make informed spill decisions, the global allocator needs an estimate of the cost of spilling each value. The cost of a spill has three components: the address computation, the memory operation, and an estimated execution frequency.

The compiler writer can choose where in memory a spilled value resides. Typically, the spilled values are kept in the current activation record (AR) to minimize the cost of the address computation, specifically, the register-save area shown in Figure 6.5. Storing spilled values in the AR lets the allocator generate an operation such as a loadAI or storeAI relative to r_{arp} for the spill. Such operations usually avoid the need for more registers to compute the address of a spill.

The cost of the memory operation is, in general, unavoidable. If the target machine has noncached on-chip local memory—as many embedded processors do—the compiler might use that memory for spilling. More typically, the compiler needs to save the value and restore it from memory when a later operation needs it. As memory latencies rise, the cost of the needed load and store operations grows. To make matters somewhat worse, the allocator inserts spill operations only when it absolutely needs a register. Thus, many spill operations occur in code where demand for registers is high, which may, in turn, keep the scheduler from moving those operations far enough to hide the memory latency. The compiler writer must hope that spill locations stay in the cache. (Paradoxically, those locations stay in the cache only if they are accessed often enough to avoid replacement—suggesting that the code is executing too many spills.)

Negative Spill Costs

A live range that contains a load, a store, and no other uses should receive a negative spill cost if the load and store refer to the same address. (Such a live range can result from transformations intended to improve the code; for example, if the use were optimized away and the store resulted from a procedure call rather than the definition of a new value.) Sometimes, spilling a live range may eliminate copy operations with a higher cost than the spill operations; such a live range also has a negative cost. Any live range with a negative spill cost should be spilled, since doing so decreases demand for registers *and* removes instructions from the code.

Infinite Spill Costs

Some live ranges are short enough that spilling them never helps. Consider a use that immediately follows its definition. Spilling the definition and use produces two short live ranges. The first contains the definition followed by a store; the second one contains a load followed by the use. Neither of these new live ranges uses fewer registers than the original live range, so the spill produces no benefit. The allocator should assign the original live range a spill cost of infinity. In general, a live range should have infinite spill cost if no other live range ends between its definitions and its uses. This condition stipulates that availability of registers does not change between the definitions and uses.

Accounting for Execution Frequencies

To account for the different execution frequencies of the basic blocks in the control-flow graph, the compiler should annotate each block (if not each reference) with an estimated execution count. Most compilers use simple heuristics to estimate execution costs. A common method is to assume that each loop executes ten times. Thus, it assigns a count of ten to a load inside one loop, and a count of one hundred to a load inside two nested loops. An unpredictable if-then-else might decrease the execution count by half. In practice, these estimates ensure a bias toward spilling in outer loops rather than inner loops.

To estimate the cost of spilling a single reference, the allocator adds the cost of the address computation to the cost of the memory operation and multiplies that sum by the estimated execution frequency of the reference. For each live range, it sums the costs of the individual references. This requires a pass over all the blocks in the code. The allocator can precompute these costs for all live ranges, or it can wait until it discovers that it must spill at least one value.

13.5.3 Interferences and the Interference Graph

The fundamental effect that a global register allocator must model is the competition among values for space in the target machine's register set. Consider two distinct live ranges, LR_i and LR_j. If there is an operation in the program during which both LR_i and LR_j are live, they cannot reside in the same register. (In general, a physical register can hold only one value at a time.) We say that LR_i and LR_j *interfere*. Formally, LR_i and LR_j interfere if one is live at the definition of the other and they have different values.

To model the allocation problem, the compiler can build an *interference graph* $I = (N E)$, in which nodes in N represent individual live ranges and edges in E represent interferences between live ranges. Thus, an undirected edge $(n_i, n_j) \in I$ exists if and only if the corresponding live ranges LR_i and LR_j interfere. Figure 13.6 shows the code from Figure 13.5 along with its interference graph. LR_a interferes with each of the other live ranges. The rest of the live ranges, however, do not interfere with each other.

If the compiler can color I with k or fewer colors, then it can map the colors directly onto physical registers to produce a legal allocation. In the example, LR_a cannot receive the same color as LR_b, LR_c, or LR_d because it interferes with each of them. However, the other three live ranges can all share a single color

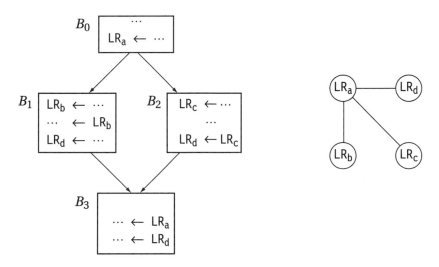

Code Fragment with Live-Range Names   Interference Graph

FIGURE 13.6   Live Ranges and Interference

because they do not interfere with each other. Thus, the interference graph is 2-colorable, and the code can be rewritten to use just two registers.

Consider what would happen if another phase of the compiler reordered the two operations at the end of B_1. This makes LR_b live at the definition of LR_d. The allocator must add the edge (LR_b, LR_d) to E, which makes it impossible to color the graph with just two colors. (The graph is small enough to prove this by enumeration.) To handle this graph, the allocator has two options: to use three registers, or, if the target machine has only two registers, to spill one of LR_b or LR_a before the definition of LR_d in B_1. Of course, the allocator could also reorder the two operations and eliminate the interference between LR_b and LR_d. Typically, register allocators do not reorder operations. Instead, allocators assume a fixed order of operations and leave ordering questions to the instruction scheduler (see Chapter 12).

Building the Interference Graph

Once the allocator has built global live ranges and annotated each basic block in the code with its LIVEOUT set, it can construct the interference graph in a simple linear pass over each block. Figure 13.7 shows the basic algorithm. As it walks the block, from bottom to top, the allocator computes the set of values that are live at the current operation. Since LIVENOW must equal the block's LIVEOUT set at the last operation in the block, the allocator initializes LIVENOW to LIVEOUT. As it works backward through the block, it adds the appropriate edges to E and updates LIVENOW.

```
for each LR i
    create a node n_i ∈ N
for each basic block b
    LIVENOW ← LIVEOUT (b)
    for o_n, o_{n-1}, o_{n-2}, ... o_1 in b
        with form op_i LR_a, LR_b ⇒ LR_c
        for each LR_i in LIVENOW
            add (LR_c, LR_i ) to E
        remove LR_c from LIVENOW
        add LR_a & LR_b to LIVENOW
```

FIGURE 13.7   Constructing the Interference Graph

The algorithm implements the definition of interference given earlier: LR_i and LR_j interfere only if one is live at a definition of the other. This definition allows the compiler to build the interference graph by adding, at each operation, an interference between the target of the operation, LR_c, and each live range that is live after the operation.

Copy operations require special treatment. The operation i2i $LR_i \Rightarrow LR_j$ does not create an interference between LR_i and LR_j, because these values can occupy the same register. This operation should not induce an edge (LR_i, LR_j). If some subsequent context forces an interference between these live ranges, that operation will create the edge. The same argument applies to ϕ-functions. Treating copies and ϕ-functions in this way gives the allocator a precise notion of when LR_i and LR_j can occupy the same register. The resulting interference graph can serve as the basis for a powerful coalescing phase that combines live ranges and eliminates unneeded copies (see Section 13.5.6).

To improve efficiency later in the allocator, the compiler should build both a lower-diagonal bit matrix and a set of adjacency lists to represent E. The bit matrix allows a constant-time test for interference, while the adjacency lists make iterating over a node's neighbors efficient. This takes more space than using a single representation, but the allocator performs both operations often enough to make this worthwhile. The compiler writer may also treat disjoint register classes as separate allocation problems to reduce both the size of E and the overall allocation time.

Building an Allocator

To build a global allocator based on the graph-coloring paradigm, the compiler writer needs two additional mechanisms. First, the allocator needs an efficient technique for discovering k-colorings. Unfortunately, the problem of determining whether a k-coloring exists for a particular graph is NP-complete. Thus, register allocators use fast approximations that are not guaranteed to find a k-coloring. Second, the allocator needs a strategy for handling the case when no color remains for a specific live range. Most coloring allocators approach this by rewriting the code to change the allocation problem. The allocator picks one or more live ranges to modify. It either spills or splits the chosen live ranges. Spilling turns the chosen live ranges into sets of tiny live ranges, one around each definition and use of each original live range. Splitting breaks each live range into smaller, but nontrivial, pieces. In either case, the transformed code performs the same computation but has a different interference graph (including more loads and stores). If the changes are effective, the new interference graph is k-colorable. If they are not, the allocator must spill more live ranges.

13.5.4 Top-Down Coloring

A top-down graph-coloring global register allocator uses low-level information to assign colors to individual live ranges and high-level information to select the order in which it colors live ranges. To find a color for a specific live range LR_i the allocator tallies the colors already assigned to LR_i's neighbors in I. If the set of neighbors' colors is incomplete—that is, one or more colors are not used—the allocator can assign an unused color to LR_i. If the set of neighbors' colors is complete, then no color is available for LR_i and the allocator must use its strategy for uncolored live ranges.

The top-down allocators try to color the live ranges in an order determined by some ranking function. The priority-based, top-down allocators assign each node a rank that is the estimated run-time savings that accrue from keeping that live range in a register. These estimates are analogous to the spill costs described in Section 13.5.2. The top-down global allocator uses registers for the most important values, as identified by these rankings.

The allocator considers the live ranges in rank order and attempts to assign a color to each of them. If no color is available for a live range, the allocator invokes the spilling or splitting mechanism to handle the uncolored live range. To improve the process, the allocator can partition the live ranges into two sets—constrained live ranges and unconstrained live ranges. A live range is *constrained* if it has k or more neighbors—that is, it has degree $\geq k$ in I. (We denote "degree of LR_i" as LR_i°, so LR_i is constrained if and only if $LR_i^\circ \geq k$.) Constrained live ranges are colored first, in rank order. After all constrained live ranges have been handled, the unconstrained live ranges are colored, in any order. Because an unconstrained live range has fewer than k neighbors, the allocator can always find a color for it; no assignment of colors to its neighbors can use all k colors.

By handling constrained live ranges first, the allocator avoids some potential spills. The alternative, working in a straight priority order, would let the allocator assign all available colors to unconstrained, but higher priority, neighbors of LR_i. This could force LR_i to remain uncolored, even though colorings of its unconstrained neighbors that leave a color for LR_i must exist.

Handling Spills

When the top-down allocator encounters a live range that cannot be colored, it must either spill or split some set of live ranges to change the problem. Since all previously colored live ranges were ranked higher than the uncolored live range, it makes sense to spill the uncolored live range rather than a previously colored one. The allocator can consider recoloring one of the previously colored live ranges, but it must exercise care to avoid the full generality and cost of backtracking.

To spill LR_i, the allocator inserts a store after every definition of LR_i and a load before each use of LR_i. If the memory operations need registers, the allocator can reserve enough registers to handle them. (For example, a register is needed to hold the spilled value when it is loaded before a use.) The number of registers needed for this purpose is a function of the target machine's instruction set architecture. Reserving these registers simplifies spilling.

An alternative to reserving registers for spill code is to look for free colors at each definition and use; this strategy can lead to a situation in which the allocator must retroactively spill a previously colored live range.[1] The paradox, of course, is that reserving registers for spilling may itself cause spills by effectively lowering k.

Splitting the Live Range

Spilling changes the coloring problem. An uncolored live range is broken into a series of tiny live ranges—so small that spilling them is counterproductive. A related way to change the problem is to take an uncolored live range and break it into pieces that are larger than a single reference. If these new live ranges interfere, individually, with fewer live ranges than the original live range, then the allocator may find colors for them. For example, if the new live ranges are unconstrained, colors must exist for them. This process, called *live-range splitting*, can lead to allocations that insert fewer loads and stores than would be needed to spill the entire live range.

The first top-down, priority-based coloring allocator, built by Chow, broke the uncolored live range into single-block live ranges, counted interferences for each resulting live range, and then recombined live ranges from adjacent blocks if the combined live range remained unconstrained. It placed an arbitrary upper limit on the number of blocks that a split live range could span. It inserted a load at the starting point of each split live range and a store at the live range's ending point. The allocator spilled any split live ranges that remained uncolored.

---

1. The allocator would recompute interferences at each spill site and compute the set of neighbors' colors for the spill site. If this process does not discover an available color at each spill site, the allocator spills the lowest-priority neighbor of the spill site. The potential for recursively spilling already colored live ranges has led most implementors of top-down, priority-based allocators to reserve spill registers instead.

13.5.5 Bottom-Up Coloring

Bottom-up graph-coloring register allocators use many of the same mechanisms as top-down global allocators. These allocators discover live ranges, build an interference graph, attempt to color it, and generate spill code when needed. The major distinction between top-down and bottom-up allocators lies in the mechanism used to order live ranges for coloring. While a top-down allocator uses high-level information to select an order for coloring, a bottom-up allocator computes an order from detailed structural knowledge about the interference graph. Such an allocator constructs a linear order in which to consider the live ranges and assign colors in that order.

To order the live ranges, a bottom-up, graph-coloring allocator relies on the fact that unconstrained live ranges are trivial to color. This fact plays a critical role in constructing an order for color assignment. Figure 13.8 shows a simple algorithm that computes such an order. The allocator repeatedly removes a node from the graph and places the node on a stack. It uses two distinct mechanisms to select the node to remove next. The first clause takes a node that is unconstrained in the graph from which it is removed. Because these nodes are unconstrained, the order in which they are removed does not matter. Removing an unconstrained node decreases the degree of each of its neighbors, possibly making them unconstrained as well. The second clause, invoked only when every remaining node is constrained, picks a node using some external criteria. When the loop halts, the graph is empty and the stack contains all the nodes in order of removal.

To color the graph, the allocator rebuilds the interference graph in the order represented by the stack—the reverse of the order in which the allocator removed them from the graph. It repeatedly pops a node n from the stack, inserts n and its edges back into I, and looks for a color that works for n. In pseudo-code, the algorithm is:

$$\textit{while (stack} \neq \emptyset \textit{)}$$
$$\textit{node} \leftarrow \textit{pop(stack)}$$
$$\textit{insert node and its edges into I}$$
$$\textit{color node}$$

To color a node n, the allocator tallies the colors of n's neighbors in the current approximation to I and assigns n an unused color.[2] If no color remains for n, it is left uncolored.

---

2. To pick a specific color, it can search in a consistent order each time, or it can assign colors in a round-robin fashion. In our experience, the mechanism used for color choice has little practical impact.

initialize stack to empty
while $(N \neq \emptyset)$
    if $\exists\, n \in N$ *with* $n° < k$
        then node $\leftarrow n$
        else node $\leftarrow n$ *picked from* N
    remove node and its edges from I
    push node onto stack

FIGURE 13.8   Computing a Bottom-Up Ordering

When the stack is empty, I has been rebuilt. If every node has a color, the allocator declares success and rewrites the code, replacing live-range names with physical registers. If any node remains uncolored, the allocator either spills the corresponding live range or splits it into smaller pieces. At this point, the classic bottom-up allocators rewrite the code to reflect the spills and splits and repeat the entire process—finding live ranges, building I, and coloring it. The process repeats until every node in I receives a color. Typically, the allocator halts in a couple of iterations. Of course, a bottom-up allocator could reserve registers for spilling, as described for the top-down allocator. This strategy would allow it to halt after a single pass.

Why Does This Work?

The bottom-up allocator inserts each node back into the graph from which it was removed. If the node representing LR_i was removed from I because it was unconstrained at the time, it is reinserted into an approximation to I in which it is also unconstrained. Thus, when the allocator inserts LR_i, it must have a color available for LR_i. The only nodes that can fail to receive colors, then, are nodes removed from I using the spill metric in the *else* clause in Figure 13.8. These nodes are inserted into a graph in which they have k or more neighbors. A color may exist for them. Assume that $n° > k$ when the allocator inserts it into I. Its neighbors cannot all have distinct colors, since they can have at most k colors. If they have precisely k colors, then the allocator finds no color for n. If, instead, they use fewer than k colors, then the allocator finds a color available for n.

The removal process determines the order in which nodes are colored. This order is crucial, in that it determines whether or not colors are available. For nodes removed from the graph because they are unconstrained, the order is unimportant with respect to the remaining nodes. The order may be important with respect to nodes already on the stack; after all, the current node may have been constrained until some of the earlier nodes were removed. For nodes removed from the graph by the *else* clause in Figure 13.8, the order is crucial. This clause executes only when every remaining node is constrained. Thus, the remaining nodes form one or more heavily connected subgraphs of I.

The heuristic used to pick the node is often called the *spill metric*. The original bottom-up graph-coloring allocator, built by Chaitin et al., used a simple spill metric. It picked the node that minimized the ratio of $\frac{cost}{degree}$, where *cost* is the estimated spill cost and *degree* refers to degree in the current graph. This metric picks a node that is relatively inexpensive to spill but lowers the degree of many other nodes. Many other spill metrics have been tried, including $\frac{cost}{degree^2}$, which emphasizes the impact on neighbors; straight *cost*, which emphasizes run-time speed; and minimizing the number of spill operations, which emphasizes code size. The first two, $\frac{cost}{degree}$ and $\frac{cost}{degree^2}$, attempt to balance cost and impact; the latter two, *cost* and spill operations, aim to optimize specific criteria. In practice, no single heuristic dominates the others. Since the actual coloring process is fast relative to building I, the allocator can try several colorings, each using a different spill metric, and retain the best result.

13.5.6 Coalescing Live Ranges to Reduce Degree

The compiler writer can build a powerful coalescing phase that uses the interference graph to determine when two live ranges that are connected by a copy can be *coalesced*, or combined. Consider the operation i2i $LR_i \Rightarrow LR_j$. If LR_i and LR_j do not otherwise interfere, the operation can be eliminated and all references to LR_j rewritten to use LR_i. Combining these live ranges has several beneficial effects. It eliminates the copy operation, making the code smaller and, potentially, faster. It reduces the degree of any LR_i that interfered with both LR_i and LR_j. It shrinks the set of live ranges, making I and many of the data structures related to I smaller. (In his thesis, Briggs shows examples where coalescing eliminates up to one-third of the live ranges.) Because these effects help in allocation, compilers often perform coalescing before the coloring stage in a global allocator.

Figure 13.9 shows an example. The original code appears on the left side, with lines to the right of the code that indicate the regions where each of the relevant values, LR_a, LR_b, and LR_c, are live. Even though LR_a overlaps both LR_b and LR_c, it interferes with neither of them because the source and destination of a copy do not interfere. Since LR_b is live at the definition of LR_c, they do interfere. Both copy operations are candidates for coalescing.

```
  add LRt, LRu ⇒ LRa                    add LRt,LRu  ⇒ LRab
       ...                    ⌐a             ...                    ⌐ab
  i2i LRa        ⇒ LRb        |  ⌐b                                 |
  i2i LRa        ⇒ LRc        ∟  |  ⌐c    i2i LRab       ⇒ LRc      |  ⌐c
                                 |  |                               |  |
       ...                       |  |          ...                  |  |
  add LRb,LRw  ⇒ LRx        ∟  |    add LRab,LRw ⇒ LRx        ∟  |
  add LRc,LRy  ⇒ LRz           ∟    add LRc,LRy  ⇒ LRz           ∟
```

Before Coalescing   After Coalescing LRa and LRb

FIGURE 13.9   Coalescing Live Ranges

The fragment on the right shows the result of coalescing LR_a and LR_b to produce LR_{ab}. Since LR_c is defined by a copy from LR_{ab}, they do not interfere. Combining LR_a and LR_b to form LR_{ab} lowered the degree of LR_c. In general, coalescing two live ranges cannot increase the degrees of any of their neighbors. It can decrease their degrees or leave their degrees unchanged, but it cannot increase their degrees.

To perform coalescing, the allocator walks each block and examines each copy operation in the block. Consider a copy i2i LR_i ⇒ LR_j. If LR_i and LR_j do not interfere $((LR_i, LR_j) \notin E)$, the allocator combines them, eliminates the copy, and updates I to reflect the combination. The allocator can conservatively update I by moving all edges from the node for LR_j to the node for LR_i—in effect, using LR_i as LR_{ij}. This update is not precise, but it lets the allocator continue coalescing. In practice, allocators coalesce every live range allowed by I, then rewrite the code, rebuild I, and try again. The process typically halts after a couple of rounds of coalescing.

The example illustrates the imprecision inherent in this conservative update to I. The update would leave an interference between LR_{ab} and LR_c when, in fact, that interference does not exist. Rebuilding I from the transformed code produces the precise interference graph, with no edge between LR_{ab} and LR_c, and allows the allocator to coalesce LR_{ab} and LR_c.

Because coalescing two live ranges can prevent subsequent coalescing of other live ranges, the order of coalescing matters. In principle, the compiler should coalesce the most frequently executed copies first. In practice, allocators coalesce copies in order by the loop nesting depth of the block where the copies are found. To implement this, the allocator can consider the basic blocks in order from most deeply nested to least deeply nested.

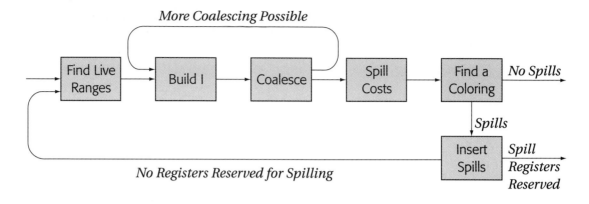

FIGURE 13.10   Structure of the Coloring Allocators

13.5.7 Review and Comparison

Both the top-down and the bottom-up coloring allocators have the same basic structure, shown in Figure 13.10. They find live ranges, build the interference graph, coalesce live ranges, compute spill costs on the coalesced version of the code, and attempt a coloring. The build-coalesce process is repeated until it finds no more opportunities. After coloring, one of two situations occurs. If every live range receives a color, then the code is rewritten using physical register names, and allocation terminates. If some live ranges remain uncolored, then spill code is inserted.

If the allocator has reserved registers for spilling, then it uses those registers in the spill code, rewrites the colored registers with their physical register names, and the process terminates. Otherwise, the allocator invents new virtual register names to use in spilling and inserts the necessary loads and stores to accomplish the spills. This changes the coloring problem slightly, so the entire allocation process is repeated on the transformed code. When each live range has a color, the allocator maps colors onto real registers and rewrites the code in its final form.

Of course, a top-down allocator could adopt the spill-and-iterate philosophy used in the bottom-up allocator. This would eliminate the need to reserve registers for spilling. Similarly, a bottom-up allocator could reserve several registers for spilling and eliminate the need for iterating the entire allocation process. Spill-and-iterate trades additional compile time for an allocation that, potentially, uses less spill code. Reserving registers produces an allocation that, potentially, contains more spills but requires less compile time to produce.

The top-down allocator uses its priority ranking to order all the constrained nodes. It colors the unconstrained nodes in arbitrary order, since the order cannot change the fact that they receive a color. The bottom-up allocator constructs an order in which most nodes are colored in a graph where they are unconstrained. Every node that the top-down allocator classifies as unconstrained is colored by the bottom-up allocator, since it is unconstrained in the original version of I and in each graph derived by removing nodes and edges from I. The bottom-up allocator, using its incremental mechanism for removing nodes and edges, classifies as unconstrained some of the nodes that the top-down allocator treats as constrained. These nodes may also be colored in the top-down allocator; there is no clear way of comparing their performance on these nodes without implementing both algorithms and running them.

The truly hard-to-color nodes are those that the bottom-up allocator removes from the graph with its spill metric. The spill metric is invoked only when every remaining node is constrained. These nodes form a strongly connected subgraph of I. In the top-down allocator, these nodes will be colored in an order determined by their rank or priority. In the bottom-up allocator, the spill metric uses that same ranking, moderated by a measurement of how many other nodes have their degree lowered by each choice. Thus, the top-down allocator chooses to spill low-priority, constrained nodes, while the bottom-up allocator spills nodes that are still constrained after all unconstrained nodes have been removed. From this latter set it picks nodes that minimize the spill metric.

13.5.8 Encoding Machine Constraints in the Interference Graph

Register allocation must deal with idiosyncratic properties of the target machine and its calling convention. Some of the constraints that arise in practice can be encoded in the coloring process.

Multiregister Values

Consider a target machine that requires an aligned pair of adjacent registers for each double-precision floating-point value and a program with two single-precision live ranges LR_a and LR_b and one double-precision live range LR_c.

With interferences (LR_a, LR_c) and (LR_b, LR_c), the techniques described in Section 13.5.3 produce the graph at left. Three registers, r_0, r_1, and r_2, with a single aligned pair, (r_0, r_1), should suffice for this graph. LR_a and LR_b can share r_2, leaving the pair (r_0, r_1) for LR_c. Unfortunately, this graph does not adequately represent the actual constraints on allocation.

Given $k = 3$, the bottom-up coloring allocator assigns colors in arbitrary order since no node has degree $\geq k$. If the allocator considers LR_c, first it will succeed, since (r_0,r_1) is free to hold LR_c. If either LR_a or LR_b is colored first, the allocator might use either r_0 or r_1, creating a situation in which the aligned register pair is not available for LR_c.

To force the appropriate order, the allocator can insert two edges to represent an interference with a value that needs two registers. This produces the graph at left. With this graph and $k = 3$, the bottom-up allocator must remove one of LR_a or LR_b first, since LR_c has degree 4. This ensures that two registers are available for LR_c.

The doubled edges produce a correct allocation because they match the degree of nodes that interfere with LR_c with the actual resource requirements. It does not ensure that an adjacent pair is available for LR_c. Poor assignment can leave LR_c without a pair. For example, in the coloring order LR_a, LR_c, LR_b, the allocator might assign LR_a to r_1. The compiler writer might bias the coloring order in favor of LR_c by choosing single-register values first among unconstrained nodes (the *then* clause in Figure 13.8). Another approach the allocator can take is to perform limited recoloring among LR_c's neighbors if an appropriate pair is not available when it tries to assign colors.

Specific Register Placement

The register allocator must also deal with requirements for the specific placement of live ranges. These constraints arise from several sources. Some operations may require their operands in particular registers; for example, the short unsigned multiply on the Intel x86 machines always writes its result into the AX register. The linkage convention dictates the placement of values that are passed in registers; this can include the ARP, some or all of the actual parameters, and the return value.

For example, if live range LR_x is passed as an actual parameter at a call site, the linkage convention might require that it reside in register r_3 across the call. Thus, we would like the allocator to assign LR_x to r_3. The compiler writer can encode such constraints in the interference graph by adding a node to N for each physical register and using edges to constrain the placement of values. For example, to force LR_x into r_3, the allocator can add an edge from LR_x to the node for every other physical register.

Of course, adding edges to physical registers can overconstrain the interference graph, forcing some of the constrained values to spill. If LR_x and LR_y are passed as parameters at different call sites and both must reside in r_3, the allocator can satisfy the constraint only if LR_x and LR_y do not interfere. The allocator must spill one or both values to produce an allocation and assignment that places each of them in r_3 across its respective call.

Another approach to this issue encodes the constraint in the code. Here, the compiler inserts a copy from LR_x to r_3 at the point where it evaluates LR_x as an argument. It does the same with LR_y when it appears as an argument. This creates small live ranges at the call sites that can be precolored to r_3. (Before assigning any colors, the allocator assigns these constrained live ranges to their mandated registers.) The allocator then relies on conservative coalescing or biased coloring to remove the copies if possible. If it cannot be removed, a copy may allow the allocator to avoid spilling an entire live range.

13.6   ADVANCED TOPICS

Because the cost of a misstep during register allocation can be high, algorithms for register allocation have received a great deal of attention. Many variations on the basic graph-coloring allocation techniques have been published. Section 13.6.1 describes several of these approaches. The global allocators, as described in this chapter, work well on many programs and many architectures. Section 13.6.2 describes three areas in register allocation where harder problems arise.

13.6.1   Variations on Graph-Coloring Allocation

Many variations on these two basic styles of graph-coloring register allocation have appeared in the literature. This section describes several of these improvements. Some address the cost of allocation. Others address the quality of allocation.

Imprecise Interference Graphs

Chow's top-down, priority-based allocator used an imprecise notion of interference: live ranges LR_i and LR_j interfere if both are live in the same basic block. This makes building the interference graph faster. However, the imprecise nature of the graph overestimates the degree of some nodes and prevents the allocator from using the interference graph as a basis for coalescing. (In an imprecise graph, two live ranges connected by a useful copy interfere because they are live in the same block.) The allocator also included a prepass to perform local allocation on values that are live in only one block.

Breaking the Graph into Smaller Pieces

If the interference graph can be separated into components that are not connected, those disjoint components can be colored independently. Since the size of the bit matrix is $O(N^2)$, breaking it into independent components saves both space and time. One way to split the graph is to consider nonoverlapping register classes separately, as with floating-point registers and integer registers. A more complex alternative for large procedures is to discover clique separators, connected subgraphs whose removal divides the interference graph into several disjoint pieces. For large enough graphs, using a hash table instead of the bit matrix may improve both speed and space.

Conservative Coalescing

When the allocator coalesces two live ranges, LR_i and LR_j, the new live range, LR_{ij}, may be more constrained than either LR_i or LR_j. If LR_i and LR_j have distinct neighbors, then $LR_{ij}^{\circ} > \max(LR_i^{\circ}, LR_j^{\circ})$. If $LR_{ij}^{\circ} < k$, then creating LR_{ij} is strictly beneficial. However, if $LR_i^{\circ} < k$ and $LR_j^{\circ} < k$, but $LR_{ij}^{\circ} \geq k$, then coalescing LR_i and LR_j can make I harder to color without spilling. To avoid this problem, some compiler writers have used a limited form of coalescing called *conservative coalescing*. In this scheme, the allocator combines LR_i and LR_j only when $LR_{ij}^{\circ} < k$. This ensures that coalescing LR_i and LR_j does not make the interference graph harder to color.

If the allocator uses conservative coalescing, another improvement is possible. When the allocator reaches a point at which every remaining live range is constrained, the basic algorithm selects a spill candidate. An alternative approach is to reapply coalescing at this point. Live ranges that were not coalesced because of the degree of the resulting live range may well coalesce in the reduced graph. Coalescing may reduce the degree of nodes that interfere with both the source and destination of the copy. Thus, this *iterated coalescing* can remove additional copies and reduce the degrees of nodes. It may create one or more unconstrained nodes and allow coloring to proceed. If it does not create any unconstrained nodes, spilling proceeds as before.

Biased coloring is another approach to coalescing copies making the graph harder to color. In this approach, the allocator tries to assign the same color to live ranges that are connected by a copy. In picking a color for LR_i, it first tries colors that have been assigned to live ranges connected to LR_j by a copy operation. If it can assign them both the same color, the allocator eliminates the copy. With a careful implementation, this adds little or no expense to the color selection process.

Spilling Partial Live Ranges

As described, both approaches to global allocation spill entire live ranges. This approach can lead to overspilling if the demand for registers is low through most of the live range and high in a small region. More sophisticated spilling techniques find the regions where spilling a live range is productive—that is, the spill frees a register in a region where a register is truly needed. The splitting scheme described for the top-down allocator achieved this result by considering each block in the spilled live range separately. In a bottom-up allocator, similar results can be achieved by spilling only in the region where interference occurs. One technique, called *interference-region spilling*, identifies a set of live ranges that interfere in the region of high demand and limits spilling to that region. The allocator can estimate the cost of several spilling strategies for the interference region and compare those costs against the standard spill-everywhere approach. By letting the alternatives compete on an estimated-cost basis, the allocator can improve overall allocation.

Live-Range Splitting

Breaking a live range into pieces can improve the results of coloring-based register allocation. In principle, splitting harnesses two distinct effects. If the split live ranges have lower degrees than the original one, they may be easier to color—possibly even unconstrained. If some of the split live ranges have high degree and, therefore, spill, then splitting may prevent spilling other portions of the same live range that have lower degree. As a final, pragmatic effect, splitting introduces spills at the points where the live range is broken. Careful selection of the split points can control the placement of some spill code—for example, outside loops rather than inside them.

Many approaches to splitting have been tried. Section 13.5.4 describes an approach that breaks a live range into blocks and coalesces them back together if doing so does not change the allocator's ability to assign a color. Several approaches that use properties of the control-flow graph to choose splitting points have been tried. Briggs showed that many have been inconsistent [45]; however, two particular techniques show promise. A method called *zero-cost splitting* capitalizes on nops in the instruction schedule to split live ranges and improve both allocation and scheduling. A technique called *passive splitting* uses a directed interference graph to determine where splits should occur and selects between splitting and spilling based on their estimated costs.

Rematerialization

Some values cost less to recompute than to spill. For example, small integer constants should be recreated with a load immediate rather than being retrieved from memory with a load. The allocator can recognize such values and rematerialize them rather than spill them.

Modifying a bottom-up graph-coloring allocator to perform rematerialization takes several small changes. The allocator must identify and tag SSA names that can be rematerialized. For example, any operation whose arguments are always available is a candidate. It can propagate these rematerialization tags over the code using one of the constant-propagation algorithms described in Chapter 10. In forming live ranges, the allocator should only combine SSA names that have identical rematerialization tags.

The compiler writer must make the spill-cost estimation handle rematerialization tags correctly, so that these values have accurate spill-cost estimates. The spill-code insertion process must also examine the tags and generate the appropriate lightweight spills for rematerializable values. Finally, the allocator should use conservative coalescing to avoid prematurely combining live ranges with distinct rematerialization tags.

13.6.2 Harder Problems in Register Allocation

This chapter has presented a selection of algorithms that attack problems in register allocation. Many harder problems remain; there is room for improvement on several fronts.

Whole-Program Allocation

The algorithms presented in this chapter all consider register allocation within the context of a single procedure. Of course, whole programs are built from multiple procedures. If global allocation produces better results than local allocation by considering a larger scope, then should the compiler writer consider performing allocation across entire programs? Whole-program optimization has the potential to move spills across procedure boundaries, in effect customizing the procedure-call convention and eliminating saves and restores.

However, the allocation problem changes significantly when it extends from single procedures to entire programs. Any whole-program allocation scheme must deal with each of the following issues.

To perform whole-program allocation, the allocator must have access to the code for the entire program. In practice, this means performing whole-program allocation at link time. (While whole-program analyses and transformations can be applied before link time, many issues that complicate an implementation of such techniques can be effectively sidestepped by performing them at link time.)

The compiler needs accurate estimates of the relative execution frequencies of all parts of the program for whole-program allocation. Within a procedure, static estimates (such as "a loop executes 10 times") have proven to be reasonable approximations to actual behavior. Across the entire program, such simple estimators may not provide good approximations to actual behavior.

A whole-program allocator must also deal with parameter-binding mechanisms. Call-by-reference parameters can link otherwise independent live ranges in distinct procedures together into a single interprocedural live range. This effect can complicate allocation by placing too many constraints on these interprocedural live ranges.

Partitioned Register Sets

New complications can arise from new hardware features. For example, consider the nonuniform costs that arise on machines with partitioned register sets. As the number of functional units rises, the number of registers required to hold operands and results rises. Limitations arise in the hardware logic required to move values between registers and functional units. To keep hardware costs manageable, some architects have partitioned the register set into smaller register files and clustered functional units around these register sets. To retain generality, the processor typically provides some limited mechanism for moving values between clusters. Figure 13.11 shows an abstract view of such a processor. Assume, without loss of generality, that each cluster has an identical set of functional units and registers, except for their distinct names.

Machines with clustered register sets layer a new set of complications onto the register-assignment problem. In deciding where to place LR_i in the register set, the allocator must deal with the availability of registers in each cluster, the cost and local availability of the intercluster transfer mechanism, and the specific functional units that will execute the operations that reference LR_i. For example, the processor might allow each cluster to generate one off-cluster register reference per cycle, with a limit of one off-cluster transfer out of each cluster each cycle. With this constraint, the allocator must pay attention to the

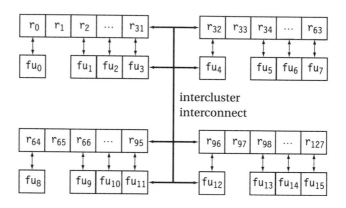

FIGURE 13.11   A Clustered Register-Set Machine

placement of operations in clusters and in time. (Clearly, this problem requires attention from both the instruction scheduler and the register allocator.) Some architectures allow a register-to-register copy operation that moves a value between clusters, with limitations on the number of values moving in and out of each cluster in a single cycle. On such systems, cross-cluster use of a value requires extra instructions; if done on the critical path, this can lengthen overall execution time.

Ambiguous Values

In code that makes heavy use of ambiguous values, the allocator's ability or inability to keep such values in registers is a serious performance issue. To improve allocation of ambiguous values, several systems have included transformations that rewrite the code to keep unambiguous values in scalar local variables, even when their "natural" home is inside an array element or a pointer-based structure. *Scalar replacement* uses array-subscript analysis to identify reuse of array-element values and to introduce scalar temporary variables that hold reused values. *Register promotion* uses data-flow analysis of pointer values to determine when a pointer-based value can safely be kept in a register throughout a loop nest and to rewrite the code so that the value is kept in a newly introduced temporary variable. Both of these transformations encode the results of analysis into the shape of the code, making it obvious to the register allocator that these values can be kept in registers. These transformations can increase the demand for registers. In fact, promoting too many values can produce spill code whose cost exceeds the the cost of the memory operations that the transformation is intended to avoid. Ideally, these techniques should be integrated into the allocator in which realistic estimates of the demand for registers can be used to determine how many values to promote.

13.7 SUMMARY AND PERSPECTIVE

Because register allocation is an important component of a modern compiler, it has received much attention in the literature. Strong techniques exist for local allocation, for global allocation, and for regional allocation. Because the underlying problems are almost all NP-hard, the solutions tend to be sensitive to small decisions, such as how ties between identically ranked choices are broken.

Progress in register allocation has come from the use of paradigms that give us leverage on the problem. Thus, graph-coloring allocators have been popular, not because register allocation is identical to graph coloring, but rather because coloring captures some of the critical aspects of the global allocation problem. In fact, most of the improvements to coloring allocators have come from attacking the points where the coloring paradigm does not accurately reflect the underlying problem, such as better cost models and improved methods for live-range splitting.

CHAPTER NOTES

Register allocation, as a problem, dates to the earliest compilers. Backus reports that Best invented the algorithm that we call "bottom-up local" in the mid-1950s, during the development of the original FORTRAN compiler [26, 25]. Best's algorithm has been rediscovered and reused in many contexts over the years [33, 173, 109, 237]. Its best-known incarnation is probably Belady's offline page-replacement algorithm [33]. The complications that arise from having a combination of clean values and dirty values are described by Horwitz [186] and by Kennedy [202]. Liberatore et al. suggest spilling clean values before dirty values as a practical compromise [237]. The example showing the problems that arise with clean values and dirty values (in Section 13.3.2) was suggested by Ken Kennedy.

The first graph-coloring global allocator described in the literature was a bottom-up allocator built by Chaitin and his colleagues at IBM for the PL.8 compiler [70, 68, 69]. It, in turn, built on the connection between graph coloring and storage-allocation problems that was originally suggested by Lavrov [232]; these ideas were used in the Alpha compiler project to pack data into memory [132, 133]. Schwartz describes early algorithms by both Ershov and Cocke [300]; these algorithms focus on reducing the number of colors used and ignore spilling.

Top-down graph coloring begins with Chow [76, 77, 78]. His implementation worked from a memory-to-memory model, used an imprecise interference graph, and performed live-range splitting as described in Section 13.5.4. The imprecise interference graph cannot support coalescing, so the compiler used a separate optimization pass to coalesce copies [76]. This style of allocation has been used in several compilers from MIPS, Silicon Graphics, and in the Gnu compiler, gcc. Larus and Hilfinger built a top-down, priority-based allocator for SPUR LISP that used a precise interference graph and operated from a register-to-register model [231].

The bottom-up allocator in Section 13.5.5 follows Chaitin's plan, as modified by Briggs [48, 49, 53]. Chaitin's contributions include the fundamental definition of interference and the algorithms for building the interference graph, for coalescing, and for handling spills. Briggs modified Chaitin's scheme by pushing constrained live ranges onto the stack rather than spilling them directly; this allowed Briggs's allocator to color a node with many neighbors that used few colors. Other significant improvements in bottom-up coloring have included better spill metrics, clean spilling, and best-of-three spilling [36], interference-region spilling [35], methods for rematerializing simple values [52], iterated coalescing [153], optimistic coalescing [270], methods for spilling partial live ranges [35], and methods for live-range splitting, such as zero-cost splitting [225] and passive splitting [100]. The large size of precise interference graphs led Gupta, Soffa, and Steele to work on splitting the graph with clique separators [168]. Harvey proposed splitting the graph by register classes [94]. Chaitin, Nickerson, and Briggs all discuss adding edges to the interference graph to model specific constraints on assignment [70, 266, 51].

Optimizations that rewrite the code to improve register allocation have been shown to be effective at reducing memory traffic. Carr's scalar replacement transformation [61, 65] uses data-dependence analysis to find array-based references that can be rewritten as scalars. Register promotion [244, 296, 241] uses data-flow analysis of pointers to rewrite pointer-based references in a similar way.

This chapter has focused on local and global allocation. Several authors have looked at allocation over regions that lie between a single block and a whole procedure. Koblenz and Callahan describe a hierarchical coloring allocator in their compiler for the Tera computer [63]. Knobe and Meltzer built an allocator with similar properties for the Compass compiler; it built a control tree and performed allocation in two passes over that tree [214]. Proebsting and Fischer developed a probabilistic approach [279]. The fusion-based technique is due to Lueh, Adl-Tabatabai, and Gross [247].

APPENDIX A

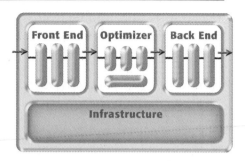

ILOC

INTRODUCTION

ILOC is the linear assembly code for a simple abstract RISC machine. The ILOC used in this book is a simplified version of the intermediate representation used in the Massively Scalar Compiler Project (MSCP) at Rice University. For example, the ILOC in this book does not differentiate between different types of numbers; they assume, for simplicity, that all numbers are integers. (Some of the examples assume that a data item is 64 bits; others assume 32 bits. The distinction, it if matters, should be clear from the example.)

The ILOC abstract machine has an unlimited number of registers. It has three-address, register-to-register operations, load and store operations, comparison operations, and branches. It supports just a few simple addressing modes—direct, address + offset, address + immediate, and immediate. Source operands are read at the beginning of the cycle when the operation issues. Result operands are defined at the end of the cycle in which the operation completes.

Other than its instruction set, the details of the machine are left unspecified. Most of the examples assume a simple machine, with a single functional unit that executes ILOC operations in their order of appearance. When other models are used, we discuss them explicitly.

An ILOC program consists of a sequential list of instructions. Each instruction may be preceded by a label. A label is just a textual string; it is separated from the instruction by a colon. By convention, we limit ourselves to labels of the form [*a–z*] ([*a–z*] | [0–9] | –)*. If some instruction needs more than one label, we insert an instruction that only contains a nop before it, and place the extra label on the nop. To define an ILOC program more formally,

$$
\begin{array}{rcl}
IlocProgram & \rightarrow & InstructionList \\
InstructionList & \rightarrow & Instruction \\
& | & \texttt{label} : Instruction \\
& | & Instruction\ InstructionList
\end{array}
$$

Each instruction contains one or more operations. A single-operation instruction is written on a line of its own, while a multioperation instruction can span several lines. To group operations into a single instruction, we enclose them in square brackets and separate them with semicolons. More formally:

$$
\begin{array}{rcl}
Instruction & \rightarrow & Operation \\
& | & [\ OperationList\ ] \\
OperationList & \rightarrow & Operation \\
& | & Operation\ \texttt{;}\ OperationList
\end{array}
$$

An ILOC operation corresponds to a machine-level instruction that might be issued to a single functional unit in a single cycle. It has an opcode, a sequence of comma-separated source operands, and a sequence of comma-separated target operands. The sources are separated from the targets by the symbol ⇒, pronounced "into."

$$
\begin{array}{rcl}
Operation & \rightarrow & NormalOp \\
& | & ControlFlowOp \\
NormalOp & \rightarrow & Opcode\ OperandList \Rightarrow OperandList \\
OperandList & \rightarrow & Operand \\
& | & Operand\ \texttt{,}\ OperandList \\
Operand & \rightarrow & \texttt{register} \\
& | & \texttt{num} \\
& | & \texttt{label}
\end{array}
$$

The nonterminal *Opcode* can be any ILOC operation, except cbr, jump, or jumpI. Unfortunately, as in a real assembly language, the relationship between an opcode and the form of its operands is less than systematic. The easiest way to specify the form of the operands for each opcode is in a tabular form. The tables that occur later in this appendix show the number of operands and their types for each ILOC opcode used in the book.

*Operand*s come in three types: register, num, and label. The type of each operand is determined by the opcode and the position of the operand in the operation. In the examples, we use both numerical (r_{10}) and symbolic (r_i) names for registers. Numbers are simple integers, signed if necessary. We always begin a label with an l to make its type obvious. This is a convention rather than a rule. ILOC simulators and tools should treat any string of the form described above as a potential label.

Most operations have a single target operand; some of the store operations have multiple target operands, as do the branches. For example, storeAI has a single source operand and two target operands. The source must be a register, and the targets must be a register and an immediate constant. Thus, the ILOC operation

$$\text{storeAI } r_i \Rightarrow r_j, 4$$

computes an address by adding 4 to the contents of r_j and stores the value found in r_i into the memory location specified by the address. In other words,

$$\text{MEMORY}(r_j + 4) \leftarrow \text{CONTENTS}(r_i)$$

Control-flow operations have a slightly different syntax. Since they do not define their targets, we write them with the single arrow $\rightarrow$, instead of $\Rightarrow$.

$$
\begin{array}{rclcl}
ControlFlowOp & \rightarrow & \text{cbr} & \text{register} \rightarrow & \text{label , label} \\
& | & \text{jumpI} & \rightarrow & \text{label} \\
& | & \text{jump} & \rightarrow & \text{register}
\end{array}
$$

The first operation, cbr, implements a conditional branch. The other two are unconditional branches, called jumps.

A.2 NAMING CONVENTIONS

The ILOC code in the text examples uses a simple set of naming conventions.

1. Memory offsets for variables are represented symbolically by prefixing the variable name with the @ character.

2. The user can assume an unlimited supply of registers. These are named with simple integers, as in r_{1776}, or with symbolic names, as in r_i.

3. The register r_0 is reserved as a pointer to the current activation record. We often write r_{arp} instead of r_0, as a reminder. Thus, the operation

$$\text{loadAI} r_0, @x \Rightarrow r_1$$

loads the contents of the variable x into r_1. The use of r_0 exposes the fact that x is stored in the current activation record. Of course, this is the same as $\text{loadAI } r_{arp}, @x \Rightarrow r_1$.

ILOC comments begin with the string // and continue until the end of a line. We assume that these are stripped out by the scanner; thus they can occur anywhere in an instruction and are not mentioned in the grammar.

A.3 INDIVIDUAL OPERATIONS

The examples in the book use a limited set of ILOC operations. The table at the end of this appendix shows the full set of ILOC operations used in the book, except for the alternate branch syntax used to discuss some branching constructs in Chapter 7.

A.3.1 Arithmetic

To support arithmetic, ILOC provides a basic set of three-address, register-to-register operations.

Opcode	Sources	Targets	Meaning
add	r_1, r_2	r_3	$r_1 + r_2 \Rightarrow r_3$
sub	r_1, r_2	r_3	$r_1 - r_2 \Rightarrow r_3$
mult	r_1, r_2	r_3	$r_1 \times r_2 \Rightarrow r_3$
div	r_1, r_2	r_3	$r_1 \div r_2 \Rightarrow r_3$

These assume that the source operands are in registers. They write the result back to a register. Any register can serve as a source or destination operand.

It is often useful to specify an immediate operand. Thus, each arithmetic operation is supported in an immediate form, or two for the noncommutative ones.

Opcode	Sources	Targets	Meaning
addI	r_1, c_1	r_2	$r_1 + c_1 \Rightarrow r_2$
subI	r_1, c_1	r_2	$r_1 - c_1 \Rightarrow r_2$
rsubI	r_1, c_1	r_2	$c_1 - r_1 \Rightarrow r_2$
multI	r_1, c_1	r_2	$r_1 \times c_1 \Rightarrow r_2$
divI	r_1, c_1	r_2	$r_1 \div c_1 \Rightarrow r_2$
rdivI	r_1, c_1	r_2	$c_1 \div r_1 \Rightarrow r_2$

These forms are useful to express the results of certain optimizations, to write down examples more concisely, and to record obvious ways to reduce demand for registers.

Note that in a real compiler using ILOC, we would need to introduce more than one data type. This would lead to typed opcodes or to polymorphic opcodes. Our preference would be for a family of typed opcodes—an integer add, a floating-point add, and so on. The MSCP compiler, where ILOC originated, has distinct arithmetic operations for integer, single-precision floating-point, double-precision floating-point, complex, and pointer data, but not for character data.

A.3.2 Shifts

ILOC supports a set of arithmetic shift operations—to the left and to the right, in both register and immediate forms.

Opcode	Sources	Targets	Meaning
lshift	r_1, r_2	r_3	$r_1 \ll r_2 \Rightarrow r_3$
lshiftI	r_1, c_2	r_3	$r_1 \ll c_2 \Rightarrow r_3$
rshift	r_1, r_2	r_3	$r_1 \gg r_2 \Rightarrow r_3$
rshiftI	r_1, c_2	r_3	$r_1 \gg c_2 \Rightarrow r_3$

A.3.3 Memory Operations

To move values between memory and registers, ILOC supports a full set of load and store operations. The load and cload operations move data items from memory to registers.

Opcode	Sources	Targets	Meaning
load	r_1	r_2	MEMORY $(r_1) \Rightarrow r_2$
loadAI	r_1, c_1	r_2	MEMORY $(r_1 + c_1) \Rightarrow r_2$
loadAO	r_1, r_2	r_3	MEMORY $(r_1 + r_2) \Rightarrow r_3$
cload	r_1	r_2	character load
cloadAI	r_1, r_2	r_3	character loadAI
cloadAO	r_1, r_2	r_3	character loadAO

The operations differ in the addressing modes that they support. The load and cload forms assume that the full address is in the single register operand. The loadAI and cloadAI forms add an immediate value to the contents of the register. We call these *address-immediate* operations. The loadAO and cloadAO forms add the contents of two registers to compute an effective address before performing the load. We call these *address-offset* operations.

As a final form of load, ILOC supports a simple load immediate operation. It takes an integer from the instruction stream and places it in a register.

Opcode	Sources	Targets	Meaning
loadI	c_1	r_2	$c_1 \Rightarrow r_2$

A complete, ILOC-like IR should have a load immediate for each distinct kind of value that it supports.

The store operations match the load operations. ILOC supports both numerical stores and character stores in its simple register form, in the address-immediate form, and in the address-offset form.

Opcode	Sources	Targets	Meaning
store	r_1	r_2	$r_1 \Rightarrow$ MEMORY (r_2)
storeAI	r_1	r_2, c_1	$r_1 \Rightarrow$ MEMORY $(r_2 + c_1)$
storeAO	r_1	r_2, r_3	$r_1 \Rightarrow$ MEMORY $(r_2 + r_3)$
cstore	r_1	r_2	character store
cstoreAI	r_1	r_2, r_3	character storeAI
cstoreAO	r_1	r_2, r_3	character storeAO

There is no store immediate operation.

A.3.4   Register-to-Register Copy Operations

To move values between registers, without going though memory, ILOC includes a set of register-to-register copy operations.

Opcode	Sources	Targets	Meaning
i2i	r_1	r_2	$r_1 \Rightarrow r_2$, for numbers
c2c	r_1	r_2	$r_1 \Rightarrow r_2$, for characters
c2i	r_1	r_2	converts character to integer
i2c	r_1	r_2	converts integer to character

The first two operations, i2i and c2c, copy a value from one register to another, with no conversion. The former is for use with integer values, while the latter is for characters. The last two operations perform conversions between characters and integers, replacing a character by its ordinal position in the ASCII character set and replacing an integer with the corresponding ASCII character.

A.4 AN EXAMPLE

To make this discussion more concrete, let's work through the example used in Chapter 1, shown again in Figure A.1. To start, notice the comments on the right end of each line. In our ILOC- based systems, comments are automatically generated by the compiler's front end to make the ILOC code more readable by humans. Since the examples in this book are intended primarily for humans to read, we continue to annotate the ILOC.

Remember, however, that the compiler cannot read the comments. Thus, the comment in

$$\text{jump} \rightarrow r_{12} \text{ // back to top of loop}$$

assists the human reader, but does not help the compiler determine what labels the jump targets.

The example assumes that w, x, y, and z are all stored in the local activation record, at fixed offsets from the ARP. The first instruction is a loadAI operation, or a *load address-immediate*. From the opcode table, we can see that it combines the contents of r_{arp} with the immediate constant @w and retrieves the value found in memory at that address; that value is w. It places the retrieved value in r_w. The next instruction is a loadI operation, or a *load immediate*. It moves the value 2 into r_2. (Effectively, it reads a constant from the instruction

1.	loadAI r_{arp}, @w $\Rightarrow$ r_w	// w is at offset 0 from r_{arp}
2.	loadAI 2 $\Rightarrow$ r_2	// constant 2 into r_2
3.	loadAI r_{arp}, @x $\Rightarrow$ r_x	// x is at offset 8
4.	loadAI r_{arp}, @y $\Rightarrow$ r_y	// y is at offset 12
5.	loadAI r_{arp}, @z $\Rightarrow$ r_z	// z is at offset 16
6.	mult r_w, r_2 $\Rightarrow$ r_w	// $r_w \leftarrow$ w $\times$ 2
7.	mult r_w, r_x $\Rightarrow$ r_w	// $r_w \leftarrow$ (w $\times$ 2) $\times$ x
8.	mult r_w, r_y $\Rightarrow$ r_w	// $r_w \leftarrow$ (w $\times$ 2 $\times$ x) $\times$ y
9.	mult r_w, r_z $\Rightarrow$ r_w	// $r_w \leftarrow$ (w $\times$ 2 $\times$ x $\times$ y) $\times$ z
10.	storeAI r_w $\Rightarrow$ r_{arp}, @w	// write r_w back to 'w'

FIGURE A.1 Introductory Example, Revisited

stream into a register.) Instructions three through five load the values of x into r_x, y into r_y, and z into r_z.

The sixth instruction multiplies the contents of r_w and r_2, storing the result back into r_w. Instruction seven multiplies this quantity by r_x. Instruction eight multiplies it by r_y, and instruction nine multiplies it by r_z. In each instruction from six through nine, the value is accumulated into r_w.

The final instruction saves the value of r_w to memory. It uses storeAI, or *store address-immediate*, to write the contents of r_w into the memory location at offset @w from r_{arp}. As pointed out in Chapter 1, this sequence evaluates the expression $w \leftarrow w \times 2 \times x \times y \times z$.

A.5 | CONTROL-FLOW OPERATIONS

In general, the ILOC comparison operators take two values and return a boolean value. If the specified relationship holds between its operands, the comparison sets the target register to the value true; otherwise the target register receives false.

Opcode	Sources	Targets	Meaning	
cmp_LT	r_1, r_2	r_3	true $\Rightarrow r_3$	if $r_1 < r_2$
			false $\Rightarrow r_3$	otherwise
cmp_LE	r_1, r_2	r_3	true $\Rightarrow r_3$	if $r_1 \leq r_2$
			false $\Rightarrow r_3$	otherwise
cmp_EQ	r_1, r_2	r_3	true $\Rightarrow r_3$	if $r_1 = r_2$
			false $\Rightarrow r_3$	otherwise
cmp_GE	r_1, r_2	r_3	true $\Rightarrow r_3$	if $r_1 \geq r_2$
			false $\Rightarrow r_3$	otherwise
cmp_GT	r_1, r_2	r_3	true $\Rightarrow r_3$	if $r_1 > r_2$
			false $\Rightarrow r_3$	otherwise
cmp_NE	r_1, r_2	r_3	true $\Rightarrow r_3$	if $r_1 \neq r_2$
			false $\Rightarrow r_3$	otherwise

The result of a comparison can be used to change control flow by using the conditional branch operation.

Opcode	Sources	Targets	Meaning
cbr	r_1	l_1, l_2	$l_1 \rightarrow$ PC if $r_1 =$ true
			$l_2 \rightarrow$ PC if $r_1 =$ false

The conditional branch operation takes a boolean as its argument and transfers control to one of two target labels. The first label is selected if the boolean is true; the second is selected if the boolean is false. Because the two branch targets are not "defined" by the instruction, we change the syntax slightly. Rather than use the arrow $\Rightarrow$, we write branches with the single arrow $\rightarrow$.

Using two labels on the conditional branch has two advantages. First, the code is somewhat more concise. In some situations, a conditional branch with only one label might need a subsequent jump. The two-label branch encodes that same combination in a single operation. Second, the code is easier to manipulate. A single-label branch depends on the layout of the code. It implicitly connects the block containing the branch with the block on the fall-through path. With single-label branches, the compiler must preserve these relationships.

The two-label conditional branch makes this implicit connection explicit and removes any possible positional dependence. This gives the compiler the freedom to lay out branches and blocks in the order that it expects to minimize execution time. Finally, it simplifies the construction of the control-flow graph.

A.5.1 Alternate Comparison and Branch Syntax

In Chapter 7, we discuss what happens when a comparison returns a value written into a condition-code register. The condition code is a value that can only be interpreted with a more complex conditional branch instruction. To talk about this mechanism, we use an alternate set of comparison and conditional branch operations.

Opcode	Sources	Targets	Meaning	
comp	r_1, r_2	cc_1	sets cc_1	
cbr_LT	cc_1	l_1, l_2	$l_1 \rightarrow$ PC	if $cc_1 =$ LT
			$l_2 \rightarrow$ PC	otherwise
cbr_LE	cc_1	l_1, l_2	$l_1 \rightarrow$ PC	if $cc_1 =$ LE
			$l_2 \rightarrow$ PC	otherwise
cbr_EQ	cc_1	l_1, l_2	$l_1 \rightarrow$ PC	if $cc_1 =$ EQ
			$l_2 \rightarrow$ PC	otherwise
cbr_GE	cc_1	l_1, l_2	$l_1 \rightarrow$ PC	if $cc_1 =$ GE
			$l_2 \rightarrow$ PC	otherwise
cbr_GT	cc_1	l_1, l_2	$l_1 \rightarrow$ PC	if $cc_1 =$ GT
			$l_2 \rightarrow$ PC	otherwise
cbr_NE	cc_1	l_1, l_2	$l_1 \rightarrow$ PC	if $cc_1 =$ NE
			$l_2 \rightarrow$ PC	otherwise

Here, the comparison operator, comp, takes two values and sets the condition code appropriately. We always designate the target of comp as a condition-code register by writing it cc_i. The corresponding conditional branch has six variants, one for each comparison result.

A.5.2 Jumps

ILOC includes two forms of the jump operation. The form used in almost all the examples is an immediate jump that transfers control to a literal label. The second, a jump-to-register operation, takes a single register operand. It interprets contents of the register as a run-time address and transfers control to that address.

Opcode	Sources	Targets	Meaning
jumpI	none	l_1	$l_1 \rightarrow$ PC
jump	none	r_1	$r_1 \rightarrow$ PC

The jump-to-register form is an ambiguous control-flow transfer. Once it has been generated, the compiler may be unable to deduce the correct set of target labels for the jump. For this reason, the compiler should avoid using jump to register, if possible.

Sometimes, the gyrations needed to avoid a jump to register are so complex that jump to register becomes attractive, despite its problems. For example, FORTRAN includes a construct that jumps to a label variable; implementing it with immediate branches would require logic similar to a case statement—a series of immediate branches, along with code to match the run-time value of the label variable against the set of possible labels. In such circumstances, the compiler should probably use a jump to register.

To reduce the loss of information from jump to register, ILOC includes a pseudo-operation that lets the compiler record the set of possible labels for a jump to register. The tbl operation has two arguments, a register and an immediate label.

Opcode	Sources	Targets	Meaning
tbl	r_1, l_2	—	r_1 might hold l_2

A tbl operation can occur only after a jump. The compiler interprets a set of one or more tbls as naming all the possible labels for the register. Thus, the following sequence asserts that the jump targets one of L01, L03, L05, or L08.

```
jump            →r_i
tbl  r_i, L01
tbl  r_i, L03
tbl  r_i, L05
tbl  r_i, L08
```

A.6 REPRESENTING SSA FORM

When a compiler constructs the SSA form of a program from its IR version, it needs a way to represent ϕ-functions. In ILOC, the natural way to write a ϕ-function is as an ILOC operation. Thus, we will sometimes write

$$\text{phi } r_i, r_j, r_k \Rightarrow r_m$$

for the ϕ-function $r_m \leftarrow \phi(r_i, r_j, r_k)$. Because of the nature of SSA form, the phi operation may take an arbitrary number of sources. It always defines a single target.

ILOC Opcode Summary

Opcode	Sources	Targets	Meaning
nop	None	None	Used as a placeholder
add	r_1, r_2	r_3	$r_1 + r_2 \Rightarrow r_3$
addI	r_1, c_1	r_2	$r_1 + c_1 \Rightarrow r_2$
sub	r_1, r_2	r_3	$r_1 - r_2 \Rightarrow r_3$
subI	r_1, c_1	r_2	$r_1 - c_1 \Rightarrow r_2$
mult	r_1, r_2	r_3	$r_1 \times r_2 \Rightarrow r_3$
multI	r_1, c_1	r_2	$r_1 \times c_1 \Rightarrow r_2$
div	r_1, r_2	r_3	$r_1 \div r_2 \Rightarrow r_3$
divI	r_1, c_1	r_2	$r_1 \div c_1 \Rightarrow r_2$
lshift	r_1, r_2	r_3	$r_1 \ll r_2 \Rightarrow r_3$
lshiftI	r_1, c_2	r_3	$r_1 \ll c_2 \Rightarrow r_3$
rshift	r_1, r_2	r_3	$r_1 \gg r_2 \Rightarrow r_3$
rshiftI	r_1, c_2	r_3	$r_1 \gg c_2 \Rightarrow r_3$
and	r_1, r_2	r_3	$r_1 \wedge r_2 \Rightarrow r_3$
andI	r_1, c_2	r_3	$r_1 \wedge c_2 \Rightarrow r_3$
or	r_1, r_2	r_3	$r_1 \vee r_2 \Rightarrow r_3$
orI	r_1, c_2	r_3	$r_1 \vee c_2 \Rightarrow r_3$
xor	r_1, r_2	r_3	$r_1\ xor\ r_2 \Rightarrow r_3$
xorI	r_1, c_2	r_3	$r_1\ xor\ c_2 \Rightarrow r_3$
loadI	c_1	r_2	$c_1 \Rightarrow r_2$
load	r_1	r_2	MEMORY $(r_1) \Rightarrow r_2$
loadAI	r_1, c_1	r_2	MEMORY $(r_1 + c_1) \Rightarrow r_2$
loadAO	r_1, r_2	r_3	MEMORY $(r_1 + r_2) \Rightarrow r_3$
cload	r_1	r_2	character load
cloadAI	r_1, r_2	r_3	character loadAI
cloadAO	r_1, r_2	r_3	character loadAO
store	r_1	r_2	$r_1 \Rightarrow$ MEMORY (r_2)
storeAI	r_1	r_2, c_1	$r_1 \Rightarrow$ MEMORY $(r_2 + c_1)$
storeAO	r_1	r_2, r_3	$r_1 \Rightarrow$ MEMORY $(r_2 + r_3)$
cstore	r_1	r_2	character store
cstoreAI	r_1	r_2, r_3	character storeAI
cstoreAO	r_1	r_2, r_3	character storeAO
i2i	r_1	r_2	$r_1 \Rightarrow r_2$
c2c	r_1	r_2	$r_1 \Rightarrow r_2$
c2i	r_1	r_2	converts character to integer
i2c	r_1	r_2	converts integer to character

ILOC Control-Flow Operations

Opcode	Sources	Targets	Meaning
cbr	r_1	l_1, l_2	$r_1 = \text{true} \Rightarrow l_1 \rightarrow PC$
			$r_1 = \text{false} \Rightarrow l_2 \rightarrow PC$
jumpI	none	l_1	$l_1 \rightarrow PC$
jump	none	r_1	$r_1 \rightarrow PC$
cmp_LT	r_1, r_2	r_3	$r_1 < r_2 \Rightarrow \text{true} \rightarrow r_3$
			(otherwise, false $\rightarrow r_3$)
cmp_LE	r_1, r_2	r_3	$r_1 \leq r_2 \Rightarrow \text{true} \rightarrow r_3$
cmp_EQ	r_1, r_2	r_3	$r_1 = r_2 \Rightarrow \text{true} \rightarrow r_3$
cmp_NE	r_1, r_2	r_3	$r_1 \neq r_2 \Rightarrow \text{true} \rightarrow r_3$
cmp_GE	r_1, r_2	r_3	$r_1 \geq r_2 \Rightarrow \text{true} \rightarrow r_3$
cmp_GT	r_1, r_2	r_3	$r_1 > r_2 \Rightarrow \text{true} \rightarrow r_3$
tbl	r_1, l_2	—	r_1 might hold l_2

ILOC Alternate Branch Syntax

Opcode	Sources	Targets	Meaning
comp	r_1, r_2	cc_1	Sets cc_1
cbr_LT	cc_1	l_1, l_2	$cc_1 = LT \Rightarrow l_1 \rightarrow PC$
			(otherwise $l_2 \rightarrow PC$)
cbr_LE	cc_1	l_1, l_2	$cc_1 = LE \Rightarrow l_1 \rightarrow PC$
cbr_EQ	cc_1	l_1, l_2	$cc_1 = EQ \Rightarrow l_1 \rightarrow PC$
cbr_GE	cc_1	l_1, l_2	$cc_1 = GE \Rightarrow l_1 \rightarrow PC$
cbr_GT	cc_1	l_1, l_2	$cc_1 = GT \Rightarrow l_1 \rightarrow PC$
cbr_NE	cc_1	l_1, l_2	$cc_1 = NE \Rightarrow l_1 \rightarrow PC$

APPENDIX B

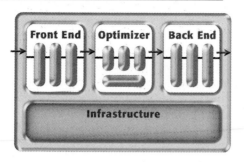

Data Structures

B.1 INTRODUCTION

Crafting a successful compiler requires attention to many details. This appendix explores some of the algorithmic issues that arise in compiler design and implementation. In most cases, these details would distract from the relevant discussion in the body of the text. We have gathered them together into this appendix, where they can be considered as needed.

This appendix focuses on the infrastructure to support compilation. Many engineering issues arise in the design and implementation of that infrastructure; the manner in which the compiler writer resolves those issues has a large impact on both the speed of the resulting compiler and the ease of extending and maintaining the compiler. As an example of the issues that arise, the compiler cannot know the size of its inputs until it has read them; thus, the front end must be designed to expand the size of its data structures gracefully in order to accommodate large input files. As a corollary, however, the compiler should know the approximate sizes needed for most of its internal data structures when it invokes the passes that follow the front end. Having generated an IR program with 10,000 names, the compiler should not begin its second pass with a symbol table sized for 1024 names. Any file that contains IR should begin with a specification of the rough sizes of major data structures.

Similarly, the later passes of a compiler can assume that the IR program presented to them was generated by the compiler. While they should do a complete job of error detection, the implementor need not spend as much time explaining errors and trying to correct them as might be expected in the front end. A common strategy is to build a validation pass that performs a thorough check on the IR program and can be inserted for debugging purposes, and to rely on less strenuous error detection and reporting when not debugging the compiler. Throughout the process, however, the compiler writers should remember that they are the people most likely to look at the code between passes. Effort spent to make the external forms of the IR more readable often reward the very people who invested the time and effort in it.

B.2 REPRESENTING SETS

Many different problems in compilation are formulated in terms that involve sets. They arise at many points in the text, including the subset construction (Chapter 2), the construction of the canonical collection of LR(1) items (Chapter 3), data-flow analysis (Chapters 8 and 9), and worklists such as the ready queue in list scheduling (Chapter 12). In each context, the compiler writer must select an appropriate set representation. In many cases, the efficiency of the algorithm depends on careful selection of a set representation. (For example, the *doms* data structure in the dominance computation represents all the dominator sets, as well as the immediate dominators, in one compact array.)

A fundamental difference between building a compiler and building other kinds of systems software—such as an operating system—is that many problems in compilation can be solved offline. For example, the bottom-up local algorithm for register allocation described in Section 13.3.2 was proposed in the mid-1950s for the original FORTRAN compiler. It is better known as Belady's MIN algorithm for offline page replacement, which has long been used as a standard against which to judge the effectiveness of online page-replacement algorithms. In an operating system, the algorithm is of only academic interest because it is an offline algorithm. Since the operating system cannot know what pages will be needed in the future, it cannot use an offline algorithm. On the other hand, the offline algorithm is practical for a compiler because the compiler can look through an entire block before making decisions.

The offline nature of compilation allows the compiler writer to use a broad variety of set representations. Many representations for sets have been explored. In particular, offline computation often lets us restrict the members of a set S to a fixed-size universe U ($S \subseteq U$). This, in turn, lets us use more efficient set representations than are available in an online situation where the size of U is discovered dynamically.

Common set operations include *member*, *insert*, *delete*, *clear*, *select*, *cardinality*, *forall*, *copy*, *compare*, *union*, *intersect*, *difference*, and *complement*. A specific application typically uses only a small subset of these operations. The cost of individual set operations depends on the particular representation chosen. In selecting an efficient representation for a particular application, it is important to consider how frequently each type of operation will be used. Other factors to consider include the memory requirements of the set representation and the expected sparsity of S relative to U.

The rest of this section focuses on three efficient set representations that have been employed in compilers: ordered linked lists, bit vectors, and sparse sets.

B.2.1 Representing Sets as Ordered Lists

In cases in which the size of each set is small, it sometimes makes sense to use a simple linked-list representation. For a set S, this representation consists of a linked list and a pointer to the first element in the list. Each node in the list contains a representation for a single element of S and a pointer to the next element of the list. The final node on the list has its pointer set to a standard value indicating the end of the list. With a linked list representation, the implementation can impose an order on the elements to create an ordered list. For example, an ordered linked list for the set $S = \{i, j, k\}, i < j < k$ might look like this:

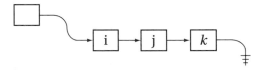

The elements are kept in ascending order. The size of S's representation is proportional to the number of elements in S, not the size of U. If $|S|$ is much smaller than $|U|$, the savings from representing just the elements present in S may more than offset the extra cost incurred for a pointer in each element.

The list representation is particularly flexible. Because nothing in the list relies on either the size of U or the size of S, it can be used in situations in which the compiler is discovering U or S or both, such as the live-range-finding portion of a graph-coloring register allocator.

The table in Figure B.1 shows the asymptotic complexities of common set operations using this representation. Most common set operations on ordered

Operation	Ordered Linked List	Bit Vector	Sparse Set
member	$O(|S|)$	$O(1)$	$O(1)$
insert	$O(|S|)$	$O(1)$	$O(1)$
delete	$O(|S|)$	$O(1)$	$O(1)$
clear	$O(1)$	$O(|U|)$	$O(1)$
select	$O(1)$	$O(|U|)$	$O(1)$
cardinality	$O(|S|)$	$O(|U|)$	$O(1)$
forall	$O(|S|)$	$O(|U|)$	$O(|S|)$
copy	$O(|S|)$	$O(|U|)$	$O(|S|)$
compare	$O(|S|)$	$O(|U|)$	$O(|S|)$
union	$O(|S|)$	$O(|U|)$	$O(|S|)$
intersect	$O(|S|)$	$O(|U|)$	$O(|S|)$
difference	$O(|S|)$	$O(|U|)$	$O(|S|)$
complement	—	$O(|U|)$	$O(|U|)$

FIGURE B.1   Asymptotic Time Complexities of Set Operations

linked lists are $O(|S|)$ because it is necessary to walk the linked lists to perform the operations. If deallocation does not require walking the list to free the nodes for individual elements, as in some garbage-collected systems or an arena-based system, *clear* takes constant time.

A variant on this idea makes sense when the universe is unknown, and the sets can grow reasonably large, as in interference-graph construction (see Chapter 13). Making each node hold a fixed number (greater than 1) of set elements significantly reduces the overhead in both space and time. With k elements per node, building a set of n elements requires $\lceil \frac{n}{k} \rceil$ allocations and $\lceil \frac{n}{k} \rceil + 1$ pointers, while a set with single-element nodes would take n allocations and $n + 1$ pointers. This scheme retains the easy expansion of the list representation but reduces the space overhead. Insertion and deletion move more data than with a single element per node; however their asymptotic complexity is still $O(|S|)$.[1]

---

1. Keeping the extra space at the front of the list rather than at the end can simplify *insert* and *delete*, assuming a singly linked list.

The *doms* array used in the dominance computation (see Section 9.3.2) is a clever application of the list representation of sets to a very special case. In particular, the compiler knows the size of the universe and the number of sets. The compiler also knows that, using ordered sets, they will have the peculiar property that if $e \in S_1$ and $e \in S_2$, then every element after e in S_1 is also in S_2. Thus, the elements starting with e can be shared. By using an array representation, the element names can be used as pointers, too. This enables a single array of n elements to represent n sparse sets as ordered lists. It also produces a fast intersection operator for those sets.

B.2.2 Representing Sets as Bit Vectors

Compiler writers often use *bit vectors* to represent sets, particularly those used in data-flow analysis (see Sections 8.6 and 9.2). For a bounded universe U, a set $S \subseteq U$ can be represented with a bit vector of length $|U|$, called the *characteristic vector* for S. For each $i \in U$, $0 \le i < |U|$; if $i \in S$, the ith element of the characteristic vector equals one. Otherwise, the ith element is zero. For example, the characteristic vector for the set $S \subseteq U$, where $S = \{i,j,k\}$, $i < j < k$ is as follows:

0		i–1	i	i+1		j–1	j	j+1		k–1	k	k+1		|U|–1
0	⋯	0	1	0	⋯	0	1	0	⋯	0	1	0	⋯	0

The bit-vector representation always allocates enough space to represent all elements in U; thus, this representation can be used only in an application where U is known—an offline application.

The table in Figure B.1 lists the asymptotic complexities of common set operations with this representation. Although many of the operations are $O(|U|)$, they can still be efficient if U is small. A single word holds many elements; the representation gains a constant-factor improvement over representations that need one word per element. Thus, for example, with a word size of 32 bits, any universe of 32 or fewer elements has a single-word representation.

The compactness of the representation carries over into the speed of operations. With single-word sets, many of the set operations become single machine instructions; for example *union* becomes a logical-or operation and *intersection* becomes a logical-and operation. Even if the sets take multiple words to represent, the number of machine instructions required to perform many of the set operations is reduced by a factor of the machine's word size.

B.2.3 Representing Sparse Sets

For a fixed universe U and a set $S \subseteq U$, S is a sparse set if $|S|$ is much smaller than $|U|$. Some of the sets encountered in compilation are sparse. For example, the LIVEOUT sets used in register allocation are typically sparse. Compiler writers often use bit vectors to represent such sets, due to their efficiency in time and space. With enough sparsity, however, more time-efficient representations are possible, especially in situations in which a large percentage of the operations can be supported in either $\mathbf{O}(1)$ or $\mathbf{O}(|S|)$ time. By contrast, bit vector sets take either $\mathbf{O}(1)$ or $\mathbf{O}(|U|)$ time on these operations. If $|S|$ is smaller than $|U|$ by a factor greater than the word size, then bit vectors may be the less efficient choice.

One sparse-set representation that has these properties uses two vectors of length $|U|$ and a scalar to represent the set. The first vector, *sparse*, holds a sparse representation of the set; the other vector, *dense*, holds a dense representation of the set. The scalar, *next*, holds the index of the location in *dense* where the next new element of the set can be inserted. Of course, *next* also holds the set's cardinality.

Neither vector needs to be initialized when a sparse set is created; set membership tests ensure the validity of each entry as it is accessed. The *clear* operation simply sets *next* back to zero, its initial value. To add a new element $i \in U$ to S, the code (1) stores i in the *next* location in *dense*; (2) stores the value of *next* in the ith location in *sparse*, and (3) increments *next* so that it is the index of the next location where an element can be inserted in *dense*.

If we began with an empty sparse set S and added the elements j, i, and k, in that order, where $i < j < k$, the set would look like this:

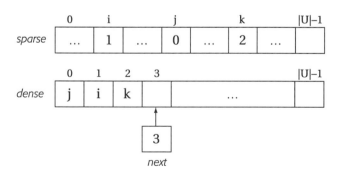

Note that the sparse-set representation requires enough space to represent all of U. Thus, it can be used only in offline situations in which the compiler knows the size of U.

Because valid entries for an element i in *sparse* and *dense* must point to each other, membership can be determined with the following tests:

$$0 \leq \textit{sparse}[i] < \textit{next} \quad \text{and} \quad \textit{dense}[\textit{sparse}[i]] = i$$

The table in Figure B.1 lists the asymptotic complexities of common set operations. Because this scheme includes both a sparse and a dense representation of the set, it has some of the advantages of each. Individual elements of the set can be accessed in $\mathbf{O}(1)$ time through *sparse*, while set operations that must traverse the set can use *dense* to obtain $\mathbf{O}(|S|)$ complexity.

Both space and time complexities should be considered when choosing between bit-vector and sparse-set representations. The sparse-set representation requires two vectors of length $|U|$ and a scalar. In contrast, a bit-vector representation requires a single bit-vector of length $|U|$. As shown in Figure B.1, the sparse-set representation dominates the bit-vector representation in terms of asymptotic time complexity. However, because of the efficient implementations possible for bit-vector set operations, bit vectors are preferred in situations where S is not sparse. When choosing between the two representations, it is important to consider the sparsity of the represented set and the relative frequency of the set operations employed.

B.3 IMPLEMENTING INTERMEDIATE REPRESENTATIONS

After choosing a specific style of IR, the compiler writer must decide how to implement it. At first glance, the choices seem obvious. DAGs are easily represented as nodes and edges, using pointers and heap-allocated data structures. Quadruples fall naturally into a $4 \times k$ array. As with sets, however, choosing the best implementation requires a deeper understanding of how the compiler will use the data structures.

B.3.1 Graphical Intermediate Representations

Compilers use a variety of graphical IRs, as discussed in Chapter 5. Tailoring the implemention of a graph to the needs of the compiler can improve both the time and space efficiency of the compiler. This section describes some of the issues that arise with trees and graphs.

Representing Trees

The natural representation for trees, in most languages, is as a collection of nodes connected by pointers. A typical implementation allocates the nodes on demand, as the compiler builds the tree. The tree may include nodes of several sizes—for example, varying the number of children in the node and some of the data fields. Alternatively, the tree might be built with a single kind of node, allocated to fit the largest possible node.

Another way to represent the same tree is as an array of node structures. In this representation, pointers are replaced with integer indexes and pointer-based references become standard array and structure references. This implementation forces a one-size-fits-all node, but is otherwise similar to the pointer-based implementation.

Each of these schemes has strengths and weaknesses.

- The pointer scheme handles arbitrarily large ASTs. The array scheme requires code to expand the array when the AST grows beyond its initially allocated size.

- The pointer scheme requires an allocation for each node, while the array scheme simply increments a counter (unless it must expand the array). Techniques, like arena-based allocation (see the sidebar, Arena-Based Allocation, in Chapter 6), can reduce the cost of allocation and reclamation.

- The pointer scheme has locality of reference that depends entirely on the behavior of the allocator at run time. The array technique uses consecutive memory locations. One, or the other, may be desirable on a particular system.

- The pointer scheme is harder to optimize because of the comparatively poor quality of static analysis on pointer-intensive code. In contrast, many of the optimizations developed for dense linear-algebra codes apply to an array scheme. When the compiler is compiled, these optimizations may produce faster code for the array scheme than for the pointer one.

- The pointer scheme may be harder to debug than the array implementation. Programmers seem to find array indexes more intuitive than memory addresses.

- The pointer system requires a way to encode pointers if the AST must be written to external media. Presumably, this includes traversing the

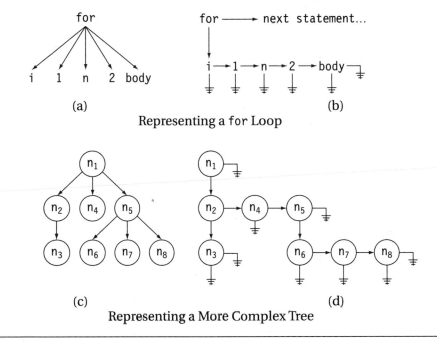

nodes, following the pointers. The array system uses offsets relative to the start of the array, so no translation is required. On many systems, this can be accomplished with a large, block I/O operation.

There are many other tradeoffs. Each must be evaluated in context.

Mapping Trees to Binary Trees

A straightforward implementation of abstract syntax trees might support nodes with many different numbers of children. For example, a typical for loop header

$$\text{for } i = 1 \text{ to } n \text{ by } 2$$

might have a node in the AST with five children—like the one shown in Figure B.2(a). The node labelled body represents the subtree for the body of the for loop.

For some constructs, no fixed number of children will work. To represent a procedure call, the AST must either custom-allocate nodes based on the number of parameters, or use a single child that holds a list of parameters. The former approach complicates all the code that traverses the AST; the variable-sized nodes must hold numbers to indicate how many children they have, and the traversal must contain code to read those numbers and modify its behavior accordingly. The latter approach separates the AST's implementation from its strict adherence to the source but uses a well-understood construct, the list, to represent those places where a fixed-arity node is inappropriate.

To simplify the implementation of trees, the compiler writer can take this separation of form and meaning one step further. Any arbitrary tree can be mapped onto a binary tree—a tree in which each node has precisely two children. In this mapping, the left-child pointer is designated for the leftmost child, and the right-child pointer is designated for the next sibling at the current level. Figure B.2(b) shows the five-child for node mapped onto a binary tree. Since each node is binary, this tree has null pointers in each leaf node. It also has a sibling pointer in the for node; in the version on the left, that pointer occurs in the for node's parent. Parts (c) and (d) in the figure show a more complex example.

Using binary trees introduces additional null pointers into the trees, as the two examples show. In return, it simplifies the implementation in several ways. Memory allocation can be done simply—with an arena-based allocator or a custom one. The compiler writer can also implement the tree as an array of structures. The code that deals with the binary tree is somewhat simpler than the code required for a tree with nodes of many different arities.

Representing Arbitrary Graphs

Several structures that a compiler must represent are arbitrary graphs, rather than trees. Examples include the control-flow graph and the data-precedence graph. A simple implementation might use heap-allocated nodes, with pointers to represent the edges. The left side of Figure B.3 shows a simple cfg. Clearly, it needs three nodes. The difficulty arises with the edges; how many incoming and outgoing edges does each node need? Each node could maintain a list of outgoing edges; this leads to an implementation that might look like the one shown on the right side of the figure.

In the diagram, the rectangles represent nodes, and the ovals represent edges. This representation makes it easy to walk the graph in the direction of the edges. It does not provide for random access to any of the nodes; to remedy this, we can add an array of node pointers, indexed by the nodes' integer names. With this minor addition (not shown), the graph is suitable for

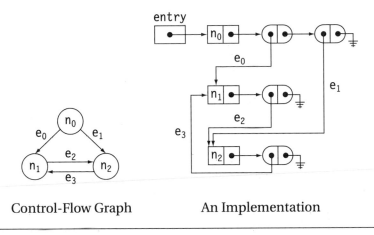

Control-Flow Graph   An Implementation

FIGURE B.3   An Example Control-Flow Graph

solving forward data-flow problems. It provides a fast means for finding all the successors of a node.

Unfortunately, compilers often need to traverse the cfg against the direction of the edges. This occurs, for example, in backward data-flow problems, where the algorithm needs a fast predecessor operation. To adapt this graph structure for backward traversal, we would need to add another pointer to each node and create a second set of edge structures to represent the predecessors of a node. This approach will certainly work, but the data structure becomes complicated to draw, implement, and debug.

An alternative, as with trees, is to represent the graph as a pair of tables—one for the nodes and one for the edges. The Nodes table has two fields: one for the first edge to a successor and one for the first edge to a predecessor. The Edges table has four fields: the first pair hold the source and sink of the edge being represented, and the other pair hold the next successor of the source and the next predecessor of the sink. Using this scheme, the tables for our example cfg are:

Nodes

Name	Successor	Predecessor
n_0	e_0	—
n_1	e_2	e_0
n_2	e_3	e_1

Edges

Name	Source	Sink	Next Successor	Next Predecessor
e_0	n_0	n_1	e_1	e_3
e_1	n_0	n_2	—	e_2
e_2	n_1	n_2	—	—
e_3	n_2	n_1	—	—

This representation provides quick access to successors, predecessors, and individual nodes and edges by their names (assuming that the names are represented by small integers).

The tabular representation works well for traversing the graph and finding predecessors and successors. If the application makes heavy use of other operations on the graph, better representations can be found. For example, the dominant operations in a graph-coloring register allocator are testing for an edge's presence in the interference graph and iterating over a node's neighbors. To support these operations, most implementations use two different graph representations (see Section 13.5.3). To answer membership questions—is the edge (i, j) in the graph?—these implementations use a bit matrix. Since the interference graph is undirected, a lower-diagonal bit matrix will suffice, saving roughly half the space required for a full bit matrix. To iterate quickly over a node's neighbors, a set of adjacency vectors is used.

Because interference graphs are both large and sparse, space for the adjacency vectors can become an issue. Some implementations use two passes to build the graph—the first pass computes the size of each adjacency vector and the second pass builds the vectors, each with the minimal required size. Other implementations use a variant of the list representation for sets from Section B.2.1—the graph is built in a single pass, using an unordered list for the adjacency vector, with multiple edges per list node.

B.3.2 Linear Intermediate Forms

Part of the conceptual appeal of linear intermediate forms, like ILOC, is that they have a simple, obvious implementation as an array of structures. For example, an ILOC program has an immediate mapping to a FORTRAN-style array—n ILOC operations map onto an $(n \times 4)$-element array of integers. The opcode determines how to interpret each of the operands. Of course, any design decision has its advantages and disadvantages, and a compiler writer who wants to use a linear IR should consider representations other than a simple array.

FORTRAN-Style Array

Using a single array of integers to hold the IR ensures fast access to individual opcodes and operands and low overhead for both allocation and access. The passes that manipulate the IR should run quickly, since all of the array accesses can be improved using the standard analyses and transformations developed to improve dense linear-algebra programs. A linear pass through the code has predictable memory locality; since consecutive operations occupy consecutive memory locations, they cannot conflict in the cache. If the compiler must write the IR to external media (between passes, for example), it can use efficient block I/O operations.

There are, however, disadvantages to the array implementation. If the compiler needs to insert an operation into the code, it must create space for the new operation. Similarly, deletions should contract the code. Any kind of code motion runs into some version of this problem. A naive implementation would create the space by shuffling operations; a compiler that takes this approach will often leave empty slots in the array—after branches and jumps—to reduce the amount of shuffling needed.

An alternative strategy is to use a detour operator that directs any traversal of the IR to an out-of-line code segment. This approach lets the compiler thread control through out-of-line segments, so an insertion can be done by overwriting an existing operation with a detour, putting the inserted code and the overwritten operation at the end of the array, and following it with a detour back to the operation after the first detour. The final piece of strategy is to linearize the detours occasionally—for example, at the end of each pass, or any time the fraction of detours exceeds some threshold.

Another complication with the array implementation arises from the need for an occasional operation, such as a ϕ-function that takes a variable number of operands. In the compiler from which our ILOC is derived, procedure calls are represented by a single complicated operation. The call operation has an operand for each formal parameter, an operand for the return value (if any), and two operands that are lists of values potentially modified by the call and potentially used by the call. This operation does not fit the mold of an $n \times 4$-element array, unless the operands are interpreted as pointers to lists of parameters, modified variables, and used variables.

List of Structures

An alternative to the array implementation is to use a list of structures. In this scheme, each operation has an independent structure, along with a pointer to the next operation. Since the structures can be allocated individually, the program representation expands easily to arbitrary size. Since order is imposed by the pointers that link operations, operations can be inserted or removed with straightforward pointer assignments—no shuffling or copying is required. Variable-length operations, like the call operation previously described, are handled by using variant structures; in fact, short operations such as loadI and jump can also use a variant to save small amounts of space.

Of course, using individually allocated structures increases the overhead of allocation—the array needed one initial allocation, while the list scheme needs one allocation per IR operation. The list pointers increase the space required. Since all the compiler passes that manipulate the IR must include many pointer-based references, the code for those passes may be slower than code that uses a simple array implementation, because pointer-based code is often harder to analyze and optimize than array-intensive code. Finally, if the compiler writes the IR to external media between passes, it must traverse the list as it writes and reconstruct the list as it reads. This slows down the I/O.

These disadvantages can be ameliorated, to some extent, by implementing the list of structures inside either an arena or an array. With an arena-based allocator, the cost of allocations drops to a test and an addition in the typical case.[2] The arena also produces roughly the same locality as a simple array implementation.

Implementing the list in an array achieves the same goals, with the additional advantage that all the pointers become integer indexes. Experience suggests that this simplifies debugging; it also makes it possible to use a block I/O operation to write and read the IR.

B.4 IMPLEMENTING HASH TABLES

The two central problems in hash-table implementation are ensuring that the hash function produces an even distribution of integers (at all the table sizes that will be used) and handling collisions in an efficient way. Finding good hash functions is difficult. Fortunately, hashing has been in use long enough that many good functions have been described in the literature.

The rest of this section describes design issues that arise in implementing hash tables. Section B.4.1 describes two hash functions that, in practice, produce good results. The next two sections present the two most widely used strategies for resolving collisions. Section B.4.2 describes *open hashing* (sometimes called *bucket hashing*), while Section B.4.3 presents an alternative scheme called *open addressing* or *rehashing*. Section B.4.4 discusses storage management issues for hash tables, while Section B.4.5 shows how to incorporate the mechanisms for lexical scoping into these schemes. The final section deals with a practical issue that arises in a compiler-development environment, namely, frequent changes to the hash-table definition.

---

2. In any pass other than the first one, the compiler should have a fairly accurate notion of how big the IR is. Thus, it can allocate an arena that holds both the IR and some space for growth and avoid the more expensive case of expanding the arena.

ORGANIZING A SYMBOL TABLE

In designing a symbol table, the first decision that the compiler writer faces concerns the organization of the table and its search algorithm. As in many other applications, the compiler writer has several choices.

Linear List A linear list can expand to arbitrary size. The search algorithm is a single, small, tight loop. Unfortunately, the search algorithm requires $O(n)$ probes per lookup, on average, where n is the number of symbols in the table. This single disadvantage almost always outweighs the simplicity of implementation and expansion. To justify using a linear list, the compiler writer needs strong evidence that the procedures being compiled have very few names, as might occur for an object-oriented language.

Binary Search To retain the easy expansion of the linear list while improving search time, the compiler writer might use a balanced binary tree. Ideally, a balanced tree should allow lookup in $O(\log_2 n)$ probes per lookup; this is a considerable improvement over the linear list. Many algorithms have been published for balancing search trees. (Similar effects can be achieved by using a binary search of an ordered table, but the table makes insertion and expansion more difficult.)

Hash Table A hash table may minimize access costs. The implementation computes a table index directly from the name. As long as that computation produces a good distribution of indexes, the average access cost should be $O(1)$. The worst case, however, can devolve to linear search. The compiler writer can take steps to decrease the likelihood of this happening, but pathological cases may still occur. Many hash-table implementations have inexpensive schemes for expansion.

Multiset Discrimination To avoid worst-case behavior, the compiler writer can use an offline technique called *multiset discrimination*. It creates a distinct index for each identifier, at the cost of an extra pass over the source text. This technique avoids the possibility of pathological behavior that always exists with hashing. (See the sidebar, An Alternative to Hashing, in Chapter 5 for more details.)

Of these organizations, the most common choice appears to be the hash table. It provides better compile-time behavior than the linear list or binary tree, and the implementation techniques have been widely studied and taught.

B.4.1 Choosing a Hash Function

The importance of a good hash function cannot be overemphasized. A hash function that produces a bad distribution of index values directly increases the average cost of inserting items into the table and finding such items later. Fortunately, many good hash functions have been documented in the literature, including the multiplicative hash functions described by Knuth and the universal hash functions described by Cormen et al.

Multiplicative Hash Functions

A *multiplicative hash function* is deceptively simple. The programmer chooses a single constant C and uses it in the following formula:

$$h(key) = \lfloor TableSize \cdot ((C \cdot key) \bmod 1) \rfloor$$

where C is the constant, *key* is the integer being used as a key into the table, and *TableSize* is, rather obviously, the current size of the hash table. Knuth suggests the value

$$0.6180339887 \approx \frac{\sqrt{5} - 1}{2} \text{ for } C.$$

The effect of the function is to compute $C \cdot key$, take its fractional part with the mod function, and multiply the result by the size of the table.

Universal Hash Functions

To implement a *universal hash function*, the programmer designs a family of functions that can be parameterized by a small set of constants. At execution time, a set of values for the constants is chosen at random—either using random numbers for the constants or selecting a random index into a set of previously tested constants. (The same constants are used throughout a single execution of the program that uses the hash function, but the constants vary from execution to execution.) By varying the hash function in each execution of the program, a universal hash function produces different distributions in each run of the program. In a compiler, if the input program produced pathological behavior in some particular compilation, it is unlikely to produce the same behavior in subsequent compilations. To implement a universal version of the multiplicative hash function, the compiler writer can randomly generate an appropriate value for C at the start of compilation.

THE PERILS OF POOR HASH FUNCTIONS

The choice of a hash function has a critical impact on the cost of table insertions and lookups. This is a case in which a small amount of attention can make a large difference.

Many years ago, we saw a student implement the following hash function for character strings: (1) break the key into 4-byte chunks, (2) exclusive-or them together, and (3) take the resulting number, e, modulo the table size, as the index. The function is relatively fast. It has a straightforward, efficient implementation. For some table sizes, it produces adequate distributions.

When the student inserted this implementation into a system that performed source-to-source translation on FORTRAN programs, several independent facts combined to create an algorithmic disaster. First, the implementation language padded character strings with blanks to the right to reach a 4-byte boundary. Second, the student chose an initial table size of 2048. Finally, FORTRAN programmers use many one- and two-character variable names, such as i, j, k, x, y, and z.

All the short variable names fit in a single word, avoiding any effect from the exclusive-or. However, taking e mod 2048 masks out all but the final eleven bits of e. Thus, all short variable names produce the same index—the last eleven bits of a pair of blanks. The hash search instantly devolves into linear search. While this particular hash function is far from ideal, simply changing the table size to 2047 eliminates the most noticeable negative effects.

B.4.2 Open Hashing

Open hashing, also called *bucket hashing*, assumes that the hash function h produces collisions. It relies on h to partition the set of input keys into a fixed number of sets, or *buckets*. Each bucket contains a linear list of records, one record per name. *LookUp(n)* walks the linear list stored in the bucket indexed by $h(n)$ to find n. Thus, *LookUp* requires one evaluation of $h(n)$ and the traversal of a linear list. Evaluating $h(n)$ should be fast; the list traversal will take time proportional to the length of the list. For a table of size S, with N names, the cost per lookup should be roughly $O(\frac{N}{S})$. As long as h distributes names fairly uniformly and the ratio of names to buckets is small, this cost approximates our goal: $O(1)$ time for each access.

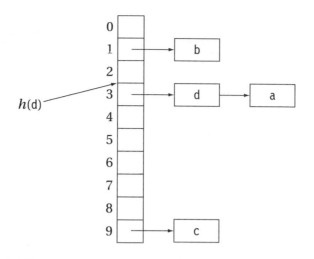

FIGURE B.4   Open-Hashing Table

Figure B.4 shows a small hash table implemented with this scheme. It assumes that $h(a) = h(d) = 3$ to create a collision. Thus, a and d occupy the same slot in the table. The list structure links them together. *Insert* should add to the front of the list for efficiency.

Open hashing has several advantages. Because it creates a new node in one of the linked lists for every inserted name, it can handle an arbitrarily large number of names without running out of space. An excessive number of entries in one bucket does not affect the cost of access in other buckets. Because the concrete representation for the set of buckets is usually an array of pointers, the overhead for increasing S is small—one pointer for each added bucket. (This makes it less expensive to keep $\frac{N}{S}$ small. The cost per name is constant.) Choosing S as a power of two reduces the cost of the inevitable mod operation required to implement h.

The primary drawbacks for open hashing relate directly to these advantages. Both can be managed.

1. Open hashing can be allocation intensive. Each insertion allocates a new record. When implemented on a system with heavyweight memory allocation, this may be noticeable. Using a lighter-weight mechanism, such as arena-based allocation (see the sidebar in Chapter 6), can alleviate this problem.

2. If any particular set gets large, *LookUp* degrades to linear search. With a reasonably behaved hash function, this occurs only when N is much

larger than S. The implementation should detect this problem and enlarge the array of buckets. Typically, this involves allocating a new array of buckets and reinserting each entry from the old table into the new table.

A well-implemented open hash table provides efficient access with low overhead in both space and time.

To improve the behavior of the linear search performed in a single bucket, the compiler can dynamically reorder the chain. Rivest and others [291, 309] describe two effective strategies: move a node up the chain by one position on each lookup, or move it to the front of the list on each lookup. More complex schemes to organize each bucket can be used as well. However, the compiler writer should assess the total amount of time lost in traversing a bucket before investing much effort in this problem.

B.4.3   Open Addressing

Open addressing, also called *rehashing*, handles collisions by computing an alternative index for the names whose normal slot, at $h(n)$, is already occupied. In this scheme, *LookUp*(n) computes $h(n)$ and examines that slot. If the slot is empty, *LookUp* fails. If *LookUp* finds n, it succeeds. If it finds a name other than n, it uses a second function $g(n)$ to compute an increment for the search. This leads it to probe the table at $(h(n) + g(n))$ mod S, then at $(h(n) + 2 \times g(n))$ mod S, then at $(h(n) + 3 \times g(n))$ mod S, and so on, until it either finds n, finds an empty slot, or returns to $h(n)$ a second time. (The table is numbered from zero to S–1, which ensures that mod S will return a valid table index.) If *LookUp* finds an empty slot, or it returns to $h(n)$ a second time, it fails.

Figure B.5 shows a small hash table implemented with this scheme. It uses the same data as Figure B.4. As before, $h(a) = h(d) = 3$, while $h(b) = 1$ and $h(c) = 9$. When d was inserted, it produced a collision with a. The secondary hash function $g(d)$ produced 2, so *Insert* placed d at index 5 in the table. In effect, open addressing builds chains of items similar to those used in open hashing. In open addressing, however, the chains are stored directly in the table, and a single table location can serve as the starting point for multiple chains, each with a different increment produced by g.

This scheme makes a subtle tradeoff of space against speed. Since each key is stored in the table, S must be larger than N. If collisions are infrequent, because h and g produce good distributions, then the rehash chains stay short and access costs stay low. Because it can recompute g inexpensively, this scheme need not store pointers to form the rehash chains—a savings of

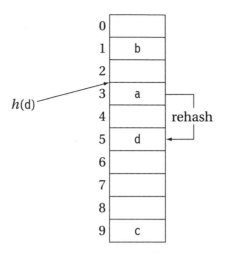

FIGURE B.5   Open-Addressing Table

N pointers. This saved space goes into making the table larger, and the larger table improves performance by lowering the collision frequency. The primary advantage of open addressing is simple: lower access costs through shorter rehash chains.

Open addressing has two primary drawbacks. Both arise as N approaches S and the table becomes full.

1. Because rehash chains thread through the index table, a collision between n and m can interfere with a subsequent insertion of some other name p. If $h(n) = h(m)$ and $(h(m) + g(m))$ mod $S = h(p)$, then inserting n, followed by m, fills p's slot in the table. When the scheme behaves well, this problem has a minor impact. As N approaches S, it can become pronounced.

2. Because S must be at least as large as N, the table must be expanded if N grows too large. (Similarly, the implementation may expand S when some chain becomes too long.) Expansion is needed for correctness; with open hashing, it is a matter of efficiency.

Some implementations use a constant function for g. This simplifies the implementation and reduces the cost of computing secondary indexes. However, it creates a single rehash chain for each value of h and has the effect of merging rehash chains whenever a secondary index encounters an already occupied table slot. These two disadvantages outweigh the cost of evaluating a second hash function. A more reasonable choice is to use two multiplicative hash functions with different constants—selected randomly at startup from a table of constants, if possible.

The table size S plays an important role in open addressing. $LookUp$ must recognize when it reaches a table slot that it has already visited; otherwise, it will not halt on failure. To make this efficient, the implementation should ensure that it eventually returns to $h(n)$. If S is a prime number, then any choice of $0 < g(n) < S$ generates a series of probes, $p_1, p_2, \ldots, p_S$ with the property that $p_1 = p_S = h(n)$ and $p_i \neq h(n), \forall i$ such that $1 < i < S$. That is, $LookUp$ will examine every slot in the table before it returns to $h(n)$. Since the implementation may need to expand the table, it should include a table of appropriately sized prime numbers. A small set of primes will suffice, due to the realistic limits on both program size and memory available to the compiler.

B.4.4 Storing Symbol Records

Neither open hashing nor open addressing directly addresses the issue of how to allocate space for the information associated with each hash table entry. With open hashing, the temptation is to allocate the records directly in the nodes that implement the chains. With open addressing, the temptation is to avoid pointers and make each entry in the index table be a symbol record. Both these approaches have drawbacks. We may achieve better results by using a separately allocated stack to hold the records.

Figure B.6 depicts this implementation. In an open-hashing implementation, the chain lists themselves can be implemented on the stack. This lowers the cost of allocating individual records—particularly if allocation is a heavyweight operation. In an open-addressing implementation, the rehash chains are still implicit in the index set, preserving the space saving that motivated the idea.

When the actual records are stored in a stack, they form a dense table, which is better for external I/O. For heavyweight allocation, this scheme amortizes the cost of a large allocation over many records. With a garbage collector, it decreases the number of objects that must be marked and collected. In either case, having a dense table makes it more efficient to iterate over the symbols in the table—an operation that the compiler uses to perform tasks such as assigning storage locations.

As a final advantage, this scheme drastically simplifies the task of expanding the index set. To expand the index set, the compiler discards the old index set,

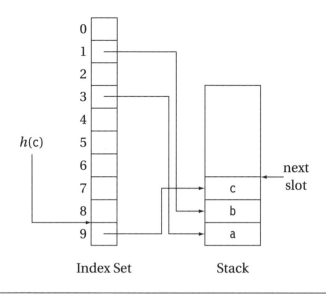

FIGURE B.6 Stack Allocation for Records

allocates a larger set, and then reinserts the records into the new table, working from the bottom of the stack to the top. This eliminates the need to have, temporarily, both the old and new table in memory. Iterating over the dense table takes less work, in general, than chasing the pointers to traverse the lists in open hashing. It avoids iterating over empty table slots, as can happen when open addressing expands the index set to keep the chains short.

The compiler need not allocate the entire stack as a single object. Instead, the stack can be implemented as a chain of nodes that each hold k records, for some reasonable k. When a node becomes full, the implementation allocates a new node, adds it to the end of the chain, and continues. This provides the compiler writer with fine-grained control over the tradeoff between allocation cost and wasted space.

B.4.5 Adding Nested Lexical Scopes

Section 5.7.3 describes the issues that arise in creating a symbol table to handle nested lexical scopes. It describes a simple implementation that creates a sheaf of symbol tables, one per level. While that implementation is conceptually clean, it pushes the overhead of scoping into *LookUp*, rather than into *InitializeScope*, *FinalizeScope*, and *Insert*. Since the compiler invokes *LookUp* many more times than it invokes these other routines, other implementations deserve consideration.

Consider again the code in Figure 5.10. It generates the following actions:

$$\uparrow \langle \mathtt{w},0 \rangle \ \langle \mathtt{x},0 \rangle \ \langle \mathtt{example},0 \rangle \ \uparrow \langle \mathtt{a},1 \rangle \ \langle \mathtt{b},1 \rangle \ \langle \mathtt{c},1 \rangle$$

$$\uparrow \langle \mathtt{b},2 \rangle \ \langle \mathtt{z},2 \rangle \ \downarrow \ \uparrow \langle \mathtt{a},2 \rangle \ \langle \mathtt{x},2 \rangle \ \uparrow \langle \mathtt{c},3 \rangle, \ \langle \mathtt{x},3 \rangle \ \downarrow \ \downarrow \ \downarrow \ \downarrow$$

where $\uparrow$ represents a call to *InitializeScope*, $\downarrow$ a call to *FinalizeScope*, and a pair $\langle \mathtt{name}, n \rangle$ a call to *Insert* that adds name at level n.

Adding Lexical Scopes to Open Hashing

Consider what would happen in an open-hashing table if we simply added a lexical-level field to the record for each name and inserted each new name at the front of its chain. *Insert* could check for duplicates by comparing both names and lexical levels. *LookUp* would return the first record that it discovered for a given name. *InitializeScope* would simply bump a counter for the current lexical level. This scheme pushes the complications into *FinalizeScope*, which must not only decrement the current lexical level, but also must remove the records for any names inserted in the scope being deallocated.

If open hashing is implemented with individually allocated nodes for its chains, as shown in Figure B.4, then *FinalizeScope* must find all records for the scope being discarded and remove them from their respective chains. If they will not be used later in the compiler, *FinalizeScope* must deallocate them; otherwise, it must chain them together to preserve them. Figure B.7 shows the table that this approach would produce, at the assignment statement in Figure 5.10.

With stack-allocated records, *FinalizeScope* can iterate from the top of the stack downward until it reaches a record for some level below the level being discarded. For each record, it updates the index-set entry with the record's pointer to the next item on the chain. If the records are being discarded, *FinalizeScope* resets the pointer to the next available slot; otherwise, the records are preserved together on the stack. Figure B.8 shows the symbol table for our example at the assignment statement.

With a little care, dynamic reordering of the chain can be added to this scheme. Since *FinalizeScope* uses the stack ordering, rather than the chain ordering, it will still find all the top-level names at the top of the stack.

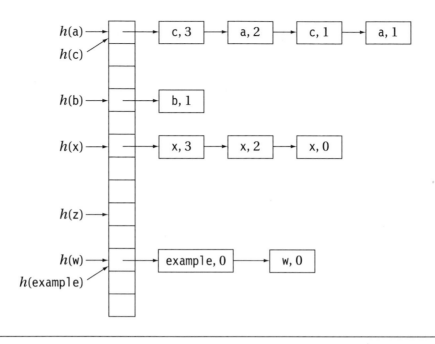

Figure B.7 Lexical Scoping in an Open-Hashing Table

With reordered chains, the compiler either needs to walk the chain to remove each deleted name record, or to doubly link the chains to allow quicker deletion.

Adding Lexical Scopes to Open Addressing

With an open-addressing table, the situation is slightly more complex. Slots in the table are a critical resource; when all the slots are filled, the table must be expanded before further insertion can occur. Deletion from a table that uses rehashing is difficult; the implementation cannot easily tell if the deleted record falls in the middle of some rehash chain. Thus, marking the slot empty breaks any chain that passes through that location (rather than ending there). This argues against storing discrete records for each variant of a name in the table. Instead, the compiler should link only one record per name into the table; it can create a chain of superseded records for older variants. Figure B.9 depicts this situation for the continuing example.

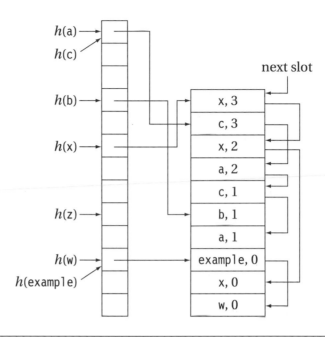

FIGURE B.8   Lexical Scoping in a Stack-Allocated Open-Hashing Table

This scheme pushes most of the complexity into *Insert* and *FinalizeScope*. *Insert* creates a new record on top of the stack. If it finds an older declaration of the same name in the index set, it replaces that reference with a reference to the new record and links the older reference to the new record. *FinalizeScope* iterates over the top items on the stack, as in open hashing. To remove a record that has an older variant, it simply relinks the index set to point to the older variant. To remove the final variant of a name, it must insert a reference to a specially designated record that denotes a deleted reference. *LookUp* must recognize the deleted reference as occupying a slot in the current chain. *Insert* must know that it can replace a deleted reference with any newly inserted symbol.

This scheme, in essence, creates separate chains for collisions and for redeclarations. Collisions are threaded through the index set. Redeclarations are threaded through the stack. This should reduce the cost of *LookUp* slightly, since it avoids examining more than one record for any single name.

Consider a bucket in open hashing that contains seven declarations for x and a single declaration for y at level zero. *LookUp* might encounter all seven records for x before finding y. With the open-addressing scheme, *LookUp* encounters one record for x and one record for y.

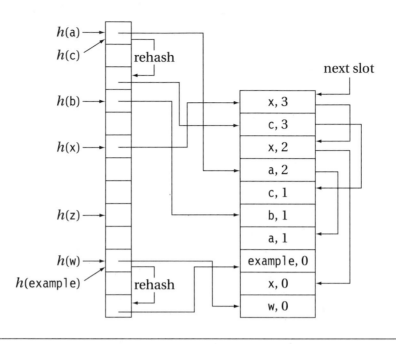

FIGURE B.9 Lexical Scoping in an Open-Addressing Table

B.5 A FLEXIBLE SYMBOL-TABLE DESIGN

Most compilers use a symbol table as a central repository for information about the various names that arise in the source code, in the IR, and in the generated code. During compiler development, the set of fields in the symbol table seems to grow monotonically. Fields are added to support new passes and to communicate information between passes. When the need for a field disappears, it may or may not be removed from the symbol-table definition. As each field is added, the symbol table swells in size and any parts of the compiler with direct access to the symbol table must be recompiled.

We encountered this problem in the implementation of the $\mathcal{R}^n$ and ParaScope programming environments. The experimental nature of these systems led to a situation where additions and deletions of symbol-table fields were common. To address the problem, we implemented a more complex but more flexible structure for the symbol table—a *two-dimensional hash table*. This eliminated almost all changes to the symbol-table definition and its implementation.

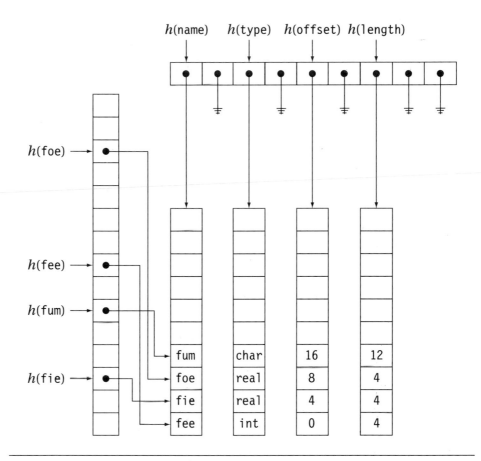

Two-Dimensional Hashed Symbol Table

The two-dimensional table, shown in Figure B.10, uses two distinct hash index tables. The first, shown along the left edge of the drawing, corresponds to the sparse index table from Figure B.6. The implementation uses this table to hash on symbol names. The second, shown along the top of the drawing, is a hash table for field names. The programmer references individual fields by both their textual name and the name of the symbol; the implementation hashes the symbol name to obtain an index and the field name to select a vector of data. The desired attribute is stored in the vector under the symbol's index. It behaves as if each field has its own hash table, implemented as shown in Figure B.6.

While this seems complex, it is not particularly expensive. Each table access requires two hash computations rather than one. The implementation need not allocate storage for a given field until a value is stored in it; this avoids the space overhead of unused fields. It allows individual developers to create and delete symbol-table fields without interfering with other programmers.

Our implementation provided entry points for setting initial values for a field (by name), for deleting a field (by name), and for reporting statistics on field use. This scheme allows individual programmers to manage their own symbol-table use in a responsible and independent way, without interference from other programmers and their code.

As a final issue, the implementation should be abstract with respect to a specific symbol table. That is, it should always take a table instance as a parameter. This allows the compiler to reuse the implementation in many cases, such as the superlocal or dominator-based value-numbering algorithms in Chapter 8.

APPENDIX NOTES

Many of the algorithms in a compiler manipulate sets, maps, tables, and graphs. The underlying implementations directly affect the space and time that those algorithms require and, ultimately, the usability of the compiler itself [54]. Algorithms and data-structure textbooks cover many of the issues that this appendix brings together [220, 4, 185, 103, 39].

Our research compilers have used almost all the data structures described in this appendix. We have seen performance problems from data-structure growth in several areas.

- Abstract syntax trees, as mentioned in the sidebar in Chapter 5, can grow unreasonably large. The technique of mapping an arbitrary tree onto a binary tree simplifies the implementation and seems to keep overhead low [220].

- The tabular representation of a graph, with lists of successors and predecessors, has been reinvented many times. It works particularly well for CFGS, for which the compiler iterates over both successors and predecessors. We first used this data structure in the PFC system in 1980.

- The sets in data-flow analysis can grow to occupy hundreds of megabytes. Because allocation and deallocation are performance issues at that scale, we routinely use Hanson's arena-based allocator [171].

- The size and sparsity of interference graphs makes them another area that merits careful consideration. We use the ordered-list variant with multiple set elements per node to keep the cost of building the graph low while managing the space overhead [94].

Symbol tables play a central role in the way that compilers store and access information. Much attention has been paid to the organization of these tables. Reorganizing lists [291, 309], balanced search trees [103, 39], and hashing [220, vol. 3] all play a role in making these tables efficient. Knuth [220, vol. 3] and Cormen [103] describe the multiplicative hash function in detail.

BIBLIOGRAPHY

[1] Philip S. Abrams. *An APL machine*. PhD thesis, Stanford University, Stanford, CA, February 1970. (Technical Report SLAC-R-114, Stanford Linear Accelerator Center, Stanford University, February 1970.)

[2] Alfred V. Aho, Mahadevan Ganapathi, and Steven W. K. Tjiang. Code generation using tree matching and dynamic programming. *ACM Transactions on Programming Languages and Systems*, 11(4):491–516, October 1989.

[3] Alfred V. Aho, John E. Hopcroft, and Jeffrey D. Ullman. On finding lowest common ancestors in trees. In *Conference Record of the Fifth Annual ACM Symposium on Theory of Computing* (STOC), pages 253–265, May 1973.

[4] Alfred V. Aho, John E. Hopcroft, and Jeffrey D. Ullman. *The Design and Analysis of Computer Algorithms*. Addison-Wesley, Reading, MA, 1974.

[5] Alfred V. Aho and Stephen C. Johnson. Optimal code generation for expression trees. *Journal of the ACM*, 23(3):488–501, July 1976.

[6] Alfred V. Aho, Stephen C. Johnson, and Jeffrey D. Ullman. Code generation for expressions with common subexpressions. In *Conference Record of the Third ACM Symposium on Principles of Programming Languages*, pages 19–31, Atlanta, GA, January 1976.

[7] Alfred V. Aho, Steven C. Johnson, and Jeffrey D. Ullman. Deterministic parsing of ambiguous grammars. In *Conference Record of the ACM Symposium on Principles of Programming Languages*, pages 1–21, Boston, MA, October 1973.

[8] Alfred V. Aho, Ravi Sethi, and Jeffrey D. Ullman. *Compilers: Principles, Techniques, and Tools*. Addison-Wesley, Reading, MA, 1986.

[9] Alfred V. Aho and Jeffrey D. Ullman. *The Theory of Parsing, Translation, and Compiling*. Prentice-Hall, Englewood Cliffs, NJ, 1973.

[10] Philippe Aigrain, Susan L. Graham, Robert R. Henry, Marshall Kirk McKusick, and Eduardo Pelegri-Llopart. Experience with a Graham-Glanville style code generator. *SIGPLAN Notices*, 19(6):13–24, June 1984. *Proceedings of the ACM SIGPLAN '84 Symposium on Compiler Construction*.

[11] Alexander Aiken and Alexandru Nicolau. Optimal loop parallelization. *SIGPLAN Notices*, 23(7):308–317, July 1988. *Proceedings of the ACM SIGPLAN '88 Conference on Programming Language Design and Implementation*.

[12] Frances E. Allen. Program optimization. In *Annual Review in Automatic Programming*, volume 5, pages 239–307. Pergamon Press, Oxford, England, 1969.

[13] Frances E. Allen. Control flow analysis. *SIGPLAN Notices*, 5(7):1–19, July 1970. *Proceedings of a Symposium on Compiler Optimization*.

[14] Frances E. Allen. The history of language processor technology in IBM. *IBM Journal of Research and Development*, 25(5):535–548, September 1981.

[15] Frances E. Allen and John Cocke. A catalogue of optimizing transformations. In R. Rustin, editor, *Design and Optimization of Compilers*, pages 1–30. Prentice-Hall, Englewood Cliffs, NJ, June 1972.

[16] Frances E. Allen and John Cocke. Graph-theoretic constructs for program flow analysis. Technical Report RC 3923 (17789), IBM Thomas J. Watson Research Center, Yorktown Heights, NY, July 1972.

[17] Frances E. Allen and John Cocke. A program data flow analysis procedure. *Communications of the ACM*, 19(3):137–147, March 1976.

[18] Frances E. Allen, John Cocke, and Ken Kennedy. Reduction of operator strength. In Steven S. Muchnick and Neil D. Jones, editors, *Program Flow Analysis: Theory and Applications*, pages 79–101. Prentice-Hall, Englewood Cliffs, NJ, 1981.

[19] John R. Allen and Ken Kennedy. *Optimizing Compilers for Modern Architectures*. Morgan Kaufmann, San Francisco, CA, October 2001.

[20] Bowen Alpern and Fred B. Schneider. Verifying temporal properties without temporal logic. *ACM Transactions on Programming Languages and Systems*, 11(1):147–167, January 1989.

[21] Bowen Alpern, Mark N. Wegman, and F. Kenneth Zadeck. Detecting equality of variables in programs. In *Conference Record of the Fifteenth Annual ACM Symposium on Principles of Programming Languages*, pages 1–11, San Diego, CA, January 1988.

[22] Stephen Alstrup, Dov Harel, Peter W. Lauridsen, and Mikkel Thorup. Dominators in linear time. *SIAM Journal on Computing*, 28(6):2117–2132, June 1999.

[23] Marc A. Auslander and Martin E. Hopkins. An overview of the PL.8 compiler. *SIGPLAN Notices*, 17(6):22–31, June 1982. *Proceedings of the ACM SIGPLAN '82 Symposium on Compiler Construction*.

[24] Andrew Ayers, Robert Gottlieb, and Richard Schooler. Aggressive inlining. *SIGPLAN Notices*, 32(5):134–145, May 1997. *Proceedings of the ACM SIGPLAN '97 Conference on Programming Language Design and Implementation*.

[25] John W. Backus. The history of Fortran I, II, and III. In Richard L. Wexelblat, editor, *History of Programming Languages*, pages 25–45. Academic Press, New York, NY, 1981.

[26] John W. Backus, R. J. Beeber, S. Best, R. Goldberg, L. M. Haibt, H. L. Herrick, R. A. Nelson, D. Sayre, P. B. Sheridan, H. Stern, I. Ziller, R. A. Hughes, and R. Nutt. The FORTRAN automatic coding system. In *Proceedings of the Western Joint Computer Conference*, pages 188–198, Institute of Radio Engineers, New York, NY, February 1957.

[27] David F. Bacon, Susan L. Graham, and Oliver J. Sharp. Compiler transformations for high-performance computing. *ACM Computing Surveys*, 26(4):345–420, 1994.

[28] John T. Bagwell, Jr. Local optimizations. *SIGPLAN Notices*, 5(7):52–66, July 1970. *Proceedings of a Symposium on Compiler Optimization*.

[29] John Banning. An efficient way to find side effects of procedure calls and aliases of variables. In *Conference Record of the Sixth Annual ACM Symposium on Principles of Programming Languages*, pages 29–41, San Antonio, TX, January 1979.

[30] William A. Barrett and John D. Couch. *Compiler Construction: Theory and Practice.* Science Research Associates, Inc., Chicago, IL, 1979.

[31] Jeffrey M. Barth. An interprocedural data flow analysis algorithm. In *Conference Record of the Fourth ACM Symposium on Principles of Programming Languages*, pages 119–131, Los Angeles, CA, January 1977.

[32] Alan M. Bauer and Harry J. Saal. Does *APL* really need run-time checking? *Software— Practice and Experience*, 4(2):129–138, 1974.

[33] Laszlo A. Belady. A study of replacement algorithms for a virtual storage computer. *IBM Systems Journal*, 5(2):78–101, 1966.

[34] C. Gordon Bell and Allen Newell. *Computer Structures: Readings and Examples.* McGraw-Hill Book Company, New York, NY, 1971.

[35] Peter Bergner, Peter Dahl, David Engebretsen, and Matthew T. O'Keefe. Spill code minimization via interference region spilling. *SIGPLAN Notices*, 32(5):287–295, May 1997. *Proceedings of the ACM SIGPLAN '97 Conference on Programming Language Design and Implementation.*

[36] David Bernstein, Dina Q. Goldin, Martin Charles Golumbic, Hugo Krawczyk, Yishay Mansour, Itai Nahshon, and Ron Y. Pinter. Spill code minimization techniques for optimizing compilers. *SIGPLAN Notices*, 24(7):258–263, July 1989. *Proceedings of the ACM SIGPLAN '89 Conference on Programming Language Design and Implementation.*

[37] David Bernstein and Michael Rodeh. Global instruction scheduling for superscalar machines. *SIGPLAN Notices*, 26(6):241–255, June 1991. *Proceedings of the ACM SIGPLAN '91 Conference on Programming Language Design and Implementation.*

[38] Robert L. Bernstein. Producing good code for the case statement. *Software—Practice and Experience*, 15(10):1021–1024, October 1985.

[39] Andrew Binstock and John Rex. *Practical Algorithms for Programmers.* Addison-Wesley, Reading, MA, 1995.

[40] Peter L. Bird. An implementation of a code generator specification language for table driven code generators. *SIGPLAN Notices*, 17(6):44–55, June 1982. *Proceedings of the ACM SIGPLAN '82 Symposium on Compiler Construction.*

[41] Rastislav Bodík, Rajiv Gupta, and Mary Lou Soffa. Complete removal of redundant expressions. *SIGPLAN Notices*, 33(5):1–14, May 1998. *Proceedings of the ACM SIGPLAN '98 Conference on Programming Language Design and Implementation.*

[42] Hans-Juergen Boehm. Space efficient conservative garbage collection. *SIGPLAN Notices*, 28(6):197–206, June 1993. *Proceedings of the ACM SIGPLAN '93 Conference on Programming Language Design and Implementation.*

[43] Hans-Juergen Boehm and Alan Demers. Implementing Russell. *SIGPLAN Notices*, 21(7):186–195, July 1986. *Proceedings of the ACM SIGPLAN '86 Symposium on Compiler Construction.*

[44] Hans-Juergen Boehm and Mark Weiser. Garbage collection in an uncooperative environment. *Software—Practice and Experience*, 18(9):807–820, September 1988.

[45] David G. Bradlee, Susan J. Eggers, and Robert R. Henry. Integrating register allocation and instruction scheduling for RISCS. *SIGPLAN Notices*, 26(4):122–131, April 1991. *Proceedings of the Fourth International Conference on Architectural Support for Programming Languages and Systems.*

[46] Preston Briggs. *Register Allocation via Graph Coloring*. PhD thesis, Rice University, Department of Computer Science, Houston, TX, April 1992. (Technical Report TR92–183, Computer Science Department, Rice University, 1992.)

[47] Preston Briggs, Keith D. Cooper, Timothy J. Harvey, and L. Taylor Simpson. Practical improvements to the construction and destruction of static single assignment form. *Software—Practice and Experience*, 28(8):859–881, July 1998.

[48] Preston Briggs, Keith D. Cooper, Ken Kennedy, and Linda Torczon. Coloring heuristics for register allocation. *SIGPLAN Notices*, 24(7):275–284, July 1989. *Proceedings of the ACM SIGPLAN '89 Conference on Programming Language Design and Implementation*.

[49] Preston Briggs, Keith D. Cooper, Ken Kennedy, and Linda Torczon. Digital computer register allocation and code spilling using interference graph coloring. United States Patent 5,249,295, March 1993.

[50] Preston Briggs, Keith D. Cooper, and L. Taylor Simpson. Value numbering. *Software—Practice and Experience*, 27(6):701–724, June 1997.

[51] Preston Briggs, Keith D. Cooper, and Linda Torczon. Coloring register pairs. *ACM Letters on Programming Languages and Systems*, 1(1):3–13, March 1992.

[52] Preston Briggs, Keith D. Cooper, and Linda Torczon. Rematerialization. *SIGPLAN Notices*, 27(7):311–321, July 1992. *Proceedings of the ACM SIGPLAN '92 Conference on Programming Language Design and Implementation*.

[53] Preston Briggs, Keith D. Cooper, and Linda Torczon. Improvements to graph coloring register allocation. *ACM Transactions on Programming Languages and Systems*, 16(3):428–455, May 1994.

[54] Preston Briggs and Linda Torczon. An efficient representation for sparse sets. *ACM Letters on Programming Languages and Systems*, 2(1–4):59–69, March–December 1993.

[55] Adam L. Buchsbaum, Haim Kaplan, Anne Rogers, and Jeffery R. Westbrook. Linear-time pointer-machine algorithms for least common ancestors, *MST* verification, and dominators. In *Proceedings of the Thirtieth Annual ACM Symposium on Theory of Computing*, pages 279–288, Dallas, TX, 1998.

[56] Michael Burke. An interval-based approach to exhaustive and incremental interprocedural data-flow analysis. *ACM Transactions on Programming Languages and Systems*, 12(3):341–395, July 1990.

[57] Michael Burke and Linda Torczon. Interprocedural optimization: Eliminating unnecessary recompilation. *ACM Transactions on Programming Languages and Systems*, 15(3):367–399, July 1993.

[58] Jiazhen Cai and Robert Paige. Using multiset discrimination to solve language processing problems without hashing. *Theoretical Computer Science*, 145(1–2):189–228, 1995.

[59] Brad Calder and Dirk Grunwald. Reducing branch costs via branch alignment. *SIGPLAN Notices*, 29(11): 242–251, November 1994. *Proceedings of the Sixth International Conference on Architectural Support for Programming Languages and Operating Systems*.

[60] David Callahan, Alan Carle, Mary W. Hall, and Ken Kennedy. Constructing the procedure call multigraph. *IEEE Transactions on Software Engineering*, 16(4):483–487, April 1990.

[61] David Callahan, Steve Carr, and Ken Kennedy. Improving register allocation for subscripted variables. *SIGPLAN Notices*, 25(6):53–65, June 1990. *Proceedings of the ACM SIGPLAN '90 Conference on Programming Language Design and Implementation.*

[62] David Callahan, Keith D. Cooper, Ken Kennedy, and Linda Torczon. Interprocedural constant propagation. *SIGPLAN Notices*, 21(7):152–161, July 1986. *Proceedings of the ACM SIGPLAN '86 Symposium on Compiler Construction.*

[63] David Callahan and Brian Koblenz. Register allocation via hierarchical graph coloring. *SIGPLAN Notices*, 26(6):192–203, June 1991. *Proceedings of the ACM SIGPLAN '91 Conference on Programming Language Design and Implementation.*

[64] Luca Cardelli. Type systems. In Allen B. Tucker, Jr., editor, *The Computer Science and Engineering Handbook*, chapter 103, pages 2208–2236. CRC Press, Boca Raton, FL, December 1996.

[65] Steve Carr and Ken Kennedy. Scalar replacement in the presence of conditional control flow. *Software—Practice and Experience*, 24(1):51–77, 1994.

[66] Roderic G. G. Cattell. Automatic derivation of code generators from machine descriptions. *ACM Transactions on Programming Languages and Systems*, 2(2):173–190, April 1980.

[67] Roderic G. G. Cattell, Joseph M. Newcomer, and Bruce W. Leverett. Code generation in a machine-independent compiler. *SIGPLAN Notices*, 14(8):65–75, August 1979. *Proceedings of the ACM SIGPLAN '79 Symposium on Compiler Construction.*

[68] Gregory J. Chaitin. Register allocation and spilling via graph coloring. *SIGPLAN Notices*, 17(6):98–105, June 1982. *Proceedings of the ACM SIGPLAN '82 Symposium on Compiler Construction.*

[69] Gregory J. Chaitin. Register allocation and spilling via graph coloring. United States Patent 4,571,678, February 1986.

[70] Gregory J. Chaitin, Marc A. Auslander, Ashok K. Chandra, John Cocke, Martin E. Hopkins, and Peter W. Markstein. Register allocation via coloring. *Computer Languages*, 6(1):47–57, January 1981.

[71] David R. Chase. An improvement to bottom-up tree pattern matching. In *Conference Record of the Fourteenth Annual ACM Symposium on Principles of Programming Languages*, pages 168–177, Munich, Germany, January 1987.

[72] David R. Chase, Mark Wegman, and F. Kenneth Zadeck. Analysis of pointers and structures. *SIGPLAN Notices*, 25(6):296–310, June 1990. *Proceedings of the ACM SIGPLAN '90 Conference on Programming Language Design and Implementation.*

[73] J. Bradley Chen and Bradley D. D. Leupen. Improving instruction locality with just-in-time code layout. In *Proceedings of the First USENIX Windows NT Workshop*, pages 25–32, Seattle, WA, August 1997.

[74] C. J. Cheney. A nonrecursive list compacting algorithm. *Communications of the ACM*, 13(11):677–678, November 1970.

[75] Jong-Deok Choi, Michael Burke, and Paul R.Carini. Efficient flow-sensitive interprocedural computation of pointer-induced aliases and side effects. In *Conference Record of the Twentieth Annual ACM Symposium on Principles of Programming Languages*, pages 232–245, Charleston, SC, January 1993.

[76] Frederick C. Chow. *A Portable Machine-Independent Global Optimizer —Design and Measurements*. PhD thesis, Department of Electrical Engineering, Stanford University, Stanford, CA, December 1983. (Technical Report CSL-TR-83-254, Computer Systems Laboratory, Stanford University, December 1983.)

[77] Frederick C. Chow and John L. Hennessy. Register allocation by priority-based coloring. *SIGPLAN Notices*, 19(6):222–232, June 1984. *Proceedings of the ACM SIGPLAN '84 Symposium on Compiler Construction*.

[78] Frederick C. Chow and John L. Hennessy. The priority-based coloring approach to register allocation. ACM *Transactions on Programming Languages and Systems*, 12(4):501–536, October 1990.

[79] Cliff Click. *Combining Analyses, Combining Optimizations*. PhD thesis, Rice University, Department of Computer Science, Houston, TX, February 1995. (Technical Report TR95-252, Computer Science Department, Rice University, 1995.)

[80] Cliff Click. Global code motion/global value numbering. *SIGPLAN Notices*, 30(6):246–257, June 1995. *Proceedings of the ACM SIGPLAN '95 Conference on Programming Language Design and Implementation*.

[81] Cliff Click and Keith D. Cooper. Combining analyses, combining optimizations. *ACM Transactions on Programming Languages and Systems*, 17(2):181–196, 1995.

[82] John Cocke. Global common subexpression elimination. *SIGPLAN Notices*, 5(7):20–24, July 1970. *Proceedings of a Symposium on Compiler Construction*.

[83] John Cocke and Ken Kennedy. An algorithm for reduction of operator strength. *Communications of the ACM*, 20(11):850–856, November 1977.

[84] John Cocke and Peter W. Markstein. Measurement of program improvement algorithms. In Simon H. Lavington, editor, *Information Processing 80*, North Holland, Amsterdam, Netherlands, pages 221–228, 1980, *Proceedings of IFIP Congress 80*.

[85] John Cocke and Peter W. Markstein. Strength reduction for division and modulo with application to accessing a multilevel store. *IBM Journal of Research and Development*, 24(6):692–694, 1980.

[86] John Cocke and Jacob T. Schwartz. Programming languages and their compilers: Preliminary notes. Technical report, Courant Institute of Mathematical Sciences, New York University, New York, NY, 1970.

[87] Jacques Cohen. Garbage collection of linked structures. *ACM Computing Surveys*, 13(3):341–367, September 1981.

[88] Robert Cohn and P. Geoffrey Lowney. Hot cold optimization of large Windows/*NT* applications. In *Proceedings of the Twenty-Ninth Annual International Symposium on Microarchitecture*, pages 80–89, Paris, France, December 1996.

[89] Stephanie Coleman and Kathryn S. McKinley. Tile size selection using cache organization and data layout. *SIGPLAN Notices*, 30(6):279–290, June 1995. *Proceedings of the ACM SIGPLAN '95 Conference on Programming Language Design and Implementation*.

[90] George E. Collins. A method for overlapping and erasure of lists. *Communications of the ACM*, 3(12):655–657, December 1960.

[91] Melvin E. Conway. Design of a separable transition diagram compiler. *Communications of the ACM*, 6(7):396–408, July 1963.

[92] Richard W. Conway and Thomas R. Wilcox. Design and implementation of a diagnostic compiler for PL/I. *Communications of the ACM*, 16(3):169–179, March 1973.

[93] Keith D. Cooper, Mary W. Hall, and Linda Torczon. An experiment with inline substitution. *Software—Practice and Experience*, 21(6):581–601, June 1991.

[94] Keith D. Cooper, Timothy J. Harvey, and Linda Torczon. How to build an interference graph. *Software—Practice and Experience*, 28(4):425–444, April 1998.

[95] Keith D. Cooper, Timothy J. Harvey, and Todd Waterman. Building a control-flow graph from scheduled assembly code. Technical Report 02-399, Department of Computer Science, Rice University, Houston, TX, June 2002.

[96] Keith D. Cooper and Ken Kennedy. Interprocedural side-effect analysis in linear time. *SIGPLAN Notices*, 23(7):57–66, July 1988. *Proceedings of the ACM SIGPLAN '88 Conference on Programming Language Design and Implementation.*

[97] Keith D. Cooper and Ken Kennedy. Fast interprocedural alias analysis. In *Conference Record of the Sixteenth Annual ACM Symposium on Principles of Programming Languages*, pages 49–59, Austin, TX, January 1989.

[98] Keith D. Cooper and Philip J. Schielke. Non-local instruction scheduling with limited code growth. In *Proceedings of the 1998 ACM SIGPLAN Workshop on Languages, Compilers, and Tools for Embedded Systems* (LCTES). *Lecture Notes in Computer Science 1474*, F. Mueller and A. Bestavros, editors, pages 193–207, Springer-Verlag, Heidelberg, Germany, 1998.

[99] Keith D. Cooper, Philip J. Schielke, and Devika Subramanian. Optimizing for reduced code space using genetic algorithms. *SIGPLAN Notices*, 34(7):1–9, July 1999. *Proceedings of the ACM SIGPLAN 1999 Workshop on Languages, Compilers, and Tools for Embedded Systems* (LCTES), May 1999.

[100] Keith D. Cooper and L. Taylor Simpson. Live range splitting in a graph coloring register allocator. In *Proceedings of the Seventh International Compiler Construction Conference, CC '98. Lecture Notes in Computer Science 1383*, pages 174–187, Springer-Verlag, Heidelberg, Germany, 1998.

[101] Keith D. Cooper, L. Taylor Simpson, and Christopher A. Vick. Operator strength reduction. *ACM Transactions on Programming Languages and Systems*, 23(5):603–625, September 2001.

[102] Keith D. Cooper and Todd Waterman. Understanding energy consumption on the C62x. In *Proceedings of the 2002 Workshop on Compilers and Operating Systems for Low Power*, pages 4–1 – 4–8, Charlottesville, VA, September 2002.

[103] Thomas H. Cormen, Charles E. Leiserson, and Ronald L. Rivest. *Introduction to Algorithms*. MIT Press, Cambridge, MA, 1992.

[104] Ron Cytron, Jeanne Ferrante, Barry K. Rosen, Mark N. Wegman, and F. Kenneth Zadeck. Efficiently computing static single assignment form and the control dependence graph. *ACM Transactions on Programming Languages and Systems*, 13(4):451–490, October 1991.

[105] Ron Cytron, Andy Lowry, and F. Kenneth Zadeck. Code motion of control structures in high-level languages. In *Conference Record of the Thirteenth Annual ACM Symposium on Principles of Programming Languages*, pages 70–85, St. Petersburg Beach, FL, January 1986.

[106] Manuvir Das. Unification-based pointer analysis with directional assignments. *SIGPLAN Notices*, 35(5):35–46, May 2000. In *Proceedings of the ACM SIGPLAN '00 Conference on Programming Language Design and Implementation.*

[107] Jack W. Davidson and Christopher W. Fraser. The design and application of a retargetable peephole optimizer. *ACM Transactions on Programming Languages and Systems*, 2(2):191–202, April 1980.

[108] Jack W. Davidson and Christopher W. Fraser. Automatic generation of peephole optimizations. *SIGPLAN Notices*, 19(6):111–116, June 1984. *Proceedings of the ACM SIGPLAN '84 Symposium on Compiler Construction.*

[109] Jack W. Davidson and Christopher W. Fraser. Register allocation and exhaustive peephole optimization. *Software—Practice and Experience*, 14(9):857–865, September 1984.

[110] Jack W. Davidson and Christopher W. Fraser. Automatic inference and fast interpretation of peephole optimization rules. *Software—Practice and Experience*, 17(11):801–812, November 1987.

[111] Jack W. Davidson and Ann M. Holler. A study of a C function inliner. *Software—Practice and Experience*, 18(8):775–790, August 1988.

[112] Alan J. Demers, Mark Weiser, Barry Hayes, Hans Boehm, Daniel Bobrow, and Scott Shenker. Combining generational and conservative garbage collection: Framework and implementations. In *Conference Record of the Seventeenth Annual ACM Symposium on Principles of Programming Languages*, pages 261–269, San Francisco, CA, January 1990.

[113] Frank DeRemer. Simple LR(k) grammars. *Communications of the ACM*, 14(7):453–460, July 1971.

[114] Frank DeRemer and Thomas J. Pennello. Efficient computation of LALR (1) look-ahead sets. *SIGPLAN Notices*, 14(8):176–187, August 1979. *Proceedings of the ACM SIGPLAN '79 Symposium on Compiler Construction.*

[115] Alain Deutsch. Interprocedural May-Alias analysis for pointers: Beyond k-limiting. *SIGPLAN Notices*, 29(6):230–241, June 1994. *Proceedings of the ACM SIGPLAN '94 Conference on Programming Language Design and Implementation.*

[116] L. Peter Deutsch. *An Interactive Program Verifier*. PhD thesis, Computer Science Department, University of California, Berkeley, Berkeley, CA, 1973. (Technical Report CSL-73-1, Xerox Palo Alto Research, May 1973.)

[117] L. Peter Deutsch and Daniel G Bobrow. An efficient, incremental, automatic, garbage collector. *Communications of the ACM*, 19(9):522–526, September 1976.

[118] Dhananjay M. Dhamdhere. On algorithms for operator strength reduction. *Communications of the ACM*, 22(5):311–312, May 1979.

[119] Dhananjay M. Dhamdhere. A fast algorithm for code movement optimisation. *SIGPLAN Notices*, 23(10):172–180, 1988.

[120] Dhananjay M. Dhamdhere. A new algorithm for composite hoisting and strength reduction. *International Journal of Computer Mathematics*, 27(1):1–14, 1989.

[121] Dhananjay M. Dhamdhere. Practical adaptation of the global optimization algorithm of Morel and Renvoise. *ACM Transactions on Programming Languages and Systems*, 13(2):291–294, April 1991.

[122] Michael K. Donegan, Robert E. Noonan, and Stefan Feyock. A code generator generator language. *SIGPLAN Notices*, 14(8):58–64, August 1979. *Proceedings of the ACM SIGPLAN '79 Symposium on Compiler Construction.*

[123] Jack J. Dongarra, James R. Bunch, Cleve B. Moler, and G. W. Stewart. *LINPACK User's Guide. SIAM*, Philadelphia, PA, 1979.

[124] Karl-Heinz Drechsler and Manfred P. Stadel. A solution to a problem with Morel and Renvoise's "Global optimization by suppression of partial redundancies." *ACM Transactions on Programming Languages and Systems*, 10(4):635–640, October 1988.

[125] Karl-Heinz Drechsler and Manfred P. Stadel. A variation of Knoop, Rüthing, and Steffen's "Lazy code motion." *SIGPLAN Notices*, 28(5):29–38, May 1993.

[126] Jay Earley. An efficient context-free parsing algorithm. *Communications of the ACM*, 13(2):94–102, February 1970.

[127] Kemal Ebcioğlu and Toshio Nakatani. A new compilation technique for parallelizing loops with unpredictable branches on a VLIW architecture. *Selected Papers of the Second Workshop on Languages and Compilers for Parallel Computing*, Pitman Publishing, London, UK, pages 213–229, 1990.

[128] John R. Ellis. *Bulldog: A Compiler for* VLIW *Architectures*. The MIT Press, Cambridge, MA, 1986.

[129] Maryam Emami, Rakesh Ghiya, and Laurie J. Hendren. Context-sensitive interprocedural points-to analysis in the presence of function pointers. *SIGPLAN Notices*, 29(6):242–256, June 1994. *Proceedings of the ACM SIGPLAN '94 Conference on Programming Language Design and Implementation.*

[130] Jens Ernst, William S. Evans, Christopher W. Fraser, Steven Lucco, and Todd A. Proebsting. Code compression. *SIGPLAN Notices*, 32(5):358–365, May 1997. In *Proceedings of the ACM SIGPLAN '97 Conference on Programming Language Design and Implementation.*

[131] Andrei P. Ershov. On programming of arithmetic expressions. *Communications of the ACM*, 1(8):3–6, August 1958. (The figures appear in volume 1, number 9, page 16.)

[132] Andrei P. Ershov. Reduction of the problem of memory allocation in programming to the problem of coloring the vertices of graphs. *Soviet Mathematics*, 3:163–165, 1962. Originally published in *Doklady Akademii Nauk S.S.S.R.*, 142(4), 1962.

[133] Andrei P. Ershov. Alpha—An automatic programming system of high efficiency. *Journal of the ACM*, 13(1):17–24, January 1966.

[134] Janet Fabri. Automatic storage optimization. *SIGPLAN Notices*, 14(8):83–91, August 1979. *Proceedings of the ACM SIGPLAN '79 Symposium on Compiler Construction.*

[135] Rodney Farrow. Linguist-86: Yet another translator writing system based on attribute grammars. *SIGPLAN Notices*, 17(6):160–171, June 1982. *Proceedings of the ACM SIGPLAN '82 Symposium on Compiler Construction.*

[136] Rodney Farrow. Automatic generation of fixed-point-finding evaluators for circular, but well-defined, attribute grammars. *SIGPLAN Notices*, 21(7):85–98, July 1986. *Proceedings of the ACM SIGPLAN '86 Symposium on Compiler Construction.*

[137] Robert R. Fenichel and Jerome C. Yochelson. A *LISP* garbage-collector for virtual-memory computer systems. *Communications of the ACM*, 12(11):611–612, November 1969.

[138] Jeanne Ferrante, Karl J. Ottenstein, and Joe D. Warren. The program dependence graph and its use in optimization. *ACM Transactions on Programming Languages and Systems*, 9(3):319–349, July 1987.

[139] Charles N. Fischer and Richard J. LeBlanc, Jr. The implementation of run-time diagnostics in Pascal. *IEEE Transactions on Software Engineering*, SE-6(4):313–319, 1980.

[140] Charles N. Fischer and Richard J. LeBlanc, Jr. *Crafting a Compiler with C*. Benjamin/Cummings, Redwood City, CA, 1991.

[141] Joseph A. Fisher. Trace scheduling: A technique for global microcode compaction. *IEEE Transactions on Computers*, C-30(7):478–490, July 1981.

[142] Joseph A. Fisher, John R. Ellis, John C. Ruttenberg, and Alexandru Nicolau. Parallel processing: A smart compiler and a dumb machine. *SIGPLAN Notices*, 19(6):37–47, June 1984. *Proceedings of the ACM SIGPLAN '84 Symposium on Compiler Construction*.

[143] Robert W. Floyd. An algorithm for coding efficient arithmetic expressions. *Communications of the ACM*, 4(1):42–51, January 1961.

[144] J. M. Foster. A syntax improving program. *Computer Journal*, 11(1): 31–34, May 1968.

[145] Christopher W. Fraser. Automatic inference of models for statistical code compression. *SIGPLAN Notices*, 34(5):242–246, May 1999. In *Proceedings of the ACM SIGPLAN '99 Conference on Programming Language Design and Implementation*.

[146] Christopher W. Fraser, David R. Hanson, and Todd A. Proebsting. Engineering a simple, efficient code generator generator. *ACM Letters on Programming Languages and Systems*, 1(3):213–226, September 1992.

[147] Christopher W. Fraser and Robert R. Henry. Hard-coding bottom-up code generation tables to save time and space. *Software—Practice and Experience*, 21(1):1–12, January 1991.

[148] Christopher W. Fraser, Eugene W. Myers, and Alan L. Wendt. Analyzing and compressing assembly code. *SIGPLAN Notices*, 19(6):117–121, June 1984. *Proceedings of the ACM SIGPLAN '84 Symposium on Compiler Construction*.

[149] Christopher W. Fraser and Alan L. Wendt. Integrating code generation and optimization. *SIGPLAN Notices*, 21(7):242–248, July 1986. *Proceedings of the ACM SIGPLAN '86 Symposium on Compiler Construction*.

[150] Christopher W. Fraser and Alan L. Wendt. Automatic generation of fast optimizing code generators. *SIGPLAN Notices*, 23(7):79–84, July 1988. *Proceedings of the ACM SIGPLAN '88 Conference on Programming Language Design and Implementation*.

[151] Mahadevan Ganapathi and Charles N. Fischer. Description-driven code generation using attribute grammars. In *Conference Record of the Ninth Annual ACM Symposium on Principles of Programming Languages*, pages 108–119, Albuquerque, NM, January 1982.

[152] Harald Ganzinger, Robert Giegerich, Ulrich Möncke, and Reinhard Wilhelm. A truly generative semantics-directed compiler generator. *SIGPLAN Notices*, 17(6):172–184, June 1982. *Proceedings of the ACM SIGPLAN '82 Symposium on Compiler Construction*.

[153] Lal George and Andrew W. Appel. Iterated register coalescing. In *Conference Record of the Twenty-Third ACM Symposium on Principles of Programming Languages*, pages 208–218, St. Petersburg Beach, FL, January 1996.

[154] Phillip B. Gibbons and Steven S. Muchnick. Efficient instruction scheduling for a pipelined architecture. *SIGPLAN Notices*, 21(7):11–16, July 1986. *Proceedings of the ACM SIGPLAN '86 Symposium on Compiler Construction.*

[155] R. Steven Glanville and Susan L. Graham. A new method for compiler code generation. In *Conference Record of the Fifth Annual ACM Symposium on Principles of Programming Languages*, pages 231–240, Tucson, AZ, January 1978.

[156] Nikolas Gloy and Michael D. Smith. Procedure placement using temporal-ordering information. *ACM Transactions on Programming Languages and Systems*, 21(5):997–1027, September 1999.

[157] Adele Goldberg and David Robson. *Smalltalk-80: The Language and Its Implementation.* Addison-Wesley, Reading, MA, 1983.

[158] James R. Goodman and Wei-Chung Hsu. Code scheduling and register allocation in large basic blocks. *Proceedings of the Second International Conference on Supercomputing*, pages 442–452, July 1988.

[159] Eiichi Goto. Monocopy and associative operations in extended Lisp. Technical Report 74-03, University of Tokyo, Tokyo, Japan, May 1974.

[160] Susan L. Graham. Table-driven code generation. *IEEE Computer*, 13(8):25–34, August 1980.

[161] Susan L. Graham, Michael A. Harrison, and Walter L. Ruzzo. An improved context-free recognizer. *ACM Transactions on Programming Languages and Systems*, 2(3):415–462, July 1980.

[162] Susan L. Graham, Robert R. Henry, and Robert A. Schulman. An experiment in table driven code generation. *SIGPLAN Notices*, 17(6):32–43, June 1982. *Proceedings of the ACM SIGPLAN '82 Symposium on Compiler Construction.*

[163] Susan L. Graham and Mark Wegman. A fast and usually linear algorithm for global flow analysis. In *Conference Record of the Second ACM Symposium on Principles of Programming Languages*, pages 22–34, Palo Alto, CA, January 1975.

[164] Susan L. Graham and Mark Wegman. A fast and usually linear algorithm for global flow analysis. *Journal of the ACM*, 23(1):172–202, 1976.

[165] Torbjörn Granlund and Richard Kenner. Eliminating branches using a superoptimizer and the *GNU* C compiler. *SIGPLAN Notices*, 27(7):341–352, July 1992. *Proceedings of the ACM SIGPLAN '92 Conference on Programming Language Design and Implementation.*

[166] David Gries. *Compiler Construction for Digital Computers.* John Wiley and Sons, New York, NY, 1971.

[167] Rajiv Gupta and Mary Lou Soffa. Region scheduling: An approach for detecting and redistributing parallelism. *IEEE Transactions on Software Engineering*, 16(4):421–431, April 1990.

[168] Rajiv Gupta, Mary Lou Soffa, and Tim Steele. Register allocation via clique separators. *SIGPLAN Notices*, 24(7):264–274, July 1989. *Proceedings of the ACM SIGPLAN '89 Conference on Programming Language Design and Implementation.*

[169] Max Hailperin. Cost-optimal code motion. *ACM Transactions on Programming Languages and Systems*, 20(6):1297–1322, November 1998.

[170] Mary W. Hall and Ken Kennedy. Efficient call graph analysis. *ACM Letters on Programming Languages and Systems*, 1(3):227–242, September 1992.

[171] David R. Hanson. Fast allocation and deallocation of memory based on object lifetimes. *Software—Practice and Experience*, 20(1):5–12, January 1990.

[172] Dov Harel. A linear time algorithm for finding dominators in flow graphs and related problems. In *Proceedings of the Seventeenth Annual ACM Symposium on Theory of Computing* STOC, pages 185–194, May 1985.

[173] William H. Harrison. A class of register allocation algorithms. Technical Report RC-5342, IBM Thomas J. Watson Research Center, Yorktown Heights, NY, 1975.

[174] William H. Harrison. A new strategy for code generation—The general purpose optimizing compiler. *IEEE Transactions on Software Engineering*, SE-5(4):367–373, July 1979.

[175] Philip J. Hatcher and Thomas W. Christopher. High-quality code generation via bottom-up tree pattern matching. In *Conference Record of the Thirteenth Annual ACM Symposium on Principles of Programming Languages*, pages 119–130, St. Petersburg Beach, FL, January 1986.

[176] Matthew S. Hecht and Jeffrey D. Ullman. Characterizations of reducible flow graphs. *Journal of the ACM*, 21(3):367–375, July 1974.

[177] Matthew S. Hecht and Jeffrey D. Ullman. A simple algorithm for global data flow analysis problems. *SIAM Journal on Computing*, 4(4):519–532, 1975.

[178] J. Heller. Sequencing aspects of multiprogramming. *Journal of the ACM*, 8(3):426–439, July 1961.

[179] John L. Hennessy and Thomas Gross. Postpass code optimization of pipeline constraints. *ACM Transactions on Programming Languages and Systems*, 5(3):422–448, July 1983.

[180] Michael Hind, Michael Burke, Paul Carini, and Jong-Deok Choi. Interprocedural pointer alias analysis. *ACM Transactions on Programming Languages and Systems*, 21(4):848–894, July 1999.

[181] Michael Hind and Anthony Pioli. Which pointer analysis should I use? *ACM SIGSOFT Software Engineering Notes*, 25(5):113–123, September 2000. In *Proceedings of the International Symposium on Software Testing and Analysis*.

[182] Christoph M. Hoffmann and Michael J. O'Donnell. Pattern matching in trees. *Journal of the ACM*, 29(1):68–95, January 1982.

[183] John E. Hopcroft. An $n \log n$ algorithm for minimizing states in a finite automaton. In Zvi Kohavi and Azaria Paz, editors, *Theory of Machines and Computations: Proceedings*, pages 189–196, Academic Press, New York, NY, 1971.

[184] John E. Hopcroft and Jeffrey D. Ullman. *Introduction to Automata Theory, Languages, and Computation*. Addison-Wesley, Reading, MA, 1979.

[185] Ellis Horowitz and Sartaj Sahni. *Fundamentals of Computer Algorithms*. Computer Science Press, Inc., Potomac, MD, 1978.

[186] Lawrence P. Horwitz, Richard M. Karp, Raymond E. Miller, and Shmuel Winograd. Index register allocation. *Journal of the ACM*, 13(1):43–61, January 1966.

[187] Susan Horwitz, Phil Pfeiffer, and Thomas Reps. Dependence analysis for pointer variables. *SIGPLAN Notices*, 24(7):28–40, July 1989. *Proceedings of the ACM SIGPLAN '89 Conference on Programming Language Design and Implementation*.

[188] Susan Horwitz and Tim Teitelbaum. Generating editing environments based on relations and attributes. *ACM Transactions on Programming Languages and Systems*, 8(4):577–608, October 1986.

[189] Brett L. Huber. Path-selection heuristics for dominator-path scheduling. Master's thesis, Computer Science Department, Michigan Technological University, Houghton, MI, October 1995.

[190] Wen-Mei W. Hwu, Scott A. Mahlke, William Y. Chen, Pohua P. Chang, Nancy J. Warter, Roger A. Bringmann, Roland G. Ouellette, Richard E. Hank, Tokuzo Kiyohara, Grant E. Haab, John G. Holm, and Daniel M. Lavery. The superblock: An effective technique for VLIW and superscalar compilation. *Journal of Supercomputing—Special Issue on Instruction Level Parallelism*, 7(1–2): 229–248, Kluwer Academic Publishers, Hingham, MA, May 1993.

[191] Edgar T. Irons. A syntax directed compiler for Algol 60. *Communications of the ACM*, 4(1):51–55, January 1961.

[192] J. R. Issaac and Dhananjay M. Dhamdhere. A composite algorithm for strength reduction and code movement optimization. *International Journal of Computer and Information Sciences*, 9(3):243–273, June 1980.

[193] Mehdi Jazayeri and Kenneth G. Walter. Alternating semantic evaluator. In *Proceedings of the 1975 Annual Conference of the ACM*, pages 230–234, 1975.

[194] Mark Scott Johnson and Terrence C. Miller. Effectiveness of a machine-level, global optimizer. *SIGPLAN Notices*, 21(7):99–108, July 1986. *Proceedings of the ACM SIGPLAN '86 Symposium on Compiler Construction.*

[195] Stephen C. Johnson. Yacc—Yet another compiler-compiler. Technical Report 32 (Computing Science), AT&T Bell Laboratories, Murray Hill, NJ, 1975.

[196] Stephen C. Johnson. A tour through the portable C compiler. In *Unix Programmer's Manual, 7th Edition*, volume 2b. AT&T Bell Laboratories, Murray Hill, NJ, January 1979.

[197] Walter L. Johnson, James H. Porter, Stephanie I. Ackley, and Douglas T. Ross. Automatic generation of efficient lexical processors using finite state techniques. *Communications of the ACM*, 11(12):805–813, December 1968.

[198] S. M. Joshi and Dhananjay M. Dhamdhere. A composite hoisting-strength reduction transformation for global program optimization. *International Journal of Computer Mathematics*, 11(1):21–44 (part I); 11(2): 111–126 (part II), 1982.

[199] John B. Kam and Jeffrey D. Ullman. Global data flow analysis and iterative algorithms. *Journal of the ACM*, 23(1):158–171, January 1976.

[200] John B. Kam and Jeffrey D. Ullman. Monotone data flow analysis frameworks. *Acta Informatica*, 7:305–317, 1977.

[201] Tadao Kasami. An efficient recognition and syntax analysis algorithm for context-free languages. Scientific Report AFRCL-65-758, Air Force Cambridge Research Laboratory, Bedford, MA, 1965.

[202] Ken Kennedy. *Global Flow Analysis and Register Allocation for Simple Code Structures.* PhD thesis, Courant Institute, New York University, October 1971.

[203] Ken Kennedy. Global dead computation elimination. SETL Newsletter 111, Courant Institute of Mathematical Sciences, New York University, New York, NY, August 1973.

[204] Ken Kennedy. Reduction in strength using hashed temporaries. SETL Newsletter 102, Courant Institute of Mathematical Sciences, New York University, New York, NY, March 1973.

[205] Ken Kennedy. Node listings applied to data flow analysis. In *Conference Record of the Second ACM Symposium on Principles of Programming Languages*, pages 10–21, Palo Alto, CA, January 1975.

[206] Ken Kennedy. Use-definition chains with applications. *Computer Languages*, 3(3):163–179, 1978.

[207] Ken Kennedy. A survey of data flow analysis techniques. In Neil D. Jones and Steven S. Muchnick, editors, *Program Flow Analysis: Theory and Applications*. Prentice-Hall, Englewood Cliffs, NJ, 1981.

[208] Ken Kennedy and Linda Zucconi. Applications of graph grammar for program control flow analysis. In *Conference Record of the Fourth ACM Symposium on Principles of Programming Languages*, pages 72–85, Los Angeles, CA, January 1977.

[209] Robert Kennedy, Fred C. Chow, Peter Dahl, Shin-Ming Liu, Raymond Lo, and Mark Streich. Strength reduction via SSAPRE. In *Proceedings of the Seventh International Conference on Compiler Construction. Lecture Notes in Computer Science 1383*, pages 144–158, Springer-Verlag, Heidelberg, Germany, March 1998.

[210] Daniel R. Kerns and Susan J. Eggers. Balanced scheduling: Instruction scheduling when memory latency is uncertain. *SIGPLAN Notices*, 28(6):278–289, June 1993. *Proceedings of the ACM SIGPLAN '93 Conference on Programming Language Design and Implementation.*

[211] Robert R. Kessler. Peep—An architectural description driven peephole optimizer. *SIGPLAN Notices*, 19(6):106–110, June 1984. *Proceedings of the ACM SIGPLAN '84 Symposium on Compiler Construction.*

[212] Gary A. Kildall. A unified approach to global program optimization. In *Conference Record of the ACM Symposium on Principles of Programming Languages*, pages 194–206, Boston, MA, October 1973.

[213] Stephen C. Kleene. Representation of events in nerve nets and finite automata. In Claude E. Shannon and John McCarthy, editors, *Automata Studies. Annals of Mathematics Studies*, 34:3–41. Princeton University Press, Princeton, NJ, 1956.

[214] Kath Knobe and Andrew Meltzer. Control tree based register allocation. Technical report, COMPASS, 1990.

[215] Jens Knoop, Oliver Rüthing, and Bernhard Steffen. Lazy code motion. *SIGPLAN Notices*, 27(7):224–234, July 1992. *Proceedings of the ACM SIGPLAN '92 Conference on Programming Language Design and Implementation.*

[216] Jens Knoop, Oliver Rüthing, and Bernhard Steffen. Lazy strength reduction. *International Journal of Programming Languages*, 1(1):71–91, March 1993.

[217] Donald E. Knuth. On the translation of languages from left to right. *Information and Control*, 8(6):607–639, December 1965.

[218] Donald E. Knuth. Semantics of context-free languages. *Mathematical Systems Theory*, 2(2):127–145, 1968.

[219] Donald E. Knuth. Semantics of context-free languages: Correction. *Mathematical Systems Theory*, 5(1):95–96, 1971.

[220] Donald E. Knuth. *The Art of Computer Programming*. Addison-Wesley, Reading, MA, 1973.

[221] Donald E. Knuth. A history of writing compilers. *Computers and Automation*, 11(12): 8–18, December 1962. Reprinted in *Compiler Techniques*, Bary W. Pollack, editor, pages 38–56, Auerbach, Princeton, NJ, 1972.

[222] Dexter C. Kozen. *Automata and Computability*. Springer-Verlag, New York, NY, 1997.

[223] Glenn Krasner, editor. *Smalltalk-80: Bits of History, Words of Advice*. Addison-Wesley, Reading, MA, August 1983.

[224] Sanjay M. Krishnamurthy. A brief survey of papers on scheduling for pipelined processors. *SIGPLAN Notices*, 25(7):97–106, July 1990.

[225] Steven M. Kurlander and Charles N. Fischer. Zero-cost range splitting. *SIGPLAN Notices*, 29(6):257–265, June 1994. *Proceedings of the ACM SIGPLAN '94 Conference on Programming Language Design and Implementation*.

[226] Monica Lam. Software pipelining: An effective scheduling technique for VLIW machines. *SIGPLAN Notices*, 23(7):318–328, July 1988. *Proceedings of the ACM SIGPLAN '88 Conference on Programming Language Design and Implementation*.

[227] David Alex Lamb. Construction of a peephole optimizer. *Software—Practice and Experience*, 11(6):639–647, June 1981.

[228] William Landi and Barbara G. Ryder. Pointer-induced aliasing: A problem taxonomy. In *Conference Record of the Eighteenth Annual ACM Symposium on Principles of Programming Languages*, pages 93–103, Orlando, FL, January 1991.

[229] David Landskov, Scott Davidson, Bruce Shriver, and Patrick W. Mallett. Local microcode compaction techniques. *ACM Computing Surveys*, 12(3):261–294, September 1980.

[230] Rudolf Landwehr, Hans-Stephan Jansohn, and Gerhard Goos. Experience with an automatic code generator generator. *SIGPLAN Notices*, 17(6):56–66, June 1982. *Proceedings of the ACM SIGPLAN '82 Symposium on Compiler Construction*.

[231] James R. Larus and Paul N. Hilfinger. Register allocation in the SPUR Lisp compiler. *SIGPLAN Notices*, 21(7):255–263, July 1986. *Proceedings of the ACM SIGPLAN '86 Symposium on Compiler Construction*.

[232] S. S. Lavrov. Store economy in closed operator schemes. *Journal of Computational Mathematics and Mathematical Physics*, 1(4):687–701, 1961. English translation in *U.S.S.R. Computational Mathematics and Mathematical Physics* 3:810-828, 1962.

[233] Charles Lefurgy, Peter Bird, I-Cheng Chen, and Trevor Mudge. Improving code density using compression techniques. In *Proceedings of the Thirtieth International Symposium on Microarchitecture*, pages 194–203, IEEE Computer Society Press , Los Alamitos, CA, December 1997.

[234] Charles Lefurgy, Eva Piccininni, and Trevor Mudge. Reducing code size with run-time decompression. In *Proceedings of the Sixth International Symposium on High-Performance Computer Architecture*, pages 218–227, IEEE Computer Society Press, Los Alamitos, CA, January 2000.

[235] Thomas Lengauer and Robert Endre Tarjan. A fast algorithm for finding dominators in a flowgraph. *ACM Transactions on Programming Languages and Systems*, 1(1):121–141, July 1979.

[236] Philip M. Lewis and Richard E. Stearns. Syntax-directed transduction. *Journal of the ACM*, 15(3):465–488, July 1968.

[237] Vincenzo Liberatore, Martin Farach-Colton, and Ulrich Kremer. Evaluation of algorithms for local register allocation. In *Eighth International Conference on Compiler Construction (CC 99)*, LNCS. *Lecture Notes in Computer Science 1575*, pages 137–152, Springer-Verlag, Heidelberg, Germany, 1999.

[238] Henry Lieberman and Carl Hewitt. A real-time garbage collector based on the lifetimes of objects. *Communications of the ACM*, 26(6):419–429, June 1983.

[239] Barbara Liskov, Russell R. Atkinson, Toby Bloom, J. Eliot B. Moss, Craig Schaflert, Robert Scheifler, and Alan Snyder CLU *Reference Manual. Lecture Notes in Computer Science 114*, Springer-Verlag, Heidelberg, Germany 1981.

[240] Jack L. Lo and Susan J. Eggers. Improving balanced scheduling with compiler optimizations that increase instruction-level parallelism. *SIGPLAN Notices*, 30(6):151–162, June 1995. *Proceedings of the ACM SIGPLAN '95 Conference on Programming Language Design and Implementation.*

[241] Raymond Lo, Fred Chow, Robert Kennedy, Shin-Ming Liu, and Peng Tu. Register promotion by sparse partial redundancy elimination of loads and stores. *SIGPLAN Notices*, 33(5):26–37, May 1998. *Proceedings of the ACM SIGPLAN '98 Conference on Programming Language Design and Implementation.*

[242] P. Geoffrey Lowney, Stefan M. Freudenberger, T. J. Karzes, W. D. Lichtenstein, Robert P. Nix, John S. O'Donnell, and John. C. Ruttenberg. The Multiflow trace scheduling compiler. *The Journal of Supercomputing—Special Issue*, 7(1–2):51–142, March 1993.

[243] Edward S. Lowry and C. W. Medlock. Object code optimization. *Communications of the ACM*, 12(1):13–22, January 1969.

[244] John Lu and Keith D. Cooper. Register promotion in C programs. *SIGPLAN Notices*, 32(5):308–319, May 1997. *Proceedings of the ACM SIGPLAN '97 Conference on Programming Language Design and Implementation.*

[245] John Lu and Rob Shillner. Clean: Removing useless control flow. Unpublished. Department of Computer Science, Rice University, Houston, TX, June 1994.

[246] Peter Lucas. Die strukturanalyse von formelübersetzern. *Elektronische Rechenanlagen*, 3:159–167, 1961.

[247] Guei-Yuan Lueh, Thomas Gross, and Ali-Reza Adl-Tabatabai. Global register allocation based on graph fusion. In *Proceedings of the Ninth International Workshop on Languages and Compilers for Parallel Computing (LCPC '96). Lecture Notes in Computer Science 1239*, pages 246–265, Springer-Verlag, Heidelberg, Germany, 1997.

[248] Bohdan S. Majewski, Nicholas C. Wormald, George Havas, and Zbigniew J. Czech. A family of perfect hashing methods. *The Computer Journal*, 39(6):547–554, 1996.

[249] Brian L. Marks. Compilation to compact code. *IBM Journal of Research and Development*, 24(6):684–691, November 1980.

[250] Peter W. Markstein, Victoria Markstein, and F. Kenneth Zadeck. Reassociation and strength reduction. Unpublished book chapter, July 1994.

[251] Henry Massalin. Superoptimizer—A look at the smallest program. *SIGPLAN Notices*, 22(10):122–126, October 1987. *Proceedings of the Second International Conference on Architectural Support for Programming Languages and Operating Systems.*

[252] John McCarthy. Lisp—Notes on its past and future. In *Proceedings of the 1980 ACM Conference on LISP and Functional Programming*, pages v–viii, Stanford University, Stanford, CA, 1980.

[253] William M. McKeeman. Peephole optimization. *Communications of the ACM*, 8(7):443–444, July 1965.

[254] Kathryn S. McKinley, Steve Carr, and Chau-Wen Tseng. Improving data locality with loop transformations. *ACM Transactions on Programming Languages and Systems (TOPLAS)*, 18(4):424–453, July 1996.

[255] Kathryn S. McKinley and Olivier Temam. A quantitative analysis of loop nest locality. In *Proceedings of the Seventh International Conference on Architectural Support for Programming Languages and Operating Systems* (ASPLOS-7), pages 94–104, Cambridge, MA, September 1996.

[256] Robert McNaughton and H. Yamada. Regular expressions and state graphs for automata. *IRE Transactions on Electronic Computers*, EC-9(1):39–47, March 1960.

[257] Terrence C. Miller. *Tentative Compilation: A design for an APL compiler*. PhD thesis, Yale University, New Haven, CT, May 1978. See also paper of same title in *Proceedings of the International Conference on APL: Part 1*, pages 88–95, New York, NY, 1979.

[258] Robin Milner, Mads Tofte, Robert Harper, and David MacQueen. *The Definition of Standard ML—Revised. MIT* Press, Cambridge, MA, 1997.

[259] Etienne Morel and Claude Renvoise. Global optimization by suppression of partial redundancies. *Communications of the ACM*, 22(2):96–103, February 1979.

[260] Robert Morgan. *Building an Optimizing Compiler*. Digital Press (an imprint of Butterworth–Heineman), Boston, MA, February 1998.

[261] Rajeev Motwani, Krishna V. Palem, Vivek Sarkar, and Salem Reyen. Combining register allocation and instruction scheduling. Technical Report 698, Courant Institute of Mathematical Sciences, New York University, New York, NY, July 1995.

[262] Steven S. Muchnick. *Advanced Compiler Design & Implementation*. Morgan Kaufmann, San Francisco, CA, August 1997.

[263] Frank Mueller and David B. Whalley. Avoiding unconditional jumps by code replication. *SIGPLAN Notices*, 27(7):322–330, July 1992. *Proceedings of the ACM SIGPLAN '92 Conference on Programming Language Design and Implementation.*

[264] Thomas P. Murtagh. An improved storage management scheme for block structured languages. *ACM Transactions on Programming Languages and Systems*, 13(3):372–398, July 1991.

[265] Peter Naur (editor), J. W. Backus, F. L. Bauer, J. Green, C. Katz, J. McCarthy, A. J. Perlis, H. Rutishauser, K. Samelson, B. Vauquois, J. H. Wegstein, A. van Wijngaarden, and M. Woodger. Revised report on the algorithmic language Algol 60. *Communications of the ACM*, 6(1):1–17, January 1963.

[266] Brian R. Nickerson. Graph coloring register allocation for processors with multi-register operands. *SIGPLAN Notices*, 25(6):40–52, June 1990. *Proceedings of the ACM SIGPLAN '90 Conference on Programming Language Design and Implementation.*

[267] Cindy Norris and Lori L. Pollock. A scheduler-sensitive global register allocator. In *Proceedings of Supercomputing '93*, pages 804–813, Portland, OR, November 1993.

[268] Cindy Norris and Lori L. Pollock. An experimental study of several cooperative register allocation and instruction scheduling strategies. In *Proceedings of the Twenty-Eighth Annual International Symposium on Microarchitecture*, pages 169–179, IEEE Computer Society Press, Los Alamitos, CA, December 1995.

[269] Kristen Nygaard and Ole-Johan Dahl. The development of the *simula* languages. In *Proceedings of the First ACM SIGPLAN Conference on the History of Programming Languages*, pages 245–272, ACM Press, New York, NY, January 1978.

[270] Jinpyo Park and Soo-Mook Moon. Optimistic register coalescing. In *Proceedings of the 1998 International Conference on Parallel Architecture and Compilation Techniques* (PACT), pages 196–204, October 1998.

[271] Eduardo Pelegrí-Llopart and Susan L. Graham. Optimal code generation for expression trees: An application of BURS theory. In *Conference Record of the Fifteenth Annual ACM Symposium on Principles of Programming Languages*, pages 294–308, San Diego, CA, January 1988.

[272] Thomas J. Pennello. Very fast LR parsing. *SIGPLAN Notices*, 21(7):145–151, July 1986. *Proceedings of the ACM SIGPLAN '86 Symposium on Compiler Construction*.

[273] Karl Pettis and Robert C. Hansen. Profile guided code positioning. *SIGPLAN Notices*, 25(6):16–27, June 1990. *Proceedings of the ACM SIGPLAN '90 Conference on Programming Language Design and Implementation*.

[274] Shlomit S. Pinter. Register allocation with instruction scheduling: A new approach. *SIGPLAN Notices*, 28(6):248–257, June 1993. *Proceedings of the ACM SIGPLAN '93 Conference on Programming Language Design and Implementation*.

[275] Gordon D. Plotkin. Call-by-name, call-by-value, and the λ-calculus. *Theoretical Computer Science*, 1(2):125–159, December 1975.

[276] Todd A. Proebsting. Simple and efficient BURS table generation. *SIGPLAN Notices*, 27(7):331–340, July 1992. *Proceedings of the ACM SIGPLAN '92 Conference on Programming Language Design and Implementation*.

[277] Todd A. Proebsting. Optimizing an ANSI C interpreter with superoperators. In *Conference Record of the Twenty-Second ACM Symposium on Principles of Programming Languages*, pages 322–332, San Francisco, CA, January 1995.

[278] Todd A. Proebsting and Charles N. Fischer. Linear-time, optimal code scheduling for delayed-load architectures. *SIGPLAN Notices*, 26(6): 256–267, June 1991. *Proceedings of the ACM SIGPLAN '91 Conference on Programming Language Design and Implementation*.

[279] Todd A. Proebsting and Charles N. Fischer. Probabilistic register allocation. *SIGPLAN Notices*, 27(7):300–310, July 1992. *Proceedings of the ACM SIGPLAN '92 Conference on Programming Language Design and Implementation*.

[280] Reese T. Prosser. Applications of boolean matrices to the analysis of flow diagrams. In *Proceedings of the Eastern Joint Computer Conference*, pages 133–138, Institute of Radio Engineers, New York, NY, December 1959.

[281] Paul W. Purdom, Jr. and Edward F. Moore. Immediate predominators in a directed graph[H]. *Communications of the ACM*, 15(8):777–778, August 1972.

[282] Brian Randell and L. J. Russell. *Algol 60 Programs Implementation; The Translation and Use of Algol 60 Programs on a Computer*. Academic Press, London, England, 1964.

[283] Bob R. Rau and C. D. Glaeser. Some scheduling techniques and an easily schedulable horizontal architecture for high performance scientific computing. In *Proceedings of the Fourteenth Annual Microprogramming Workshop on Microprogramming*, pages 183–198, December 1981.

[284] John H. Reif. Symbolic programming analysis in almost linear time. In *Conference Record of the Fifth Annual ACM Symposium on Principles of Programming Languages*, pages 76–83, Tucson, AZ, January 1978.

[285] John H. Reif and Harry R. Lewis. Symbolic evaluation and the global value graph. In *Conference Record of the Fourth ACM Symposium on Principles of Programming Languages*, pages 104–118, Los Angeles, CA, January 1977.

[286] Thomas Reps. Optimal-time incremental semantic analysis for syntax-directed editors. In *Conference Record of the Ninth Annual ACM Symposium on Principles of Programming Languages*, pages 169–176, Albuquerque, NM, January 1982.

[287] Thomas Reps and Bowen Alpern. Interactive proof checking. In *Conference Record of the Eleventh Annual ACM Symposium on Principles of Programming Languages*, pages 36–45, Salt Lake City, UT, January 1984.

[288] Thomas Reps and Tim Teitelbaum. *The Synthesizer Generator: A System for Constructing Language-Based Editors*. Springer-Verlag, New York, NY, 1988.

[289] Martin Richards. The portability of the BCPL compiler. *Software—Practice and Experience*, 1(2):135–146, April–June 1971.

[290] Steve Richardson and Mahadevan Ganapathi. Interprocedural analysis versus procedure integration. *Information Processing Letters*, 32(3): 137–142, August 1989.

[291] Ronald Rivest. On self-organizing sequential search heuristics. *Communications of the ACM*, 19(2):63–67, February 1976.

[292] Anne Rogers and Kai Li. Software support for speculative loads. *SIGPLAN Notices*, 27(9):38–50, September 1992. *Proceedings of the Fifth International Conference on Architectural Support for Programming Languages and Operating Systems*.

[293] Barry K. Rosen, Mark N. Wegman, and F. Kenneth Zadeck. Global value numbers and redundant computations. In *Conference Record of the Fifteenth Annual ACM Symposium on Principles of Programming Languages*, pages 12–27, San Diego, CA, January 1988.

[294] Daniel J. Rosenkrantz and Richard Edwin Stearns. Properties of deterministic top-down grammars. *Information and Control*, 17(3):226–256, October 1970.

[295] Barbara G. Ryder. Constructing the call graph of a program. *IEEE Transactions on Software Engineering*, SE-5(3):216–226, May 1979.

[296] A. V. S. Sastry and Roy D. C. Ju. A new algorithm for scalar register promotion based on SSA form. *SIGPLAN Notices*, 33(5):15–25, May 1998. *Proceedings of the ACM SIGPLAN '98 Conference on Programming Language Design and Implementation*.

[297] Randolph G. Scarborough and Harwood G. Kolsky. Improved optimization of FORTRAN object programs. *IBM Journal of Research and Development*, 24(6):660–676, November 1980.

[298] Philip J. Schielke. *Stochastic Instruction Scheduling*. PhD thesis, Rice University, Department of Computer Science, Houston, TX, May 2000. (Technical Report TR00-370, Computer Science Department, Rice University, 2000.)

[299] Herb Schorr and William M. Waite. An efficient machine-independent procedure for garbage collection in various list structures. *Communications of the ACM*, 10(8):501–506, August 1967.

[300] Jacob T. Schwartz. On programming: An interim report on the SETL project. Installment II: The SETL language and examples of its use. Technical report, Courant Institute of Mathematical Sciences, New York University, New York, NY, October 1973.

[301] Ravi Sethi and Jeffrey D. Ullman. The generation of optimal code for arithmetic expressions. *Journal of the ACM*, 17(4):715–728, October 1970.

[302] Marc Shapiro and Susan Horwitz. Fast and accurate flow-insensitive points-to analysis. In *Conference Record of the Twenty-Fourth ACM Symposium on Principles of Programming Languages*, pages 1–14, Paris, France, January 1997.

[303] Robert M. Shapiro and Harry Saint. The representation of algorithms. Technical Report CA-7002-1432, Massachusetts Computer Associates, February 1970.

[304] Peter B. Sheridan. The arithmetic translator-compiler of the IBM FORTRAN automatic coding system. *Communications of the ACM*, 2(2):9–21, February 1959.

[305] Olin Shivers. Control flow analysis in Scheme. *SIGPLAN Notices*, 23(7):164–174, July 1988. *Proceedings of the ACM SIGPLAN '88 Conference on Programming Language Design and Implementation*.

[306] L. Taylor Simpson. *Value-Driven Redundancy Elimination*. PhD thesis, Rice University, Department of Computer Science, Houston, TX, 1996.(Technical Report TR 96–308, Computer Science Department, Rice University, 1996.)

[307] Michael Sipser. *Introduction to the Theory of Computation*. PWS Publishing Co., Boston, MA, December 1996.

[308] Richard L. Sites and Daniel R. Perkins. Universal P-code definition, version 0.2. Technical Report 78-CS-C29, Department of Applied Physics and Information Sciences, University of California at San Diego, San Deigo, CA, January 1979.

[309] Daniel Dominic Sleator and Robert Endre Tarjan. Amortized efficiency of list update and paging rules. *Communications of the ACM*, 28(2): 202–208, February 1985.

[310] Michael D. Smith, Mark Horowitz, and Monica S. Lam. Efficient superscalar performance through boosting. *SIGPLAN Notices*, 27(9): 248–259, September 1992. *Proceedings of the Fifth International Conference on Architectural Support for Programming Languages and Operating Systems*.

[311] Mark Smotherman, Sanjay M. Krishnamurthy, P. S. Aravind, and David Hunnicutt. Efficient DAG construction and heuristic calculation for instruction scheduling. In *Proceedings of the Twenty-Fourth Annual Workshop on Microarchitecture* (MICRO-24), pages 93–102, Albuquerque, NM, August 1991.

[312] Arthur Sorkin. Some comments on "A solution to a problem with Morel and Renvoise's 'Global optimization by suppression of partial redundancies.' " *ACM Transactions on Programming Languages and Systems*, 11(4):666–668, October 1989.

[313] Thomas C. Spillman. Exposing side-effects in a PL/1 optimizing compiler. In *Information Processing 71*, pages 376–381. North-Holland, Amsterdam, Netherlands, 1972. *Proceedings of IFIP Congress 71*.

[314] Guy Lewis Steele, Jr. Rabbit: A compiler for Scheme. Technical Report AI-TR-474, MIT Artificial Intelligence Laboratory, Massachusetts Institute of Technology, Cambridge, MA, May 1978.

[315] Philip H. Sweany and Steven J. Beaty. Post-compaction register assignment in a retargetable compiler. In *Proceedings of the Twenty-Third Annual Workshop and Symposium on Microprogramming and Microarchitecture* (MICRO-23), pages 107–116, Orlando, FL, November 1990.

[316] Philip H. Sweany and Steven J. Beaty. Dominator-path scheduling—A global scheduling method. *ACM SIGMICRO Newsletter*, 23(1–2): 260–263, December 1992. *Proceedings of the Twenty-Fifth Annual International Symposium on Microarchitecture.*

[317] Robert Endre Tarjan. Testing flow graph reducibility. *Journal of Computer and System Sciences*, 9(3):355–365, December 1974.

[318] Robert Endre Tarjan. Fast algorithms for solving path problems. *Journal of the ACM*, 28(3):594–614, July 1981.

[319] Robert Endre Tarjan. A unified approach to path problems. *Journal of the ACM*, 28(3):577–593, July 1981.

[320] Robert Endre Tarjan and John H. Reif. Symbolic program analysis in almost-linear time. *SIAM Journal on Computing*, 11(1):81–93, February 1982.

[321] Ken Thompson. Programming Techniques: Regular expression search algorithm. *Communications of the ACM*, 11(6):419–422, 1968.

[322] Steven W. K. Tjiang. TWIG reference manual. Technical Report CSTR 120, Computing Sciences, AT&T Bell Laboratories, Murray Hill, NJ, January 1986.

[323] Jeffrey D. Ullman. Fast algorithms for the elimination of common subexpressions. *Acta Informatica*, 2(3):191–213, 1973.

[324] David Ungar. Generation scavenging: A non-disruptive high performance storage reclamation algorithm. *ACM SIGSOFT Software Engineering Notes*, 9(3): 157–167, May 1984. *Proceedings of the First ACM SIGSOFT/SIGPLAN Software Engineering Symposium on Practical Software Development Environments.*

[325] Victor Vyssotsky and Peter Wegner. A graph theoretical FORTRAN source language analyzer. Manuscript, AT&T Bell Laboratories, Murray Hill, NJ, 1963.

[326] William Waite and Gerhard Goos. *Compiler Construction*. Springer-Verlag, New York, NY, 1984.

[327] Scott Kipling Warren. *The Coroutine Model of Attribute Grammar Evaluation*. PhD thesis, Department of Mathematical Sciences, Rice University, Houston, TX, April 1976.

[328] Mark N. Wegman and F. Kenneth Zadeck. Constant propagation with conditional branches. In *Conference Record of the Twelfth Annual ACM Symposium on Principles of Programming Languages*, pages 291–299, New Orleans, LA, January 1985.

[329] Mark N. Wegman and F. Kenneth Zadeck. Constant propagation with conditional branches. *ACM Transactions on Programming Languages and Systems*, 13(2):181–210, April 1991.

[330] William E. Weihl. Interprocedural data flow analysis in the presence of pointers, procedure variables, and label variables. In *Conference Record of the Seventh Annual ACM Symposium on Principles of Programming Languages*, pages 83–94, Las Vegas, NV, January 1980.

[331] Clark Wiedmann. Steps toward an APL compiler. *ACM SIGAPL APL Quote Quad*, 9(4):321–328, June 1979. *Proceedings of the International Conference on APL.*

[332] Paul R. Wilson. Uniprocessor garbage collection techniques. In *Proceedings of the International Workshop on Memory Management. Lecture Notes in Computer Science 637,* pages 1–42, Springer-Verlag, Heidelberg, Germany, 1992.

[333] Robert P. Wilson and Monica S. Lam. Efficient context-sensitive pointer analysis for C programs. *SIGPLAN Notices,* 30(6):1–12, June 1995. *Proceedings of the ACM SIGPLAN '95 Conference on Programming Language Design and Implementation.*

[334] Michael E. Wolf and Monica S. Lam. A data locality optimizing algorithm. *SIGPLAN Notices,* 26(6):30–44, June 1991. *Proceedings of the ACM SIGPLAN '91 Conference on Programming Language Design and Implementation.*

[335] Michael Wolfe. *High Performance Compilers for Parallel Computing.* Addison-Wesley, Redwood City, CA, 1996.

[336] D. Wood. The theory of left-factored languages, part 1. *The Computer Journal,* 12(4):349–356, November 1969.

[337] D. Wood. The theory of left-factored languages, part 2. *The Computer Journal,* 13(1):55–62, February 1970.

[338] D. Wood. A further note on top-down deterministic languages. *The Computer Journal,* 14(4):396–403, November 1971.

[339] William Wulf, Richard K. Johnsson, Charles B. Weinstock, Steven O. Hobbs, and Charles M. Geschke. *The Design of an Optimizing Compiler.* Programming Languages Series. American Elsevier Publishing Company, Inc., New York, NY, 1975.

[340] Cliff Young, David S. Johnson, David R. Karger, and Michael D. Smith. Near-optimal intraprocedural branch alignment. *SIGPLAN Notices,* 32(5):183–193, May 1997. *Proceedings of the ACM SIGPLAN '97 Conference on Programming Language Design and Implementation.*

[341] Daniel H. Younger. Recognition and parsing of context-free languages in time n^3. *Information and Control,* 10(2):189–208, 1967.

[342] F. Kenneth Zadeck. Incremental data flow analysis in a structured program editor. *SIGPLAN Notices,* 19(6):132–143, June 1984. *Proceedings of the ACM SIGPLAN '84 Symposium on Compiler Construction.*

EXERCISES

CHAPTER 1

1. Consider a simple web browser that takes as input a textual string in HTML format and displays the specified graphics on the screen. Is the display process one of compilation or interpretation?

2. In designing a compiler, you will face many tradeoffs. What are the five qualities that you, as a user, consider most important in a compiler that you purchase? Does that list change when you are the compiler writer? What does your list tell you about a compiler that you would implement?

3. Compilers are used in many different circumstances. What differences might you expect in compilers designed for the following applications?

   a. A *just-in-time* compiler used to translate user interface code downloaded over a network

   b. A compiler that targets the embedded processor used in a cellular telephone

   c. A compiler used in an introductory programming course at a high school

   d. A compiler used to build wind-tunnel simulations that run on a massively parallel processor (where all processors are identical)

   e. A compiler that targets numerically intensive programs to a large number of diverse machines

CHAPTER 2

Section 2.2

1. Describe informally the languages accepted by the following FAs:

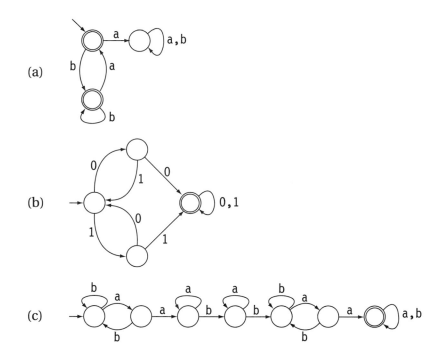

(a)

(b)

(c)

2. Construct an FA accepting each of the following languages:

   a. $\{w \in \{a, b\}^* \mid w$ starts with 'a' and contains '$baba$' as a substring$\}$

   b. $\{w \in \{0, 1\}^* \mid w$ contains '111' as a substring and does not contain '00' as a substring$\}$

   c. $\{w \in \{a, b, c\}^* \mid$ in w the number of 'a's modulo 2 is equal to the number of 'b's modulo 3$\}$

3. Create FAs to recognize (a) words that represent complex numbers and (b) words that represent decimal numbers written in scientific notation.

Section 2.3

1. Different programming languages use different ways to represent integers. Construct a regular expression for each one of the following:

   a. Nonnegative integers in C represented in bases 10 and 16

   b. Nonnegative integers in VHDL that may include underscores

      (An underscore cannot occur as the first or last character.)

   c. Currency, in dollars, represented as a positive decimal number rounded to the nearest one-hundredth. Such numbers begin with the character $, have commas separating each group of three digits to the left of the decimal point, and end with two digits to the right of the decimal point, for example, $8,937.43 and $7,777,777.77

2. Write a regular expression for each of the following languages.

   (*Hint:* not all the specifications describe regular languages.)

   a. Given an alphabet $\Sigma = \{0, 1\}$, L is the set of all strings of alternating pairs of 0s and pairs of 1s.

   b. Given an alphabet $\Sigma = \{0, 1\}$, L is the set of all strings of 0s and 1s that contain an even number of 0s or an even number of 1s.

   c. Given the lowercase English alphabet, L is the set of all strings in which the letters appear in ascending lexicographical order.

   d. Given an alphabet $\Sigma = \{a, b, c, d\}$, L is the set of strings *xyzwy*, where *x* and *w* are strings of one or more characters in Σ, *y* is any single character in Σ, and *z* is the character z, taken from outside the alphabet.

      (Each string xyzwy contains two words *xy* and *wy* built from letters in Σ. The words end in the same letter, *y*. They are separated by *z*.)

   e. Given an alphabet $\Sigma = \{+, -, \times, \div, (,), \text{id}\}$, L is the set of algebraic expressions using addition, subtraction, multiplication, division, and parentheses over ids.

3. Write a regular expression to describe each of the following programming language constructs:

   a. Any sequence of tabs and blanks (sometimes called *white space*)

   b. Comments in the programming language C

   c. String constants (without escape characters)

   d. Floating-point numbers

Section 2.4

1. Consider the three regular expressions:

$$(ab \mid ac)^*$$

$$(0 \mid 1)^* \, 1100 \; 1^*$$

$$(01 \mid 10 \mid 00)^* \; 11$$

   a. Use Thompson's construction to construct an NFA for each RE.

   b. Convert the NFAs to DFAs.

   c. Minimize the DFAs.

2. One way of proving that two REs are equivalent is to construct their mini-mized DFAs and then to compare them. If they differ only by state names, then the REs are equivalent. Use this technique to check the following pairs of REs and state whether or not they are equivalent.

   a. $(0 \mid 1)^*$ and $(0^* \mid 10^*)^*$

   b. $(ba)^+ \, (a^* \; b^* \mid a^*)$ and $(ba)^* \; ba^+ \, (b^* \mid \epsilon)$

3. Consider the following regular expression

$$r0 \mid r00 \mid r1 \mid r01 \mid r2 \mid r02 \mid \cdots \mid r09 \mid r10 \mid r11 \mid \cdots \mid r30 \mid r31$$

Apply the constructions to build:

   a. The NFA from the RE

   b. The DFA from the NFA

   c. The RE from the DFA

Explain any differences between the REs produced in parts (a) and (c).

How does the DFA that you produced compare with the DFA built in Chapter 2 from the following RE?

$$r((0 \mid 1 \mid 2) \, ([0 \cdots 9] \mid \epsilon) \mid (4 \mid 5 \mid 6 \mid 7 \mid 8 \mid 9) \mid (3 \, (0 \mid 1 \mid \epsilon)))$$

4. Minimize the DFA that you derived in the previous exercise. After minimization, what is the penalty in size and speed for using the simpler register specification?

5. In some cases, two states connected by an ϵ-move can be combined.

   a. Under what set of conditions can two states connected by an ϵ-move be combined?

   b. Give an algorithm for eliminating ϵ-moves.

   c. How does your algorithm relate to the ϵ-closure function used to implement the subset construction?

6. Show that the set of regular languages is closed under intersection.

Section 2.5

1. Construct a DFA for each of the following C language constructs, and then build the corresponding table for a table-driven implementation for each of them:

   a. Integer constants

   b. Identifiers

   c. Comments

2. For each of the DFAs from the previous exercise, build the corresponding direct-coded scanner.

3. This chapter described two styles of DFA implementations: a table-driven implementation that uses a case or switch statement, and a direct-coded scanner that uses branches and jumps. A third alternative is to use mutually recursive functions to implement a scanner. Discuss the advantages and disadvantages of such an implementation.

Chapter 3

Section 3.2

1. Write a context-free grammar for the syntax of regular expressions.

2. Write a context-free grammar for the Backus-Naur Form (BNF) notation for context-free grammars.

3. When asked about the definition of an *unambiguous context-free grammar* on an exam, two students gave different answers. The first defined it as "a grammar where each sentence has a unique syntax tree by leftmost derivation." The second defined it as "a grammar where each sentence has a unique syntax tree by any derivation." Which one is correct?

Section 3.3

1. The following grammar is not suitable for a top-down predictive parser. Identify the problem and correct it by rewriting the grammar. Show that your new grammar satisfies the LL(1) condition.

$$
\begin{array}{llllll}
L & \rightarrow & R\,a & R & \rightarrow & aba & Q & \rightarrow & bbc \\
  & | & Q\,ba &   & | & caba &   & | & bc \\
  &   &   &   & | & R\,bc &   &   &
\end{array}
$$

2. Consider the following grammar:

$$
\begin{array}{llllll}
A & \rightarrow & B\,a & C & \rightarrow & c\,B \\
B & \rightarrow & dab &   & | & A\,c \\
  & | & C\,b &   &   &
\end{array}
$$

Does this grammar satisfy the LL(1) condition? Justify your answer. If it does not, change the grammar to make it LL(1) without changing the language that it describes.

3. Grammars that can be parsed top-down, in a linear scan from left to right, with a k word lookahead are called LL(k) grammars. In the text, the LL(1) condition is described in terms of FIRST sets. How would you define the FIRST sets necessary to describe an LL(k) condition?

4. Suppose an elevator is controlled by two commands: ↑ to move the elevator up one floor and ↓ to move the elevator down one floor. Assume that the building is arbitrarily tall and that the elevator starts at floor x.

   Write an LL(1) grammar that generates arbitrary command sequences that (1) never cause the elevator to go below floor x and (2) always return the elevator to floor x at the end of the sequence. For example, ↑↑↓↓ and ↑↓↑↓ are valid command sequences, but ↑↓↓↑ and ↑↓↓ are not. For convenience, you may consider a null sequence as valid. Prove that your grammar is LL(1).

Section 3.4

1. Each move of a bottom-up, shift-reduce parser is called an *action*. The actions include a shift, a reduce, an accept, and the error action. A *parsing conflict* arises when multiple actions are possible at a given point in a parse.

   Consider all the kinds of conflict that can occur among the parser's actions. Which kinds of conflict are possible and which are impossible? Justify each answer.

2. Top-down and bottom-up parsers construct a syntax tree in different orders. Write a pair of programs, TopDown and BottomUp, that take a syntax tree and print out the nodes in order of construction. TopDown should display the order for a top-down parser, while BottomUp should show the order for a bottom-up parser.

Section 3.5

1. The ClockNoise language (*CN*) is represented by the following grammar:

$$
\begin{array}{lcl}
\textit{Goal} & \rightarrow & \textit{ClockNoise} \\
\textit{ClockNoise} & \rightarrow & \textit{ClockNoise}\ \texttt{tick tock} \\
& | & \texttt{tick tock}
\end{array}
$$

a. What are the LR(1) items of *CN*?

b. What are the FIRST sets of *CN*?

c. Construct the Canonical Collection of Sets of LR(1) Items for *CN*.

d. Derive the ACTION and GOTO tables.

2. The following grammar describes a language of matched parentheses.

$$
\begin{array}{lcl}
\textit{Goal} & \rightarrow & \textit{Parens} \\
\textit{Parens} & \rightarrow & \textit{(Parens) Parens} \\
& | & \epsilon
\end{array}
$$

a. Construct the Canonical Collection of Sets of LR(1) Items for this grammar.

b. Derive the ACTION and GOTO tables.

c. Is the grammar LR(1)?

3. Consider the following grammar:

$$
\begin{array}{lcl}
\textit{Start} & \rightarrow & S \\
S & \rightarrow & A\ \texttt{a} \\
A & \rightarrow & B\ C \\
& | & B\ C\ \texttt{f} \\
B & \rightarrow & \texttt{b} \\
C & \rightarrow & \texttt{c}
\end{array}
$$

a. Construct the Canonical Collection of Sets of LR(1) Items for this grammar.

b. Derive the ACTION and GOTO tables.

c. Is the grammar LR(1)?

4. Consider a robot arm that accepts two commands: ▽ puts an apple in the bag and △ takes an apple out of the bag. Assume the robot arm starts with an empty bag.

A valid command sequence for the robot arm should have no prefix that contains more △ commands than ▽ commands. As examples, ▽▽△△ and ▽△▽ are valid command sequences, but ▽△△▽ and ▽△▽△△ are not.

a. Write an LR(1) grammar that represents all the value command sequences for the robot arm.

b. Prove that the grammar is LR(1).

Section 3.6

1. Write a grammar for expressions that can include binary operators (+ and ×), unary minus (-), autoincrement (++), and autodecrement (- -) with their customary precedence. Assume that repeated unary minuses are not allowed, but that repeated autoincrement and autodecrement operators are allowed.

Section 3.7

1. Consider the task of building a parser for the programming language Scheme. Contrast the effort required for a top-down recursive descent parser with that needed for a table-driven LR(1) parser. (Assume that you already have an LR(1) table-generator.)

2. The text describes a manual technique for eliminating useless productions in a grammar.

a. Can you modify the LR(1) table-construction algorithm so that it automatically eliminates the overhead from useless productions?

b. Even though a production is syntactically useless, it may serve a practical purpose. For example, the compiler writer might associate a syntax-directed action (as in Chapter 4) with the useless production. How should your modified algorithm handle an action associated with a useless production?

CHAPTER 4

Section 4.2

1. In Scheme, the + operator is overloaded. Given that Scheme is a dynamically typed language, describe a method to type check an operation of the form (+ a b) where a and b may be of any type that is valid for the + operator.

2. Some languages, such as APL or PHP, neither require variable declarations nor enforce consistency between assignments to the same variable. (A program can assign the integer 10 to x and later assign the string value "book" to x in the same scope.) This style of programming is sometimes called *type juggling*.

   Suppose that you have an existing implementation of a language that has no declarations but requires type-consistent uses. How could you modify it to allow type juggling?

Section 4.3

1. Based on the following evaluation rules, draw an annotated parse tree to show how the syntax tree for a - (b + c) is constructed.

Production	Evaluation Rules
$E_0 \rightarrow E_1 + T$	{ E_0.nptr $\leftarrow$ mknode(+,E_1.nptr,T.nptr) }
$E_0 \rightarrow E_1 - T$	{ E_0.nptr $\leftarrow$ mknode(-,E_1.nptr,T.nptr) }
$E_0 \rightarrow T$	{ E_0.nptr $\leftarrow T$.nptr }
$T \rightarrow (E)$	{ T.nptr $\leftarrow E$.nptr }
$T \rightarrow$ id	{ T.nptr $\leftarrow$ mkleaf(id,id.entry) }

2. Use the attribute grammar paradigm to write an interpreter for the classic expression grammar. Assume that each ident has a value attribute and a name attribute. Assume that all attributes are already defined and that all values will always have the same type.

3. Write a grammar to describe all binary numbers that are multiples of four. Add attribution rules to the grammar that will annotate the start symbol of a syntax tree with an attribute value that contains the decimal value of the binary number.

4. Using the grammar defined in the previous exercise, build the syntax tree for the binary number 11100.

   a. Show all the attributes in the tree with their corresponding values.

   b. Draw the attribute dependence graph for the syntax tree and classify all attributes as being either synthesized or inherited.

Section 4.4

1. In Pascal, a programmer can declare two integer variables a and b with the syntax

$$\text{var a, b: int}$$

   This declaration might be described with the following grammar:

$$
\begin{array}{rcl}
VarDecl & \rightarrow & \text{var } IDList : TypeID \\
IDList & \rightarrow & IDList, ID \\
& | & ID
\end{array}
$$

   where *IDList* derives a comma-separated list of variable names and *TypeID* derives a valid Pascal type. You may find it necessary to rewrite the grammar.

   a. Write an attribute grammar that assigns the correct data type to each declared variable.

   b. Write an ad hoc syntax-directed translation scheme that assigns the correct data type to each declared variable.

   c. Can either scheme operate in a single pass over the syntax tree?

2. Sometimes, the compiler writer can move an issue across the boundary between context-free and context-sensitive analysis. Consider, for exam-

ple, the classic ambiguity that arises between function invocation and array references in FORTRAN 77 (and other languages). These constructs might be added to the classic expression grammar using the productions:

$$
\begin{array}{rcl}
Factor & \rightarrow & \texttt{ident} \; (\; ExprList \;) \\
ExprList & \rightarrow & ExprList \; \texttt{,} \; Expr \\
& | & Expr
\end{array}
$$

Here, the only difference between a function invocation and an array reference lies in how the `ident` is declared.

In previous chapters, we have discussed using cooperation between the scanner and the parser to disambiguate these constructs. Can the problem be solved during context-sensitive analysis? Which solution is preferable?

3. Sometimes, a language specification uses context-sensitive mechanisms to check properties that can be tested in a context-free way. Consider the grammar fragment in Figure 4.15. It allows an arbitrary number of *StorageClass* specifiers when, in fact, the standard restricts a declaration to a single *StorageClass* specifier.

   a. Rewrite the grammar to enforce the restriction grammatically.

   b. Similarly, the language allows only a limited set of combinations of *TypeSpecifier*. `long` is allowed with either `int` or `float`; `short` is allowed only with `int`. Either `signed` or `unsigned` can appear with any form of `int`. `signed` may also appear on `char`. Can these restrictions be written into the grammar?

   c. Propose an explanation for why the authors structured the grammar as they did. (*Hint*: the scanner returned a single token type for any of the *StorageClass* values and another token type for any of the *TypeSpecifiers*.)

   d. Do your revisions to the grammar change the overall speed of the parser? In building a parser for C, would you use the grammar like the one in Figure 4.15, or would you prefer your revised grammar? Justify your answer.

Section 4.5

1. Object-oriented languages allow operator and function overloading. In these languages, the function name is not always a unique identifier, since you can have multiple related definitions, as in

```
void Show(int);
void Show(char *);
void Show(float);
```

For lookup purposes, the compiler must construct a distinct identifier for each function. Sometimes, such overloaded functions will have different return types, as well. How would you create distinct identifiers for such functions?

2. Inheritance can create problems for the implementation of object-oriented languages. When object type A is a parent of object type B, a program can assign a "pointer to B" to a "pointer to A," with syntax such as a ← b. This should not cause problems since everything that A can do, B can also do. However, one cannot assign a "pointer to A" to a "pointer to B," since object class B can implement methods that object class A does not.

   Design a mechanism that can use ad-hoc syntax-directed translation to determine whether or not a pointer assignment of this kind is allowed.

CHAPTER 5

Section 5.3

1. Show how the code fragment

```
if (c[i] ≠ 0)
    then a[i] ← b[i] ÷ c[i];
    else a[i] ← b[i];
```

might be represented in an abstract syntax tree, in a control-flow graph, and in quadruples. Discuss the advantages of each representation. For what applications would one representation be preferable to the other?

2. Examine the following program. Draw its CFG and show its SSA form as a linear code.

```
...
x ← ...
y ← ...
a ← y + 2
b ← 0
while(x < a)
    if (y < x)
        x ← y + 1
        y ← b × 2
    else
        x ← y + 2
        y ← a ÷ 2;
    w ← x + 2
    z ← y × a
    y ← y + 1
```

Section 5.4

1. Show how the expression x - 2 × y might be translated into an abstract syntax tree, static single-assignment form, one-address code, two-address code, and three-address code.

Section 5.5

1. Consider the following three procedures written in C:

```
static int max = 0;
void A(int b, int e)
{
  int a, c, d, *p;
  a = B(b);
  if (b > 100) {
    c = a + b;
    d = c * 5 + e;
  }
  else
    c = a * b;
  *p = c;
  C(&p);
}
```

```
int B(int k)
{
  int x, y;
  x = 2 ^ k;
  y = x * 5;
  return y;
}

void C(int *p)
{
  if (*p > max)
    max = *p;
}
```

a. Suppose a compiler works from a register-to-register memory model. Which variables in procedures A, B, and C would the compiler be forced to store in memory? Justify your answers.

b. Suppose a compiler works from a memory-to-memory model. Consider the execution of the two statements that are in the if clause of the if-else construct. If the compiler has two registers available at that point in the computation, how many loads and stores would the compiler need to issue in order to bring values to registers and get them back to memory during execution of those two statements? What if it has three registers available?

2. In FORTRAN, two variables can be forced to begin at the same storage location with an equivalence statement. For example, the following statement forces a and b to share storage:

equivalence (a,b)

Can the compiler keep a local variable in a register throughout the procedure if that variable appears in an equivalence statement? Justify your answer.

Section 5.7

1. Some part of the compiler must be responsible for entering each identifier into the symbol table.

   a. Should the scanner or the parser enter identifiers into the symbol table? Each has an opportunity to do so.

   b. Is there an interaction between this issue, declare-before-use rules, and disambiguation of subscripts from function calls in a language with the FORTRAN 77 ambiguity?

2. The compiler must store information in the IR version of the program that allows it to get back to the symbol table entry for each name. Among the options open to the compiler writer are pointers to the original character strings and subscripts into the symbol table. Of course, the clever implementor may discover other options.

   What are the advantages and disadvantages of each of these representations for a name? How would you represent the name?

3. You are writing a compiler for your favorite lexically-scoped language.

   Consider the following example program:

```
 1    procedure main
 2        integer a, b, c;
 3        procedure f1(w,x);
 4            integer a,x,y;
 5            call f2(w,x);
 6            end;
 7        procedure f2(y,z)
 8            integer a,y,z;
 9            procedure f3(m,n)
10                integer b, m, n;
10                c = a * b * m * n;
11                end;
12            call f3(c,z);
13            end;
14        ...
15        call f1(a,b);
16        end;
```

a. Draw the symbol table and its contents at line 10.

b. What actions are required for symbol table management when the parser enters a new procedure and when it exits a procedure?

4. Determine the output of the following C++ program:

```
int i = 2;
  while (i == 2) {
     i--;
     int i = 2;
     i++;
     cout << i << " ";
}
cout << i << "\n";
```

5. The most common implementation technique for a symbol table is a hash table, where insertion and deletion are expected to have $O(1)$ cost.

a. What is the worst-case cost for insertion and for deletion in a hash table?

b. Suggest an alternative implementation scheme that guarantees $O(1)$ insertion and deletion.

CHAPTER 6

Section 6.2

1. Consider the following C program.

```
int Sub(int i, int j) {
   return i - j;
}
int Mul(int i, int j) {
   return i * j;
}
```

```
int Delta(int a, int b, int c) {
   return Sub(Mul(b,b), Mul(Mul(4,a),c));
}
void main() {
   int a, b, c, delta;

   scanf("%d %d %d", &a, &b, &c);
   delta = Delta(a, b, c);
   if (delta == 0)
     puts("Two equal roots");
   else if (delta > 0)
     puts("Two different roots");
   else
     puts("No root");
}
```

Show its call tree and its execution history.

2. Consider the following C program.

```
void Output(int n, int x) {
   printf("The value of %d! is %s.\n", n, x);
}
int Fat(int n) {
   int x;
     if (n > 1)
   x = n * Fat(n - 1);
   else
     x = 1;
   Output(n, x);
   return x;
}
void main() {
   Fat(4);
}
```

Show its call tree and its execution history.

Section 6.3

1. Some programming languages allow the programmer to use functions in the initialization of local variables but not in the initialization of global variables.

   a. Is there an implementation rationale to explain this seeming quirk of the language definition?

   b. What mechanisms would be needed to allow initialization of a global variable with the result of a function call?

2. The compiler writer can optimize the allocation of ARs in several ways. For example, the compiler might:

   a. Allocate ARs for leaf procedures (those that make no procedure calls) statically.

   b. Combine the ARs for procedures that are always called together. (When α is called, it always calls β.)

   c. Use an arena-style allocator in place of heap allocation of ARs.

   For each scheme, consider the following questions:

   a. What fraction of the calls might benefit? In the best case? In the worst case?

   b. What is the impact on run-time space utilization?

3. Consider the following Pascal, in which only procedure calls and variable declarations are shown.

```
1   program Main(input, output);
2     var a, b, c : integer;
3     procedure P4; forward;
4     procedure P1;
5       procedure P2;
6         begin
7         end;
```

```
 8        var b, d, f : integer;
 9        procedure P3;
10          var a, b : integer;
11          begin
12             P2;
13             end;
14        begin
15          P2;
16          P4;
17          P3;
18          end;
19    var d, e : integer;
20    procedure P4;
21      var a, c, g : integer;
22      procedure P5;
23        var c, d : integer;
24        begin
25           P1;
26           end;
27      var d : integer;
28      begin
29        P1;
30        P5;
31        end;
32    begin
33      P1;
34      P4;
35      end.
```

a. Construct a static coordinate table, similar to the one in Figure 6.3.

b. Construct a graph to show the nesting relationships in the program.

c. Construct a graph to show the calling relationships in the program.

4. Draw the structures that the compiler would need to create to support an object of type Dumbo, defined as follows:

```
class Elephant {
   private int Length;
   private int Weight;
   static int type;

   public int GetLen();
   public int GetTyp();
}

class Dumbo extends Elephant {
   private int EarSize;
   private boolean Fly;

   public boolean CanFly();
}
```

Section 6.4

1. The possibility that two distinct variables refer to the same object (memory area) is considered undesirable in programming languages. Consider the following Pascal procedure, with parameters passed by reference.

```
procedure mystery(var x, y : integer);
  begin
    x := x + y;
    y := x - y;
    x := x - y;
  end;
```

If no overflow or underflow occurs during the arithmetic operations:

a. What result does mystery produce when it is called with two distinct variables a and b?

b. What would be the expected result if mystery is invoked with a single variable a passed to both parameters? What is the actual result in this case?

2. Consider the following program in a Pascal-like pseudo–programming language. Simulate its execution under call-by-value, call-by-reference, call-by-name, and call-by-value-result parameter binding rules. Show the results of the print statements in each case.

```
1    procedure main;
2       var a : array[1...3] of int;
3           i : int;
4       procedure p2(e : int);
5         begin
6           e := e + 3;
7           a[i] := 5;
8           i := 2;
9           e := e + 4;
10          end;
11      begin
12        a := [1, 10, 77];
13        i := 1;
14        p2(a[i]);
15        for i := 1 to 3 do
16          print(a[i]);
17        end.
```

Section 6.5

1. Suppose that the ARs for a Pascal implementation are stack allocated with the form shown in diagram (a). (Some fields have been omitted for simplicity.) The ARP is the only pointer to the AR, so access links are previous values of the ARP. The stack grows toward the top of the page. Diagram (b) shows the initial AR for a computation.

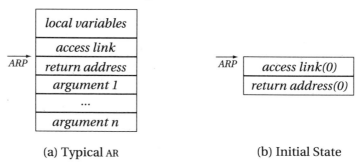

(a) Typical AR   (b) Initial State

For the following Pascal program, draw the set of ARs that are on the stack just prior to the return from function F1. Include all entries in the ARs. Use line numbers for return addresses. Draw directed arcs for access links. Clearly label the values of local variables and parameters. Label each AR with its procedure name.

```
1    program main(input, output);
2      procedure P1( function g(b: integer): integer);
3        var a: integer;
4        begin
5          a := 3;
6          writeln(g(2))
7          end;
8      procedure P2;
9        var a: integer;
10       function F1(b: integer): integer;
11         begin
12           F1 := a + b
13           end;
14       procedure P3;
15         var a:integer;
16         begin
17           a := 7;
18           P1(F1)
19           end;
20       begin
21         a := 0;
22         P3
23         end;
24     begin
25       P2
26       end.
```

2. Consider the following Pascal program. Assume that the ARs follow the same layout as in the previous question, with the same initial condition, *except* that the implementation uses a global display rather than access links.

```
 1   program main(input, output);
 2     var x : integer;
 3         a : float;
 4     procedure p1();
 5       var g:character;
 6       begin
 7         ...
 8       end;
 9     procedure p2();
10       var h:character;
11       procedure p3();
12         var h,i:integer;
13         begin
14           p1();
15         end;
16       begin
17         p3();
18       end;
19     begin
20       p2();
21     end
```

Draw the set of ARs that are on the run-time stack when the following program reaches line 7 in procedure p1.

Section 6.6

1. What is the relationship between the notion of a linkage convention and the construction of large programs? Of interlanguage programs? How can the linkage convention provide for an interlanguage call?

2. Assume that the compiler is capable of analyzing the code to determine facts such as *"from this point on, variable v is not used again in this procedure"* or *"variable v has its next use in line 11 of this procedure,"* and that the compiler keeps all local variables in registers for the following three procedures.

```
procedure main
    integer a, b, c
    b = a + c;
    c = f1(a,b);
    call print(c);
    end;
procedure f1(integer x, integer y)
    integer v;
    v = x * y;
    call print(v);
    call f2(v);
    return -x;
    end;
procedure f2(integer q)
    integer k, r;
    ...
    k = q / r;
    end;
```

a. Variable x in procedure f1 is live across two procedure calls. For fastest execution of the compiled code, should the compiler keep it in a caller-saves or callee-saves register? Justify your answer.

b. Consider variables a and c in procedure main. Should the compiler keep them in caller-saves or callee-saves registers, again assuming that the compiler is trying to maximize the speed of the compiled code. Justify your answer.

Section 6.7

1. Consider a tail-recursive function with local variables and parameters. Describe a storage mechanism that eliminates the need for stack-allocated activation records.

2. What property or properties of C's type system make automatic garbage collection difficult?

CHAPTER 7

Section 7.2

1. Memory layout affects the addresses assigned to variables. Assume that character variables have no alignment restriction, short integer variables must be aligned to halfword (2 byte) boundaries, integer variables must be aligned to word (4 byte) boundaries, and long integer variables must be aligned to doubleword (8 byte) boundaries. Consider the following set of declarations.

```
char a;
long int b;
int c;
short int d;
long int e;
char f;
```

Draw a memory map for these variables:

a. Assuming that the compiler cannot reorder the variables

b. Assuming the compiler can reorder the variables to save space

2. For each of the following types of variable, state where in memory the compiler might allocate the space for such a variable. Possible answers include registers, activation records, static data areas (with different visibilities), and the run-time heap.

a. A variable local to a procedure

b. A global variable

c. A dynamically allocated global variable

d. A formal parameter

e. A compiler-generated temporary variable

Section 7.3

1. Use the treewalk code generation algorithm from Section 7.3 to generate naïve code for the following expression tree. Assume an unlimited set of registers.

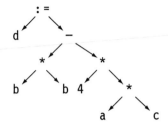

2. Find the minimum number of registers required to evaluate the following trees using the ILOC instruction set. For each nonleaf node, indicate which of its children must be evaluated first in order to achieve this minimum number of registers.

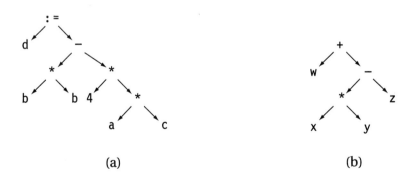

(a)   (b)

3. Build expression trees for the following two arithmetic expressions, using standard precedence and left-to-right evaluation. Compute the minimum number of registers required to evaluate each of them using the ILOC instruction set.

   a. ((a + b) + (c + d)) + ((e + f) + (g + h))

   b. a + b + c + d + e + f + g + h

Section 7.4

1. Generate predicated ILOC for the following code sequence. (No branch instructions should appear in the solution.)

```
if (x < y)
    then z = x * 5;
    else z = y * 5;
w = z + 10;
```

2. As mentioned in Section 7.4, short-circuit code for the following expression in C avoids a potential division-by-zero error.

```
a != 0 && b / a > 0.5
```

If the source-language definition does not specify short-circuit evaluation for boolean-valued expressions, can the compiler generate short-circuit code as an optimization for such expressions? What problems might arise?

Section 7.5

1. For a character array A[10...12,1...3] stored in row-major order, calculate the address of the reference A[i,j] using at most four arithmetic operations in the generated code.

2. What is a dope vector? Give the contents of the dope vector for the character array in the previous question. Why does the compiler need a dope vector?

3. When implementing a C compiler, is it advisable to have the compiler perform range checking for array references. Assuming range checks are used and that all array references in a C program have successfully passed them, is it possible for the program to access storage outside the range

of an array, for example, accessing A[-1] for an array declared with lower bound zero and upper bound N?

Section 7.6

1. Consider the following character-copying loop from Section 7.6.2:

```
                          loadI  @b    ⇒ r@b  // get pointers
                          loadI  @a    ⇒ r@a
                          loadI  NULL  ⇒ r₁   // terminator
                    L₁: cload  r@b   ⇒ r₂   // get next char
                          cstore r₂    ⇒ r@a  // store it
do {
  *a++ = *b++;            addI   r@b,1 ⇒ r@b  // bump pointers
} while (*b!='\0')        addI   r@a,1 ⇒ r@a

                          cmp_NE r₁,r₂ ⇒ r₄
                          cbr    r₄    → L₁,L₂

                    L₂: nop                  // next stmt
```

Modify the code so that it branches to an error handler at L_{sov} on any attempt to overrun the allocated length of a. Assume that the allocated length of a is stored as an unsigned four-byte integer at an offset of –8 from the start of a.

2. Consider the following implementation of the string assignment a = b; as shown in Section 7.6. It assumes that the actual length of a string is stored at offset –4 from the start of the string, for both a and b. and that the allocated length of a string is stored at offset –8 from the start of a string.

```
                    loadI    @b       ⇒ r@b
                    loadAI   r@b,-4  ⇒ r₁      // get b's length
                    loadI    @a       ⇒ r@a
                    loadAI   r@a,-8  ⇒ r₂      // get a's length

                    cmp_LT   r₂,r₁   ⇒ r₃      // will b fit in a?
                    cbr      r₃       → Lsov,L₁ // Lsov raises error

            L₁: loadI    0        ⇒ r₄      // counter
 a = b;             cmp_LT   r₄,r₁   ⇒ r₅      // more to copy ?
                    cbr      r₅       → L₂,L₃

            L₂: cloadAO  r@b,r₄  ⇒ r₆      // get char from b
                    cstoreAO r₆       ⇒ r@a,r₄ // put it in a
                    addI     r₄,1    ⇒ r₄      // increment offset

                    cmp_LT   r₄,r₁   ⇒ r₇      // more to copy ?
                    cbr      r₇       → L₂,L₃

            L₃: nop                           // next statement
```

It uses two cmp/cbr pairs to implement the end-of-loop tests—one in the block labelled L_1 and the other in the block labelled L_2.

In an environment where the size of compiled code is critical, the compiler might replace the cmp/cbr pair at the end of the loop with a jumpI to L_1.

How would this change affect execution time for the loop? Are there machine models on which it runs faster? Are there machine models on which it runs slower?

3. Figure 7.9 shows how to use word-oriented memory operations to perform a character string assignment for two word-aligned strings. Arbitrary assignments can generate misaligned cases.

   a. Write the ILOC code that you would like your compiler to emit for an arbitrary PL/I-style character assignment, such as

```
fee(i:j) = fie(k:l);
```

where j-i = l-k. This statement copies the characters in fie, starting at location k and running through location l into the string fee, starting at location i and running through location j.

Include versions using character-oriented memory operations and versions using word-oriented memory operations. You may assume that fee and fie do not overlap in memory.

b. The programmer can create character strings that overlap. In PL/I, the programmer might write

```
fee(i:j) = fee(i+1:j+1);
```

or, even more diabolically,

```
fee(i+k:j+k) = fee(i:j);
```

How does this complicate the code that the compiler must generate for the character assignment?

c. Are there optimizations that the compiler could apply to the various character-copying loops that would improve run-time behavior? How would they help?

Section 7.7

1. Consider the following type declarations in C:

```
struct S2 {          union U {              struct S1 {
    int i;               float r;               int a;
    int f;               struct S2;             double b;
};                   };                         union U;
                                                int d;
                                            };
```

Build a structure-element table for S1. Include in it all the information that a compiler would need to generate references to elements of a variable of type S1, including the name, length, offset, and type of each element.

2. Consider the following declarations in C:

```
struct record {
   int StudentId;
   int CourseId;
   int Grade;
} grades[1000];
int g, i;
```

Show the code that a compiler would generate to store the value in variable g as the grade in the ith element of grades, assuming:

a. The array grades is stored as an array of structures.

b. The array grades is stored as a structure of arrays.

Section 7.8

1. As a programmer, you are interested in the efficiency of the code that you produce. You recently implemented, by hand, a scanner. The scanner spends most of its time in a single while loop that contains a large case statement.

   a. How would the different case statement implementation techniques affect the efficiency of your scanner?

   b. How would you change your source code to improve the run-time performance under each of the case statement implementation strategies?

2. Convert the following C tail-recursive function to a loop.

```
List * last(List *l) {
  if (l == NULL)
      return NULL;
  else if (l->next == NULL)
      return l;
  else
      return last(l->next); }
```

Section 7.9

1. Assume that x is an unambiguous, local, integer variable and that x is passed as a call-by-reference actual parameter in the procedure where it is declared. Because it is local and unambiguous, the compiler might try to keep it in a register throughout its lifetime. Because it is passed as a call-by-reference parameter, it must have a memory address at the point of the call.

   a. Where should the compiler store x?

   b. How should the compiler handle x at the call site?

   c. How would your answers change if x was passed as a call-by-value parameter?

2. The linkage convention is a contract between the compiler and any outside callers of the compiled code. It creates a known interface that can be used to invoke a procedure and obtain any results that it returns (while protecting the caller's run-time environment). Thus, the compiler should only violate the linkage convention when such a violation cannot be detected from outside the compiled code.

   a. Under what circumstances can the compiler be certain that using a variant linkage is safe? Give examples from real programming languages.

   b. In these circumstances, what might the compiler change about the calling sequence and the linkage convention?

Section 7.10

1. Explain the purpose of the first field in a class record, such as the records for sc, mc, and giant in Figure 7.13.

2. In Java, the access rule is different for data members than for method members. For example, suppose class b inherits from a, and that both classes define a member named foo. Further suppose that an object o is allocated as an instance of class b, but it is treated as an object of class a when accessing its member foo. If foo is a method member, the call will resolve to the method defined in class b. But if foo is a data member, the access will be made to the field defined in class a.

   Explain how you would implement a Java compiler that supports these two distinct access rules.

3. Some implementations of multiple inheritance use "trampoline functions" to adjust the object-record pointer, as described in Section 7.10.2.

   a. When does the code need to adjust the object-record pointer, known as this in Java?

   b. Describe a situation in which a class needs multiple trampoline functions—that is, trampoline functions with distinct offsets.

4. In a programming language that features a dynamic class structure—that is, a class structure that can change at run-time—the number of method invocations that must be dispatched dynamically can be large. A method cache, as described in Section 7.10.2, can reduce the runtime cost of these lookups by short-circuiting them.

   As an alternative to a global method cache, the implementation might maintain a single entry method cache at each call site. It would record the address of the method most recently dispatched from that site, along with its class.

   Develop pseudocode to use and maintain such an inline method cache. Be sure to explain the initialization of the inline method caches and any modifications to the general method lookup routine required to support inline method caches.

CHAPTER 8

Section 8.3

1. Many optimization and code generation algorithms are designed to operate on DAGs. Even a compiler that used a low-level IR such as ILOC might have occasion to build a DAG.

   a. Sketch an algorithm for building a DAG from a basic block expressed in ILOC.

   b. Compare your algorithm with the value numbering algorithm shown in Figure 8.3.

   c. Sketch an algorithm to regenerate ILOC from your DAG.

   d. Can you extend your DAG-construction algorithm to include some of the other features of value numbering, such as constant folding or handling algebraic identities?

2. Consider the following two basic blocks:

$$
\begin{array}{ll}
\text{a} \leftarrow \text{b} + \text{c} & \quad \text{a} \leftarrow \text{b} + \text{c} \\
\text{d} \leftarrow \text{c} & \quad \text{e} \leftarrow \text{c} + \text{c} \\
\text{e} \leftarrow \text{c} + \text{d} & \quad \text{f} \leftarrow \text{a} + \text{c} \\
\text{f} \leftarrow \text{a} + \text{d} & \quad \text{g} \leftarrow \text{b} + \text{e} \\
\text{g} \leftarrow \text{b} + \text{e} & \quad \text{h} \leftarrow \text{b} + \text{c} \\
\text{h} \leftarrow \text{b} + \text{d} &
\end{array}
$$

   a. Build a DAG for each block.

   b. Value number each block.

   c. Explain any differences in the redundancies found by these two techniques.

   d. At the end of each block, f and g have the same value. Why do the algorithms have difficulty discovering this fact?

3. Given a linear list of ILOC operations, develop an algorithm that finds basic blocks. Extend your algorithm to build a control-flow graph to represent the connections between blocks.

Section 8.4

1. Consider the following control-flow graph:

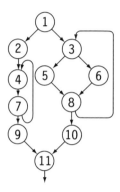

a. Identify the extended basic blocks in the graph.

b. Identify the loops in the graph.

c. Write a procedure in C that might generate this control-flow graph.

2. Give an efficient algorithm for determining the set of basic blocks contained within a loop L. Assume that you are given the loop-closing edge in the control-flow graph (an edge whose destination dominates its source). For example the edge from 7 to 4 and the edge from 8 to 3 are loop-closing edges in the CFG for the previous problem.

Section 8.5

Use the following control-flow graph when solving problems 1 and 2:

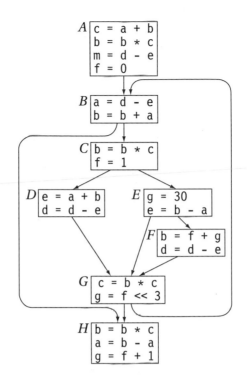

1. Using the CFG shown above:

   a. Find the extended basic blocks in the CFG.

   b. Find the dominator set for each basic block.

   c. Build the dominance tree for the CFG.

2. Using the CFG from the previous exercise:

   a. Apply superlocal value numbering to the CFG.

   b. Apply dominator-based value numbering to the CFG.

Section 8.6

Use the following control-flow graph for problems 1 and 2.

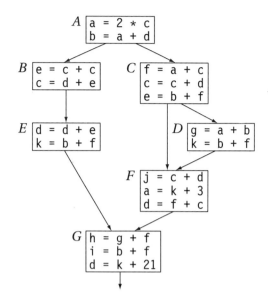

1. The global redundancy elimination algorithm (GRE), using available expressions, discovers a different set of redundancies than the value-numbering techniques.

   a. In the previous CFG, which expressions does GRE find as redundant?

   b. Which redundant expressions does dominator-based value numbering find that GRE cannot find?

2. Compute DEEXPR, EXPRKILL, and AVAIL sets for the blocks in the CFG above. Rewrite the code to replace the redundant expressions with copy expressions.

3. As shown in Figure 8.8, the computation of EXPRKILL is more complex than the computation of DEEXPR sets. Sketch algorithms that

   a. Construct the name space for expressions.

   b. Construct the mapping from VARKILL to EXPRKILL.

   Estimate the asymptotic complexity of your algorithms. How fast can you make them?

4. Section 8.6.2 shows one scheme for inserting the copy operations that global redundancy elimination needs. That scheme inserts some copies that are useless (and will be removed by the dead code eliminator).

Develop another technique for inserting copies that creates fewer useless copies.

Section 8.7

1. This section describes two forms of code replication, cloning and inline substitution.

    a. What programming language features prevent the compiler from cloning a block or substituting a called procedure inline?

    b. Both cloning and inline substitution have benefits and overheads. Sketch a strategy that the compiler might use to determine when to clone a block. Sketch a strategy that the compiler might use to determine when to substitute a call inline.

2. In some circumstances, code replication always makes sense. For example, a procedure that is only called from one call site is a strong candidate for inline substitution, unless inlining makes the caller too large to fit in some layer of the memory hierarchy.

    a. Under what circumstances should the compiler always clone a block?

    b. Under what circumstances should the compiler always inline substitute a call?

CHAPTER 9

Section 9.2

1. The algorithm for live analysis in Figure 9.2 initializes the LiveOut set of each block to ϕ. Are other initializations possible? Do they change the result of the analysis? Justify your answer.

2. The algorithm for live analysis in Figure 9.2 iterates over all the nodes in the CFG, but it does not specify the order in which those blocks are processed. Does the order matter?

3. In live variable analysis, how should the compiler treat a block containing a procedure call? What should the block's UEVar set contain? What about its VarKill set?

4. Consider the following control-flow graph:

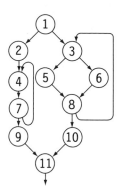

a. Compute a reverse preorder numbering for the nodes in the graph.

b. Compute a reverse postorder numbering for the nodes in the graph.

Section 9.3

1. Consider the following control-flow graphs:

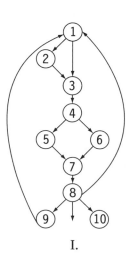

I.

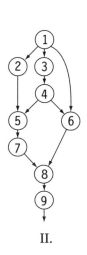

II.

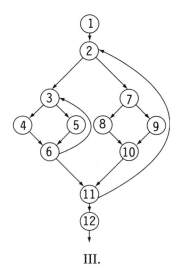

III.

   a. Compute the dominator trees for CFGs I, II, and III.

   b. Compute the dominance frontiers for nodes 3 and 5 of CFG I, nodes 4 and 5 of CFG II, and nodes 3 and 11 of CFG III.

2. Translate the code in the following control-flow graph to SSA form. Show only the final code, after both ϕ-insertion and renaming.

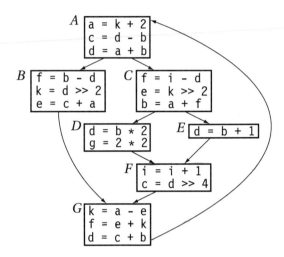

3. Consider the set of all blocks that receive a ϕ-function because of an assignment $x \leftarrow \ldots$ in some block b. The algorithm in Figure 9.11 inserts a ϕ-function in each block in DF(b). Each of those blocks is added to the worklist; they, in turn, can add nodes in their DF sets to the worklist. The algorithm uses a checklist to avoid adding a block to the worklist more than once. Call the set of all these blocks $DF^{+}(b)$.

We can define $DF^{+}(b)$ as the limit of the sequence

$$\mathbf{DF}_1(b) = DF(b)$$

$$DF_2(b) = DF_1(b) \cup_{x \in DF_1(b)} DF(x))$$

$$\ldots$$

$$DF_{i+1}(b) = DF_i(b) \cup_{x \in DF_i(b)} DF_i(x))$$

Using these extended sets, $DF^+(b)$, leads to a simpler algorithm for inserting ϕ-functions.

a. Develop an algorithm for computing $DF^+(b)$.

b. Develop an algorithm for inserting ϕ-functions using these DF^+ sets.

c. Compare the overall cost of your new algorithm, including the computation of the DF^+ sets, to the cost of the ϕ-insertion algorithm given in Section 9.3.3.

4. The "maximal" SSA construction is both simple and intuitive. However, it can insert many more ϕ-functions than the "semipruned" algorithm. In particular, it can insert both redundant ϕ-functions $(x_i \leftarrow \phi(x_j, x_j))$ and dead ϕ-functions—where the result is never used.

a. Propose a method for detecting and removing the extra ϕ-functions that the maximal construction inserts.

b. Can your method reduce the set of ϕ-functions to just those that the semipruned construction inserts?

c. Contrast the asymptotic complexity of your method against that of the semipruned construction.

Section 9.4

1. For each of the following control-flow graphs, show whether or not it is reducible.

(a)

(b)

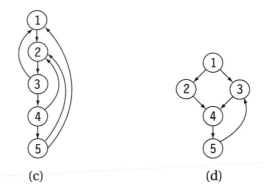

(c)   (d)

2. Prove that the following definition of a reducible graph is equivalent to the definition that uses the transformations T_1 and T_2: "A graph G is reducible if and only if removing its back edges produces an acyclic graph G'." (Recall that a back edge is one whose destination dominates its source.)

3. Show a sequence of reductions, using T_1 and T_2, that reduce the graph labelled "After" in Figure 9.21.

CHAPTER 10

Section 10.3

1. One of the primary functions of an optimizer is to remove overhead that the compiler introduced during the translation from source language into IR.

   a. Give four examples of inefficiencies that you would expect an optimizer to improve, along with the source-language constructs that give rise to them.

   b. Give four examples of inefficiencies that you would expect an optimizer to miss, even though they can be improved. Explain why an optimizer would have difficulty improving them.

2. A compiler can find and eliminate redundant computations in many different ways. Among these are value numbering, global common subex-

pression elimination based on available expressions (GCSE), and lazy code motion (LCM).

    a. Give two examples of redundancies eliminated by value numbering that cannot be found by GCSE or LCM.

    b. Give an example that LCM finds that is missed by value numbering and GCSE.

    c. Can GCSE find any redundancies that LCM misses? Give an example, or prove your answer.

3. Figure 10.3 shows the algorithm for DEAD. The marking pass is a classic fixed-point computation.

    a. Explain why this computation terminates.

    b. Is the fixed-point that it finds unique? Prove your answer.

    c. Derive a tight time bound for the algorithm.

4. Consider the algorithm CLEAN from Section 10.3.1. It removes useless control flow and simplifies the CFG.

    a. Why does the algorithm terminate?

    b. Give an overall time bound for the algorithm.

5. Hoisting replaces multiple evaluations of an expression with a single one, located "above" the originals in the CFG. An analogous transformation, called *sinking*, might find points in the code where (1) every path leading to a block b contains an evaluation of e; (2) evaluating e at b produces the same result; and (3) the result of e is not used before b.

    a. Formulate the data-flow problem needed to locate opportunities for sinking and to prove its safety.

    b. Sketch an efficient algorithm for inserting the new evaluations and eliminating the earlier evaluations.

Section 10.4

1. A simple form of operator strength reduction replaces a single instance of an expensive operation with a sequence of operations that are less

expensive to execute. For example, some integer multiply operations can be replaced with a sequence of shifts and adds.

   a. What conditions must hold to let the compiler safely replace an integer operation $x \leftarrow y \times z$ with a single shift operation?

   b. Sketch an algorithm that replaces a multiplication of a known constant and an unsigned integer with a sequence of shifts and adds in cases where the constant is not a power of two.

2. A compiler can use procedure abstraction to shrink the size of the code that it produces.

   a. What conditions must hold for a repeated code sequence in order for the compiler to safely apply procedure abstraction?

   b. Your compiler has found two code sequences that have identical operations and register names. However, the sequence has a branch in the middle of it and the two instances branch to different targets. How might the compiler handle this situation? Can you generalize your idea?

   c. What is the overhead of procedure abstraction? Are there situations in which the overhead makes the transformation unprofitable?

CHAPTER 11

Section 11.2

1. The treewalk code generator shown in Figure 7.2 uses a `loadI` for every number. Rewrite the treewalk code generator so that it uses `addI`, `subI`, `rsubI`, `multI`, `divI` and `rdivI`. Explain any additional routines or data structures that your code generator needs.

Section 11.3

1. Using the rules given in Figure 11.5, generate two tilings for the AST shown in Figure 11.4.

2. Build a low-level abstract syntax tree for the following expressions, using the tree in Figure 11.4 as a model.

   a. y ← a × b + c × d

   b. w ← x × y × z - 7

   Use the rules given in Figure 11.5 to tile these trees and generate ILOC.

3. Tree-pattern matching assumes that its input is a tree.

   a. How would you extend these ideas to handle DAGs, where a node can have multiple parents?

   b. How do control-flow operations fit into this paradigm?

4. In any tree-walk scheme for code generation, the compiler must choose an evaluation order for the subtrees. That is, at some binary node n, does it evaluate the left subtree first or the right subtree first?

   a. Does the choice of order affect the number of registers required to evaluate the entire subtree?

   b. How can this choice be incorporated into the bottom-up tree-pattern matching schemes?

Section 11.4

1. A real peephole optimizer must deal with control-flow operations, including conditional branches, jumps, and labelled statement.

   a. What should a peephole optimizer do when it brings a conditional branch into the optimization window?

   b. Is the situation different when it encounters a jump?

   c. What happens with a labelled operation?

   d. What can the optimizer do to improve this situation?

2. Write down concrete algorithms for performing the simplification and matching functions of a peephole transformer.

   a. What is the asymptotic complexity of each of your algorithms?

   b. How is the running time of the transformer affected by a longer input program, by a larger window, and by a larger pattern set (both for simplification and for matching)?

3. Peephole transformers simplify the code as they select a concrete implementation for it. Assume that the peephole transformer runs before either instruction scheduling or register allocation and that the transformer can use an unlimited set of virtual register names.

   a. Can the peephole transformer change the demand for registers?

   b. Can the peephole transformer change the set of opportunities that are available to the scheduler for reordering the code?

CHAPTER 12

Section 12.2

1. Develop an algorithm that builds the precedence graph for a basic block. Assume that the block is written in ILOC and that any values defined outside the block are ready before execution of the block begins.

2. If the primary use for a precedence graph is instruction scheduling, then accurate modeling of actual delays on the target machine is critical.

   a. How should the precedence graph model the uncertainty caused by ambiguous memory references?

   b. In some pipelined processors, write-after-read delays can be shorter than read-after-write delays. For example, the sequence

$$[\text{ add } r_{10}, r_{12} \Rightarrow r_2 \mid \text{ sub } r_{13}, r_{11} \Rightarrow r_{10}]$$

would read the value from r_{10} for use in the add before writing the result of the sub into r_{10}. How can a compiler represent antidependences in a precedence graph for such an architecture?

   c. Some processors bypass memory to reduce read-after-write delays. On these machines, a sequence such as

$$\text{storeAI } r_{21} \qquad \Rightarrow r_{arp}, 16$$
$$\text{loadAI } \ r_{arp}, 16 \Rightarrow r_{12}$$

forwards the value of the store (in r_{21} at the beginning of the sequence) directly to the result of the load (r_{12}). How can the dependence graph reflect this hardware bypass feature?

Section 12.3

1. Extend the local list-scheduling algorithm shown in Figure 12.3 to handle multiple functional units. Assume that all functional units have identical capabilities.

2. A critical aspect of any scheduling algorithm is the mechanism for setting initial priorities and for breaking ties when several operations with the same priority are ready at the same cycle. Some of the tiebreakers suggested in the literature include:

   a. Take the operation with the most descendants in the precedence graph.

   b. Take the operation with the longest latency.

   c. Take the operation with the fewest operands that are live after its execution.

   d. Take a randomly chosen operation.

   e. Take a load before any computation.

   For each tiebreaker, suggest a rationalization—a guess as to why someone suggested it. Which tiebreaker would you use first? Which would you use second? Justify (or rationalize) your answers.

3. Most modern microprocessors have *delay slots* on some or all branch operations. With a single delay slot, the operation immediately following the branch executes while the branch processes; thus, the ideal slot for scheduling a branch is in the second-to-last cycle of a basic block. (Most processors have a version of the branch that does not execute the delay slot, so that the compiler can avoid generating a nop instruction in an unfilled delay slot.)

a. How would you adapt the list scheduling algorithm to improve its ability to "fill" delay slots?

b. Sketch a post-scheduling pass that would fill delay slots.

c. Propose a creative use for the branch-delay slots that cannot be filled with useful operations.

Section 12.4

1. The order in which operations occur determines when values are created and when they are used for the last time. Taken together, these effects determine the lifetime of the value.

   a. How can the scheduler reduce the demand for registers? Suggest concrete tiebreaking heuristics that would fit into a list scheduler.

   b. What is the interaction between these register-oriented tiebreakers and the scheduler's ability to produce short schedules?

2. Software pipelining overlaps loop iterations to create an effect that resembles hardware pipelining.

   a. What impact do you expect software pipelining to have on the demand for registers?

   b. How can the scheduler use predicated execution to reduce the code-space penalty for software pipelining?

CHAPTER 13

Section 13.3

1. Consider the following ILOC basic block. Assume that r_{arp} and r_i are live on entry to the block.

```
loadAI    r_arp,12  ⇒  r_a
loadAI    r_arp,16  ⇒  r_b
add       r_i,r_a   ⇒  r_c
sub       r_b,r_i   ⇒  r_d
mult      r_c,r_d   ⇒  r_e
multI     r_b,2     ⇒  r_f
add       r_e,r_f   ⇒  r_g
storeAI   r_g       ⇒  r_arp,8
jmp                 →  L_003
```

   a. Show the result of using the top-down local algorithm on it to allocate registers. Assume a target machine with four registers.

   b. Show the result of using the bottom-up local algorithm on it to allocate registers. Assume a target machine with four registers.

2. The top-down local allocator is somewhat naive in its handling of values. It allocates one value to a register for the entire basic block.

   a. An improved version might calculate live ranges within the block and allocate values to registers for their live ranges. What modifications would be necessary to accomplish this?

   b. A further improvement might be to split the live range when it cannot be accommodated in a single register. Sketch the data structures and algorithmic modifications that would be needed to (1) break a live range around an instruction (or range of instructions) where a register is not available and to (2) reprioritize the remaining pieces of the live range.

   c. With these improvements, the frequency count technique should generate better allocations. How do you expect your results to compare with using the bottom-up local algorithm? Justify your answer.

Section 13.4

1. Consider the following control-flow graph:

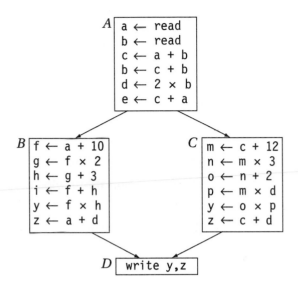

Assume that read returns a value from external media and that write transmits a value to external media.

a. Compute the LiveIn and LiveOut sets for each block.

b. Apply the bottom-up local algorithm to each block, *A*, *B*, and *C*. Assume that three registers are available to the computation. If block *b* defines a name *n* and $n \in \text{LiveOut}(b)$, the allocator must store *n* back to memory so that its value is available in subsequent blocks. Similarly, if block *b* uses name *n* before any local definition of *n*, it must load *n*'s value from memory. Show the resulting code, including all loads and stores.

c. Suggest a scheme that would allow some of the values in LiveOut(*A*) to remain in registers, avoiding their initial loads in the successor blocks.

Section 13.5

1. Consider the following interference graph:

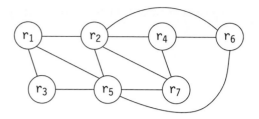

Assume that the target machine has just three registers.

a. Apply the bottom-up global coloring algorithm to the graph. Which virtual registers are spilled? Which are colored?

b. Does the choice of spill node make a difference?

c. Earlier coloring allocators spilled any live range that is constrained when it is selected. Rather than applying the algorithm shown in Figure 13.8, they used the following method:

> *initialize stack to empty*
> *while (N = ϕ)*
>   *if ∃ n ∈ N with n° < k then*
>   *remove n and its edges from I*
>   *push n onto stack*
>   *else*
>   *pick a node n from N*
>   *mark n to be spilled*

If this marks any node for spilling, the allocator inserts spill code and repeats the allocation process on the modified program. If no node is marked for spilling, it proceeds to assign colors in the manner described for the bottom-up global allocator.

What happens when this algorithm is applied to the example interference graph? Does the mechanism used to choose a node for spilling change the results?

2. After register allocation, a careful analysis of the code may discover that, in some stretches of the code, there are unused registers. In a bottom-up, graph-coloring, global allocator, this occurs because of detailed shortcomings in the way that live ranges are spilled.

    a. Explain how this situation can arise.

    b. How might the compiler discover if this situation occurs and where it occurs?

    c. What might be done to use these unused registers, both within the global framework and outside of it?

Section 13.6

1. When a graph-coloring global allocator reaches the point where no color is available for a particular live range, LR_i, it spills or splits that live range. As an alternative, it might attempt to recolor one or more of LR_i's neighbors. Consider the case where $\langle LR_i, LR_j \rangle \in I$ and $\langle LR_i, LR_k \rangle \in I$, but $\langle LR_j, LR_k \rangle \notin I$. If LR_j and LR_k have already been colored, and have received different colors, the allocator might be able to recolor one of them to the other's color, freeing up a color for LR_i.

    a. Sketch an algorithm for discovering if a legal and productive recoloring exists for LR_i.

    b. What is the impact of your technique on the asymptotic complexity of the register allocator?

    c. Should you consider recursively recoloring LR_k's neighbors? Explain your rationale.

2. The description of the bottom-up global allocator suggests inserting spill code for *every* definition and use in the spilled live range. The top-down global allocator first breaks the live range into block-sized pieces, then combines those pieces when the result is unconstrained and, finally, assigns them a color.

    a. If a given block has one or more free registers, spilling a live range multiple times in that block is wasteful. Suggest an improvement to the spill mechanism in the bottom-up global allocator that avoids this problem.

    b. If a given block has too many overlapping live ranges, then splitting a spilled live range does little to address the problem in that block. Suggest a mechanism (other than local allocation) to improve the behavior of the top-down global allocator inside blocks with high demand for registers.

INDEX